DATE DUE

DEMCO 38-296

Merriam-Webster's
Legal Secretaries
Handbook

R

Merriam-Webster's
Legal Secretaries
Handbook

SECOND EDITION

Austin G. Anderson, Esq.
Consulting Editor

Merriam-Webster, Incorporated
Springfield, Massachusetts

®

A GENUINE MERRIAM-WEBSTER

The name *Webster* alone is no guarantee of excellence. It is used by a number of publishers and may serve mainly to mislead an unwary buyer.

Merriam-Webster™ is the name you should look for when you consider the purchase of dictionaries or other fine reference books. It carries the reputation of a company that has been publishing since 1831 and is your assurance of quality and authority.

Copyright © 1996 by Merriam-Webster, Incorporated
Philippines Copyright 1996 by Merriam-Webster, Incorporated

Library of Congress Cataloging-in-Publication Data

Merriam-Webster's legal secretaries handbook / Austin G. Anderson,
    consulting editor.—2nd ed.
        p.   cm.
    Rev. ed. of: Webster's legal secretaries handbook. © 1981.
    Includes index.
    ISBN 0-87779-134-1 (cloth)
    1. Legal secretaries—United States—Handbooks, manuals, etc.
I. Anderson, Austin G., 1931-   II. Webster's legal secretaries
handbook.
KF319.M47   1996
651'.934973—dc20   96-19829
                                                                CIP

Made in the United States of America

123456RRD010099989796

SECOND EDITION

Consulting Editor
AUSTIN G. ANDERSON, Esq.
AndersonBoyer Group
Ann Arbor, Michigan

General Editor
MICHAEL SHALLY-JENSEN
Merriam-Webster, Inc.

Contributors

EARL W. BRICKNER II
Administrator
May, Oberfell & Lorber
South Bend, Indiana

WILLIAM L. COOPER, Esq.
Head of Research and Instructional
  Services
Law Library
William and Mary School of Law
Williamsburg, Virginia

MARY JO GAMBLE
Office Manager
Nicholas Critelli Associates
Des Moines, Iowa

J. LARRY GREEN
Administrator
Blasingame, Burch, Garrard & Bryant
Athens, Georgia

PAMELA K. GREER
Director of Administration
Bottum & Feliton
Los Angeles, California

WESLEY P. HACKETT JR., Esq.
Attorney at Law
East Lansing, Michigan

JANE ANN HARTNETT
President
RHT Bay
Mt.Clemens, Michigan

LESLIE NOWACKI
Application Support Specialist
Murtha, Cullina, Richter and Pinney
Hartford, Connecticut

PATRICK E. PLEISS
Administrator
Herbolsheimer, Lannon, Henson,
  Duncan and Reagan
La Salle, Illinois

JULIE WICK
Administrator
Tricia A. Smith, Esq.
Del Mar, California

MAXINE WILLITS
Administrator
Finley, Alt, Smith, Sharnberg & May
Des Moines, Iowa

FIRST EDITION

Consulting Editor
Austin G. Anderson, Esq.

General Editor
Coleen K. Withgott

Contributors

Cleijo J. Bates
Roger W. Dow
Thomas More Griffin
John G. Iezzi, CPA
Lorraine A. Kulpa

Sheryl L. Lindsell
Frances J. Mahan
Dorothy Mangum
Eunice Miller
Estelle M. Sherry

Herbert S. Schwab, Esq.
Willoughby Ann Walshe
Sandra Yost

Contents

.

Preface

It is with pride and pleasure that Merriam-Webster, Inc., publisher of Merriam-Webster dictionaries and reference books, offers this newly revised edition of what has come to be a standard reference source in the legal-administrative field. *Merriam-Webster's Legal Secretaries Handbook, Second Edition,* is the product of a collaborative effort between selected specialists in the legal field—both lawyers and administrators—and the Merriam-Webster editorial department, who bring to the work the same thorough research and careful editing that have distinguished Merriam-Webster publications for over 150 years.

The present volume is intended to serve as both a thorough introductory guide to the workings of the modern law office and a highly practical day-to-day reference book for secretaries and managers. A glance at either the Table of Contents or the list below should be enough to convince you of the book's practical focus and comprehensive coverage. Users should find here concise, accurate, and practical information about virtually every aspect of law-office administration. The contents of the book are as follows:

- *Chapter 1* provides an overview of the American legal system, including information about the types and sources of law, federal and state court systems, judicial and law-enforcement offices, and criminal and civil court procedures.

- *Chapter 2* describes the roles and functions of law-office personnel, including lawyers, paralegals, legal assistants, and legal secretaries, and discusses the practicalities of obtaining work and carrying out one's duties as a legal secretary in today's work environment. It also contains information about professional ethics, continuing education, and opportunities for professional certification.

- *Chapter 3* covers basic office design, equipment, and supplies. It discusses optimal workstation design, including equipment, lighting, and acoustical considerations, and provides advice on assessing and operating photocopying and other equipment. The last section is an overview of managing office supplies.

- *Chapter 4* is a user-friendly treatment of computer technology as used in today's law office. The chapter covers hardware and software, word processing and database operation, and specialized legal-applications products such as case-management programs.

- *Chapter 5* presents the latest information regarding the quickly evolving field of telecommunications, including wire-based and wireless telephone systems, pagers and data assistants, fax machines, and e-mail. It also reviews the handling of office mail and describes services available from the U.S. Postal Service and private carriers.

- *Chapter 6* offers guidance on coordinating schedules and managing appointments, communicating with and receiving clients, and participating in business meetings and conferences. It also describes how to set up business trips for the lawyer.

- *Chapter 7* presents the standard letter formats and stylings used in law offices today. It offers guidelines on letter writing and reviews the various elements of an effective business letter. In addition to including over 25 sample letters, it includes a detailed chart that lists proper forms of address to use in greeting or corresponding with clients.

- *Chapter 8* expands the coverage of written communications to include the subject of punctuation and style. It offers detailed guidance on the correct use of punctuation, capitalization, plurals, possessives, compounds, abbreviations, and numbers in written work. It also includes a final section on understanding and using legal citations.
- *Chapter 9* introduces the subject of dictation and transcription, including information about selecting and using dictation equipment, handling various types of dictation, preparing for and performing transcription, and recording and preparing meeting minutes.
- *Chapter 10* provides information regarding the preparation and execution of legal documents, including the use of standard legal forms and the signing, recording, and filing of legal instruments.
- *Chapter 11* describes the techniques and procedures that are used to ensure court and other legal deadlines are met, including the use of manual and computer calendaring systems. It introduces the more general subject of law-office records management, including automated and manual systems, and discusses issues of confidentiality and security.
- *Chapter 12* presents the various types of financial records that law offices keep and reviews their basic application and use. It includes information about balance sheets, income statements, cash-flow analysis, payroll and tax forms, and—of particular relevance to law firms—trust accounts. The final section covers the use of computerized accounting systems.
- *Chapter 13* is a description of the various types of legal publications used by law firms and the kinds of information they contain. The chapter includes information about computer-assisted legal research and basic library management for the secretary.

Every paragraph of the previous edition has been subjected to review and reconsideration, and major changes have been made throughout the book in order to make it the most up-to-date and authoritative guide of its kind.

This second edition has benefited from the contributions of several members of the Merriam-Webster staff. Mark A. Stevens, senior editor, read the entire manuscript and offered many valuable comments and criticisms. Linda Picard Wood, associate editor, reviewed portions of the manuscript and provided useful advice, as did Stephen J. Perrault, senior editor, and Amy West, assistant editor. Keyboarding was done by Georgette B. Boucher. The text was proofread by Rebecca R. Bryer, Deanna Chiasson, and Jennifer S. Goss, assistant editors, under the direction of Madeline L. Novak, senior editor. A freelance editor, Robie Grant, prepared the index.

Michael Shally-Jensen

Merriam-Webster's
Legal Secretaries
Handbook

Chapter 1

American Law and the Judicial System

The legal secretary is aware of the existence of law long before entering the law office. The contact has been made in many ways—observing the speed limit, registering to vote, taking out a marriage license, or paying taxes. However, in your position as legal secretary, it will be helpful if you are familiar with the origins of the law and with the agencies and individuals that administer and interpret the law. The documents prepared in your law office will have greater meaning if you can relate client to legal matter and legal matter to court or agency.

Although laws affect much of what we do and how we do it, rarely do we think of what law is. In simplest terms, laws are the rules and principles of conduct that are recognized, applied, and enforced by a court. If there is a single word that may be used to describe the science or philosophy of law, it is *jurisprudence*. Jurisprudence differs from *justice*, the principle or ideal of legal fairness. It is justice that is sought by any party bringing a dispute to a court. Jurisprudence, on the other hand, is a formal analytical science dealing with the principles on which legal rules are based. It is jurisprudence that lawyers and other legal professionals are schooled in.

Classifications of Law

Law may be classified in several ways: by system (common and civil law), by source (constitutional, statutory, and case law), by the parties involved (public and private law), by substance (civil and criminal law), and by function (substantive and adjective law). Each of these classifications is discussed in the sections that follow.

Common- and Civil-Law Systems

The two primary systems of American law are the common-law system and the civil-law system. The common-law system, which developed in England, is the most prevalent system of law in North America. The civil-law system in North America is strongest in Louisiana in the United States and in Quebec in Canada; it is also prevalent in Mexico.

The common-law system is based on precedent. Although the legislative bodies at the federal, state, and provincial levels enact written statutes, and sometimes collect portions of those statutes into "codes," there is no formal, comprehensive code of its laws. Instead, the courts build the law by attempting to follow earlier recorded decisions *(precedents)* in deciding subsequent cases.

The civil-law system may be traced back to the Roman law from which most European law systems originated. It was brought to the Western Hemisphere by the French, Spanish, and Portuguese. The civil-law system as it exists in Europe is the result of Napoleon Bonaparte's efforts: he provided for the drafting of the *Code Civil* or *Code Napoléon*, which restated the earlier principles of Roman law in more modern terms. In the civil-law system, the Code Civil is a general statement of legal principles that is looked to in the interpretation of statutes and cases.

Constitutional Law

A constitution is the basic framework for a legal and governmental system. It defines basic principles of law and delegates authority to various officials and agencies. Constitutions are created by the people acting in their collective capacity as sovereign in the nation or state in which they live.

The United States Constitution is the supreme law of the United States. No other law, statute, or case may impose upon its provisions. The Constitution provides in Article VI, Section 2, that it "shall be the supreme Law of the Land; and the Judges in every State shall be bound thereby, any Thing in the Constitution or Laws of any State to the Contrary notwithstanding."

The U.S. Constitution is divided into three parts. The first part, the original text of the Constitution, divides governmental power among the three branches of government (legislative, executive, and judicial) and between the federal and state governments. Powers not reserved by the U.S. Constitution reside with the states.

The second part of the Constitution is the Bill of Rights, which consists of the first ten amendments. The first nine amendments provide for and protect individual freedoms. The First Amendment provides for freedom of religion, speech, press, assembly, and petition for redress of grievances. Other amendments protect the ability to keep arms, the freedom from unreasonable searches and seizures, and the right to speedy and public jury trials in criminal cases and jury trials in civil cases. These have been among the most widely debated concepts in constitutional law.

The third part of the Constitution—the additional amendments that have been added over the past 200 years—reflects the efforts to keep it current with respect to changing social and political needs. These amendments cover a wide range of subjects. The Thirteenth Amendment abolished slavery in 1865. The Fourteenth Amendment granted the equal protection of the laws and due process of law to all the citizens and residents of the various states. The Fifteenth, Nineteenth, Twenty-fourth, and Twenty-sixth Amendments extended the right to vote. The Eighteenth Amendment prohibited the manufacture and sale of intoxicating beverages, and the Twenty-first Amendment repealed the Eighteenth Amendment.

Article V of the original Constitution defines how amendments to the Constitution may be made:

> The Congress, whenever two thirds of both Houses shall deem it necessary, shall propose Amendments . . . or, on the Application of the Legislatures of two thirds of the several States, shall call a Convention for proposing Amendments, which . . . shall be valid . . . when ratified by the Legislatures of three fourths of the several States, or by Conventions in three fourths thereof. . . .

Thus, two methods are provided for proposing amendments (two thirds of both houses of Congress, or a Constitutional Convention called for by the legislatures of two thirds of the states) and two methods are provided for ratifying the proposed amendments (three fourths of the legislatures or three fourths of the conventions called in each state). By requiring a supermajority (i.e., at least two thirds), the framers made sure that any constitutional changes would have such general acceptance throughout the nation that the possibility of a legal challenge or outright rebellion would be minimized.

States also have constitutions, which are often more detailed than the U.S. Constitution. When a court is interpreting a state constitution, it may find correctly that the state constitution gives people within that state more rights than the same language contained in the U.S. Constitution. Because of the supremacy clause of the U.S. Constitution, however, no state can give its people *fewer* rights than the same language of the U.S. Constitution.

Statutory Law

Statutes are enacted by the legislative branch of government (whether federal or state) to regulate areas within the legislature's jurisdiction, as granted by the Constitution.

The United States Congress (by authority of Article I, Section 8, of the Constitution) has reserved to itself the power to regulate certain activities, including patents, trademarks, copyrights, federal taxation, customs matters, the postal system, admiralty matters, bankruptcy, and diplomatic matters. It has the exclusive right to pass laws affecting these subjects. Congress also has power to pass legislation not specifically reserved to it by the Constitution, such as labor laws, pollution-control laws, and laws in many other areas.

Laws passed by Congress are not effective until they are signed into law by the President or have been repassed over the President's veto by a two-thirds majority of each house of the Congress. These laws are published annually in the *Statutes at Large (Stat.)* and *Public Laws (P.L.)* and are compiled in the *United States Code (U.S.C.)*—all official government publications. Various private publishers publish annotated editions of the United States Code, which have become popular research tools for lawyers working in the law office or at the law library. This Code is organized into 50 titles or general subject areas. When citing (referring) to the United States Code or to one of the commercial annotated sets, the title number appears first, followed by the abbreviation *U.S.C.* and the appropriate section number. For example, 50 U.S.C. § 1511 cites to Title 50 (War and National Defense), Section 1511, of the *United States Code*.

Titles of the United States Code

1. General Provisions	28. Judiciary and Judicial Procedure
2. The Congress	29. Labor
3. The President	30. Mineral Lands and Mining
4. Flag and Seal, Seat of Government and the States	31. Money and Finance
5. Government Organization and Employees	32. National Guard
	33. Navigation and Navigable Waters
6. Surety Bonds (repealed and most provisions covered under title 31)	34. Navy (eliminated by the enactment of Title 10)
7. Agriculture	35. Patents
8. Aliens and Nationality	36. Patriotic Societies and Observances
9. Arbitration	37. Pay and Allowances of the Uniformed Services
10. Armed Forces	
11. Bankruptcy	38. Veterans' Benefits
12. Banks and Banking	39. Postal Service
13. Census	40. Public Buildings, Property, and Works
14. Coast Guard	
15. Commerce and Trade	41. Public Contracts
16. Conservation	42. The Public Health and Welfare
17. Copyrights	43. Public Lands
18. Crimes and Criminal Procedure	44. Public Printing and Documents
19. Customs Duties	45. Railroads
20. Education	46. Shipping
21. Food and Drugs	47. Telegraphs, Telephones, and Radiotelegraphs
22. Foreign Relations and Intercourse	
23. Highways	48. Territories and Insular Possessions
24. Hospitals and Asylums	
25. Indians	49. Transportation
26. Internal Revenue Code	50. War and National Defense (with Appendix)
27. Intoxicating Liquors	

Each year the legislature in each state passes many laws, which are then approved by the governor or passed over the governor's veto. The exact titles of the session laws—that is, the collections of statutes passed in each session of the legislature—vary, as do the titles given to the compilations of laws. Statutory compilations, which are collections of all the laws in force in a particular state, are ordinarily known as *codes, revisions,* or *compilations.* In Michigan, for example, they are known as *Michigan Compiled Laws;* in Minnesota they are called *Minnesota Statutes Annotated;* in North Dakota they are called the *North Dakota Century Code.* Like the United States Code, these compilations are published in annotated editions by private law-book publishers.

Annotated statutes will include the text of each statute along with legislative history, prior laws on the subject, references to cases construing the statute, references to law-review articles and other legal-research sources, and other pertinent information about the statute. Commercial statute compilations are kept up to date by cumulative annual supplements (called "Pocket Parts," because they are filed in a pocket in the back cover of the book) and interim pamphlets.

Relationship of constitutions, statutes, and the courts   The so-called federal-supremacy doctrine declares any federal law or constitutional provision to be dominant when a state and a federal interest are at odds. Federal laws must comply only with the federal Constitution, but the laws of any state must comply with provisions of both the state constitution and the federal Constitution. In a clash between a federal and a state law, the federal law prevails.

When a state legislature has spoken clearly on a subject through the passage of a law signed by the governor, the courts ordinarily will not overrule the legislature. However, if a state legislature were to pass a law in violation of the state constitution—for example, a law requiring that all textbooks be submitted to a review board—the appellate court in the state could declare the law unconstitutional.

Except in the matter of constitutionality of laws or statutes, the legislative body has the last word. Courts will, however, interpret statutes and supply legal principles when no rule exists. Once the court decides what the legislature intended, the court's ruling has as much validity and importance as the statute itself, and it becomes part of the case law on the subject.

Case Law

Case law or *common law* is the law made by courts. It is known as case law because it derives from judicial decisions in legal cases rather than from written statutes. This means that as a court decides and reports its decision concerning a particular suit, this reported case becomes part of the body of law and is consulted in later cases involving similar problems.

Prior to the development of constitutional and statutory law, controversies were decided on the basis of established customs. If there were no established customs, judges decided a case on the basis of what they considered to be right and wrong. As these decisions began to be recorded, judges were directed to look for guidance to the decision in a prior case that had similar facts. This is known as the *doctrine of precedents*, or *stare decisis*—literally, "to stand by (previous) decisions." The doctrine of precedents is important because it provides for consistency in the application of common law and offers some assurance to a person seeking relief in the courts as to the rules governing the likely outcome of the case.

Case law consists of reported decisions of both federal and state courts. These decisions may be divided into three primary categories: (1) interpretation of the U.S. Constitution and the various state constitutions, (2) interpretation of federal and state statutes, and (3) decisions based on British and American precedents involving matters in which no constitution or statutory enactment seems to apply.

Equity law   A review of the common law is not complete without examining *equity law*. Equity law and its origins in English common law can be summarized as follows:

> Since legal rules cannot be formulated to deal adequately with every possible contingency, applying them mechanically can sometimes result in injustice. To remedy such injustices, the law of equity was developed. The principle of equity was as old as the English common law, but it was hardly needed until the 14th century, since the law was still relatively fluid and informal. As the common law became firmly established, however, its strict rules of proof began to cause hardship. Power to grant relief in situations involving potential injustices lay with the king and the lord chancellor. Eventually the chancellor's jurisdiction developed into the Court of Chancery, whose function was to administer equity. The chancellor

decided each case on its merits and had the right to grant or refuse relief without giving reasons, but common grounds for relief, such as fraud and breach of confidence, came to be recognized. And because the defendant could file an answer, a system of written pleadings developed.

Although a few states in the United States still have separate courts of equity and courts of law, most jurisdictions have merged the procedures of law and equity courts. But, although the procedures were merged, the intention was to keep the remedies separate. While the historical justifications for equity law are declining, equity techniques continue to provide unusual and personal remedies for legal disputes of a civil nature. Two of the most familiar equity decrees are the *injunction* and *specific performance*. An injunction restrains a party from doing something that would cause irreparable harm if not enjoined or temporarily halted. For example, an injunction may order a manufacturer to stop dumping certain chemicals into a river. Specific performance requires the performance of a duty agreed on in a contract or other agreement.

Public and Private Law

Another classification of laws evolving from both constitutional and statutory sources is based on the scope of the laws, that is, on the parties to whom they apply. This classification includes public and private law.

Private law governs the relationship between private citizens. Disputes may involve property, contracts, negligence, wills, and any number of other matters. Occasionally, as in marriage and divorce, the state may be involved indirectly, but, as it is not itself a litigant, the matter remains one of private law.

Public law is a branch of law concerned with regulating the relations of individuals among themselves and with the government as well as the organization and conduct of government itself. Public-law disputes involve the state or its agencies in a direct manner. Usually the state is a litigant; it is often the plaintiff, the party bringing the suit to court. Examples of public law are municipal law, township law, criminal law, admiralty law, securities law, social security law, and aviation law.

When individual laws are referred to, however, there is a different kind of distinction between public and private laws. Specifically, a private law is a law that affects only selected individuals or localities, while a public law affects the welfare of the whole governed unit. A private law provides a kind of exception to the public rule.

Administrative law   Administrative law has become a major part of public law. Administrative law comprises the rules and regulations framed and enforced by an administrative agency created by Congress or a state legislature to carry out a specific statute. Administrative bodies, while primarily executive in nature, may also have powers to exercise legislative or judicial authority. For example, the Federal Aviation Administration not only issues regulations for air transportation but also adjudicates some disputes between airlines and their customers. Among the areas of concern covered by federal administrative agencies are taxation and revenue collections, civil rights, the environment, banks and banking, labor relations, veterans, railroads, and securities. Some of the federal administrative agencies with which law firms come into contact are the Commodity Futures Trading Commission, the Consumer Product Safety Commission, the Environmental Protection Agency, the Federal Deposit Insurance Corporation, the National Labor Relations Board, the Occupational Safety and Health Administration, the Internal Revenue Service, and the Federal Trade Commission.

The best single source of information in the field of federal administrative procedures is the *United States Government Manual*. The official handbook of the federal government, this manual provides comprehensive information on the agencies of the legislative, judicial, and executive branches of government as well as quasi-official agencies; international organizations in which the United States participates; and boards, committees, and commissions. The manual is published annually by the Office of the Federal Register, and is available from the Superintendent of Documents, P.O. Box 371954, Pittsburgh, PA 15250-7954.

State and local governments also have administrative agencies. They may be a part of an executive department of the state government or they may be independent entities. These agencies tend to function in areas not preempted by federal agencies, but they may also be found in fields subject to both federal and state regulation. State administrative agencies often have jurisdiction over these areas: unemployment and workers' compensation, taxation, education, motor vehicles, and health and safety. States generally publish their own directories similar to the *United States Government Manual,* and it is helpful to have a copy available in the office. Examples of local administrative agencies include zoning boards and sewer commissions.

Administrative law is becoming an important legal specialty. As government agencies proliferate and their rules and regulations increase (even during periods of streamlining or downsizing), it is a rare business client who is not affected by one or more agencies. It is important for the law office to keep abreast of developments taking place in administrative law.

Civil and Criminal Law

Cases that come before a court may generally be divided into two categories: *civil* and *criminal*. *Civil law* is concerned with civil or private rights and remedies, as contrasted with criminal laws. Civil law is in essence the law of private rights. Civil law deals with conflicts of interest between individuals or groups at least one of whom has a complaint against another. The complaint may be caused by the failure of a party to carry out an agreement or by a different kind of injury, called a tort, that does not involve a contractual relationship. When a civil case is brought, a private party seeks resolution of a personal rather than a public dispute. The civil law has several subcategories, including real estate, domestic relations, partnership, taxes, contracts, wills and trusts, probate, employment, personal injury, water, oil and gas, schools, local government, securities, commerce, banking, and labor.

Criminal law declares what conduct is criminal and prescribes the punishment to be imposed for it. A criminal action is always brought in the name of the federal government ("The United States of America"), the state ("The People of the State of . . ."; "The State of . . ."), or a political subdivision, because the case is based on the alleged violation of the rights of *all* the people. The remedy sought in a criminal case is intended to punish the offender. The major categories of crimes are murder and manslaughter, assault and battery, rape, larceny, robbery, burglary, embezzlement, and false pretenses.

Substantive and Adjective Law

Substantive law consists of the principal rules that a court will apply in considering the rights and obligations set forth in federal and state statutes, whereas *adjective* or *procedural* law states the procedural rules by which a person can secure his or her substantive rights. Thus, adjective law consists of the rules of procedure or practice according to which the substantive law is administered. Adjective law deals with *pleadings*, which are papers that pass between the parties; *practice*, which refers to the guides to the conduct of litigation; and *evidence*, or the distillation of traditional doctrine governing the admissibility of evidence to achieve fairness while avoiding unnecessary expense or delay.

Although adjective law does not state the law, it outlines the procedures that must be followed in applying the substantive law. Adjective law enables the attorney to decide whether a case should go to federal or state court. Adjective law will tell the attorney when a lawsuit must be started, what pleadings are required of all parties, and what kind of evidence can be presented at trial. It can be as important as the substantive law in determining the outcome of a case. A knowledge of adjective law is generally more useful to the legal secretary than a knowledge of substantive law. It is necessary that the secretary be aware of the procedures and pleadings involved in a civil case to ensure that deadlines are met and papers are properly served and filed.

The American Judicial System

Article III, Section 1, of the U.S. Constitution creates the federal judicial system. It says: "The judicial Power of the United States, shall be vested in one supreme Court, and in such inferior Courts as the Congress may from time to time ordain and establish." Sections 2 and 3 spell out the extent of the judicial power afforded the Supreme Court and the subordinate federal courts. In turn, the constitutions of the various states have created state judicial systems, many of them similar to the federal judicial system. The complexity of a state judicial system is normally in direct proportion to the population of the governmental unit. The judiciaries of many states with small populations are much less complex than the judiciaries of some large cities. Furthermore, some of the municipal judicial systems are nearly as autonomous within the state system as the state system is within the federal system.

The Courts

The term *court* has several meanings. One meaning encompasses all the persons who are assembled for the administration of justice; these include the judge or judges, clerk, marshal, bailiff, court reporter or public stenographer, jurors, and attorneys. Court may also refer to the hall, chamber, or place where a judicial proceeding is being held. The courthouse includes the offices occupied by many of the persons associated with the administration of justice. And frequently the judge or judges themselves are referred to as "the Court."

The two principal functions of courts are settling controversies between parties and deciding the rules of law applicable in a particular case. In general, the judicial process as carried out by the courts consists of interpreting the laws and applying them justly to all cases arising in litigation. Most courts do not give advisory opinions. Exceptions exist, however, where the constitutions of some states permit the supreme courts of those states to render advisory opinions to the legislature or governor concerning the constitutionality of a statute.

Jurisdiction

Jurisdiction may be defined as the authority of a court to hear a controversy or dispute. Affirmative answers to the following questions will determine that a court has jurisdiction over a particular case:

1. Has the court been vested by law with authority to decide this kind of case?
2. Does the court have authority over the parties in the case?
3. Has adequate notice been given to the parties, so that the court can make a valid judgment affecting them?
4. Has the court acquired jurisdiction over any property involved in the case?

Another way of testing the jurisdiction of the court over a matter is to determine whether it has *in personam* jurisdiction over the litigants (who may live in different geographical areas) or *in rem* jurisdiction over the subject matter (usually physical property such as real estate) in a controversy.

Original and appellate jurisdiction   Jurisdiction is either original or appellate. A court of *original jurisdiction* has the authority to receive the case when begun, to try the case, and to render a decision based on the law and facts presented. *Appellate jurisdiction,* which is set by statute or constitution, is the authority to review, overrule, or revise the action of a lower court.

The American judicial system, at both the state and federal level, is pyramidal and hierarchical. The courts at the top of the pyramid are supreme courts. Supreme courts are normally appellate courts, although they may have original jurisdiction in some matters. Below the supreme appellate courts are usually intermediate appellate courts. These courts generally hear most initial appeals and have appellate jurisdiction and supervisory control over the trial courts except as laws provide otherwise, but they are also courts of original jurisdiction in certain areas prescribed by constitution or statute. Trial courts are courts of either general or limited jurisdiction whose decisions are subject to review and correction by appellate courts.

Concurrent and exclusive jurisdiction   Jurisdiction is exclusive when only one court is empowered by law to hear the case in question. It is concurrent when the plaintiff has a choice of courts in which to initiate litigation.

Diversity jurisdiction   The federal courts have constitutional authority to try cases under diversity jurisdiction, which occurs when the litigants are residents of different states. Congress has added other stipulations, however—such as a minimum economic threshold involved in the dispute—before diversity cases may be decided in federal trial courts.

Equity   Most courts of general jurisdiction serve as both courts of common law and courts of equity. When these courts maintain separate dockets (agendas) for law and equity cases, they will follow different procedures for each docket. When these courts are allowed to combine law and equity cases, they may award both money damages (financial compensation) and equitable relief (remedial measures). Some states continue to maintain completely separate courts of equity known as *chancery courts,* or courts with chancery divisions that have equity jurisdiction. The judges in these courts of equity are called *chancellors,* and the judgments they render are usually called *decrees.*

Courts of limited jurisdiction   Some trial courts are courts of limited jurisdiction. Courts of limited jurisdiction are ordinarily created by statute, and their jurisdiction is limited to those matters set forth in the statute. Courts of limited jurisdiction include *district courts, county courts, municipal courts, justice courts, county district courts, juvenile courts,* or *probate courts.* Courts of limited jurisdiction may have exclusive jurisdiction where the amount in controversy does not exceed a fixed amount. They may also have jurisdiction over minor criminal matters, such as misdemeanors or ordinance violations. A record may be kept in courts of limited jurisdiction. However, in small-claims divisions of district courts and in justice-of-the-peace courts, municipal courts, or magistrate's courts, it may be that no verbatim record of the proceedings will be kept.

The Federal Court System

The federal courts form a part of the federal judicial system, the jurisdiction of which is prescribed by Article III of the Constitution. The federal court system consists of a large number of district courts that are courts of general jurisdiction, 13 courts of appeals, a Supreme Court, and a number of specialized courts.

The Supreme Court of the United States   The Supreme Court of the United States was created in accordance with Article III, Section 1, of the U.S. Constitution and was organized on February 2, 1790. The Supreme Court is made up of the Chief Justice of the United States and a number of associate justices set by statute. Currently there are eight associate justices. The President has the power to nominate the justices, and appointments are made with the advice and consent of the Senate. The Supreme Court's term runs from the first Monday in October of each year until business is completed, usually about the end of June. The nine justices sit *en banc* (in full court). Six justices constitute a quorum (minimum number required to constitute a lawful bench), but certain cases can be acted upon by a single justice.

Article III, Section 2, of the Constitution defines the original and exclusive jurisdiction of the Supreme Court as (1) all controversies between states, and (2) all actions or proceedings against ambassadors or other public ministers of foreign states or their domestic servants, not inconsistent with the law of nations. The Court has original but *not* exclusive jurisdiction over (1) all actions or proceedings brought by ambassadors or other public ministers of foreign states or to which consuls or vice consuls of foreign states are parties, (2) all controversies between the United States and a state, and (3) all actions or proceedings by a state against the citizens of another state or against aliens.

The Court only occasionally hears cases in original jurisdiction, however; its chief function is as an appellate court. The Supreme Court may review cases from the U.S. courts of appeals either by writ of certiorari (a written mandate to call up the records of a subordinate court) granted to petitioners that are party to any civil or criminal case, or by appeal of a party relying on a state statute that has been held by the court of appeals to be unconstitutional or illegal. A majority of Supreme Court cases come on petition for certiorari.

The Supreme Court also has appellate jurisdiction over the final judgment of the highest court of a state in which a decision on a case may be rendered if (1) there is a question as to the validity of a treaty or statute of the United States and the state court has decided against its validity, or (2) the state court rendered a decision approving a state statute that is questioned as being unconstitutional or illegal. More than 40 percent of the Supreme Court's cases come from state supreme courts.

The Supreme Court normally reviews fewer than 200 cases each year. By contrast, it refuses to review about 2,000 cases each year: the majority of its decisions consist of denials of certiorari to review decisions of courts of appeals or state supreme courts.

The Supreme Court also possesses statutory power to prescribe rules of procedure to be followed in the lower federal courts. Studies are carried out and rules recommended by the Judicial Conference of the United States, the main policy-making group for the federal judiciary. The Supreme Court has set rules of procedure governing such matters as bankruptcy proceedings, copyright cases, appellate proceedings, civil law, and criminal law. These rules of procedure for the federal courts are published with the decisions of the Supreme Court in the *United States Reports* (abbreviated *U.S.*) and also with the statutes of Congress in the *United States Code*.

United States Courts of Appeals   The courts of appeals were created in 1891, to relieve the Supreme Court of the task of considering all appeals for cases originally decided by the federal trial courts. By statute , they are empowered to review all final decisions and certain provisional decisions of federal district courts, although there are exceptions where direct review by the Supreme Court is provided for. The courts of appeals are also empowered to review and enforce orders of many federal administrative bodies, such as the National Labor Relations Board and the Federal Trade Commission, and also to review appeals from the Tax Court of the United States. Decisions of the courts of appeals are final, except as to discretionary review by or appeal to the Supreme Court. Each of the 50 states is assigned to one of 11 judicial circuits (see Fig. 1.1). There is an additional circuit for the District of Columbia, and another for the Federal Circuit. Each court of appeals usually hears cases in divisions consisting of a panel of three judges; however, it may sit *en banc* with all judges present. The number of judges assigned to each court of appeals is fixed by statute. Individual judges make decisions for the court only in procedural matters.

United States District Courts   The district courts are federal trial courts with general federal jurisdiction. There is at least one district court in each state, while some larger states have as many as four. There are in all 92 federal district courts in the 50 states plus one in the District of Columbia and one in

Fig. 1.1   Circuits of the United States Courts of Appeals

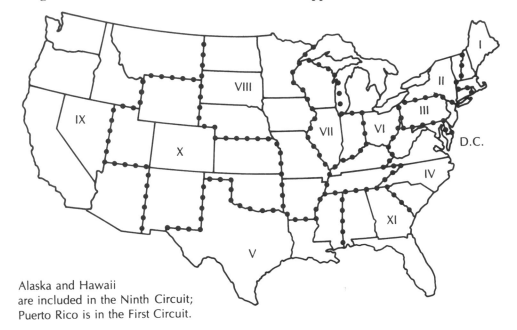

Alaska and Hawaii
are included in the Ninth Circuit;
Puerto Rico is in the First Circuit.

Puerto Rico. The number of federal district court judges is fixed by statute. Normally only one judge hears a case, but in certain cases a three-judge panel is required.

Each district court is served by a clerk, a U.S. attorney, a U.S. marshal, and one or more U.S. magistrates, bankruptcy judges, probation officers, and court reporters. Magistrates are federal judicial officers who serve under the general supervision of the federal district, but who also have some responsibilities as defined in the Federal Magistrate Act of 1979. These responsibilities include the power to conduct some trials, to enter sentences for misdemeanors or infractions, to conduct hearings (including evidentiary hearings), and to hear and determine pretrial matters pending before the court.

The jurisdiction of the federal district courts is set forth in the *United States Code*. These courts possess only original jurisdiction. Among the cases tried are those involving crimes against the United States, cases involving diversity of citizenship (cases in which a citizen of one state brings a suit against a citizen of another state), admiralty and maritime cases, cases involving review and enforcement of orders of most federal administrative agencies, and civil cases arising under federal statutes, treaties, or the Constitution if the value in controversy is in excess of $50,000. When the federal district court exercises diversity jurisdiction, it is not necessary for a federal question to be involved. In the diversity cases, the district court applies the law of the state in which the case arose. Bankruptcy and parole cases form a large part of their work in addition to the regular civil and criminal cases.

In each district court, the bankruptcy judges constitute a unit of the court known as the bankruptcy court for that district. Each bankruptcy court may have its own clerk. The bankruptcy court has exclusive jurisdiction to hear all matters arising under the bankruptcy code and any matters concerning the administration of a bankruptcy estate. Decisions of a bankruptcy court may be reviewed first by the district court, then by a federal court of appeals.

Special U.S. Courts   In addition to the courts discussed above, Congress has created special courts from time to time to deal with particular kinds of cases. Appeals from decisions of these courts may ultimately be reviewed by the Supreme Court. Among those courts are two created for the District of Columbia—the Superior Court and the District of Columbia Court of Appeals. Other courts include the U.S. Court of Appeals for the Armed Forces, which is concerned exclusively with criminal law, and the Territorial Courts. The three major special courts—the U.S. Court of Federal Claims, the Court of International Trade, and the U.S. Tax Court—are described below. The former U.S. Court of Customs and Patent Appeals has been superseded by the Court of Appeals for the Federal Circuit. (See Fig. 1.2.)

U.S. Court of Federal Claims   The U.S. Court of Federal Claims was originally established in 1855. It has original jurisdiction to render judgment on claims against the United States. Examples are claims for compensation for the taking of property, claims arising under construction and supply contracts, claims by civilian and military personnel for back pay and retirement pay, and claims for the refund of federal income and excise taxes. The demonstrated purpose of the court was to relieve Congress of pressure to pass private bills to resolve claims. If the monetary amount of damages is small, claims may be settled by the federal executive departments involved; but large claims are filed either in

Fig. 1.2   Federal Court System

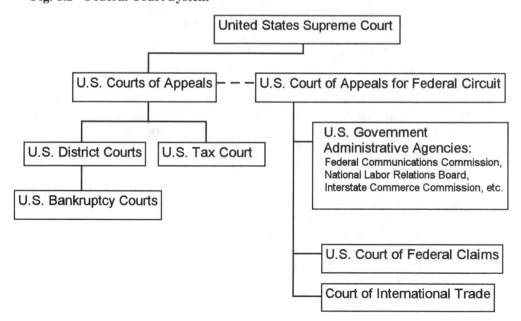

the district courts or in the Court of Federal Claims, which have concurrent jurisdiction. Judgments of the court are final and conclusive, subject to review by the Court of Appeals for the Federal Circuit.

Court of International Trade   The Court of International Trade was created in 1926 as the U.S. Customs Court. Through subsequent legislation it was integrated into the federal court system and became a court of record. This court deals with questions of external revenue, while the U.S. Tax Court deals with questions of internal revenue. The Court of International Trade has exclusive jurisdiction of civil actions under the tariff laws, such as controversies over the appraised value of imported merchandise . The court has a chief judge and eight judges, not more than five of whom can belong to the same political party. The Chief Justice of the United States may temporarily designate and assign any of its judges as a federal-circuit or district-court judge. Ordinarily cases are tried before a single judge, although a three-judge panel may be used. Appeals are taken to the Court of Appeals for the Federal Circuit. The principal offices of the court are in New York City, but its nine judges are divided among three divisions that can conduct trials in ports other than New York.

U.S. Tax Court   The U.S. Tax Court is a court of record under Article I of the Constitution, and consists of 19 members. The Tax Court tries and decides controversies involving deficiencies or overpayment in income, estate, gift, and personal-holding-company surtaxes in cases where deficiencies have been determined by the Commissioner of Internal Revenue. It hears taxpayers' claims against the Internal Revenue Service after the machinery of administrative adjudication within the Treasury Department has been exhausted. Other than in small tax cases, all decisions are subject to review by the federal courts of appeals and ultimately by the Supreme Court. The Tax Court, which is located in Washington, D.C., has 19 divisions, one for each of its judges. Trials are public and are conducted by single judges in locations throughout the country.

State Court Systems

The judicial power of the states is qualified by the U.S. Constitution, which states: "Full Faith and Credit shall be given in each State to the public Acts, Records, and judicial Proceedings of every other State." It is further qualified by the Fourteenth Amendment, which states: "No State shall make or enforce any law which shall abridge the privileges or immunities of citizens of the United States; nor shall any State deprive any person of life, liberty, or property, without due process of law; nor deny to any person within its jurisdiction the equal protection of the laws."

Federal courts have exclusive jurisdiction in those areas provided by the Constitution—conflicts between states, conflicts between a state and the United States, petitions for federal regulatory agencies to enforce a decision, and prosecution of national criminal laws—and by federal statutes; state courts cannot invade this jurisdiction. State courts, in turn, usually have exclusive jurisdiction over matters not held by the federal courts. Two areas that have remained exclusive to the states are probate and domestic relations. However, state courts may hold concurrent jurisdiction with federal courts in many other areas; there are many situations where claims may be litigated in either a federal or state court. If there is no overriding federal provision for cases involving diversity jurisdiction, federal and state courts are equally available. It is in the state courts, however, that most of the litigational problems that arise in the lives of most U.S. citizens are resolved. Conflicts resolved by state courts include those involving domestic relations, common crimes and misdemeanors, business relationships, morals offenses, personal injury and property damage, real estate, and aspects of business practice such as sales and secured transactions.

The states frequently experiment with restructuring their court systems, although the basic structure of a supreme court, an intermediate appellate court, and a trial court of general jurisdiction is usually maintained. (See Fig. 1.3.)

State supreme courts The highest court in a state is usually called the Supreme Court, although in some states it is called the Court of Appeals (New York and Maryland), the Supreme Court of Appeals (West Virginia), or the Supreme Judicial Court (Maine and Massachusetts).

The supreme court in most states is given supervisory control over and appellate jurisdiction from all other courts in the state judicial system, limited only by the constitution and statutes. The supreme appellate court draws its authority from the state constitution. Appeals to the supreme court from lower state courts may be either *of right* or *on leave* (permission) granted by the court. The court rules and/or statutes will set forth the grounds on which either may be accomplished. In a few states that do not have an intermediate appellate court, appeals are made directly to the supreme appellate court. States with an intermediate appellate court usually require that an appeal from a court of

Fig. 1.3 State Court Systems

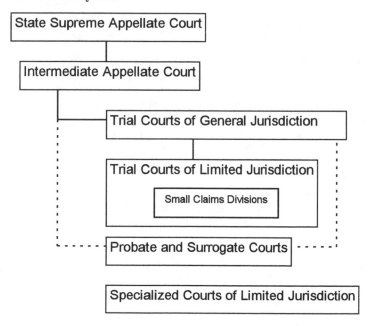

original jurisdiction go to the intermediate court, but in very limited situations they may provide for direct appeal to the supreme appellate court. In states with an intermediate appellate court, the supreme court may have complete control over those cases that it is willing to hear. For example, in Illinois direct appeal to the state supreme court is possible in cases in which a circuit court imposes the death penalty. Ordinarily the state supreme court has very few areas of original jurisdiction.

Intermediate appellate courts   Most states have intermediate courts of appeal. In most cases the intermediate appellate court was created to lessen the caseload of the supreme appellate court. Intermediate appellate courts ordinarily have initial appellate jurisdiction over the final judgments of a state's trial court of general jurisdiction. Other courts may, by leave to appeal, reach the intermediate appellate court. The jurisdiction of the intermediate court of appeal may be established by statute, by rule of the supreme appellate court, or both. Intermediate courts of appeal may exercise original jurisdiction when it is required for the complete determination of a case on review and may issue certain writs when permitted by statute or court rule.

Trial courts of general jurisdiction   Below the supreme and intermediate appellate courts in the state judicial hierarchy is the trial court of general jurisdiction. It may be called the *circuit court,* the *superior court,* the *district court,* the *court of common pleas,* or, in New York, the *supreme court.*
    This court ordinarily has the authority to try both civil and criminal cases except where the constitution or a statute has limited that jurisdiction; it is also normally empowered to try cases arising under both equity and common law. The circuit court usually has appellate jurisdiction and supervisory control over subordinate courts except as provided by law, and it ordinarily possesses the power to issue extraordinary writs. A basic rule to remember is that the circuit court has original jurisdiction in any matter unless that jurisdiction has been specifically placed in some other court by the state constitution or by statute.
    Circuit courts are geographically organized, with each circuit serving one or more counties. Each circuit may have one or more judges assigned to it, although each case is usually heard by a single judge.
    State courts of general jurisdiction are courts of record. This means that their acts, decisions, and proceedings are documented in a written record that is maintained by the clerk of the court. Records of court decisions and the processes that led to those decisions are important. Without such records it is difficult to challenge a decision successfully in a higher court.

Trial courts of limited jurisdiction   Whether called *municipal courts* or *district courts* or by some other name, most states have trial courts of limited jurisdiction. The jurisdiction of these courts may vary from matters of the type usually handled by the circuit court to lesser matters such as traffic offenses, minor criminal matters, ordinance violations, and probable-cause hearings. These courts may also be given exclusive jurisdiction over common-law claims up to a determined monetary limit, such as $10,000 or $25,000. The jurisdiction of these courts will ordinarily determine whether it is a court of record, and that in turn determines whether and to what court an appeal may be taken. The territorial authority of these courts is ordinarily confined to the city or county in which the court is located. /

These courts may also have a *small-claims division*. Cases heard in the small-claims division are limited as to the amount that the court may award as damages. Lawyers are usually prohibited from representing litigants in small-claims cases, and no juries and no appeals are permitted.

Specialized courts of limited jurisdiction Specialized courts of limited jurisdiction include *probate* or *surrogate courts, family courts, traffic courts,* and in some instances, subordinate courts variously designated as *justice courts, justice-of-the-peace courts, magistrate's courts,* and *police courts.*

Many states have separate *probate* or *surrogate courts.* Probate courts are courts of limited jurisdiction. Their jurisdiction is limited in subject matter but not by geographical or monetary restrictions. In some states probate courts may be organized into districts, with a single court serving more than one county. The jurisdiction of the probate court is ordinarily limited to the settlement of estates, wills, and guardianship of minors and legally incompetent persons. In some states the probate courts also have jurisdiction over juvenile delinquents, neglected children, dependents, and the adoption of children, and other matters such as name changes. Appeals from probate court may be taken to the intermediate appellate court or to the trial court of general jurisdiction.

Several states have either *juvenile* or *family-law courts.* Juvenile courts standing alone will ordinarily have exclusive original jurisdiction over all neglected, dependent, or delinquent children under a certain age. Family-law courts will have exclusive jurisdiction over divorce, separation, annulment, support actions, suits involving temporary custody of children, and adoption. In some cases, the functions of the juvenile and family-law courts are combined and the court has original jurisdiction over all of these matters.

Traffic courts are courts of limited jurisdiction geographically, monetarily, and with respect to the punishment that may be meted out. Jurisdiction is ordinarily limited to misdemeanors and traffic violations. While the traffic court is not a court of record, the right to appeal depends on the statute creating the court.

A few states have retained the *police court.* Jurisdiction is limited to misdemeanor offenses and to the conduct of preliminary examinations determining whether there is sufficient evidence to bind the case over to the court with jurisdiction for further proceeding. In some states the police court has jurisdiction to try civil cases within geographical and monetary limits.

Native American Tribal Courts

Outside the structure of the federal and state courts are the Native American *tribal courts.* These courts function under their own enabling structures, statutes, and court rules, and are limited only by the most fundamental concepts of U.S. Constitutional law.

In any divorce case in a state court, if any of the children of the marriage are Native American, the state court must surrender jurisdiction regarding issues of custody and visitation to a tribal court for decision. Similarly, a state court cannot exercise jurisdiction over a Native American child for purposes of adoption or other issues determinative of the child's familial status.

Tribal courts also adjudicate matters arising on or concerning tribal lands, such as hunting and fishing rights, oil and gas rights, development rights, and rights of ownership and rental. Some of these rights may be granted by treaties with the federal government. Contracts with Native American tribes may require that disputes or enforcement be brought before tribal courts. In recent years Native American tribes have become increasingly engaged in gambling enterprises as a way of generating needed revenues for their communities, and cases involving gambling debts owed by non-Native Americans may be adjudicated in tribal courts. Similarly, criminal cases arising from violation of tribal laws may be adjudicated in tribal courts.

Issues involving Native American law and court jurisdiction may be significant in such states as Wisconsin, Michigan, Florida, New York, and the New England and Western States. The legal secretary working for a lawyer practicing in any of these areas needs to be aware of the potential substantive and procedural claims of Native American law and tribal courts.

Court and Law-Enforcement Personnel

Officers of the Court

The officers of the court are persons assembled at the court to administer justice. They include the judge, who is the principal officer of the court, lawyers, the clerk of the court, the sheriff, the marshal, the bailiff, and possibly a constable or court officer.

Judges   The judge may be elected or appointed. Judges in the federal judiciary are appointed for life by the President with the advice and consent of the Senate. Candidates for the federal judiciary are cleared through the office of the Deputy U.S. Attorney General, who receives reports of each candidate from the F.B.I. and the American Bar Association. The Senate Judiciary Committee then conducts hearings on the nomination and makes a recommendation to the full Senate.

There are five methods of selecting judges in the states. The leading method is selection by partisan election, often following nomination at party primaries or conventions. Slightly less common is the nonpartisan election. The remaining states use either elections by the legislature, gubernatorial appointments, or the Missouri Plan. The Missouri Plan, so called because of its place of origin, was designed to overcome the weaknesses of the elective system. It permits the governor to select a judge from a list of nominees recommended by a special commission but also requires the judge to be voted on in a public referendum after serving a period of time.

At trials and hearings the judge presides and rules on issues occurring during the trial. In jury cases, the judge presides over the selection of the jury and instructs the jury concerning the law of the case. The judge may also be called upon to rule on motions made before the start of the trial.

From the time the oath of office is taken, judges at all levels are bound to conduct themselves in an ethical manner and to adhere to a code of judicial conduct. An official Code of Judicial Conduct was adopted by the American

Bar Association in 1972, and has been amended since. Its seven basic canons are as follows:

Canon 1   A judge should uphold the integrity and independence of the judiciary.

Canon 2   A judge should avoid impropriety and the appearance of impropriety in all activities.

Canon 3   A judge should perform the duties of office impartially and diligently.

Canon 4   A judge may engage in activities to improve the law, the legal system, and the administration of justice.

Canon 5   A judge should regulate extra-judicial activities to minimize the risk of conflict with judicial duties.

Canon 6   A judge should regularly file reports of compensation received for quasi-judicial and extra-judicial activities and of monetary contributions.

Canon 7   A judge or a candidate for judicial office should refrain from political activity inappropriate to judicial office.

State laws determine whether the court officers are referred to as judges or justices. In most states, as in the federal judiciary, the term *justice* is reserved for the members of the supreme appellate court. It is important for the legal secretary to know the correct terminology when preparing court orders, judgments, and decrees for the court's approval.

Administration of the courts   The Chief Justice of the United States is the chief administrative officer of the federal judiciary. As the title implies, that he or she is not merely the Chief Justice of the Supreme Court, but the Chief Justice of the entire United States. Each federal court of appeals and district court has a chief judge. With the assistance of a circuit executive, the chief judge of a circuit administers most of the work of the court of appeals. The chief judge of a federal district court usually takes responsibility for most of the administration of that court. However, chief judges do not have authority over the decisions of cases made by their fellow judges. In deciding cases, the authority of chief judges is the same as that of any other judge.

Chief justices of the state supreme appellate courts, depending upon the language of the state constitution, may or may not be the chief judicial officers in the state. As chief justices, however, they do have influence over the administration of the entire court system through the supreme appellate court's superintending or rule-making power. They are also responsible for the administration of the appellate courts.

Chief judges of intermediate appellate courts are responsible for the administration of those courts according to the constitution, statute, or court rule describing their responsibilities. Within the power given it, each court establishes rules to assist in the administration of the court.

Attorneys   Attorneys are also officers of the court. They are responsible for the preparation, management, and trial of their clients' cases. Like judges, they are held to a code of professional conduct. The Model Rules of Professional Conduct, adopted by the American Bar Association in 1983, seek to guide the attorney in the conduct of his or her various roles in relation to clients, the court, the public, and society in general.

If a lawyer is found guilty of violating these ethical standards, he or she is subject to discipline, including reprimands, fines, suspension, and even disbarment. For this reason, the legal secretary should assist the lawyer in adhering to these rules.

Rule 5.3 governs the lawyer's responsibilities regarding nonlawyer assistants, and provides:

> With respect to a nonlawyer employed or retained by or associated with a lawyer:
> (a) a partner in a law firm shall make reasonable efforts to ensure that the firm has in effect measures giving reasonable assurance that the person's conduct is compatible with the professional obligations of the lawyer;
> (b) a lawyer having direct supervisory authority over the nonlawyer shall make reasonable efforts to ensure that the person's conduct is compatible with the professional obligations of the lawyer; and
> (c) a lawyer shall be responsible for conduct of such a person that would be a violation of the Rules of Professional Conduct if engaged in by a lawyer if:
> (1) the lawyer orders or, with the knowledge of the specific conduct, ratifies the conduct involved; or
> (2) the lawyer is a partner in the law firm in which the person is employed, or has direct supervisory authority over the person, and knows of the conduct at a time when its consequences can be avoided or mitigated but fails to take reasonable remedial action.

The employee's obligations under the Rules of Professional Conduct extend beyond the term of the employee's employment with the lawyer or the law firm. In order to assist the lawyer and the legal secretary in solving potential problems of legal ethics, the Center for Professional Responsibility of the American Bar Association has published an *Annotated Model Rules of Professional Conduct*.

Other court personnel   Other officers assigned to the court include the clerk and the sheriff. The *clerk* schedules trials and officially records all court business. The clerk is responsible for maintaining the completeness, accuracy, and integrity of the court files, and in that capacity receives and files all court papers, including summonses, complaints, answers, amendments, motions, and appearances. The court clerk is also responsible for the care of the jury. The *sheriff*, in addition to keeping the peace in the jurisdiction, serves summonses, complaints, and other court documents and carries out court orders. Some of the civil functions of the sheriff may be performed by a designated court officer.

Marshals in federal courts are appointed by the President, with the advice and consent of the Senate, to serve four-year terms. They are responsible for (1) serving as marshals of the federal district court and of the federal court of appeals when those courts are sitting in the district; (2) executing all writs, processes, and orders issued under the authority of the United States, including those of the courts; and (3) paying the salaries and expenses of the U.S. attorneys and their staffs, and the marshals' own staffs. Marshals and their deputies may also exercise the same powers as sheriffs of the state in which they are located.

The *bailiff* is responsible for the protection of everyone in the courtroom and for maintaining the dignity and decorum of court proceedings.

Courts of record also employ a *court reporter*, who is responsible for making a complete and accurate verbatim record of every word spoken during a trial or hearing before the court. This record may be taken down by sound recording or stenography, or by using a stenotype machine.

Additional court personnel may include law clerks and secretaries assigned to judges, a vast number of office workers in the office of the clerk of court, probation officers with their clerical staffs, and law clerks to the court reporters. In the federal district courts there are bankruptcy trustees with their staffs. The larger courts may also employ a number of messengers and librarians.

Law-Enforcement Agencies

The U.S. Department of Justice The U.S. Department of Justice, created in 1870, is headed by the U.S. Attorney General, who directs all the affairs and activities of the department. The Department of Justice conducts all Supreme Court suits in which the United States is involved; the Solicitor General usually argues special cases for the government in the Supreme Court, while members of his or her staff represent the government in other Supreme Court cases in which the United States is a litigant. The Justice Department also represents the government in legal matters generally, giving legal advice and opinions to the President and the heads of executive departments when requested.

The Attorney General supervises these activities and also directs the U.S. attorneys and U.S. marshals in the judicial districts around the country. (There is one U.S. district attorney and one U.S. marshal for every federal judicial district.) The Deputy Attorney General is primarily concerned with criminal law or investigative matters; he or she also directs the Executive Office of United States Attorneys. The Associate Attorney General generally supervises criminal matters. An Assistant Attorney General for Administration is responsible for matters relating to the internal administration of the department. The assistant attorney general in charge of the Office of Legal Counsel serves as legal adviser to the President and the heads of executive branch agencies.

Divisions within the Department of Justice include the Antitrust Division, the Civil Rights Division, the Civil Division, the Criminal Division, the Land and Natural Resources Division, and the Tax Division. The divisions may institute investigations or supervise or direct litigation in federal courts. Other bureaus and administrative units within the Department of Justice are the Federal Bureau of Investigation, the Bureau of Prisons, the United States Marshals Service, the Immigration and Naturalization Service, the Drug Enforcement Administration, the Law Enforcement Assistance Administration, the Board of Immigration Appeals, and the Parole Commission.

State law-enforcement offices The *state attorney general* is the principal law-enforcement officer in a state. The office brings actions in the name of the state when appropriate, serves as legal counsel to the legislative and executive branches, and issues opinions clarifying or interpreting statutes. The attorney general may also intervene in suits where it is felt the state's interest should be represented. The office, however, is much weaker than that of the U.S. Attorney General.

The chief local law-enforcement officer may be called the *prosecuting attorney, state attorney,* or *district attorney.*

The office of the *public defender* is now active in many states. Public defenders provide legal counsel for people of limited means in both trial and appellate courts.

Court Procedures

Legal procedures vary from state to state and from court to court. This lack of uniformity has led legislatures and bar associations to try to reduce the number of disparities among various jurisdictions by standardizing court procedures, legal terminology, and legal documents. Standardizing legal procedures is of great value to the courts and the legal profession in the efficient administration of justice and the handling of cases in court.

In an effort to simplify common law pleading, Congress in 1938 adopted a set of rules known as the *Federal Rules of Civil Procedure*. These rules set out each step in a civil proceeding, including the method of preparing required documents in all federal courts. Since then, the majority of the states have adopted similar rules. Consequently, the rules of procedure in the state courts are to a certain extent now uniform.

Types of Court Action

The courts have responsibility in three general areas—criminal, civil, and equity law. In most jurisdictions, the same courts try cases in all three areas. In a few jurisdictions, special courts known as chancery courts hear equity cases, and some states have separate courts for civil and criminal cases. Under the Federal Rules of Civil Procedure, there is no longer a distinction between law and equity in the preparation of pleadings in civil law cases.

Criminal actions   An individual or a group breaking a law designed to protect society from harm is considered to have committed a crime. Because the public has suffered as a result of the crime, the people of the state or of the United States bring the action; they are represented in court by a public official who may be known as a *district attorney, a public prosecutor,* or a *United States attorney.* The jurisdiction of each court determines the types of crimes that are to be prosecuted there. Courts of limited jurisdiction generally hear lesser crimes, or misdemeanors, while courts of general jurisdiction try the more serious crimes, or felonies.

Civil actions   A civil case may arise when the actions of an individual or a group cause harm to another, who then goes to court seeking compensation for that harm. The injured party, called the *plaintiff* or *complainant,* asks the court to grant damages in the form of a payment of money. In some jurisdictions, if either party in the case requests it, a jury may hear the trial. If neither party requests a jury, the judge renders judgment after hearing both sides. In civil actions the party who brings the action must present a *preponderance of evidence* or the action will fail.

Equity actions   In most jurisdictions equity actions are encompassed within civil actions, although a few states provide separate courts of equity. In equity cases the party who brings suit is called the *petitioner* or *complainant*. The petitioner asks the court to order the opposing party, usually known as the *respondent*, to perform or to cease from performing a specific act. Equity will be sought when relief is not available to the petitioner through money damages. No jury can be requested in equity matters; the judge alone makes the decision. The decision of the judge in a case in equity is, technically, a *decree* rather than a judgment; in practice, however, the words are commonly interchanged.

Steps in Criminal Procedure

Arrest An individual may file an informal complaint with a law enforcement officer, after which a judge signs a warrant, which is written authority for a law-enforcement officer to make an arrest. The officer may also make an arrest without a warrant if there is probable cause to do so. In some cases a grand jury must be convened to determine whether there is cause to indict (charge) an alleged criminal perpetrator.

Bail Bail is a deposit of money that helps to guarantee that an accused person will appear for trial at the time and date specified. When the accused has been taken into custody, the court may set bail and release the accused person. If he or she does not appear, bail is forfeited. If the accused can reasonably be expected to appear when ordered, the court may release the accused on his or her own recognizance (that is, without bail), depending on local rules and the seriousness of the crime.

Preliminary hearing A preliminary hearing is held to determine whether there is probable cause for holding the accused for trial. A preliminary hearing may also be held to fix bail. In the case of certain less serious crimes the preliminary hearing may follow the arraignment (see below).

Arraignment The next step in a criminal procedure is an arraignment. Arraigning an accused person has three purposes: (1) to establish the identity of the accused, (2) to inform the accused of the charges, and (3) to allow the court to hear the plea of the accused—that is, the answer to the charge, or a declaration of guilt or innocence.

Trial If the trial is to be held before a jury, it is selected and sworn. A trial jury typically consists of 12 citizens who listen to the facts and present their decision, the verdict. In criminal actions a unanimous vote of the jurors is usually necessary. In a jury trial, the judge rules on points of law and the jury decides questions of fact.

After the jury has been sworn in, the trial usually follows this sequence: (1) opening statement by the prosecutor; (2) opening statement by the defendant's lawyer (this may be delayed, however, until the beginning of step 4); (3) presentation of evidence by the prosecutor; (4) presentation of evidence by the defendant's lawyer; (5) closing argument by the prosecutor; (6) closing argument by the defendant's lawyer; and (7) the judge's charge to the jury.

The judge charges the jury, instructing them regarding the law that relates to the case, and provides guidance in reaching a verdict. The judge prepares the instructions, but prior to the trial each attorney prepares and submits to the judge a set of requested *jury instructions*. In this way, each attorney can make sure that the judge does not overlook any point that the attorney considers important.

Verdict   The jury retires to a private room and considers the case. A vote of the jury is taken to arrive at a decision. If the defendant is found guilty, the court has the authority to impose sentence, although in some jurisdictions the jury will determine the sentence. The sentence is based on specific findings of fact and conclusions of law. The verdict is signed by the judge and recorded so that it may be included in the transcript of the case. If the accused is found guilty, the case may be appealed. An *appeal* is a proceeding by which the decision of a lower court is reviewed by a higher court.

Steps in Civil Procedure

Civil procedure consists of four fairly well-defined phases: (1) pleadings, (2) discovery, (3) trial and judgment, and (4) conclusion of litigation.

Phase 1: Pleadings   The general term *pleadings* refers to the series of written claims and defenses that form the first phase of a lawsuit. During this phase the attorneys prepare and file various documents to initiate the action and narrow the issues.

Complaint   As the first step in a civil lawsuit, the plaintiff's attorney files a *complaint*, which may also be known as a *petition* or a *declaration*, against the defendant. Where courts of equity exist, the first pleading in an equity action is called a *bill of complaint* or a *bill in equity*. The complaint states the specific kind and amount of damages suffered by the plaintiff and the acts of the defendant alleged to have caused those damages.

Summons   The defendant must be given positive notice that a complaint has been filed and that a response to the complaint must be made. This notice is called a *summons*, and in most states it must be served with a copy of the complaint. Once the action has been initiated by filing and serving the complaint and summons, it cannot be terminated unless specified legal steps are taken.

Appearance   Taking the correct legal steps to respond to a complaint or summons within the specified time limit is known as making an *appearance*.

Objections   Rules of court procedure require that a complaint be clear, definite, and complete and that it be prepared in accordance with the law and the rules of the court. When the defense believes that the complaint is not in accordance with court rules or the law, the attorney may object to it by means of various documents such as a *demurrer*, a *motion to strike*, a *motion to quash*, or a *motion to make complaint more definite and certain*. These documents, and others, attempt to invalidate the complaint on the grounds that it is not legally supported. As these documents are based on points of law, most courts require a supporting document to be prepared and attached. This document may be a brief, a legal memorandum, or a memorandum of points and authorities.

Answer   The next step in a civil action is the preparation of an answer, in which the defendant responds to the allegations in the complaint. Court rules in many jurisdictions permit the answer to contain a *counterclaim* against the plaintiff. This counterclaim arises out of the subject of the complaint; it is not merely an answer to the charge but a separate charge against the plaintiff. Though it could be the subject of a separate lawsuit, it is often more conveniently included in the answer.

Cross-complaint or cross-claim   If the defendant believes that another party is responsible, the attorney will respond to the complaint with an *answer and cross-claim* or *cross-complaint*. The cross-claim or cross-complaint may be filed and served as a document separate from the answer, or it may be combined with the answer into one document.

Phase 2: Discovery   When the initial pleading stage of litigation is concluded, the attorneys will attempt to locate all witnesses and uncover all evidence while learning as much as possible about the issues. This process is known as discovery.

Numerous discovery devices are available, and the attorney must decide which devices to use and when. The legal secretary will be primarily involved in arranging for depositions of parties and witnesses and for preparing necessary notices, motions, written interrogatories, and other documents that may be specifically related to discovery. Some of these discovery devices are discussed below.

Interrogatories   Information may be obtained by means of a written set of questions in a court document, usually entitled *interrogatories,* that require written answers. Testimony may also be taken by asking witnesses oral questions. This discovery activity is known as taking a *deposition* or using *oral interrogatories*. The manner in which the questioning can be conducted is precisely determined by the rules governing procedure in civil cases.

Subpoena   When witnesses are required to give testimony in court, they must receive official notice that they are to appear. This notice is called a *subpoena*. Some states require that witnesses who are to give depositions be subpoenaed. If an attorney knows that a witness may refer to certain documents or other evidence in the testimony—either in court or in a deposition—or if the attorney wants certain items admitted as evidence, a document called a subpoena duces tecum ("under penalty you shall bring with you") is required. This document tells a person to appear at a specified time and place with those particular exhibits (documents, photographs, or other items) related to the suit.

Other discovery devices   The attorney may petition the court for the right to inspect evidence or documents and also for the right to order a physical or mental examination of a party.

Pretrial conference   After all preliminary work has been completed and the case has been set for trial, the attorneys of record may meet informally with the judge to discuss the issues involved in the lawsuit. These conferences are not required in all states. At a pretrial conference the attorneys discuss the issues, the allegations, and the facts involved in the case. As the issues are discussed, information is exchanged; and sometimes evidence is produced that results in a request to dismiss the litigation without trial. Sometimes certain aspects of the case can be settled by *stipulation,* or agreement, between the attorneys with the approval of the judge. Because trials are expensive in terms of time, emotion, and money, both parties may reevaluate the situation and decide to settle out of court.

Conclusion of litigation without trial   Many lawsuits never go to court. Sometimes the reason is personal, having to do with the attitude of the parties. On the other hand, a high percentage of lawsuits are terminated before trial for legal reasons. Sometimes evidence is uncovered that is so significant that a judge may decide a trial is not required. Sometimes one of the parties or the attorney deliberately does not respond within the time specified. At other times the parties mutually agree to terminate the suit. Whatever the reason for concluding a case without trial, the attorneys of record must prepare, file, and serve certain documents in order to bring the case to a conclusion.

Summary judgment   The attorney for either party to a case may bring a motion for summary judgment. The moving party must show that there is no real dispute as to any facts in the case and thus no need for a trial. The moving party must show that an application of the law to the facts in the case results in a judgment in his or her favor. Motions for summary judgment are usually accompanied by supporting affidavits of potential witnesses. The opposing party may also file documents challenging the motion. After reviewing these documents, the judge decides either for or against the motion.

Discontinuance   For a variety of reasons, a lawsuit may be discontinued. To obtain a discontinuance, the lawyer must file and serve appropriate documents that set forth the reason for stopping the action. Discontinuance may be voluntary or involuntary. When the parties agree to settle out of court, *voluntary abatement* occurs. If the plaintiff fails to meet certain legal requirements, the law requires that an action be discontinued. In this case, the court mandates the discontinuance, which is sometimes referred to as *involuntary dismissal.*

Statute of limitations and dismissal   The statute of limitations in each state precisely prescribes the time allowed a potential party to commence a lawsuit. If a party fails to meet these statutory deadlines, the lawsuit must be terminated.

Motion to dismiss for failure to prosecute   After a complaint has been issued, if a plaintiff's attorney fails to cause a date to be set for an action to come for trial, the defendant's attorney may file a motion to dismiss the action for failure to prosecute. This motion is accompanied by a supporting document that states significant dates and claims that the plaintiff did not take the steps necessary to bring the matter to court for trial.

Dismissal with and without prejudice   Dismissal may be filed with prejudice or without prejudice. The plaintiff may file for dismissal without prejudice at any time before the commencement of the trial. In this case, the plaintiff has the option of filing suit against the same defendant on the same matter at a later date. However, if the action is terminated *after* the trial has begun, it is by dismissal with prejudice, which prevents the plaintiff from filing at a later date on the same matter.

Release When a case is dismissed as the result of a settlement out of court, the party who is to make restitution usually will not do so unless given a properly executed agreement most often called *release* or *release of all claims*. In this document, the person who receives the settlement agrees never again to bring suit for additional costs on the matter in dispute.

Phase 3: Trial and judgment If a case cannot be settled by mutual agreement and if there are no grounds for dismissal or default, the case must go to trial for a decision on the merits. Rules have been developed which carefully prescribe the procedures to be followed for setting the matter for trial, conducting the trial, and entering the judgment of the court.

Trial When either attorney feels that the case is ready for trial, the clerk of the court is notified through the filing of a *note of issue*, a *memorandum setting for trial*, or a *notice of trial*. The calendar clerk places the trial on the calendar, meaning that it is added to the list of cases that are going to be tried. The clerk notifies the parties to the action when and where the trial will be held. For the customary sequence of a trial, refer to the preceding section on steps in a criminal proceeding. In civil cases the plaintiff's attorney rather than a prosecutor argues the case, and in most jurisdictions the plaintiff's attorney is permitted a rebuttal immediately following the defense lawyer's final argument.

Judgment When there is no jury, the judge hears the case, applies the law, and issues a judgment in favor of one party or the other based on the facts and the merits of the case. When a case is heard before a jury, the jury decides in favor of one of the parties on the basis of the facts presented and sets the amount of damages. In civil cases the judgment or decree is issued in favor of the party judged to have the preponderance of evidence. The party in whose favor judgment is made is the *prevailing party*.

Phase 4: Conclusion of litigation After the court hands down a judgment, the losing party has several options: (1) to perform satisfaction, thereby taking the final step in litigation; (2) to fail to perform satisfaction, in which case the prevailing party may have to take measures to obtain what is owed; or (3) to appeal the case to a higher court. If the losing party chooses to appeal, no payment is made to the prevailing party. The attorney for the losing party must make the appeal within the time limit prescribed by law or lose the right to appeal.

Satisfaction The judgment is a court order requiring the losing party to provide satisfaction in some manner to the prevailing party. Satisfaction may take several forms: the losing party may be required to pay court costs and monetary damages to the prevailing party, to perform a specified action requested by the other party, or to stop a certain action to which the other party objects. Once satisfaction has been made, the court must be given a document indicating that the judgment has been satisfactorily carried out.

In settling court costs the prevailing party must submit for the court's approval a statement of all recoverable expenses incurred in the course of litigation. The appropriate motion is filed and served on opposing counsel. The opposing party may object to the costs indicated and file a motion to that effect. The court will rule on both motions. If the court allows all costs, the order signed by the judge is filed, and official copies are served on opposing counsel.

When the prevailing party has been paid all money owed, both damages and costs, the prevailing attorney files a document stating the amount of money received and declaring that full satisfaction of claims has been made. It also shows that judgment was entered into the official records. The document must be signed by the prevailing party, filed, and served on opposing counsel.

If the losing party fails to provide satisfaction as adjudged, various special proceedings may take place that could result in the seizure of person or property by the court.

Chapter 2

Employment in a Law Office

Beside every successful lawyer there is a professional legal secretary who helped pave the road to success. This phenomenon is not new; nor is the role of the legal secretary. The role is at least 350 years old, going back to the time of the traditional English barrister's clerk. As recounted in history books and novels, the clerk functioned as the lawyer's personal assistant and office manager. And now as in the past, it is the clerk or legal secretary who schedules appointments with clients, maintains case calendars, prepares court and client documents, handles contacts with court officials and other attorneys' offices, maintains financial records, and performs a myriad of other duties and responsibilities. So important is the position that in some sense the secretary becomes the lawyer's silent partner.

Making the commitment to be a legal secretary requires an appreciation for the professional responsibility to be undertaken. The position is not just a job; it is potentially a lifetime career. Law firms are important offices that deal with serious issues, sometimes life-or-death matters. Because of the importance of the position, the legal secretary is held to a higher standard of conduct than is required of secretaries in general. This expectation of absolute professionalism forms the very essence of the legal-secretarial position.

This chapter provides an overview of the legal profession, the nature of law firms, the role of the legal secretary, and professional ethics and human relations. It also discusses opportunities for employment and for professional training and education.

The Legal Profession

Law in the United States is basically an adaptation of the common law of England. As described in Chapter 1, our law may be divided into two major categories: statutory law and case law. Laws written by the various state legislatures and by the United States Congress, as well as ordinances passed by local authorities, constitute statutory law. Case law is the vast body of law based on legal precedents.

In our complex business world, many honest differences arise between competitors, or between suppliers and purchasers, or between landlords and tenants. In the settlement of these differences, the businessperson first consults counsel—i.e., a lawyer. The lawyer, after gathering the facts, examines the applicable statutory law and then reviews past cases to discover how similar disputes have been decided in the courts. Upon concluding the research, the lawyer forms an opinion and advises the client accordingly.

The Lawyer

Problem solver   The lawyer is a professional problem solver. The client or potential client walking through the door is typically a person with a problem. The problem may involve the client's property, well-being, liberty, or any number of other areas that pertain to the person's existence in society. It is the lawyer's job to solve such problems to the best of his or her ability, whether this entails only a simple interview or a full-fledged lawsuit with appeals to the Supreme Court.

Success is not always possible, of course. Indeed, lawyers can make no guarantees. A manufacturer can put a warranty upon its product because the manufacturing process involves known properties of physical objects that will act with predictable results. The lawyer, on the other hand, works with the human equation: the lawyer is human, the client is human, the opponents are human, the judge is human, and the jury is human. Even the laws in the books have been written and interpreted by humans who inevitably will have brought to their tasks the prejudices, shortsightedness, wisdom, and compassion of their all-too-human backgrounds. The great Oliver Wendell Holmes once wrote, "The life of the law has not been logic: it has been experience." Thus, the lawyer's work is one of art that only occasionally takes on the appearance of science. Although the lawyer can make no guarantees in his or her work and will be found to be wrong on occasion, with care and attention to detail he or she can minimize error and try to satisfy the client's legal needs.

Fiduciary   The lawyer is expected to respect the confidences of the client, not only the verbal confidences expressed in the course of any action but also the client's property—including money—if deposited with the lawyer. To many lawyers, the key rule of the generally accepted Model Rules of Professional Conduct has to do with avoiding the commingling of client moneys with the firm's own. The lawyer has the right to place a lien upon the client's property to secure payment of the lawyer's fees, but the lawyer may not arbitrarily mix the client's funds with those of the firm.

With respect to verbal confidences, there are certain limits that the legal secretary should be aware of. No lawyer is permitted to keep silent when he or she knows the client is about to commit a crime or is in the process of such an act. It makes no difference whether the client tells the lawyer he or she wants to commit a crime and asks the lawyer's advice on how to do it without punishment, or whether the client is on the witness stand and is in the process of committing perjury. In all such events, the lawyer is duty-bound not to the client but to the court and to society (which in this instance takes precedence over the client) to speak up and expose the errant client.

Advocate   The lawyer represents the client; the lawyer advises the client; the lawyer speaks for the client and on the client's behalf. Yet, for all this, the lawyer and the client are not one and the same. It is wrong to infer, for example, that a lawyer is a criminal simply because he represents criminals. The lawyer may well be one, but not because of the clients he or she represents. Most of us have experienced the situation in which we presume to speak on someone else's behalf only to find that we do not have the whole story, for which we are subsequently embarrassed. The lawyer, in his or her role as advocate, invites this problem but seeks to separate those who can truly use the lawyer's help from those who have little or no case to be made on their behalf.

It is often asked how a lawyer can defend a person who he or she knows is guilty of a crime. The answer is that, under our system of government, a person is presumed innocent until proven guilty beyond a reasonable doubt by the government. In defending a person charged with crime, however clear the facts may *seem* to be (even given a confession by the suspect) the person so charged is entitled to require that his or her guilt be proven and to have his or her rights fully protected while that proof is being made. Thus, the lawyer makes the state prove its case and seeks to protect the client's rights.

Law School

The study of the law—statutory law and case law—constitutes the principal portion of the law-school curriculum. As a general rule, law schools require full attendance for three academic years. Requirements for admission to law school usually include a baccalaureate degree from a recognized college. In other words, a prospective lawyer must generally spend four years in college followed by three years in law school.

The law-school curriculum varies from school to school, but certain required courses are common to almost all. Such required courses include those in contracts, property, civil procedure, evidence, criminal law, and torts. In addition, the law student takes elective courses as a way to gain some understanding of or entry into a particular field of law. These subjects may include trusts, wills and estates, energy, antitrust, environmental, labor, and family law.

Upon the successful completion of the three years of study, most schools now confer the J.D. (*Juris Doctor,* or Doctor of Jurisprudence) degree. Many years ago, the LL.B. (Bachelor of Laws) was the standard degree conferred by law schools.

A few law schools do not require a baccalaureate degree for admission. Several of these schools will also accept less than the three full years of day study, substituting evening study and some work experience. However, prospective students must verify ahead of time whether completion of the courses at such a school will qualify them to take the state bar examination. The degree conferred by such schools is usually an LL.B. rather than a J.D.

Law schools are accredited by the American Bar Association, which establishes certain minimum requirements for law-school curricula, facilities, and faculty.

It is possible to continue legal education beyond the J.D. degree. The master's degree (LL.M.) usually involves one year of additional study that combines coursework and research. The Doctorate of Juridical Sciences (S.J.D.) is a graduate degree that involves advanced academic work, while the Master's in Comparative Law (M.C.L.) involves advanced work for foreign-educated lawyers.

Admission to the Bar

Most law-school graduates are interested in practicing law, and in order to do so they must be licensed. Admission to the bar is ordinarily governed by the supreme appellate courts of the individual states, and the procedure varies from state to state. In most cases, passing a written bar examination is required. The bar examination includes both a multistate portion, which is given nationally, and an examination prepared by the law examiners in the state where the examination is taken. The bar examination is intended to be a comprehensive inquiry into the applicant's legal education. It may include such subjects as real property; wills and trusts; contracts; constitutional law; criminal law and procedure; corporations, partnerships, and agency; evidence; creditors' rights; practice and procedure in trial and appellate courts at the state and federal levels; and equity, torts, and sales. The examinations are usually held twice a year, shortly after the academic year ends and again shortly after the end of the calendar year. Most persons taking bar examinations find it useful, after completing law school, to take special six- to eight-week courses designed to prepare them for the bar examinations. These courses are conducted in many cities and are also available for programmed home study.

In addition to successfully passing the bar examination, an applicant must satisfy the state bar committee on character and moral fitness to practice law. Once applicants have met these requirements, they appear in court to take the oath as a lawyer.

Admission to practice in one state does not necessarily qualify a lawyer to practice in another state. Ordinarily a lawyer admitted in one state must take a separate bar examination to be admitted in the second state; however, depending on the length of time the lawyer has practiced in the first state, the second state may either waive the examination or require only a short professional examination rather than the full new-graduate examination. The lawyer who is considering practicing in another state must check these requirements.

In addition to the requirement of admission to the various state bars, there are special requirements for admission to practice in the federal courts. The requirements for the federal courts and courts of appeals vary. To be admitted to the United States Supreme Court, an attorney must have practiced for three years in the highest court in his or her state and also be nominated by a member of the Supreme Court bar.

Continuing Legal Education

After admission to the bar, lawyers often attend continuing-education courses to maintain and sharpen their skills. Several states have adopted rules that require all members of the bar to attend a minimum number of hours of continuing legal education each year. Every state, through its state bar association, law schools, or a combination of organizations, has continuing legal education

courses available. Lawyers who have been certified as specialists usually are obligated to attend a fixed number of hours of continuing-education courses annually.

Most law offices also encourage their secretaries, legal assistants, and other
staff members to continue their educations, often at the firm's expense.

The Practice of Law

The vast majority of lawyers in the nineteenth century, like the doctors, were
general practitioners. The lawyer who hung out his shingle in 1890 was usually
prepared to accept any legal problem that came his way. And almost without
exception, lawyers were men. As with doctors, all this has changed. Today
there are many, many women practicing law, and there are many, many specialists in the profession.

Law specialties   The complexity of the law requires many lawyers to focus on a
single area of the law. The prospect of a malpractice action being brought for
handling a matter beyond one's competence has contributed to this movement.
While most lawyers would still regard themselves as general practitioners, many
today limit their practice to one or more major specialties such as corporate, tax,
antitrust, criminal, family, aviation, customs-and-immigration, real-estate, probate, medical-malpractice, personal-injury, administrative, patent, and bankruptcy law. Fields that have emerged more recently are those of energy and environmental law. In addition, the number of public-interest law firms has
increased, and many lawyers work in legal-aid societies and organizations such
as the American Civil Liberties Union. Among the specialties practiced by these
firms are housing, child-welfare, mental-health, and prison law.

The rapid expansion of the need for lawyers and legal specialists began
during the Great Depression of the 1930s. The impetus came from the legislation enacted during that decade that was aimed, in particular, at preventing
another depression. The corporate securities market became carefully regulated, social security legislation was enacted, the National Labor Relations
Board was established, and the entry of government into other fields required
the ordinary citizen unsophisticated in matters of law to seek legal help. Enter
the specialist lawyer.

Although little official sanction was given to the various specialties for
many years, some bar associations have now recognized certain of them and
formed sections to help practitioners keep current with developments in their
fields. Today, some state bodies governing the practice of law have recognized
particular specialties, set out the requirements for certification, and certified
lawyers who met the requirements and applied for certification. Among the
certified specialties at the present are those in the fields of workers' compensation, family law, criminal law, and tax law. The American Bar Association has
begun to accredit national organizations (both within and outside of the ABA)
with programs designed to provide national certification of specialties. It is important to note that certification as a specialist in a field is not a prerequisite to
practicing law in that field. Any lawyer admitted to the bar in a particular jurisdiction who feels qualified to handle a matter in a specialty field is free to do
so; the certification is merely a recognition by the jurisdiction's governing body
that the lawyer has met its requirements for specialization in the field.

Bar associations   As noted earlier, the practice of law in each state is regulated by the state's supreme appellate court. To carry out this responsibility, many such courts have established boards and delegated to them the duty to set the requirements for admission to the bar and to certify persons for admission to the bar. In some states, this responsibility is carried out by a recognized state bar association. In such instances, all lawyers must belong to the bar association in order to practice law in that state. In states where this situation exists and the lawyer is automatically a dues-paying member of the bar association, the bar is referred to as an integrated or unified bar. Among the states having integrated bar associations are Florida, California, Texas, and Michigan. In those states where admission to the bar does not require dues-paying membership in the state bar association, membership is purely voluntary. Even in these latter instances, however, the vast majority of lawyers belong to the state bar association. In a few states both integrated and voluntary bar associations exist.

In addition to state bar associations, lawyers may belong to local bar associations. These associations are generally interested in the administration of justice in a city, county, or judicial district. Membership in local bar associations is voluntary.

There are several national bar associations. The two largest are the American Bar Association and the Association of Trial Lawyers of America. At the time when black lawyers were excluded from membership in the American Bar Association, the National Bar Association was formed to reflect their interests. Membership in these national bar associations is voluntary. The American Bar Association (ABA), with headquarters in Chicago and with membership throughout the 50 states, is the largest. Membership in the ABA does not carry with it the authority to practice law, but membership is a valuable means of keeping current with developments taking place in the law and maintaining relations with fellow lawyers throughout the country. In addition to providing a number of services for its members, it serves as an umbrella for a number of groups that are interested in the general practice of law or in a single legal specialty. The Association of Trial Lawyers of America is of particular interest to trial lawyers throughout the nation. Many of these organizations offer continuing-education programs for lawyers. Some of them also allow nonlawyers who work in the legal field to hold associate memberships.

The ABA recommends rules for the ethical conduct of lawyers, rules that have been adopted and followed by many of the state bar associations and legislative bodies. The ABA and the state bar groups are vigilant in seeking to maintain high standards of professional conduct on the part of all lawyers in their respective jurisdictions. It is through these bodies that disciplinary proceedings may be carried out which result in the censure, suspension, or disbarment of lawyers who fail to meet the code of professional conduct.

Directories   One important source of information about lawyers and law firms is the *Martindale-Hubbell Law Directory*, published by Martindale-Hubbell, Inc., New Providence, N.J., and available in print (25 vols., 1995 ed.) or CD-ROM in most law libraries and many city public libraries. It gives the size of the law office, the educational background of each lawyer, and the areas of the law in which he or she practices; it also includes coverage of corporate law departments. A useful part of the Martindale-Hubbell directory is the section containing digests, or summaries, of the law of the various states and foreign countries.

Other directories such as the ABA directory and your state bar directory are also important reference books. West Publishing Company (St. Paul, MN) offers a national legal directory on-line through the Internet or in CD-ROM format.

Professional Liability

Lawyers, like other professionals, can be sued for professional malpractice. In recent years, lawyers and members of the general public have placed increasing emphasis on the lawyer's responsibility to represent clients properly and with due care. There is no question but that some lawyers are more skillful and aggressive than others, but the fact that one lawyer may not be as skillful as his or her adversary in a case is not a cause for legal action. On the other hand, the lawyer who, through gross negligence or criminal act, causes a client to be penalized may be charged with the financial responsibility to reimburse the client. The most common example of negligence is failure to meet a statutory deadline. This would include the failure to start an action before the statute of limitations ran out, the failure to answer or to move for a new trial in a timely manner, or the failure to file a tax return or secure an extension for filing. If a penalty and interest are assessed against the client because the lawyer failed to meet a deadline, the lawyer may be required to make good the sum so lost.

An example of criminality on the part of a lawyer is the diversion of clients' funds entrusted to the lawyer's safekeeping. If those funds are expended in the lawyer's personal interest, not only is the lawyer financially liable but he or she may be subject to criminal prosecution and may be suspended or expelled from the profession.

Preventing liability claims   Many lawyers now carry professional liability (malpractice) insurance, often through a bar association–sponsored insurance company. As claims against lawyers increase and are sustained, the cost of this insurance increases. It is expensive and sometimes difficult to obtain. Many insurance companies, for instance, refuse to provide professional liability insurance to law firms until they are shown, among other things, proof of an efficient docket-control system within the firm that prevents the missing of deadlines.

The lawyer's secretary is in a good position to help prevent instances that give rise to liability claims and that raise the cost of the lawyer's malpractice coverage. Among the many ways that a secretary can contribute to safeguarding the lawyer's and clients' interests are (1) by ensuring that the lawyer and all law-office staff members maintain good client contact, (2) by ensuring that the law office has a good calendar and docket system and that important dates are called to the attention of the responsible person, (3) by continually working to improve the efficiency of the law office, and (4) by ensuring a sharp and complete separation between the lawyer's personal funds and the funds of clients. This is accomplished by the creation of a client trust account. In the small office where responsibility for handling funds devolves upon the secretary, top priority must be given to preserving the integrity of client funds. (See chapters 12 and 13 for more on docket-control systems and client trust accounts.)

The Law Office

Growth and Specialization of Law Firms

Law firms have changed a great deal since Abraham Lincoln practiced with one partner more than a century ago. Despite predictions that the solo practice of law would vanish in America, in the 1990s about 45 percent of all the practicing lawyers in the United States continued to be solo practitioners. Over three fifths of practicing lawyers work in small firms of one to five lawyers. Starting in the late 1980s many large firms dissolved or began to reduce their staffs. As a result, many lawyers who expected lifetime careers in large firms found themselves entering the ranks of the solo practitioners and the small-firm lawyers. Also, because of reduced employment opportunities in government offices and large firms, many recent law-school graduates have been forced into solo practice. At the same time, however, solo practitioners sometimes combine their practices, and small firms may hire associates in order to grow and better serve their clients. Legal practices in the United States are thus very fluid, and generalizations about law-firm size or ability are difficult to make.

The interesting thing about law firms is that, essentially, they all function in the same way. The client comes to the firm, whether it has one lawyer or 125, discusses a legal problem with a lawyer who will prosecute the matter, and is billed for services performed on an agreed-upon basis. The basic services that a lawyer provides have changed little in the last century. They still include researching the law, providing information about the law, and giving advice to clients on the basis of the law; representing clients in litigation and in nonlitigation matters such as negotiations with a third party; and preparing documents such as contracts and wills.

Lawyers in firms of all sizes have begun, in varying degrees, to specialize. Solo practitioners set up "boutique" practices restricted to certain types of cases. Large firms, in contrast, can engage in the "general practice" of law because they can cover more areas and because individual members of the firm who specialize in particular fields often share their knowledge with their partners.

Multiple offices   As law firms grow, especially in the big cities, they find it highly desirable to establish and maintain multiple offices. In New York City, for example, a number of firms have their main office in the financial or Wall Street area and branch offices several miles away in the midtown area. Similarly, many firms with primary offices in New York or Chicago or San Francisco or Los Angeles find it helpful to their clients and productive of additional business to establish offices in the suburban areas of those cities. Additionally, those firms representing clients with interests closely connected with state or federal government often establish an office in the state capital or in Washington, D.C., so as to be better prepared to represent their clients before government agencies in those cities.

A major contributor to the proliferation of offices of large firms is the nature of their clients' business. As American business grows, it grows both nationally and internationally. There are corporations in the fields of automobile manufacturing, pharmaceuticals, petroleum, and communications with interests on almost every continent and in 30 or 40 nations. Since protection and prosecution of these interests requires the intervention of lawyers, the firms representing such corporations have found it necessary to establish national and foreign offices. As a result, we find law firms with main offices in major U.S. cities maintaining offices not only in other states but also in London, Paris, Abu Dhabi, Brussels, Tokyo, Beijing, Hong Kong, Moscow, and elsewhere as their clients' needs dictate.

An even more recent phenomenon is the merger of law firms with established firms in other states in order to create national law firms. Although such mergers are far from common, they are increasing and contributing to the acceptance of the multioffice practice of law as a professional way of life.

Law-Office Organization

Just as the structure and nature of business organizations have become more complex, so have the structure and nature of legal organizations, whether they are one-lawyer or 100-lawyer firms.

The smallest law office is that of the sole practitioner. Most lawyers can engage profitably in such a practice, usually with at least one nonlawyer employee. The nonlawyer employee may fill many roles, including secretary/typist, receptionist, telephone-answering service, supply clerk, and librarian. As the volume of business grows and the single lawyer takes on additional lawyer help, the nonlegal functions increase and additional personnel may be employed to fill a variety of positions—but there is always a need for the legal secretary. With the growth of computer literacy among lawyers, the role of the secretary is evolving from that of typist and dictation-taker to that of general office manager.

At the other extreme from the single-lawyer office is the very large firm. Before examining the structure of such organizations, however, we must understand how law firms function as businesses.

Partners and associates   The majority of lawyers practice either as sole practitioners or in partnerships. A *partner* is one of the proprietors of a law firm. He or she owns a percentage of the firm's capital (leasehold, furniture, accounts receivable, and goodwill) and is liable for the firm's obligations. An *associate* is an employed lawyer. The associate owns no part of the firm, is not obligated for any of the firm's liabilities, and is paid a salary. In some instances, depending upon the firm's prosperity, the associate may also receive a bonus. In many firms there is a middle level between partner and associate—the *junior partner.* Some firms also employ lawyers as regular staff; unlike associates, these lawyers are not in line to become partners of the firm.

Types of firms   Most states today allow lawyers to form professional corporations, professional associations, or professional limited-liability companies (hence the abbreviations P.C., P.A., or P.L.C. in a firm's name). A *professional corporation* is composed of a group of professionals practicing not as individuals or in partnership but in corporate form. A *professional association* is a group of individuals who share facilities and other resources but do not carry a corporate charter. A *limited-liability company* is a hybrid of corporate and partnership characteristics. A corporation or limited-liability company enjoys limited liability but individual lawyers are liable for professional negligence.

Staff personnel   In law firms of any size, the support or nonlawyer personnel may outnumber the lawyers, particularly if the nature of the practice lends itself to the use of paralegals. In the smaller firms, those under about 25 lawyers, the person in charge of the support personnel may be one of the senior secretaries or a legal assistant. As firms increase in size, these responsibilities begin to require the exclusive attention of one individual. When the firm reaches about 25 lawyers, its structure usually will be firmly fixed more or less along the lines of the chart shown in Fig. 2.1. Office structures will vary in detail, of course, and may be influenced by individual capabilities and personalities. Despite such differences, however, they will all encompass the areas depicted in the chart.

The key person in the chart is often called the Director of Administration. As late as the 1970s, a lawyer in the firm often did double duty, serving both as a practicing attorney and as the managing partner or lawyer-administrator. However, larger firms began to recognize that the assignment of administrative duties to a practicing lawyer was a waste of legal talent, and turned to finding and employing business managers to run the business part of the organization.

The chart indicates that the three major areas in the administrative organization have to do with personnel, office services, and finance. With the extensive use of the personal computer, computer services are now likely included in the "office services" area.

Personnel, both support and legal, are the heart of the firm. Usually the lawyers are not directed by the administrator but rather by the professional-personnel committee consisting of partners or, in some instances, by a lawyer who has been designated as the managing or senior partner. Support personnel are under the authority of the chief administrator. Depending upon the size of the firm, the top administrator may employ a number of assistants. The qualifications of these assistants often depend upon the qualifications of the

Fig. 2.1   Personnel Organization in a Large Law Firm

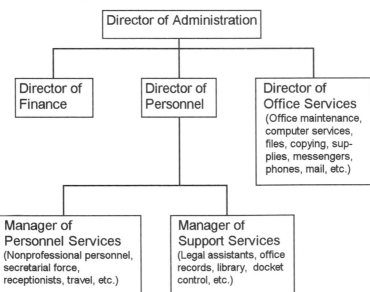

administrator. For example, if the administrator is an accountant, it is likely that the top assistant will be qualified in the personnel field. Conversely, if the administrator is qualified primarily in the personnel field, the assistant may be a specialist in accounting or finance.

The legal secretary   Except for those positions listed within the finance department, an ambitious and qualified legal secretary can fill any position named on the chart. A secretary should determine his or her qualifications to fill any of them and, if reassignment is desired, prepare for a particular job by study and training. One way for a legal secretary to prepare for a supervisory position is to take college classes in the area of business administration or management.

Assignments within the finance department are quite different, since this area requires special education and training. Some legal secretaries with an interest or skills in finance have become qualified as accountants while carrying their secretarial assignments and have moved up to positions analogous to that of Director of Finance.

The Legal Secretary

The days when the legal secretary spent the better part of the day sitting before the lawyer's desk, steno pad in hand, taking dictation and then transcribing it, by means of a manual typewriter, onto several carbon copies are fortunately a thing of the past. The lawyer today will likely have a computer at his or her own desk; may prepare a document or brief himself or herself; check for E-mail and send or receive fax documents by computer; and perform legal research using hypertext research techniques with CD-ROM and on-line research systems, downloading text directly to the brief or document. If, in addition. the lawyer works in a nonoffice environment using scheduled facilities and electronic connections, the work of the secretary will depart that much more from the traditional role.

Nevertheless, the well-organized lawyer will usually have a very clear concept of how the legal secretary should function. Much of this will depend on the lawyer's type of practice. For example, the litigator or trial lawyer often spends most of the working day in court or handling depositions. This means that the secretary will be expected to "keep the office running" by scheduling appointments and litigation events for the lawyer and keeping the lawyer informed of his or her schedule. The result is that the secretary may be required to arrive early and leave late in order to properly carry out these tasks. In many cases the secretary must try to organize the lawyer's work so that the hours it consumes can be reduced and overtime kept to a minimum.

Perhaps the most prized attribute of a legal secretary—or of any employee in a law office, for that matter—is accuracy. The business of the law office is words and ideas. The employee who is careless with spelling, does not know the basic rules of grammar, has a weak vocabulary, or persists in using nonstandard English either orally or in writing can be a liability to the office and should not expect to advance to the highest levels of responsibility.

Duties of a Legal Secretary

The secretary working in a single-lawyer office may do everything from preparing documents to brewing coffee. Depending on the size and nature of the office and the preferences of the attorney-employer, a legal secretary may be expected to perform any combination of the following tasks:

- Keyboarding correspondence
- Composing routine business letters
- Answering the telephone
- Transferring calls to the attorney
- Taking messages accurately
- Placing telephone calls
- Keeping a master telephone list
- Filing and maintaining office records
- Greeting clients and other callers
- Making appointments and appointment reminders
- Maintaining daybooks, diaries, and tickler files
- Maintaining the court docket or suit register for the office
- Following court cases on court calendars
- Serving as a notary public
- Maintaining financial records: bookkeeping, billing, banking, and collection for the firm
- Keeping time sheets for the attorney
- Transcribing, keyboarding, and proofreading documents on electronic media
- Taking live instructions and following through on them
- Preparing documents for clients (real estate, tax, wills, etc.)
- Preparing documents for filing with courts (litigation)
- Making copies of documents
- Operating telecommunications equipment
- Receiving and sending electronic mail (e-mail)
- Using legal forms properly in preparing documents
- Filing documents in the offices of the clerks of the courts
- Handling incoming and outgoing mail
- Serving court documents on opposing parties and attorneys
- Ensuring that the office is clean and orderly
- Maintaining office and file security
- Handling the storage and circulation of library materials
- Inventorying and ordering supplies
- Verifying citations
- Doing library and on-line research
- Making travel arrangements for the attorney
- Arranging meetings and conferences for the attorney

In the best of relationships between attorney and secretary, the two function as a team: while each performs those functions for which he or she has been trained and has demonstrated competence, both need to work together in carrying out these functions and completing the firm's work. If a firm expands with more lawyers, more space, and more support personnel, the secretary may share or drop altogether many of the collateral assignments. The professional legal secretary's primary responsibilities, however, remain the same: to be familiar with all aspects of the lawyer's professional work, including the needs of the lawyer's clients; to handle written communications of all types; and—an overriding requirement—to see that all legal deadlines are met.

Office routine   Almost immediately after being employed, especially in a well-structured law firm, the new secretary will likely be briefed by someone of authority. The secretary will often be furnished with a manual of information about the firm and the position. If no manual exists, the secretary should make extensive notes about office procedures; and, once he or she is fully integrated into the operation of the office, should consider creating a draft of an office-operations manual. The office or personnel manual should contain information about working hours, lunch periods, sick days, sick leave, vacations, employee benefits, overtime procedures, banking facilities, how to answer the telephone, how and where to have copies made, and procedures for controlling work sent to the word-processing center. These are topics that apply to all the office staff. In addition, the lawyer to whom the secretary is assigned should outline any routines or procedures peculiar to the assignment. If this is not done, the secretary should ask whether there are any special requirements. For example, does the lawyer wish to take all phone calls personally or is the secretary expected to screen incoming calls? Should the home telephone number of the lawyer be given to clients? If so, which clients? Lawyers, like everyone else, have their personal preferences and idiosyncrasies. By identifying such requirements and learning to accommodate them, the secretary can contribute immeasurably to building a strong lawyer-secretary team and creating a pleasant working relationship. To the extent that special requirements are not already incorporated into the office or personnel manual, the secretary might eventually suggest modifications of the manual to include them. In a firm of more than one lawyer, general information should be maintained in one portion of the manual and the specific requirements of the individual lawyers in another.

Job Qualifications

Education   The *minimum* educational background necessary for successfully performing legal-secretarial duties is attainment of a high-school diploma with a strong background in English, mathematics, social studies, and business. The average applicant, however, will have a degree from a business college or a two-year community college, preferably an associate's degree (A.A.) in legal-secretarial studies plus further courses in economics, political science, and business law. The applicant with *maximum* qualifications will have a bachelor's degree (B.A.) plus secretarial and business skills.

Dictation and keyboarding skills   The secretary is responsible for the appearance of the lawyer's end product, the legal document. Even if the content of the document is superb, the enthusiasm and degree of acceptance with which the document is received will depend to a large extent on how well the secretary has prepared it. Lawyers with years of experience have stated that 50 percent of their success is attributable to solid secretarial support, and a large part of that support is the production of accurate, attractive documents.

As education, training, equipment, and work spaces have improved, the speed and accuracy of secretarial typing and keyboarding have advanced. At present, an acceptable keyboarding speed is 60 to 70 words per minute, error-free.

Person-to-person dictation has largely vanished from the law office, although lawyers will still frequently give person-to-person instructions about anything from a single file to a large set of files or other office matters. Dictating machines have generally replaced the former person-to-person dictation. Small portable dictating machines have allowed lawyers to record their instructions in almost any setting, including automobile and air travel or during a conference with a client. As with keyboarding, dictation transcription needs to be error-free. (For more on dictation and transcription, see Chapter 9.)

Other skills   A prospective legal secretary will also find the following skills useful when applying for a position:

1. *Business-machine operation* Familiarity with and the ability to operate computers, electronic dictating/transcribing machines, adding machines, photocopiers, telephone equipment, facsimile machines, and printers.
2. *Records management* A good grasp of filing systems, both the alphabetic and the numeric methods, and how to set them up and use them.
3. *Business math* A strong background in bookkeeping, billing, banking, and collection procedures as well as tax recordkeeping.
4. *Legal forms* The ability to select and fill in legal forms with a minimum of attorney supervision.
5. *Language arts* A sound command of the English language—its grammar, syntax, and style—including an understanding of the conventions of punctuation and capitalization peculiar to law. Familiarity with Latin or French phrases and locutions peculiar to the law. Excellent spelling ability.
6. *Social skills* The ability to function intelligently and maturely within the social organization of the office as well as with clients.

The fully prepared applicant for a legal-secretarial position will also have secured his or her commission through the state as a notary public with a permanent (metal) seal. The prospective employer may not expect applicants to have completed this step, and may even be willing to pay for commissioning and a seal, but the applicant who already has them will signal to the prospective employer that he or she possesses the job preparedness that will serve the lawyer and the firm well.

The Legal Assistant

In recent decades there has been a marked development of the legal-assistant or paralegal field as a career. This position is somewhat analogous to that of the medical assistant. Many tasks formerly performed by doctors are now performed by paramedics and medical assistants, leaving the doctor free to concentrate on complex problems requiring highly specialized skills. Assigned to the paramedics are those problems requiring specialized education of shorter duration and a different level from that required of the fully trained physician. In this respect, paralegals are like paramedics.

The duties of paralegals vary widely from office to office, and no nation-wide certification program has yet been established. In fact, many legal secretaries perform paralegal tasks. The National Association of Legal Assistants (NALA) in Tulsa, Oklahoma, has adopted the following description of the legal assistant's work:

> *Under the supervision of a lawyer,* the legal assistant shall apply knowledge of law and legal procedures in rendering direct assistance to lawyers, clients and courts; design, develop and modify procedures, techniques, services and processes; prepare and interpret legal documents; detail procedures for practicing in certain fields of law; research, select, assess, compile and use information from the law library and other references; and analyze and handle procedural problems that involve independent decisions.

The NALA manual further clarifies these duties by describing what the assistant may not do:

> With the exception of *not accepting cases, not setting fees, not representing the client in court, nor giving legal advice to the client,* the legal assistant may perform any task delegated and *supervised by a lawyer.* The lawyer, of course, is and must be responsible to the client for the final work product.

Legal assistants were first extensively employed in the probate field. They were generally secretaries who had been working for lawyers in the wills and probate fields drawing wills, qualifying executors, preparing estate tax returns, and preparing accounts in estates. Lawyers and their secretaries in this specialty soon discovered that after working together for a while the secretary was often as qualified to carry out the administrative acts as was the lawyer. The estate tax return, for example, could be prepared initially by an experienced probate secretary with review by the lawyer, some possible discretionary revisions, and signature. When this task was assigned to the secretary, the lawyer time involved was reduced, as was the fee charged the client. The secretary's value to the firm was concurrently increased, and the compensation paid the secretary reflected this greater value. Finally, the firm profited, since, as the time burden on the probate lawyer was reduced, the lawyer became available to handle additional matters.

Following the remarkable success of the probate paralegal movement, openings occurred in real-estate, corporate, litigation, and antitrust law. In this last field, for example, much of the tedious, burdensome search through hundreds of thousands of documents can be accomplished at relatively low cost by paralegals, working with or without computers, compared with the very expensive conduct of such a search by qualified lawyers. These lawyers are also deprived of the opportunity to use their time and education more profitably in other matters. Other specialty practices that rely heavily on legal assistants are admiralty law, bankruptcy, criminal law, domestic relations, labor relations, oil and gas law, patent and trademark law, personal injury and medical malpractice, public utilities, tax law, and workers' compensation.

Legal Assistants, Paralegals, and Legal Secretaries

Because legal assistants only arrived on the scene fairly recently, their status in relation to the lawyer and the legal secretary is not yet clearly defined, and exactly where each position fits within the office organizational scheme may vary from office to office. The relationship between the legal assistant and the legal secretary should be close and cordial, since how well they mesh will determine how well they serve the lawyer and the clients for whom they both work.

Within the profession, the terms *paralegal* and *legal assistant* are often treated as synonymous, but certain differences are recognized. The legal assistant can be viewed as a generalist, capable of handling a wide range of activities for the lawyer, from litigation management to office operations. The legal assistant is in this sense a highly qualified legal secretary, particularly with regard to certain firm- or officewide duties and responsibilities. Thus, while the legal assistant is a legal-administrative generalist, the legal secretary typically retains a more personal relationship with a specific lawyer in the office. In contrast, the paralegal is usually a person who has been specially trained in one or more legal fields and is capable of processing cases within those fields. Paralegals will find employment in those offices with sufficient specialization to warrant employing a trained paraprofessional in those fields. The legal secretary and the legal assistant then, are both generalists by comparison to the paralegal. Much of what is contained in this book, in fact, is applicable to both the legal secretary and the legal assistant. Indeed, the more the legal secretary can absorb and apply in his or her employment, the more valuable he or she will be and the more likely it is that an employer will consider him or her more a legal assistant than a secretary.

A legal secretary who is interested in becoming a legal assistant should be cautioned, however. Competent and experienced legal secretaries are becoming a rare commodity, while competent and experienced paralegals and legal assistants are becoming more plentiful. As the need for good legal secretaries continues to increase and their numbers decrease, each one becomes more valuable. The same may not apply to paralegals since, although the fields in which they are employed may continue to increase, the number of competent persons in the various specialties may well increase at a greater rate. Employment as a paralegal may prove harder to find in the years to come than employment as an experienced legal secretary.

Employment Opportunities

A qualified legal secretary will find a wide choice of opportunities in the job market. Which path to follow will be a matter of personal preference, and before making the decision it is well to examine the major paths. The choices lie in both the private sector (law firms and corporate legal departments) and the public sector (courts and public governmental or quasi-governmental agencies).

The Private Sector

Law firms   Private law firms offer the widest variety of work and the greatest opportunity for individual initiative. A legal secretary working for a sole practitioner or a small group of lawyers will find a myriad of tasks that may be undertaken (or tactfully rejected). For example, a legal secretary who has some bookkeeping or accounting knowledge may become responsible for this area of the firm management if the firm has not employed someone in or out of the firm to do it. When such responsibilities are voluntarily assumed, the secretary's value to the firm is enhanced and should be reflected in the salary. The secretary should not undertake such additional duties, however, without consulting with the lawyer/employer and reaching an agreement as to the tasks to be performed and the potential impact this will have on the performance of previously assigned tasks.

A legal secretary may also be asked to take on menial tasks such as tidying the conference room or reshelving books in the library or straightening out a file storage area. These tasks clearly do not constitute work for which a secretary is employed, and to allocate the valuable time of a qualified and well-paid legal secretary to them is a waste of money and talent. For this reason, secretaries ordinarily should not perform such tasks routinely but should bring to the attention of the employer the need to hire a person or a service to take care of them.

Many secretaries prefer the atmosphere of a large organization and contribute more in such a situation than when they work for one or two lawyers. Large firms may offer excellent training for the secretary with basic skills, permitting their development and the acquisition of additional skills such as those required in a litigation or probate practice. In the probate area, for example, it is not at all unusual for a legal secretary to reach a point of proficiency where more than half of the work associated with the estate is performed by the secretary and referred to the lawyer for minor revision and approval.

On the other hand, secretaries working for the sole practitioner or small firm will find the wide variety of activities challenging and the more personal relationship that can develop rewarding. A big problem for many sole practitioners and small firms is liquidity or cash flow, that is, having sufficient cash revenues to meet financial obligations, including salaries. The secretary who is able to discover ways to increase cash flow and make the proper recommendation can be very valuable indeed to the lawyer(s) in the firm.

Legal secretaries relocating to a new city or initially coming on the job market should first look up the names and makeup of the local firms in a good law directory. Many local directories are published, but the most comprehensive and widely used directory is the *Martindale-Hubbell Law Directory,* referred to earlier in this chapter (page 34). The biographical section, arranged by state and city, lists the major firms alphabetically and indicates their specialties. By learning the size of the office and the age level, educational background, and legal areas of the lawyers, the secretary can make a first judgment as to whether the firm should be considered as an employer.

Corporate law departments   Many corporations have law departments, usually directed by a general counsel. Financial institutions such as banks and trust companies usually have large legal departments and ordinarily seek qualified legal secretaries.

Two advantages of working for a corporate legal department are the well-defined work and the regular hours. This situation differs from that of the law firm, where after-hours and weekend work may sometimes be required for several weeks at a time.

Another advantage of corporate legal work is the possibility of assignment to a particular field, such as real estate, with the opportunity to refine skills, establish a daily routine, and be free from numerous unwelcome shifts.

Legal clinics   A legal clinic is a law office that offers routine legal services at reasonable prices to people of low or moderate means. It does this by limiting its practice to certain routine matters that lend themselves to heavy reliance on paralegals and efficient systems for processing cases. Legal clinics are usually located conveniently to their prospective clients—in a shopping district or mall or even next to the local courthouse—and they frequently advertise in order to maintain a high-volume practice.

Although some clinics specialize in fields like bankruptcy or domestic relations, most of them offer a range of basic services needed by the ordinary citizen. Family law is their main service, followed in order by criminal law, wills, trusts and probate, landlord-tenant relations, real estate, consumer problems, bankruptcy, and personal-injury cases.

Despite á high failure rate in recent years, legal clinics have apparently become a permanent part of the legal scene.

The Public Sector

The legal departments of towns, cities, and states offer employment to legal secretaries, as do numerous federal agencies. The courts and the public agencies associated with them have a constant need for qualified legal secretaries. One of the most demanding jobs is that of secretary to a judge whose court docket is crowded. In the public prosecutor's office or the public defender's office, legal secretaries will be doing work similar to that performed in private law firms. The advantage of working in a public office is chiefly one of job security, since most of these positions are in the civil service. After seniority is attained, the prospect of being terminated for reasons other than cause is very slim. On the other hand, the chances of rapid advancement tend to be limited since most civil-service positions require time in grade at each step on the career ladder.

One should not overlook job opportunities with elected public officials. Many legislators, state and federal, prefer and even demand hometown employees for jobs in the legislator's hometown or state capital or Washington, D.C. One should never be unnecessarily awed by these positions; any applicant who has the intelligence, skills, and personality to fit the job may be hired.

Jobs Overseas

A number of legal secretarial jobs exist overseas in government agencies such as the State Department or for U.S. corporations doing business in foreign countries. The large automobile manufacturing companies, for example, maintain a number of offices overseas, as do the major oil companies and a number of other business corporations. Many of these corporations pursue a policy whereby secretarial help in the foreign country is found in the country itself. Despite this practice, many corporations make necessary exceptions and arrange for work permits so that a competent legal secretary employed by the corporation in, say, its Chicago office may be assigned for a specified period to its branch office in Paris or London. Secretaries interested in such assignments should ascertain the location of the branch offices and make known their desire for foreign assignment.

In the case of agencies of the U.S. government that maintain offices overseas, employment is easier since U.S. citizenship is usually a prerequisite. Legal secretaries interested in government assignments abroad may explore the opportunities available by writing to the government department involved, usually headquartered in Washington, D.C. For example, a letter of inquiry may be addressed to the employment office for the Department of State concerning the availability of State Department jobs abroad. Addresses of the employment offices of departments in the federal government are listed in the annual *United States Government Manual,* available from the Government Printing Office or a GPO bookstore.

A great personal asset when seeking employment abroad is facility with the language of the host country. Knowledge of a second language can also be an asset to the secretary working in the United States, particularly in a firm with an international-law focus or one that regularly represents clients who speak English only as a second language. The legal secretary with facility in a second language should therefore make a reasonable effort to maintain ability in that language in order to be able to apply it to the job as necessary.

Salaries abroad are generally competitive within the particular local market. They may be greater or smaller than salaries in the United States. Before accepting a job overseas, the secretary should ascertain not only the precise salary that will be paid but also general information concerning applicable taxes, cost of living, and other special factors that might affect the decision to take overseas employment. Another item to take into consideration is the opportunity for advancement overseas. As a general rule, employment overseas is for a particular job, and the opportunities for advancement at the foreign station are limited. However, outstanding performance in an overseas office may result in transfer back to the United States at a substantially higher level than that enjoyed when the overseas assignment was made.

Applying for a Job

Although there is no such thing as complete job security, we are often told that there is security in knowing how to go about finding a job. The various ways in which you can obtain a position will differ according to (1) your educational background and the professional contacts you have made during your studies, (2) your past or current on-the-job experience, and (3) the nature of your geographical area. If, for example, you live in a small town or rural area where most of the inhabitants know one another, you may depend on personal contacts with the local lawyers. If, on the other hand, you live in a city or in a large suburb, you will likely rely more on employment agencies and on advertisements in your search. Competition for the available jobs will obviously directly affect the likelihood of securing employment.

If you are responsible for the care of children, it is best to make arrangements for their long-term care *before* you start looking for a job. The employer that hires you will not consider it acceptable for you to take time out from your job to be with your children during routine childhood illnesses or because you have not found satisfactory child care. This is *your* responsibility, not your employer's. If an employer offers day care, that is an added benefit; but you should not assume that such a program is available when starting to seek employment.

In seeking a position, it is always best to explore and evaluate every possible opportunity. Do not settle for the first offer that comes along unless you are absolutely sure that the job is right for you and that you are the right person for the job. Think of moving laterally as well as up the career ladder. Looking for a job in the right way takes time, energy, thoroughness, and organization. In addition to reviewing the section below on sources of employment information, inquire within the legal and secretarial community regarding law offices in the area and employment conditions within them.

Sources of Employment Information

There are a number of sources of information on legal-secretarial positions. First, there is the classified section of the local newspaper, where positions will be listed under the heading of "Secretary" or "Legal Secretary." In addition to daily general-interest newspapers, a number of large metropolitan areas have daily or weekly newspapers devoted exclusively to the legal community. These also list positions in law offices.

Newspaper advertisements may be placed by employment agencies (discussed below) or directly by law offices. The ads may be blind or signed. A blind ad is one that lists and describes the job and sometimes the salary, and then gives a post office or newspaper box to which to send a letter of application, a résumé, and any other required material. A signed ad, on the other hand, gives not only the above information about the job but also the name, address, and possibly the telephone number of the prospective employer. (If you are answering a blind ad, be sure that your name and address are on the envelope, the letter, and the résumé.) If references are asked for, supply them. Be certain that your application materials are letter-perfect, as this is your initial chance to make a positive impression.

When responding to a signed ad requesting that you telephone the office for an appointment, make sure that you call only during the hours specified. Have your background material at hand so that you can respond concisely, coherently, and completely to all questions. You may be telephone-interviewed by another secretary, by an office manager, or by the lawyer, and your responses and your own questions ought to be tailored to the individual conducting the interview. For example, in talking with a lawyer, you should keep your responses and questions brief but inclusive so as to convey all necessary information but not waste the lawyer's valuable time. On the other hand, you can pursue important matters with the lawyer such as his or her personal expectations of the successful candidate—matters that you ordinarily would not bring up with a staff member. If the interviewer is an office manager or another secretary, you can discuss details of office routines.

Local legal-secretarial associations may be helpful in locating job opportunities, but usually they are not the most appropriate for first-time job applicants. The association usually makes the vacancies known to its members, and the positions are filled before the newcomer is aware of them. Local bar associations and chambers of commerce are good contact points for general information about the job market for legal secretaries, but they do not ordinarily list particular jobs. The publications of large metropolitan bar associations, however, often list secretarial openings, and a few local bar associations run legal-secretarial hiring services. Some law firms and many corporations have installed electronic "information centers" on the Internet (see Chapter 4, pp. 108–09), and many of those centers include information on employment opportunities.

Employment Agencies

The source of employment information and assistance most often used by newcomers to the job market is the professional employment agency. Usually an employment agency places newspaper ads for its clients regarding job openings that they need to fill. The agency interviews and screens the candidates for the jobs and then refers the qualified candidates to the prospective employer. Depending on the job and the geographical location, the employment agency may charge you a fee for placing you in a position; or the fee may be charged entirely to your ultimate employer or split on a percentage basis between you and the employer. It is wise to investigate what you must pay the agency when it finds you a job. If the agency claims that the employer will be charged for all or part of the fee, you should confirm this with the prospective employer when an offer of employment is made so that no problems arise with regard to fee payments.

Employment agencies are listed in the telephone Yellow Pages of the areas where they are located. If you are canvassing all of the opportunities and sources of information in a particular geographical location, you can make unsolicited inquiries about potential jobs by simply calling or writing to the agencies. If you write, be sure to include your résumé with your letter of inquiry so that the agency can act on it right away or call you later when any suitable openings come up.

Employment agencies usually represent to the employer that they "prescreen" applicants and administer certain tests so as to be able to report an applicant's qualifications to the employer. An agency that does not work to fit its applicants to available positions is doing no more for either party than they could do themselves with newspaper ads. Certainly, if an employment agency that you are using reports objective "qualifications" (such as keyboarding or dictation-transcription speeds) for which no testing or other basis exists, you should advise a prospective employer and offer to take a test so as to be able to substantiate your claim of proficiency.

Employment agencies, as noted earlier, advertise their listings in newspapers and in some legal periodicals. If you see an advertised job for which you are qualified, call the agency that placed the ad right away. Be sure to have on hand your résumé and references. This material is important because the initial screening will take place over the telephone. You will make a better impression with the account representative if you can supply all needed data quickly, crisply, and completely without delays or paper shuffling. Remember, the agency will want to interview you in person before recommending you or sending you to a prospective employer. Arrive on time for the agency interview, and follow the guidelines for interview etiquette outlined later in this chapter (see pages 57–59). Take with you to the agency two copies of your résumé and reference list, one for the agency and another for the agency to send ahead to its client. Also be prepared to ask your high school and/or college to submit transcripts of your grades to the agency if requested. This is your responsibility. (You may have to pay the schools a nominal fee for this service.)

Never forget that undoubtedly you are only one among many applicants being screened by the agency for a position. Therefore, be sure to show real interest in the job. Find out as much as you can about the tasks and responsibilities involved. Ask about the nature of the law practice. Find out the office hours and whether weekend work, night work, or other overtime is required. And most importantly—ask *exactly* what duties you will be expected to perform. Find out, if you can, whether any specialized skills (such as machine transcription) are required. Ask whether the lawyer expects to train you further in specialized procedures on the job. While the employment agency may not be able to give you all of the answers to these questions, you will have found out which questions to ask the employer later on, and you will also have demonstrated genuine interest in the job and a thorough knowledge of your field. After you have explored what the job entails, you can then discuss further with the agency the salary range and the benefits offered by the employer.

Apart from responding to advertisements, consider writing letters of application and enclosing résumés to particular firms or companies you would like to work for, even if you are not aware of any vacancy in those organizations. Before responding to advertisements or writing letters of application on your own, however, review your contract with the employment agency to determine whether you or your prospective employer will have to pay the agency for a job that you obtain directly. Depending upon the size of the firm, the résumé should be addressed to the office manager, the personnel director, or the managing partner. If the résumé discloses a job applicant who appears to be of top quality, the hiring official may well invite the applicant in for an interview and offer employment even if a full vacancy does not then exist, in order to build up a reserve of legal-secretarial talent.

Inquiring About a Job

When inquiring about a job that may be open or responding to an employment ad by telephone, be polite and coherent. After all, one of a legal secretary's prime responsibilities is the easy handling of telephone calls. Thus, the members of the law office team will be evaluating your telephone performance from the beginning to the end of the conversation. If an applicant shows that he or she cannot converse with aplomb during an initial interview, it is obvious that the applicant may not be able to deal effectively with all of the many calls that come into or originate from a busy law office. Take into consideration the fact that clients can be demanding and often impatient. It is necessary, therefore, to project a smile in your voice and a relaxed, confident self-assurance.

Be sure to prepare yourself before placing your call. If necessary, jot down any special questions you want to ask and any particular points you wish to make. Have your personal information on hand by the telephone. Keep these materials at hand, even if you are simply waiting for the lawyer to call you. Since you can never know what kinds of questions will be asked, you must be ready for anything.

In all telephone conversations with a prospective employer, remember that your telephone demeanor is being judged at all times, either directly or subconsciously. Use your most pleasant voice and use only standard conversational English. Except in the most unusual circumstances, colloquialisms, slang, and unconventional usages are out of place in the law office.

The following guidelines will help make a positive impression on your telephone interviewer:

1. In your concern about the job, do not forget to say hello and good-bye.
2. Identify yourself at once and state your reason for calling.
3. Use the other person's name in the conversation; if for some reason it has not been mentioned, ask "To whom am I speaking, please?"
4. Give straightforward, complete, concise answers to all questions.
5. Ask the questions that *you* have, but keep in mind that there may be some questions that only the lawyer can answer.
6. Be polite and enthusiastic without becoming emotional.
7. If you have small children at home, do not try to call when they are in the room making noise. Such a practice indicates that you aren't well organized. Make your call when they are outside or napping.
8. If, for some reason, you discover during the conversation that you really are not qualified for the job or that you do not want to pursue the matter further, say so politely.
9. If the interviewer sounds rushed, ask if you can call at another time, or if the interviewer could call you back at his or her convenience.
10. It is usually pointless to discuss salary matters during an initial telephone conversation.

Sometimes the lawyer or office manager will return a phone call after reviewing your résumé and consulting your references. The following are suggestions for handling this type of telephone call:

1. If you are expecting a call or calls regarding employment, don't just answer the telephone with "Hello"; give your name as well.
2. Answer all questions politely and thoroughly, but do not ramble; lawyers are too busy to waste time with irrelevant conversations.
3. If the lawyer suggests a personal interview save most of your questions for then. You can, however, ask one or two general questions about the size of the firm or the nature of the practice. That way, you will show your interest but not at the expense of the lawyer's valuable time. Also, jot down your questions (and the responses) for future reference.
4. Verify your appointment date, time of day, and location. Ask directions if necessary.
5. Let the caller terminate the conversation by being the first to say good-bye.

The Job-Application Letter

A properly formatted and well-written letter of application will greatly assist in preselling you to a prospective employer. This type of letter is a concrete indication of your verbal and technical skills and of your general personality and intelligence.

The letter should be on plain bond paper. (*Do not* use social stationery or notepaper.) Using a word processor will make the job easier. Exotic typefaces should be avoided. Any of the letter formats discussed in Chapter 7 (pages

158–69) in this book are appropriate. The letter ought not to exceed one page. (See Fig. 2.2.) Under no circumstances should you prepare and photocopy a form letter to be sent to numerous law offices, although individually prepared letters using a word-processing merge feature are allowable. The applicant lacking the time and the common courtesy to write a personal letter will probably not receive careful consideration.

Fig. 2.2 Letter of Application

```
                                      Caroline C. Elkin
                                      123 Yurok Lane
                                      Lynwood, CA 98765
                                      (310) 123-4567

                    June 1, 19--

Ms. Anna Stone-Calvert
Director, Personnel
Brown, Black, Green & Gray, P.L.C.
Suite 112
81 Esquire Towers
Los Angeles, CA 90663

Dear Ms. Stone-Calvert:

     The Brown, Black, Green & Gray employment ad in
the May 30 edition of the Sunday Times-Republican has
attracted my interest.  Because I believe that I am
qualified for the secretarial position in your office,
I am sending you a copy of my résumé.

     My keyboarding rate is 70 wpm.  I am experienced
in the use of machine dictation and transcription
equipment.  I have been commissioned a Notary Public
and have a seal.  I am also proficient in Spanish.

     I am currently employed as secretary to Selma S.
Addington, who is retiring from her law practice at the
end of July.  I believe that the experience gained in
this position would be useful in your law office.

     I look forward to a personal interview at your
convenience.  Brown, Black, Green & Gray is a fine law
firm--one for which I know I would enjoy working.

                         Sincerely yours,



                         Caroline C. Elkin

enc.
```

Before preparing the letter, plan your approach in detail. Make an outline or a draft of the points to be made . If the letter is solicited (i.e., if you are responding to an advertisement), mention in the first paragraph the specific position for which you are applying and the date and source of the advertisement. If the letter is unsolicited (i.e., if you are applying on your own initiative), say as much in the first paragraph and state why you are interested in working for the particular practice. Next, focus on and develop your best assets. A concise statement of your technical skills (such as dictation and keyboarding rates) may be given along with mention of any more specialized skills (such as operation of computer spreadsheet programs). Another sentence or even a paragraph expanding on some aspect of your education or your previous employment not already developed fully in the résumé can be included. The tone throughout should be straightforward yet modest and sincere. The text should be carefully proofread for grammatical and typographical errors. Keep a copy of the letter for your records.

The Résumé

The lawyer, or the personnel director of a law firm or corporate legal office, may invite you to submit a résumé prior to setting up an interview.

Because your résumé is the complete statement of your professional advancement and accomplishments to date, it is a key factor in achieving your employment objectives. Although books have been written on this subject, the elements essential to all well-written résumés can be set down here. These elements are as follows:

1. *Personal identification:* your full name, address, and telephone number (home and/or office).
2. *Employment experience:* each job that you have held, listed chronologically from present to past, including, for each employer, the name and address of the employer, employment dates, your job title, a *brief* job description if the responsibilities are not obvious from the title itself, and perhaps a concise summary of your special accomplishments in each position if space permits.
3. *Educational background:* a list of the institutions that you have attended or from which you have graduated, starting with the most recent and concluding with high school.
4. *Special skills:* a list of special skills that might be valued by a prospective employer.
5. *References:* the sentence "References will be provided on request."

If you have no previous employment experience, supplement your education category with a list of the business and secretarial courses that completed, mention your keyboarding and transcription rates, and list any academic or professional honors that you have been awarded. If you have completed any special freelance secretarial projects (e.g., typing manuscripts and theses), you can mention them under the heading "Special Projects" following the educational section. Work in the medical field should also be mentioned, as well as fluency in languages other than English. A sample résumé is illustrated in Fig. 2.3.

Employers are prohibited from inquiring about age, sex, marital status, race, religion, or national origin. References to this information, including

Fig. 2.3   Sample Résumé

CAROLINE C. ELKIN
123 Yurok Lane
Lynwood, CA 98765
(310) 123-4567

EXPERIENCE

9/92–Present   Addington & Associates, P.L.C., Los Angeles
    Legal Secretary, Corporate Practice

9/88–9/92   Jones, Robinson & Burgin, P.C., Los Angeles
    Legal Secretary, Litigation Practice

6/85–9/88   Security Pacific National Bank, Los Angeles
    Secretary for Loan Officer

4/83–6/85   Western Gear Corporation, Lynwood, Cal.
    Accounting Clerk (part-time)

EDUCATION

2/94–Present   Pasadena City College, Pasadena, Cal.
    Currently enrolled in paralegal courses

9/81–6/85   Lynwood High School, Lynwood, Cal.
    Top 10% of class; Bank of America Award in
    Business

SKILLS   WordPerfect 6.X
    QuattroPro
    Notary Public commission with seal
    Proficient in Spanish

REFERENCES   References will be provided upon request

---

photographs, should not be included in the résumé. Other data that should not be given on the résumé are as follows:

1. *Names and addresses of references* References should be listed separately and should be provided by you at the interview or in an interview follow-up letter (see Fig. 2.4).

2. *Salary expectations* It is best to discuss salary requirements and ranges during the interview itself, since you will not want to undersell yourself ahead of time or possibly price yourself out of a job market that you may be unfamiliar with.

3. *Your reasons, if any, for changing jobs* Since wording can often be misunderstood without personal clarification, it is best to discuss this matter with the interviewer, and only if you are asked, rather than committing yourself on paper.

4. *Your reasons for present unemployment, if applicable* This topic is also tricky and is therefore best dealt with in person or in a telephone conversation, since adequate explanations often require valuable page space that can be better used to highlight your assets.

Your résumé normally should not exceed one page. However, quality and comprehensiveness should not be sacrificed for brevity. A two-page résumé may be best for certain individuals. In order to achieve both maximum brevity and comprehensiveness, you should plan the material and then expect to prepare several drafts before settling on the final form. All facts should be double-checked. Use plain, straightforward, standard English devoid of technical jargon and superlatives. The suggestions given above regarding the appearance of the job application letter apply to the résumé as well.

Although there are many acceptable résumé formats, the simplest and cleanest treatment is to block all the material flush left. Entries should be single-spaced internally, with double- or triple-spacing between entries, depending on the page space available. Main and secondary headings may be introduced with underscoring, capital letters, or bold print.

Once you have prepared your initial résumé (preferably using a word-processing program), save it or a copy of it. When the time comes to prepare a new résumé, you should only need to update the information.

References The references best suited for a future employer are those furnished by past employers. Many former employers, out of real or imagined fear of litigation, are severely limiting the type and amount of information they are willing to supply regarding former employees. Consequently, it is very important that you *not* give a person's name as a reference to a prospective employer without first getting permission from that person. You may be asked to provide a release to the former employer if that employer is going to do more than confirm that you were an employee.

If you have no prior work experience, the chief source for references is the instructors in the schools you have attended. Avoid using relatives as references, since most employers feel that opinions obtained from relatives are not objective.

In some cases, references may write blanket "To whom it may concern" letters of introduction and recommendation that you can take with you in sealed envelopes to prospective employers. These letters are generally not as effective as letters written directly to each prospective employer, however.

When you prepare a list of references, follow the general format and style that you have used for your résumé. Head the list "REFERENCES." Single-space each entry and double- or triple-space between entries. Include the full name, title, address, and telephone number of each person who has consented to recommend you. Include at least one supervisor and/or attorney from each former place of employment. Include one former instructor if possible. No un-explained gaps should show up when the résumé and reference list are compared. Personal character references can be listed at the bottom of the sheet, if necessary. Give the employer the reference list when it is asked for, but do not staple this list to your résumé. A sample list of references is shown in Fig. 2.4.

There may be instances when you do not want a present or former employer to be contacted for a reference. That fact should be noted. Be prepared, however, to explain fully and candidly to the prospective employer *why* you do not want the person contacted. You should also be prepared to explain the circumstances under which you would withdraw that request, such as a decision by the prospective employer to make an offer of employment subject to the report of the reference.

Tests and Application Forms

Many law firms or employment agencies test the skills of applicants in one or more of the following areas: keyboarding, dictation transcription, spelling, vocabulary, grammar, proofreading, punctuation, and basic mathematics. If a test is administered as part of the job application procedure, do your best and don't worry about the results. Remember that accuracy may be regarded as

Fig. 2.4   References

CAROLINE C. ELKIN

REFERENCES

Selma S. Addington, Esq.
Addington & Associates
783 W. First Street
Los Angeles, CA 90031
(213) 880-1374

Gary Wayne Cole
Assistant Treasurer
Western Gear Corporation
777 Pullman Street
Lynwood, CA 98761
(213) 876-0543

Brian R. Burgin, Esq.
Jones, Robinson & Burgin
Suite 2
9837 Avenue S
Los Angeles, CA 90560
(213) 999-1234

John L. Stimson
Assistant Vice President
Security Pacific
   National Bank
Los Angeles, CA 90111
(213) 690-6129

Personal Reference

The Reverend Donald D. O'Leary
The Rectory
St. Mary's Church
6 Northwood Street
Lynwood, CA 98761
(213) 876-1112

more valuable than speed. If the results are sufficiently bad, you are not ready for the job and should aim your search elsewhere. Perhaps additional coursework, or a review of prior coursework, will solve the problem. Otherwise you can prepare by using various basic skill–enhancement booklets or paralegal test aids available at bookstores and libraries. If the results are not top-notch but still acceptable, you may well be offered the job on the bias of your appearance, personality, and general qualifications. In other words, relax and do your best.

Many employers use application forms as a means of obtaining information about a prospective employee prior to an interview. You may be expected to fill out an application form for the prospective employer. Be prepared by bringing a copy of your résumé with you as a reference. Write down the necessary information—details about past employment, including company addresses, supervisors' names, employment dates, and salaries; details of your education, with dates; addresses and telephone numbers of references—writing "N/A" (for *not applicable*) or a dash on those blanks that are not relevant. Some application forms have a space in which to write the salary you expect. It is better to write a salary *range* rather than a specific amount.

The Job Interview

Once you reach the interview stage, you should prepare for it carefully. First impressions—whether created on the telephone, in writing, or in person—are lasting impressions.

Dress carefully for your interview. Clothing should be clean, pressed, and conservative. Exotic attire is definitely out of place. Be especially careful in cleaning your hands and manicuring your fingernails. Clean, neatly arranged hair should add to your appearance. Strong scents should be avoided, although subtle scents may be beneficial. If you are a woman, avoid excessive makeup. Dress simply and comfortably in a manner suitable for secretarial work. The dress need not be on the masculine side but should convey the image of a professional, skilled person. Men applying for secretarial positions are expected to wear a suit, or at a minimum slacks and jacket, with shirt and tie. On the job itself it may not always be necessary to wear a tie or jacket, but undoubtedly this outfit is best for the interview. Shoes must be shined. A sloppy, unkempt appearance is often taken as an indicator of a sloppy worker.

Lawyers are in the business of persuading other people, whether judges, juries, opponents, witnesses, or clients; that is why they dress as they do. If you want to persuade the lawyer or law firm that you should be hired, you need to dress accordingly. You must meet or exceed the office's expectations regarding personal appearance.

Since the secretary is usually the first and last member of the law-office team seen by clients and other visitors, it is essential that he or she be a credit to the practice. Thus, impeccable manners are requisite. Since an applicant's manners will be carefully observed by an interviewer, the following are some of the most important points to remember:

1. *Punctuality* Be on time for your interview. If you don't know exactly where the office is located, get directions beforehand. If the office is in a large city where traffic and parking are a problem, ask a staff member for the best driving or public-transportation route and find out where you can park. This

can be done when your appointment is being made. If you are still unsure of the directions, make a dry run in advance. In any event, give yourself plenty of time to get there.

2. *Arrival* When you enter the office, identify yourself to the receptionist and state your business ("I'm Frank Sowell, and I have a 4:30 appointment with Ms. Tanner.") Be cheerful and polite. If the weather is bad and you need to doff heavy outerwear, find out where to hang it up so that you won't be burdened with coat, scarf, mittens, hat, or the like during the interview.

3. *Waiting to see the lawyer* If you have to wait for a while before seeing the lawyer or personnel manager, sit quietly and observe the office routine without appearing nosy. This will provide you with additional questions to ask in the interview, and it will also give you a fairly accurate sense of the practice itself.

4. *Introductions* When introduced to the lawyer or personnel manager, as well as to other staff members, smile, repeat their names ("How do you do, Mr. Lee," or "It's nice to meet you, Ms. Smith"), and appear enthusiastic but not gushy. The other extreme to avoid is appearing glum or sick (even if you *feel* that way!).

5. *Posture* When sitting, do not sprawl. On the other hand, do not sit rigidly like a store mannequin. Try to relax and enjoy the experience.

6. *Smoking and gum-chewing* Most offices are now no-smoking areas. Even where smoking is permitted, it is best not to smoke. Gum-chewing is strictly taboo at an interview.

During the interview, bear in mind not only that you are being interviewed but that you should be interviewing the prospective employer. In addition to answering questions fully and frankly, do not hesitate to ask questions that will help you determine whether you want the job if it is offered. While it is impossible to offer cut-and-dried guidelines to cover every eventuality in interviews, the following suggestions should help make your experience more positive:

1. *Eye contact* Look directly at the interviewer when you are speaking or are being spoken to. Avoiding someone's eyes, especially when you are answering questions, can be interpreted as evasiveness. On the other hand, don't stare blankly at the interviewer.

2. *Speech mannerisms* Try to avoid those annoying verbal tics that many people use to cover up pauses or to give themselves time to think of what to say next. Some of the more irritating mannerisms are the use of "ah" or "uh," sentences starting with "Like, . . . ," and repeating "you know" or "OK" throughout a conversation.

3. *Asking questions* Don't try to lead the conversation, since the lawyer undoubtedly will have decided what is to be asked and discussed. Follow the lawyer's lead. You can interject your own questions during lulls or save them for the end when you will probably be asked if you have any questions.

4. *Job description and on-the-job training* Be sure that you get a clear idea of just what you will be doing in the office. Understand the expected hours of work and any required overtime. Find out if the lawyer intends to give you any on-the-job training and, if so, what kind.

5. *Questions you can't answer* Many people are embarrassed when they discover during an interview that they don't know everything an interviewer expects them to know. If you are asked something that you cannot answer, say so honestly. Sometimes interviewers ask questions that they know you can't answer just to see whether they will get an honest reaction.

6. *Weaknesses in your skills* If the lawyer mentions a required skill in which you know you are weak, admit it right away. Be prepared to say that you are willing to improve in that area, whether by programmed self-study, by taking a refresher course, or by learning on the job.

7. *Handicaps* Under the Americans with Disabilities Act (applicable to employers with 15 or more employees), employers are prohibited from discriminating against you because of your handicap. If you are handicapped, it may be obvious when you appear for your interview. If the handicap is not visible, you should make sure that your interviewer knows of its existence before the interview is over. Disclosure of the handicap should open a discussion regarding (1) any job requirements that the handicap would prevent you from performing and/or (2) any accommodations that the employer would have to make in order to meet your specific needs. Even though you may be handicapped and may have been to dozens of job interviews without getting the job, never assume that you will fail to get the job for which you are interviewing before the interview is concluded, as this will negatively color the interview and lessen your chance.

Salary, fringe benefits, and insurance The interviewer will tell you your base pay and will undoubtedly outline the firm's fringe benefits. Feel free to bring up any of these topics if the interviewer doesn't. Ascertain the precise details of the position in question rather than relying on information furnished by your employment agency, since in many instances the agency will not have the exact data. It is bad practice to argue with a prospective employer about a salary that you feel is too low. You can ask about the employer's raise policy (for example, what is a standard raise and when are employees considered for them?). If the office is large enough to accommodate a large staff, you can ask about staff promotions. Sometimes an employment ad that you are responding to will have stipulated that the salary is *open* (i.e., open to negotiation). If you have familiarized yourself beforehand with the usual salary range for legal secretaries in your area, you ought to be able to discuss the issue intelligently with the lawyer. In cases like this, it is even more important to highlight any education, experience, and specialized skills that you feel would place you as close as possible to the top of the range.

If you can see that the interview is about to end with the lawyer's still not having brought up the matter of salary, you might say, "Oh, by the way, Ms. ———, what do you feel is a reasonable salary, based on your expectations and my qualifications?" Other ways of wording your question are "What will the starting salary be for this position?" and "May I ask what the salary will be?" You can also convey your knowledge of the usual salary range in the area by mentioning the figures in round numbers: "When I spoke recently with the bar association, it was suggested that the going salary for this type of position is currently ———." Avoid being pushy or insistent; just state the facts pleasantly and objectively.

Determine during the interview whether or not you will be covered in the lawyer's professional liability insurance policy. This is very important, for as an agent of the lawyer you too can be liable to litigation. (See the section "Professional Liability," p. 35.)

The closing At the conclusion of an interview, the interviewer will often ask if you have any questions. In addition to asking any you may have, it may also be appropriate and beneficial at this point to encourage the interviewer to summarize your qualifications for the position or clear up any concerns by asking, "What do you see as my strengths for this position?" and "Are there any concerns about my background that I can clear up?"

At the end of the interview, you may be offered a job on the spot or the interviewer may tell you that he or she will get back to you in a week or so, after

Fig. 2.5   Interview Follow-Up Letter

```
                                   Caroline C. Elkin
                                   123 Yurok Lane
                                   Lynwood, CA 98765
                                   (310) 123-4567


                   June 15, 19--



Ms. Anna Stone-Calvert
Director, Personnel
Brown, Black, Green & Gray, P.L.C.
Suite 112
81 Esquire Towers
Los Angeles, CA 90663

Dear Ms. Stone-Calvert:

     It was a pleasure talking with you yesterday
about the secretarial position at Brown, Black, Green
& Gray.  I was very impressed with the job as you
described it and with the professionalism of the
staff.

     I hope you will give me the opportunity to put
my skills and enthusiasm to work for you.  I think my
transcription experience and general secretarial
skills would serve the firm well as it looks to
expand.  I am excited about the challenges I see
ahead with Brown, Black, Green & Gray and look
forward to having the chance to make a major
contribution to its efforts.

                         Yours truly,



                         Caroline C. Elkin
```

all other applicants have been interviewed. If you would like a day or two to think about the offer, say so. However, you should set a specific day and hour when you will call the interviewer back. Do not delay your return call more than one or two days. If the interviewer says that you will be called regarding a possible offer, accept this decision politely. Try to get some idea of when you will be contacted so that you will be at home. You might also mention that you need to complete your own plans rather soon.

If your prospects look good or if you have been offered the job, try to get a brief tour of the office suite. Another good idea is to borrow an extra copy of the procedures manual, if there is one, so that you can familiarize yourself with the actual management of the office before your first day on the job.

Let the interviewer end the interview. When he or she stands up, then you may do the same. Shake hands, thank the interviewer for the time spent with you, express your interest in the position, say that the interview has been enjoyable or whatever seems most appropriate, and then say good-bye. Do not forget to say good-bye to the assistant or receptionist on your way out.

If, at the close of the interview, you are told that you are not quite qualified for the position, thank the interviewer for the candid evaluation and be sure to mention that the interview has been a pleasant as well as an informative experience. Say good-bye politely. Do not be needlessly discouraged: appreciate the honest evaluation, work to improve any indicated deficiencies, and keep looking for the right position. Each interviewing experience will bring you added confidence and ease in answering the interviewer's questions.

If the possibility of employment is left open, follow the interview with a thank-you letter. You can use this opportunity to restate your interest in the position or to add anything you omitted during the interview. (See the sample thank-you letter in Fig. 2.5.)

Successful Human Relations

The Lawyer-Secretary Team

A lawyer and secretary working together are like a duo of musicians. With practice, and by recognizing and accommodating to each other's strengths, weaknesses, and idiosyncrasies, the musicians can give a performance of grace and beauty, whereas failure to make such an accommodation leads to a breakdown of harmony and results in discord. The same discord can occur between lawyer and secretary when the two fail to become attuned to each other.

In order to achieve harmony with the lawyer to whom you are assigned, try to learn exactly what he or she expects. For instance, how does the lawyer wish to be addressed? Is a formal *Mr. Brown* expected? If the lawyer is female, does she prefer *Miss, Mrs.,* or *Ms. Brown*? Don't trust to guesswork on this point—ask the question. Even if first-name informality is permitted, the more formal form of address should always be used when clients or other similar persons are present. Until you are sure of yourself, lean toward a formal relationship with the lawyer and observe it until the lawyer clearly indicates that a more informal relationship is in order. The same principle applies to the manner in which you wish to be addressed. The best way to realize your wishes is by making them known at the very outset of the job. A common means of communicating by written notes or memoranda within the law office is to use the other person's initials.

Ascertain the work habits of the lawyer. Is he or she an early starter, a late worker, a workaholic? Is the lawyer methodical and well organized? Seek to come to an understanding of how your work schedule may be dovetailed with these habits for the sake of maximum efficiency. For example, if the lawyer is a late starter and works late, consider whether to have your working hours changed to accommodate his or her schedule and whether office policy permits such a change. Ascertain such things as the following: how the lawyer wishes to have you answer the telephone, how to determine the clients' wishes, to which clients you may give the lawyer's home phone number, to which clients you are free to disclose where the lawyer is at a particular time, and the best time of day to schedule appointments. In other words, become an extension of the lawyer in all matters affecting the office—*except* the furnishing of legal advice. *Never* advise a client in the law; this is a commandment that must be observed at all times.

How to help increase a lawyer's billable time   Perhaps the best way to begin to achieve success as a member of the lawyer-secretary team is by understanding how a lawyer earns fees. Fees make up the fund from which the lawyer pays the rent for the office, the myriad bills that represent operating costs, and the salaries of secretaries, paralegals, associates, file clerks, and messengers. After all of these are paid, what is left is the income of the lawyer or, if there is more than one, the income of the members of the firm, to be divided on the basis of some agreed formula.

In order to bill for fees, the lawyer keeps a record of time spent on a matter and bills the client at an appropriate rate. If the lawyer's billable time is valued at $100 per hour and ten hours are spent on the matter, the bill will be $1000, absent some other understanding or special agreement. For reasons that need not be detailed here, even when the lawyer is retained on a flat-fee or contingent-fee basis, he or she should maintain time records.

Assume the lawyer arrives at 9:00 a.m., takes an hour for lunch, and leaves at 5:00 p.m., thereby putting in seven office hours. If the lawyer's rate is $100 per hour and 60 minutes of each one of the seven hours is charged to a client and collected, the lawyer's production for that day will be $700. If, however, the lawyer spends half an hour looking for a file, another half hour waiting for the secretary to arrive in the morning, a quarter hour waiting while the secretary changes the printer ribbon and gets a notebook, half an hour waiting for the secretary to return from lunch, and three quarters of an hour correcting typed copy and then rereading it, the potential of seven chargeable hours is reduced to four and one-half hours, and office productivity for the day falls from $700 to $450. If each day follows the same pattern, in a five-day week this will result in a loss of $1,250.

An understanding of this system of billing indicates clearly how the secretary may best serve in a lawyer-secretary team—by doing everything possible to relieve the lawyer of all unnecessary detail and by maximizing the lawyer's chargeable time. In this way the lawyer's income goes up, the secretary's value is recognized, and the secretary's income goes up.

One way in which the secretary can improve the productivity of the lawyer is by ganging up office appointments and telephone calls. The secretary, in consultation with the lawyer, should try to string together appointments and telephone calls so as to free up blocks of time for the lawyer to use on projects requiring lengthier time commitments. If this method is used, the secretary should check with the lawyer from time to time to assess the success of the effort.

The Office Team

In addition to being part of a lawyer-secretary team, the secretary is usually part of an office team. Since much of a secretary's working life is spent with an "office family," it is a good idea to contribute to making it a happy family. Be courteous and helpful to your fellow workers. Stay on a friendly but somewhat formal basis until informality is clearly invited. Respect the privacy of others in the firm and try to prevent the formation of cliques that pit one group against another. Office politics waste time and impair morale. Finally, do more than your share of work whenever it is feasible. If you are not busy and your coworker is swamped, lend a helping hand. The favor will be repaid and over a period of time will be recognized by office management and the members of your office family.

By following these precepts, the secretary can begin to demonstrate the qualities of leadership that are desirable in higher, supervisory positions. If your goal is to climb the office ladder, the fastest and best way to the top rung is by demonstrating outstanding ability and leadership starting at the bottom rung and continuing on each step up.

Relations With Clients

The legal secretary is usually the first and last member of the office staff whom a client sees and can contribute a great deal to the client's favorable impression of the office. The following guidelines will help you project a positive image of the law firm:

1. Be courteous to all clients and prospective clients on the telephone and in person. When clients enter the office, make them feel at home. It is always gracious to walk a new client to the lawyer's office and introduce him or her to the lawyer.

2. Learn the client's name and get it right—both its spelling and pronunciation. Make an effort to remember the name by using it in conversation. If you are responsible for filling out intake forms, print the information in all capital letters for the sake of accuracy, consistency, and readability.

3. When clients try to discuss their affairs with you, be sympathetic but don't get overly involved. You may have to tactfully change the topic of conversation.

4. Never attempt to offer legal advice, even if the client tries to draw you into a conversation about it.

5. Make no comment if the client criticizes another attorney.

6. Make sure the client understands that you regard all matters as confidential. One way to do this is never to leave telephone messages for the client other than asking him or her to return the call.

7. Have on hand in the office one or more books devoted to the subject of business etiquette.

8. Keep clients informed. Even if you have nothing to report, you may give the client a call to say that, while nothing new has occurred, the attorney will let him or her know as soon as something does develop.

   9. Avoid unnecessary delays in preparing a client's legal papers and correspondence.
  10. Always be discreet.

For more information regarding contact with clients see the section "Client Appointments" in Chapter 6, pp. 128–36.

Ethics

What takes place in a lawyer's office between the lawyer and the client is always confidential. Regardless of how important it is—and all matters are important to the client—neither the lawyer nor the secretary is at liberty to reveal or discuss it except as a necessary part of the lawyer's prosecution of the matter in behalf of the client. Conversations concerning client matters should not be indulged in in the office, at home, in the elevators, in the rest rooms, over lunch at a restaurant—anywhere or at any time. Even the way you maintain your work area is important. Never create the opportunity for an unauthorized person to read the papers on your desk.

Code of Ethics

The confidential nature of a lawyer's practice comes under the general heading of ethics. Confidentiality is but one of the tenets of the codes of ethics applicable to lawyers and legal secretaries. The aim of these codes is to ensure that lawyers and legal secretaries adhere to the highest standards of professional conduct. As one means to this end, the National Association of Legal Secretaries (NALS) has promulgated a code of ethics. According to the code, every member shall:

- encourage respect for the law and the administration of justice;
- observe rules governing privileged communications and confidential information;
- promote and exemplify high standards of loyalty, cooperation, and courtesy;
- perform all duties of the profession with integrity and competence; and
- pursue a high order of professional attainment.

The legal profession, acting through the American Bar Association (ABA), has adopted and promulgated *Model Rules of Professional Conduct* that set forth in detail guidelines for the conduct of all members of the profession. Secretaries as well as attorneys are bound by these rules, and taking time to review them periodically is worthwhile. The attorney has serious ethical responsibilities; if a secretary should undermine them, even unwittingly, it could result in harming a client, subjecting the lawyer to disciplinary action, or even ruining the lawyer's career.

By keeping the following precepts in mind at all times, a legal secretary can prevent such disasters:

- All client matters are confidential information and may not be divulged to anyone.
- All written office documents are confidential and may not be divulged without the attorney's permission.

- Cases should not be commented on or discussed outside the office.
- The ABA's *Model Rules of Professional Conduct* apply to secretaries as well as to lawyers.
- The secretary must be absolutely loyal to the attorney.
- The secretary must at all times refrain from giving legal advice, since this could be construed as the illegal practice of law.

Training and Education

Law offices are becoming more and more sophisticated, both in terms of the equipment operated and the administrative functions performed. Legal secretaries today are typically required to:

- operate networked computers housing several varieties of software;
- use complex telecommunications systems;
- oversee detailed docketing, scheduling, and record-tracking systems;
- manage office accounting and bookkeeping systems; and
- maintain good human relations with clients, lawyers, and fellow staff members.

All these professional duties and responsibilities require a high degree of competency and commitment on the part of the secretary. In order to take full advantage of a firm's resources and best serve its needs, the secretary needs to be properly trained and to keep current regarding new developments in the field. The more you can expand your knowledge, the more valuable you will become to the firm and the more satisfying your work will be.

Varieties of Training

There are several different varieties of secretarial training available. Such training may be obtained through:

- individual equipment vendors,
- in-house training-and-development departments,
- professional training organizations,
- off-the-shelf training packages, and
- courses of study.

A word of caution: With any kind of training you undertake, plan ahead to make sure that your daily responsibilities will be taken care of in your absence. Arrangements can be made to have a temporary secretary come in, or the firm may have another secretary on staff who can assume your responsibilities. The attorney should always be advised of your temporary absences for training so that he or she can plan accordingly.

Training by equipment vendors Most vendors offer training as part of the purchase price of new equipment and software. They also offer training-maintenance packages to provide ongoing training for new hires and refresher courses for working secretaries. These maintenance packages usually provide a predetermined number of training hours at a flat rate, to be used at the firm's discretion.

Vendor training may consist of on- or off-site instruction. The vendor provides the instructor and the equipment, software, and other materials. The training can last anywhere from a few hours for simple equipment or software to several days for more sophisticated software packages and office equipment.

Training sessions should be scheduled according to the skill level or the practice area of the trainees. Those who have had previous experience or who readily absorb new knowledge and skills, for example, could be scheduled together. This will ensure that everyone derives the maximum benefit from the classes. Organizing classes around a specific practice area, on the other hand, may help focus the training. In either case, arrangements should be made with the vendor to use actual firm documents, procedures, and other materials to help make the training more productive. The vendor should also provide on-site follow-up support once the training is over in order to give trainees a technological "cushion" as they return to the workplace and apply their new skills.

In-house training departments   A large firm will probably have an in-house training department to handle training for both new hires and existing staff. The department typically issues a manual that provides information on office procedures, policies, equipment, software, and facilities, and is used as a training text by new hires and as a reference by existing employees. It is normally updated as changes occur, and training is often scheduled to take account of these changes.

Training personnel also usually keep records to track the development of each employee and to schedule ongoing training according to need. Training classes may be held either on- or off-site, depending on the firm's facilities and the nature of the training. Classes may be taught by either an in-house or an outside trainer, depending on the subject and the expertise of the firm's internal trainers.

Professional training organizations   Firms that are too small to accommodate an in-house training department, or larger firms that for one reason or another cannot deliver a particular type of training to their staff, may utilize the services of a professional training group. As with equipment vendors, professional training organizations provide either outside classroom facilities or in-house training, depending on the subject, number of trainees, equipment needed, and so on. They should be able to provide high-quality training and also offer on-site follow-up support to help trainees in applying their new skills on the job. Once again, firm documents, procedures, and similar materials should be used to make the training more effective.

A member of the law firm should perform a reference check before retaining the services of an outside training company. The training organization should provide a fee structure that fits the firm's training budget. Such organizations may charge by the employee, by the hour, or by the project; they may also be able to offer a flat-rate service or maintenance contract that specifies a given amount of training to be used at the firm's discretion.

Off-the-shelf training packages   Another source of training is the so-called off-the-shelf training packages available through catalogs or directly from companies that specialize in training. Individual law firms may even produce their own training packages for in-house use. Off-the-shelf (and in-house) training packages typically include videotapes, instruction manuals and workbooks, computer diskettes or CD-ROMs, audiotapes, and other components. Usually the package contains instructions (audio or written) accompanied by a video-tape or computer program and a workbook containing practice applications. Instruction is thus reinforced through sample problems or practice situations.

It is wise to learn about the reputability of a company offering off-the-shelf products by checking with other law firms that may have used these products, by consulting product reviews in trade magazines, or by attending professional conferences or trade shows in which you can see a product demonstration and do some comparative shopping. Sample packages are also sometimes available by mail order.

Courses of study   In addition to in-house and outside training programs, credit and noncredit courses are offered in many areas by high-school exten-sion services, community colleges, and state universities. Some courses teach practical skills such as how to prepare legal documents; others introduce the student to particular areas of law such as real estate or probate. In some cases, these studies may also overlap with paralegal training and so can further en-hance the secretary's career prospects. Self-programmed guides or interactive computer programs may also be purchased for home study either for credit or for a certificate of completion. Check trade magazines such as *The Docket* (pub-lished by the National Association of Legal Secretaries, 2250 E. 73rd St., Suite 550, Tulsa OK 74136) and *Legal Assistant Today* (published by James Publishing, 3520 Cadillac Avenue, Suite E, Costa Mesa, CA 92626) for information regard-ing these and other programs.

The Secretary as Trainer

Experienced secretaries in a law firm are often responsible for training new hires and other less experienced members of the support staff. Sometimes this responsibility includes assisting in the training of new attorneys, law clerks, and other members of the professional staff. The secretary may even partici-pate in developing an overall training-and-development program, a role that can add to the secretary's career prospects and make the job more satisfying.

In creating a training program, the first and most important step is *plan-ning*. You must determine the firm's training needs and the equipment, in-structional material, and facilities that can be made available to attain the re-sults desired. You might start by interviewing both professional and support staff to determine their needs and expectations. It is a good idea to obtain a complete set of views or else use a group that represents a cross-section of the firm in compiling your findings. Before deciding on any particular program, review these findings with the staff to help ensure that you have properly iden-tified their needs and to allow them to become part of the training-develop-ment process.

A practical next step (one that could also take place simultaneously with the first) is a review of the firm's office manual with an eye toward updating or revising it as necessary. Here too you should enlist the aid of secretaries, attor-neys, legal assistants, and other staff members in order to get a balanced set of opinions. The goal should be to ensure a comprehensive and useful document that reflects effective policies and procedures.

In implementing any kind of training, keep in mind the needs of the end users. Always begin with the most basic information and steadily take trainees through more advanced applications. All training should include exercises that mirror actual firm usage. Training sessions should be long enough to guarantee that trainees can return to the workplace ready to apply their new skills, but not so long as to cause their attention to wander. It may be better to schedule several short training sessions than one or two lengthy ones. Properly delivered training can mean the difference between the trainees mastering new skills and their remaining ignorant and frustrated.

Once the training is completed, you should continuously monitor employees' progress to determine whether the training has been effective. This can be done through personal interviews or, in the case of larger firms, a short questionnaire that asks staff members to assess how much the training has helped them in their work. You should continually seek out information regarding any procedures, policies, or equipment that have been causing problems for people, and use such information to update and enhance the firm's training program and its office manual.

A law firm should be a creative environment. The secretary and the lawyer should routinely meet to discuss not only work in progress and client relations but the overall operation of the office. A well-managed firm does not become complacent and is always seeking new ways to improve its practice. The more you can do to keep yourself current on developments in the field and assist others in learning and applying new skills, the higher your value will be to the firm and the better your prospects for advancement.

Professional Associations

Professional Secretaries International (PSI), located at 10502 NW Ambassador Drive, P.O. Box 20404, Kansas City, MO 64195, and the National Association of Legal Secretaries (NALS; see address above) offer programs to help you continue to advance your professional education. There may also be local secretarial associations or societies in your area.

Whether you join a professional secretarial association is naturally a personal decision. But membership and participation in at least one of these organizations can generate benefits similar to those that membership in a bar association can generate for lawyers. In addition to continuing-education opportunities, participation will enable you to develop a professional network and allow you to exchange ideas about problem-solving and issues facing the profession. There are also additional benefits such as social activities, making new friends, and being alerted to job opportunities in your area. Participation usually reflects credit upon both you and your firm.

Professional certification   NALS offers two certification programs that, when successfully completed, designate a person as either an Accredited Legal Secretary (ALS) or a Professional Legal Secretary (PLS). The first program is for "apprentice-level" legal support staff and involves a one-day exam (given in March and September) covering (1) written-communication comprehension and application; (2) office administration, legal terminology, and accounting; and (3) ethics, human relations, and applied office procedures. The second program is for "professional-level" legal secretaries and involves a two-day exam (given in March and September) covering (1) written-communication skills and knowledge; (2) ethics; (3) legal-secretarial procedures; (4) accounting; (5) legal terminology, techniques, and procedures; (6) judgment; and (7) legal-secretarial skills. Exam preparation materials are available from NALS.

As emphasis on continuing legal education increases, the programs and materials available to legal secretaries will likely also increase in both quantity and quality. Professional associations can offer a wide variety of benefits and opportunities that are to your advantage to explore.

Community involvement   Educational programs are often on the lookout for lecturers and adjunct instructors. Students want to see and hear the "real thing" when it comes to learning about the career. To legal students, the professional will be someone they hope to emulate, someone who has been on the "front line" and can relate valuable firsthand experiences. With the legal secretary acting as educator and ambassador, the firm maintains a community presence and serves to promote the profession.

Because the occupation of legal secretary is a valued one, the experienced secretary should welcome the opportunity to sit on secretarial advisory boards at local community and career colleges. As an extension of the law firm into the community, a seat on such a board signals to other law firms and members of the community that you and your employer are committed to quality and community service. You will, as a board member, be in a position to share valuable experience and offer concrete suggestions about programs that enable schools to educate future legal secretaries.

Chapter 3

Office Design, Equipment, and Supplies

The job of a legal secretary encompasses many routine but important responsibilities, including organizing your own workstation and assisting in general office design, operating photocopying and other equipment, and handling supplies. These are the topics covered in the present chapter. Various other topics relating to the broad subject of work environment and office equipment are discussed in individual later chapters: for example, computers in the law office (Chapter 4), communications technology (Chapter 5), dictation and transcription equipment (Chapter 9), and records management and filing equipment (Chapter 11).

Office Design

Designing and furnishing a law office is a challenging undertaking. Naturally the scope of the task depends on the size of the office planned. For a firm that numbers more than 25 people (lawyers and support staff), it is almost essential that a professional interior designer be employed. A designer should also be employed when innovative designs are contemplated in smaller firms. Either case calls for a task force consisting of the designer, the chief office administrator, and, for particular work areas, the individual users.

Office Atmosphere and Landscaping

The designer is responsible for developing a space plan that makes optimal use of the space to be occupied and provides each occupant with comfortable and adequate working quarters. A common approach to office arrangement is called *office landscaping*, whereby the office becomes a large open space with no walls except movable panels and screens of various heights to give some privacy. Furniture can be assembled in a variety of modules to create whatever working arrangement best suits any particular employee. However, a careful study of work flow must be made before remaking the office. Handbooks and textbooks of office management have a wealth of information on office layouts and can instruct you in experimenting with space and furniture templates made to scale. (See bibliography, Appendix III.)

The plan should take into account adequate lighting as a key consideration—not only for the lawyers but for each member of the staff. Insufficient lighting can cause eyestrain, headache, fatigue—and mistakes. High-intensity light is vital for areas where close work such as proofreading is done. Evenness of illumination, absence of glare, (particularly on computer screens), and contrast should be considered. Natural light is always best if it is available. Desks, chairs, and especially visitors' chairs should be placed so that they do not face directly into a light source.

Ventilation and noise levels are other important environmental factors. Hot, stale, or humid air slows down productivity and contributes to illness. Excessive noise may cause stress and fatigue. Pads under office machines, carpets on the floor, and acoustical tiles on the ceiling can reduce office noise.

Some firms rent paintings and works of art that may be exchanged for others periodically. If no effort is made by your firm to provide anything but basic furniture, your own attractive hangings or art objects may provide welcome relief from monotony. It should be emphasized, however, that decals, amateur artwork, overly elaborate floral arrangements, pictures drawn by a five-year-old niece, and brightly colored inexpensive "junque" will make your office appear gaudy and cheap. Your objective should be to produce a restful and pleasing effect on clients, legal staff, and the attorney for whom you work, while at the same time retaining a businesslike atmosphere in which you can work efficiently.

Lawyers usually know how their individual professional offices should be designed and furnished, since they do not work in the staff areas, however, advice on the design and furnishing of these spaces should come from the respective staff members. Many firms place such importance on comfortable, attractive, and adequate secretarial workstations that, before giving approval to final plans, they insist that a mock-up of a typical secretarial workstation be built, reviewed, and revised as appropriate by a team of the firm's secretaries. This can result in invaluable suggestions being incorporated into the final design. Consequently, if you are asked to comment on the design of a new workstation or the revision of an old one, you should not feel constrained to agree with the designer, the administrator, or the lawyer but instead should offer constructive criticism aimed at improving the work area for all secretaries.

Layout

The layout of a law office depends almost entirely upon its size. A single practitioner's office may consist of only two or three rooms: (1) the lawyer's private office, (2) another room divided into a reception area, a file room, and a secretarial work area, and perhaps (3) a conference room. If the reception area is adjacent to a work area, care should be taken to separate waiting clients from the work area. This is important not only for the comfort of the clients but also to prevent visitors from viewing the work that is being done for other clients. Large firms may have separate rooms for the library, files, copying and duplicating equipment, word-processing center, bookkeeping department, lounge, and the like. A private secretarial office may be attached to the private office of each lawyer.

Whether the firm is large or small, the attorney's office is always separate in order that the client's affairs may be conducted in privacy. And whether the secretary has a private office or a workstation, it must be easily accessible to both the secretary and the lawyer. The secretary will probably prefer to conduct most of his or her work, whether keyboarding or using the telephone, in a position such that the lawyer's comings and goings can be readily observed.

Your workstation   Even if you cannot control major office-design decisions, your desk and the office space immediately adjacent to it are yours to organize for maximum efficiency and attractiveness. Your desk is the place to begin. Try this: Sit in your chair and face your working surface. Stretch your arms straight out over it about 6″ above the surface with thumbs together. Now swing them carefully out to each side, making a wide arc, and watch to see what areas of the desk your arms cover. This is the surface on which you should have all of the articles that you work with frequently—and *only* those articles. The far corners that you cannot reach without effort should be clean and free from clutter and may house your nameplate or even a plant or a small, unobtrusive decorative item or two. A nonglare working surface will be easier on your eyes than glass or shiny plastic.

If your telephone is not installed where it is handy for you to use, request permission to have it moved. Your essential reference books should be readily available on your desktop or on a shelf within your "working arc." A lazy Susan can hold several books in a small space.

Keep a work organizer of some kind on your desk. It may be an open-faced cabinet with thinly spaced shelves, a multilevel desk tray, or a vertical sorting rack. Separate labeled folders placed in the organizer should hold dictation to be transcribed, items ready for the attorney to sign, reading to be done, projects in progress, and other such materials. A folder devoted to pending work is useful, especially if you review it each day and attach a note to each piece of work stating exactly what has to be done with it. It is always a good idea to keep documents that must be signed in a separate folder marked in some way so that the attorney can immediately identify it.

Your computer or typewriter should be protected with a dust cover at the end of each day and cleaned at regular intervals. Store all loose papers at the day's end *inside* your desk. If they must be left on top of your desk, put them out of sight.

Of equal importance is your organization of the contents of your desk drawers. The large center drawer that holds small things is the one most likely to become jumbled unless you corral loose items in a desk organizer, plastic containers, or something similar. (Sticky tape or a dab of glue will hold containers in place and keep them in order.)

Word-processing stations   In older offices the L-shaped desk arrangement, consisting of a basic desk and a smaller and somewhat lower typing table attached to the desk at a 90-degree angle, was popular. Today, because so many secretaries are working with word processors or computers made up of several component parts, an entire industry has developed to supply customized computer furniture to organize all these parts. The furniture ranges from movable carts, which hold all the devices associated with a computer or word processor, to complete modular systems, which encompass desks, storage shelves, and movable partitions. (In many offices, unfortunately, furnishings have not caught up with technology and the equipment often must be set down wher-ever it fits.)

For maximum convenience, you should be able to sit at your word-pro-cessing equipment and comfortably reach your telephone, your diskettes and CD-ROMs, and your printer, while still having an accessible flat surface on which to open a manual or other reference book. (If you are connected to a lo-cal area network, in which several people share a centralized printer, you will not have to accommodate a printer in your immediate area.)

Important accessories for your workstation are *wrist rests*, which attach to your keyboard to enable you to rest your wrists during prolonged periods of keyboarding; *footrests*, to support your legs and improve circulation; a *copy-holder*, which holds papers so that they can be easily viewed for keyboarding; and ancillary computer components such as a *mouse pad*, a *power strip* (a heavy-duty extension cord with outlets), and a *keyboard cover*.

The open landscape design discussed in the first part of this chapter has had a number of positive effects; however, it has also created some problems with respect to working with word-processing equipment. The pattern of ceil-ing lights, which is generally a symmetrical grid for the entire office space, may have no relation to where individual desks and workstations are placed. As a result, you may find that your overhead light is off to the side, while your neighbor may get no direct light at all. To compensate, additional light is often needed, either permanently or just for specific tasks.

Space planning   Space planners and lawyers have traditionally allocated too little space to support activities and more than enough space to individual lawyers' offices. In the past, and continuing into the present, the status of a lawyer in a law firm was generally measured by length of tenure with the firm, reputation in the community, and size of the lawyer's private office. Successful lawyers near the top of their firms occupied the largest offices, often located in the corner of the building. More recently, however, it has become common to find most lawyers in a firm occupying offices of about equal size, as firms rec-ognize the need for increased space for support activities—data and word pro-cessing, library, files, mail services, copying, and the like. The staff providing these important services must have adequate space to operate efficiently. Here, again, input by both lawyers and staff is necessary before design and construc-tion can proceed.

The reception area   A law office should have a sober, dignified appearance. A clean, comfortable reception area with a subdued color scheme and well-coor-dinated furnishings makes a positive impression on a client. Pop music and junk art are taboo.

Law books can be used as a design element in the reception area. To the client these volumes represent the authority of the law and the professionalism of the firm. A client sitting in a waiting area surrounded by legal publications is more likely to be impressed than one sitting in a stark room containing only dog-eared, out-of-date magazines.

The following are a few further suggestions:

- Seating accommodations should be comfortable, attractive, and inviting.
- Current reading material should be available and in good order. Lighting should be adequate for reading.

- Accommodations for coats, hats, and other miscellaneous items should be provided.
- Books in bookcases must present a neat appearance; bookends can help when a shelf is not filled.
- Fresh flowers will add a delightful and refreshing touch to the waiting area.
- If possible, the staff should not pass through the reception area. The area should be kept relatively private and the operations of the general office should be obscured from visitors.

Other Considerations

Ergonomics As office operations have become increasingly automated, concern for the effects all this automation has on the humans who use it has spawned an entire discipline: *ergonomics*, the study of the effects of the physical design of equipment on the physical and emotional well-being of its users. An engineer or designer schooled in ergonomics may be as much concerned with the size and shape of an on/off switch as with whether the switch actually works. Can it be reached without the user having to stretch, bend, or risk injury? Is it too large or small to be used conveniently? Is it clearly labeled?

Once regarded as an esoteric field, ergonomics has now moved into the mainstream of design. The European Union, for example, has established uniform rules that make employers responsible for removing health risks from the workplace and require them to be knowledgeable about advances in workstation design.

Specialists in ergonomics have studied the effects of all the various office technologies and accessories, examining everything from the color of a computer screen to the shape of a chair. You can profit from the considerable body of knowledge that now exists when selecting or recommending products for your office.

The virtual office With the increasing pervasiveness of computer technology, a view is developing that the amount of office space needed in the recent past is no longer necessary. Much of the work that lawyers and secretaries do, it is thought, can be accomplished at home or elsewhere outside the office using a personal computer with a modem linked to the main office. The lawyer can then occasionally schedule the use of a shared office as necessary to meet clients or conduct other routine business. The secretary too could make productive use of flexible office hours, or flextime. Ongoing and future changes such as these will undoubtedly affect law-office design.

Reprographic and Other Equipment

Reprographic equipment includes any machines used for making copies of documents. In the office environment, it generally refers to photocopiers.

The Photocopier

The photocopier is similar to a laser printer for a computer in that its paper is electrostatically charged to attract inklike *toner* to its surface. The toner may be

in powder or liquid form and can be refilled as needed right in the office. Photocopiers are classified according to capacity: copies per minute (that is, speed)
and copies per month (that is, expected heaviness of use). Here are typical
ranges for standard types of copiers:

Type	Copies per minute	Copies per month
Low-volume	10–20	2,000–20,000
Medium-volume	20–50	20,000–50,000
High-volume	50–100	50,000–100,000

Low-volume copiers tend to have few special features and may even be
desktop models. They are most useful in areas where only a few pages at a time
are copied and no large documents have to be collated. Medium-volume
copiers are generally equipped with an automatic document feeder and a col-
lator, and are adequate for most routine office copying needs. High-volume
copiers, sometimes referred to as high-speed copier-duplicators, often provide
advanced features such as two-sided printing and stapling. Their high price
makes them economical only in offices where large quantities of reports and
other documents are frequently needed.

The weakest aspect of copiers is their potential for paper jams. Most
copiers will indicate where the jam has occurred so that office workers can
clear it themselves. The potential for jams increases with the length and route
of the paper path.

In some offices, for security or budget reasons, you may need an access
code to use the copier. This prevents unauthorized use and allows firm administrators to track the usage of the copier. The access code is generally for a department or practice area rather than an individual, especially where a copier
may be used by several different areas and the expenses need to be charged
back accordingly. The American Bar Association has recently cautioned that,
while law firms have the right to recoup from clients expenses associated with
copying equipment, such equipment should not be considered a source of
profit. It therefore becomes important that the firm determine the actual cost
involved in operating copying equipment so as to be able to justify charges to
clients if necessary.

Photocopier features vary by manufacturer and, to an even greater extent,
by the volume of work the machine was designed to perform. If your firm is
considering the purchase of a new machine, the following questions should be
addressed:

- What *volume* of work is the machine capable of handling? (See table above.)
- How many *paper trays* for different sizes of paper does the machine have?
  (You will generally need at least two, one for letter-sized paper and one for
  legal-sized.)
- Can the machine *collate* when several copies of a multipage document are
  needed?
- Does the machine allow for *reduction/enlargement* of original documents?
- Can the machine generate *two-sided copies* automatically, or must you manu-
  ally turn over and reinsert the partially printed copies?
- Can the machine copy facing pages of *books* when material from law books or
  other texts is needed?

- Does the machine make *good-quality copies* on all types of paper that the office uses—e.g., letterhead, card stock, and labels?
- Are *parts and supplies* available from vendors other than the seller? Is local and on-site *repair service* available?

Other Copying and Printing Processes

Film carbon and carbonless packs   There is relatively little need today for making traditional carbon copies, but they are still useful in some types of typing projects. If you are filling out special court forms or documents relating to real estate or vehicle transfers, for example, carbon may still be needed when multiple copies are required.

Film carbon is the material of preference for secretaries using loose carbon. This is a tough polyester sheet coated with a special film. The increased durability of the material prevents tearing, wrinkling, and curling. It is strong but pliant and will produce numerous copies from one sheet. You use film carbon in the same way you use ordinary carbon paper, placing a sheet between blank originals and inserting the set in your typewriter as you would an ordinary sheet of paper. Placing the top edge of the carbon set under the flap of an envelope before insertion will help to align the paper and carbon.

Offices that need carbon copies also sometimes use *carbonless packs*. A carbonless pack contains an original blank form or document and copy sheets that are treated to allow copying without the use of carbon. These packs are used in the same way regular carbon sets or film are used.

Care must be taken when using carbon to correct errors both on the original and the copies. First, proofread the material while it is still in the typewriter. When an error has been spotted, remove it from the original by using a correcting typewriter if available (if not, remove it by erasure). Next, remove the pack or set from the typewriter and use a soft eraser to erase the error from the copies. Finally, reinsert the set into the typewriter and type the correction on the original so that it passes through to the copies. While this may be a somewhat tedious process, it is necessary if you want your work to be top-quality.

Printing processes   *Offset printing* is often used when results of higher quality than those produced by photocopying are needed; it can also be more economical when printing thousands of copies. The process involves using a printing plate to make an inked impression on a rubber-blanketed cylinder and then transferring the impression to the paper. (The same process is used in book and magazine printing.) Offset printing can be used to print announcements, business cards, stationery, and many other commonly used business documents, but many law firms prefer to use higher-quality thermographic or engraving processes to print their best stationery. Offset printing should be available in your local retail copying shop (see your Yellow Pages under "Printing").

Thermography is similar to old-fashioned letterpress, only in this case a special ink containing a yeast-like powder is applied by the press and heated slightly to cause the printed lettering to rise—hence its more common name, *raised-letter printing*. Thermography is used to create a slightly more sophisticated look than that produced by offset, and it is slightly more expensive too. Check your Yellow Pages under "Thermographers" for services in your area.

Engraving is the highest-quality—and most costly—printing process. It is generally used to convey an image of the firm as prestigious. In engraving, an engraved metal die to which ink is applied is firmly pressed onto the paper being printed, leaving slightly raised lettering on the sheet's front and slightly indented lettering (in reverse) on the back. For the names of engravers in your area, check your local Yellow Pages under "Engraving—Stationery."

In an effort to control supply costs, some firms use both engraved letterhead and thermographically printed letterhead. The former is used for correspondence with outside counsel and with important clients; the latter is used for correspondence with government agencies, courts, administrative agencies, and others.

Software programs are now available that allow you to print letterhead using a laser printer in the office. Usually you must first send a copy of the firm's letterhead to the software manufacturer, who then writes a short program and sends it to you on a diskette. Once the program is installed, you simply tell the computer whether you are printing a letter, envelope, pleading, or similar document. A little training and experience are usually needed to master the use of the software, but offices using this technology have found the savings in letterhead and envelopes to be worth the small effort and expense.

Other Office Equipment

Most of the equipment commonly used in law offices is treated separately in later chapters: for example, computers (Chapter 4), communications technology (Chapter 5), dictation and transcription equipment (Chapter 9), and records-management and filing equipment (Chapter 11). This section reviews three other pieces of equipment commonly found in the law office.

Electronic typewriters The electronic typewriter occupies a place between the older electric typewriter and the word processor. It can be useful for various tasks—letters and envelopes, forms, memorandums, brief reports, etc.—that do not require advanced features. It is also useful as a backup in the event of computer failure.

Electronic typewriters usually lack a separate monitor or printer; however, a line or two of text just typed may appear on a small electronic display in order to be checked by the typist before printing. They generally have such features as quick correction (of a word or an entire line), wordwrap (automatic carriage return), automatic centering and underscoring, quick tabulation (for creating columns and tables), boldface type, right justification, and automatic letterspacing. The most sophisticated typewriters, with their sizable memory capacities and numerous word-processing features, are almost indistinguishable from actual word processors. Study the accompanying manual carefully until every useful feature is familiar to you.

Combination fax machines/copiers/printers/scanners These devices are becoming more popular because they save space and cost only slightly more than basic individual machines. They can receive and send fax messages, make copies, print material from a computer, and, in the more sophisticated units equipped with scanners, scan in printed text to a computer system.

Paper shredders Paper shredders are used principally as security devices for destroying sensitive documents. Shredders vary in size from compact models that fit on top of wastebaskets to large floor models. Like photocopiers, they are rated according to the volume of work they can handle.

Maintenance and Repair

It is wise—and in the long run more economical—to maintain all equipment in good working order. Having to replace defective equipment sooner than expected is both inconvenient and expensive. Follow the preventive-maintenance procedures outlined in the manuals accompanying all products. Have the equipment serviced at once when failures occur. Good preventive maintenance often makes replacing the equipment unnecessary.

Many basic office machines do not require service contracts. However, as the equipment becomes more complex and is asked to perform more tasks, service contracts become not only reasonable but necessary. Consult your vendor and other law firms about the advisability of maintaining service contracts for particular pieces of equipment.

Office Supplies

One of your responsibilities will likely be office supplies and inventory control. A large firm may have an administrator in charge of purchasing, in which case you will simply draft order requests as necessary and give them to the administrator. At a small firm, you may make the purchases yourself from a local office-supply shop or catalog. In either case, you must keep track of the supplies on hand and know when and how frequently to reorder.

Choosing Suppliers

Business supplies can be obtained from office-supply houses or from stationers. Legal supplies may occasionally have to be ordered from more specialized houses, but more and more office-supply houses are becoming full-service companies that offer specialized as well as general products.

The decision to do business with a particular supply house may rest with the lawyer, the administrator, or the secretary. In any case, it is your responsibility to establish and maintain good credit and good business relationships with the designated suppliers. Likewise, it is prudent to continue to deal with the established supply houses and not to move from one to another without good reason. Most houses will try to please their longtime customers by expediting orders or offering reduced rates. If you have been dealing with a particular supplier on a regular basis, the supplier will often allow your office to examine or test new products before they are purchased.

Receiving Supplies

Immediately check any supplies received against the original order and the invoice. (An invoice is a statement from the company listing the items shipped, the price, and the terms of sale.) Make sure that the listed items and the amounts are correct. Ensure that no part of the shipment has been damaged. If a mistake has been made, notify the supply house; be prepared to provide the company with the invoice number, the date of order, the name of the product and manufacturer, and the complaint. After you have returned the defective items, you should receive a credit slip stating that the items have been received and that you are due a replacement, refund, or credit in the amount shown on the slip.

Standard Office Supplies

The following is a list of items a secretary must often keep on hand:

Paper, Filing, and Related Products
Letterhead and second sheets
Letterhead envelopes
Legal forms
Copier/printer paper
Scratch paper
Ruled notepads
Memo pads
Self-stick notes
Dictation notebooks
Telephone message pads
Lawyer's time sheets
Index cards
Manila and mailing envelopes
File folders
Index tabs (or preprinted file guides)
Labels
Hanging file folders (and tabs)
Calendar/appointment-book refills
Bookkeeping forms
Loose-leaf binders
Report folders
Office-equipment paper (for calculators, fax machines, etc.)
Sheet protectors
Easel pads
Expanding files
Film carbon

Desk Supplies
Staplers, staples, and staple removers
Tape and tape dispensers
Liquid glue or glue sticks
Pens, felt-tip pens, and pencils
Erasers
Scissors
In and Out baskets
Rulers
Rubber bands
Paper clips and fasteners, binder clips

Pushpins
Bookends
Letter openers
Envelope moisteners
Ink pads for rubber stamps
Correction fluid
Postage stamps

Desk References
Dictionaries (English, legal, medical)
Thesaurus
Legal-citations manual
Secretarial handbook
Legal-forms binder
Zip-code directory
Rotary card files
Postal and courier rate charts
Telephone books
Office-supply catalogs

Computer Supplies
Printer ribbons or cartridges
Diskettes
Diskette holders
CD-ROM holders

Dictation Supplies
Cassette tapes
Tape storage unit
Cleaning cartridges
Batteries

Miscellaneous
Toner
Replacement drums
Clipboards
Packaging tape
Punches
Magazine racks
First-aid kit
Fire extinguisher
Pencil sharpeners
Easels
Collapsible storage boxes
Maps
Coffee (tea, etc.) supplies

Handling Supplies

Consider ordering in bulk those items for which there is a steady demand. It is a good idea to keep a sheet near the supply area so that employees can write down what they need and what supplies are getting low.

Storage   Most offices have a supply cabinet of some kind, and you may be charged with keeping it orderly. Grouping similar things together and labeling the shelves should help keep the supply cabinet neat. Items that can spill should be stored on bottom shelves. Paper and other heavy supplies should be stored on lower shelves, with the labels facing the front. Open a ream of paper on the end that has no label; in this way, you will preserve the label so that everyone will know what kind of paper is in the package. (This is also helpful for reordering.) Smaller items should be on shelves at eye level, stored in labeled boxes; do not allow small loose items to scatter about the shelves. Computer diskettes should be stored in their original packaging at temperatures no lower than 50° F, away from any magnetic field.

Distribution   It is crucial to monitor the distribution of supplies, since they have a tendency to "walk away," especially expensive items such as diskettes. Keep the supplies under lock and key if possible, and maintain a list of the supplies you distribute and to whom they are distributed.

Computerized inventory control   If you are responsible for the inventory in a large office, there are software packages available that can track, follow up, and summarize reports; produce price quotations, invoices, vendor lists, and mailing labels; track purchase orders; and automatically add inventory to the reorder report when items fall below a designated level. Ask your local software vendor for information on such packages.

Recycling paper products   The computer explosion was supposed to create a "paperless office," but if you look around you will realize that offices are using at least as much paper as ever. Approximately 70 to 80 percent of all office paper is waste. Recycling paper products makes both environmental and economic sense. If your company has not started a recycling program, perhaps you can initiate one. Place recycling bins or paper cartons near every desk, photocopier, printer, and bulletin board. Affix a label on each bin that indicates it is for recycling purposes. Enlist the help of the custodial staff. You can arrange collection with a wastepaper broker or with your local municipality if it has a recycling program.

The following white and colored paper products can generally be recycled together:

- bond paper
- envelopes without windows or self-stick labels
- copier/printer paper (but not the wrapping)
- telephone message slips
- greenbar paper
- adding-machine/calculator paper
- newsletters

Such a list should appear on each bin. (You may be able to get list labels from your recycling vendor.) Newspapers should be put in a separate bin.

To learn more about office paper recycling, contact the American Forest and Paper Association, 1111 19th Street NW, Suite 700, Washington, D.C. (800-878-8878).

Chapter 4

The Computer and the Law Office

The emergence of computer technology designed to serve the needs of secretaries and other office professionals has produced a revolution in the work environment. Computers are now an integral part of almost every law office, facilitating citation research and document assembly as well as the production of routine memorandums and correspondence. Computer technology is continuously changing, and the "leading edge" of today will not necessarily be the "state of the art" tomorrow. But since the emergence of personal computers in the 1970s, at least some elements of even this most dynamic of technologies have remained more or less constant. The average user is still primarily concerned with entering or "capturing" data, manipulating or enhancing it using the computer's memory and other functions, and storing it for later reference or for output in one form or another. These are some of the topics taken up in this chapter.

Although this chapter will not teach you how to use any particular brand of computer technology, it will introduce you to the fundamentals of using the computer in the law office. Its purpose is to familiarize you with the basic tools and applications as well as the basic vocabulary that is used. Various other topics relating to computer technology are discussed elsewhere in this book. See Chapter 5, "Communications Systems," for a discussion of computer-based communications technology; see Chapter 11, "Docket Control and Records Management," for a discussion of computerized calendaring and records management; see Chapter 12, "Financial Management," for a discussion of computerized accounting; and see Chapter 13, "The Law Library," for a discussion of computerized legal research.

The basic computer system, as almost anyone who has used a computer in school or at work will know, is composed of physical components called *hardware* and sets of electronically coded programs and procedures called *software*. The hardware supports and physically runs the software, while the software in turn translates instructions from the user to run the machinery and perform programming functions. We will discuss the major elements of computer hardware and software in separate sections below. Note that sans-serif type is used to represent individual keys on the computer keyboard.

Computer Hardware

The computer is a multicomponent device made up of five primary parts:

1. The *computer* itself, which is made up of boards and circuits that process information.
2. The *monitor,* which displays the information.
3. The *keyboard* and other user input devices such as the mouse, which are used to enter information.
4. The *printer,* which prints the information on paper.
5. The *disk drives* and *disks,* which allow you to store the information electronically.

See the illustration in Fig. 4.1.

The Computer

The computer itself depends on a series of *chips,* integrated circuits made from silicon that store and process information. Chips are attached to *boards* inside the computer, which generally should be removed and replaced only by technicians. The most important board is called the *system board* or *motherboard,* and the most important chip on the system board is the *central processing unit,* or CPU. The CPU is the computer's "traffic cop," controlling all the information flowing between the keyboard, the computer itself, the printer, and various other devices you may have connected. Computers are often identified by their CPUs. Some common CPUs include Intel's 486 and Pentium chips,

Fig. 4.1   Desktop Computer

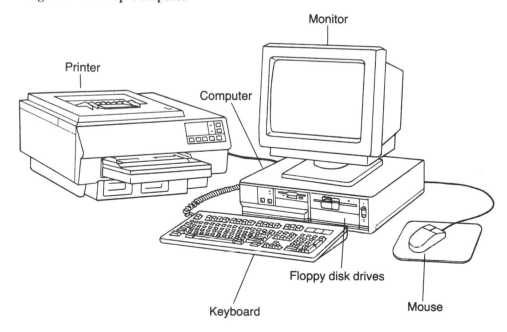

which are found in IBM-compatible computers. Macintosh computers use CPUs made by Motorola, such as the 68LC040 and the PowerPC.

Computer memory   The computer has two kinds of memory: ROM and RAM. ROM, or *read-only memory,* contains the computer's own internal operating instructions. The computer "reads," or uses, the information in ROM to run itself. The user has no access to anything stored in ROM. RAM, or *random-access memory,* is a temporary work space in which the computer runs your software program. Unlike ROM, which is permanent memory, anything in RAM is wiped out as soon as you turn off the computer (or experience a power outage).

Memory, in the computer's terms, is measured in thousands or millions of bytes. A byte holds one character. A thousand bytes is a *kilobyte,* or K for short; a million bytes is a *megabyte,* or MB for short. (Actually, because of the method of quantifying information, these figures are rounded; a kilobyte is really 1,024 bytes, and a megabyte is really 1,048,576 bytes.) A computer with 4MB of memory can hold about 4 million bytes in its "temporary work space" at one time. Since different software programs require different amounts of memory to run, the amount of memory your computer contains will determine what software you will be able to use on it. Memory requirements are usually listed on the software packaging and in the program documentation.

Modern so-called graphical software requires large amounts of memory to run efficiently. Although Microsoft Windows and Apple Macintosh System software can run on as little as 4MB of RAM, it is recommended that all office computers running such software have at least 8MB.

Math coprocessor   Many computers contain an extra chip or microprocessor that is designed to perform specialized tasks such as complex mathematical calculations. Such a chip, which contains an arithmetic/logic unit (ALU), is known as a *math coprocessor.* Some models of computer that do not already contain a coprocessor allow you to add one if this becomes necessary.

Input/Output ports   The CPU is connected to the outside world by input/output (I/O) ports, electronic channels through which it can send the results of its processing to a display, a printer, or a storage device. It is also through these ports that the CPU receives and responds to special user commands, such as CANCEL and **Escape**. I/O ports can be either *serial* or *parallel.* Serial ports transmit information sequentially through a single channel. Parallel ports transmit information through separate channels at the same time and therefore are faster than serial ports. A typical modern computer has both serial and parallel ports. When adding printers, modems, and other peripheral equipment to your computer, check to be sure that the required I/O port is available for use.

The Monitor

Most monitors will display up to 80 characters, or columns of characters, across the screen. With proportional spacing, in which each character occupies a different amount of space, that number may be smaller. The vertical length of the display varies even more. Most monitors display about half of a standard 11-inch page at once; full-page displays are also available, but are more likely to be used for special applications.

Most monitors today are color monitors, though monochrome units are still in use. The screen's resolution and the number of colors the monitor can display are determined by a special video card, which is inserted into the appropriate slot in the computer's motherboard. Also available are video accelerator boards that increase the speed at which the screen registers changes.

Unless your screen requires special cleaning, a household glass-cleaning fluid and paper towel should be all you need. Always spray fluid onto the cloth and *not* onto the screen, since excess fluid there could stain the casing or seep inside the monitor and damage it.

The Keyboard

The central part of the computer keyboard, containing the alphabet letter keys, the punctuation keys, and the space bar, is essentially the same as the traditional typewriter keyboard. But in addition to these standard keys, a typical keyboard for an IBM-compatible PC will also include (1) the function keys: F1–F12; (2) the numeric keypad, with numerals 0–9 and other keys; (3) the cursor-control and editing keys: ↑, ↓, →, ←, Insert, Delete, Backspace, Home, End, Page Up, Page Down; (4) the control-panel keys: Alt, Ctrl, Delete, Enter; and (5) the command keys: Print Screen, Scroll Lock, Pause/Break, Esc. (See Fig. 4.2.) A keyboard designed specifically for Macintosh computers will differ in some respects, having, for example, an Option key instead of an Alt key, and a command or Apple key (with the symbol ⌘) in addition to the Ctrl key. Some of these keys' placement on the keyboard will vary depending on the make or model. How they function may also vary depending on the software used. Some basic applications, however, are virtually identical industry-wide.

As thousands of coffee spillers can attest, the keyboard is the most easily damaged part of the computer. Keep any liquids well away from the computer. If a spill occurs, disconnect the keyboard, invert it over a trash can, and let it dry out before using it again.

Fig. 4.2 Computer Keyboard

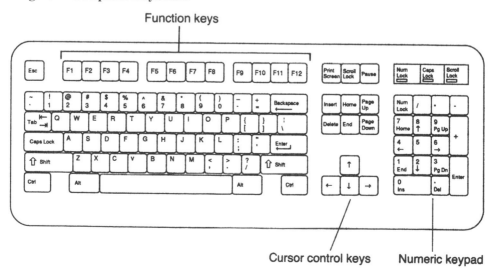

The function keys   Function keys are used for quickly entering frequently used information or for specifying that certain routine tasks be performed. The WordPerfect for DOS program, for example, uses the F7 key to issue the command to stop processing and exit the program. The File Manager in Microsoft Windows uses the F7 key to move files or directories. Check your software manual to learn exactly what the function keys will do.

The numeric keypad   The numeric keypad can be used either for entering numbers, especially in statistical or mathematical applications, or for editing text. Use the Num Lock key to switch, or "toggle," between these two different modes. With Num Lock on, use the keypad to enter numerical data. In this mode the keypad consists of the number keys 0–9, the arithmetical function keys +, −, * (multiply), / (divide), . (the decimal-point key), and Enter.

Never use a capital *O* in place of *0* (zero) or a lowercase *L* in place of *1* (one). In doing calculations and in other applications, the computer "knows" the difference and will not perform correctly if the proper data has not been entered.

With Num Lock off, use the keypad function keys to edit text. The keypad performs three editing functions in this mode: (1) delete and insert (Del, Ins); (2) control cursor (↑, ↓, →, ←); and (3) control page/position (Pg Up, Pg Dn, End, Home). See below for more on cursor control, positioning, and editing.

The cursor-control and editing keys   The arrow keys, ↑, ↓, →, ←, are used for moving the cursor around on the screen. The character following the cursor can be deleted by using the Delete key and the character preceding the cursor can be deleted with the Backspace key. Typed characters are normally inserted into the existing string of characters ("insert" mode), but characters can also be overwritten (i.e., deleted and replaced) by using the Insert key to shift to the "overstrike" mode. The Home and End keys send the cursor to the start or end of a line, while the Page Up and Page Down keys relocate the cursor to a point earlier or later in the document, usually by an increment of one screen or one page. Some of these keys can be used in combination with other keys; for example, pressing Ctrl + Home at the same time returns you to the start of the document in many Microsoft Windows programs.

It is a good idea to learn exactly what actions your keyboard can perform rather than rely on old habits. By neglecting to read the manual, you may be missing valuable shortcuts or otherwise failing to take full advantage of the keyboard's functions.

The control-panel keys   The control-panel keys are usually used or with other keys to execute special commands. Check your manual to see precisely how these keys function with your software. For example, on IBM-compatible computers running MS-DOS, if your system freezes up you can reboot (restart) it by pressing the control-panel keys Ctrl + Alt + Delete.

The command keys   The Print Screen key is used in MS-DOS to print the contents of the current screen. The Scroll Lock key is used to stop a screen from scrolling. The Pause/Break key is used to stop the output of a command given to the computer. Press Ctrl and Pause/Break at the same time to stop the execution of any command in MS-DOS; to resume the function, press any key but the **Pause/Break** key.

The mouse and other input devices   The *mouse* is basically a pointing device that allows input of processing commands without the use of a keyboard. For example, it may be possible to open and close programs and files with a mouse simply by pointing to a small icon on the screen and clicking the mouse's button. The mouse is an essential tool for much modern software.

Less commonly used input devices include the *touch screen,* which allows the user to enter commands by touching an icon on the screen. A *light pen* is a device that looks like an ordinary pen but is connected to the computer and allows for on-screen editing and drawing.

A *digital scanner,* finally, "reads" hard copy or "paper" material and converts it into electronic data accessible to the user (see below).

The Printer

Printers vary widely in their cost, speed, and print quality. The most common types of printer are (1) dot-matrix, (2) laser, (3) inkjet, and (4) plotter.

The *dot-matrix* printer forms characters by means of impact pins that produce dots arrayed in the shape of letters. This type of printer is noisy but cheap and fast and can be an office workhorse, producing draft or near-letter-quality print. *Inkjet* printers form an image by spraying ink from a matrix of tiny jets. This type of printer is quiet and inexpensive and can produce excellent copy. The *laser* printer is the fastest and most expensive. Laser printers use office-copier technology to produce typeset-quality text. *Plotter* printers transfer computer-generated drawings to paper using a movable carriage. Printers are also available that produce high-resolution *color* imaging and offer additional fonts for working with presentation graphics, or charts and graphs that are prepared for an audience.

Printers are usually connected to the computer by a parallel port, although serial printers are also available. The parallel connection is much faster, but the cable making the connection cannot be more than about ten feet long.

Printer components or accessories include *sheet feeders,* which allow separate sheets of paper such as letterhead to print continuously; *envelope feeders,* which feed envelopes continuously; *printer trays,* which allow you to use different sizes and quantities of paper; *memory-expansion boards,* which enhance your printer's capacity for processing documents; *font programs* and cartridges; which provide for the use of various typefaces and other enhancements; *color kits,* which can convert black-ink printers to black-and-color printers; and *utility stands,* which give you varying degrees of freedom in positioning your printer and printer supplies.

The Disk Drives and Disks

A disk drive is a device that copies information from or records new information onto a reusable storage disk—either a *hard disk* or a *floppy disk.* The drive for the hard disk is usually a nonremovable unit built into the computer. The floppy-disk drive operates with removable user disks of either 3½" or 5¼" (though the latter are disappearing from the market). In MS-DOS, each drive is assigned an identifying alphabetical letter: *c* for the hard drive, *a* and *b* for the floppy drives. Any additional drives, such as CD-ROM drive, are designated *d, e,* and so on.

Using disks   Disks need to be properly *formatted* (electronically prepared) to enable them to store information. Formatting is usually a simple procedure that should be described in your user manual. Take care not to format a disk that contains information of use to you, as the formatting procedure will erase the contents of the disk. Preformatted disks are also available; these can be timesavers and can eliminate the potential hazard of erasing valuable files.

To *write-protect* a disk, that is, to prevent disk files from being changed or erased, use the small tab and/or notch on the floppy disk. On 3½" disks you *uncover* the notch (i.e., reposition the tab) to protect the disk; on 5¼" disks you *cover* the notch using the tab (if present) or a piece of tape. If there is no tab or notch, this probably means that the disk is a program disk and is permanently write-protected.

Always *store* your disks in a safe place, away from dust, moisture, and extreme temperatures. Magnetic fields, such as are generated by dictating machines, should also be avoided, since these fields can erase or garble information stored on disk. It is best to keep disks in a storage box specifically designed for this purpose. Disks should always be *labeled* with the contents of the disk and the user. Always use a soft, felt-tip pen to label your disks; pressing down with pencils or ballpoint pens can damage the disk.

CD-ROMs   The CD-ROM disk drive is a read-only device designed to access data on compact disks. Compact disks can store more than 500MB of data; one CD-ROM disk can hold 250,000 pages of text. Currently dictionaries, encyclopedias, and many legal publications are available on CD-ROM.

Other Hardware

A computer will be fully operable with the hardware described above, but there are a few other devices that are used in many law offices.

The modem   A modem enables you to transmit data from one computer to another over ordinary telephone lines. It converts the computer's digital language into the telephone's analog language for transmission. At the other end, a receiving modem converts it back to a digital signal. This is where the modem's name comes from: it is a device that *mo*dulates and *dem*odulates data.

There are two forms of modem: the *internal modem,* a board that fits into a slot in the computer, and the *external modem,* a small box that attaches to one of the computer's ports by a cable.

Modems are rated according to the speed at which they transmit data. The measurement is in bits per second, or bps, sometimes also referred to as the *baud rate.* Here are some common modem speeds:

9600 bps	72,000 characters (14,400 words) per minute
14400 bps	108,000 characters (21,600 words) per minute
28800 bps	200,000 characters (43,200 words) per minute

In the context of word processing, modems are frequently used to exchange text files between computers. It is not unusual for one person to draft a document, transmit it electronically to someone else who may edit or comment on it, and then return the file to the originator for more work. The electronic transmission may only take seconds, and is far more convenient and economical than exchanging paper, especially across long distances.

There are a number of factors to consider in using modems to exchange files.

1. In addition to word-processing software, both the sender and the receiver must have communications software to drive the modem.

2. The sender and receiver may also need to be using the same word-processing software, so that files loaded at either end preserve the same formatting characteristics (underlines, boldface, type fonts, and so forth). Otherwise, you may have to exchange "text-only" (unformatted) files.

3. Outside third-party vendors, such as electronic-mail services, will generally provide for hardware compatibility so that entirely different computers or word processors can exchange files with each other. Differences in software, however, may continue to be a problem.

Every improvement in hardware and software requires a corresponding improvement in transmission capability. If you have a modem, consult your user manual for setup and operating instructions, and do not be surprised or discouraged if you find that you need some technical assistance from the vendor to make it work.

The fax modem   With a fax modem it is possible to send and receive telefaxes from a fax machine or a computer attached to a modem. You can view a document being sent or received electronically before, or instead of, printing it out on either a computer printer or a fax machine. In this way both time and paper can be saved. A fax modem does require communications software and a dedicated (single-purpose) telephone line to operate; consult your local vendor. A large hard drive is recommended for use of a fax modem, particularly if you expect to be receiving many fax messages. Each fax can use 50kb–1MB of disk space.

Laptop, notebook, and subnotebook computers   The need to communicate and work while away from the office is a phenomenon that is here to stay. Today's computer is not only a desktop appliance but a portable productivity tool.

The first portable computer was the *laptop computer*—a battery-powered computer, keyboard, and monitor packaged in a briefcase-sized unit that weighed about 20 pounds. The laptop computer soon led to the *notebook computer,* a smaller and lighter version weighing four to six pounds. Further advances have led to the *subnotebook computer,* a slim, easily portable device weighing two pounds or less. Each of these computers is available with the full range of features that can be found on their desktop counterparts, including hard disks, floppy disk drives, CD-ROM drives, fax modems, and built-in mouse devices.

Portable computers have tended to be less powerful and more expensive than full-sized desktop computers, but continuing rapid development and cost reduction have narrowed the gap considerably. More and more people are now using compact portable computers on their desktops as well as on the road, and with the latest *docking-system* technology the two kinds of units can work together as one.

The following is a list of the kinds of documents and software that lawyers often keep on their portable computers:

Trial notebook/outline	The full text of statutes and cases
Depositions and deposition summaries	Research notes
	Rules of evidence
Transcripts of prior hearings	Rules of court
Document databases	Search software
Briefs	Word-processing software
Pleadings	Spreadsheet software
Discovery requests and responses	Presentation graphics
Pretrial motions and orders	Legal research software
Documentary exhibits	Fax/modem software
Demonstrative charts and graphs	

Power converter   A power converter will allow you to plug your portable computer, modem, or telefax machine into an auto cigarette lighter.

The scanner   Computer technology enables a user to transfer existing printed material directly into a computer file. This requires a *scanner,* a device that copies the image of the text from a piece of paper to a digitized file, essentially treating the text as a picture; *optical character recognition* (OCR) software then converts it into a document file. Scanners are also used to reproduce photographs and graphic images. A scanner's success can vary considerably depending on the size, type, and quality of reproduction of the material scanned. (See also Chapter 3, p. 77, for information on combination fax/copier/printer/scanner units.)

Tape drive   It is particularly important in a law office to back up work produced on the computer. The most widely used backup device is a tape-drive unit, which automatically records files from the computer onto magnetic tape. Other such devices use optical and/or audio technology to accomplish the same end. Consult your dealer to identify the best system for your needs.

Equipment for the disabled   There are a number of hardware devices available for the disabled. For the visually impaired, there are Braille keyboards, Braille printers, voice-recognition systems, voice synthesizer/read-back machines, and word-processing programs that provide automatic spelling correction. For the physically impaired, there are hardware adapters and ergonomically designed keyboards. Software programs such as KeyLock allow you to use one command key at a time to execute key sequences such as Ctrl + Delete and Alt + F1. MySpeech is a program that reads keystrokes and speaks them through a synthesizer. DLK software is a text-to-speech package that allows the visually impaired to have access to computers. The Magnify system is a set of programs that double the size of characters on the screen.

Computer Software

Software is the entire set of programs, procedures, and related documentation associated with a computer system. Most computer systems come with their own basic built-in software, which the user then may enhance or replace with off-the-shelf, commercially available software packages. Software ranges from the very basic to the highly complex. Most programs offer more features than any one user would ever need. Prices range widely depending on the program's sophistication. A *site license*—essentially, a discount for multiple purchases—may be available if your organization wants many people to be able to use the same program.

Some software programs can be run from floppy disks or CD-ROMs, but most programs—particularly those sold on floppy disks—will need to be installed on the hard disk of a computer. Your manual will contain instructions for installing the program. You may have to copy each individual file, but usually the program will include a built-in installation program that does most of the work for you. Either way, you should not find this a difficult task. You will be instructed to make a set of backup disks first, in case the original disks are lost or damaged. Programs that are copy-protected by the manufacturer allow you to make one set of backup disks, but no more.

The Operating System

The operating system of a computer is software that controls the operation of the computer and directs the processing of programs, such as by assigning storage space in memory and controlling input and output functions. The most popular of today's commercially available operating systems for personal computers (PCs) are Microsoft's MS-DOS, IBM's Operating System/2 (OS/2), and the operating system of the Apple Macintosh. Special operating-system software is used with computers connected through a local area network (LAN) and with mainframe computers that serve sophisticated user workstations.

MS-DOS   MS-DOS is a command-driven operating system for IBM and IBM-compatible PCs, meaning that the user is required to type commands to make the computer system operate. For example, to run a program in MS-DOS the user types the program's name (or an abbreviated version of the name) and presses **ENTER**. Although MS-DOS is in many ways an old-fashioned operating system, it is still very widely used.

Microsoft Windows   Microsoft Windows provides what is known as a graphical user interface for IBM-compatible computers running MS-DOS. The program divides your computer's display into different areas (windows) on which are displayed different types of information and computer functions represented in the form of menus, icons, text, scrollbars, and other visual elements. The usual method of giving commands in windows is by pointing and clicking with the mouse. To run a program in Windows the user points to the program's icon and clicks the mouse's button twice. Windows permits access to several programs or files simultaneously and lets you transfer data between them.

Operating System/2 (OS/2)   IBM's OS/2 operating system is a *multitasking* program for IBM-compatible machines, a program under which several jobs can be performed concurrently. Like Windows, it offers menus, icons, and other graphical elements to facilitate access to information and to make it easier to transfer text and graphics from one application to another. It can run its own applications as well as MS-DOS and Windows applications.

The Macintosh   The Macintosh was the first widely available computer to use the mouse- and menu-driven interface (access system) and other features that have become standards in the industry. Its operating system still offers a state-of-the-art graphical user interface that serves a wide variety of applications. Macintosh computers are especially popular for use in desktop publishing and in creating and editing graphics.

Network Operating System   A network is a system of computers, and associated peripheral devices (such as printers) connected by communication lines. The operating system for a network initiates and sustains the link between the various components and provides administrative and security functions to facilitate the effective use of shared information. A typical network requires (1) a CPU designated as the *file server,* or main unit, with file-server software; (2) software for each of the other computers (called *clients*) connected to the server; and (3) a special board called a *network interface card* installed in each computer on the network. Although simple networks can be set up by the experienced user, it is usually better to work with a reputable dealer or installer who can advise you about the proper equipment and software and can service the system once it is installed.

UNIX   UNIX is an operating system that was originally developed for mainframe computers but today is increasingly used in a personal-computer or LAN (Local Area Network) environment. UNIX is especially suited to use with larger networks or with networks that run specialized programs such as database management or corporate-accounting applications. The system offers concurrent processing by which several processors operate simultaneously on the same information.

A law office may use personal computers to do one kind of work (e.g., producing letters, tracking clients and contacts, scheduling appointments, and calendaring court dates) and a mainframe computer to do another kind of work (e.g., creating invoices, generating financial reports, managing cash flow, and billing and accounting). However, it is possible to integrate the two systems and achieve better coordination of efforts through use of a network.

Word Processing

Five word-processing programs dominate today's market: WordPerfect for DOS, WordPerfect for Windows, Microsoft Word for Windows, Microsoft Word for the Macintosh, and Lotus AmiPro for Windows.

Word-processing programs are designed to make the creation, formatting, editing, and printing of text easier. The benefits of word processing include (1) reduced time spent on repetitive tasks such as rekeying and reproofreading, and (2) increased productivity through better quality and increased speed. Some word-processing programs have page-layout capabilities that allow you to use your system as a desktop publisher to produce well-designed, camera-ready (i.e., ready-to-copy) material for newsletters, advertisements, brochures, and the like.

The basic functions of word-processing software are

- Creating documents
- Editing text
- Formatting text

- Saving files
- Printing documents

Creating documents   Creating a document is very much like typing on a standard typewriter. Two notable differences are that (1) the screen does not usually hold a full page of text, and (2) words extending beyond the right-hand margin will automatically "wrap around" to the line below—a feature known as *word wrap.*

Editing text   One of the many advantages that word processors have over typewriters is that they make it a simple matter to correct mistakes and otherwise revise and edit text. Word-processing programs allow you to use the keyboard and the mouse to insert, copy, move, and delete individual characters, words, or large blocks of text.

Formatting text   The formatting features in word-processing software enable you to style text in the manner desired (by applying boldface or italic formatting, for example, or employing a variety of fonts and typesizes) and to arrange the elements of a page or document in a suitable way preparatory to printing. Such formatting is done by adjusting, among other things, margins and tabs, line spacing, typesize and typeface, text alignment, text layout (as in columns and tables), page size and length, headings, footnotes, rules, and page numbers.

Saving files   When a document is saved, it is given a name and copied to a specified location on a hard disk or floppy disk. Before it has been saved, it is stored only in the computer's temporary memory (RAM), where even a momentary power failure or any of a variety of software problems could cause the document to be lost. Most word processors include an automatic-save feature, which can be set to save at regular intervals. You should get in the habit of saving your work frequently, however, and not rely exclusively on the automatic-save feature.

Printing documents   Your word processor should allow you to easily change the settings for the size and orientation—"portrait" (upright) or "landscape" (oblong)—of the paper you are printing on. Most word-processing programs also allow you to print envelopes and labels.

Word-Processing Features

Some word-processing features affect page setup and appearance, while others affect the arrangement of the text itself. The following features are available in a variety of programs. Most good word-processing programs will contain all or nearly all of the features listed.

Append   This feature permits you to take text from one file and add it to another file.

Automatic file backup   Just as you should always back up your files to protect against accidental damage or loss, you should also have a system for saving the previous version of any file you have revised, in case it becomes necessary to have access to the earlier version. Some programs offer a system for automatically saving the previous version.

Automatic formatting   This feature allows the user to format, or design, an entire document at once. After you type a document with minimal formatting, the software reviews the document's structure and suggests formatting that seems appropriate, choosing, for example, a particular typeface, character size, and indent to apply to different kinds of paragraphs and headings. You can then review the appearance of the formatted document and choose to accept or reject any or all of the suggested changes.

Automatic text insertion   This feature enables you to create your own list of frequently used words, phrases, sentences, and paragraphs, and add them to any document with a few keystrokes. Stock sentences and paragraphs, informally known as "boilerplate," can be especially helpful when you need to modify form letters. If your program does not have an automatic insertion function, you can get the same result by storing your boilerplate language as separate files or macros (see "Macros" below) and then loading them into any file as needed.

Boldface   Characters and words can be printed in boldface type for emphasis or to serve as a heading.

Boxes   The ability to create boxes around text, especially when combined with the ability to create horizontal and vertical lines, enables you to design charts, tables, attractive headings, and much else. Boxes can usually be plain, drop-shadowed, or filled with various degrees of shading.

Capitalization   Many programs allow you to select and automatically capitalize any text you have already entered in lowercase. You may also specify that it be set in SMALL CAPITALS.

Centering   Any word, line, or paragraph can be automatically centered between the margins of the documents. This is useful for headings, quotations, or any other material that should stand out from the main body of the text.

Columns   This page-layout capability is useful for charts, documentation, and many other applications. It generally permits you to divide your page into a desired number of columns and specify the amount of space between the columns. The most common types of column are newspaper columns, in which the text simply wraps to the top of the next column, and side-by-side columns, in which specific items are lined up directly across from each other.

Copy   Within a file, the Copy feature allows you to select any block of text and duplicate it (see the "Cut and paste" section, below). At the directory or menu level of the program, a Copy feature enables you to duplicate an entire file so that an alternative version can be created without losing the original.

Cross-reference   This feature is valuable in creating internal references to page numbers, figures, and footnotes—and in updating the references if the document is revised. In pleadings, contracts, or even correspondence, the text may refer to another portion of the same document—for example, "(*See* Liens, page 3)." If you revise the document, the *Liens* section may move to page 4; by using the cross-reference feature, the page number within the cross-reference will automatically change to the correct one.

Cut and paste   Also called simply *moving copy,* this fundamental feature of all word-processing programs enables you to select any amount of text and move it to another location in the document. The process requires you to "cut" the text after highlighting it, locate the new insertion point with the cursor, and then "paste" it in by using the keys designated by your software. Text that is cut is held in temporary memory until you move it. From temporary memory, it may be pasted into the document multiple times if desired. If you choose not to paste the text back in—which amounts to deleting it—it will remain in the temporary memory only until you either turn off the computer or displace it by cutting some other text (since there is normally only room for one piece at a time in the temporary memory).

Date and time   The current date and time, in various formats, can be easily inserted at any point in your document.

Delete   In the process of editing and correcting, you will probably be deleting text as often as you add it, so this feature is one of the most fundamental capabilities of word processing. Minor deletions are often accomplished by merely backspacing over the last text that was entered. To remove a large block of text, you will have to highlight the entire block and then press the Delete key.

File notation and finding   Because the names given to computer files can often be very cryptic, you may sometimes forget the name and location of a particular file. The file notation feature allows you to store information about a file—such as a longer and more descriptive name, the author of the document, and certain keywords (such as a client's name)—that can be used in locating the file by means of the software's file finding feature.

Find and replace   The find feature allows you to specify a word or phrase that occurs anywhere in the document and then have the software locate that spot for you instantly. This is a tremendous time-saver when you are trying to locate something in a long document. Using the replace feature, you can specify another word or phrase to substitute for the original. You can use this feature to make global changes (that is, changes throughout a given document), such as replacing an incorrect name or title wherever it occurs without having to find and retype every instance of it.

Graphics   Word-processing programs allow you to add, or "import," graphics created through a separate graphics program into your document. This capability has further blurred the lines between word processing and desktop publishing.

Headers and footers   In any document you may need to display repetitive identification at the top or bottom of each page: the name of the document or file, the title of a presentation or proposal, or chapter or section numbers, as well as page numbers. For convenience or attractiveness, you may want these lines to appear as *headers* (that is, lines running across the top of the page, as on the page you are reading) or as *footers* (lines running across the bottom of the page).

Indent   Any word processor makes it easy to adjust the indention on lines and paragraphs, either individually or for an entire document.

Indexing   This feature automates the job of preparing alphabetical indexes. After you have gone through a lengthy document and highlighted or identified those words or phrases that you want included in the index, the program takes over, pulling together the entire index with appropriate page numbers and formatting.

Italic   Italics are useful especially to set off titles, to emphasize words and phrases, and to provide stylistic variation in captions and headings.

Justification   This feature controls line width by adjusting the spacing between words. Most typed documents have lines of varying length, depending on the number of words in the line; the left margin is flush but the right margin varies, in the style usually called "ragged right." Full justification, also called "right justification," creates equal margins on both sides by inserting extra space as needed between words. Full justification has a more formal look and is desirable for certain kinds of documents, but it is harder to read because of the unequal spacing.

Kerning   When a document's design is important, sometimes the spacing between letters in a word (often in a title, heading, or other element) seems too loose or too tight. Increasing or reducing that spacing is called kerning or simply *letter spacing*, and it can be easily done on a word processor.

Leading   The space between lines on a page, called leading (pronounced "ledding") or simply *line spacing*, is determined by the software and may vary according to the font (that is, the style or design of type) being used and the point size of the letters. The feature that permits you to increase or decrease the standard leading is particularly useful for desktop publishing.

Macros   A macro is a miniature computer program you may write by yourself to direct the software to perform one or more repetitive tasks. For example, rather than pressing a series of keys to print, close, and save a file, you could write a macro that would enable you to do all those things with one keystroke. Macros can be used to create form letters, pleading formats, letter formats, memorandums, signature blocks, second-page headings, and other forms.

Mail merge   The ability to automate multiple mailings can be one of the great benefits of a word-processing program. This feature allows you to create a form letter in one file and an address list in another and then merge them to produce personalized letters using each individual's name and address. You will need to embed instructions in the document file telling it where to insert the address and salutation, and you will also have to follow strict rules for formatting the address list so that the information merges correctly.

Master documents   Documents of a hundred pages or more can be difficult to scroll through, spell-check, and cross-reference. The *master document* function allows you to break down a larger document into smaller units to make it easier to handle. A good application of master documents is in pleadings. The master document would contain a Notice of Motion, Memorandum of Points and Authorities, and various declarations. By defining the whole as a master document, each section could be treated as a separate document (or subdocument) for ease in editing, spell-checking, and formatting but would act as one document for cross-referencing and printing.

Pagination   Once you set the page size of a document, the software will automatically begin a new page whenever necessary. If you later edit the document, making it longer or shorter, the system will repaginate for you. You can override this by manually inserting a page break wherever you want one. Page breaks are normally displayed on-screen so that you can always see where they occur.

Password protection   Some programs allow you to establish your own access code so that no one else can get into your files. If this is not part of your word-processing program, you can probably purchase a separate program that does the same thing.

Print preview   This feature saves paper by allowing the user to see exactly how a printed document will look before printing it. It is often possible to make adjustments to the layout of a document while viewing it in print preview. Some word processors also include a "fit in" capability so that if a document is seen in print preview to be running a few lines long, the software will look for ways to fit it onto one less page (such as by reducing the size of the font or widening the margins slightly).

Redlining   Redlining refers to the practice of showing revisions within a document. Deletions are typically struck-through with a line, while additions are shown as highlighted or underlined text (see Fig. 4.3). This is a useful function when more than one attorney is working on a document, since each can easily

Fig. 4.3   Redlined Document

> The exchange of information and/or documents ~~respecting~~ ~~plaintiff's~~ among counsel for the insurers concerning the prosecution or ~~cross-defendants'~~ defense of this action, ~~among~~ ~~any of the cross-defendants and/or plaintiff~~ irrespective of whether principals for the insurers receive such information or documents, is deemed to be a communication for the limited purpose of assisting in a common cause and shall not constitute a waiver of whatever attorney-client privilege, work product doctrine, or other privilege or doctrine would otherwise apply if such information and/or documents were not exchanged.

see what the other has done. While many word-processing programs include this function, commercially available software specific to law-firm applications is also available (e.g., from JuriSoft, Inc. in Cambridge, Mass.).

Sorting   If you ever need to produce documents with long lists that must appear in either numerical or alphabetical order, look for the sorting feature. It allows you, for example, to take an unordered list of name-and-address files or subjects for an index and instantly alphabetize it—and painlessly update it whenever new entries are added.

Spell check and thesaurus   A spell-check program will find and highlight misspelled words and make suggestions for correcting them. An electronic thesaurus will assist you in finding the word you want by displaying synonyms and related words. (See also "Lexicons and Grammar Checkers," page 108.)

Styles   If you prepare documents containing multiple sections, each with its own characteristics—margins, type font, italics, boldface, or underlining, for example—your word-processing program should offer you the option of creating reusable styles—that is, formats for individual sections. This feature, usually called Styles or Style Sheets, lets you define individual styles, or collections of formatting characteristics, and then apply them to different blocks of text in the document. A standard application in a law firm is the creation of pleadings.

Superscript and subscript   Various mathematical formulas and chemical notations employ characters printed slightly above or below the regular line of text, which are termed *superscripts* and *subscripts,* respectively. Trademark and registration symbols are also generally written as superscripts or subscripts.

Table of authorities   A table of authorities is an alphabetical listing of all the legal sources cited in a document. The list may be divided into categories such as cases, articles, and texts. The table-of-authorities function in word-processing software supports this application by allowing you to mark citations in the text that will then be copied onto the correct section of the table of authorities with the appropriate page numbers.

Table of contents   Tables of contents are used in filing motions as well as in requests for proposals and office handbooks. You can create a table of contents in much the same way that you prepare a table of authorities. Mark the headings you want to appear in the table of contents; when the function is activated, a table of contents with page numbers is automatically generated.

Tables   Word processors make it simple to create customized tables, allowing easy adjustments to the number and size of columns and rows as well as to the overall style and appearance of the table. For multipage tables, you may specify headings that will be automatically inserted in the row at the top of each page.

Templates   In the language of word processing, a template is a file containing a number of predefined settings and automatically generated elements to be used as a starting point in the creation of a particular type of document. A template for business letters, for example, might include such elements as a company logo at the top of the first page, a particular paragraph style and typeface for the body of the letter, and preset margins. A more elaborate template to be used for data entry might open on the screen with the appearance of a printed form. Word processors come with a selection of predefined templates for the user to choose from in creating a new document. It should also be possible to create your own templates, customized to meet your specific needs.

Underline   Underlining is useful for highlighting words or phrases for emphasis or for designating subheadings in a document.

Undo/redo   One of the great advantages of word processors is that they allow you to correct your mistakes. If you accidentally delete all the text in your document or commit some other major computing blunder, you can almost always save yourself by making use of the undo feature, which reverses your previous action. Most programs allow the user to undo dozens of changes at a time. Using this feature, you can experiment with formatting changes to see how they will look and then quickly return to the original formatting by undoing those changes. If you then want to see the modified formatting again, you can do so with the redo function, which reapplies previously undone changes.

Widow and orphan control   In typesetting terminology, a widow is the last line of a paragraph that spilled over to the top of the next page. An orphan is the opposite: the first line of a paragraph at the bottom of a page, when the rest of the paragraph is on the next page. Both are considered unattractive, and word-processing programs have a feature to prevent them by bringing over an additional line from the previous page to keep the widow company and moving the orphan line to the next page to join the rest of its "family."

Spreadsheet Programs

Spreadsheet programs are computer-based financial planning and calculating tools. A spreadsheet consists essentially of an electronic "page" of columns and rows—as in an accountant's ledger—into which data and mathematical formulas are entered. The program uses the formulas and data to perform calculations. Two of the most commonly used programs are Lotus 1-2-3 and Microsoft Excel; but several others exist, including those that come with word-processing packages such as WordPerfect and Microsoft Word.

The worksheet   The *worksheet* is the ledger-like layout that appears on-screen to the user. Columns are identified by letter across the top of the worksheet. Rows are identified by number down the left margin of the worksheet. The intersection of each column and row is called a *cell*, which is identified by an "address" consisting of the column letter and row number. The upper left cell of a worksheet, for example, bears the address A1 (see Fig. 4.4). (The worksheet can, however, extend beyond the range of the alphabet by doubling or even tripling letters, e.g., AAA110.) Cells in the worksheet can be filled in with labels (words), numbers (data), or mathematical formulas.

Formulas   A *formula*, or combination of mathematical signs, must be entered if you want a calculation to be performed. In Fig. 4.5, for example, a formula has been entered (or "embedded") in cell E18 for summing (adding) the amounts

Fig. 4.4 Worksheet (with Cell A1 Highlighted)

	A	B	C	D	E	F
1						
2						
3						
4						
5						
6						
7						
8						
9						
10						
11						
12						
13						
14						
15						
16						
17						
18						
19						
20						

in column E ($15.00 + $7.50 + $65.00). The formula itself does not show up in the cell; only the result ($87.50) does.

What-if analysis One of the major advantages of spreadsheet programs is their ability to perform "what-if" analyses. This means that once you have created a worksheet, you can then ask the program "what if" you were to use different data instead? In Fig. 4.5, for example, if you were to change the amount in cell E15 from $65.00 to $165.00 (or any of the other amounts in column E),

Fig. 4.5 Worksheet with Data Entered and Results of Calculations Shown

	A	B	C	D	E	F
1						
2						
3						
4				EXPENSE	LOG	
5						
6						
7	DATE: 9/12/XX		I.D.: SLP			
8						
9						
10	MATTER NAME		CLIENT	MATTER	AMOUNT	DESCRIPTION
11						
12						
13	Smith vs. Brown		1600	120	$15.00	Parking at deposition
14	Green vs. Hamilton		2300	010	$7.50	Mileage/parking court
15	Reed vs. Simon		2110	057	$65.00	Jury lunch
16						
17						
18	Total				$87.50	
19						
20						

Fig. 4.6 Worksheet Showing Results of "What-if" Analysis

	A	B	C	D	E	F
1						
2						
3						
4				EXPENSE	LOG	
5						
6						
7	DATE: 9/12/XX		I.D.: SLP			
8						
9						
10	MATTER NAME		CLIENT	MATTER	AMOUNT	DESCRIPTION
11						
12						
13	Smith vs. Brown		1600	120	$15.00	Parking at deposition
14	Green vs. Hamilton		2300	010	$7.50	Mileage/parking court
15	Reed vs. Simon		2110	057	$165.00	Jury lunch
16						
17						
18	Total				$187.50	
19						
20						

the corresponding result in cell E18 would automatically change to reflect the new data ($187.50 instead of $87.50). (See Fig. 4.6)

Database Programs

Database programs are tools for amassing, organizing, and retrieving data. The effective operation of a database program requires (1) preparing records, (2) sorting and searching, and (3) updating files.

Preparing records A *record*, in computer terms, is a collection of related information treated as a unit. A client's name, address, phone number, and related information is an example of a single database record. Each of the elements within a record (name, address, etc.) is termed a *field*. Records and fields are the basic building blocks of database programs. In Fig. 4.7, for example, record 1 contains the fields (1) Company, (2) Address, (3) Phone number, (4) Contact, and so on. The *data* consist of the entries assigned to each of these fields ("John Brown & Company," "300 Business Center Lane," etc.).

Sorting and searching *Sorting*, as described earlier, is the process by which information is reordered by the user according to priorities specified in advance. Sorting is usually done by field, and the results may be presented in alphabetical or numerical order, either ascending or descending. Figure 4.8 illustrates a simple sort that specified fields 1–7 (company, address, phone number, contact, title, type of business, size of company) arranged in descending order by size of company. (This information would typically print out on wide continuous-sheet paper.)

Searching involves telling a database program to present information selectively. An example would be specifying "all clients whose *type of business* is real estate and who are located in the *908* calling area."

The real power of a database program becomes evident when you can ask questions and learn something you didn't know before, or ask questions that help you to ask even more important questions.

Fig. 4.7   Database Records

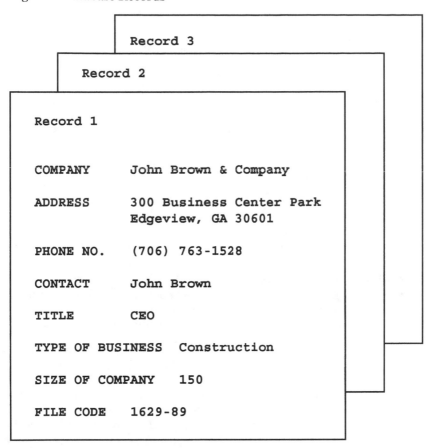

Law-office applications   Database programs are used in law offices principally for litigation support, marketing support, and human-resources management. *Litigation support* can be provided by various special database programs:

- *Full-text retrieval* Programs that enable you to retrieve the complete text (or relevant portion thereof) of a legal case, ruling, or similar type of information.
- *Document abstracts* Programs that enable you to access summaries of key information.
- *Work-product retrieval* Programs that enable you to call up earlier or current versions of documents.
- *Discovery tracking* Programs that assist you in the creation of expert and witness lists.

A typical litigation-support program offers the following benefits:

- Documents can be stored to be readily accessible for use in discovery or as exhibits during depositions and trial.
- Transcripts can be entered full-text and are searchable by word, allowing quick referencing.

Fig. 4.8 Sample Sort

FILE NAME: CLIENTS

SIZE	COMPANY	ADDRESS	PHONE	CONTACT	TITLE	RECORD
4,000	BIGCO	3 PARK WAY DALLAS, TX 75331	214-239- 5368	PETER BEST	PRES	12
2,750	MEDCO	17 COWPER LN DALLAS, TX 76207	817-556- 9482	SHARON EARL	GEN COUNSEL	33
2,200	DOE PUBLISHING	33 RIVER DR BULTON,TX 76610	903-765- 0032	STEVEN TUNNEY	CEO	17
1,700	BRADFORD INDUSTRIES	8 ASSEMBLY DR HARRISON, TX 77535	817-366- 0876	SAMUEL BRADFORD	PRES	15

- Chronologies of events can be produced to develop a timeline.
- Biographical information and relevant notes and summaries of testimony can be collected in a witness notebook.
- Court file and work-product documents can also be stored and accessed.

Marketing support is available from basic database applications that can help in creating client records, compiling mailing lists, and keeping historical information on clients.

Human-resources management is assisted by means of database records containing such information as Social Security numbers, salaries, titles, review dates, vacations and sick leaves, emergency information, and educational achievements.

For more advanced applications, a *relational database system* may be used to access data stored in separate files or programs. Such programs can sometimes take a little time to learn properly, but the user is often rewarded by the results.

Work-Product Retrieval

One of the most efficient means by which the firm can improve its services is to reuse work product that it has produced in the past. The firm's ability to provide excellent, reliable work in less time and at less cost to the client will confer a business advantage. Whether the organization is a large corporate staff or a small private firm, investing time in carefully storing the results of legal work will increase efficiency as later projects call for similar types of information. Arranging office work product using a popular database program such as *Quattro Pro* or *Folio Views* will allow you to retrieve work by date, client, or subject matter. If you also include the client number or other of the firm's filing codes, you will make retrieval all the easier.

Memorandums, briefs, opinion letters, and transactional documents should all be reviewed and preserved for retrieval. If these are stored in a computer, they can be reused without significant new research or manual retyping being required. Some firms also retain copies of legal instruments particular to their areas of practice—e.g., buy-sell agreements, lease provisions, or estate-planning provisions. Court papers, interrogatories, the depositions of expert witnesses—anything that might save time or improve your effectiveness in a later undertaking—should be considered candidates for work-product retrieval. A few firms add unpublished opinions, useful articles, and research tools developed for earlier cases to the same system.

There are at least three elements that can contribute to the success of such a system:

1. *Incentive* There should be an appropriate incentive for the attorney's and other staff members to submit their work product to the system. (Some firms have reported a reluctance on the part of lawyers to contribute work to such systems.) If your attorney-compensation system is set up to reward individuals for generating billable hours, both the document author and the lawyer who later reuses the document can be given credit for some billable hours when the document is reused. (The amount might represent the savings realized.)

2. *Usability* The work submitted should be of practical value and be readily accessible. Summaries of the document, notes about where or how it will be useful, and information about indexing (i.e., how it has been subject-coded and/or filed) should be made available to users if possible. This will aid the inexperienced lawyer who may need help choosing the document that best suits the intended application.

3. *Currency* Once material is in the system, it should be reviewed periodically to make certain that it is based on current law. As documents are made obsolete by changes in the law, the dated material must be purged or at least flagged for deletion or alteration.

Case-Management Programs

It is no longer possible to rely solely on manual procedures to make important calendar entries, maintain dockets, and check for conflicts of interest. Some legal insurers now require automated systems for all these functions. While separate calendar, time-and-billing, and conflict-of-interest programs are available, a comprehensive case-management package will include these and other functions, as described below.

Calendar Electronic calendars have begun to replace the printed kind in the law office. Typical calendar menu choices include event entry, recurring-event entry, inquiry by date, time and billing, client/matter, and report; reports can give you information sorted in any number of ways.

Docket While a manual docket consists of a ledger of information about documents that enter or leave the office, an automated docket system performs the same function but offers an electronic menu in place of the manual ledger sheet. Automation permits reports to be run that show the whereabouts of a document or list all hearings that pertain to a particular matter. Docket systems can also interface with calendar programs. (See also Chapter 11, "Docket Control and Records Management.")

Conflict of interest In today's law firm, automated conflict-of-interest software is a must; the secretary's or attorney's memory cannot be relied on to identify professional conflicts. Conflict-of-interest programs provide menu choices that include name search, information verification, inquiries by client/matter, synonym definition, address entry, and data linking. The data fields should include the *client*, the client's *corporate affiliates*, the *officers* of the client, the *directors* of the client, the *ownership* of the client, and the *particulars* of the case, including information on *opposing counsel*.

A number of specialized or general database programs may be used for conflict-of-interest applications. One key consideration is that fields should be *repeatable* so that you can list several entities if necessary.

Other functions   In addition to the functions described above, case-management software should assist you in keeping track of the following information:

Client matter (or file number)	Opposing counsel
Case type	Date file received
Court case number	Date response due
Trial type	Discovery deadlines
Case caption	Trial dates
Presiding judge	Statute of limitations
Jurisdiction	Other deadlines

Citation-Recognition and Document-Comparison Programs

Software programs are available that are capable of working with word-processing software to check citations, verify quotations, and compare documents to identify changes from one version to the next. While some word-processing programs are capable of "redlining" a document and preparing a table of authorities, add-on programs designed specifically for these purposes can be cost-effective in that they generally do more and work faster. Pleadings and briefs can be run through such programs to extract tables of authorities without citations having been marked beforehand. Citations can be automatically checked for correct format against a standard legal authority, and quotations can be automatically verified for accuracy by using CheckCite from LEXIS or WestCheck from West Publishing. Documents can be compared using CompareWrite from Jurisoft, which highlights revisions so that all parties can take note of them. (See "Redlining," pp. 98–99.)

Forms

One type of software that is gaining popularity in law firms is the *forms* package, which contains electronically laid-out forms for completing court papers and jury instructions. With forms software, the proper form is simply called up onto the screen and the information is typed into the form just as if you were using a typewriter. In some cases you can even purchase printer paper that is perforated according to the court's requirements. Using these programs, it is no longer necessary to store numerous printed forms that can become outdated before they are used. Rather, current forms can be stored in your computer by form type or name and may be updated as necessary. (See Chap. 10.)

Computer-Assisted Document Assembly

Computer-assisted document assembly (CADA) is the creation of commonly used documents by means of software programming that "asks" the user a series of questions or otherwise allows for the input of document specifications ("specs"). Documents that carry a checklist of standard requirements—such as wills, contracts, foreclosures, pension accounts, and routine pleadings and correspondence—lend themselves particularly well to this application. Documents are created using predefined criteria for input, thus reducing the possibility for error and increasing the speed with which the task is accomplished.

Supplementary Technologies

Desktop-Publishing Programs

Desktop publishing (DTP) is the creation of typesetter-quality text and graphics using a desktop computer. It is one of the fastest-growing areas in modern computing. DTP can be used for newsletters, brochures, stock offers, award certificates, seminar announcements, printed advertisements, training manuals, corporate logos, and survey forms, among other uses.

In conventional publishing, the author traditionally types a manuscript and pastes any necessary artwork in place. The editor then edits it and sends it out for typesetting, and the typeset galleys return for proofreading by the author and editor. These are sent back to the typesetter to be corrected and (usually) pasted up with the artwork into pages. These must again be checked and corrected; errors caught at a late stage can be time-consuming and expensive to correct.

Using DTP technology, you become more directly responsible for the whole production cycle—especially if you are also the author. Most changes that need to be made can be implemented instantly right at your computer. The most popular programs are QuarkXpress (Macintosh) and PageMaker (IBM), but there are numerous others available.

Below is a series of guidelines that should help you to save time and increase productivity as you embark on a desktop-publishing project. Before you start such a project, consider the following elements:

- *Planning* Ask yourself who is the intended audience and what is the message you wish to convey.
- *Experimentation* Try out ideas by sketching them first.
- *Inspiration* Look for good and bad designs in newspapers, magazines, and direct-mail pieces.
- *Relevance* Design elements (e.g., a logo or letterhead) should reflect the best of the firm and be distinct.
- *Proportion* The size and layout of text and graphics indicate their relative importance and as such must be balanced.
- *Direction* The design should help guide the reader through the piece.
- *Consistency* Typeface, margins, spacing, paragraphs, and indents should generally be uniform unless a particular item element (e.g., a headline) is meant to stand out.
- *Contrast* Light and dark areas (e.g., regular text and spacing vs. shaded text and graphics) should be used to make the piece visually more interesting.
- *Restraint* It is generally best to strive for simplicity.
- *Detail* Everything on the page should be carefully considered and checked.

Your desktop-publishing system may not include everything you need to complete every assignment. If so, there are outside vendors or service bureaus that will perform particular functions, such as electronic imaging (scanning artwork), laser color-copying, and producing 35-mm slides and high-resolution output from a floppy disk or data sent from your office by modem. Check under "Computer Graphics," "Desktop Publishing," or "Graphic Designers" in the local Yellow Pages.

Lexicons and Grammar Checkers

As noted above, most of today's word-processing programs come with some sort of spell-check function and a basic thesaurus. In addition, you can get an electronic dictionary and a grammar checker. Because communication is so important in the law, use these programs judiciously to enhance your written work.

Use a *spell checker* when you are unsure about the spelling of a word or want to check an entire document or section for misspellings or typographical errors. (CAUTION: Spell checkers cannot identify words that are correctly spelled but misused—for example, "there" in place of "their.") Use a *thesaurus* when you are unsure about which word to use in a particular context and want to see a list of synonyms and antonyms. (CAUTION: Thesauruses do not usually give the *meaning* of a word, so avoid using synonyms about whose precise meaning you are unsure.) Use a *dictionary* when you want to find out the meaning of a word, learn how to pronounce it, discover its roots in the language, check how it should break at the end of a line, or find similar information. (CAUTION: Some electronic dictionaries are abridged versions of printed dictionaries and may not contain all the information you need.) Use a *grammar checker* to check for correct sentence structure, punctuation, and mechanical errors such as mixed capitalization or transposed words. (CAUTION: Grammar checkers are a relatively recent development and still operate at a fairly primitive level. *They cannot substitute for a sound knowledge of English.*)

The Internet and World Wide Web

The *Internet* is a global network of computer networks, the computer equivalent of the global network of regional phone networks. The primary uses of the Internet are e-mail (see Chapter 5), file transfer (using ftp, or file transfer protocol), electronic bulletin boards and newsgroups, and remote computer access (telnet). Other applications include book and magazine publishing, video conferencing, and audio broadcasts.

The *World Wide Web* (also known as *WWW* and *the Web*) is a network of hypertext and hypermedia documents (i.e., electronic documents containing direct links or cross-references to other data and media) located on computers on the Internet. World Wide Web documents, called *Web pages*, are accessed by using a *browser* (communications software) on your networked personal computer or central system. See your Yellow Pages under "Computers—Systems Designers and Consultants" or "Computer Networks" for the names of service providers in your area.

Electronic bulletin boards   Bulletin-board systems (BBSs) have become very popular over the past few years. Such systems are maintained by personal-computer enthusiasts or other interested persons who want to join a forum to discuss issues, often free of charge but sometimes at a small cost. You can use your communications software to dial a BBS. Legal-specific bulletin boards can be particularly helpful. Two legal bulletin boards are LawMug (312-661-1740) and Legalese (509-326-3238). You can also make use of public-domain software and shareware (software that is still in development but is offered to users to test its capabilities) that have been posted to a BBS.

Although bulletin-board systems are a good way to keep abreast of the legal field and to experiment with new software, it is generally wise to avoid downloading information to your disk or to do so with great caution, as computer viruses can be imported.

Other law-office applications A number of law *mailing lists* are available through the Internet. You can subscribe and post information to them from an account established through a commercial provider. There are lists for business law, family law, advertising law, civil rights law, and many others. Some list publishers also maintain an archive site where past discussions and even programs are stored.

Many legal *sources* (e.g., case law and statutes) are available through the World Wide Web, and more and more law firms have established Web pages to announce and make available their services to Internet users. (See also Chapter 13, "The Law Library.")

Chapter 5

Telecommunications and Office Mail

The first three sections of this chapter cover the practical and technical aspects of telephone and telecommunications services commonly found in law firms, including teleconferencing, voice mail, cellular phones and other mobile technologies, fax machines, and e-mail.

As a secretary you will need to know how to operate some of the telecommunications equipment found in your office. The more you understand about telephones, telecommunications, and computers, the more valuable you will be to your employer. In most firms, technology is underused because no one really understands the full range of its available practical uses. Consult your user manual, talk with technicians, or, if necessary, contact the supplier or the account representative who sold the equipment or service to your firm. (For a discussion of telephone manners, see Chapter 6, pp. 132–33.)

The last section of the chapter covers the processing of incoming and outgoing mail through services offered by the U.S. Postal Service and commercial carriers.

The processing of office mail may be one of your most important responsibilities. Due to its timely nature and its significance as a communication link, all mail must be handled quickly and efficiently. You must be familiar with the various mail classifications and special services offered by the various postal carriers.

Telecommunications

Telecommunications systems may be broken down into two main categories based on the technology and services that are used: (1) wire-based systems and (2) wireless systems.

Wire-Based Systems

Wire-based systems include telephone systems, commercial teleconferencing, and voice-mail services.

Telephone systems   One of the most common problems plaguing law firms to-day is the failure to provide the most basic of tools—a dependable, easy-to-use telephone system. If the average law firm were to consider the amount of aggravation and wasted time caused by its outmoded or cut-rate telephone system, perhaps there would be fewer secretaries saying, "Hold on while I try to transfer you; and if you get cut off, please dial ——— or call back," which provides the clearest indication that a new telephone system is needed.

Telephone systems are of two basic types, *hybrid-key systems* and *PBX systems.*

1. *Hybrid-key systems* These systems developed from an older variety known as *key telephone systems,* which were designed for small offices needing multiline telephones with a private interoffice communications arrangement and signaling capability. The hybrid systems are basically key systems with extra features similar to those found in PBX systems. For example, specially designed telephones may be used to place and answer calls and perform functions such as transferring and forwarding calls and making conference calls. A central answering switchboard is usually provided with hybrid systems.

2. *PBX systems* Private Branch Exchange, or PBX, systems are telephone exchanges serving an individual organization and having direct connections to a public telephone exchange. They are used in offices that require over a hundred telephones. PBX systems include a central console where an operator answers incoming calls. Direct dialing to a specific extension is also available. PBX systems are either analog or digital in design; analog systems are designed primarily for voice transmission, while digital systems also allow for high-speed data and facsimile transmission and teleconferencing services.

Hybrid-key and PBX systems are necessary to provide high-quality voice, facsimile, and data communications between you and your firm's clients. These modern systems offer various programmable features and sophisticated workstation features that can greatly improve call handling. Basic features available on older or more primitive systems, such as a hold button and a call-transfer button, may help prevent the disconnected or lost call. But for true flexibility, potential for growth, improved internal communications, timesaving features, and fail-safe methods of providing security and moving calls through the firm, a more sophisticated hybrid-key or PBX system is recommended.

There are many books on the market that discuss phone-system selection and use, and such books may be helpful if your office is considering upgrading its system (see bibliography, Appendix III).

Commercial teleconferencing   Many legal staff members and attorneys are unaware of the many teleconferencing services available and the benefits and auxiliary services they provide. You may save money and will receive better service by using a commercial teleconferencing service than by trying to arrange a conference call yourself using your telephone system as the central connection point or "bridge."

These companies offer a variety of features, such as "meet me" services, where participants dial a specific telephone to join a group conference; operators who will contact participants for a conference call; audioconferencing supervisors who silently monitor your conference call to insure consistently balanced volumes and noise-free telephone lines; high-quality audio recording of a telephone conference; and sophisticated electronic connections (bridges) that improve voice quality, allow disconnected participants to easily rejoin a conference, and provide instant access to a conference-assistance operator. They may even allow you to select the music played during the holding period while the operator contacts the remaining participants.

To obtain more information about teleconferencing, contact your local telephone company or long- distance carrier, or look in the Yellow Pages under "Teleconferencing Service."

Voice mail and other features   If your firm does not already have a voice-mail system, you should recommend that it consider purchasing one. In a voice-mail system, calls to an employee's number are recorded if the employee cannot answer the phone. He or she can retrieve the messages from any telephone by dialing a given number and entering a personal identification code. Most larger firms now buy or lease voice-mail systems. However, many phone companies offer simple voice-mail systems to their customers. These may be preferable to individual answering machines, since there is less concern over power failures and broken message tapes, and messages can be taken if the caller is busy with another conversation.

Some firms create guest voice-mail boxes for important clients who require a high degree of attorney-client interaction. These mail boxes provide a means for the attorney to leave confidential, detailed messages whenever the client (who may not have a voice-mail system of his or her own) is unavailable. By providing such a service, the firm demonstrates its willingness to extend itself for its clients.

One feature that can dramatically increase the attorney's availability to his or her clients is *call forwarding*. This feature lets you program your phone to redirect incoming calls to another phone (and, when desired, to return them to the original phone). With *call waiting*, a short tone will let you know when someone is trying to call you while you are on the phone. You can quickly press down on the switch hook, putting your original conversation on hold, in order to talk to the second caller.

Wireless Systems

Wireless systems include cellular phones, personal communications devices, special mobile radiotelephone services (SMRS), and pagers.

Cellular phones   These are wireless phones that can be carried anywhere; they have become established as a standard tool in business. The cellular system is a sophisticated mix of radiotelephone and computer technology, in which a geographic area (such as a city) is divided into small sections that are each served by a short-range transmitter. As the user leaves one cell area and enters another, the computerized system immediately transfers a call in progress to the new site. Thus, as the user drives through a metropolitan area, he or she may leave and enter several cells.

When you dial a cellular-phone number, you may receive a recorded message saying that the phone is not within reach of the base transmitter; if so, you can only keep trying the number until the phone owner returns to the region. Many cellular phone owners also use voice mail so that they can pick up messages that arrived while they were out of range. Attorneys who need to connect their portable computers to their offices or to commercial on-line information services (e.g., CompuServe, America Online) may use an inexpensive cellular-phone-to-computer interface.

Although cellular service has become a necessary tool for the active attorney, users often fail to take the necessary security precautions. Conversations conducted over cellular phone systems can be listened to by persons using scanners to monitor frequency bands. Sensitive information should therefore never be passed over cellular phone systems. (The same caution applies to home cordless phones.) Additionally, certain electronic identifying information is stored and periodically transmitted by every cellular telephone. This allows your cellular service provider's equipment to know that your telephone is on and how the call should be routed over their network to the appropriate cell in which you are then traveling. This information also acts as a type of key that allows you to utilize your carrier's services. Thieves can receive this electronic key and sell it so that it can be used to reprogram stolen cellular phones. The user must therefore watch for large increases in his or her cellular service bill, and consult with the service provider about what additional security measures might be taken.

Personal data assistants   Personal data assistants, or PDAs, provide an additional communications tool. A PDA is a small, portable device that can be connected to a telephone (wire-based or cellular) to allow the attorney to call into the office to transmit or receive digital information. Since many PDAs do not have a keyboard, users communicate with a "pen" that activates PDA features and allows brief handwritten messages to be faxed.

The most commonly used features on a PDA are appointment book/calendaring, scratch pad, communications to another computer, telephone/address book, and scheduling. Additionally, most PDAs can easily be attached to a personal computer, thus allowing you to exchange data between the two devices.

Personal communication devices   Personal communication devices (PCDs) are low-powered handheld units that communicate, like cellular phones, via small cells distributed widely within metropolitan areas. Though a still-emerging technology, PCDs are eventually expected to be less expensive to operate than their cellular predecessor. Depending on your locale, a PCD system may already be close to completion, or be planned for your area. Contact your cellular service provider for more information, as its representatives will likely know about your area's potential for a PCD system.

SMRS   The acronym SMRS stands for *special mobile radiotelephone service*, which is a somewhat older technology but one that still fills a niche in many areas. SMRS offers high-quality, long-range radiotelephone communications services in many parts of the United States where cellular service is not available. From the user's perspective, SMRS operates very much like a cellular system. SMRS is likely to remain available in these areas until either cellular or satellite-facilitated radiotelephone services are offered to the public at an affordable cost.

Pagers   Pagers offer one simple but very practical feature, namely, reliable local, and in some cases nationwide, notification. While cellular phones and certain pagers must be operated in the vicinity of a transmission facility, some pagers can receive signals from a distant transmitter that emits low-frequency tones or a digital sequence. Signal quality is not nearly as important for pagers as for cellular phones, and even pagers with display screens can tolerate weak or poor-quality signals.

The most common pager receives activation signals from a local transmission facility serving a designated area. These pagers are generally very reliable as long as the user stays within the physical limits of the service provider's transmission area. More recently, the small, nationwide pager has become the pager of choice for the traveling attorney. With this system, satellite technology is used to activate a local transmitter. Even in this case, however, if the user is too far away from the local transmitter (usually located in a large metropolitan area), the pager will not be able to receive the signal.

There are two basic types of paging devices: *beepers* and *full-display pagers*.

1. *Beepers* Perhaps the most widely used pager today is the beeper or vibrating (silent call) pager. This simple, lightweight box emits an audible signal or a vibrating sensation to alert the user that someone is attempting to contact him or her. The user can then either call his or her voice-mail service to receive a detailed voice message from the caller or, with some units, see the caller's phone number displayed to enable it to be dialed directly.

2. *Digital full-display pager* The digital full-display pager allows the caller not only to enter a telephone number that displays on the pager's liquid crystal display (LCD) panel, but to include a short message with each page. To provide this service, the caller's office must have a vendor-provided software program loaded on a personal computer. This configuration then allows the user's office to page him or her and simultaneously send a short message. New two-way pagers allow the user to communicate back.

Fax Machines

The facsimile, or fax, machine has dramatically changed the way business and law firms exchange documents and other information. For certain kinds of material, they have replaced overnight couriers, first-class mail, local messengers, and even the telephone as the means of choice for communicating rapidly. Today few if any law firms can conduct routine business without a fax machine.

Currently the market offers three basic methods of displaying transmitted images or facsimiles: *thermal-paper* fax machines, *plain-paper* fax machines, and *computer-based* fax transmission.

Thermal-Paper Fax Machines

Although these machines are dropping from the market, they still appeal to those buyers who have very tight budgets and anticipate very low volumes of fax transmissions and receipts. A thermal-paper fax machine reproduces an image by means of a hot stylus that burns black dots into thermally sensitive paper. The problems associated with these machines are expensive paper, clumsiness, slow speed, and low reproduction quality. Thermal paper, used on a roll, often presents the user with several yards of continuous paper that represents many pages of a large document transmission. Faxes printed on thermal paper fade in a few months and become difficult, if not impossible, to read; thus, if a received fax on thermal paper needs to be filed, you should copy it first. The addition of an automatic paper cutter makes these machines attractive to a small and diminishing market.

Plain-Paper Fax Machines

The waning of the thermal-paper fax machine is best understood by appreciating the features of its successor, the plain-paper fax. Using inexpensive photocopier paper, and offering superior reproductions of the original documents, these machines can be had for a reasonable price—although the lowest-priced machines will lack certain features reviewed below. These machines require toner, and often a component or two must be replaced during their lifetime, but even with these expenses the per-copy cost can be less than that of thermal-paper machines for frequent users.

In addition to the characteristics noted above, plain-paper fax machines:

- can easily print on letter-sized or legal-sized paper (depending on features),
- do not require received documents to be cut since they use standard sheets of paper,
- transmit and receive more quickly,
- provide durable, nonfading reproductions with the same life as photocopies,
- are more reliable since their paper paths are straighter and less likely to jam, and
- are not expected to become obsolete in the foreseeable future, so parts, supplies, and other consumables will remain readily available.

Choosing a Fax Machine

During your review of any fax machine, gain a practical understanding of how it works, what *features* it offers, the kind of *consumables* it uses, and how good its *image quality* is.

Features The following list is intended to serve as a guide to choosing a new fax machine or reviewing what your current machine is capable of.

- Does the machine have paper trays for both letter-sized and legal-sized paper? If not, how is a legal-sized page received on the machine? Is the copy broken onto two letter-sized pages or reduced onto one? Are the trays manually switched or automatically switched?
- Does the machine have memory to store incoming documents in the event that it is depleted of toner or paper or is otherwise inoperable? If yes, is this memory protected until someone makes the machine operational again? When memory is filled, what happens to incoming documents? Does the machine give a busy signal when it is out of paper or toner or at the onset of other problems?
- Does the machine provide for undersized or nonstandard-sized document transmission? If it accepts oversized documents, does it automatically reduce the image sent or decrease one or both margins?
- Does the machine have memory for transmitting documents? Will this memory allow users to enter a telephone number and charge code and scan in a document before transmission begins (sometimes called *walk-away fax capability*)? If yes, how many pages of single-spaced text on a standard letter-sized

paper will the machine store for transmission? What happens when memory is full? Can the machine scan in a document for transmission while it is busy receiving and reproducing another document?

- Can the machine's memory be increased? If it can, what are the additional memory increments and how much do they cost?

- Can the machine store a document and send it later? What happens if the number you enter is incorrect or for some other reason the transmission fails?

- Does the machine offer speed-dialing for commonly used numbers? If so, how many numbers will it store? Can you program several numbers to a specific speed-dial number for group distribution? If so, how many numbers can be programmed to a single button? Does this affect other buttons?

- How do you stop or remove a job? What are the consequences?

- Can the machine dial other fax machines to determine if a receivable document is stored and then proceed to receive it?

- Can the machine receive a confidential document and store it until its intended recipient enters a personal identification number (PIN)? Does this feature work with all other fax machines with which your machine is in contact or only on similar makes and models?

- Will the machine allow you to notify someone at the other fax machine that you want him or her to pick up the handset and speak with you over the phone line (which is one of the principal uses of the fax phone, the other being to serve as an ordinary phone set when you want to notify the recipient of an incoming fax)?

- Does the machine include document stamping, so that you know when a document was sent or received?

- Does the machine provide a time, date, and number-dialed log or registry for all outgoing documents, or does it print a "confirmation" page that includes this information following each transmission?

Consumables   Always ask the salesperson about the various types of supplies you will need (e.g., toner, paper), the cost of each supply item, and how many full pages of text each supply item will support. Be sure that you and the salesperson understand that you are asking for any items that will be consumed or diminished as the machine is used, including the photoreactive drum or similar component that must be replaced after a specified number of copies have been made.

Image quality   Obtain several images produced on the fax machine while you watch. Do not accept prefabricated "test" or photocopied images from the salesperson; instead, you should ideally have an assistant at another location fax a few documents to the demonstration model, and then transmit a set of originals back to your assistant. Make sure that you and your assistant mark each set of documents as to brand and type of machine tested, and whether the documents were received or transmitted from the test machine.

Operating the Fax Machine

Fax machines work by scanning your document and creating a digitized "bit map" of the information. That information is then sent over telephone lines, and the receiving fax machine prints a copy of the image by reading the digitized map.

When a fax machine calls up another fax machine, they go through a process called "training" or "handshaking." The sending machine also typically prints out a company identification (if it has been programmed into the machine), along with the time, date, and page number, and these appear as headers on each page.

Here are a few suggestions for successfully operating your fax machine:

- Get the proper training. Too often law firms will purchase an expensive, sophisticated fax machine but fail to allocate time or money for training. As a consequence, only a select few employees are shown the basic operations and very few if any learn the full range of options available. Unless everyone knows how to take advantage of the technology, the firm will not be getting its money's worth.

- Prepare a cover sheet. It should include the name of the recipient and the number of pages being sent. (The cover sheet itself will usually be included in the number of pages.) If the recipient is in a large organization, it is useful to include his or her department and personal phone number. You should also include your firm's fax number and the sender's name and phone number, so that the recipient can call if the fax is not received clearly or pages are missing. Law firms commonly include a note regarding the confidentiality of the material as well. A sample cover sheet is shown in Fig. 5.1.

- Number the pages you are sending, especially if they are part of a larger document or need to be referred to by other than the numbering provided by the fax machine. This will make it easier for the recipient to make sure he or she has received all the pages. Also, since some fax machines just drop received pages on a table or large bin, numbering the pages will help the recipient put the received document in the correct order.

- If a document contains small type or pictures or graphics, test the transmittal quality by using the machine's copy function. If the copy is not clear, try using the "Fine" mode. This will increase the transmittal time but should add to the document's clarity.

- When receiving a fax, check to see that all the pages have been sent and that they are readable. If pages are missing or some are unreadable, notify the sender. Always make sure received faxes are delivered quickly; faxes should be handled with the same urgency as telephone messages.

Security

When the information being sent is confidential, you will need to use your judgment about using a fax machine for delivery, since many fax machines are shared. If you are concerned, you should ask your employer. An alternative means of delivery, such as overnight courier, may be better. Some firms have "executive" fax machines or other fax machines that are monitored to allow for private transmission. In all cases, the fax cover sheet should contain a note regarding confidentiality (see Fig. 5.1).

Misdirected faxes You may occasionally come across a misdirected fax document—just as you will occasionally receive misdirected mail or phone calls to the wrong number. The real problem is when such documents show up in opposing counsel's office. This serious error is usually due to a misunderstanding of who the proper recipients are. Great care must be exercised in getting the correct recipient's name and number so that your fax is not misdirected.

Fig. 5.1 Fax Cover Sheet

Sims, Borstein, Gomez & Lang, P.C.
304 North Mountain Road
St. Louis, MO 44327-1432
PH (314) 512-8876
FX (314) 512-8213

FAX TRANSMITTAL SHEET

TO: Mr. Sunil Tamabara   DATE: Aug. 16, 19--
     Bateson Enterprises
     Fax: (314) 631-7732

FROM: Francis Williams

TOTAL PAGES (INCLUDING THIS COVER SHEET): 2

ADDITIONAL COMMENTS/DIRECTIONS:

_____

_____

_____

_____

_____

NOTE: This message is intended only for the use of the individual or entity to which it is addressed and may contain information that is privileged, confidential, and exempt from disclosure under applicable law. If the reader of this message is not the intended recipient, or the employee or agent responsible for delivering the message to the intended recipient, you are hereby notified that any dissemination, distribution, or copying of this communication is strictly prohibited. If you have received this communication in error, please notify us immediately by telephone and return the original message to us at the above address via the U.S. Postal Service. Thank you.

IF YOU HAVE QUESTIONS OR TRANSMITTAL IS INCOMPLETE, PLEASE CALL

_____ AT (314) 512-8876, EXT. _____.

Your firm should establish standard procedures for handling incoming misdirected documents. In general, such documents should:

- be treated with the utmost confidentiality in accordance with the strictest ethical standards,
- not be used to the advantage of the recipient or any other parties,
- never be used to intimidate or harass the sending attorney or firm, and

- be immediately returned to the sender, with a cover letter stating that you have used all possible measures to preserve the document's confidentiality (including not having read it).

Commercial Fax Services

If you anticipate a large volume of transmissions of the same document to a specified group, you should consider using a commercial fax-distribution service. Such services allow you to send one copy of the document to a central receiving computer and then direct the fax to go to a list of recipients that you maintain with the service provider. This type of service will save wear and tear on your fax machine and keep it open for incoming documents. For information, check the Yellow Pages under "Fax Transmission Service."

Computer-Based Fax Transmission

By installing a fax board and communications software on your networked computer, you can send electronic faxes directly, bypassing the need to create paper documents. Check with your local computer-service vendor for details concerning your machine.

E-mail

Electronic mail, or e-mail, provides a means of data communications between computers. E-mail can be on private systems or public networks, or be specialized for a particular function such as Electronic Data Interchange (EDI). Some of the key characteristics of the various types of e-mail systems are explained in the following pages.

Private E-Mail Systems

Many larger firms have e-mail systems as part of their computer systems. Some e-mail systems are on local area networks (LANs), while others are on minicomputer or mainframe computer systems.

E-mail systems let users send messages created on their computers to one or more electronic "mailboxes" belonging to other individuals in the firm that have access to the mail system. Some private e-mail systems are also linked into public e-mail systems so that users can have access to individuals outside of their firm. A system administrator is usually responsible for registering system users and for maintaining the system, and he or she should be able to teach new users how to use the system and provide a directory of in-house mailbox addresses.

If you are an e-mail user, you will usually have a sign-on identification code as well as a mailbox address. Often the mailbox address will include your name or a code similar to your name. You should check your mailbox periodically to see if you have received an electronic message. When sending a message for the attorney, you may need to use his or her sign-on identification. If you use your own sign-on identification to send a message for the attorney, be very clear in the message about who it is from, since many mail systems will automatically attach to the message the name of the person whose sign-on identification is being used. If someone has asked you to read his or her mailbox, you must sign on as that individual. Make sure you transfer or save the mailbox messages to a computer file or print them out.

Public E-Mail Systems

There are several major providers of e-mail systems in the United States, including AT&T, MCI, Sprint, and CompuServe. These systems provide e-mail through your office computer. If you are connected through a minicomputer or a mainframe computer to one of these public systems, the service vendor and the technical advisor within your firm will have made all the connections for you.

You will need communications software and a modem to equip a personal computer to use a public e-mail system. You can obtain such software from your e-mail provider or purchase one of several available brands. A modem is needed to enable your computer to dial up the e-mail system so that it can connect with the host computer.

When you send a message through public e-mail service, you should be able to obtain notification that the message was delivered. The service should also provide you with a daily summary report of sent messages.

You should not assume that you can send a regular word-processing file through an e-mail system, since it could only be read by someone with the same word-processing program. Instead, you must send what are known as *ASCII* (pronounced "as-key") or *text files*. You create an ASCII or text file by taking the document you have created in your word-processing program and following the procedures found in your word-processing manual for saving documents as ASCII or text files. (This serves to eliminate formatting from the file so that it is more easily transferred.)

However, some e-mail systems will let you send word-processing or other computer files such as spreadsheets. This type of service is called *file transfer*. File transfer should only be used when the recipient of the file has the same kind of application program. You would not use this method for sending regular messages, but only for sending a document that another individual needed to work on. This process is the equivalent of giving a file on a disk to another individual to work on.

When you receive messages in a mailbox, you can save them in a computer file or by printing them out. If you want to edit the file in your word-processing program, you will have to consult your word-processing manual on how to edit an ASCII or text file.

When sending an e-mail message, be sure to give it the same attention and care you would any other correspondence. After writing a message, check it for proper spelling, grammar, and punctuation before sending it.

There are many private and public e-mail systems available, each of which was designed independently. The result is that it may be difficult for these systems to "talk" to each other. During the 1980s, an international committee devised a set of rules to enable e-mail systems to interconnect with each other by using the same technical rules or "protocols." As more private and public e-mail systems start using these interfaces, e-mail will become more far-reaching.

The same international committee realized that if a truly universal e-mail network was to become a reality, e-mail users would need to know who has electronic mailboxes and what their addresses are. Accordingly, it devised a set of rules for creating an automated directory of all e-mail addresses. Unfortunately, a universal directory has not actually been developed yet. For the most part, you still must get mailbox addresses directly from the individuals with whom you want to communicate. Many public e-mail users include their mailbox address on their business cards and stationery. If your public e-mail service does not provide an on-line directory to subscribers, you may be able to call the service for directory information.

Postal Services

Even with the increasing use of e-mail, fax machines, and other computerized means of communication, the services offered by the U.S. Postal Service (USPS) and commercial delivery services such as United Parcel Service (UPS) and Federal Express (FedEx) will continue to be indispensable for effective lawyer-client communications. The wise secretary will thus develop a thorough understanding of these mail services in order to ensure that the attorney's and client's documents arrive in the right place at the right time and at a reasonable cost.

Incoming Mail

In large corporations and law firms, the mailroom personnel receive the mail directly from the carrier or a messenger picks it up from the post office. The mail is sorted in the mailroom and delivered to the various departments (or practice sections) by messenger. Within individual departments, one person may be assigned to sort the mail further and then deliver it to each attorney or attorney's secretary. The mail will then be sorted by the secretary just as in a one-attorney/secretary law office. The steps outlined in the following pages apply to mail processing in virtually all law offices.

Preliminary sorting   Incoming mail is commonly sorted into six categories: top-priority (overnight, express, and priority mail, certified, registered, and special-delivery letters), first-class (primarily letters and cards), periodicals (newspapers and magazines), standard mail "A" (circulars, booklets, catalogs, and other printed materials), and standard mail "B" (ordinary parcels).

Opening   Unless specifically authorized, you should not open letters marked "Personal" or "Confidential." (If you open such a letter unintentionally, mark the envelope "Opened by mistake," initial it, and reseal it with tape.) Other, routine mail should be opened (if it is office policy to have the secretary do so). Be certain that you completely empty each envelope. Check the letter's enclosure notations to be sure that nothing is missing; if an item has been omitted, make a note of it on the letter or on a self-stick note. You should follow your firm's procedures regarding the attachment of the envelope to the letter. Always check the letterhead to ensure that your address list is current and accurate.

Dating   The date of receipt must be stamped on the back or front of each document received by the law firm. If a date stamp is temporarily unavailable, the document should be hand-dated and initialed.

Secondary sorting   The next step is the secondary sorting of opened mail for presentation to the attorney. Top-priority items should be placed on top, so that the attorney may deal with the most important mail first.

Reading   In some law offices you may be asked to read letters and highlight important passages or dates for the attorney. Dates should also be calendared as appropriate (see Chapter 11, "Docket Control and Records Management" for more on calendaring).

Recording   In some law firms, the receipt of each letter and document is recorded in a central register or log. (Only important mail is recorded in this register; items like circulars and ads are not.) The following data are usually recorded: date and time received, the date of the letter itself, the writer, the addressee, a brief description of the subject (or matter/case), and the disposition of the letter. Such a log may also be kept on a word processor. See Fig. 5.2.

Fig. 5.2   Mail Register or Log

DATE REC'D	TIME	DATED	FROM	ADDRESSEE	SUBJECT	DISPOSITION
7/2/-	9 A.m.	7/1/-	ADA MERCK	S. GERSTEIN	LETTER - INFO	REPLY SENT 7/6
7/2/-	9 A.m.	6/30/-	SAMUELS + MARK	T. COOKE	DISCOVERY SOMERS CASE	FILED 7/2
7/2/-	2 A.m.	6/30/-	R. DOW	S. SMYTHE	LETTER-APPOINTMENT	PHONE CALL 7/2
7/3/-	9 A.m.	7/1/-	COLE, INC.	PERSONNEL	SEMINAR ANNOUNCEMENT	REFERRED TO T. COOKE 7/4

Delivery to the attorney   The opened and sorted mail should be placed on the attorney's desk immediately, as should incoming overnight mail and faxed documents. Client checks should also be processed immediately, according to your firm's accounting procedures.

Handling mail during the attorney's absence   You may be asked to acknowledge client correspondence when the attorney is out of the office. An acknowledgment should explain that the attorney is temporarily away but has been apprised of the correspondence and will take whatever action is necessary upon his or her return (see Chapter 7, Fig. 7.14, p. 208). Under no circumstances should you send correspondence to a client or other party without the prior consent of the lawyer.

Outgoing Mail

In most law firms and corporate law departments you will be responsible for processing outgoing mail. You will assemble the necessary documents, check for the proper addresses, signatures, enclosures, and reference-copy notations, and place the mail in an envelope for delivery to the mailroom or mail pickup site.

Addresses   The address on the letter and envelope should be the same. To reduce the chance of error, some firms use window envelopes, thus eliminating the need for typing the address on the envelope. Whatever kind of envelope is used, it must contain a complete address, including the name of the recipient, the street address and/or post-office box number (in that order, if both are used), the city and state, and the zip code (see below).

Zip-code information   Use of the proper zip code—preferably the full "zip + 4," which consists of the standard zip code followed by a hyphen and four digits, such as 03060-1234—will greatly speed the handling of your mail by the U.S. Postal Service. You might consider the use of electronic zip-code products, of which several are available. These are either off-the-shelf software packages that are updated frequently or on-line services that provide access to a U.S. postal center. Most postal centers allow for 24-hour computer dial-up access to zip-code information. In either case, you simply enter a street address or post-office box number and the city and state, and the computer will provide the full zip + 4 code. The better dial-up services and software packages can also generate envelope bar coding that can be printed directly onto the envelope by most laser or impact printers. This bar coding will further speed your document through the mail system.

   If you do not own the software or subscribe to the on-line services noted above, you should keep a copy of the current *U.S. Postal Service National ZIP Code and Post Office Directory,* which is available at your local post office or through the Government Printing Office (GPO) for a nominal cost.

State abbreviations   The USPS prefers that senders use the standard two-letter abbreviation system for U.S. states and dependencies and for Canadian provinces. See the table of abbreviations on page 183.

Mailing notices   Two types of mailing notices or directions may appear on an envelope: (1) mailing-service directions such as "CERTIFIED MAIL" or "SPECIAL DELIVERY," and (2) on-arrival notices such as "CONFIDENTIAL" or "PERSONAL." Either type of notification should be typed in capital letters on both the envelope and the enclosed letter. On-arrival notations are usually typed four lines below the return address or nine lines below the top edge of the envelope, starting at least ½" from the left edge of the envelope. Postal directions or special mailing notations are placed on the same line at least ½" from the *right* edge of the envelope. Check with your local post office for more detailed instructions. (See also Chapter 7, pp. 182–85, for envelope addressing instructions.)

Signatures   It is your responsibility to check all outgoing letters and legal documents for proper signatures and/or execution. If you are authorized to sign on behalf of the attorney, sign using the lawyer's name and clearly print your own initials next to the signature.

Enclosures   It is very important that all enclosures cited in the enclosure notation at the bottom of the letter be included with the letter. Some secretaries type visual reminders, such as three hyphens or three periods, in the left margin by each line in which mention is made of the item or items to be enclosed, to alert themselves to include the enclosures with the letter.

Reference and copy notations   If you are answering a letter that is identified by a reference number, be sure that the number is repeated in the reference line of your reply letter.

The copy notation (*cc*) indicates to whom additional copies of the letter should be sent. Check carefully to see that envelopes have been addressed to the individuals mentioned in regular (*cc*) and blind (*bcc*) copy notations. The blind copy notation appears *only* on the copies, usually in the upper-left corner; however, it may also be placed below the reference and enclosure notations. Also make sure that the appropriate number of file copies have been retained.

Final processing   So that your office will receive faster service, it is suggested that you (or your mailing department) handle outgoing mail as follows:

1. Sort the mail. Your mail can skip an entire sorting operation at the post office if you separate it into major categories such as local, out-of-town, state, and precanceled, or by zip code. Each bundle should have a label identifying its category or zip code. Check with your local postmaster to determine the preferred method for presorting.

2. Use a postage meter or an electronic postage scale. The postage meter automatically stamps an envelope with the designated postage, while an electronic postage scale allows you to weigh an item to determine the correct rate. Check with your local post office or office-supply vendor for information on purchasing or leasing such machines.

3. If your staffing permits, schedule two daily trips to the post office, the first to deposit mail before the early-afternoon sorting, and the second to deposit mail before the end-of-the-day sorting. Contact your local postmaster to determine optimal times to deposit mail for your area.

It is your responsibility to know the range of services offered by the USPS and to keep abreast of any changes to rates, sorting requirements, postage-machine operation, and so on. Your best source of information will be your local postmaster and official USPS publications.

USPS Services

Although USPS services are subject to change, a brief overview of some of the more commonly used services is provided in the following pages. For additional information, check with your local post office and obtain a copy of the useful USPS publication Pub. 123, *Ratefold*.

Express Mail   This category is for next- or second-day delivery to most destinations. All packages must use an Express Mail label, and weight and size limitations apply. Flat-rate envelopes are available for letter-packages up to two pounds. Check with your local post office for current prices, time schedules, weight limits, and any restrictions.

Priority Mail   This category is for two-day service to most domestic destinations. Flat-rate envelopes are available for letter-packages up to two pounds; for other items, weight and size limitations may apply.

First-Class Mail   This category is for ordinary correspondence, bills and statements of account, postcards and postal cards (postal cards are the ones printed by the USPS), canceled and uncanceled checks, and business reply mail. First-class mail is normally sealed and may not be opened for postal inspection. Large envelopes or packages sent as first-class mail should be stamped "FIRST CLASS" just below the postage area to avoid confusion with standard mail A at the post office. Envelopes with green diamond edging are useful because they immediately identify the contents as first-class mail.

Periodicals   This category, used primarily by publishers and news agencies, includes magazines and newspapers issued at least four times a year. A permit is required to mail material at the periodicals rate.

Standard Mail (A)   This category includes circulars, booklets, catalogs, and similar printed materials commonly referred to as "advertising mail" or "direct mail." Standard mail (A) has a weight limit of 16 ounces. (Any item sent as standard mail A but exceeding 16 ounces will be reclassified by the USPS as standard mail B). Standard mail (A) is usually left unsealed so that it can be opened easily for postal inspection. It is generally slower than other types of mail, including standard mail (B).

Standard Mail (B)   This category consists mainly of domestic parcel post, but it may also include special catalog mailings (bulk), library mailings ("book rate"), and other specialized mailings. It is used to send packages weighing 16 ounces or more. Upper weight limits also apply; check with your local post office for the specific limits.

International mail   International mail generally includes letters, letter packages (which in this case means packaged material with a letter enclosed), printed matter, small packages of merchandise or samples, and parcel post destined for foreign countries. For further information regarding international mail services, contact your local postmaster and ask for Pub. 51, *International Postal Rates and Fees.*

Special services   The USPS offers other services such as business reply mail, certificates of mailing, certified mail, registered mail, special delivery, special handling, Collect On Delivery (COD), insured mail, money orders, and post-office boxes. You should investigate these and other USPS services by contacting your local postmaster and asking for Pub. 201, *A Consumer's Guide to Postal Services and Products.*

Commercial Carriers

Law firms, like most other businesses, frequently make use of delivery services other than those of the USPS. Companies such as United Parcel Service (UPS) and Federal Express (FedEx) specialize in full-service domestic and international express and regular ground services. Other carriers may also be listed in your local Yellow Pages under "Delivery Services" or "Courier Services." In choosing commercial carriers, you should obtain complete information about the services they provide and the fees they charge. It may also be useful to get opinions from other law firms regarding a courier's record of efficiency and reliability. The two most widely used services, UPS and FedEx, are outlined below.

United Parcel Service   United Parcel Service (UPS) provides ground and air service within the United States and to over 185 countries and territories worldwide for delivery of letters and packages weighing up to 150 pounds and measuring up to 130″ in combined length and girth, with a maximum length of 108″. You should not use string, cellophane tape, or masking tape. All packages are automatically insured against loss or damage up to $100; higher insurance protection may be obtained for an additional charge. For information on service, rates, and restrictions, and to order the service guides, contact your local UPS office or check the UPS home page on the World Wide Web.

Domestic ground service, including package tracking, is available to any address in the 48 contiguous states. There are two types of air service, and one combination air-ground service.

UPS Next Day Air service guarantees delivery of letters and packages on the next business day to all addresses in the 50 states and Puerto Rico. Most of these deliveries, including those to major metropolitan areas, are made by 10:30 a.m., and many others by noon. Electronic package tracking is included. Saturday deliveries can also be scheduled for an additional charge.

UPS 2nd Day Air service guarantees delivery of packages on the second business day, except in rural Alaska, which may require one or more extra days.

UPS 3 Day Select service guarantees delivery of special or multipiece packages within three business days in the 48 contiguous states. A 24-hour phone-in tracking system is available through an 800 number.

Special services include address correction, COD and third-party billing service, delivery confirmation service (which provides proof of delivery), tracking software and Call Tag service (which allows for return of merchandise previously delivered by UPS from anywhere in the 48 contiguous states).

UPS ground service to Canada and Mexico includes standard service to any address in the ten Canadian provinces and most major metropolitan areas in Mexico.

Export documentation is required for shipments to Puerto Rico and Canada, except for UPS Next Day Air letters to Puerto Rico and UPS Air Express letters to Canada.

International service consists of two door-to-door service levels: UPS Worldwide Express service, which serves 185 countries and territories and generally provides delivery of letters and packages in two business days, and UPS Worldwide Expedited service, which provides precisely scheduled delivery of packages to major cities in Europe and Asia within four business days. Export documentation is required for all packages. For information on international shipments, including customs brokerage information, call the UPS International Information Center at 800-782-7892.

Federal Express   Federal Express provides fast delivery of letters and packages up to 150 pounds, and measuring up to 130″ in combined length and girth, with a maximum length of 108″, within the United States and to more than 170 countries worldwide. Freight service is also available for larger and heavier packages. Automatic insurance against loss or damage is provided up to $100, with additional coverage available. For general information or to order a service guide, call 800-463-3339.

Domestic services include FedEx Same Day service, which provides same-day delivery to most U.S. destinations, and FedEx Priority Overnight service, which provides delivery of letters and packages by 10:30 a.m. or by noon to most locations in the United States. FedEx Standard Overnight service offers delivery by 3 p.m. or 4:30 p.m. to most areas. FedEx 2Day service provides delivery of packages by 4:30 p.m. (7 p.m. for residential addresses) on the second business day. Other special services include COD service, proof of performance, free shipping software, on-line package tracking, and volume discounts.

International services include FedEx International Priority service, which provides scheduled door-to-door delivery, including customs clearance, in one to three days, and FedEx International Economy service, which provides customs-cleared shipment of documents and packages to or from Canada in two to three days. Export documentation is required for other international shipments.

Chapter 6

Appointments, Meetings, and Trips

This chapter covers the essentials of arranging appointments and meeting clients and provides an overview of business meetings and trips for the secretary whose role includes supporting these activities.

An ability to deal effectively with clients is one of those skills that distinguishes the experienced legal secretary from the novice and is of paramount importance to the firm. With practice, though, even the new secretary can develop the requisite tact and propriety and begin to convey a sense of competence and professionalism. You must be able to satisfy clients that their matter is in good hands and display to the attorney that you know the value of good client relations for the success of the firm.

A similar set of skills is required to set up successful business meetings and conferences. Whether a private meeting between partners in the firm or a large gathering of legal professionals, a meeting must be properly planned and smoothly executed. You must become an expert event coordinator. Accurate notes or minutes must also be kept in many cases.

Finally, today's lawyers, like their counterparts in business, have become increasingly mobile. For this reason you must have a fairly broad understanding of what types of travel information are needed, know where to obtain current information quickly, and be able to extract the essential data for the attorney. In short, you must be able to expedite a business trip from the initial planning stages through the post-trip follow-up.

Client Appointments

A daily calendar for your desk, one for the attorney's desk, and a small pocket diary for the attorney to carry are essential for scheduling appointments. A weekly or monthly desk calendar can also be useful, especially for scheduling far in advance. Regularly scheduled events such as weekly meetings and monthly report deadlines should be penciled in at the beginning of each week or month. (For more on calendar systems, see Chapter 11.)

Client appointments may be made in several ways:

1. The attorney schedules an appointment and tells you about it. You make sure it is recorded both on your calendar and on his or her desk calendar.

(In offices where a large number of daily appointments are made, all appointments may be recorded in a separate appointment book or calendar rather than on the desk calendars.)

2. You schedule an appointment with someone over the telephone or in person, check with the attorney to confirm it, and then add it to the calendars.

3. Someone writes to secure a time for an appointment. Once the time is set, you notify the person seeking the appointment and then record it on the calendars.

4. Your employer may, while conferring with a client, ask that you schedule a future appointment with that client. After doing so, you give the client a written or oral reminder of the appointment and enter it on the calendars.

5. You or your employer may schedule tentative appointments with out-of-town visitors by mail. These should be entered on the calendars in pencil, since they are subject to change.

The following is a list of essential information that must be obtained in setting up an appointment—particularly with a new client. As clients become known to you, you may ignore points 2 and 6.

1. The caller's *name,* spelled correctly. If the name is difficult to pronounce or does not correspond to the spelling, note in parentheses how to pronounce it (e.g., "sounds like ———").

2. The caller's full *address.*

3. The caller's work and home *telephone numbers.* (For every appointment, it is important to ask where the caller can be reached the *day of the appointment* in case the appointment must be rescheduled at the last minute.)

4. The *nature of the appointment*—e.g., will, personal injury, divorce, tax problem, etc.

5. The *date and time of the appointment.* (See "Scheduling Appointments," below.)

6. The *person who referred* the caller. A letter of thanks should be sent to this person for the referral and for their confidence and trust in your firm.

Scheduling Appointments

In scheduling appointments, the legal secretary is faced with a number of problems that other business secretaries do not have to consider. The complexity of legal questions, the urgent nature of many cases, and erratic court dockets (agendas) require flexible schedules. For example, a trial lawyer may be in court for weeks instead of just a few days. A tax lawyer must meet tax deadlines to avoid the assessment of penalties. A lawyer may have to prepare a will for a client who is near death. A real-estate deal may fail if sales contracts are not immediately prepared and signed. These are a few of the reasons why a legal secretary must carefully assist the lawyer in timing and keeping appointments. The secretary should study the professional practice and personal habits of the lawyer and make appointments accordingly. Some items to consider in scheduling appointments are these:

- Bear in mind the lawyer's workday habits. Some lawyers arrive early and some late. Some function best in the morning, some in the afternoon; observe the lawyers in your firm for their best working time. Some like to set aside a period each day when they have no calls and appointments; others like to set aside certain times to see clients.

- Always check the calendar and docket-control report before making appointments.
- When the lawyer is in trial, limit appointments to those specifically requested by the attorney. When possible, leave free time on the lawyer's schedule calendar before and after the trial in order to allow for trial preparation and follow-up.
- Avoid late-afternoon appointments that might run past the office closing time.
- Keep Monday and Friday appointments as light as possible. Limit the number of appointments on the first day after vacation, as the lawyer will need time to review matters that have accumulated during his or her absence.
- Always be careful not to make appointments on weekends, on national and court holidays, or during other events that have already been calendared!
- If an appointment takes the lawyer outside the office, always call to confirm the appointment and allow time in the schedule for travel.
- If the lawyer is going to be late for an appointment outside the office, always call the waiting party to give an expected arrival time.
- If there is any question about the lawyer's schedule when setting up an appointment, get alternative dates and advise the caller that the appointment must be tentative until you confirm it with the attorney.
- If your law firm employs legal assistants, advise them of any appointments in which they need to be included.
- When an appointment is made with a client or a witness for a court appearance or deposition, call the individual the preceding day as a reminder. If possible, have the client come early to the office to meet with the lawyer so that they can go to court together.
- Unless approved by the lawyer, do not make appointments with vendors. Large firms commonly assign one person in management to meet with all salespeople. In smaller firms, after gathering the information the secretary should discuss the matter with the lawyer before making an appointment or referring a vendor to the lawyer.
- For appointments requiring several lawyers, be sure to coordinate all the individual calendars. This can at times be a difficult task; the form shown in Fig. 6.1 should facilitate such coordination.

You may discover, much to your embarrassment, that the attorney has scheduled appointments that you know nothing about because he or she has forgotten to tell you about them. Therefore, it is extremely important that you ask the attorney each morning to check his or her pocket diary for any appointments you may not be aware of. Be smilingly persistent about this, for your calendar and the attorney's *must* coincide. (The two calendars are not duplicates, however; your calendar should include reminders of secretarial tasks that the attorney would not want to be bothered with.) As you get to know your employer better, you will be able to screen and classify visitors according to his or her preferences.

Reminders   Attorneys need to be reminded of their appointments even though they have a marked calendar before them each day. This may be done by simply giving them cards from the tickler file (see Chapter 11). Some prefer to be reminded by a typed and detailed list of the day's appointments on their desk when they arrive in the morning; others prefer that a list of the next day's appointments be given to them before they leave in the evening. Make a copy

Fig. 6.1   Request for Scheduling

```
                    REQUEST FOR SCHEDULING

  ┌───────────────┐ ┌───────────────────┐ ┌──────────────────────────┐
  │ Date          │ │ File No:          │ │ Case Name:               │
  └───────────────┘ └───────────────────┘ └──────────────────────────┘

  PLEASE SCHEDULE THE FOLLOWING MATTER:

  ┌────────────────────────────────────────────────────────────┐
  │                                                              │
  │                                                              │
  │                                                              │
  └────────────────────────────────────────────────────────────┘

  THE SCHEDULED EVENT SHOULD OCCUR BEFORE THE FOLLOWING DEADLINE:

          ┌──────────────────────────────────┐
          │                                  │
          └──────────────────────────────────┘

  OTHERS   INVOLVED IN THE SCHEDULING EVENT ARE:
  NAME_____ PHONE _____ FAX NO. _____
  NAME_____ PHONE _____ FAX NO. _____
  NAME_____ PHONE _____ FAX NO. _____
  NAME_____ PHONE _____ FAX NO. _____
  NAME _____ PHONE _____ FAX NO. _____
  NAME _____ PHONE _____ FAX NO. _____
  NAME _____ PHONE _____ FAX NO. _____
  NAME _____ PHONE _____ FAX NO._____

  ┌────────────────────────────────────────────────────────────┐
  │              MISCELLANEOUS COMMENTS                         │
  │                                                              │
  │                                                              │
  │                                                              │
  │                                                              │
  │                                                              │
  └────────────────────────────────────────────────────────────┘

     Date_____        Attorney_____
```

of the reminder list so that you can check it at the end of the day to delete all appointments that were not kept and insert any that were added. If you do not file appointment books permanently, it is wise to keep these reminder lists as a log of visitors seen and a record of places the attorney went during the year. Such records are invaluable for tax purposes.

New clients   It will be most helpful to set aside more time than usual for the new client, as these appointments generally will take longer. If you work for a large firm that has specialized areas of practice, make the appointment with the lawyer whom the caller has specifically requested; however, try to coordinate it with the specialty lawyer, as this lawyer may be called into the meeting.

Some law firms have standard policies regarding new-client calls, and you must become familiar with these policies. For instance, when an appointment has been made with a new client, immediately check your client cross-index system to see if any name or information indicates a possible conflict of interest, and advise the lawyer if the information reveals such a possible conflict.

Referrals

A recent American Bar Association survey indicated that 52 percent of a firm's new clients are referred through existing clients. Obviously a firm's clients are a potentially strong base on which to continue to build business: satisfied clients will not only return for additional legal services but will also refer their friends and colleagues; law firms lose business when clients perceive problems with quality, cost, or responsiveness to their concerns. You must be able to communicate high-quality service in everything you do, from using the telephone to meeting clients in person and handling their case materials in a confidential and conscientious way.

Legal professionals with whom you interact—including other lawyers— are also a potential source of client referrals. Depending on the type of law your firm practices and the firm's size, you may be in contact with various other professionals, agencies, and businesspeople on a routine basis. If an outside attorney is unqualified to handle a particular matter, he or she may be in a position to refer the matter to your firm as one that specializes in that area. Thus, in your interactions with outside lawyers and other legal personnel, the golden rule for ensuring the best professional working relationship is to treat people as you yourself would wish to be treated.

There may be times when you cannot make an appointment because your own office does not handle certain types of cases. In these situations the caller should first be directed to the lawyer he or she has requested, who can then personally refer the caller to another firm. Sometimes the lawyer requested by the caller will not be available; for such cases, you may have been given a list of referral telephone numbers to use to refer the caller yourself. Request the caller to please inform the lawyer to whom you have referred him or her that the referral came through your office. You should also keep the numbers of your Lawyer Referral Service or Legal Aid Office handy, when appropriate.

Telephone Manners

The ability to handle telephone calls properly is a secretarial skill that lawyers consider extremely important. The correct use of the telephone can speed business, build goodwill, project the best possible image of your firm, elevate your office in the eyes of your superiors, and thus be important to your own success. If you learn to recognize frequent callers' voices at once so that you can address them by name, you will gain the reputation of being exceptionally keen.

Knowing your equipment is essential. You must know what each button and switch on your telephone is for and how to use it. You must also be aware that telephone systems have made remarkable technological advances in the past decades, providing a wealth of equipment designed for special needs in the office. Telephone-company representatives will be glad to answer questions about automatic dialers, call forwarding and call pickup features, special signaling devices, and a wide variety of other options (see Chapter 5).

Although a single set of rules or guidelines will not be able to cover every situation, the following suggestions will be helpful:

- Develop the habit of picking up a pen and reaching for a pad as soon as the telephone rings.
- Try to pick up no later than the third ring.
- Smile when you answer the telephone. Your voice will be more cheerful.
- When answering, always identify your firm, yourself, or the lawyer for whom you work: "Good morning, this is Gore, Bechansky & Steele law firm (or "this is Kathy Wertalik," or "Ms. Robertson's office"). How may I help you?"
- Learn the client's name as soon as possible and, if a new client, make sure of its correct spelling. Use the name in discussing matters with the client.
- Unless you are instructed to screen calls, do not say, "May I ask what this concerns?" It can make the caller feel unimportant if he or she is not put through to the lawyer.
- To the caller, refer to the attorney as "Mr." or "Ms."
- Should the caller ask for someone who is unavailable, you could say, "I'm sorry, she's talking on another line. May I help you, or would you care to speak to someone else?" Never say "She hasn't come back from lunch yet" (and it's 3 p.m.), or "He's playing golf today," or "I don't know where she went," or "He isn't in" without elaboration. Courtesy requires that you give the correct information, but do not state facts that could lead to a misunderstanding or divulge information you are not authorized to give.
- When taking telephone messages, repeat the name and number for accuracy.
- When making an appointment with a client, be sure to note his or her name, what the appointment is for, and, in the case of a new client, who referred him or her to the attorney. In case an appointment might have to be rescheduled, ask the client the number where he or she can be reached on the day of the appointment.
- Never give legal advice.
- Before you place a call, be certain you have the information you need. It is rude to put someone you have called on hold while you are thumbing through a file.
- Always end a call with "Good-bye." As a courtesy, wait for the client to hang up first.

Receiving Clients

The typical law-office client, particularly the new client, knows very little about the law and law firms and tends to fear the unknown. It is therefore important to remember that it can be uncomfortable for the client to visit a law office, and that the following four questions may be in the client's mind at the initial conference:

1. Can these people be trusted?
2. Will they be sensitive to my matter?
3. Are they capable?
4. Will my matter be held in strict confidence?

Greeting   The secretary should seek to ease any fears the client might have and tend to his or her comfort. When a client arrives for an appointment, be friendly, pleasant, and professional; and immediately notify the lawyer that the client has arrived. The client should not ordinarily be kept waiting; if a delay is unavoidable, you should explain the situation. The client may be offered a cup of coffee or a soft drink during the wait. The attorney should come to the waiting area to greet the client; if the attorney and client have never met, you are expected to formally introduce them.

Depending on the custom of your office, the legal assistant might also be introduced at the time of the client's first visit. Often the preliminary, routine information can be recorded by the legal assistant rather than the attorney. Explain to the client that this enables the lawyer to spend more time on strictly legal problems.

Conference   Before the client arrives, files and papers relative to the appointment should be ready. If the meeting is to be in a conference room instead of the lawyer's office, it may be necessary to reserve the room. Be sure the room is in order and any loose papers or stray client files are removed. Supplies such as pencils and legal pads, along with the client file or new-client intake sheet (see below), should be available for the attorney.

When the conference is taking place, care should be taken that the conference areas remain quiet, private, and free from any interruptions in order that the client be granted the attorney's undivided attention. Unless instructed otherwise, you should route all incoming calls for the attorney to you or someone else the attorney designates. If the conference goes on for some time, deliver fresh coffee, tea, or water to the conference room. The message should be that this is the only client the lawyer has.

In some cases, you may be asked to sit in on the meeting and takes notes for the attorney. Usually verbatim accuracy is not necessary, but all key points should be noted. (See also Chapter 9.)

When the client departs the office at the end of the conference, after the lawyer has escorted him or her back to the reception room, thank the client by name and offer parting regards.

Handling Client Documents

Often clients will leave important or even irreplaceable items or documents with their attorney. Such items should be accepted from the client with the utmost care, and the client should be assured that these important materials will be thoroughly safeguarded. A written receipt or log should be kept for tracking the items (see Fig. 5.2, p. 122), and the firm should use burglary- and fireproof filing equipment (see Chapter 11). Take care that *other* client's documents are not in view in order to protect *their* privacy and demonstrate the firm's integrity on security matters.

New-client intake   When a new client first visits the office, a new-client file should be prepared and entered into the office's filing system. One way to accomplish this is through a two-stage process. When the client first visits the office, a colored "preliminary" file folder is opened (the colored file indicating that the firm has not yet decided whether it will represent the client) and a client intake form, such as the one in Fig. 6.2, is attached to the file for the

Fig. 6.2   Client Intake Form

```
                        File No._____

 Preliminary File No._____        Date File Opened_____

 Multiple File: 1 of _____         Atty:_____


                   _____

 Client:_____
 Address:_____
 City/State/Zip_____
 Telephone:_____    Work:_____

 Nature of the Case:_____

 Case Name:_____vs. _____

 Conflict of Interest Control: Adverse Party_____

                        Fee Arrangements

 Hourly Rate $_____ Trust Acct Max. $_____ Min. $_____
 Contingency %_____ Retainer $_____    Expense Retainer $_____
 Flat Fee $_____ Expense Retainer $_____

                   LIMITATIONS AND DEADLINES

             Statute of Limitations _____
                   215.1_____

 Discovery Deadlines _____
 Expert Witness Deadlines:_____
 Pleading Deadlines:_____

                     TELEPHONE DIRECTORY

 Opposing Counsel Name:_____Phone:_____

 Opposing Counsel Name:_____Phone:_____

 Other Attorney:_____Phone:_____

 Other Attorney:_____Phone:_____

 Adverse Insurance Carrier:_____

 Clerk of Court: Case No.:_____  Phone No._____

 Assignment Clerk:_____

 Judge: Name:_____ Phone No._____

 Other: Name:_____ Phone No._____

 Other: Name:_____ Phone No._____

 Other: Name:_____ Phone No._____
```

lawyer's or the legal assistant's notes. The file serves as a tracking system and as a depository for such items as preliminary letters, memos, intake notes, and documents taken from the client. When a determination is made about whether the firm will handle the client's matter, either the papers are transferred to the general file system or a letter of declination is sent to the client and the preliminary file is closed.

Appointment-Related Situations

All appointments with clients are important and must be scheduled carefully. A lawyer's actions are governed by strict rules of professional responsibility set by the ABA and the states in which lawyers have been licensed to practice; special grievance committees investigate complaints filed against lawyers. Missed appointments, lack of punctuality, and frequent rescheduling of appointments by the lawyer might result in the client's rights being affected, for which a complaint may be filed. Even if a complaint is groundless and is eventually dismissed, no lawyer wants to suffer the embarrassment of having to appear before a grievance committee. The legal secretary must be alert to clients' reactions and attitudes. Because a good client relationship is essential to a successful law practice, any criticism of the lawyer made by a client must be immediately reported to the lawyer and steps should be taken to rectify the situation with the client.

Handling appointments competently and developing a good rapport with clients and other visitors is important. You will be confronted daily with different and often difficult situations that require tact and diplomacy. You will be challenged to handle each with the professionalism required of your position, for your conduct in the office and your handling of each client affect the reputation of the lawyer and your firm.

If a client arrives without an appointment, explain that the lawyer is unavailable, engaged in a difficult briefing, preparing for a trial, or whatever the reasonable explanation is. Offer to make an appointment at a time when the lawyer can give the client's problem the undivided attention it deserves. If another lawyer is in the office and available, ask the client if he or she would like to see that lawyer. When a client sees that you are being truthful and genuinely helpful, other arrangements can usually be made agreeably.

Appointments, court hearings, and other matters involving the lawyer frequently run past the allotted time. If this occurs and the client is left waiting, apologize for the delay and explain that a lawyer's schedule cannot always be controlled. Make every effort to make the client comfortable and, if the wait becomes lengthy, consult with the lawyer about the possibility of rescheduling the appointment.

The legal office receives visitors and callers from all walks of life and in a wide range of emotional states. The professional legal secretary must develop the skills and the confidence to handle any situation that might arise from contact with this great variety of people seeking legal assistance. Meeting this challenge is one of the rewards of being a legal secretary.

Business Meetings and Conferences

The scope of your responsibility in assisting with business meetings and conferences will vary, depending on the size of the event. A business *meeting* or *conference* may be anything from a brief intraoffice parley to a gathering on a national or international scale whereas a *convention* is always a large, formal gathering. Regardless of the magnitude of the event, you may be assigned duties involving helping to get ready for the meeting, providing services during the meeting, and assisting with post-meeting follow-ups. (For a discussion of taking and transcribing meeting minutes, see Chapter 9, pp. 333–38.) Flexibility and adaptability will be necessary to cope with the last-minute changes that frequently occur.

Invitations to In-House Meetings

You will often be responsible for getting the right people together at the right time for business meetings. Legal secretaries sometimes say that their most difficult task is to find enough time in the busy schedules of three or four lawyers to arrange special meetings among them.

When picking a time for an in-house meeting, avoid scheduling it on a religious holiday or early Monday morning or late Friday afternoon. Bear in mind also that people are generally more alert in the morning than in the afternoon.

In-house invitations must be prepared for regular staff meetings, special staff meetings, annual stockholders' meetings (and proxies), corporate directors' meetings, and other meetings and conferences.

Regular staff meetings   For weekly or monthly meetings that are on a regular schedule, remind the participants about the meeting by means of a memorandum containing the following information (see also Fig. 6.3):

- Names of the individuals attending or name of the group.
- Day of the week, date, time, and place of the meeting.
- Agenda (including names of persons who are to speak on given topics).
- Any advance preparation required of the participants, or materials they should bring.

You may also telephone lawyers' offices to make a quick check on the availability of professional staff for regularly scheduled meetings. The person chairing the meeting should be notified of any member's anticipated absence, so that voting on key issues will not be hampered by lack of a quorum.

Special staff meetings   Attorneys sometimes find themselves in crisis situations that call for immediate action, and special meetings may be required to deal with these situations. In such situations, you must contact the professional staff quickly, either in person or by telephone. If the meeting is not to be held immediately, a follow-up written reminder should be sent.

Annual stockholders' meetings (and proxies)   Invitations to or notices of the annual meeting of the stockholders of a corporation must meet certain legal requirements. The formal notices are usually issued in printed form by the corporate secretary or corporate counsel, with the assistance of the legal secretary. (See Fig. 6.4.) A reply card and a proxy card and a proxy form are routinely mailed with the annual meeting notice about three or four weeks before the event, or as stipulated in the corporate bylaws. If a stockholder is unable to attend, he or she may vote by completing and returning the proxy form (see Fig. 6.5).

Corporate directors' meetings   Individual corporate bylaws may stipulate how the directors are to be notified of upcoming meetings. Even if written notification for regular meetings is not required, it is nonetheless advisable. You may also have to notify directors of special meetings by telephoning them. Have a list of the directors' names available for each meeting and indicate on it whether or not they will be present. A printed notification and attendance form such as the one shown in Fig. 6.6 will be a time-saver. Frequently the by-

Fig. 6.3   Notice of Staff Meeting

Rutledge & Singh
Law Offices

MEMORANDUM

TO: Staff

FROM: Anwit Singh

DATE: January 10, 19--

SUBJECT: Staff meeting

This is to remind you that the regularly scheduled staff meeting to discuss the topics noted below will be held at 10 a.m. on **Wednesday, January 12**, in the office conference room.

The following topics are on the agenda:

1. New medical plan options.
2. Streamlining billing procedures.

Please bring your copy of the medical-plan summary (circulated last week) with you to the meeting.

Please notify Julia Chang if you cannot attend.

---

laws require the secretary to prepare an affidavit such as the one shown in Fig. 6.7, certifying that notices were properly mailed. Should the call for a special meeting not allow time to meet the notice requirements of the bylaws, a corporate director might execute a Waiver of Notice of the Special Meeting, a signed form that would be filed in the corporate records. Waivers of Notice may also

Fig. 6.4   Shareholders' Notice

Jones & Lebenthal, P.C.
416 Powhatan Lane
Commerce Corner, VA 22133

**CALL AND NOTICE OF ANNUAL
MEETING OF SHAREHOLDERS**

TO THE SHAREHOLDERS OF JONES & LEBENTHAL, P.C.

NOTICE IS HEREBY GIVEN that the annual meeting of the shareholders of JONES & LEBENTHAL, a Virginia professional corporation, is hereby called and will be held at the corporate offices at 416 Powhatan Lane, in the city of Commerce Corner, Virginia, on the eighteenth day of February, 19--, at the hour of 9 a.m. for the purpose of electing directors and transacting such other business as may come before the meeting.

Dated:_____   _____
                                                 William Bates
                                                 Secretary

Fig. 6.5   Proxy Form

KNOW ALL MEN BY THESE PRESENTS   that the undersigned shareholder of seventy-five (75) shares of PDQ CORPORATION does hereby appoint EMMA DOUGLASS, of 367 Highview Road, Grandee, Illinois, or the bearer of this proxy, to be his true and lawful attorney-in-fact and agent to vote as proxy at the meeting of shareholders of PDQ CORPORATION to be held on September 7, 19--, at the Chalfont Hotel, or any adjournment of such meeting, and to act as fully as the undersigned could do if personally present at such meeting. By this proxy the undersigned does hereby revoke any proxy previously given.

Dated:_____   _____
                                                 Burton D. Grover
                                                 742 Lawton Drive
                                                 Grandee, Illinois 50638

Fig. 6.6   Directors' Meeting Notification and Attendance Form

---

DATACO SERVICES, INC.

Directors' Meeting

DATE: March 17, 19--

TIME: 2 p.m.

PLACE: Boardroom

CHAIR: Earl Saunders, Presiding Officer

BOARD MEMBERS	NOTICE SENT	WILL ATTEND	WILL NOT ATTEND
Waylon Sevier	3/4/--	X	
Carleton Langley	"	X	
Melissa Hecht	"	X	
Kirby Rainwater	"	X	
Monica Shiffler	"		X
George Caitlan	"	X	
Jan Hanawalt	"	X	
Jacqueline Frank	"	X	
Harold Kay Long	"	X	
Martin Blum	"	X	
Arlo Kleinbauer	"	X	
Ada Puig	"	X	
Simon Rosser	"	X	
Eugene Dudley	"	X	
Christian Sullivan	"	X	

Total Attending: *14*

Quorum Assured: Yes *X*   No_____

Alicia Green
Secretary

---

be signed and filed when directors are in close touch and agree that a formal notice is not required.

Other meetings and conferences   Announcements of other in-house meetings should be distributed well before the meeting date. Meeting notices to be sent to large groups of company personnel are normally printed or duplicated.

Fig. 6.7 **Affidavit of Mailing**

AFFIDAVIT OF MAILING OF
NOTICE OF SPECIAL MEETING
OF SHAREHOLDERS
of
Crowley Law Offices, P.C.

STATE OF KENTUCKY)
COUNTY OF FAYETTE) ss.:

MARIE NORRIS being duly sworn deposes and says:

I am the Administrative Secretary of Crowley Law Offices, that on the fifteenth day of September, 19–, I deposited in an official depository maintained under the exclusive care and custody of the United States Postal Service located in the State of Kentucky, a true and complete copy of the Notice of Special Meeting of the shareholders of Crowley Law Offices, each enclosed in a sealed, postage-paid wrapper to each shareholder whose name appears on the attached list at the respective address adjacent to each name.

_____
Marie Norris

Sworn to before me this

_____ day of _____, 19___

_____
Notary Public

Your initial task will be to assemble all pertinent data and arrange it in an attractive format. Notices of in-house committee meetings and other routine meetings may be issued on interoffice correspondence paper. Headings such as "All Attorneys," "Personal-Injury Attorneys and Staff," or "Financial Staff" may be used to address particular groups. Frequently an invitation asks that the recipient notify the chairperson if he or she cannot attend. Depending upon the size of the group and the importance of the event, you may be requested to send separate letters to specific individuals.

The day of the week, the time of day, the location, and the subject of the meeting must be clearly spelled out. If the participants are to bring any special materials with them, that should be specified. Invitations to seminars, workshops, training sessions, and other specialized in-house activities may use color and unusual design to gain attention and spark interest.

Invitations to Outside Conferences and Other Functions

Various styles are used for the announcements of outside business meetings and functions ranging from those for major conventions to those for minor social gatherings.

Outside conferences   Printed invitations designed in an original way are useful in attracting attention and in developing interest in large-scale conferences. In preparing the invitations, be sure to double-check the day of the week, the date, the time of day, the room location, and the names of all participants in the various programs and sectional meetings. No participant should have to telephone the sponsors for vital information inadvertently omitted, or to protest the omission or misspelling of his or her name.

Outside professional and community meetings   If your employer is a leader in professional or community affairs, he or she may be asked to send out informal meeting notices, perhaps as part of a newsletter. An illustration of this kind of meeting notice is shown in Fig. 6.8. A self-addressed postal card such as the one shown in Fig. 6.9 may also be included, so that the participants in the meeting can respond to the invitation quickly. These cards will later serve as the basis for the reservation list (as for a luncheon or dinner meeting).

Outside social/business functions   You will likely be involved at some time in preparing invitations to social/business functions, often as part of a conference. Such invitations are usually extended to lawyers and their spouses. Reply (R.S.V.P.) cards may be included with the invitation. (Today the reply to a business invitation is rarely handwritten, although handwritten replies are still conventional for formal social invitations.)

Using Mailing Lists for Invitations and Notices

Devise a system for keeping mailing lists current. In most offices, you will keep your mailing lists as word-processing or database files. Updating can be done rapidly on computer, and mailing labels can be printed out with great speed.

   In offices where the only mailings are extremely small, a simple card system may be used. Each card will show the name and address of a regular mailing recipient, and the cards can be arranged by geographical region, by company, or by individual name. However, typing out more than one or two dozen addresses onto labels or envelopes can become very laborious.

Preparing for Conferences

If you work closely with the attorney who is directing or sponsoring a conference, the principal areas of conference preparation in which you may be involved are the following: (1) meeting-site and speaker confirmation, (2) preparing conference materials, and (3) special arrangements for services, including publicity.

Meeting-site and speaker confirmation   If hotel rooms will be needed for conference participants, you should contact the site manager for block reservations. Room size (single or double) and price range should be specified. The site manager should be asked to reserve the appropriate meeting rooms.

Fig. 6.8   Newsletter Meeting Notice

Twin Cities Regional Chapter

LAW OFFICE ADMINISTRATOR S' GROUP

SEMIANNUAL FORUM

Thursday, May 18, 19--, 6:00–9:00 p.m.

TOPIC: Total Quality Management in the Law Office

SPEAKER: Marcia B. Kolve, Administrative Partner, Bemberg &
            Kolve, P.C., Minneapolis

PANEL: Thomas Fulton, Anderson Associates
            Arlene Basarab, Pilson & Curie
            Cecilia Orr, Legal Services, Ltd.
            Ola Knapp, Latch Insurance Co.
            Frederic Sauvage, Mercer, Mason & Otto
            Vivian Heald, Legal Consultants, Inc.

PLACE: Bardwick Tower Hotel, Suite 111, St. Paul

EVENTS: 6:00 Social
            6:30 Dinner
            7:15 Presentation
            8:00 Discussion

MENU: Smorgasbord

COST: $25.00

Please return enclosed reservation card by May 11

It is a good idea to inspect unfamiliar meeting sites, if possible, to be certain that there is adequate space for the event. Firsthand knowledge of the meeting or conference layout will be helpful in accommodating your guests. A letter confirming the reservation of all conference facilities should be sent to the site manager. In the case of in-house requests, this may be done by telephone and confirmed by a memorandum.

Fig. 6.9   Reservation Postal Card

```
PLEASE send this reservation card to our Secretary on
or before Tuesday of next week (5/11).

_____    YES.  I plan to attend the LOAG Semiannual
          Forum.  I will be bringing ____ guests.

Guest names: _____


_____

_____    NO.  I will not be attending the meeting this
          time.

      Signature _____

      Firm/Company _____
```

After the meeting date is set, letters of invitation to speakers may be composed or dictated, unless the lawyer chooses to telephone the invitations to the speakers. Such invitations should be taken care of as soon as possible. When each invitation is accepted, a follow-up letter requesting information about the speaker's background and experience may be sent.

Preparing conference materials   A meeting should never be held without an agenda. An agenda distributed in advance may encourage participants to gather material and ideas to contribute. As the meeting proceeds, the Chair can use the agenda to keep discussions on the subject at hand and then check off each item as it is completed. An informal agenda is shown in Fig. 6.10.

Fig. 6.10   An Informal Agenda

A G E N D A

Partners' Meeting

Tuesday, Oct. 5, 9:30 a.m.

1.   Review of last quarter's business activity.

2.   Recent SEC filing change.

3.   Litigation strategy in Sedgewick case.

4.   Possible public-relations activities for firm's 50th anniversary.

Supporting materials such as tables, reports, financial statements, or advertisements may be needed, and you may be asked to prepare copies for the meeting participants. These items are often assembled and distributed in a folder or envelope. Double-check that all names, titles, topics, sections, and meeting times are correct.

When the conference speakers have submitted their résumés or autobiographical sketches, a news release may be prepared. If the firm has a public-relations officer, you should forward the information to him or her; if the firm does not have such an officer, you may be asked to draft a press release describing the conference and speakers. (See Figure 7.29, p. 223, for an example of a press release.)

Trip itineraries will be necessary for meetings and conferences held outside the firm. At least two copies of the itinerary are needed: one for the attorneys travel folder, and at least one office copy. (For a sample itinerary and discussion of travel arrangements, see "Making Travel Arrangements," beginning on page 146.)

Special arrangements for services   Large-scale conventions and conferences require a wide variety of special services. You may be asked to do any of the following:

> Arrange for printing and engraving services.
> Organize tours and special events for conferees.
> Arrange for refreshments and meals.
> Handle pre-registration and registration arrangements.
> Assemble conference folders or packets.
> Request audiovisual equipment and materials.
> Arrange for translation services (for international conferences).
> Mail prework conference materials (to be studied in advance by participants).
> Ship supplies and printed materials to conference site.
> Arrange for press coverage.
> Inform security officers and parking attendants of pertinent conference details.
> Prepare meeting file folders.

For a detailed discussion of these services, consult a book on conference planning (see bibliography) or see Chapter 4 of *Merriam-Webster's Secretarial Handbook, 3d ed.*

Duties During Conferences

The following list identifies some services that you may have to provide at a conference:

- Check the meeting room(s) and oversee final arrangements.
- Greet conference guests.
- Supervise the registration desk. Alert registration-desk personnel as to the identity and the arrival time of speakers and special guests so that badges, programs, and complimentary tickets for luncheons and other events may be presented to them.
- Provide statistics on the number of participants who will attend each event.

- Prepare a list of participants with the names and addresses of their companies, to be duplicated and distributed.
- Take minutes of certain meetings.
- Handle correspondence requests for conference officers, executives, or special guests.
- Assemble and prepare information for a conference news sheet. Print and distribute news sheet to participants.
- Coordinate conference events by transmitting messages and reaching individuals sought by others.
- Meet media representatives and photographers and direct them to room locations for group pictures and other events. Distribute press releases.
- Arrange place cards for seating officers and guests on the dais or at the head table for luncheons and banquets.

Following Up After Conferences

The follow-up duties after a conference often become your responsibility. You may be asked to perform the following duties at the meeting site:

- Remove any surplus conference-related literature (such as reports or minutes) from the meeting room.
- Notify the catering manager to collect water glasses and any food-service items from the meeting room.
- Request that any equipment or materials that have been borrowed or rented be removed and arrange for their prompt return.
- Return any lost-and-found items to the company receptionist or the appropriate conference authorities.

Making Travel Arrangements

A successful business trip requires careful preparations carried out methodically. Even if your firm has an in-house travel department, you yourself should know what information will be needed and where it may be obtained. You should know *in advance* the following:

1. *Office policies and procedures*
   - Whether travel arrangements are to be made by an in-house travel department, a travel agent, or you and the attorney.
   - The procedure for making a formal travel request.
   - The procedure for requesting cash advances and/or prepayment or reimbursement of expenses.
   - How to coordinate office schedules in the attorney's absence.
2. *The attorney's personal preferences and needs*
   - Means of transportation—specific carrier, class, time of day, meal service, and special services
   - Hotel accommodations—chain affiliation, required facilities, smoking or nonsmoking room, and special arrangements.
   - Entertainment and sightseeing.
   - Ground transportation services.

- Amount of leisure time.
- Personal interests.
- Medical problems.
3. *Methods for keeping records of the trip*
   - Portable dictation equipment, telephone, fax, E-mail, outside clerical assistance, or dictation upon return.

Although gathering and organizing this information may involve a great deal of time, the result will make the investment worthwhile.

In addition, you must determine the following:

- Purpose of the trip, departure and return dates, and number of people traveling.
- Most convenient and expedient means of transportation, mileage, and estimated travel time.
- Hotel most completely equipped and closest to trip activities.
- Arrangements and facilities for meetings.
- Forms to be completed before departure.
- Memoranda and background information for cocounsel or opposing attorney.
- Information or instructions to give to clients.
- Availability of necessary supplies (dictation equipment, reference books or research facilities, files, handout materials, etc.) and services (clerical, reproduction, etc.)
- Allocation of free time and designated activities.
- Additional arrangements for family and traveling companions.
- Notes on climate, time zones, and accepted modes of dress.

Commercial Travel Agencies

Reputable travel agencies are staffed with skilled employees who can provide assistance at no cost to the traveler. A call to a travel agent will save time and assure a minimum of confusion from the beginning to the end of the trip. Travel agents make travel reservations, issue tickets, recommend hotels and make hotel reservations, arrange for car rentals, and assist in obtaining passports and visas. They sometimes give additional help with incidentals such as tickets for the theater or sporting events. They have at their fingertips data about airline flight schedules and prices, air distances and travel times to principal cities around the globe, luggage limitations, and air freight.

The selection of a travel agent may be based on personal recommendations, established reputation, or spot usage. Some agencies offer discounts for corporate clients. Once an agent has been chosen, try to use the same agent to arrange all trips, so that he or she can become familiar with the traveler's habits.

Names of accredited travel agencies are available from the American Society of Travel Agents (ASTA), 1101 King Street, Suite 200, Alexandria, VA 22314. You can also get a list of Certified Travel Agencies in your area by sending a self-addressed, stamped envelope to the Institute of Certified Travel Agents (ICTA), 148 Linden Street, P.O. Box 812059, Wellesley, MA 02181-0012.

Have all necessary information at hand before calling the agent, and be courteous and friendly yet completely candid about the attorney's desires. Be ready to supply the following information:

1. The attorney's office address and home and office telephone numbers.
2. The desired dates and times of departure and return.
3. The attorney's travel preferences—first-class or coach, aisle or window seat, special diet, etc.

The agent will provide confirmation, suggest an acceptable method of payment, and arrange either to send the tickets to you or have you pick them up.

International travel   The travel agent is indispensable for an attorney who travels to other countries. The secretary should verify with the agent such things as passport and visa regulations, required inoculations, luggage restrictions, currency exchange rates, political conditions in the host country, consulate facilities, and entry and departure requirements. For further information see Chapter 15 of *Merriam-Webster's Secretarial Handbook, 3d ed.*

In-House Travel Departments

Some large law firms and many companies have in-house travel departments that monitor travel requests and provide a detailed tracking system of moneys spent. Some companies have special policies regarding returning frequent-flyer mileage to the company, and this too can be monitored by an in-house travel department.

Electronic Reservation Systems

If you are making reservations through an in-house travel department or on your own, there are on-line services such as Prodigy, CompuServe, Eaasy Sabre, and The Travel Index through which you can make reservations and obtain tickets. The *Official Airline Guide* (Official Airline Guides, 2000 Clearwater Dr., Oak Brook, IL 60521; 800-323-3537) has an Electronic Edition (OAGEE). The following services are literally at your fingertips by means of a computerized travel service: latest flight information, ticketing arrangements, credit-card arrangements, meal selections, seating preferences, hotel and motel reservations, restaurant information, banquet and conference facilities, weather conditions in cities throughout the world, and travel tips.

Making Travel Arrangements Directly

If you make travel reservations without the help of an agent, preparation is more complex. It may involve obtaining current schedules and brochures from airlines, bus lines, railroads, travel clubs, motor clubs, and various travel agencies. If you make extensive arrangements directly, you will need to have access to the *Official Airline Guide* (see address above), *The Hotel and Travel Index* (HTM/Reed Travel Group, 500 Plaza Dr., Secaucus, NJ 07096; 800-360-0015), or on-line resources.

Know the full particulars of the trip before making any reservations. Contact the chamber of commerce, convention bureau, or tourism office of the destination city for brochures and special information. Another source of information is the local newspaper or the monthly magazine of the destination city, where you can find special-events calendars, weather reports, and service and facility advertisements.

Most of the major airlines, hotels, and car-rental agencies have toll-free numbers. If you do not have access to a directory of toll-free 800 numbers, call the toll-free information number, 800-555-1212, for the listing you need.

Airline reservations If you do not rely on an agent for airline reservations, a call to the airline will provide information about its schedules and rates. Reservations and even seat assignments may be made instantly. You can confirm flights and sometimes make hotel reservations through the airline, but you should always confirm hotel reservations yourself. Clip the special service announcements and schedules that are often published in newspapers. Allot enough time between connecting flights. Inquire specifically as to methods of payment and how to pick up the ticket.

Most major airlines have private clubroom facilities in the larger airports. An annual membership charge enables the club member to avoid the turmoil of a busy airport, find a quiet place to work during layovers, change reservations if necessary, and obtain seat assignments well in advance of the gate's opening. Information about such facilities is available from ticket agents and flight attendants.

Railroad travel Rail travel is limited to certain cities at certain times of the day and is feasible only when time and access to Amtrak terminals are available. Rail travel generally requires more time than the attorney is likely to have, but some people prefer to travel by train. You can obtain a schedule for Amtrak trains as well as for connecting or commuter lines from the nearest Amtrak station; Amtrak schedules are also accessible through the Internet.

Automobile travel In some instances the attorney may choose to travel by automobile. Membership in an automobile or oil-company travel club provides guides and maps, towing and repair service, and detailed road trip plans. If the attorney will be renting a car, the type of car and rate should be guaranteed with the agency. You should determine the method of payment, special discounts available, and insurance requirements. The attorney's return-trip arrival time or time of arrival at the drop-off site should be specified so that no unnecessary delays are encountered in checking out. Some car-rental agencies use the term "unlimited mileage" to indicate that the driver pays a set amount for a designated period of time, regardless of the number of miles the car is driven. The term "drop-off charges" refers to the fee the driver must pay when the car is rented at one location but returned to another.

Hotel reservations It is essential to make hotel reservations as soon as the dates of the trip are definite, since hotels in major cities may be fully booked several weeks in advance. *The Hotel & Motel Red Book,* published by the American Hotel and Motel Association, 1201 New York Avenue, NW, Suite 600, Washington, DC 20005, provides descriptions of selected hotels and motels throughout the United States. Reservations are normally made by telephone and confirmed in writing. Specify whether the traveler will desire a smoking or nonsmoking room. Many hotels hold reservations only until a certain hour, usually 6 p.m. You may frequently hold a reservation beyond that hour by guaranteeing payment whether or not the guest arrives. To guarantee a room, you will need to give the name and address of the firm or the number and expiration date of a major credit card.

Advise the hotel by telephone as to the attorney's preferences and inquire about a guarantee that such accommodations will be available. Find out about meal plans, valet and laundry services, barber/hairdressers, masseurs, health clubs, and shoe shining and repair facilities, and make notes of these services on the itinerary. It may be desirable to make advance appointments for certain services. Request written confirmation of all hotel reservations, including arrival and departure dates, guarantee, room rates, and tax. In addition, ask about check-out times, payment procedures, credit and check-cashing privileges, fax machines, meeting facilities, and other needed services.

Ask about complimentary limousine service from the airport or railway station and the comparative rates and times of other means of ground transportation. The clerk should also be able to tell you how to find ground transportation upon arrival if arrangements cannot be made beforehand. There may be a direct telephone line to the hotel from the baggage-claim area of the airport, for example, or an agent at a desk or curbside, or posted notices of available transportation.

Special Arrangements

Selecting cocounsel   It may be necessary for the attorney to engage another attorney in the destination city as cocounsel to advise as to applicable state laws and local rules of practice and perhaps make many of the arrangements at the destination city. In choosing cocounsel the attorney may rely on acquaintances in the area, or the local bar association may have referral lists. The name of a competent attorney may also be obtained from the *Martindale-Hubbell Law Directory* or from individual state and regional directories.

If the trip involves the deposing of a key witness, the attorney must confirm that the requested subpoenas or notices have been served and that cocounsel has arranged for conference rooms and a court reporter.

Health problems   The attorney with health problems may have to wear appropriate identification, carry medication, and arrange for access to a local physician. Provision for special diets or other needs may also have to be made.

The Travel Folder

File all notes on the various arrangements in one folder to facilitate the preparation of an itinerary and appointment schedule. When the arrangements are completed, mark a deadline on the calendar for receipt of confirmations. If confirmations are not received by that date, a follow-up phone call must be made.

The itinerary   An itinerary is invaluable in guiding an attorney through a hectic day in a distant city. The itinerary should be logically and neatly arranged so that he or she can review it at a glance. It should include a brief description of activities, with dates and times; departure and arrival times, with terminals specified; hotel names and addresses, and confirmed reservations (official con-

Fig. 6.11 Sample Itinerary

ITINERARY

Deposition of Brower case witnesses

Grant Law Offices, Denver, Co.

Sept. 17-18

WEDNESDAY, SEPT. 17

Departure

Lv. San Diego International Airport	4:30 p.m.	American Flight #167A	One stop in Phoenix; dinner served
Ar. Denver International Airport	8:45 p.m.		McCaffrey Transport Services to Hotel

Accommodations

Radisson Hotel	One night: Sept. 17
65 Sunderland Avenue	Guaranteed for late arrival (confirmation attached)
Denver, CO	
(719) 776-3888	

THURSDAY, SEPT. 18

Breakfast Meeting—Atty. Grant	8:00 a.m.	Radisson Club Rm.	Grant cocounsel, Mr. Saunders

Depositions—Grant Law Offices, 123 State Street, Denver
James Brower (10:00 a.m.–12:30 p.m.)
Trevor Donnelly (2:30 p.m.–4:30 p.m.)

Return

Lv. Denver International Airport	6:00 p.m.	United Flight #213B	Non-stop; dinner served
Ar. San Diego International Airport	9:15 p.m.		

---

firmations are usually attached); and social engagements, with comments as to dress. A detailed itinerary may also contain pertinent information about individuals, reference to files or reports and correspondence, reminders to reconfirm flight reservations and meeting arrangements, and comments on climate and social amenities. A simple itinerary is illustrated in Fig. 6.11.

In preparing the itinerary, confer with the attorney and make careful notes about desired dates and times of departure and return, the time needed for each meeting or appointment, and any need for free time to relax or attend to personal matters. The traveler should be told the details of any flight—what meals will be served, whether the flight is nonstop, the distance between terminals if a change of planes is involved, and the approximate distance between the airport and the hotel. Errors in planning can result in costly delays and needless confusion.

Travel agents also provide itineraries, but these are usually in the form of a printout from a computerized reservation service and thus should be carefully reviewed and supplemented with additional appointments and information. In some cases a separate appointment schedule is advisable, with notes for each meeting—participants, papers needed, and so on. After the draft itinerary is approved by the attorney, the final itinerary is typed and filed in the travel folder, and copies may be distributed as needed within the office.

Expense-account records   In preparing the travel folder, be sure to include the appropriate expense-account records. These contain ledger space for expenses such as transportation, personal mileage, taxi fares and fares for other local transport, room, meals (including tips), business entertainment, and business-related telephone calls. There is also space for recording cash advances and the total amount expended from such advances. Such records are needed to charge travel expenses to the proper client and to comply with Internal Revenue Service regulations. Many law firms design their own expense-account records. However, the secretary might wish to examine I.R.S. Publication 463, *Travel, Entertainment, and Gift Expenses,* which sets forth the conditions for making deductions on federal tax returns and also outlines bookkeeping rules. Copies of this booklet are available from the Government Printing Office (G.P.O.) in Pittsburgh, PA.

Business travelers bringing home gifts from abroad must be able to substantiate the following information: cost, date of purchase, description, and reason for giving it.

Time sheets   Lawyers should keep records of their working time away from the office. Be sure to add to the travel folder a pad of the firm's standard time sheets, which will look something like the one illustrated in Fig. 6.12. Arrangements should be made for the attorney to fax or mail time sheets to the office on a regular basis.

Travel diaries   A separate diary may be provided for each trip, or the same one may be used for successive trips. Within the diary the efficient secretary will list items from the itinerary and the addresses and telephone numbers of contacts in the destination city. Care should be taken to list the information correctly and to provide ample space for notes and comments by the attorney. Upon return, the diary may be filed in the client's file or in a general travel folder by geographical location. If the attorney prefers not to take notes during the trip, you should provide portable dictation equipment and ask him or her to return the tapes periodically so that transcription can begin prior to his or her return.

Fig. 6.12 Attorney's Time Sheet

ATTY. NO.	CLIENT		DATE		TIME
MATTER		CLIENT / MATTER NO.			
		CODE	START		
			STOP		.
			START		
			STOP		.
			START		
			STOP		.
			TOTAL		.

ATTY. NO.	CLIENT		DATE		TIME
MATTER		CLIENT / MATTER NO.			
		CODE	START		
			STOP		.
			START		
			STOP		.
			START		
			STOP		.
			TOTAL		.

ATTY. NO.	CLIENT		DATE		TIME
MATTER		CLIENT / MATTER NO.			
		CODE	START		
			STOP		.
			START		
			STOP		.
			START		
			STOP		.
			TOTAL		.

The travel checklist The final step is to assemble all the necessary materials and equipment. The following checklist may be helpful:

_____ tickets
_____ frequent-flyer number
_____ hotel information
_____ car-rental confirmation
_____ itinerary
_____ addresses and phone numbers of contact persons at destination
_____ all necessary client files and other case/matter information
_____ diary or journal
_____ time sheets
_____ expense-account record forms
_____ copy of notice of deposition or hearing
_____ agenda and advance publicity for conferences/meetings
_____ speeches, reports
_____ slides or transparencies
_____ business cards
_____ law-firm letterhead and envelopes
_____ gummed note tags, paper clips, manila folders, etc.

_____ laptop computer with fax modem and printer
_____ portable dictating equipment, extra tapes
_____ reference books for destination city and country
_____ traveler's checks
_____ medical prescriptions
_____ passport, visa, international driving permit, immunization certificates

Maintaining the Office

Maintaining office efficiency and decorum in the attorney's absence is a vital part of the secretary's role. You should see that clients' problems receive the necessary attention and that ongoing work does not fall behind. Be aware of the attorney's travel schedule and organize the office workload to minimize disruption.

Checklist of Follow-Up Procedures

As soon as possible upon the attorney's return, the secretary needs to attend to the following:

1. Read any instructions from the attorney regarding transcription of dictated material or the reworking of computer-generated materials.
2. Review the travel folder for notes and comments.
3. Review the client file or seminar materials for labeling and filing.
4. Arrange receipts chronologically, cross-checking with expense-account records; arrange billing to the proper client; and submit for reimbursement.
5. Review the trip diary and make notes for future reference.
6. File all materials.

Canceling a Planned Trip

When a planned trip is canceled, you must notify all parties as quickly as possible. Transportation and hotel arrangements should be canceled promptly by telephone, and a follow-up letter should confirm the cancellation. Meeting arrangements should be canceled with the concierge, catering manager, or meeting coordinator.

If the tickets have been prepaid, application for a refund (accompanied by the unused tickets if you have them) is made directly to the carrier or travel agent. If hotel accommodations have been paid for in advance, apply for a refund to the hotel by letter promptly after telephoning the cancellation. If hotel reservations are guaranteed, *prompt* cancellation is crucial to avoid charges. If any payment has been made by charge card, application for credit should be made through the carrier, the hotel reservations clerk, or the travel agent. When the following monthly statement arrives, be sure that the correct credit has been allowed.

Chapter 7

Business Letters and Forms of Address

This chapter focuses on questions of letter format—that is, the design, punctuation, and styling that apply specifically to letter-writing—and on the etiquette of letter-writing. (For more on punctuation, capitalization, and other mechanics of writing, see Chapter 8. For information about legal forms, see Chapter 10.) The chapter includes over 25 sample letters to be used as models in preparing correspondence and a chart that lists proper forms of address.

All of the elements of letter style come together to produce a reflection on paper not only of the writer's ability and knowledge and the typist's competence but also of an organization's total image. Well-prepared letters reflect a firm's pride and its concern for quality, whereas poorly prepared correspondence can create such a negative impression that its recipients may have second thoughts about pursuing business with the firm. This is a special consideration for small firms. The business letter, then, is actually an indicator of overall organizational style, regardless of the size of the firm. Thus, the impression created by clearly written, logically ordered, and attractively and accurately typed letters can be a crucial factor in the success of any firm.

A lawyer may devote as much as 50 percent of the workday to correspondence. This includes conceiving the tone and content of outgoing letters and reading and acting on incoming letters. Secretaries may spend an even higher proportion of their time on correspondence. And all this time costs money. However, the time and money will have been well spent if both writer and typist keep in mind the following general rules:

1. The stationery should be of high-quality paper.
2. The typing or keyboarding should be neat and accurate, and any corrections or erasures should be rendered invisible.
3. The elements of the letter (dateline, inside address, message, signature block) should conform in placement and style with one of the generally accepted business letter formats (such as the Full Block, the Modified Block, or the Semiblock format).

4. The language should be clear, concise, grammatically correct, and devoid of padding and clichés.
5. The ideas should be logically presented, and the tone should be appropriate to the reader.
6. All numerical data should be accurate and complete.
7. All names should be correctly spelled and styled.

NOTE: Throughout this chapter, wherever lines of type are counted ("six lines from the top," "two lines below," etc.), the number refers to the number of times you must press the Return (or Enter) key. Thus, the number of *blank* lines will always be one less than the number specified. Wherever spaces are counted ("indented five spaces," "five spaces to the right of center," the number refers to letter spaces, not the half-letter spaces that some computer-keyboard space bars and word-processing programs produce.

Material and Design Considerations

Paper

Paper size, quality, and basis weight vary according to application. The table below lists various paper sizes along with their uses.

Good-quality paper is essential to the production of attractive, effective letters. Paper with rag content is considerably more expensive than sulfite bond papers; nevertheless, many law offices use rag-content paper because it suggests the merit and stature of the firm. Since the cost of paper has been estimated at less than five percent of the total cost of the average business letter, it is easy to understand why many firms consider high-quality paper to be worth the added expense—at least for certain types of correspondence.

Stationery and Applications

Stationery	Stationery size	Application
Standard	8½″ × 11″ *also* 8″ × 10½″	general business correspondence and some legal documents
Legal	8½″ × 14″	some legal documents
Executive *or* Monarch	7¼″ × 10½″ *or* 7½″ × 10″	high-level officer's correspondence
Half-sheet *or* Baronial	5½″ × 8½″	extremely brief notes

The paper grain, or fiber direction, should be parallel to the type. In addition, every sheet of high-quality stationery has a *felt* side, or top side, from which a watermark may be read; the letterhead should be printed or engraved on this side.

The weight of the paper must also be considered when ordering stationery supplies. *Basis weight,* also called *substance number,* is the weight in pounds of a ream of paper cut to a basic size. Basis 24 is the heaviest for stationery and is used for important correspondence; basis 13 is the lightest and is used for overseas airmail letters.

In some offices, carbon copies are still made. The paper used for carbon copies is lighter in weight and is available as inexpensive *manifold* paper, a stronger and more expensive onionskin, or a lightweight letterhead with the word COPY printed on it.

Continuation sheets and envelopes must match the letterhead sheet in color, basis weight, texture, size, and quality. Therefore, they should be ordered along with the letterhead to ensure a good match.

Letterhead and continuation sheets as well as envelopes should be stored in their original boxes to prevent soiling. A small supply of these materials may be kept in your drawer or near your printer, but it should be arranged carefully so as to protect the materials from wear and tear.

Letter Balance

It has often been said that an attractive letter should look like a symmetrically framed picture, with even margins working as a frame for the typed lines, which should be balanced under the letterhead. Word processors have features such as standard settings for text pages and options for print previewing that can help you prepare letters that are properly formatted and pleasing to the eye. However, regardless of the kind of equipment available to you, the following steps will help you create letters with the desired appearance:

1. Estimate the number of words in the letter or the general length of the message by looking over the writer's rough draft or your own shorthand notes, or by checking the length of a dictated source.
2. Make mental notes of any long quotations, tables, long lists, or footnotes that may require margin adjustments or a different typeface.
3. Set the left and right margins according to the estimated letter length: about 1″ for long letters (300 words or more, or at least two pages), about 1½″ for medium-length ones (about 100–300 words), and about 2″ for short ones (100 words or less). Some offices use a standard 6″ typing line (i.e., 1¼″ left and right margins) for all letters on full-size stationery, regardless of length, because it eliminates the need to reset margins.
4. Remember that the closing parts of a letter take 10-12 lines (2″) or more and that the bottom margin should be at least six lines (1″).
5. Single-space within paragraphs; double-space between paragraphs. Very short letters (up to three sentences) may be double-spaced throughout.
6. Carry over at least three lines of the message to any continuation sheet.

Short letters may be typed or printed on half-sheets, on Executive-size stationery, or on full-size stationery with wide margins. When typing very short letters on full-size stationery consider the following formatting possibilities:

1. Use the standard 1¼″ left/right margins but increase the space between the date and the inside address, between the complimentary close and the signature, and between the signature and the transcriber's initials or enclosure notations.
2. Use the standard left/right margins but double-space. Double-spacing should be used only in very short letters (about six lines or less, or up to three sentences). If a double-spaced letter contains more than one paragraph, indent the paragraph openings.
3. Use wider margins and/or a combination of points 1 and 2 above.

Letterhead Design

Letterhead designs vary. Some letterheads are confined to the center of the page, others extend across the top from the left to the right margin, and still others are positioned to the right or left of center. Sometimes a firm's name (or a corporate name and logo) appear at the top of the page and its address and other data at the bottom.

Regardless of layout and design, a typical letterhead contains some or all of the following elements, including at least items 1, 2, 5, and 6.

1. Full name of the firm or organization (and logo, if a corporate entity)
2. Street address
3. Suite, room, or building number
4. Post-office box number
5. City, state, and zip code
6. Telephone and fax numbers
7. Other data (such as branch offices, names of partners and associates, states admitted in, or services offered)

The names of particular departments, practice areas, or divisions may be printed on the letterhead of extremely large or diversified firms or organizations. Elaborate letterhead layouts require careful letter planning to avoid an unbalanced look. For example, a letterhead with a long list of names on the left side might be best balanced by use of the Modified Block format, where the date, reference numbers, and signature appear on the right side of the page.

High corporate officers frequently use a personalized or executive letterhead. Here the standard letterhead design is supplemented with the name of the office (such as "Office of the President") or with the full name and business title of the officer (such as "John M. Dennehy, Jr., Chief Counsel") printed or engraved in small letters one or two lines beneath the letterhead at or near the left margin. The officer's title may appear on the same line as his or her name if space permits and if both name and title are short, or it may be blocked directly below the name. For executive stationery, the letterhead is often not printed but instead engraved on a better grade of paper than that of the standard stationery. Executive stationery is also smaller than the standard, as shown in the table on page 156. Envelopes should match the paper and should be printed with the executive's name and return address.

Standard Letter Formats

The choice of letter format, like the choice of letterhead design, is usually determined by the firm. However, it is important to be familiar with the various formats so that you can apply them when necessary to particular types of letters and do so consistently and accurately. The three most common letter formats used by law offices are the *Full Block* (also called *Block*), the *Modified Block,* and the *Semiblock* (also called *Modified Semiblock*) formats. Also used are the *Simplified* letter, the *Official* letter, and the *Half-sheet*. All of these formats are described and illustrated below.

The various elements, or parts, of a standard business letter are shown in Figure 7.1. Those elements shown (see labels) are common to most business

Fig. 7.1   The Parts of a Business Letter

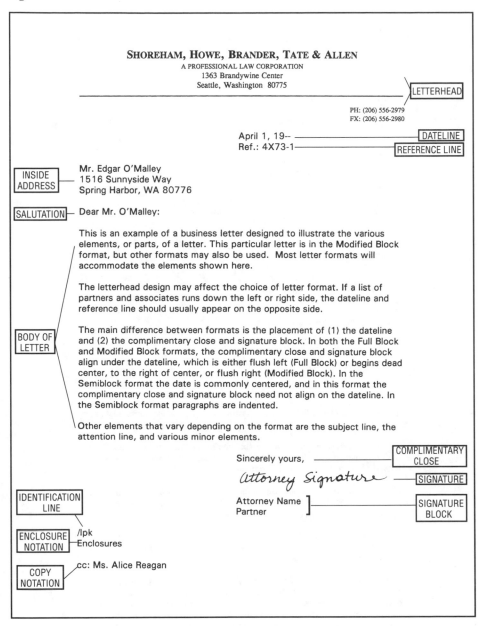

letters, but, as explained in the sections that follow, some may or may not be included, depending on the letter format used and the nature of the letter itself. For more on the individual elements, including some that are not shown here, see the explanations below and the section "Letter Elements and Styling" beginning on p. 169.

Many word-processing programs offer various letter templates that can be used to format or even compose standard business letters, but before using such programs make sure that their substance and style are appropriate to your office and that true time savings can be realized; otherwise it may be better to simply compose your own letters individually according to the situation.

Fig. 7.2   The Full Block Letter

NEWMAN, LAWTON & SHANE
A PROFESSIONAL CORPORATION
632 RIORDAN BOULEVARD
PROVIDENCE, RHODE ISLAND 10623
TELEPHONE (401) 636-2190
TELEFAX (401) 636-2110

January 1, 19--
X-123-4

Consumer Relations Department
LKJ Corporation
1234 Thomas Boulevard
Warwick, RI 10655

Attention Mr. James Green

Ladies and Gentlemen:

SUBJECT: FULL BLOCK LETTER

This is a facsimile of the Full Block letter, all of whose elements begin flush left.

The dateline may be typed two to six lines below the last letterhead line; here it is placed three lines below the letterhead. The reference line, if any, is typed immediately below the dateline.

Placement of the inside address varies according to letter length; here it is typed two lines below the reference line. An attention line, if required, is typed two lines below the last inside-address line.

The salutation is typed two lines below the attention line, or two to four lines below the last inside-address line. An optional subject line may be typed two lines below the salutation.

The message begins two lines below the salutation, or two lines below the subject line if there is one. The message is single-spaced with a blank line between paragraphs. At least three message lines must be carried over to a continuation sheet; the complimentary close and signature block should never stand alone on such a sheet. The last word on a sheet should not

The Full Block Letter

Letters using the Full Block format (see Fig. 7.2) exhibit the following characteristics:

1. All elements aligned flush left.
2. No indentations (with the exception of tables and displayed quotations).

Fig. 7.2   The Full Block Letter (continued)

Consumer Relations Department
LKJ Corporation
January 1, 19--
X-123-4
Page 2

be divided. The continuation-sheet heading is typed about one inch from the top edge of the page. Any reference line from the first sheet must be repeated in the continuation-sheet headings. The message continues four lines below the last line of the heading.

The complimentary close is typed two lines below the last message line and may be followed by the optional firm name in all-capitals. At least four blank lines are allowed for the written signature, followed by the writer's typed name. The writer's title and/or department may be included in the typed signature block if they do not appear in the printed letterhead.

Initials identifying the typist are typed two lines below the last signature-block line. (The author's initials usually do not appear in the Full Block letter.) Any enclosure notation is typed immediately below the identification initials. The courtesy-copy notation, if needed, is placed one or two lines below any other notation, depending on available space.

Sincerely yours,

NEWMAN, LAWTON & SHANE, P.C.

attorney Signature
Attorney Name

gbb
Enclosures (2)

cc: Marlene T. Hansen, Esq.

The Modified Block Letter

Letters using the Modified Block format (see Fig. 7.3) exhibit the following characteristics:

1. Dateline, complimentary close, and signature block aligned ("blocked") either (a) at dead center, (b) to the right of center, or (c) with the longest line

Fig. 7.3   The Modified Block Letter

COURTLAND & CARRERA, P.L.C.
8777 BERGLUND AVENUE
SUITE 200
SACRAMENTO, CALIFORNIA 97654
(916) 432-9000
FAX 432-9800

January 1, 19--

REGISTERED MAIL
PERSONAL

Mr. William B. Gerard, III
Treasurer
XYZ Corporation
1234 Langley Boulevard
Boyleston, CA 97735

Dear Mr. Gerard:

RE Modified Block Letter

This is a facsimile of the Modified Block letter. It differs from the Full Block letter chiefly in the placement of its dateline, complimentary close, and signature block, all of which are aligned and positioned either (1) at center, (2) toward the right margin, or (3) at the right margin.

While the dateline may be positioned from two to six lines below the last line of the letterhead, its standard position is three lines below the letterhead. In this facsimile, the dateline begins at dead center. If a reference line is required, it is blocked on the line above or below the date.

Special mailing notations and on-arrival notations such as the two shown above are all-capitalized and aligned flush left about two lines below the dateline.

The inside address begins about four lines below the dateline except where there are special notations, in which case it begins two lines below the last notation. This spacing can be expanded or contracted according to the letter length. The inside address, the salutation, and all paragraphs of the message are aligned flush left. The salutation is typed two to four lines below the last line of the inside address. A subject line, if used, is typed two lines below the salutation in capital letters and is either blocked flush left or, as shown here, centered on the page.

The message begins two lines below the salutation or the subject line. The message is single-spaced within each paragraph and double-spaced between paragraphs; however, in very short letters, the paragraphs may be double-spaced within each paragraph and triple-spaced between paragraphs.

Continuation sheets should contain at least three message lines. The last word on a sheet should not be divided. The continuation-sheet heading may be blocked flush left

flush right). All other elements (with the exceptions noted below) positioned flush left.

2. No paragraph indentations.
3. Attention line (if used) usually flush left, but sometimes centered.
4. Subject line (if used) usually flush left, but sometimes centered.

Fig. 7.3   The Modified Block Letter (continued)

Mr. Gerard   -2-   January 1, 19--

as in the Full Block letter or laid out across the top of the page as here. It is positioned about one inch from the top edge of the sheet, and the message is continued four lines beneath it.

The complimentary close is typed two lines below the last line of the message and is aligned vertically with the dateline--in this case, beginning dead center.

The signature line is typed at least four lines below the complimentary close. The writer's title and department name may be included if they do not already appear in the printed letterhead. All elements of the signature block align with each other and with the complimentary close and dateline.

Identification initials are usually only those of the secretary, providing that the writer and the signer are the same person. These initials appear two lines below the signature block. Any enclosure notation is typed on the line below the initials, and any courtesy-copy notation appears one or two lines below any other notations, depending on space available.

Sincerely yours,

Attorney Signature

Attorney Name
Attorney Title

gbb
Enclosures (5)

cc Ms. Santucci
     Dr. Franklin

The Semiblock Letter

Letters using the Semiblock format (see Fig. 7.4) exhibit the following characteristics:

    1. Dateline commonly (a) centered, less commonly (b) beginning dead center, (c) beginning to the right of center, or (d) flush right; complimentary close and signature block need not be aligned with the date, but are themselves

Fig. 7.4   The Semiblock Letter

WALTON, SHINER, LaFORGE, ARDEN & PALIN
22 CARMELINA DRIVE
SAVANNAH, GEORGIA 33210

A PROFESSIONAL LAW CORPORATION
PHONE (912) 775-8723
FAX (912) 775-8620

January 1, 19--

Ms. Carol D. Felkins
Sales Manager
Radin Company
234 Sundry Boulevard
Millborough, GA 33215

Dear Ms. Felkins:

    SEMIBLOCK LETTER

    This is a facsimile of the Semiblock letter. In this style, the dateline is commonly centered or begins at dead center, slightly to the right of center, or flush right. The inside address and salutation are aligned flush left, while the paragraph openings are indented. The complimentary close and signature block need not be aligned under the date. Identification initials, enclosure notations, and courtesy-copy notations are aligned flush left.

    A reference line would be blocked on the line above or below the date. Any special mailing notation or on-arrival notation would be typed flush left about two lines below the dateline and two lines above the inside address. An attention line, if required, is usually aligned flush left, two lines below the inside address; it may also be centered. The subject line, if any, is typed two lines below the salutation and usually centered on the page but may also be indented to match paragraph indentations, as shown here.

    The text is single-spaced within paragraphs and double-spaced between paragraphs unless the letter is extremely short, in which case it may be double-spaced throughout.

    Continuation sheets should contain at least three message lines, and the last word on a sheet should never be divided. The heading for a

usually blocked and begin at or to the right of center or with the longest line flush right.

2. Paragraphs indented five to ten spaces.

3. Attention line (if used) usually flush left, but sometimes centered.

4. Subject line (if used) usually centered, but sometimes indented to match paragraph indentations.

Fig. 7.4   The Semiblock Letter (continued)

Ms. Felkins   -2-   January 1, 19--

continuation sheet begins at least one inch from the top edge of the page and follows the format shown in this letter.

The complimentary close is typed two lines below the last line of the message. The signature line, four lines below the complimentary close, is aligned with it if possible. If the name or title will be long, the complimentary close should begin at dead center or about five spaces to the right of center to ensure enough room for the signature block.

Yours,

Attorney Signature

Attorney Name

gbb

Enclosures: 2

cc: Dr. Edgar Dinnerston
     Crane Engineering Associates
     91011 Jones Street
     Savannah, GA 33289

A postscript, if needed, is typically positioned two to four lines below the last notation. In the Semiblock letter, the first line is indented like the message paragraphs. It is not necessary to head the postscript with the abbreviation *P.S.* The postscript should be initialed by the writer.

a.S.

The Simplified Letter

Letters using the Simplified format (see Fig. 7.5) exhibit the following characteristics:

1. All elements aligned flush left; no indentations (with the exception of displayed quotations and unnumbered lists).

Fig. 7.5   The Simplified Letter

GLADWIN & THOMPSON, P.C.
577 FULTON PARK ROAD
KANSAS CITY, MISSOURI 44370
PHONE (816) 655-9103
FAX (816) 654-4432

January 1, 19--

Mr. George I. Needham
Director of Marketing
TLC Corporation
1234 Exeter Boulevard
Kansas City, MO 44371

SIMPLIFIED LETTER

Mr. Needham, this is the Simplified letter, which is used mostly for general business applications such as mass mailings and relatively impersonal form letters. Its main features--block format, fewer internal parts, and the absence of punctuation in the heading and closing--reduce the number of keystrokes and formatting adjustments you must make, thus saving time and decreasing the possibility of error.

The dateline is typed four to six lines below the last letterhead line, so that the inside address, also flush left, about three lines below the dateline, can be seen through a window envelope when the letter is folded. The official Postal Service state abbreviation should be used, followed by one space and the zip code.

The traditional salutation has been replaced by an all-capitalized subject line (without the heading SUBJECT) typed flush left, three lines beneath the inside address.

The message begins three lines below the subject line. The first sentence includes a greeting to the reader by name, as shown above. The last paragraph should repeat the reader's name. All paragraphs are blocked flush left, single-spaced internally, with a blank line between paragraphs. Tables and numbered lists are also blocked flush left and set off from the rest of the message

---

2. Salutation replaced by the subject line (all-capitalized, unpunctuated).
3. Addressee's name in the first sentence of the message.
4. No complimentary close.
5. Typed signature all-capitalized and followed on the same line by the writer's title (if used).

Fig. 7.5   The Simplified Letter (continued)

Mr. Needham
Page 2
January 1, 19--

by blank lines at top and bottom. Long quotations and unnumbered lists should be indented five to ten spaces from the left and right margins and similarly set off from the rest of the message by blank lines at top and bottom.

If a continuation sheet is required, at least three message lines must be carried over. Continuation-sheet format and margins must match those of the first sheet. At least six blank lines are left from the top edge of the page to the first line of the heading, which is blocked flush left, single-spaced internally, and typically composed of the addressee's courtesy title and last name, the page number, and the date. The rest of the message begins four lines beneath the last heading line.

There is no complimentary close in the Simplified letter, although a warm closing sentence may end the message. The writer's name (and title if needed) is typed flush left all in capitals at least five lines below the last message line. Some companies use a spaced hyphen between the writer's surname and professional title; others prefer a comma instead. The writer's department name may be typed flush left all in capitals one line below the signature line.

The identification initials, flush left and two lines below the signature block, are the typist's initials only. An enclosure notation may be typed on the next line below. Courtesy-copy notation may be typed one or two lines below the last notation, depending on available space. If, Mr. Neeedham, there is no enclosure line, the courtesy-copy notation is typed two lines below the last line above.

Writer's Signature
NAME - BUSINESS TITLE

gbb
Enclosures (2)

cc: Alice L. Barnes

The Official Letter

Letters using the Official format (see Fig. 7.6) exhibit the following characteristics:

1. Written on personalized Executive (7½″ × 10½″) letterhead.
2. Inside address below the signature.

Fig. 7.6   The Official Letter

UREY, BEEL & STANLEY

LAW ASSOCIATES
119 SCOTT CIRCLE
MILWAUKEE, WISCONSIN 64981

TELEPHONE (414) 342-1171
TELEFAX (414) 342-1185

Officer's Name
Officer's Title

January 1, 19--

Dear Ms. Washington:

This is a facsimile of the Official letter format, often used by an officer of the firm or corporate executive for personal correspondence written on his or her own personalized company stationery. The paper size is Executive or Monarch.

The Official letter is characterized by the page placement of the inside address: It is typed flush left, two to five lines below the signature block or the written signature. Paragraphs may be either indented or blocked.

A typed signature block is not needed on personalized Executive or Monarch stationery. However, if the writer's signature either is difficult to decipher or might be unfamiliar to the addressee, it may be typed four lines below the complimentary close.

The secretary's initials, if included, are typed two lines below the inside address. Any enclosure notation appears two lines below the initials, or two lines below the inside address, also flush left.

Sincerely,

Officer's Signature

Ms. Mary Washington
490 Jay Street
Abbeyville, WI 64921

The Half-Sheet

Letters written on half-sheet (5½″ × 8½″) stationery exhibit the following characteristics (see Fig. 7.7):

1. Written on half-sheet paper.
2. Full Block, Modified Block, or Semiblock format.

Fig. 7.7   The Half-sheet

Pfizer & Barbeau
Attorneys at Law

January 1, 19--

Mr. Theodore R. Manfred
235 Plimsoul Place
Sheldrake, AL 55321

Dear Ted:

This is a facsimile of the half-sheet, which is
used for the briefest of notes-- those containing one
or two sentences or two very short paragraphs.

The Full Block, Modified Block, or Semiblock
format may be used.

Sincerely yours,

Attorney Signature

gbb

Letter Elements and Styling

The various elements of a business letter are listed below in order and described in the sections that follow.

Dateline	Salutation	Identification initials
Reference line	Subject line	Enclosure notation
Special mailing notations	Message	Copy notation
On-arrival notations	Continuation sheets	Postscript
Inside address	Complimentary close	Path name
Attention line	Signature block	

Many firms establish standard letter formats and stylings in order to save time, and these standards should always be followed. However, certain applications of common letter elements will still require an individual decision by the secretary.

Dateline

The dateline may be typed two to six lines below the printed letterhead; three lines below is recommended as a standard for most letters.

The dateline consists of the month, the day, and the year (January 1, 19—). Ordinals (1st, 2d, 24th, etc.) should not be used, and the months should not be represented with abbreviations or numerals. The dateline should never overrun the margin.

The dateline is commonly placed in one of five positions, depending on the letter format or the letterhead layout. The dateline is typed flush *left* in the Full Block and Simplified formats. It may be typed flush *right* or begin at dead center or about five spaces to the right of center in the Modified Block or Semiblock formats. In the Semiblock format it may also be centered.

Reference Line

A numerical reference line—showing the number of a file, correspondence, order, invoice, or policy—is included when the addressee has specifically requested that correspondence on a subject contain such a line, or when it is needed for your own filing. Most offices require that it be vertically aligned with (i.e., blocked on) the date and typed one line directly above or below the date line, though it can also be positioned elsewhere (such as centered) to call attention to it. Some firms use the abbreviation *Ref* (or *Ref.*) and a colon preceding the reference number. (See also "Subject Line," pp. 174–75).

Reference line blocked left	*Reference line blocked right*
January 1, 19—	January 1, 19—
X-123-4	Ref: X-123-4
or	*or*
X-123-4	Ref: X-123-4
January 1, 19—	January 1, 19—

A reference line on the first sheet must be carried over to the continuation sheets. The style should match the style used on the first page. For example, if the reference line appears on a line below the date on the first sheet, it should be typed there on the continuation sheet. The following example illustrates a continuation-sheet reference line as used in the Simplified or Full Block format.

Mr. Carlton B. Jones
January 1, 19—
X-123-4
Page 2

The next example illustrates the positioning of a reference line on the continuation sheet of a Modified Block or Semiblock letter. (See also "Continuation Sheets," p. 176.)

Mr. Carlton B. Jones   -2-   January 1, 19—
                                            Ref: X-123-4

Special Mailing Notations

If a letter is to be sent by any method other than regular mail, that fact may be indicated on the letter itself as well as on the envelope (see page 184 for details on envelope style). The all-capitalized special mailing notation, such as CERTIFIED MAIL, SPECIAL DELIVERY, or AIRMAIL (for foreign mail only), is always aligned flush left about four lines below the dateline, and about two lines above the inside address. Some organizations prefer that these notations appear on all copies, others prefer that they be typed only on the original, and many omit them altogether.

Vertical spacing (such as between the dateline and the special mailing notation) may vary with letter length, more space being left for short or medium-length letters.

On-Arrival Notations

The on-arrival notations that may be included on the letter itself are PERSONAL and CONFIDENTIAL. The first indicates that the letter may be opened and read only by its addressee; the second indicates that the letter may also be opened and read by any other persons authorized to view such material. These all-capitalized notations are usually positioned four lines below the dateline and usually two but not more than four lines above the inside address. They are blocked flush left in all letter styles. If there is a special mailing notation, the on-arrival notation is blocked on the line beneath it.

If either PERSONAL or CONFIDENTIAL appears on the letter, it must also appear on the envelope (see page 184 for envelope style).

Inside Address

An inside address typically includes the following elements:

1. Addressee's courtesy title and full name
2. Addressee's business title, if required
3. Full name of addressee's business affiliation
4. Full address

If the letter is addressed to an organization in general but to the attention of a particular individual, the inside address typically includes the following elements:

1. Full name of the organization
2. Department name, if required
3. Full address

(See also "Attention Line," below)

The inside address is placed two to eight lines below the date. The inside address in the Simplified letter is typed three lines below the date. The placement of the inside address in relation to the date may vary according to letter length or organization policy. The inside address is blocked flush left and is single-spaced.

A courtesy title (such as *Mr., Ms., Dr.,* or *The Honorable*) precedes the addressee's full name, even if a business or professional title (such as *Treasurer* or *Chief of Staff*) follows the surname. No courtesy title, however, should ever precede the name when *Esquire* or an abbreviation for a degree follows the name. (See also "Forms of Address," beginning on p. 186.)

Before typing the addressee's name, refer to the signature block of previous correspondence from that person to confirm its exact spelling and style. This may also be obtained from printed executive letterhead. A business or professional title, if included, should also match the title used in previous correspondence or in official literature (such as an annual report or a business directory). If an individual holds more than one office (such as Vice President and General Manager) within an organization, the title shown in the signature block of previous correspondence should be copied, or the title of the individual's highest office (in this case, Vice President) may be selected. Business and professional titles should not be abbreviated. If a title is so long that it might overrun the center of the page, it may be typed on two lines with the second line indented two spaces:

> Mr. John P. Hemphill, Jr.
> Vice President and Director
>   of Research and Development

Special attention should be paid to the spelling, punctuation, and official abbreviations of company names. Note, for example, whether an ampersand (&) is used for the word *and*, whether series of names are separated by commas, and whether the word *Company* is spelled in full or abbreviated.

The addressee's title may be placed on the same line as the name. Alternatively, it may be put on the second line either by itself or followed by the name of the organization. The following are acceptable inside-address styles for business and professional titles:

> Mr. Arthur O. Brown
> General Counsel
> XYZ Corporation
> 1234 Peters Street
> Jonesville, ZZ 56789

> Dr. Joyce A. Cavitt, Dean
> School of Business and Finance
> Stateville University
> Stateville, ST 98765

> Anna B. Kim, Esquire
> Powell, Smith & Klein, P.C.
> 67 Green Street
> North Bend, XX 12345

> Mrs. Juanita Casares
> President, C & A Realty
> Johnson Beach, ZZ 56789

Street addresses should be typed in full and not abbreviated unless window envelopes are being used. Numerals are used for all building, house, apartment, room, and suite numbers except for *One*, which is written out.

> One Bayside Drive   6 Link Road   1436 Fremont Avenue

Numbered street names from *First* through *Twelfth* are usually written out; numerals are usually used for all numbered street names above *Twelfth*.

> 167 West Second Avenue   One East Ninth Street   19 South 22nd Street

An apartment, building, room, or suite number, if required, follows the street address on the same line.

> 62 Park Towers, Suite 9   Rosemont Plaza Apartments, Apt. 117

Note that the word *Number,* and its abbreviation *No.,* and the symbol # are not used after the words *Suite, Apartment,* or *Building,* which themselves may nevertheless be abbreviated.

Names of cities (except those including the word *Saint,* such as *St. Louis* or *St. Paul*) should be typed out in full (e.g., *Fort Wayne, Mount Prospect*). The name of the city is followed by a comma, the name of the state, and the zip code. Names of states (not including the District of Columbia, which is always written *DC* or *D.C.*) may or may not be abbreviated. If a window envelope is being used, the official Postal Service State abbreviation, followed by one space and the zip code, must be used. Most firms now use the official abbreviations on all inside addresses. See page 183 for a list of these abbreviations.

An inside address should comprise no more than six lines. No line should overrun the center of the page; lengthy organization names, like lengthy business titles, may be carried over to a second line and indented two spaces.

Sometimes a single letter will have to be sent to two persons at different addresses, both of whom should receive an original. In these cases, the inside address should consist of two complete names and addresses separately by a line of space. The names should be in alphabetical order unless one person is obviously more important than the other. An alternative method is to place the inside addresses side by side, beginning on the same line. For salutations used in letters to multiple addressees, see pages 199–205.

Attention Line

If the writer wishes to address a letter to an organization in general but bring it to the attention of a particular individual, an attention line may be typed two lines below the last line of the inside address and two lines above the salutation if there is one. The attention line is usually blocked flush with the left margin; however, some organizations prefer that it be centered on the page. This placement is acceptable in all letters except the Simplified and the Full Block, in which the attention line must be typed flush left. This line should be neither underlined nor entirely capitalized. The word *Attention* is not abbreviated. A colon after the word *Attention* is optional unless the Simplified format is being used, in which case the colon should be omitted:

> Attention Mr. James Chang
> Attention: Mr. James Chang

Even though the attention line routes the letter to a particular person, such a letter is still considered to be written to the organization, so a collective-noun salutation (e.g., Ladies and Gentlemen) should be used.

Salutation

The salutation—used with all letter styles except the Simplified—is typed flush left two lines beneath the inside address or the attention line, if any. Additional space may be added after the inside address of a short letter that is to be enclosed in a window envelope. The salutation is followed by a colon; only in informal personal correspondence is it followed by a comma.

One of the most frequently asked questions today is what salutation to use when addressing an organization, or when addressing a person whose name and gender are unknown to the letter-writer. The traditional "Dear Sir" (when addressing a particular individual) and "Gentlemen" (when addressing a group or organization) have been largely replaced by "Dear Sir or Madam" and "Ladies and Gentlemen," respectively.

"To whom it may concern" is very impersonal and is usually used only when the writer is unfamiliar with both the person and the organization that is being addressed, such as when one is addressing a letter of recommendation.

A different type of salutation now being used to solve the problem of addressing a company or a company officer whose name and sex are unknown simply addresses the company ("Dear XYZ Company") or the title or department of the intended recipient ("Dear Personnel Supervisor," "Dear Personnel Department," "Dear XYZ Engineers"). The use of this type of salutation has increased markedly in recent years.

Occasionally a letter-writer is faced with an addressee's name that gives no clue as to the addressee's sex. Traditionally in these uncertain cases, convention has required the writer to use the masculine courtesy title in the salutation; for example, "Dear Mr. Lee Schmidtke," "Dear Mr. T. A. Gagnon." However, most writers now prefer to express their uncertainty by using such forms as "Dear Mr. or Ms. Schmidtke" or "Dear T. A. Gagnon."

The most convenient way of avoiding the problem of gender is to use the Simplified letter, which eliminates the salutation altogether.

The salutation for a married couple may be written in one of the following ways:

> Dear Mr. and Mrs. Hathaway
> Dear Dr. and Mrs. Simpson
> Dear Dr. and Mr. Singh

For more information about choosing appropriate salutations, including salutations for two or more persons and for people with specialized titles, see "Forms of Address" beginning on page 186.

Subject Line

A subject line gives the gist of a letter. It must be succinct and should not require more than one line. The subject line serves as an immediate point of reference for the reader as well as a convenient filing aid for the secretaries at both ends of the correspondence.

In the Simplified letter, which does not include a salutation, the subject line (an essential element) is positioned flush left, three lines below the last line of the inside address. It may be entirely capitalized and not underlined, or the main words may begin with capital letters and every word be underlined.

If a subject line is included in a letter with a salutation, it is frequently positioned flush left, two lines beneath the salutation, and may be entirely capitalized. In the Modified Block and Semiblock formats, the subject line may be centered or even indented to match the indention of the paragraphs. A growing number of law offices prefer to position the subject line two lines above the salutation rather than below it.

The subject line may be entirely capitalized or capitalized headline-style; that is, the initial letter of the first word and the initial letter of all other words except coordinating conjunctions, articles, and short prepositions are capitalized. The words *Subject Reference, Re,* and *In re* are sometimes also used to introduce the line.

> SUBJECT: PROPOSED SALE OF ROE PROPERTY
> Subject: Proposed Sale of Roe Property

Reference: Proposed Sale of Roe Property
Re: Proposed Sale of Roe Property
In re: Proposed Sale of Roe Property

The subject line should not be confused with the reference line (see page 170), even though the subject line often begins with the word *Reference*. They differ not only in position but also in appearance and purpose: the reference line indicates a numerical classification, whereas the subject line identifies the content of the letter.

Message

The body of the letter—the message—should begin two lines below either the salutation or the subject line, if the latter follows the salutation. In the Simplified letter, however, the message is typed three lines below the subject line.

Paragraphs are single-spaced internally. Double-spacing is used to separate paragraphs. If a letter is extremely brief, it may be double-spaced throughout, with indented paragraphs, or triple-spaced between paragraphs.

The first lines of indented paragraphs (as in the Semiblock letter) should begin five or 10 spaces (½"– 1") from the left margin; five spaces (½") is most common. (On a word processor you can set the automatic tab stop to any measure you want.)

Long quotations should be indented and blocked five to 10 spaces (½"–1") from the left and right margins, singled-spaced, with a blank line above and below. Long enumerations should also be indented and set off with a blank line above and below. Enumerations with items requiring more than one line apiece may require single-spacing within each item and double-spacing between items. Tables should be centered on the page. See Fig. 7.8.

Fig. 7.8   Page Placement of Items Inset within the Message

Page Placement of a Long Quotation   **Page Placement of an Enumeration**

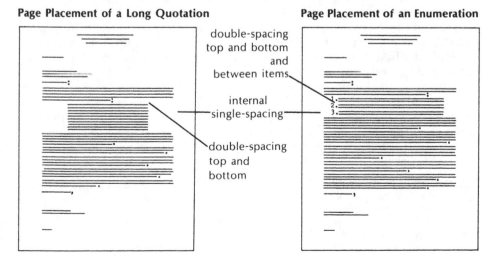

Rules for end-of-line division in business letters include the following:

1. Do not divide a word at the end of the first line.
2. Do not divide a word if it will leave part of the word by itself as the last line of a paragraph.
3. Do not divide a person's name from his or her courtesy title.

Continuation Sheets

If a letter is long enough to require a continuation sheet or sheets, at least three message lines must be carried over to the next page. The complimentary close and/or typed signature block should never stand alone on a continuation sheet. The last word on a page should not be divided.

At least a 1″ margin should be left at the top of the continuation sheet, followed by the continuation-sheet heading. The two most common types of continuation-sheet heading are illustrated in Figs. 7.2 and 7.3. The format shown in Fig. 7.2 is used with the Simplified and Full Block letter. The flush-left heading begins with the addressee's courtesy title and full name, continues on the next line with the date, repeats the reference number (if used) on the third line, and ends with the page number. Some companies prefer that the page number appear as the first line of the continuation-sheet heading, especially if a reference number is not used.

Another style is illustrated in Fig. 7.3. Here the heading extends across the page, 1″ from the top edge of the sheet. The addressee's full name is typed flush left, the page number is centered and enclosed with spaced hyphens, and the date is aligned flush right—all on the same line; if a reference line is used, it is typed flush right one line below the date. This format is often used with the Modified Block and the Semiblock letters.

Complimentary Close

A complimentary close is used with all letter formats except the Simplified letter. It is typed two lines below the last line of the message. Its horizontal placement depends on the letter format being used. In the Full Block letter, the complimentary close is typed flush left (see Fig. 7.2). In the Modified Block and the Semiblock letters, it may be aligned under the dateline (e.g., about five spaces to the right of center, or flush right) or under some particular part of the printed letterhead. It should never overrun the right margin. (See Figs. 7.3 and 7.4.)

Only the first word of the complimentary close is capitalized. The complimentary close ends with a comma.

Always use the complimentary close that is dictated, because the writer may have a special reason for the choice of phrasing. If the writer does not specify a particular closing, you should select the one that best reflects the general tone of the letter and the state of the writer-reader relationship. The table below lists the most commonly used complimentary closes.

Complimentary Closes for Business Correspondence

General Tone and Degree of Formality	Complimentary Close
Highly Formal (used in diplomatic, governmental, or ecclesiastical correspondence)	Respectfully yours Respectfully Very respectfully

General Tone and Degree of Formality	Complimentary Close
Polite, Formal (used in general correspondence)	Very truly yours Yours very truly Yours truly
Less Formal (used in general correspondence)	Very sincerely Very sincerely yours Sincerely yours Yours sincerely Sincerely Yours Cordially Cordially yours
Informal, Friendly (used when writer and reader are on a first-name basis)	As ever Best wishes Best regards Kindest regards Warmest personal regards Regards

Complimentary closes on letters written over a period of time to a particular person may become gradually more informal and friendly; once an informal pattern has been established, they should not revert to a more formal style.

Signature Block

The first line of the signature block indicates responsibility for the letter. Either the name of the writer or the name of the firm may appear there. In the former case, the writer's name is typed at least four lines below the complimentary close; in the latter, the firms name is typed all in capital letters two lines below the complimentary close and the writer's name at least four lines below the firm's name (See Fig. 7.9).

Note (Fig. 7.9) that some attorneys ask that the heading *By* (or *By:* or *by*) be added to the signature line when the firm name is used, in order to emphasize that they are writing as a representative of the firm. Attorneys may also wish to sign correspondence manually using the firm's name, especially when the letters give opinions about legal matters.

In the Simplified letter, the name of the writer is typed entirely in capitals, flush left, at least five lines below the last line of the message. If the writer's professional title is not included in the printed letterhead, it may be typed on the same line as the name entirely in capitals and separated from the last element of the name by a spaced hyphen. Some organizations prefer to use a comma in place of the hyphen. A combination of the two may be used if the title is complex.

JOHN P. HEWETT - CHIEF ADMINISTRATOR
JOHN P. HEWETT, CHIEF ADMINISTRATOR
JOHN P. HEWETT - CHIEF ADMINISTRATOR, FINANCIAL DIVISION
   or
JOHN P. HEWETT - CHIEF ADMINISTRATOR
FINANCIAL DIVISION

Fig. 7.9   Common Signature-block Styles

Sincerely yours,

Stanley R. Grudin

Stanley R. Grudin

Very truly yours,

HALLOWAY & GRUDIN

By: *Janice T. Jones*

Janice T. Jones
Associate Partner

Sincerely yours,

Stanley R. Grudin

STANLEY R. GRUDIN

Very truly yours,

Janice T. Jones

HALLOWAY & GRUDIN

In the Full Block letter, the signature block is aligned flush left. The first letter of each element of the writer's name and each major element of the writer's title and department name, if included, are capitalized. The title and department name may be omitted if they appear in the letterhead:

If title and dept. needed for identification:	John D. Russell, Director Corporate Litigation Division
If dept. appears on letterhead:	John D. Russell Director
If both title and dept. appear on letterhead:	John D. Russell

In the Modified Block and the Semiblock letters, the signature block begins with the name of the writer typed at least four lines below the complimentary close. The signature block is aligned (blocked) directly below the complimentary close; in the Semiblock letter, however, it may be centered under the complimentary close, particularly if it would otherwise overrun the right margin.

The name of the firm may be typed in capitals on the second line beneath the complimentary close, with the first letter of the firm's name aligned directly underneath and the writer's name typed in capitals and lowercase at least four lines below the firm's name. The writer's title, if needed, is typed in capitals and lowercase on the line below the signature line. If the company name is long enough to overrun the right margins, it may be centered beneath the complimentary close in the Semiblock letter.

A letter may occasionally be written and signed by two individuals. In these cases, it is generally best to place the names side by side, with the first name flush left in block formats or beginning left of center in other letter formats in

Fig. 7.10   Signature Block When Two People Sign a Letter

Very truly yours,

Barton K. Wheeler   *Marilyn S. Gomes*

Barton K. Wheeler   Marilyn S. Gomes
President   Treasurer

Fig. 7.11   Signature When Secretary Signs the Writer's Name

Barton K. Wheeler/as   *Barton K. Wheeler*
                                                            as

Fig. 7.12   Signature Block When Secretary Signs as a Representative

Sincerely yours,   Sincerely yours,

Paula K. Seymour   *James P. Kim*

Paula K. Seymour   James P. Kim
Secretary to Ms. Langley   Assistant to Senator Bales

order to leave enough room for two horizontally aligned signatures. (See Fig. 7.10.) If horizontal positioning is not feasible, the names may be placed one under the other.

If you sign a letter for the writer, the writer's name is followed by your initials immediately below and to the right of the surname, or centered under the full name. (See Fig. 7.11).

If you sign a letter in your own name for someone else, your name and title are typed in the signature block. (See Fig. 7.12).

Identification Initials

The initials of the typist and sometimes those of the writer are placed two lines below the signature block and are aligned flush left in all letter formats. Most offices formerly preferred that three capitalized initials be used for the writer's name and two lowercase initials be used for the typist's. Today, however, the writer's initials are usually omitted if the name is already typed in the signature block or if it appears in the printed letterhead. In many organizations the typist's initials appear only on office copies for record-keeping purposes, and the writer's initials are omitted unless another individual signs the letter. The following are the most common styles:

hol
hl
/hol
FCM/hol
FCM:hl
FCM:hol

Enclosure Notation

If a letter is to be accompanied by an enclosure or enclosures, a notation such as one of the following should be typed flush left one or two lines beneath the identification initials or, if there are no initials, one or two lines beneath the signature block. The unabbreviated form Enclosure is usually preferred.

Enclosure	Enclosures (3)
enc. *or* encl.	3 encs. *or* Enc. 3

If the enclosures are of special importance, they should be numerically listed and briefly described, with single-spacing between the items.

Enclosures: 1. Lease for signature (2 copies)
            2. Itemization of May 24 bill

The following type of notation then may be typed in the top right corner of each page of each of the enclosures:

Enclosure (1) to Johnson Associates letter No. 1-234-X, dated January 1, 19—, page 2 of 8

If the enclosure is bound, a single notation attached to its cover sheet will suffice.

When additional material is being mailed separately, a notation such as the following may be used:

Separate mailing: ZYX Corp. Annual

Copy Notation

Copies of letters and memos, traditionally called *carbon copies*, are now often called *courtesy copies* or simply *office copies*. In some offices, *c* for *copy* or *pc* for *photocopy* is used instead of the traditional *cc* for *carbon copy* or *courtesy copy*.

A copy notation showing the distribution of courtesy copies to other individuals should be aligned flush left and typed two lines below the signature block if there are no other notations or initials, or two lines below any other notations. If space is very tight, the courtesy-copy notation may appear on the line below any notations or initials.

cc	cc:
c	Copy to

Multiple recipients of copies should be listed alphabetically. Sometimes only their initials are shown.

cc: WPB
       TLC
       CNR

More often, the individual's names are shown and sometimes also their addresses, especially if the writer feels that such information can be useful to the addressee.

cc: William L. Ehrenkreutz, Esq.   cc Ms. Lee Jamieson
    45 Park Towers, Suite 1
    Smithville, ST 56789   Copy to Mr. Javier Linares

    Dr. Daniel I. Maginnis   Copies to Mr. Houghton
    1300 Dover Drive   Mr. Rhys
    Jonesville, ZZ 12345   Mr. Smythe

If the recipient of the copy is to receive an enclosure or enclosures as well, that individual's full name and address as well as a description of each enclosure and the total number of enclosed items should be shown in the carbon-copy notation.

cc: Ms. Barbara S. Lee (2 copies, Signed Agreement)
    123 Jones Street
    Smithville, ST 56789

    Mrs. Sara T. Torchinsky
    Mrs. Laura E. Yowell

If the first names or initials are given along with the last names, courtesy titles *(Mr., Mrs., Miss,* and *Ms.)* may be omitted.

cc: William L. Ehrenkreutz   cc: W. L. Ehrenkreutz
    Daniel I. Maginnis   D. I. Maginnis

Typists usually leave either one or two spaces between the cc: and the names that follow. If only one name follows the cc: and it is given in all initials, the space or spaces may be omitted.

cc: JBH

If the writer wishes that copies of the letter be distributed without the list of recipients being shown on the original, the blind-courtesy-copy notation *bcc* or *bcc:,* followed by an alphabetical list of the recipients' initials or names, may be typed on the copies only, either in the same page position as a regular copy notation or in the upper left corner.

Carbon or courtesy copies are not usually signed. The secretary may type the signature, preceded by the symbol /S/ or /s/, to indicate that the writer signed the original copy.

Postscript

A postscript is aligned flush left two to four lines below the last notation (depending on space available). If the paragraphs are blocked flush left, the postscript should also begin flush left; if the paragraphs are indented, the first line of the postscript should also be indented. All postscripts are single-spaced. The writer should initial a postscript. While it is not incorrect to head a postscript with the initials *P.S.* (for an initial postscript) or *P.P.S.* (for subsequent ones), these headings are redundant and can be omitted.

Path Name

Some firms include as the last element in business letters the *path name,* indicating the location of a letter on the secretary's computer or the firm's computer network. The path name is usually entered as a word-processing footer (end-of-document note) and appears in small lowercase type below the copy notation, postscript, or identification initials (whichever is last), usually positioned flush left.

Envelope Addresses

The following information may appear on any envelope regardless of its size. Items 1 and 2 are essential; items 3 and 4 are optional, depending on the requirements of the particular letter.

1. The addressee's full name and address, typed approximately in the vertical and horizontal center
2. The sender's name and address, printed or typed in the upper left corner
3. Special mailing notation or notations, typed below the stamp
4. On-arrival notation or notations, typed about nine lines below the top edge on the left side

The address block on a regular envelope should be no larger than $1\frac{1}{2}'' \times 3\frac{3}{4}''$. There should be $\frac{5}{8}''$ from the bottom line of the address block to the bottom edge of the envelope, which should be free of print. On regular envelopes, the address block usually begins about five spaces to the left of center. It should be single-spaced. Block style should be used. Unusual or italic typefaces should be avoided.

If a window envelope is being used, all address data must appear within the window space, with $\frac{1}{4}''$ margins between the address and the edges of the window.

Position of Elements

The elements of the address block should be styled and positioned as shown in the following examples. Though the initial examples below are shown in traditional capital-and-lowercase style, the U.S. Postal Service recommends an all-capitals style for any letters intended for automated processing (such as with mass mailings). Check with your local post office for details.

First line The addressee's courtesy title and full name are typed on the first line. If his or her business title is included in the inside address, it may be typed either on the first line of the address block or alone on the next line, depending on the length of title and name.

Mr. Lee O. Idlewild, President   Mr. Lee O. Idlewild
                                          President

If the addressee is an organization, its full name is typed on the first line. If a particular department is specified, its name is typed under the name of the organization.

>XYZ Corporation
>Sales Department

Next line(s)   The full street address should be typed out (although it is acceptable to abbreviate such designations as *Street, Avenue, Boulevard*). Type the room, suite, or apartment number immediately after the last element of the street address on the same line with it. A building name, if used, goes on a separate line above the street address.

A post-office box number, if used, is typed on the line immediately above the last line in order to assure delivery to the box rather than the street address. (The box number precedes the station name when a station name in included.) Both street address and post-office box number may be written in the address, but the letter will be delivered to the location specified on the next-to-last line.

Last line   The last line contains the city, state, and zip-code. Allow one space between the state abbreviation and the zip code, which should never be on a line by itself. The zip code is mandatory, as are the official Postal Service State abbreviations. See the table of abbreviations below.

Two-letter Abbreviations for States and U.S. Dependencies

Alabama	AL	Kentucky	KY	Ohio	OH
Alaska	AK	Louisiana	LA	Oklahoma	OK
Arizona	AZ	Maine	ME	Oregon	OR
Arkansas	AR	Maryland	MD	Pennsylvania	PA
California	CA	Massachusetts	MA	Puerto Rico	PR
Colorado	CO	Michigan	MI	Rhode Island	RI
Connecticut	CT	Minnesota	MN	South Carolina	SC
Delaware	DE	Mississippi	MS	South Dakota	SD
District of Columbia	DC	Missouri	MO	Tennessee	TN
Florida	FL	Montana	MT	Texas	TX
Georgia	GA	Nebraska	NE	Utah	UT
Guam	GU	Nevada	NV	Vermont	VT
Hawaii	HI	New Hampshire	NH	Virginia	VA
Idaho	ID	New Jersey	NJ	Virgin Islands	VI
Illinois	IL	New Mexico	NM	Washington	WA
Indiana	IN	New York	NY	West Virginia	WV
Iowa	IA	North Carolina	NC	Wisconsin	WI
Kansas	KS	North Dakota	ND	Wyoming	WY

When a post-office box number is part of an address, you can usually include the full zip + four code by simply adding the box number (or zeros and the box number) to the regular zip code.

>XYZ Corporation
>P. O. Box 600
>Smithville, ST 56788-0600

Fig. 7.13   Envelope Showing On-Arrival and Special Mailing Notations

```
Sarton, Small & Idres, P.C.
72 Grover Avenue
Bridgeport, CT 10246


CONFIDENTIAL                                              SPECIAL DELIVERY



                      Ms. Pamela F. Kerman
                      1716 E. South Street
                      Bridgeport, CT 10246
```

Other elements   The on-arrival notations PERSONAL and CONFIDENTIAL must be typed entirely in capital letters, about nine lines below the top left edge of the envelope. Any other on-arrival instructions, such as Hold for Arrival or Please Forward, may be typed in capitals and lowercase, underlined, about nine lines below the top left edge.

If an attention line is used in the letter itself, it too must appear on the envelope, as the third-to-last line in the address block.

XYZ Corporation
Sales Department
Attention Mr. E. R. Bailey
1234 Smith Boulevard
Smithville, ST 56789

A special mailing notation such as CERTIFIED, REGISTERED MAIL, or SPECIAL DELIVERY is typed entirely in capitals just below the stamp or about nine lines from the top right edge. It should not overrun a ½″ margin. (See Fig. 7.13.)

A printed return address may be supplemented by the name of the writer typed in above or below. The return address on a plain envelope should be typed at least two lines below the top edge of the envelope and ½″ from the left edge.

See Chapter 5 for a detailed treatment of mailing procedures.

Foreign Addresses

When typing a foreign address, refer to the return address on the envelope of previous correspondence for the correct ordering of the elements. The letterhead on previous correspondence may be checked if an envelope is not available. If neither is available, the address should be typed as it appears in the inside address of the dictated letter. The following guidelines may be of assistance:

1. All foreign addresses should be typed in English or in English characters. If an address must be in foreign characters (such as Russian), and English translation should be inserted between the lines in the address block.
2. Foreign courtesy titles may be substituted for the English, but they are not necessary.
3. The name of the country should be spelled out in capital letters by itself on the last line. Canadian addresses always carry the name CANADA after the name of the province.
4. When applicable, foreign postal-district numbers should be included. These are positioned either before or after the name of the city, never after the name of the country.

Canadian addresses should adhere to the form requested by the Canada Post for quickest delivery through its automated handling system. As shown in the following examples, the name of the city, fully capitalized, is followed by the name of the province, spelled out with initial capitals and lowercase letters on the same line. The Postal Code follows on a separate line. For mail originating in the United States, CANADA is added on a final line. Note that capitalization and punctuation differ slightly in French-language addresses.

Mr. F. F. MacManus	Les Entreprises Optima Ltée
Fitzgibbons and Brown	6789, rue Principale
678 Main Street	OTTAWA (Ontario)
HALIFAX, Nova Scotia	K1A 0B3
B3J 2N9	CANADA
CANADA	

The Canadian Postal Code consists always of letter-digit-letter (space) digit-letter-digit. Failure to include the correct code number may result in considerable delay in delivery. When space is limited, the Postal Code may be typed on the same line with the province, separated from it by at least two spaces.

OTTAWA, Ontario K1A 0B3

or

OTTAWA, ON K1A 0B3

The following two-letter provincial and territorial abbreviations may also be used when space is limited.

Two-letter Abbreviations for Canadian Provinces, Territories, and Islands

Alberta	AB	Newfoundland	NF	Quebec	PQ
British Columbia	BC	Northwest Territories	NT	Saskatchewan	SK
Labrador	LB	Nova Scotia	NS	Yukon Territory	YT
Manitoba	MB	Ontario	ON		
New Brunswick	NB	Prince Edward Island	PE		

Forms of Address

The following pages contain a chart of categorically grouped and alphabetically listed forms of address for individuals whose offices, ranks, or professions warrant special courtesy. (For information about choosing complimentary closes, see pages 176–77.) The main categories in the chart are listed below in the order of their appearance.

1. Government Officials—Federal
2. Government Officials—State
3. Government Officials—Local
4. Clerical and Religious Orders
5. Colleges and University Faculty and Officials
6. Diplomats and Consular Officers
7. Military Personnel
8. Miscellaneous Professional Titles
9. Multiple Addresses

A more detailed discussion of special titles and abbreviations (*Doctor, Esquire, Honorable,* etc.) begins on page 200. For the use of gender-neutral salutations, see pages 173–74.

When two or more styles are shown in the Forms of Address chart, the most formal appears first.

Approximately half of the entries are illustrated with a man's name and half with a woman's name. The female equivalent of *Sir* is *Madam* (or *Madame* when the addressee is foreign). The female equivalent of *Mr.* when it immediately precedes a name is *Ms.* (or *Mrs.* or *Miss* if either is known to be preferred by the addressee). The male equivalent of *Madam* standing alone is *Sir.* When *Madam* precedes another title, the male equivalent is *Mr.,* and vice versa. The male equivalent of *Ms.* is *Mr.* The terms *Her Excellency* and *His Excellency* are similarly equivalent.

Lack of space has made it necessary to exclude lower-ranking officials, such as city water commissioners. Addressing these minor officials should present no problem, however. The official's title should appear in the address only if the official *heads* an agency or department; otherwise, only the name of the agency or department is included. The salutation on letters to minor officials should consist simply of courtesy title + surname.

Mrs. Joan R. Zaricki, Chair Smithville School Board	Dear Mrs. Zaricki
Mr. James McPhee Smithville School Board	Dear Mr. McPhee

The substitution of a professional title for the courtesy title is correct only for high-ranking officials such as governors and judges, for military officers, and for certain police and fire officers.

Dear Governor Serafino
Dear Senator Scott
Dear Judge Dvorak
Dear Major Stearns
Dear Chief Rodriguez
Dear Sheriff Robbins *but also* Dear Mr. Robbins

Military officers retain their highest rank upon retirement and are addressed in the same way as active officers.

Inside-Address Style	*Salutation Style*

Government Officials—Federal

Attorney General
The Honorable Amelia R. Smith / Madam
The Attorney General / Dear Madam Attorney General

Cabinet officer (other than Attorney General)
The Honorable John R. Smith / Sir
Secretary of ——— / Dear Mr. Secretary
  or
The Secretary of ——— / (same)

Cabinet officer, former
The Honorable Amelia R. Smith / Dear Ms. Smith

Chairman of a (sub)committee, U.S. Congress (styles shown apply to both House of
  Representatives and Senate)
The Honorable John R. Smith / Sir
Chairman / Dear Mr. Chairman
Committee on ——— / Dear Senator Smith
United States Senate

Chief justice—see SUPREME COURT, FEDERAL; STATE

Commissioner
 if appointed
The Honorable Amelia R. Smith / Dear Madam Commissioner
Commissioner / Dear Ms. Smith
 if career
Ms. Amelia R. Smith / Dear Ms. Smith
Commissioner / Dear Commissioner Smith

Congressman—see REPRESENTATIVE, U.S. CONGRESS

Director (as of an independent federal agency)
The Honorable John R. Smith / Dear Mr. Smith
Director / Dear Director Smith
———Agency

District attorney
The Honorable Amelia R. Smith / Dear Ms. Smith
District Attorney

Federal judge
The Honorable John R. Smith / Sir
Judge of the United States District / Dear Judge Smith
  Court of the ——— District
  of ———

Justice—see SUPREME COURT, FEDERAL; STATE

Librarian of Congress
The Honorable Amelia R. Smith / Madam
Librarian of Congress / Dear Ms. Smith

Inside-Address Style	*Salutation Style*
Postmaster General	
The Honorable John R. Smith	Sir
The Postmaster General	Dear Mr. Postmaster General
President of the United States	
The President	Mr. President
	Dear Mr. President
President of the United States (former)	
The Honorable John R. Smith	Sir
	Dear Mr. Smith
President-elect of the United States	
The Honorable Amelia R. Smith	Dear Madam
President-elect of the United States	Dear Ms. Smith
Representative, U.S. Congress	
The Honorable Amelia R. Smith	Madam
United States House of Representatives	Dear Representative Smith
	Dear Ms. Smith
Representative, U.S. Congress (former)	
The Honorable John R. Smith	Dear Mr. Smith
Senator, U.S. Senate	
The Honorable Amelia R. Smith	Madam
United States Senate	Dear Senator Smith
Senator-elect	
The Honorable John R. Smith	Dear Mr. Smith
Senator-elect	
Senator (former)	
The Honorable Amelia R. Smith	Dear Senator Smith
Speaker, U.S. House of Representatives	
The Honorable Speaker of the House	Madam
of Representatives	
or	
The Honorable Amelia R. Smith	Madam
Speaker of the House of Representatives	Dear Madam Speaker
	Dear Ms. Smith
Speaker, U.S. House of Representatives (former)	
The Honorable Amelia R. Smith	Madam
	Dear Madam Speaker
	Dear Ms. Smith
Special assistant to the President of the United States	
Mr. John R. Smith	Dear Mr. Smith
Supreme Court, associate justice	
Mr. Justice Smith	Sir
The Supreme Court of the United States	Dear Mr. Justice
	Dear Justice Smith
Supreme Court, chief justice	
The Chief Justice of the United States	Sir
	Dear Mr. Chief Justice
or	
The Chief Justice	(same)

Inside-Address Style	*Salutation Style*
Supreme Court, retired Justice	
The Honorable Amelia R. Smith	Madam
	Dear Justice Smith
Territorial delegate	
The Honorable Amelia R. Smith	Dear Ms. Smith
Delegate of ———	
House of Representatives	
Undersecretary of a department	
The Honorable John R. Smith	Dear Mr. Smith
Undersecretary of ———	
Vice President of the United States	
The Vice President of the United States	Madam
United States Senate	Dear Madam Vice President
or	
The Honorable Amelia R. Smith	(same)
Vice President of the United States	

Government Officials—State

Assemblyman—see REPRESENTATIVE, STATE

Attorney general
The Honorable John R. Smith   Sir
Attorney General of the State of ———   Dear Mr. Attorney General

Clerk of a court
Amelia R. Smith, Esq.   Dear Ms. Smith
Clerk of the Court of ———

Delegate—See REPRESENTATIVE, STATE

Governor
The Honorable John R. Smith   Sir
Governor of ———   Dear Governor
          Dear Governor Smith

  or in some states
His Excellency, the Governor of ———   (same)

Governor (acting)
The Honorable Amelia R. Smith   Madam
Acting Governor of ———   Dear Ms. Smith

Governor-elect
The Honorable John R. Smith   Dear Mr. Smith
Governor-elect of ———

Governor (former)
The Honorable Amelia R. Smith   Dear Ms. Smith

Judge, state court
The Honorable John R. Smith   Sir
Judge of the ——— Court   Dear Judge Smith

Judge/justice, state supreme court—see SUPREME COURT, STATE

Inside-Address Style	*Salutation Style*
Lieutenant governor	
The Honorable Lieutenant Governor of ———	Madam
or	
The Honorable Amelia R. Smith	Madam
Lieutenant Governor of ———	Dear Ms. Smith
Representative, state (includes assemblyman, delegate)	
The Honorable John R. Smith	Sir
House of Representatives (State Assembly, House of Delegates, etc.)	Dear Mr. Smith
Secretary of state	
The Honorable Secretary of State of ———	Madam
or	
The Honorable Amelia R. Smith	Madam
Secretary of State of ———	Dear Madam Secretary
Senate, state, president of	
The Honorable John R. Smith	Sir
President of the Senate of the State of ———	Dear Mr. Smith
	Senator
Senator, state	
The Honorable Amelia R. Smith	Madam
The Senate of ———	Dear Senator Smith
Speaker, state assembly (house of delegates, house of representatives)	
The Honorable John R. Smith	Sir
Speaker of ———	Dear Mr. Smith
State's attorney	
The Honorable Amelia R. Smith	Dear Ms. Smith
(title)	
Supreme court, state, associate justice	
The Honorable Amelia R. Smith	Madam
Associate Justice of the Supreme Court of ———	Dear Justice Smith
Supreme court, state, chief justice	
The Honorable John R. Smith	Sir
Chief Justice of the Supreme Court of ———	Dear Mr. Chief Justice
Supreme court, state, presiding justice	
The Honorable Amelia R. Smith	Madam
Presiding Justice ——— Division Supreme Court of ———	Dear Madam Justice

Government Officials—Local

Alderman	
The Honorable John R. Smith	Dear Mr. Smith
	Dear Alderman Smith
or	
Alderman John R. Smith	(same)

Inside-Address Style	*Salutation Style*

City attorney (includes city counsel, corporation counsel)
The Honorable Amelia R. Smith — Dear Ms. Smith

Councilman—see ALDERMAN

County clerk
The Honorable John R. Smith — Dear Mr. Smith
Clerk of ——— County

County treasurer—see COUNTY CLERK

Judge
The Honorable Amelia R. Smith — Dear Judge Smith
Judge of the ——— Court of ———

Mayor
The Honorable John R. Smith — Sir
Mayor of ——— — Dear Mr. Mayor
Dear Mayor Smith

Selectman—see ALDERMAN

Clerical and Religious Orders

Abbot
The Right Reverend John R. Smith, — Right Reverend and dear Father
  O.S.B. (O.F.M., etc.) — Dear Father Abbot
Abbot of ——— — Dear Father

Archbishop
The Most Reverend Archbishop — Your Excellency
  of ——— — Most Reverend Sir
  or
The Most Reverend John R. Smith — Your Excellency
Archbishop of ——— — Dear Archbishop Smith

Archdeacon
The Venerable The Archdeacon — Venerable Sir
  of ——— — Dear Archdeacon Smith
  or
The Venerable John R. Smith — (same)
Archdeacon of ———

Bishop, Catholic
The Most Reverend John R. Smith — Most Reverend Sir
Bishop of ——— — Your Excellency
— Dear Bishop Smith

Bishop, Episcopal
The Right Reverend The Bishop — Right Reverend Sir
  of ———
  or
The Right Reverend John R. Smith — Right Reverend Sir
Bishop of ——— — Dear Bishop Smith

Bishop, Episcopal, Presiding
The Most Reverend John R. Smith — Most Reverend Sir
Presiding Bishop — Dear Bishop
— Dear Bishop Smith

Inside-Address Style	*Salutation Style*
Bishop, Protestant (excluding Episcopal)	
The Reverend John R. Smith	Reverend Sir
	Dear Bishop Smith
Brotherhood, member of	
Brother John, S.J. (O.F.M., O.S.B., etc.)	Dear Brother John
	Dear Brother
Canon	
The Reverend John R. Smith	Dear Canon Smith
Canon of ——— Cathedral	
Cardinal	
His Eminence John Cardinal Smith	Your Eminence
	Dear Cardinal Smith
or	
His Eminence Cardinal Smith	(same)
or if also an archbishop	
His Eminence John Cardinal Smith	(same)
Archbishop of ———	
or	
His Eminence Cardinal Smith	(same)
Archbishop of ———	

Chaplain, college or university—see COLLEGE AND UNIVERSITY FACULTY AND OFFICIALS

Clergy, Protestant	
The Reverend Amelia R. Smith	Dear Ms. Smith
or with a doctorate	
The Reverend Dr. Amelia R. Smith	Dear Dr. Smith
Dean (of a cathedral)	
The Very Reverend John R. Smith	Very Reverend Sir
——— Cathedral	Dear Dean Smith
or	
Dean John R. Smith	(same)
——— Cathedral	
Monsignor, domestic prelate	
The Reverend Monsignor John R. Smith	Reverend and dear Monsignor
or	Smith
The Rev. Msgr. John R. Smith	Dear Monsignor Smith
Monsignor, papal chamberlain	
The Very Reverend Monsignor John R.	Very Reverend and dear Monsignor
Smith	Smith
	Dear Monsignor Smith
or	
The Very Rev. Msgr. John R. Smith	(same)
Mother superior (of a sisterhood)	
The Reverend Mother Superior	Reverend Mother
Convent of ———	Dear Reverend Mother
or	
Reverend Mother Mary Angelica, O.S.D.	(same)
(S.M., S.C., Etc.)	
Convent of ———	
or	
Mother Mary Angelica, Superior	(same)
Convent of ———	

Inside-Address Style	*Salutation Style*
Patriarch (of an Eastern Orthodox Church)	
His Beatitude the Patriarch of ———	Most Reverend Lord Your Beatitude
Pope	
His Holiness the Pope	Your Holiness Most Holy Father
or	
His Holiness Pope John	(same)
President, Mormon	
The President Church of Jesus Christ of Latter-day Saints	Dear President Smith
Priest, Catholic	
The Reverend Father Smith	Reverend Father Dear Father Smith Dear Father
or	
The Reverend John R. Smith	(same)

Priest, president (of a college or university)—see COLLEGE AND UNIVERSITY FACULTY AND OFFICIALS

Rabbi	
Rabbi John R. Smith	Dear Rabbi Smith
or with a doctorate	
Rabbi John R. Smith, D.D.	Dear Dr. Smith
Sisterhood, member of	
Sister Mary Angelica, S.C. (S.M., O.S.D., etc.)	Dear Sister Dear Sister Mary Angelica

College and University Faculty and Officials

Chancellor	
Dr. Amelia R. Smith Chancellor	Dear Dr. Smith
Chaplain	
The Reverend John R. Smith Chaplain	Dear Chaplain Smith Dear Father Smith Dear Mr. Smith
Dean	
Dean Amelia R. Smith	Dear Dr. Smith Dear Dean Smith
or	
Dr. Amelia R. Smith Dean	(same)
Instructor	
Mr. John R. Smith Instructor	Dear Mr. Smith
President	
Dr. Amelia R. Smith	Dear Dr. Smith

Inside-Address Style	*Salutation Style*
President	
or	
President Amelia R. Smith	Dear President Smith
President, priest	
The Very Reverend John R. Smith	Dear Father Smith
President	
Professor, assistant or associate	
Ms. Amelia R. Smith	Dear Professor Smith
Assistant/Associate Professor of ———	Dear Ms. Smith
or with a doctorate	
Dr. Amelia R. Smith	Dear Dr. Smith
Assistant/Associate Professor of ———	
Professor, full	
Professor John R. Smith	Dear Professor Smith
or	
Dr. John R. Smith	Dear Dr. Smith
Professor of ———	

Diplomats and Consular Officers

Ambassador, American	
The Honorable Amelia R. Smith	Madam
American Ambassador	Dear Madam Ambassador
	Dear Ambassador Smith
or if in Central or South America	
The Honorable Amelia R. Smith	(same)
Ambassador of the United States of	
America	
Ambassador, foreign	
His Excellency John R. Smith	Excellency
Ambassador of ———	Dear Mr. Ambassador
Chargé d'affaires ad interim, American	
Amelia R. Smith, Esq.	Madam
American Chargé d'Affaires ad Interim	Dear Ms. Smith
or if in Latin America or Canada	
Amelia R. Smith, Esq.	(same)
United States Charge d'Affaires ad	
Interim	
Chargé d'affaires ad interim, foreign	
Mr. John R. Smith	Sir
Chargé d'Affaires ad Interim of ———	Dear Mr. Smith
Chargé d'affaires, foreign	
Ms. Amelia R. Smith	Madame
Chargé d'Affaires of ———	Dear Ms. Smith
Consulate, American	
The American Consulate	Ladies and Gentlemen

Inside-Address Style	*Salutation Style*
or if in Central or South America	
The Consulate of the United States of America	(same)

Consul, American (covers all consular grades such as *Consul, Consul General, Vice-Consul,* and *Consular Agent*)

The American Consul	Sir or Madam
or if in Central or South America	
The Consul of the United States of America	(same)
or if individual name is known	
Amelia R. Smith, Esq.	Madam
American Consul	Dear Ms. Smith
or if in Central or South America	
Amelia R. Smith, Esq.	(same)
Consul of the United States of America	

Consulate, foreign

The ——— Consulate	Ladies and Gentlemen
or	
The Consulate of ———	(same)

Consuls, foreign (covers all consular grades)

The ——— Consul	Sir or Madame
or	
The Consul of ———	(same)
or if individual name is known	
The Honorable John R. Smith	Sir
——— Consul	Dear Mr. Smith

Minister, American

The Honorable John R. Smith	Sir
American Minister	Dear Mr. Minister
or if in Latin America or Canada	
Minister of the United States of America	(same)

Minister, foreign

The Honorable Amelia R. Smith	Madame
Minister of ———	Dear Madame Minister

Representative to the United Nations, American

The Honorable Amelia R. Smith	Madam
United States Permanent Representative to the United Nations	Dear Madam Ambassador

Representative to the United Nations, foreign

His Excellency John R. Smith	Excellency
Representative of ——— to the United Nations	Dear Mr. Ambassador

Secretary-General of the United Nations

Her Excellency Amelia R. Smith	Excellency
Secretary-General of the United Nations	Dear Madam (*or* Madam) Secretary-General

Undersecretary of the United Nations

The Honorable John R. Smith	Sir
Undersecretary of the United Nations	Dear Mr. Smith

Military Personnel

The first entry below describes an appropriate form of address for any member of the armed forces. Abbreviations for each rank and the branches of service using them are shown at individual entries. In actual practice, salutations will differ according to degree of formality. The most formal will often employ the addressee's full title. The salutations shown generally represent a level of formality between the highly formal and the familiar.

Inside-Address Style	*Salutation Style*
For any rank	
full or abbreviated rank + full name +	*Dear + full rank + surname*
comma + abbreviation of the branch of	
service (USA, USN, USAF, USMC, USCG)	
Admiral [coast guard, navy (ADM)]	
Admiral Amelia R. Smith, USCG (etc)	Dear Admiral Smith
or	
ADM Amelia R. Smith, USCG (etc)	(same)

—a similar pattern is used for **rear admiral** (RADM), **vice admiral** (VADM), and **fleet admiral** (FADM), with the full rank given in the salutation line.

Airman [air force (Amn)]	
Airman John R. Smith, USAF	Dear Airman Smith
or	
Amn John R. Smith, USAF	(same)

—a similar pattern is used for **airman basic** (AB) and **airman first class** (A1C), with the full rank given in the salutation line.

Cadet [U.S. Air Force Academy, U.S. Military Academy]	
Cadet Amelia R. Smith	Dear Cadet Smith
Captain [army (CPT); coast guard, navy (CAPT); air force, marine corps (Capt)]	
Captain John R. Smith, USAF (etc)	Dear Captain Smith
or	
Capt John R. Smith, USAF (etc)	(same)
Chief master sargeant [air force (CMSgt)]	
Chief Master Sergeant John R. Smith, USAF	Dear Chief Smith
or	
CMSgt John R. Smith, USAF	(same)

—a similar pattern is used for **chief master sergeant of the air force** [air force (CMSAF)].

Chief petty officer [coast guard, navy (CPO)]	
Chief Petty Officer Amelia R. Smith	Dear Chief Smith
or	
CPO Amelia R. Smith, USN (etc)	(same)
Chief warrant officer [army (CW2, CW3, CW4, CW5); navy, coast guard, air force (CWO-2, CWO-3, CWO-4); marine corps (CWO2, CWO3, CWO4)]	
Chief Warrant Officer Amelia R. Smith,	Dear Ms. Smith
USA (etc)	Dear Chief Warrant Officer Smith
or	
CW4 Amelia R. Smith, USA (etc)	(same)

Inside-Address Style	*Salutation Style*

Colonel [army (COL); air force, marine corps (Col)]
Colonel Amelia R. Smith, USMC (etc)   Dear Colonel Smith
or
Col Amelia R. Smith, USMC (etc)   (same)

—a similar pattern is used for **lieutenant colonel** [army (LTC); air force, marine corps (LtCol)], with the full rank given in the salutation line.

Commander [coast guard, navy (CDR)]
Commander John R. Smith, USN (etc)   Dear Commander Smith
or
CDR John R. Smith, USCG (etc)   (same)

—a similar pattern is used for **lieutenant commander** [coast guard, navy (LCDR)], with the full rank given in the salutation line.

Corporal [army (CPL); marine corps (Cpl)]
Corporal Amelia R. Smith, USA (etc)   Dear Corporal Smith
or
CPL Amelia R. Smith, USA (etc)   (same)

—a similar pattern is used for **lance corporal** [marine corps (L/Cpl)], with the full rank given in the salutation line.

Ensign [coast guard, navy (ENS)]
Ensign John R. Smith, USN (etc)   Dear Ensign Smith
                                            Dear Mr. Smith
or
ENS John R. Smith, USN (etc)   (same)

First lieutenant [army (1LT); air force, marine corps (1stLt)]
First Lieutenant Amelia R. Smith, USMC   Dear Lieutenant Smith
  (etc)
or
1stLt Amelia R. Smith, USMC (etc)   (same)

General [army (GEN); air force, marine corps (Gen)]
General Amelia R. Smith, USAF (etc)   Dear General Smith
or
Gen Amelia R. Smith, USAF (etc)   (same)

—a similar pattern is used for **brigadier general** [army (BG); air force (BGen), marine corps (BrigGen)], **major general** [army (MG); air force, marine corps (MajGen)], and **lieutenant general** [army (LTG); air force, marine corps (LtGen)], with the full rank given in the salutation line.

Lieutenant [coast guard, navy (LT)]
Lieutenant John R. Smith, USN (etc)   Dear Lieutenant Smith
                                            Dear Mr. Smith
or
LT John R. Smith, USN (etc)   (same)

Lieutenant junior grade [coast guard, navy (LTJG)]
Lieutenant (j.g.) Amelia R. Smith, USCG   Dear Lieutenant Smith
  (etc)   Dear Ms. Smith
or
LTJG Amelia R. Smith, USCG (etc)   (same)

Inside-Address Style	*Salutation Style*

Major [army (MAJ); air force, marine corps (Maj)]

Major John R. Smith, USAF (etc)	Dear Major Smith
or	
Maj John R. Smith, USAF (etc)	(same)

Master chief petty officer [coast guard, navy (MCPO)]

Master Chief Petty Officer Amelia R.	Dear Master Chief Smith
Smith, USN (etc)	
or	
MCPO Amelia R. Smith, USN (etc)	(same)

Midshipman [coast guard and naval academies]

| Midshipman John R. Smith | Dear Midshipman Smith |

Petty officer first class [coast guard, navy (PO1)]

Petty Officer First Class John R. Smith,	Dear Petty Officer Smith
USN (etc)	
or	
PO1 John R. Smith, USN (etc)	(same)

—a similar pattern is used for **petty officer second class** (PO2) and **petty officer third class** (PO3).

Private [army (PVT); marine corps (Pvt)]

Private John R. Smith, USMC (etc)	Dear Private Smith
or	
Pvt John R. Smith, USMC (etc)	(same)

—a similar pattern is used for **private first class** [army, marine corps (PFC)].

Seaman [coast guard, navy (Seaman)]

| Seaman Amelia R. Smith, USCG (etc) | Dear Seaman Smith |

—a similar pattern is used for **seaman apprentice** (SA) and **seaman recruit** (SR).

Second lieutenant [army (2LT); air force, marine corps (2ndLt)]

Second Lieutenant John R. Smith, USA	Dear Lieutenant Smith
(etc)	
or	
2LT John R. Smith, USA (etc)	(same)

Senior chief petty officer [coast guard, navy (SCPO)]

Senior Chief Petty Officer John R. Smith,	Dear Senior Chief Smith
USCG (etc)	
or	
SCPO John R. Smith, USCG (etc)	(same)

Sergeant [army (SGT); air force, marine corps (Sgt)]

Sergeant Amelia R. Smith, USAF (etc)	Dear Sergeant Smith
or	
Sgt Amelia R. Smith, USAF (etc)	(same)

—a similar pattern is used for other sergeant ranks, including **first sergeant** [army (1SG); marine corps (1stSgt)]; **gunnery sergeant** [marine corps (GySgt)]; **master gunnery sergeant** [marine corps (MGySgt)]; **master sergeant** [army (MSG); air force, marine corps (MSgt)]; **senior master sergeant** [air force (SMSgt)]; **sergeant first class** [army (SFC)]; **staff sergeant** [army (SSG); air force, marine corps (SSgt)]; and **technical sergeant** [air force (TSgt)], with the full rank given in the salutation line.

Inside-Address Style	Salutation Style

Sergeant major [army (SGM); marine corps (SgtMaj)]
Sergeant Major Amelia R. Smith, USMC   Dear Sergeant Major Smith
  (etc)
  or
SgtMaj Amelia R. Smith, USMC (etc)   (same)

—a similar pattern is used for **command sergeant major** [army (CSM)], **sergeant major of the army** [army (SMA)], and **sergeant major of the marine corps** [marine corps (SgtMaj)].

Specialist [army (SPC)]
Specialist John R. Smith, USA   Dear Specialist Smith
  or
SPC John R. Smith, USA   (same)

Warrant officer [army (WO1, WO2); navy (WO-1); air force, marine corps (WO)]
Warrant Officer John R. Smith, USA (etc)   Dear Warrant Officer Smith
                                           Dear Mr. Smith
  or
WO1 John R. Smith, USA (etc)   (same)

Miscellaneous Professional Titles

Attorney
Ms. Amelia R. Smith, Attorney-at-Law   Dear Ms. Smith
  or
Amelia R. Smith, Esq.   (same)

Certified public accountant
Amelia R. Smith, C.P.A.   Dear Ms. Smith

Dentist
John R. Smith, D.D.S. (D.M.D., etc.)   Dear Dr. Smith
  or
Dr. John R. Smith   (same)

Physician
Amelia R. Smith, M.D.   Dear Dr. Smith
  or
Dr. Amelia R. Smith   (same)

Veterinarian
John R. Smith, D.V.M.   Dear Dr. Smith
  or
Dr. John R. Smith   (same)

Multiple Addressees (See also pages 200–205)

Two or more men (with same or different surnames)
Mr. Arthur W. Jones   Gentlemen
Mr. John H. Jones
  or   *or*
Messrs. Arthur W. Jones and John H. Jones
  or
The Messrs. Jones   Dear Messrs. Jones

Inside-Address Style	*Salutation Style*
Two or more women (with same or different surnames)	
Ms. Barbara F. Lee	Dear Ms. Lee and Ms. Kay
Ms. Helen G. Kay	
or	
Mss. (or Mses.) Barbara F. Lee and	
Helen G. Kay	
or	
Mss. (or Mses.) Lee and Kay	

Special Titles, Designations, and Abbreviations

Initials representing academic degrees, religious orders, and professional ratings may appear after a name, separated from each other by commas, in the following order: (1) religious orders (such as *S.J.*); (2) theological degrees (such as *D.D.*); (3) academic degrees (such as *Ph.D.*); (4) honorary degrees (such as *Litt.D.*); (5) professional ratings (such as *C.P.A.*).

Initials that represent academic degrees (with the exception of *M.D.*, *D.D.S.*, and other medical degrees) are not commonly used in addresses, and two or more sets of such letters appear even more rarely. Only when the initials represent achievements in different fields that are relevant to one's profession should more than one set be used. On the other hand, initials that represent earned professional achievements (such as *C.P.A.*, *C.A.M.*, *C.P.S.*, or *P.E.*) are often used in business addresses. When any of these sets of initials follow a name, however, the courtesy title *(Mr., Mrs., Ms., Miss, Dr.)* is omitted.

> Nancy Robinson, P.L.S.
> Mary R. Lopez, C.P.A.
> Jordan R. Dodds, J.D., C.M.C.
> The Rev. Seamus McMalley, S.J., D.D., LL.D.
> Chaplain, Smithville College

Below are discussed, in alphabetical order by title or designation, additional issues concerning forms of address.

Doctor   If *Doctor* or *Dr.* is used before a person's name, academic degrees (such as *D.D.S.*, *D.V.M.*, *M.D.*, or *Ph.D.*) are not included after the surname. The title *Doctor* may be either typed out in full or abbreviated in a salutation, but it is usually abbreviated on an envelope and in an inside address in order to save space. When *Doctor* appears in a salutation, it must be used in conjunction with the addressee's surname.

> Dear Doctor Smith *or* Dear Dr. Smith (*not* Dear Doctor)

If two or more doctors are associated in a joint practice, the following styles may be used:

| Drs. Francis X. Sullivan and | *formal:* |
| Philip K. Ross | My dear Drs. Sullivan and Ross |

informal:

Francis X. Sullivan, M.D.	Dear Drs. Sullivan and Ross
Philip K. Ross, M.D.	Dear Doctors Sullivan and Ross
	Dear Dr. Sullivan and Dr. Ross
	Dear Doctor Sullivan and Doctor Ross

Esquire The abbreviation *Esq.* for *Esquire* is often used in the United States after the surnames of attorneys, and also of court officials such as clerks of court and justices of the peace. *Esquire* may be written in addresses and signature lines but not in salutations. It is used regardless of sex. Some people, however, object to the use of *Esquire* as a title for a woman professional, and you should follow the recipient's wishes, if they are known, using an alternative form such as "Amy Lutz, Attorney-at-Law."

In Great Britain *Esquire* is generally used after the surnames of people who have distinguished themselves in professional, diplomatic, or social circles. For example, when addressing a letter to a British surgeon or to a high corporate officer of a British firm, one should include *Esq.* after the surname, both on the envelope and in the inside address. If a courtesy title such as *Dr., Hon., Miss., Mr., Mrs.,* or *Ms.* is used before the addressee's name, *Esquire* or *Esq.* is omitted.

The plural of *Esq.* is *Esqs.,* and it is used with the surname of multiple addresses.

Carolyn B. West, Esq.	Dear Ms. West
or	
Ms. Carolyn B. West	
Attorney-at-Law	
Samuel A. Sebert, Esq.	Gentlemen
Norman D. Langfitt, Esq.	Dear Mr. Sebert and Mr. Langfitt
or	Dear Messrs. Sebert and Langfitt
Sebert and Langfitt, Esqs.	
or	
Messrs. Sebert and Langfitt	
Attorneys-at-Law	
Simpson, Tyler, and Williams, Esqs.	Dear Ms. Tyler and Messrs. Simpson and Williams
or	
Scott A. Simpson, Esq.	
Annabelle W. Tyler, Esq.	
David I. Williams, Esq.	

Honorable In the United States, *The Honorable* or its abbreviated form *Hon.* is used as a title of distinction (but not rank) for elected or appointed (but not career) government officials such as judges, justices, congressmen, and cabinet officers. Neither the full form nor the abbreviation is ever used by its recipient in written signatures, letterhead, business or visiting cards, or typed signature blocks. While it may be used in an envelope address block and in the inside address of a letter, it is never used in the salutation. *The Honorable* should never appear before a surname standing alone: there must always be an intervening first name, an initial or initials, or a courtesy title. A courtesy title should not be added, however, when *The Honorable* is used with a full name.

The Honorable John R. Smith
The Honorable J. R. Smith
The Honorable J. Robert Smith
The Honorable Mr. Smith
The Honorable Dr. Smith
  not
The Honorable Smith
  and not
The Honorable Mr. John R. Smith

When an official and his wife are being addressed, his full name should be typed out.

The Honorable John R. Smith   Dear Mr. and Mrs. Smith
  and Mrs. Smith
  or
The Honorable and Mrs. John R.
  Smith

The styles "Hon. and Mrs. Smith" and "The Honorable and Mrs. Smith" should never be used. If a married woman holds the title and her husband does not, her name appears first on business-related correspondence addressed to both persons. However, if the couple is being addressed socially, the woman's title may be dropped unless she has retained her maiden name for use in personal as well as business correspondence.

in business correspondence:
The Honorable Harriet O.   Dear Mrs. (*or* Governor, etc.)
  Johnson and Mr. Johnson   Johnson and Mr. Johnson
The Honorable Harriet A. Ott   Dear Ms. Ott and Mr. Johnson
  and Mr. Robert Y. Johnson
in social correspondence:
Mr. and Mrs. Robert Y. Johnson   Dear Mr. and Mrs. Johnson
Ms. Harriet A. Ott   Dear Ms. Ott and Mr. Johnson
Mr. Roger Y. Johnson

When *The Honorable* occurs in running text, the *T* in *The* is lowercased.

A speech by the Honorable Charles H. Patterson, the American Consul in Athens . . .

Jr. and Sr.   The designations *Jr.* and *Sr.* may or may not be preceded by a comma, depending on office policy or writer preference; however, one style should be selected and adhered to for the sake of uniformity.

John K. Walker Jr. *or* John K. Walker, Jr.

Jr. and *Sr.* may be used in conjunction with courtesy titles, academic degrees abbreviations, or professional rating abbreviations.

Mr. John K. Walker, Jr.
General John K. Walker, Jr.
The Honorable John K. Walker, Jr.

John K. Walker, Jr., Esq.
John K. Walker, Jr., M.D.
John K. Walker, Jr., C.A.M.

Madam The title *Madam* should be used only in salutations of highly impersonal or high-level governmental and diplomatic correspondence. The title may be used to address women officials in other instances only if the writer is certain that the addressee is married.

Messrs. The plural abbreviation of *Mr.* is *Messrs.* (short for *Messieurs*). It is used before the surnames of two or more men associated in a professional partnership or business. *Messrs.* may appear on an envelope, in an inside address, and in a salutation, but never without the surnames.

Messrs. Archlake, Smythe, and
  Dabney
Attorneys-at-Law
	Dear Messrs. Archlake, Smythe, and
	  Dabney
	Gentlemen

(For additional usage examples, see "Multiple Addresses," pages 199–200.)

Messrs. should never be used before a compound corporate name formed from two surnames such as *Lord & Taylor* or *Woodward & Lothrop* or a corporate name like *H. L. Jones and Sones.* For the use of *Messrs.* with *The Reverend,* see pages 204–205.

Mss. or Mses. The plural form of *Ms.* is *Mss.* or *Mses.*, and either may be used before the names of two or more women who are being addressed together. It may appear on an envelope, in an inside address, and in a salutation. Like *Messrs., Mss.* or *Mses.* should never stand alone but must occur in conjunction with a name or names. (For other examples in this category, see "Multiple Addressees," pages 199–200.)

Mss. Hay and Middleton Attorneys-at-Law	Dear Mss. Hay and Middleton

Professor If used only with a surname, *Professor* should be typed out in full; however, if used with a given name or a set of initials as well as a surname, it may be abbreviated to *Prof.* It is therefore usually abbreviated in envelope address blocks and in inside addresses, but typed out in salutations. *Professor* should not stand alone in a salutation.

Prof. Florence C. Marlowe Department of English	Dear Professor Marlowe Dear Dr. Marlowe Dear Ms. Marlowe *but not* Dear Professor

When addressing a letter to a professor and his wife, the title is usually written out in full unless the name is unusually long.

Professor and Mrs. Lee Dow
Prof. and Mrs. Henry Talbott-
  Smythe
	Dear Professor and Mrs. Dow
	Dear Professor and Mrs. Talbott-
	  Smythe

Letters addressed to couples in which the wife is the professor and the husband is not may follow one of these patterns:

business correspondence:

Professor Diana Goode and
  Mr. Goode
	Dear Professor Goode and
	  Mr. Goode

business or social correspondence:

Mr. and Mrs. Lawrence F. Goode	Dear Mr. and Mrs. Goode

if wife has retained her maiden name:

Professor Diana Falls Mr. Lawrence F. Goode	Dear Professor (*or* Ms.) Falls and Mr. Goode

When addressing two or more professors—male or female, whether having the same or different surnames—type *Professors* and not *Profs.:*

Professors Albert L. Smith and Charlene L. Doe	Dear Professors Smith and Doe Dear Drs. Smith and Doe Dear Mr. Smith and Ms. Doe

Reverend   In formal or official writing, *The* should precede *Reverend;* however, *The Reverend* is often abbreviated to *The Rev.* or just *Rev.,* especially in unofficial or informal writing, and particularly in business correspondence where space is a factor. The typed-out full form *The Reverend* must be used in conjunction with the full name, as in the following examples:

The Reverend Philip D. Asquith

The Reverend Dr. Philip D. Asquith

The Reverend may appear with just a surname only if another courtesy title intervenes:

The Reverend Mr. Asquith

The Reverend Professor Asquith

The Reverend Dr. Asquith

The Reverend, The Rev., or *Rev.* should not be used in the salutation, although any of these titles may be used on the envelope and in the inside address. In salutations, the following titles are acceptable: *Mr. (Ms., Miss, Mrs.), Father, Chaplain,* or *Dr.* See the Forms of Address chart under "Clerical and Religious Orders" for examples. The only exceptions are in letters addressed to high prelates (bishops, monsignors, etc.); see the Forms of Address chart. When addressing a letter to a member of the clergy and his or her spouse, follow the following style:

The Reverend (*or* Rev.) and Mrs.
   Philip D. Asquith
	Dear Mr. (*or with a doctorate,* Dr.) and
	   Mrs. Asquith

The Reverend (*or* Rev.) Marcia
   Ogden and Mr. James Ogden
	Dear Mrs. (Ms., *or with a doctorate,*
	   Dr.) and Mr. Ogden

Two members of the clergy should not be addressed in letters as "The Reverends," "The Revs.," or "Revs." They may, however, be addressed as *The Reverend* (or *The Rev.*) *Messrs.* if both are male, or *The Reverend* (or *The Rev.*) *Drs.* if both have doctorates, or the titles *The Reverend, The Rev.,* or *Rev.* may be repeated before each name.

The Rev. Simon J. Stephens and the Rev. Barbara O. Stephens	Dear Mr. and Mrs. Stephens
Rev. Simon J. Stephens and Rev. Barbara O. Stephens	
The Reverend (*or* Rev.) Messrs. Philip A. Francis and Lanford Beale	Gentlemen Dear Father Francis and Father Beale
The Rev. Philip A. Francis The Rev. Lanford Beale	

In formal lists of names, "The Reverends," "The Revs.," and "Revs." are not acceptable as collective titles. *The Reverend* (or *Rev.*) *Messrs.* (*Drs., Professors*) may be used if appropriate, or *The Reverend* or *The Rev.* or *Rev.* may be repeated before each name. If the term *clergyman, clergywoman,* or *the clergy* is mentioned in introducing the list, a single title *the Reverend* or *the Rev.* may be used to serve all of the names. While it is true that "The Revs." is often seen in newspapers and elsewhere, it is still not recommended for formal, official writing.

> . . . were the Reverend Messrs. Jones, Smith, and Bennett, as well as . . .
>
> Among the clergy present were the Reverend John G. Jones, Mr. Smith, and Dr. Bennett.
>
> Prayers were offered by the Rev. J. G. Jones, the Rev. Mr. Smith, and the Rev. Dr. Bennett.

Second, third, fourth These designations after surnames may take the form of Roman numerals (II, III, IV) or ordinals (2nd/2d, 3rd/3d, 4th). There should be no comma between the name and the number.

> Mr. Jason T. Cabot III (*or* 3rd *or* 3d)

Letter-Writing Guidelines

Your ability to write routine correspondence can make you a valuable asset to your firm. To the extent that you can perform this quasi-managerial function, you will free the attorney for other work. How much correspondence you are entrusted with will depend greatly on your understanding of the attorney's responsibilities and his or her confidence in your capacities and judgment.

All business letters should not sound alike. The tone of each letter—formal or informal, objective or partial, friendly or critical, and so on—will depend on your relationship with your recipient. However, the language should almost always be polite and pleasant, and *never* less than civil. Always keep the reader's point of view and possible reactions in mind, even when you are intent on setting forth your own objectives. Except when special formality is required or when you are very friendly with the recipient, try to use language that is slightly more formal and concise than your everyday speech.

Highlight or underscore significant facts and requests in any letter you are responding to. If necessary, make your own notes in the margin of the previous letter—meeting dates, appointments, brochure titles, and so on.

Jot down in order the topics you have to cover, producing a basic outline before beginning to write, even if the outline amounts to no more than four or five scrawled subject headings.

Bear in mind that your degree of familiarity with the subject matter will often be different from your reader's. Avoid writing on too low a level to experts in a given field, and avoid writing over the heads of nonexperts.

Feel free to vary the length of your paragraphs. Generally keep them as short as appropriate, with few longer than five sentences. However, breaking all your paragraphs up into one- and two-sentence lengths defeats the purpose of paragraphing, which is to organize the material for the sake of easier comprehension.

Open most paragraphs with a topic sentence, which should usually correspond to a heading in your outline. This will greatly assist the reader to scan the material initially and later to absorb it more easily and thoroughly. It will also help you keep your paragraphs focused in an appropriately narrow way.

Use natural, easy-to-understand language, while avoiding overly casual or slangy expressions. Short, clear, direct words are easier to read and understand than long words and should generally be used in place of their longer synonyms except where they risk making the tone too abrupt or the sentence too graceless. They will also prevent your sounding self-important, insecure, or bureaucratic.

Prefer the active voice to the passive. Active voice usually sounds more natural, direct, and honest and takes fewer words. However, the passive can sometimes be useful, particularly for disguising the identity of the person doing something, whether for reasons of tact or prudence.

Avoid clichés. Business-letter clichés (see list in Appendix I) have unfortunately become fixtures in the prose of many writers who think they are somehow appropriate and desirable. A busy reader can easily become impatient with them. However, there is no need to avoid many standard phrases that are as useful and irreplaceable as individual words.

Employ the personal pronouns—*I, we, you, my, our, your*, etc.—in order to give a communication a warmer tone. Avoiding them can make a letter less cordial—which in certain cases may be desirable.

Use contractions when you want to achieve a somewhat informal tone. Sometimes contractions will be all that is needed to soften a letter's formality.

Avoid padding your letter with overlong or repetitious material. Your reader will be grateful.

Give accurate and adequate information, and respond to any questions that have been raised. Neglecting to answer a question from previous correspondence is a serious omission; double-check by rereading the previous correspondence against your response.

Avoid ambiguous language, and scan your prose for unintended ambiguity. If a statement *can* be misunderstood, it *will* be.

Use specifics rather than abstractions where possible. Abstractions not only tend to bore the reader but may indicate that the writer hasn't actually visualized the subject adequately or is generalizing beyond his or her knowledge.

Exercise tact. Try to introduce unfavorable comments with favorable ones and to present the positive aspects of a situation before making any negative observations. Soften your language with euphemisms, if necessary, to avoid a negative tone.

Use humor where it seems natural and appropriate; there is no law that business and professional letters have to be humorless. For some writers, however, it is hard to find a good humorous tone, and there is often the possibility that the recipient won't think the humor successful or, more seriously, will fail to understand that it is even intended as humor. If you are uncertain about its effect, be sure to put the letter aside before rereading it.

Avoid sexist and other biased language. You risk offending or at least distracting many readers today if you are not attentive to problems of discriminatory usage. In particular, try to avoid using *he, him,* or *his* when referring to a person who could be either male or female.

State or restate any request clearly and pleasantly in the last paragraph. If no request is being made, use the final paragraph of an informal letter for a pleasant closing thought (for instance, an allusion to the season or to a recent or upcoming event in the recipient's life).

Edit your first draft. Ask yourself if each word is necessary or desirable and cross out all those that aren't.

Set your letter aside for a while, if possible, so that you can come back to it with a fresh eye. Pretend that you are the recipient and have just opened it. (To make the exercise more realistic, you could even try putting it in an envelope and then opening the envelope to read it.)

When giving your letter a final rereading, ask yourself the following questions:

- Has every question, request, and issue raised in the preceding communication been dealt with, or at least acknowledged?
- Is the tone appropriate, given the particular relationship between writer (or signer) and reader?
- Will the recipient be able to grasp the essence of the letter almost immediately?
- Is it obvious why each paragraph *is* a paragraph? Does it hang together, or does it instead contain material that really belongs elsewhere or omit material that instead shows up in another paragraph?
- Is the meaning of each sentence unambiguous?
- Is there still any unnecessary or undesirable verbiage?
- Have you used the word *I* too much?
- Is any intended humor both appropriate and funny?
- Have you actually enclosed all the enclosures referred to?

Be sure you know whose signature is to appear at the end. Normally, only letters of general information and routine requests may bear a secretary's or assistant's signature, except when special authorization has been given.

Proofread the letter for misspelled words, incorrect figures and dates, lack of agreement between subject and verb, misplaced commas, and other such pitfalls. Check to see that each of the necessary parts or elements of the letter has been included.

Sample Letters

This section includes sample business letters that are appropriate for a range of situations and occasions in a law office. Those letters that bear the signature of an attorney represent the kinds of letter that a secretary might compose for an attorney to sign. Other letters shown here bear the signature of a secretary and represent the kinds of letter that a secretary might compose for his or her own business purposes.

Fig. 7.14   Acknowledgment or Deferral

LAI   **Legal Assistance Institute**

Nina R. Ramirez	Brent A. Porteris	**Law Associates**
Kevin B. Jansen	Sondra O. Melines	
Sherwood T. Baines	Frank P. Jeremiah	**Oakland / San Jose**
Eric I. Linowitz	Linda Dena Sanchez	
Sheryl Paolo DeBlanc	Bartlett Z. Walton	
Henry G. Dawkins	Isaiah C. Garvey	
Oriana Meagher	Priscilla S. Nieman	
Lawrence R. Leavy	Jonathan E. Collins	
Peter S. Lopez	Alan G. Batanabaras	

June 14, 19--

Ms. Alana R. McDermott
Chairperson
Eardry Commons Planning Association
1515 Fitzwilliams Road
Oakland, CA 93042

Dear Ms. McDermott:

    Your letter to Ms. DeBlanc concerning the
community housing initiative arrived during her
absence on business from the office. She will be
returning early next week, and I'll be sure to
bring your letter to her attention then.

    Please accept my apology for any inconvenience
this brief delay may have caused.

                        Yours sincerely,

                        Margery B. Foster

                        Margery B. Foster
                        Office Administrator

    cc: SPD

355 Marianas Drive, Suite 100, Oakland, CA 90246 Telephone: 415-753-4467 / Fax 415-754-4467
177 Greenbelt Road, Suite 390, San Jose, CA 90355 Telephone: 408-566-2233 / Fax 408-567-2231

Fig. 7.15   Adjustment or Apology

**Burton, DeCarlo,
Gatineau & Deledda, P.C.**

54 Corenda Lake Drive   Phone: (371) 989-5385
Bloomington, IN 45337   Fax: (371) 989-5384

February 18, 19--
REF: Bill #305-SS

Mr. Anton Shockley, Jr.
444 Ledgerfield Way
Chambray, IN 45352

Dear Mr. Shockley:

Thank you for bringing to our attention the most recent bill (dated Feb. 12) you received from this office.

I have checked our records and discovered that indeed an error occurred in listing the length of time for a phone conversation between Mr. Deledda and you on January 28. The time should have been listed as .5 hours, not 1.5 hours.

I sincerely regret this mistake and will take every precaution to ensure that it does not happen again. Your account has been adjusted to reflect the proper charges, and a revised bill is enclosed.

Once again, please accept my apology, and let me or Mr. Deledda know if you have any further questions or problems concerning our services.

Yours truly,

Selina Teagarten

Selina Teagarten
Assistant to Mr. Deledda

Enclosure

Fig. 7.16   Announcement, Printed

The Law Firm of

KRAVITZ & SARANIN

is pleased to announce

that

STEWART J. RECOSTA

and

MARVIN B. SHORE

have joined the firm as partners.

MR. RECOSTA's practice will include antitrust,
banking, bankruptcy, and health care litigation.

MR. SHORE's practice will include securities,
franchise, employment, and contract litigation.

February 19--

Fig. 7.17 Appointment Confirmation

KOFFLER & MANNING
ATTORNEYS AT LAW

DANIEL C. KOFFLER

BARRY L. MANNING
—
MEMBERS PA & NJ BAR

1200 LOGAN SQUARE
PHILADELPHIA, PA. 19011
(215) 433-5000
FAX (215) 433-5001
—
400 SHOSTAK AVENUE
HADDONFIELD, N.J. 08024
(609) 344-2500
FAX (609) 344-2237

REPLY TO:

Haddonfield

June 17, 19--

Mr. & Mrs. Patrick Keneally
763 Rumsford Drive
Camden, NJ 08035

Dear Brenda and Patrick:

    Re: Court Hearing

This is to confirm that the Preliminary Court Hearing regarding Thomas Glass Keneally has been scheduled for June 24, 19--, at 10:30 a.m. before Judge Jameson in the Camden County Juvenile Court, Room No. 35, Fifth and Mickle Boulevard, Camden, New Jersey. It is important that you arrive at least 20 minutes prior to the scheduled time in order to register with the bailiff.

For your convenience, I have enclosed a set of directions to the courthouse. I will, of course, be available if you have any questions prior to the Hearing. Thanks and best regards.

Very truly yours,

Daniel C. Koffler

DANIEL C. KOFFLER

DCK:lpk
Enclosure

Fig. 7.18   Cease and Desist

MARCIA G. CLIBURN
Attorney at Law

218 NORTH STREET
POST OFFICE BOX 361
SYRACUSE, NEW YORK 13956
PH (422) 341-5347
FX (422) 342-5350

August 12, 19--

Mr. Mark L. Clemens
Collections Manager
Homelife Finance Corp.
1000 Liberty Avenue
Albany, NY 13557

    Re: Acct. No. 1-97-00175

Dear Mr. Clemens:

    I am writing on behalf of my clients Mr. and Mrs. Harvey Novato. The Novatos report that they are still receiving billing notices regarding the above account.

    This account was settled on April 22, 19--, and my clients are under no further obligation to your firm. I ask that you take the proper steps to suspend the mailing of any further notices to my clients. Future questions you have regarding the account should be directed to me.

           Sincerely,

           Marcia G. Cliburn

           Marcia G. Cliburn
           Attorney at Law

MGC/cm

cc: Harvey and Shirley Novato

Fig. 7.19   Condolence or Sympathy

**Turnowski, Brill, Upton,
Frankl & Weber, P.C.**
3335 Cayman Boulevard
Miami Beach, FL 66210
(305) 633-2100

Harry R. Brill
Senior Partner

January 1, 19--

Dear George:

My staff and I wish to extend our heartfelt sympathy to you during this period of your bereavement since the passing of your wife, Grace.

She will be warmly remembered here as a woman of exceptional elegance and dignity. We fondly recall the many occasions on which we welcomed her to the office over the past twenty years, and will miss the opportunity to do so again.

It must be a comfort to have your family visiting from the north. May the memories of your years together sustain you all and bring you strength and peace.

Very sincerely,

Harry Brill

Mr. George Parkman
Apt. 3C
Sandy Towers West
Miami Beach, FL 66210

Fig. 7.20   Congratulation

**Minone, Fallon,
Theroux & Hardy, P.L.C.**

—

66 Atticus Foundry Road
Toledo, Ohio 40307
Phone: (419) 544-3210
Fax: (419) 545-3210

*Granville K. Fallon
Senior Partner*

> January 1, 19--

Dear Anne:

Yesterday's Toledo *Sampler-Record* announced the pleasant news of your appointment as General Counsel at Ambley Corporation. Congratulations!

It is well known that you provided outstanding legal counsel to the corporate clients of your former firm, Blanchard & Sembley. Your selection for this new position is certainly well deserved, and the task it represents is in excellent hands.

Again, you have my sincere congratulations and best wishes for continued success.

> Cordially,
>
> *Granville Fallon*

Anne Marie McBundy, Esq.
14 Seeley Lane
Cordone, Ohio 40366

Fig. 7.21   Declination of Client Matter

Franklin M. Richler James S. Talbrook Carolyn R. Menninger	**THE LAW OFFICES OF RICHLER & TALBROOK** 99 Main Street Groton, CT 02310

Tel: (203) 446-6100
Fax: (203) 446-6110

February 1, 19--

Mr. John C. Falconer
555 Broadview Court
Groton, CT 02310

Dear Mr. Falconer:

This letter is to formalize our recent discussions regarding your complaint against Boatyard Manufacturing Company. As we discussed, this Firm has a conflict of interest in the matter and therefore cannot represent you. We disclaim any duty or obligation to do so. Should you wish to pursue the matter, we urge that you consult with another attorney.

We would, of course, be pleased to discuss any new opportunities to serve you. We will confirm any future business relationships in an engagement letter for your review and approval.

We wish you well in the above-mentioned matter and request that you sign the enclosed copy of this letter and return it in the self-addressed envelope provided.

Very truly yours,

RICHLER & TALBROOK

Franklin M. Richler

Franklin M. Richler

_____   Date: _____
     John C. Falconer

tse
Enclosures (2)

Fig. 7.22   Disengagement of Services

Drummond & Drummond, P.L.C.
One Sioux Highway, Suite 1000
Des Moines, IA 53867
Phone: (515) 766-9722
Fax: (515) 766-9723

October 11, 19--

Mr. and Mrs. Ronald P. Wilson
517 Lamberton Place
Des Moines, IA 58867

Dear Mr. and Mrs. Wilson:

This letter is to confirm that, as we discussed in previous telephone
conversations, your matter has been successfully concluded and, as of
October 10, 19--, this Firm is no longer providing you legal representation
regarding it. The Firm's responsibility to you for representation, advice,
counseling, or legally-required responses regarding this matter has terminated
as of the above date.

If you wish to retain the Firm for future representation, we will naturally be
pleased to serve you after you have executed a letter of engagement affirming
your decision to retain the Firm.

To date, we show outstanding on your account the sum of $600 in
disbursements and $150 in legal fees as represented in the enclosed final bill,
and we would appreciate your giving this matter your attention.

Thank you for the opportunity to have served you, and we hope that such an
opportunity might arise again in the future.

Yours truly,

Espy L. Drummond

Espy L. Drummond

ELD/rvi
Enclosure

Fig. 7.23   Employment Refusal

COUNSEL
WAYNE S. LEARSON
JACK R. CATRILL
CURTIS F. KILBORNE
—
SENIOR SHAREHOLDERS
R. GEORGE CURZON
HARRIET P. SAYLES
ARLO S. CROWLEY
—
PHILIP H. DeMARCO
CLIFTON Z. RICHARDS
DEREK L. WELLMAN
SHARON S. OLDENBURG
RUSSELL T. HOUSE
DAVID P. OUSPENSKI
STEPHEN J. MIRSHEN
WILLIAM D. HARTMAN
DEBORAH R. STANTON
JACOB D. TRUMBULL
JAMIE C. KENDRAKE

WATTS CRANE
A PROFESSIONAL CORPORATION

**500 MARWICK CENTER
SUITE 1300
RALEIGH, NC 35885**

PHONE (919) 775-3195
FAX (919) 775-6434

March 22, 19--

BENJAMIN L. WATTS (1894-1953)
AMBROSE H. CRANE (1911-1962)
—

WASHINGTON, D.C. OFFICE
1674 K STREET, N.W.
WASHINGTON, D.C. 20040
PHONE (202) 371-0880
FAX (202) 971-3202
—
DURHAM, N.C. OFFICE
206 E. FALCON LANE
DURHAM, N.C. 36522
PHONE (919) 454-3300
FAX (010) 454 32100
—
GREENSBORO, N.C. OFFICE
317 TUFTON AVENUE
GREENSBORO, N.C. 36280
PHONE (919) 599-0023
FAX (919) 553-9077

Ms. Jacqueline W. Lemke
644 Rombarton Avenue
Raleigh, NC 35886

Dear Ms. Lemke:

Thank you for your letter of March 15. Your experience, education, and skills are impressive. Unfortunately, we do not have an opening for a legal secretary at this time.

I will keep your resume on file for future reference. In the event that a suitable opening does arise, I will attempt to contact you.

Thank you for considering Watts Crane. I wish you success in finding a position.

Sincerely,

Jason F. Lawrence
Director of Administration

/pgp

Fig. 7.24   Engagement Letter

F & P	**FREYLY & PALGRAVE, P.C.**	15 WARD ROAD
	ATTORNEYS AND COUNSELORS	AMHERST, MA 01067
		(413) 577-2103
		FAX (413) 576-2300

August 31, 19--

Ms. Marion B. Southall
14 Addison Lane
Belchertown, MA 01367

Re: Hafner Properties, Inc.

Dear Ms. Southall:

We are pleased that you have chosen to retain our firm to represent you in the above matter. This engagement letter will serve as an agreement about the nature and scope of our relationship, and set forth the fee arrangements.

The firm is dedicated to the highest ethical standards. We will hold strictly confidential all proprietary information obtained from you during the course of our dealings. We will also keep you reasonably informed about the status of your matter.

We typically bill on a monthly basis. The bill will specify the individual providing the service, the date, and the work performed. My rate is currently $_____ per hour; rates for associates and legal assistants range from $___ to $___ per hour. Bills are expected to be paid monthly, with interest to accrue on any unpaid balance. In order that we may begin serving you, I ask that you provide us a $____ retainer payment, which will be applied against fees and expenses incurred on your behalf.

It is extremely difficult to estimate the total cost for this type of engagement. The work needed to properly represent you depends on numerous issues, including, in this case, the responses of the examining IRS personnel.

If the foregoing arrangements are satisfactory to you, please sign the duplicate copy of this letter to indicate your acceptance of our firm's engagement, and return the signed letter and your retainer check to the above address.

Once again, we are pleased that you have selected Freyly & Palgrave to assist you in this matter, and look forward to establishing a mutually rewarding and enduring relationship with you as your legal counsel.

Yours very truly,

Adrian J. Palgrave

Adrian T. Palgrave

AGREED: _____   DATE: _____
          Marion B. Southall

Fig. 7.25   Follow-up or Reminder

BASEDOW AND SKELLEY

Attorneys at Law

245 MADISON STREET
P.O. BOX 322
SPRINGFIELD, ILLINOIS 44763

THOMAS I. BASEDOW
BRANDON T. SKELLEY*
*ILL. AND FLA. BARS
— —

OF COUNSEL
JOHN P. BASEDOW

TEL: (217)-443-6700
FAX: (217) 443-2879

FILE NO. 31755

June 5, 19--

Ms. Sherry L. Fogerty
Fogerty Products, Inc.
771 Hambley Road
Springfield, IL 44767

Dear Ms. Fogerty:

I am following up on our May 20 meeting concerning your Annual Report. I trust that by now you will have had a chance to review the changes and are ready to file the report with the State. I should remind you that the filing deadline, June 15, is rapidly approaching. If the report is acceptable, please sign it at the bottom (section 7), fill in the date, and return it to my attention with a corporate check in the amount of $25.00 payable to the Illinois Secretary of State.

You recall too that I prepared a form for the consent of shareholders in lieu of an annual meeting. Copies of this form need to be signed by the shareholders and received by us no later than June 14.

Finally, I note that the original stock certificates in your possession need to be signed by you as president and embossed with the corporate seal.

Please contact me so that we can make arrangements to complete all the neccessary steps for filing prior to the deadline.

Very truly yours,

Brandon T. Skelley

Brandon T. Skelley

BS/sry

Fig. 7.26   Inquiry or Request

LAW OFFICES OF

P. D. JESPERSON
16 SAN RAFAEL AVENUE
KLAMATH, CALIFORNIA 96744

A PROFESSIONAL CORPORATION
MEMBER OF
CALIFORNIA & OREGON BARS

PHONE 707-331-2898
FAX 707-332-4467
E-MAIL PDJLAW@HIGHLANDS.COM

October 8, 19--

William Marburg, Esq.
Marburg Sully & Duphrene, P.C.
532 Billings Way
Humbolt, CA 96321

RE: Freemont Co., Licensing Agreement

Dear Mr. Marburg:

In your letter of September 29 to Mr. Jesperson you wrote that you were enclosing an edited draft of the Licensing Agreement in the Freemont matter. The copy we received, however, appears to be an earlier partially edited draft that is missing some of the items you had discussed with Mr. Jesperson.

Mr. Jesperson would appreciate it if you would send the completed draft to him right away so that he may review the changes and help advance this matter toward its conclusion.

Thank you very much, Mr. Marburg.

Sincerely,

Sylvia K. Paul

Sylvia K. Paul
Assistant to Mr. Jesperson

Fig. 7.27   Invitation, Formal

The Law Offices of

MASANTE & DURHAM

request the pleasure of your company at the

Annual Summer Dinner Dance

on Saturday, the 14th of July, 19—

at seven o'clock

at the Pontchartrain Hotel

414 Aubrey Way

New Orleans

Please respond by June 30th
Lorraine Elsevier (504) 599-8700

Fig. 7.28   Job Offer

COLBY & MANNION   A PROFESSIONAL CORPORATION   TEL (503) 666-3211
33 INLAND BROOK MANOR   FAX (503) 666-3200
PORTLAND, OREGON 87010

September 15, 19--

Ms. Darcy K. Sebastian
875 Bolton Lane
Portland, OR 87011

Dear Ms. Sebastian:

   This letter constitutes our formal offer to you of the position of Assistant
Legal Administrator at Colby & Mannion, P.C. Your duties will consist of
assisting the Director of Administration in all professional areas of law-firm
administration and in carrying out special projects that relate to client
communications and staff development, as assigned by the Director.

   This is a full-time position, paying a salary of $31,500 a year less the
deductions for federal and state taxes and Social Security. You will receive a
salary review after three months and annually thereafter. Increases will depend
on the firm's general policy and on your contributions to our administrative
activities. Fringe benefits and other details regarding employment are explained
in the employee manual that is being sent to you separately.

   We have agreed that you will begin work on September 30, 19--. On that
day, please bring with you proof of your U.S. citizenship or resident-alien status.
A driver's license with photo or a state-issued identification card with photo will
suffice. If one of these is not available, you may bring alternative documents as
explained on the enclosed form I-9. Without the appropriate documents, you will
not be able to begin work.

   If this offer is acceptable to you, please sign and date the enclosed copy of
this letter and return it to us for our files.

                              Yours sincerely,

                              Barbara W. Peters

                              Barbara W. Peters
                              Director of Administration

Enclosures (2)

Fig. 7.29   Press Release

LAWRENCE NICHOLSON ASSOCIATES, p.c.
LAWYERS

February 5, 19-_

Contact: Arial Medford
           (402)639-2177

FOR IMMEDIATE RELEASE

Edward C. Baker, an Associate Attorney with Lawrence Nicholson Associates, P.C., has written an article entitled "Holding Down Insurance Costs in the Medium-Sized Firm," which will appear in the March issue of *Law Practice Management*.

Mr. Baker specializes in Tax and Insurance Law, and has contributed several articles to professional law journals in the past few years.

He joined Lawrence Nicholson three years ago. Previously he worked for a well-known financial management corporation as an in-house counsel.

Mr. Baker and his family live in Omaha.

---

12 STRAWSON LANE, OMAHA, NEBRASKA 53241 PH: 402-887-5535 FAX: 402-887-5581

Fig. 7.30   Reference or Recommendation

BURRIDGE, DALBY, ELLMAN, FRIED & EBERT
ATTORNEYS AT LAW
THE GRANT BUILDING
466 CHESTERFIELD WAY
PITTSBURGH, PENNSYLVANIA 19370

SANDRA T. GIMBLE
OFFICE MANAGER

(412) 829-9600
FAX: 829-9610

December 5, 19—

Ms. Gloria F. Calabrese
Director of Personnel
Donnelley & Herbert, P.C.
300 Massachusetts Ave., N.W.
Washington, D.C. 07302

Dear Ms. Calabrese:

I am delighted to respond to your request for a reference for Helena
Zellman, who served as secretary to two of our attorneys for the past three
years.

As she leaves to relocate to the Washington, D.C., area, we are extremely
disappointed to see her go but at the same time wish her well in her new
endeavor.

Helena was responsible for a wide range of duties here, including providing
day-to-day administrative support for two attorneys, coordinating
docketing information in our Family Law practice area, assisting the Chief
Administrator with client development, and training part-time clerical
staff. She was almost single-handedly responsible for implementing a
productive and efficient client-tracking system in our office.

Her word-processing and database skills are exceptional. She provides
timely and accurate keyboarding and and is knowledgeable and insightful
about many different aspects of database management. Helena's approach
to her job can be characterized as truly professional.

If you need an Assistant Office Manager who is responsible, industrious,
and talented, you should hire Ms. Zellman.

Yours sincerely,

Sandra T. Gimble

Fig. 7.31   Request for Payment (Level I)

HEDGES, SANDERSON & REASON
Attorneys at Law
13 Hampton Court
Cincinnati, Ohio 55413
(513) 724-8811
FAX 724-8200

September 23, 19--

Mr. Charles T. Avakian
922 Perdido Drive
Cincinnati, OH 55411

RE: Account No. H-733-98

Dear Mr. Avakian:

This is to remind you that your account with this firm shows an outstanding balance which is now past due. We have enclosed a copy of the bill for your convenience.

We would appreciate your prompt attention to this matter and remittance of your past due balance within five (5) business days from the date of this letter.

If you have any questions regarding this matter, please contact me.

Very truly yours,

Glenda R. James

Glenda R. James
Assistant to Mr. Sanderson

Enclosure

Fig. 7.32   Request for Payment (Level II)

HEDGES, SANDERSON & REASON
Attorneys at Law
13 Hampton Court
Cincinnati, Ohio 55413
(513) 724-8811
FAX 724-8200

November 1, 19--

Mr. Charles T. Avakian
922 Perdido Drive
Cincinnati, OH 55411

RE: Account No. H-733-98

Dear Mr. Avakian:

Your account for legal services rendered by this firm is over 60 days past due. The balance of $___ has been outstanding since the work was completed in August .

We would still like to resolve this on amicable terms, but we need to receive payment promptly. Otherwise, we will refer this matter to collections, which could result in litigation with all its attendant costs and inconvenience.

To avoid collection action, please remit payment for the total balance due immediately upon receipt of this letter, or contact me at the number listed above.

Sincerely,

Glenda R. James

Glenda R. James
Assistant to Mr. Sanderson

Chapter 8

A Guide to Punctuation and Style

Punctuation

Punctuation marks are used to help clarify the structure and meaning of sentences. They separate groups of words for meaning and emphasis; they convey an idea of the variations in pitch, volume, pauses, and intonation of the spoken language; and they help avoid ambiguity. The choice of what punctuation to use, if any, will often be clear and unambiguous. In other cases, a sentence may allow for several punctuation patterns. In cases like these, varying notions of correctness have developed, and two writers might, with equal correctness, punctuate the same sentence quite differently, relying on their individual judgment and taste.

APOSTROPHE

The apostrophe is used to form most possessives and contractions as well as some plurals and inflections.

1. The apostrophe is used to indicate the possessive of nouns and indefinite pronouns. (For details, see the section beginning on page 281.)

   the girl's shoe   anyone's guess
   the boys' fathers   the Browns' house
   Simmons's role   Arkansas's capital
   children's laughter

2. Apostrophes are sometimes used to form plurals of letters, numerals, abbreviations, symbols, and words referred to as words. (For details, see the section beginning on page 277.)

   cross your *t*'s   two L.H.D.'s *or* two L.H.D.s
   three 8's *or* three 8s   used &'s instead of *and*'s

3. Apostrophes mark omissions in contractions made of two or more words and in contractions of single words.

wasn't	she'd rather not	ass'n
they're	Jake's had it	dep't

4. The apostrophe is used to indicate that letters have been intentionally omitted from a word in order to imitate informal speech.

"Singin' in the Rain," the popular song and movie
"Snap 'em up" was his response.

Sometimes such words are so consistently spelled with an apostrophe that the spelling becomes an accepted variant.

rock 'n' roll [*for* rock and roll]
ma'am [*for* madam]
sou'wester [*for* southwester]

5. Apostrophes mark the omission of digits in numerals.

class of '98
fashion in the '90s

If the apostrophe is used when writing the plurals of numerals, either the apostrophe that stands for the missing figures is omitted or the word is spelled out.

90's *or* nineties *but not* '90's

6. In informal writing, apostrophes are used to produce forms of verbs that are made of individually pronounced letters. An apostrophe or a hyphen is also sometimes used to add an *-er* ending to an abbreviation; if no confusion would result, the apostrophe is usually omitted.

OK'd the budget	4-H'er
X'ing out the mistakes	49er

BRACKETS

Outside of mathematics and chemistry texts, brackets are primarily used for insertions into carefully handled quoted matter. They are rarely seen in general writing but are common in historical and scholarly contexts.

1. Brackets enclose editorial comments, corrections, and clarifications inserted into quoted matter.

Surely that should have peaked [sic] the curiosity of a serious researcher.

Here they much favour the tiorba [theorbo], the arclute [archlute], and the cittarone [chitarrone], while we at home must content ourselves with the lute alone.

In Blaine's words, "All the vocal aristocracy showed up—Nat [Cole], Billy [Eckstine], Ella [Fitzgerald], Mabel Mercer—'cause nobody wanted to miss that date."

2. Brackets enclose insertions that take the place of words or phrases.

And on the next page: "Their assumption is plainly that [Durocher] would be the agent in any such negotiation."

3. Brackets enclose insertions that supply missing letters.

> A postscript to a December 17 letter to Waugh notes, "If D[eutsch] won't take the manuscript, perhaps someone at Faber will."

4. Brackets enclose insertions that alter the form of a word used in an original text.

> He dryly observes (p. 78) that the Gravely investors had bought stocks because "they want[ed] to see themselves getting richer."

5. Brackets are used to indicate that capitalization has been altered. This is generally optional; it is standard practice only where meticulous handling of original source material is crucial (particularly legal and scholarly contexts).

> As Chief Justice Warren held for the Court, "[T]he Attorney General may bring an injunctive action . . .
>
> *or in general contexts*
>
> "The Attorney General may bring . . ."

Brackets also enclose editorial notes when text has been italicized for emphasis.

> But tucked away on page 11 we find this fascinating note: "In addition, we anticipate that *siting these new plants in marginal neighborhoods will decrease the risk of organized community opposition*" [italics added].

6. Brackets function as parentheses within parentheses, especially where two sets of parentheses could be confusing.

> Posner's recent essays (including the earlier *Law and Literature* [1988]) bear this out.

7. In mathematical copy, brackets are used with parentheses to indicate units contained within larger units. They are also used with various meanings in chemical names and formulas.

> $x + 5[(x + y)(2x - y)]$
>
> $Ag[Pt(NO_2)_4]$

With Other Punctuation

8. Punctuation that marks the end of a phrase, clause, item in a series, or sentence follows any bracketed material appended to that passage.

> The report stated, "if we fail to find additional sources of supply [of oil and gas], our long-term growth will be limited."

When brackets enclose a complete sentence, closing punctuation is placed within the brackets.

> [Since this article was written, new archival evidence of documented falsification has come to light.]

COLON

The colon is usually a mark of introduction, indicating that what follows it—generally a clause, a phrase, or a list—has been pointed to or described in what precedes it. (For the use of capitals following a colon, see paragraphs 7–8 on pages 259–60.)

With Phrases and Clauses

1. A colon introduces a clause or phrase that explains, illustrates, amplifies, or restates what has gone before.

> An umbrella is a foolish extravagance: if you don't leave it in the first restaurant, a gust of wind will destroy it on the way home.
>
> Dawn was breaking: the distant peaks were already glowing with the sun's first rays.

2. A colon introduces an appositive.

> The issue comes down to this: Will we offer a reduced curriculum, or will we simply cancel the program?
>
> That year Handley's old obsession was replaced with a new one: jazz.

3. A colon introduces a list or series, often following a phrase such as *the following* or *as follows*.

> She has trial experience on three judicial levels: county, state, and federal.
>
> Anyone planning to participate should be prepared to do the following: hike five miles with a backpack, sleep on the ground without a tent, and paddle a canoe through rough water.

It is occasionally used like a dash to introduce a summary statement following a series.

> Baseball, soccer, skiing, track: he excelled in every sport he took up.

4. Although the colon usually follows a full independent clause, it also often interrupts a sentence before the clause is complete.

> The nine proposed program topics are: offshore supply, vessel traffic, ferry services, ship repair, . . .
>
> Information on each participant includes: full name, date of birth, complete mailing address, . . .
>
> For example: 58 percent of union members voted, but only 44 percent of blue-collar workers as a whole.
>
> The association will:
> > Act with trust, integrity, and professionalism.
> > Operate in an open and effective manner.
> > Take the initiative in seeking diversity.

With Quotations

5. A colon usually introduces lengthy quoted material that is set off from the rest of a text by indentation but not by quotation marks.

> The *Rumpole* series has been nicely encapsulated as follows:
> > Rumpled, disreputable, curmudgeonly barrister Horace Rumpole often wins cases despite the disdain of his more aristocratic colleagues. Fond of cheap wine ("Château Thames Embankment") and Keats's poetry, he refers to his wife as "She Who Must Be Obeyed" (an allusion to the title character of H. Rider Haggard's *She*).

6. A colon is often used before a quotation in running text, especially when (1) the quotation is lengthy, (2) the quotation is a formal statement or is being given special emphasis, or (3) a full independent clause precedes the colon.

Said Murdoch: "The key to the success of this project is good planning. We need to know precisely what steps we will need to take, what kind of staff we will require, what the project will cost, and when we can expect completion."

The inscription reads: "Here lies one whose name was writ in water."

This was his verbatim response: "At this time Mr. Wilentz is still in the company's employ, and no change in his status is anticipated imminently.

Other Uses

7. A colon separates elements in bibliographic publication data and page references, in biblical citations, and in formulas used to express time and ratios. No space precedes or follows a colon between numerals.

> Stendhal, *Love* (New York: Penguin, 1975)
> *Paleobiology* 3:121
> John 4:10
> 8:30 a.m.
> a winning time of 3:43:02
> a ratio of 3:5

8. A colon separates titles and subtitles.

> *Southwest Stories: Tales from the Desert*

9. A colon follows the salutation in formal correspondence.

> Dear Judge Wright: Dear Product Manager:
> Dear Laurence: Ladies and Gentlemen:

10. A colon follows headings in memorandums, government correspondence, and general business letters.

> TO: VIA:
> SUBJECT: REFERENCE:

11. An unspaced colon separates the writer's and typist's initials in the identification lines of business letters.

> WAL:jml

A colon also separates copy abbreviations from the initials of copy recipients. (The abbreviation *cc* stands for *carbon* or *courtesy copy; bcc* stands for *blind carbon* or *courtesy copy*.) A space follows a colon used with the fuller name of a recipient.

> cc:RSP
>   JES
> bcc:MWK
> bcc: Mr. Jones

With Other Punctuation

12. A colon is placed outside quotation marks and parentheses that punctuate the larger sentence.

> The problem becomes most acute in "Black Rose and Destroying Angel": plot simply ceases to exist.
> Wilson and Hölldobler remark on the same phenomenon in *The Ants* (1990):

COMMA

The comma is the most frequently used punctuation mark in English and the one that provides the most difficulties to writers. Its most common uses are to separate items in a series and to set off or distinguish grammatical elements within sentences.

Between Main Clauses

1. A comma separates main clauses joined by a coordinating conjunction, such as *and, but, or, nor,* or *so.*

> She knew very little about the new system, and he volunteered nothing.
> The trial lasted for nine months, but the jury took only four hours to reach its verdict.
> We will not respond to any more questions on that topic this afternoon, nor will we respond to similar questions in the future.
> All the first-floor windows were barred, so he had clambered up onto the fire escape.

2. When one or both of the clauses are short or closely related in meaning, the comma is often omitted.

> They said good-bye and everyone hugged.

If commas set off another phrase that modifies the whole sentence, the comma between main clauses is often omitted.

> Six thousand years ago, the top of the volcano blew off in a series of powerful eruptions and the sides collapsed into the middle.

3. Commas are sometimes used to separate short and obviously parallel main clauses that are not joined by conjunctions.

> One day you're a successful corporate lawyer, the next day you're out of work.

Use of a comma to join clauses that are neither short nor obviously parallel, called *comma fault* or *comma splice,* is avoided. Clauses not joined by conjunctions are normally separated by semicolons. For details, see paragraph 1 on page 255.

4. If a sentence is composed of three or more clauses that are short and free of commas, the clauses are occasionally all separated by commas even if the last two are not joined by a conjunction. If the clauses are long or punctuated, they are separated with semicolons; the last two clauses are sometimes separated by a comma if they are joined by a conjunction. (For more details, see paragraph 5 on page 256.)

> Small fish fed among the marsh weed, ducks paddled along the surface, an occasional muskrat ate greens along the bank.
> The kids were tired and whiny; Napoleon, usually so calm, was edgy; Tabitha seemed to be going into heat, and even the guinea pigs were agitated.

With Compound Predicates

5. Commas are not normally used to separate the parts of a compound predicate.

> The firefighter tried to enter the burning building but was turned back by the thick smoke.

However, they are often used if the predicate is long and complicated, if one part is being stressed, or if the absence of a comma could cause a momentary misreading.

> The board helps to develop the financing and marketing strategies for new corporate divisions, and issues periodic reports on expenditures, revenues, and personnel appointments.
>
> This is an unworkable plan, and has been from the start.
>
> I try to explain to him what I want him to do, and get nowhere.

With Subordinate Clauses and Phrases

6. Adverbial clauses and phrases that begin a sentence are usually set off with commas.

> Having made that decision, we turned our attention to other matters.
>
> In order to receive a high school diploma, a student must earn 16 credits from public or private secondary schools.
>
> In addition, staff members respond to queries, take new orders, and initiate billing.

If the sentence can be easily read without a comma, the comma may be omitted. The phrase will usually be short—four words or less—but even after a longer phrase the comma is often omitted.

> As cars age, they depreciate. *or* As cars age they depreciate.
>
> In January the firm will introduce a new line of investigative services.
>
> On the map the town appeared as a small dot in the midst of vast emptiness.
>
> If nobody comes forward by Friday I will have to take further steps.

7. Adverbial clauses and phrases that introduce a main clause other than the first main clause are usually set off with commas. If the clause or phrase follows a conjunction, one comma often precedes the conjunction and one follows the clause or phrase. Alternatively, one comma precedes the conjunction and two more enclose the clause or phrase, or a single comma precedes the conjunction. Short phrases, and phrases in short sentences, tend not to be enclosed in commas.

> They have redecorated the entire store, but[,] to the delight of their customers, it retains much of its original flavor.
>
> We haven't left Springfield yet, but when we get to Boston we'll call you.

8. A comma is not used after an introductory phrase if the phrase immediately precedes the main verb.

> From the next room came a loud expletive.

9. A subordinate clause or phrase that modifies a noun is not set off by commas if it is *restrictive* (or *essential*)—that is, if its removal would alter the noun's meaning.

> The man who wrote this obviously had no firsthand knowledge of the situation.
>
> They entered through the first door that wasn't locked.

If the meaning would not be altered by its removal, the clause or phrase is considered *nonrestrictive* (or *nonessential*) and usually is set off by commas.

The new approach, which was based on team teaching, was well received.

Wechsler, who has done solid reporting from other battlefronts, is simply out of his depth here.

They tried the first door, which led nowhere.

10. Commas set off an adverbial clause or phrase that falls between the subject and the verb.

The Clapsaddle sisters, to keep up appearances, rode to the park every Sunday in their rented carriage.

11. Commas set off modifying phrases that do not immediately precede the word or phrase they modify.

Scarbo, intent as usual on his next meal, was snuffling around the butcher's bins.

The negotiators, tired and discouraged, headed back to the hotel.

We could see the importance, both long-term and short-term, of her proposal.

12. An absolute phrase (a participial phrase with its own subject that is grammatically independent of the rest of the sentence) is set off with commas.

Our business being concluded, we adjourned for refreshments.

We headed southward, the wind freshening behind us, to meet the rest of the fleet in the morning.

I'm afraid of his reaction, his temper being what it is.

With Appositives

13. Commas set off a word, phrase, or clause that is in apposition to (that is, equivalent to) a preceding or following noun and that is nonrestrictive.

It sat nursing its front paw, the injured one.

Aleister Crowley, Britain's most infamous satanist, is the subject of a remarkable new biography.

A cherished landmark in the city, the Hotel Sandburg has managed once again to escape the wrecking ball.

The committee cochairs were a lawyer, John Larson, and an educator, Mary Conway.

14. Restrictive appositives are not set off by commas.

He next had a walk-on role in the movie *The Firm*.

Longfellow's poem *Evangeline* was a favorite of my grandmother's.

The committee cochairs were the lawyer John Larson and the educator Mary Conway.

Lord Castlereagh was that strange anomaly[,] a Labor-voting peer.

With Introductory and Interrupting Elements

15. Commas set off transitional words and phrases.

Indeed, close coordination will be essential.

Defeat may be inevitable; however, disgrace is not.

The second report, on the other hand, shows a strong bias.

When such words and phrases fall in the middle of a clause, commas are sometimes unnecessary.

They thus have no chips left to bargain with.
The materials had indeed arrived.
She would in fact see them that afternoon.

16. Commas set off parenthetical elements, such as authorial asides.

All of us, to tell the truth, were completely amazed.
It was, I should add, not the first time I'd seen him in this condition.

17. Commas are often used to set off words or phrases that introduce examples or explanations, such as *namely, for example,* and *that is.*

He expects to visit three countries, namely, France, Spain, and Germany.
I would like to develop a good, workable plan, that is, one that would outline our goals and set a timetable for accomplishing them.

Such introductory words and phrases may also often be preceded by a dash, parenthesis, or semicolon. Regardless of the punctuation that precedes the word or phrase, a comma usually follows it.

Sports develop two valuable traits—namely, self-control and the ability to make quick decisions.
In writing to the manufacturer, be as specific as possible (i.e., list the missing or defective parts, describe the malfunction, and identify the store where the unit was purchased).
Most had traveled great distances to participate; for example, three had come from Australia, one from Japan, and two from China.

18. Commas set off words in direct address.

This is our third and final notice, Mr. Sutton.
The facts, my fellow Americans, are very different.

19. Commas set off mild interjections or exclamations.

Ah, the mosaics in Ravenna are matchless.
Uh-oh, His Eminence seems to be on the warpath this morning.

With Contrasting Expressions

20. A comma is sometimes used to set off contrasting expressions within a sentence.

This project will take six months, not six weeks.

21. When two or more contrasting modifiers or prepositions, one of which is introduced by a conjunction or adverb, apply to a noun that follows immediately, the second is set off by two commas or a single comma, or not set off at all.

A solid, if overly wordy, assessment
   or a solid, if overly wordy assessment
   or a solid if overly wordy assessment
This street takes you away from, not toward, the capitol.
   or This street takes you away from, not toward the capitol.
grounds for a civil, and maybe a criminal, case
   or grounds for a civil, and maybe a criminal case
   or grounds for a civil and maybe a criminal case

Dashes or parentheses are often used instead of commas in such sentences.

grounds for a civil (and maybe a criminal) case

22. A comma does not usually separate elements that are contrasted through the use of a pair of correlative conjunctions such as *either . . . or, neither . . . nor,* and *not only . . . but also.*

Neither my brother nor I noticed the error.

He was given the post not only because of his diplomatic connections but also because of his great tact and charm.

When correlative conjunctions join main clauses, a comma usually separates the clauses unless they are short.

Not only did she have to see three salesmen and a visiting reporter, but she also had to prepare for next day's meeting.

Either you do it my way or we don't do it at all.

23. Long parallel contrasting and comparing clauses are separated by commas; short parallel phrases are not.

The more that comes to light about him, the less savory he seems.

The less said the better.

With Items in a Series
24. Words, phrases, and clauses joined in a series are separated by commas.

Men, women, and children crowded aboard the train.

Her job required her to pack quickly, to travel often, and to have no personal life.

He responded patiently while reporters shouted questions, flashbulbs popped, and the crowd pushed closer.

When the last two items in a series are joined by a conjunction, the final comma is often omitted, especially where this would not result in ambiguity. In individual publications, the final comma is usually consistently used, consistently omitted, or used only where a given sentence would otherwise be ambiguous or hard to read. It is consistently used in most nonfiction books; elsewhere it tends to be used or generally omitted equally often.

We are looking for a house with a big yard, a view of the harbor[,] and beach and docking privileges.

25. A comma is not generally used to separate items in a series all of which are joined with conjunctions.

I don't understand what this policy covers or doesn't cover or only partially covers.

They left behind the fogs and the wood storks and the lonesome soughing of the wind.

26. When the elements in a series are long or complex or consist of clauses that themselves contain commas, the elements are usually separated by semicolons, not commas. See paragraph 7 on page 257.

With Coordinate Modifiers
27. A comma is generally used to separate two or more adjectives, adverbs, or phrases that modify the same word or phrase.

She spoke in a calm, reflective manner.
They set to their work again grimly, intently.

The comma is often omitted when the adjectives are short.

one long thin strand   skinny young waiters
a small white stone   in this harsh new light
little nervous giggles

The comma is generally omitted where it is ambiguous whether the last modifier and the noun-or two of the modifiers-constitute a unit.

the story's stark dramatic power
a pink stucco nightclub

In some writing, especially works of fiction, commas may be omitted from most series of coordinate modifiers as a matter of style.

28. A comma is not used between two adjectives when the first modifies the combination of the second plus the noun it modifies.

the last good man   the only fresh water
a good used car   the only freshwater lake
his protruding lower lip   their black pickup truck

A comma is also not used to separate an adverb from the adjective or adverb that it modifies.

this formidably difficult task

In Quotations

29. A comma usually separates a direct quotation from a phrase identifying its source or speaker. If the quotation is a question or an exclamation and the identifying phrase follows the quotation, the comma is replaced by a question mark or an exclamation point.

She answered, "I'm afraid it's all we've got."
"The comedy is over," he muttered.
"How about another round?" Elaine piped up.
"I suspect," said Mrs. Horowitz, "we haven't seen the last of her."
"You can sink the lousy thing for all I care!" Trumbull shouted back.
"And yet . . . ," she mused.
"We can't get the door op——" Captain Hunt is heard shouting before the tape goes dead.

In some cases, a colon can replace a comma preceding a quotation; see paragraph 6 on page 230.

30. When short or fragmentary quotations are used in a sentence that is not primarily dialogue, they are usually not set off by commas.

He glad-handed his way through the small crowd with a "Looking good, Joe" or "How's the wife" for every beaming face.
Just because he said he was "about to leave this minute" doesn't mean he actually left.

Sentences that fall within sentences and do not constitute actual dialogue are not usually set off with commas. These may be mottoes or maxims, unspoken or imaginary dialogue, or sentences referred to as sentences; and they may or may not be enclosed in quotation marks. Where quotation marks are not used, a comma is often inserted to mark the beginning of the shorter sentence clearly. (For the use of quotation marks with such sentences, see paragraph 6 on page 252.)

> "The computer is down" was the response she dreaded.
> He spoke with a candor that seemed to insist, This actually happened to me and in just this way.
> The first rule is, When in doubt, spell it out.

When the shorter sentence functions as an appositive (the equivalent to an adjacent noun), it is set off with commas when nonrestrictive and not when restrictive.

> We had the association's motto, "We make waves," printed on our T-shirts.
> He was fond of the slogan "Every man a king, but no man wears a crown."

31. A comma introduces a directly stated question, regardless of whether it is enclosed in quotation marks or if its first word is capitalized. It is not used to set off indirect discourse or indirect questions introduced by a conjunction (such as *that* or *what*).

> I wondered, what is going on here?
> The question is, How do we get out of this situation?
> *but*
> Margot replied quietly that she'd never been happier.
> I wondered what was going on here.
> The question is how do we get out of this situation.

32. The comma is usually omitted before quotations that are very short exclamations or representations of sounds.

> He jumped up suddenly and cried "I've got it!"

Replacing Omitted Words
33. A comma may indicate the omission of a word or phrase in parallel constructions where the omitted word or phrase appears earlier in the sentence. In short sentences, the comma is usually omitted.

> The larger towns were peopled primarily by shopkeepers, artisans, and traders; the small villages, by peasant farmers.
> Seven voted for the proposal, three against.
> He critiqued my presentation and I his.

34. A comma sometimes replaces the conjunction *that*.

> The smoke was so thick, they were forced to crawl.
> Chances are, there are still some tickets left.

With Addresses, Dates, and Numbers
35. Commas set off the elements of an address except for zip codes.

> Write to Bureau of the Census, Washington, DC 20233.
> In Needles, California, their luck ran out.

When a city name and state (province, country, etc.) name are used together to modify a noun that follows, the second comma may be omitted but is more often retained.

> We visited their Enid, Oklahoma plant.
> *but more commonly*
> We visited their Enid, Oklahoma, plant.

36. Commas set off the year in a full date.

> On July 26, 1992, the court issued its opinion.
> Construction for the project began on April 30, 1995.

When only the month and year are given, the first comma is usually omitted.

> In December 1903, the Wright brothers finally succeeded in keeping an airplane aloft for a few seconds.
> October 1929 brought an end to all that.

37. A comma groups numerals into units of three to separate thousands, millions, and so on.

> 2,000 case histories   a population of 3,450,000
> 15,000 units   a fee of $12,500

Certain types of numbers do not contain commas, including decimal fractions, street addresses, and page numbers. (For more on the use of the comma with numbers, see paragraphs 1–3 on page 306.)

> 2.5544
> 12537 Wilshire Blvd.
> page 1415

With Names, Degrees, and Titles

38. A comma separates a surname from a following professional, academic, honorary, or religious degree or title, or an abbreviation for a branch of the armed forces.

> Amelia P. Artandi, M.D.
> Robert Hynes Menard, Ph.D., L.H.D.
> John L. Farber, Esq.
> Sister Mary Catherine, S.C.
> Admiral Herman Washington, USN

39. A comma is often used between a surname and the abbreviations *Jr.* and *Sr.*

> Douglas Fairbanks, Sr. *or* Douglas Fairbanks Sr.
> Dr. Martin Luther King, Jr. *or* Dr. Martin Luther King Jr.

40. A comma is often used to set off corporate identifiers such as *Incorporated, Inc., Ltd., P.C.,* and *L.P.* However, many company names omit this comma.

> StarStage Productions, Incorporated
> Hart International Inc.
> Walsh, Brandon & Kaiser, P.C.
> The sales manager from Doyle Southern, Inc., spoke at Tuesday's meeting.

Other Uses

41. A comma follows the salutation in informal correspondence and usually follows the complimentary close in both informal and formal correspondence.

> Dear Rachel,
>
> Affectionately,
>
> Very truly yours,

42. The comma is used to avoid ambiguity when the juxtaposition of two words or expressions could cause confusion.

> Under Mr. Thomas, Jefferson High School has flourished.
>
> He scanned the landscape that opened out before him, and guided the horse gently down.

43. When normal sentence order is inverted, a comma often precedes the subject and verb. If the structure is clear without it, it is often omitted.

> That we would succeed, no one doubted.
>
> And a splendid occasion it was.

With Other Punctuation

44. Commas are used next to brackets, ellipsis points, parentheses, and quotation marks. Commas are not used next to colons, dashes, exclamation points, question marks, or semicolons. If one of the latter falls at the same point where a comma would fall, the comma is dropped. (For more on the use of commas with other punctuation, see the sections for each individual mark).

> "If they find new sources [of oil and gas], their earnings will obviously rebound . . . ."
>
> "This book takes its place among the most serious, . . . comprehensive, and enlightened treatments of its great subject."
>
> There are only six small files (at least in this format), which take up very little disk space.
>
> According to Hartmann, the people are "savage," their dwellings are "squalid," and the landscape is "a pestilential swamp."

DASH

The dash can function like a comma, a colon, or a parenthesis. Like commas and parentheses, dashes set off parenthetical material such as examples, supplemental facts, and explanatory or descriptive phrases. Like a colon, a dash introduces clauses that explain or expand upon something that precedes them. Though sometimes considered a less formal equivalent of the colon and parenthesis, the dash may be found in all kinds of writing, including the most formal, and the choice of which mark to use is often a matter of personal preference.

The common dash (also called the *em dash*, since it is approximately the width of a capital M in typeset material) is usually represented by two hyphens in typed and keyboarded material. (Word-processing programs make it available as a special character.)

Spacing around the dash varies. Most newspapers insert a space before and after the dash; many popular magazines do the same; but most books and journals omit spacing.

The *en dash* and the *two-* and *three-em dashes* have more limited uses, which are explained in paragraphs 13–15 on page 243.

Abrupt Change or Suspension

1. The dash marks an abrupt change or break in the structure of a sentence.

> The students seemed happy enough with the new plan, but the alumni—there was the problem.

2. A dash is used to indicate interrupted speech or a speaker's confusion or hesitation.

> "The next point I'd like to bring up—" the speaker started to say.
>
> "Yes," he went on, "yes—that is—I guess I agree."

Parenthetical and Amplifying Elements

3. Dashes are used in place of commas or parentheses to emphasize or draw attention to parenthetical or amplifying material.

> With three expert witnesses in agreement, the defense can be expected to modify its strategy—somewhat.
>
> This amendment will finally prevent corporations—large and small—from buying influence through exorbitant campaign contributions.

When dashes are used to set off parenthetical elements, they often indicate that the material is more digressive than elements set off with commas but less digressive than elements set off by parentheses. For examples, see paragraph 16 on page 235 and paragraph 1 on page 247.

4. Dashes set off or introduce defining phrases and lists.

> The fund sought to acquire controlling positions—a minimum of 25% of outstanding voting securities—in other companies.
>
> Davis was a leading innovator in at least three styles—bebop, cool jazz, and jazz-rock fusion.

5. A dash is often used in place of a colon or semicolon to link clauses, especially when the clause that follows the dash explains, summarizes, or expands upon the preceding clause in a somewhat dramatic way.

> The results were in—it had been a triumphant success.

6. A dash or a pair of dashes often sets off illustrative or amplifying material introduced by such phrases as *for example, namely,* and *that is,* when the break in continuity is greater than that shown by a comma, or when the dash would clarify the sentence structure better than a comma. (For more details, see paragraph 17 on page 235.)

> After some discussion the motion was tabled—that is, it was removed indefinitely from the board's consideration.
>
> Lawyers should generally—in pleadings, for example—attempt to be as specific as possible.

7. A dash may introduce a summary statement that follows a series of words or phrases.

> Crafts, food booths, children's activities, cider-making demonstrations—there was something for everyone.

Once into bankruptcy, the company would have to pay cash for its supplies, defer maintenance, and lay off workers—moves that could threaten its future.

8. A dash often precedes the name of an author or source at the end of a quoted passage—such as an epigraph, extract, or book or film blurb—that is not part of the main text. The attribution may appear immediately after the quotation or on the next line.

Only the sign is for sale.
                                    —Søren Kierkegaard

"I return to her stories with more pleasure, and await them with more anticipation, than those of any of her contemporaries."—William Logan, *Chicago Tribune*

With Other Punctuation

9. If a dash appears at a point where a comma could also appear, the comma is omitted.

Our lawyer has read the transcript—all 1,200 pages of it—and he has decided that an appeal would not be useful.

If we don't succeed—and the critics say we won't—then the whole project is in jeopardy.

In a series, dashes that would force a comma to be dropped are often replaced by parentheses.

The holiday movie crowds were being entertained by street performers: break dancers, a juggler (who doubled as a sword swallower), a steel-drummer, even a three-card-monte dealer.

10. If the second of a pair of dashes would fall where a period should also appear, the dash is omitted.

Instead, he hired his mother   an odd choice by any standard.

Much less frequently, the second dash will be dropped in favor of a colon or semicolon.

Valley Health announced general improvements to its practice—two to start this week: evening office hours and a voice-mail message system.

His conduct has always been exemplary—near-perfect attendance, excellent productivity, a good attitude; nevertheless, his termination cannot be avoided.

11. When a pair of dashes sets off material ending with an exclamation point or a question mark, the mark is placed inside the dashes.

His hobby was getting on people's nerves—especially mine!—and he was extremely good at it.

There would be a "distinguished guest speaker"—was there ever any other kind?—and plenty of wine afterwards.

12. Dashes are used inside parentheses, and vice versa, to indicate parenthetical material within parenthetical material. The second dash is omitted if it would immediately precede the closing parenthesis; a closing parenthesis is never omitted.

We were looking for a narrator (or narrators—sometimes a script call for more than one) who could handle a variety of assignments.

The wall of the Old City contains several gates—particularly Herod's Gate, the Golden Gate, and Zion Gate (or "David's Gate")—with rich histories.

En Dash and Long Dashes

13. The *en dash* generally appears only in typeset material; in typed or key-boarded material the simple hyphen is usually used instead. (Word-processing programs provide the en dash as a special character.) Newspapers similarly use the hyphen in place of the en dash. The en dash is shorter than the em dash but longer than the hyphen. It is most frequently used between numbers, dates, or other notations to signify "(up) to and including."

pages 128–34 September 24–October 5
1995–97 8:30 a.m.–4:30 p.m.

The en dash replaces a hyphen in compound adjectives when at least one of the elements is a two-word compound. It replaces the word *to* between capitalized names, and is used to indicate linkages such as boundaries, treaties, and oppositions.

post–Cold War era
Boston–Washington train
New Jersey–Pennsylvania border
male–female differences *or* male-female differences

14. A *two-em dash* is used to indicate missing letters in a word and, less frequently, to indicate a missing word.

The nearly illegible letter is addressed to a Mr. P—— of Baltimore.

15. A *three-em dash* indicates that a word has been left out or that an unknown word or figure is to be supplied.

The study was carried out in ———, a fast-growing Sunbelt city.

ELLIPSIS POINTS

Ellipsis points (also known as *ellipses, points of ellipsis,* and *suspension points*) are periods, usually in groups of three, that signal an omission from quoted material or indicate a pause or trailing off of speech. A space usually precedes and follows each ellipsis point. (In newspaper style, spaces are usually omitted.)

1. Ellipsis points indicate the omission of one or more words within a quoted sentence.

We the People of the United States . . . do ordain and establish this Constitution for the United States of America.

2. Ellipsis points are usually not used to indicate the omission of words that precede the quoted portion. However, in some formal contexts, especially when the quotation is introduced by a colon, ellipsis points are used.

He ends with a stirring call for national resolve that "government of the people, by the people, for the people shall not perish from the earth."

Its final words define the war's purpose in democratic terms: ". . . that government of the people, by the people, for the people shall not perish from the earth."

Ellipsis points following quoted material are omitted when it forms an integral part of a larger sentence.

She maintained that it was inconsistent with "government of the people, by the people, for the people."

3. Punctuation used in the original that falls on either side of the ellipsis points is often omitted; however, it may be retained, especially if this helps clarify the sentence.

> Now we are engaged in a great civil war testing whether that nation . . . can long endure.
>
> But, in a larger sense, we can not dedicate, . . . we can not hallow this ground.
>
> We the People of the United States, in Order to . . . promote the general Welfare, and secure the Blessings of Liberty . . . , do ordain and establish this Constitution for the United States of America.

4. If an omission includes an entire sentence within a passage, the last part of a sentence within a passage, or the first part of a sentence other than the first quoted sentence, the period preceding or following the omission is retained (with no space preceding it) and is followed by three ellipsis points. When the first part of a sentence is omitted but the quoted portion acts as a sentence, the first quoted word is usually capitalized.

> We have come to dedicate a portion of that field, as a final resting place for those who here gave their lives that this nation might live. . . . But, in a larger sense, we can not dedicate—we can not consecrate—we can not hallow—this ground.
>
> Now we are engaged in a great civil war. . . . We are met on a great battlefield of that war.
>
> The brave men, living and dead, who struggled here, have consecrated it, far above our poor power to add or detract. . . . From these honored dead we take increased devotion to that cause for which they gave the last full measure of devotion. . . .

Alternatively, the period may be dropped and all omissions may be indicated simply by three ellipsis points.

5. If the last words of a quoted sentence are omitted and the original sentence ends with punctuation other than a period, the end punctuation often follows the ellipsis points, especially if it helps clarify the quotation.

> He always ends his harangues with some variation on the question, "What could you have been thinking when you . . . ?"

6. When ellipsis points are used to indicate that a quotation has been intentionally left unfinished, the terminal period is omitted.

> The paragraph beginning "Recent developments suggest . . ." should be deleted.

7. A line of ellipsis points indicates that one or more lines have been omitted from a poem. (For more on poetry and extracts, see the section on pages 253–54.)

> When I heard the learned astronomer,
> . . . .
> How soon unaccountable I became tired and sick,
> Til rising and gliding out I wandered off by myself,
> In the mystical moist night-air, and from time to time,
> Looked up in perfect silence at the stars.

8. Ellipsis points are used to indicate faltering speech, especially if the faltering involves a long pause or a sentence that trails off or is intentionally left unfinished. Generally no other terminal punctuation is used.

The speaker seemed uncertain. "Well, that's true . . . but even so . . . I think we can do better."

"Despite these uncertainties, we believe we can do it, but . . ."

"I mean . . ." he said, "like . . . How?"

9. Ellipsis points are sometimes used informally as a stylistic device to catch a reader's attention, often replacing a dash or colon.

They think that nothing can go wrong . . . but it does.

10. In newspaper and magazine columns consisting of social notes, local events listings, or short items of celebrity news, ellipsis points often take the place of paragraphing to separate the items. (Ellipsis points are also often used in informal personal correspondence in place of periods or paragraphing.)

Congratulations to Debra Morricone, our up-and-coming singing star, for her full scholarship to the Juilliard School this fall! . . . And kudos to Paul Chartier for his winning All-State trumpet performance last Friday in Baltimore! . . . Look for wit and sparkling melody when the Lions mount their annual Gilbert & Sullivan show at Syms Auditorium. This year it's . . .

EXCLAMATION POINT

The exclamation point is used to mark a forceful comment or exclamation.

1. An exclamation point can punctuate a sentence, phrase, or interjection.

There is no alternative!

Without a trace!

My God! It's monstrous!

2. The exclamation point may replace the question mark when an ironic, angry, or emphatic tone is more important than the actual question.

Aren't you finished yet!

Do you realize what you've done!

Why me!

Occasionally it is used *with* the question mark to indicate a very forceful question.

How much did you say?!

You did what!?

3. The exclamation point falls within brackets, dashes, parentheses, and quotation marks when it punctuates only the enclosed material. It is placed outside them when it punctuates the entire sentence.

All of this proves—at long last!—that we were right from the start.

Somehow the dog got the gate open (for the third time!) and ran into the street.

He sprang to his feet and shouted "Point of order!"

At this rate the national anthem will soon be replaced by "You Are My Sunshine"!

4. If an exclamation point falls where a comma could also go, the comma is dropped.

"Absolutely not!" he snapped.

They wouldn't dare! she told herself over and over.

If the exclamation point is part of a title, it may be followed by a comma. If the title falls at the end of a sentence, no period follows it.

Hello Dolly!, which opened in 1964, would become one of the ten longest-running shows in Broadway history.

His favorite management book is still *Up the Organization!*

HYPHEN

Hyphens have a variety of uses, the most significant of which is to join the elements of compound nouns and modifiers.

1. Hyphens are used to link elements in compound words. (For more on compound words, see the section beginning on page 283.)

secretary-treasurer   fund-raiser
cost-effective   spin-off

2. In some words, a hyphen separates a prefix, suffix, or medial element from the rest of the word. Consult a dictionary in doubtful cases. (For details on using a hyphen with a prefix or a suffix, see the section beginning on page 291.)

anti-inflation
umbrella-like
jack-o'-lantern

3. In typed and keyboarded material, a hyphen is generally used between numbers and dates with the meaning "(up) to and including." In typeset material it is replaced by an en dash. (For details on the en dash, see paragraph 13 on page 243.)

pages 128–34
the years 1995–97

4. A hyphen marks an end-of-line division of a word.

In 1975 smallpox, formerly a great scourge, was declared totally eradicated by the World Health Organization.

5. A hyphen divides letters or syllables to give the effect of stuttering, sobbing, or halting speech.

"S-s-sammy, it's my t-toy!"

6. Hyphens indicate a word spelled out letter by letter.

l-i-a-i-s-o-n

7. Hyphens are sometimes used to produce inflected forms of verbs made of individually pronounced letters or to add an *-er* ending to an abbreviation. However, apostrophes are more commonly used for these purposes. (For details on these uses of the apostrophe, see paragraph 6 on page 228.)

DH-ing for the White Sox   *or*   DH'ing for the White Sox
a dedicated UFO-er   *or*   a dedicated UFO'er

PARENTHESES

Parentheses generally enclose material that is inserted into a main statement but is not intended to be an essential part of it. For some of the cases described below, commas or dashes are frequently used instead. (For examples, see paragraph 16 on page 235 and paragraph 3 on page 241.) Parentheses are particularly used when the inserted material is only incidental. Unlike commas and dashes, an opening parenthesis is always followed by a closing one. Because parentheses are almost always used in pairs, and their shapes indicate their relative functions, they often clarify a sentence's structure better than commas or dashes.

Parenthetical Elements

1. Parentheses enclose phrases and clauses that provide examples, explanations, or supplementary facts or numerical data.

   > Nominations for principal officers (president, vice president, treasurer, and secretary) were heard and approved.
   > Four computers (all outdated models) will be replaced.
   > First-quarter sales figures were good (up 8%), but total revenues showed a slight decline (down 1%).

2. Parentheses sometimes enclose phrases and clauses introduced by expressions such as *namely, that is, e.g.,* and *i.e.,* particularly where parentheses would clarify the sentence's structure better than commas. (For more details, see paragraph 17 on page 235.)

   > In writing to the manufacturer, be as specific as possible (i.e., list the defective parts, describe the malfunction, and identify the store where the unit was purchased), but also as concise.

3. Parentheses enclose definitions or translations in the main part of a sentence.

   > The company announced plans to sell off its housewares (small-appliances) business.
   > The *grand monde* (literally, "great world") of prewar Parisian society consisted largely of titled aristocracy.

4. Parentheses enclose abbreviations that follow their spelled-out forms, or spelled-out forms that follow abbreviations.

   > She cited a study by the Food and Drug Administration (FDA).
   > They attended last year's convention of the ABA (American Booksellers Association).

5. Parentheses often enclose cross-references and bibliographic references.

   > Specialized services are also available (see list at end of brochure).
   > The diagram (Fig. 3) illustrates the action of the pump.
   > Subsequent studies (Braxton 1990; Roh and Weinglass 1993) have confirmed these findings.

6. Parentheses enclose numerals that confirm a spelled-out number in a business or legal context.

   > Delivery will be made in thirty (30) days.
   > The fee is Four Thousand Dollars ($4,000), payable to UNCO, Inc.

7. Parentheses enclose the name of a state that is inserted into a proper name for identification.

> the Kalispell (Mont.) Regional Hospital
> the *Sacramento* (Calif.) *Bee*

8. Parentheses may be used to enclose personal asides.

> Claims were made of its proven efficacy (some of us were skeptical).
> *or*
> Claims were made of its proven efficacy. (Some of us were skeptical.)

9. Parentheses are used to enclose quotations that illustrate or support a statement made in the main text.

> After he had a few brushes with the police, his stepfather had him sent to jail as an incorrigible ("It will do him good").

Other Uses

10. Parentheses enclose unpunctuated numbers or letters indicating individual elements or items in a series within a sentence.

> Sentences can be classified as (1) simple, (2) multiple or compound, and (3) complex.

11. Parentheses indicate alternative terms.

> Please sign and return the enclosed form(s).

12. Parentheses may be used to indicate losses in accounting.

> Operating Profits
> (in millions)
> Cosmetics 26.2
> Food products . . . 47.7
> Food services 54.3
> Transportation . . . (17.7)
> Sporting goods . . . (11.2)
> Total 99.3

With Other Punctuation

13. When an independent sentence is enclosed in parentheses, its first word is capitalized and a period (or other closing punctuation) is placed inside the parentheses.

> The discussion was held in the boardroom. (The results are still confidential.)

A parenthetical expression that occurs within a sentence—even if it could stand alone as a separate sentence—does not end with a period but may end with an exclamation point, a question mark, or quotation marks.

> Although several trade organizations opposed the legislation (there were at least three paid lobbyists working on Capitol Hill), the bill passed easily.
> The conference was held in Portland (Me., not Ore.).
> After waiting in line for an hour (why do we do these things?), we finally left.

A parenthetical expression within a sentence does not require capitalization unless it is a quoted sentence.

> He was totally confused ("What can we do?") and refused to see anyone.

14. If a parenthetical expression within a sentence is composed of two independent clauses, a semicolon rather than a period usually separates them. Independent sentences enclosed together in parentheses employ normal sentence capitalization and punctuation.

> We visited several showrooms, looked at the prices (it wasn't a pleasant experience; prices in this area have not gone down), and asked all the questions we could think of.
>
> We visited several showrooms and looked at the prices. (It wasn't a pleasant experience. Prices in this area have not gone down.)

Entire paragraphs are rarely enclosed in parentheses; instead, paragraphs of incidental material often appear as footnotes or endnotes.

15. No punctuation (other than a period after an abbreviation) is placed immediately before an opening parenthesis within a sentence; if punctuation is required, it follows the final parenthesis.

> I'll get back to you tomorrow (Friday), when I have more details.
> Tickets cost $14 in advance ($12 for seniors); the price at the door is $18.
> The relevant figures are shown below (in millions of dollars):

16. Parentheses sometimes appear within parentheses when no confusion would result; alternatively, the inner parentheses are replaced with brackets.

> Checks must be drawn in U.S. dollars. (*Please note:* We cannot accept checks drawn on Canadian banks for amounts less than four U.S. dollars ($4.00). The same regulation applies to Canadian money orders.)

17. Dashes and parentheses may be used together to set off parenthetical material. (For details, see paragraph 12 on page 242.)

> The orchestra is spirited, and the cast—an expert and enthusiastic crew of Savoyards (some of them British imports)—comes through famously.

PERIOD

Periods almost always serve to mark the end of a sentence or abbreviation.

1. A period ends a sentence or a sentence fragment that is neither a question nor an exclamation.

> From the Format menu, choose Style.
> Robert decided to bring champagne.
> Unlikely. In fact, inconceivable.

Only one period ends a sentence.

> The jellied gasoline was traced to the Trenton-based Quality Products, Inc.
> Miss Toklas states categorically that "This is the best way to cook frogs' legs."

2. A period punctuates some abbreviations. No space follows an internal period within an abbreviation. (For details on punctuating abbreviations, see the section beginning on page 294.)

Assn.	Dr.	p.m.
Ph.D.	e.g.	etc.

3. Periods are used with a person's initials, each followed by a space. (Newspaper style omits the space.) If the initials replace the name, they are unspaced and may also be written without periods.

> J. B. S. Haldane
> L.B.J. *or* LBJ

4. A period follows numerals and letters when they are used without parentheses in outlines and vertical lists.

> 1. Objectives   Required skills are:
>   A. Economy   1. Shorthand
>   1. Low initial cost   2. Typing
>   2. Low maintenance cost   3. Transcription
>   B. Ease of operation

5. A period is placed within quotation marks, even when it did not punctuate the original quoted material. (In British practice, the period goes outside the quotation marks whenever it does not belong to the original quoted material.)

> The founder was known to his employees as "the old man."
>
> "I said I wanted to fire him," Henry went on, "but she said, 'I don't think you have the contractual privilege to do that.'"

6. When brackets or parentheses enclose an independent sentence, the period is placed inside them. When brackets or parentheses enclose a sentence that is part of a larger sentence, the period for the enclosed sentence is omitted.

> Arturo finally arrived on the 23rd with the terrible news that Katrina had been detained by the police. [This later proved to be false; see letter 255.]
>
> I took a good look at her (she was standing quite close to me).

QUESTION MARK

The question mark always indicates a question or doubt.

1. A question mark ends a direct question.

> What went wrong?
> "When do they arrive?" she asked.

A question mark follows a period only when the period punctuates an abbreviation. No period follows a question mark.

> Is he even an M.D.?
> "Will you arrive by 10 p.m.?"
> A local professor would be giving a paper with the title "Economic Stagnation or Equilibrium?"

2. Polite requests that are worded as questions usually take periods, because they are not really questions. Conversely, a sentence that is intended as a question but whose word order is that of a statement is punctuated with a question mark.

> Could you please send the necessary forms.
> They flew in yesterday?

3. The question mark ends a question that forms part of a sentence. An indirect question is not followed by a question mark.

> What was her motive? you may be asking.
> I naturally wondered, Will it really work?
> I naturally wondered whether it would really work.
> He asked when the report was due.

4. The question mark punctuates each element of a series of questions that share a single beginning and are neither numbered nor lettered. When the series is numbered or lettered, only one question mark is generally used.

> Can you give us a reasonable forecast? Back up your predictions? Compare them with last year's earnings?
> Can you (1) give us a reasonable forecast, (2) back up your predictions, and (3) compare them with last year's earnings?

5. The question mark indicates uncertainty about a fact or the accuracy of a transcription.

> Homer, Greek epic poet (9th-8th? cent. B.C.)
> He would have it that Farjeon[?] is the onlie man for us.

6. The question mark is placed inside brackets, dashes, parentheses, or quotation marks when it punctuates only the material enclosed by them and not the sentence as a whole. It is placed outside them when it punctuates the entire sentence.

> I took a vacation in 1992 (was it really that long ago?), but I haven't had time for one since.
> What did Andrew mean when he called the project "a fiasco from the start"?
> Williams then asks, "Do you realize the extent of the problem [the housing shortage]?"

QUOTATION MARKS

The following paragraphs describe the use of quotation marks to enclose quoted matter in regular text, and for other, less frequent uses. For the use of quotation marks to enclose titles, see paragraph 70 on page 273.

Basic Uses

1. Quotation marks enclose direct quotations but not indirect quotations or paraphrases.

> Dr. Mee added, "We'd be grateful for anything you could do."
> "We just got the lab results," he crowed, "and the blood types match!"
> "I'm leaving," she whispered. "This meeting could go on forever."
> "Mom, we *tried* that already!" they whined in unison.
> "Ssshh!" she hissed.
> She said she was leaving.
> Algren once said something like, Don't ever play poker with anyone named Doc, and never eat at a diner called Mom's.

2. Quotation marks enclose fragments of quoted matter.

> The agreement makes it clear that he "will be paid only upon receipt of an acceptable manuscript."
>
> As late as 1754, documents refer to him as "yeoman" and "husbandman."

3. Quotation marks enclose words or phrases borrowed from others, and words of obvious informality introduced into formal writing. Words introduced as specialized terminology are sometimes enclosed in quotation marks but more often italicized.

> Be sure to send a copy of your résumé—or as some folks would say, your "biodata summary."
>
> They were afraid the patient had "stroked out"—had had a cerebrovascular accident.
>
> referred to as "closed" or "privately held" corporations
> *but more frequently*
> referred to as *closed* or *privately held* corporations
>
> New Hampshire's only "green" B&B

4. Quotation marks are sometimes used to enclose words referred to as words. Italics are also frequently used for this purpose.

> changed every "he" to "she"
> *or*
> changed every *he* to *she*

5. Quotation marks may enclose representations of sounds, though these are also frequently italicized.

> If it sounds like "quank, quank" [*or* like *quank, quank*], it may be the green treefrog.

6. Quotation marks often enclose short sentences that fall within longer sentences, especially when the shorter sentence is meant to suggest spoken dialogue. Mottoes and maxims, unspoken or imaginary dialogue, and sentences referred to as sentences may all be treated in this way.

> On the gate was the inscription "Arbeit macht frei" [*or Arbeit macht frei*]—"Work will make you free."
>
> The fact was, the poor kid didn't know "C'mere" from "Sic 'em."
>
> In effect, the voters were saying "You blew it, and you don't get another chance."
>
> Their reaction could only be described as "Kill the messenger."
>
> She never got used to their "That's the way it goes" attitude.
> *or*
> She never got used to their that's-the-way-it-goes attitude.

Quotation marks are often omitted in sentences of this kind when the structure is clear without them. (For the use of commas in such sentences, see paragraphs 29–30 on page 237.)

> The first rule is, When in doubt, spell it out.

7. Direct questions are enclosed in quotation marks when they represent quoted dialogue, but usually not otherwise.

> She asked, "What went wrong?"
>
> The question is, What went wrong?

We couldn't help wondering, Where's the plan?
> *or*

We couldn't help wondering, "Where's the plan?"

8. Quotation marks enclose translations of foreign or borrowed terms.

> This is followed by the Dies Irae ("Day of Wrath"), a climactic movement in many settings of the Requiem.
>
> The term comes from the Latin *sesquipedalis,* meaning "a foot and a half long."

They also frequently enclose definitions.

> *Concupiscent* simply means "lustful."
> *or*
> *Concupiscent* simply means lustful.

9. Quotation marks sometimes enclose letters referred to as letters.

> The letter "m" is wider than the letter "i."
>
> Put an "x" in the right spot.

However, such letters are more frequently italicized (or underlined), or left undifferentiated from the surrounding text where no confusion would result.

> How many *e*'s are in her name?
>
> a V-shaped blade
>
> He was happy to get a B in the course.

With Longer Quotations

10. Quotation marks are not used with longer passages of prose or poetry that are indented as separate paragraphs, called *extracts* or *block quotations.* Quoted text is usually set as an extract when it is longer than a sentence or runs to at least four lines, but individual requirements of consistency, clarity, or emphasis may alter these limits. Extracts are set off from the normal text by (1) indenting the passage on the left, and often on the right as well, and (2) usually setting it in smaller type. Extracts are usually preceded by a sentence ending with a colon, and they usually begin with a capitalized first word. The first line of an extract has no added indention; however, if the extract consists of more than one paragraph, the subsequent paragraphs are indented. (For the use of ellipsis points to show omissions within extracts, see the section beginning on page 243.)

> The chapter begins with a general description of memos:
> The interoffice memorandum or memo is a means of informal communication within a firm or organization. It replaces the salutation, complimentary close, and written signature of the letter with identifying headings.

If the extract continues the flow of an incomplete sentence, no punctuation is required and the extract begins with a lowercase letter.

> They describe the memo as
> a means of informal communication within a firm or organization. It replaces the salutation, complimentary close, and written signature of the letter with identifying headings.

If the sentence preceding the extract does not refer directly to it, the sentence usually ends with a period, though a colon is also common.

As of the end of April she believed that the product stood a good chance of success.
Unit sales are strong, revenues are better than forecast, shipments are being made on schedule, and inventory levels are stable.

11. When an extract itself includes quoted material, double quotation marks enclose the material.

The authors recommend the following procedure:
The presiding officer will call for the appropriate report from an officer, board member, standing committee, or special committee by saying, "Will the chairperson of the Ways and Means Committee please present the committee's report?"

12. When poetry is set as an extract, the lines are divided exactly as in the original. A spaced slash separates lines of run-in poetry.

The experience reminded them of Pope's observation:
A little learning is a dang'rous thing;
Drink deep, or taste not the Pierian spring:
There shallow draughts intoxicate the brain,
And drinking largely sobers us again.

When the poet Gerard Manley Hopkins wrote that "Nothing is so beautiful as spring— / When weeds, in wheels, shoot long and lovely and lush," he probably had my yard in mind.

13. Quotation marks are not used with epigraphs. However, they are generally used with advertising blurbs.

The whole of science is nothing more than a refinement of everyday thinking.
—Albert Einstein

"A brutal irony, a slam-bang humor and a style of writing as balefully direct as a death sentence."—*Time*

With Other Punctuation

14. When a period or comma follows text enclosed in quotation marks, it is placed within the quotation marks, even if the original language quoted was not followed by a period or comma.

He smiled and said, "I'm happy for you."
But perhaps Pound's most perfect poem was "The Return."
The cameras were described as "waterproof," but "moisture-resistant" would have been a better description.

In British usage, the period or comma goes outside the quoted matter whenever the original text did not include the punctuation.

15. When a colon or semicolon follows text enclosed in quotation marks, the colon or semicolon is placed outside the quotation marks.

But they all chimed in on "O Sole Mio": raw adolescents, stately matrons, decrepit old pensioners, their voices soaring in passion together.
She spoke of her "little cottage in the country"; she might better have called it a mansion.

16. The dash, question mark, and exclamation point are placed inside quotation marks when they punctuate the quoted matter only, but outside the quotation marks when they punctuate the whole sentence.

"I can't see how—" he started to say.

He thought he knew where he was going—he remembered her saying, "Take two lefts, then stay to the right"—but the streets didn't look familiar.

He asked, "When did they leave?"

What is the meaning of "the open door"?

She collapsed in her seat with a stunned "Good God!"

Save us from his "mercy"!

Single Quotation Marks

17. Single quotation marks replace double quotation marks when the quoted material occurs within quoted material.

> The witness said, "I distinctly heard him say, 'Don't be late,' and then I heard the door close."
>
> "We'd like to close tonight with that great Harold Arlen wee-hours standard, 'One for My Baby.'"
>
> This analysis is indebted to Del Banco's "Elizabeth Bishop's 'Insomnia': An Inverted View."

When both single and double quotation marks occur at the end of a sentence, the period falls within both sets of marks.

> The witness said, "I distinctly heard him say, 'Don't be late.'"

British usage often reverses American usage, enclosing quoted material in single quotation marks, and enclosing quotations within quotations in double quotation marks. In British usage, commas and periods following quoted material go inside only those quotation marks that enclose material that originally included the period or comma.

18. A quotation within a quotation within a quotation is usually enclosed in double quotation marks. (Such constructions are usually avoided by rewriting.)

> As the *Post* reported it, "Van Houten's voice can be clearly heard saying, 'She said "You wouldn't dare" and I said "I just did."'"
>   *or*
> The *Post* reported that Van Houten's voice was clearly heard saying, "She said 'You wouldn't dare' and I said 'I just did.'"

SEMICOLON

The semicolon may be used much like the comma, period, or colon, depending on the context. Like a comma, it may separate elements in a series. Like a period or colon, it frequently marks the end of a complete clause, and like a colon it signals that the remainder of the sentence is closely related to the first part. However, in each case the semicolon is normally used in a distinctive way. It serves as a higher-level comma; it connects clauses, as a period does not; and it does not imply any following exemplification, amplification, or description, as a colon generally does.

Between Clauses

1. A semicolon separates related independent clauses joined without a coordinating conjunction.

> Cream the shortening and sugar; add the eggs and beat well.
>
> The river rose and overflowed its banks; roads became flooded and impassable; freshly plowed fields disappeared from sight.

2. A semicolon often replaces a comma between two clauses joined by a coordinating conjunction if the sentence might otherwise be confusing—for example, because of particularly long clauses or the presence of other commas.

> In a society that seeks to promote social goals, government will play a powerful role; and taxation, once simply a means of raising money, becomes, in addition, a way of furthering those goals.

3. A semicolon joins two clauses when the second includes a conjunctive adverb such as *accordingly, however, indeed,* or *thus,* or a phrase that acts like a conjunctive adverb such as *in that case, as a result,* or *on the other hand.*

> Most people are covered by insurance of some kind; indeed, many don't even see their medical bills.
>
> It won't be easy to sort out the facts; a decision must be made, however.
>
> The case could take years to work its way through the courts; as a result, many plaintiffs will accept settlements.

When *so* and *yet* are treated as conjunctive adverbs, they are often preceded by a semicolon and followed by a comma. When treated as coordinating conjunctions, as they usually are, they are generally only preceded by a comma.

> The new recruits were bright, diligent, and even enthusiastic; yet[,] the same problems persisted.
>
> His grades improved sharply, yet the high honor roll still eluded him.

4. A semicolon may join two statements when the second clause is elliptical, omitting essential words that are supplied by the first. In short sentences, a comma often replaces the semicolon.

> The conference sessions, designed to allow for full discussions, were much too long; the breaks between them, much too short.
>
> The aged Scotch was haunting, the Asiago piquant.

5. When a series of clauses are separated by semicolons and a coordinating conjunction precedes the final clause, the final semicolon is sometimes replaced with a comma.

> The bars had all closed hours ago; a couple of coffee shops were open but deserted[; *or* ,] and only a few lighted upper-story windows gave evidence of other victims of insomnia.

6. A semicolon is often used before introductory expressions such as *for example, that is,* and *namely,* in place of a colon, comma, dash, or parenthesis. (For more details, see paragraph 17 on page 235.)

> On one point only did everyone agree; namely, too much money had been spent already.
>
> We were fairly successful on that project; that is, we made our deadlines and met our budget.

In a Series

7. A semicolon is used in place of a comma to separate phrases or items in a series when the phrases or items themselves contain commas. A comma may replace the semicolon before a conjunction that precedes the last item in a series.

> The assets in question include $22 million in land, buildings, and equipment; $34 million in cash, investments, and accounts receivable; and $8 million in inventory.
>
> The votes against were: Precinct 1, 418; Precinct 2, 332; Precinct 3, 256.
>
> The debate about the nature of syntactic variation continues to this day (Labov 1991; Dines 1991, 1993; Romaine 1995).
>
> The Pissarro exhibition will travel to Washington, D.C.; Manchester, N.H.; Portland, Ore., and Oakland, Calif.

When the items in a series are long or are sentences themselves, they are usually separated by semicolons even if they lack internal commas.

> Among the committee's recommendations were the following: more hospital beds in urban areas where there are waiting lines for elective surgery; smaller staff size in half-empty rural hospitals; and review procedures for all major purchases.

With Other Punctuation

8. A semicolon that punctuates the larger sentence is placed outside quotation marks and parentheses.

> I heard the senator on yesterday's "All Things Considered"; his views on Medicare are encouraging.
>
> She found him urbane and entertaining (if somewhat overbearing); he found her charmingly ingenuous.

SLASH

The slash (also known as the *virgule, diagonal, solidus, oblique,* and *slant*) is most commonly used in place of a short word or a hyphen or en dash, or to separate numbers or text elements. There is generally no space on either side of the slash.

1. A slash represents the words *per* or *to* when used between units of measure or the terms of a ratio.

> 40,000 tons/year
> 29 mi/gal
> price/earnings ratio   *or*   price–earnings ratio
> cost/benefit analysis   *or*   cost–benefit analysis
> a 50/50 split   *or* a 50-50 split
> 20/20 vision

2. A slash separates alternatives, usually representing the words *or* or *and/or.*

> alumni/ae
> his/her
> the *affect/effect* problem   *or*   the *affect-effect* problem

3. A slash replaces the word *and* in some compound terms.

> air/sea cruise *or* air-sea cruise
> the May/June issue *or* the May-June issue
> 1996/97 *or* 1996–97
> travel/study trip *or* travel-study trip

4. A slash is sometimes used to replace certain prepositions such as *at, versus,* and *for.*

> U.C./Berkeley *or* U.C.–Berkeley
> parent/child issues *or* parent–child issues
> Vice President/Editorial *or* Vice President, Editorial

5. A slash punctuates a few abbreviations.

> w/o [*for* without]
> c/o [*for* care of]
> I/O [*for* input/output]
> d/b/a [*for* doing business as]
> w/w [*for* wall-to-wall]
> o/a [*for* on or about]

6. The slash separates the elements in a numerical date, and numerators and denominators in fractions.

> 11/29/95
> 2 3/16 inches wide *or* 2 3/16 inches wide
> a 7/8-mile course *or* a 7/8-mile course

7. The slash separates lines of poetry that are run in with the text around them. A space is usually inserted before and after the slash.

> The great Alexander Pope once observed: "'Tis with our judgments as our watches, none / Go just alike, yet each believes his own."

Capitals and Italics

Words and phrases are capitalized or italicized (underlining takes the place of italics in typed or handwritten text) to indicate that they have a special significance in particular contexts. (Quotation marks sometimes perform the same functions; see paragraphs 69–71 on pages 272–73 and the section on quotation marks beginning on page 251.)

BEGINNINGS

1. The first word of a sentence or sentence fragment is capitalized.

> They make a desert and call it peace.
> So many men, so many opinions.
> O times! O customs!

2. The first word of a sentence contained within parentheses is capitalized. However, a parenthetical sentence occurring inside another sentence is not capitalized unless it is a complete quoted sentence.

No one answered the telephone. (They were probably on vacation.)

The road remains almost impassable (the locals don't seem to care), and the journey is only for the intrepid.

After waiting in line for an hour (what else could we do?), we finally left.

In the primary election Evans placed third ("My campaign started late").

3. The first word of a direct quotation is capitalized. However, if the quotation is interrupted in mid-sentence, the second part does not begin with a capital.

The department manager explained, "We have no budget for new computers."

"We have no budget for new computers," explained the department manager, "but we may next year."

4. When a quotation, whether a sentence fragment or a complete sentence, is syntactically dependent on the sentence in which it occurs, the quotation does not begin with a capital.

The brochure promised a tour of "the most exotic ancient sites."

His first response was that "there is absolutely no truth to the reports."

5. The first word of a sentence within a sentence that is not a direct quotation is usually capitalized. Examples include mottoes and rules, unspoken or imaginary dialogue, sentences referred to as sentences, and direct questions. (For the use of commas and quotation marks with such sentences, see paragraphs 30–31 on pages 237–38 and paragraphs 6–7 on pages 252–53.)

You know the saying "Fools rush in where angels fear to tread."

The first rule is, When in doubt, spell it out.

One ballot proposition sought to enforce the sentencing rule of "Three strikes and you're out."

My question is, When can we go?

6. The first word of a line of poetry is traditionally capitalized. However, in the poetry of this century line beginnings are often lowercased. The poem's original capitalization is always reproduced.

Death is the mother of beauty, mystical,
Within whose burning bosom we devise
Our earthly mothers waiting, sleeplessly.
                              —Wallace Stevens

        If tributes cannot
be implicit,
give me diatribes and the fragrance of iodine,
the cork oak acorn grown in Spain . . .
                              —Marianne Moore

7. The first word following a colon is lowercased when it begins a list and usually lowercased when it begins a complete sentence. However, when the sentence introduced is lengthy and distinctly separate from the preceding clause, it is often capitalized.

In the early morning they broadcast an urgent call for three necessities: bandages, antibiotics, and blood.

The advantage of this system is clear: it's inexpensive.

The situation is critical: This company cannot hope to recoup the fourth-quarter losses that were sustained in five operating divisions.

8. If a colon introduces a series of sentences, the first word of each sentence is capitalized.

> Consider the steps we have taken: A subcommittee has been formed to evaluate past performance. New sources of revenue are being explored. Several candidates have been interviewed for the new post of executive director.

9. The first words of items that form complete sentences in run-in lists are usually capitalized, as are the first words of items in vertical lists. However, numbered phrases within a sentence are lowercased. For details, see the section beginning on page 313.

10. The first word in an outline heading is capitalized.

> I. Editorial tasks
> II. Production responsibilities
>   A. Cost estimates
>   B. Bids

11. In minutes and legislation, the introductory words *Whereas* and *Resolved* are capitalized (and *Resolved* is also italicized). The word immediately following is also capitalized.

> Whereas, Substantial benefits ...
> *Resolved,* That ...

In legal documents, full capitalization is often used for introductory words and phrases.

> IN WITNESS WHEREOF, I have hereunto . . .

12. The first word and certain other words of the salutation of a letter and the first word of a complimentary close are capitalized.

> Dear Sir or Madam: Sincerely yours,
> Ladies and Gentlemen: Very truly yours,
> To whom it may concern:

13. The first word and each subsequent major word following a SUBJECT or TO heading in a memorandum are capitalized.

> SUBJECT: Pension Plans
> TO: All Department Heads and Editors

PROPER NOUNS AND ADJECTIVES

The following paragraphs describe the ways in which a broad range of proper nouns and adjectives are styled. Capitals are always employed, sometimes in conjunction with italics or quotation marks.

Abbreviations

1. Abbreviated forms of proper nouns and adjectives are capitalized, just as the spelled-out forms would be. (For details on capitalizing abbreviations, see the section beginning on page 294.)

> Jan. [*for* January]
> NATO [*for* North Atlantic Treaty Organization]

Abstractions and Personifications
2. Abstract concepts and qualities are sometimes capitalized when the concept or quality is being personified. If the term is simply used in conjunction with other words that allude to human characteristics or qualities, it is not capitalized.

> as Autumn paints each leaf in fiery colors
> the statue of Justice with her scales
> hoping that fate would lend a hand

Academic Degrees
3. The names of academic degrees are capitalized when they follow a person's name. The names of specific degrees used without a person's name are usually lowercased. More general names for degrees are lowercased.

> Lawton I. Byrne, Doctor of Laws
> earned his associate in science degree
> *or* earned his Associate in Science degree
> completed course work for his doctorate
> working for a master's degree

Abbreviations for academic degrees are always capitalized. (For details, see paragraphs 11–12 on page 299.)

> Susan L. Wycliff, M.S.W.
> received her Ph.D. in clinical psychology

Animals and Plants
4. The common names of animals and plants are not capitalized unless they contain a proper noun, in which case the proper noun is usually capitalized and any name element preceding (but not following) it is often capitalized. When in doubt, consult a dictionary. (For scientific names, see the section on page 271.)

the springer spaniel	a Great Dane	mayflower
Holstein cows	Queen Anne's lace	jack-in-the-pulpit
California condor	black-eyed Susan	

Awards and Prizes
5. Names of awards and prizes are capitalized. Words and phrases that are not actually part of the award's name are lowercased.

Academy Award	Nobel Prize winner
Emmy	Nobel Prize in medicine
Rhodes Scholarship	*but*
Rhodes scholar	Nobel Peace Prize
Pulitzer Prize-winning novelist	

Derivatives of Proper Names
6. Derivatives of proper names are capitalized when used in their primary sense. If the derived term has taken on a specialized meaning, it is often lowercased. Consult a dictionary when in doubt.

Roman sculpture	pasteurized milk
Viennese culture	french fries
Victorian prudery	*but*
a Britishism	American cheese
Hodgkins disease	Dutch door
chinaware	

Geographical and Topographical References

7. Terms that identify divisions of the earth's surface and distinct areas, regions, places, or districts are capitalized, as are derivative nouns and adjectives.

the Pacific Rim	the Golan Heights	the Highlands
the Great Lakes	Burgundy	Highland attitudes
Arnhem Land	Burgundians	

8. Popular names of localities are capitalized.

Little Italy	the Sunbelt
the Left Bank	the Big Easy

9. Compass points are capitalized when they refer to a geographical region or form part of a street name. They are lowercased when they refer to a simple direction.

the Southwest	North Pole
West Coast	north of the Rio Grande
North Atlantic	born in the East
East Pleasant Street	driving east on I-90

10. Nouns and adjectives that are derived from compass points and that designate or refer to a specific geographical region are usually capitalized.

Southern hospitality	Southwestern recipes
Easterners	Northern Europeans

11. Words designating global, national, regional, and local political divisions are capitalized when they are essential elements of specific names. They are usually lowercased when they precede a proper name or are not part of a specific name.

the Roman Empire	the state of New York
British Commonwealth nations	the Third Precinct
New York State	voters in three precincts

In legal documents, such words are often capitalized regardless of position.

    the State of New York

12. Common geographical terms (such as *lake, mountain, river,* or *valley*) are capitalized if they are part of a proper name.

Lake Tanganyika	Mount Everest	Cayman Islands
Great Salt Lake	Cape of Good Hope	Yosemite Valley
Atlas Mountains	Massachusetts Bay	

13. Common geographical terms preceding names are usually capitalized.

> Lakes Huron and Erie
> Mounts McKinley and Whitney

When *the* precedes the common term, the term is lowercased.

> the river Nile

14. Common geographical terms that are not used as part of a single proper name are not capitalized. These include plural terms that follow two or more proper names, and terms that are used descriptively or alone.

> the Indian and South Pacific oceans   Caribbean islands
> the Mississippi and Missouri rivers   the river delta
> the Pacific coast of Mexico

15. The names of streets, monuments, parks, landmarks, well-known buildings, and other public places are capitalized. However, common terms that are part of these names (such as *street, park,* or *bridge*) are lowercased when they occur after multiple names or are used alone.

> State Street   Golden Gate Bridge
> the Lincoln Memorial   Empire State Building
> Statue of Liberty   Beverly Hills Hotel
> the Pyramids   back to the hotel
> Grant Park   Main and Oak streets

Well-known shortened forms of place-names are capitalized.

> the Hill [*for* Capitol Hill]
> the Channel [*for* English Channel]
> the Street [*for* Wall Street]

Governmental, Judicial, and Political Bodies

16. Full names of legislative, deliberative, executive, and administrative bodies are capitalized, as are easily recognizable short forms of these names. However, nonspecific noun and adjective references to them are usually lowercased.

> United States Congress   the Fed
> Congress   congressional hearings
> the House   a federal agency

When words such as *department, committee,* or *agency* are used in place of a full name, they are most often capitalized when the department or agency is referring to itself, but otherwise usually lowercased.

> This Department welcomes constructive criticism . . .
> The department claimed to welcome such criticism . . .

When such a word is used in the plural to describe more than one specific body, it is usually capitalized when it precedes the names and lowercased when it follows them.

> involving the Departments of State and Justice
> a briefing from the State and Justice departments

17. Full names of high courts are capitalized. Short forms of such names are often capitalized in legal documents but lowercased otherwise.

> ... in the U.S. Court of Appeals for the Ninth Circuit
> International Court of Justice
> The court of appeals [*or* Court of Appeals] held ...
> the Virginia Supreme Court
> a federal district court
> the state supreme court

However, both the full and short names of the U.S. Supreme Court are capitalized.

> the Supreme Court of the United States
> the Supreme Court
> the Court

18. Names of city and county courts are usually lowercased.

> the Springfield municipal court   the county court
> small-claims court   juvenile court

19. The noun *court,* when it applies to a specific judge or presiding officer, is capitalized in legal documents.

> It is the opinion of this Court that ...
> The Court found that ...

20. The terms *federal* and *national* are capitalized only when they are essential elements of a name or title. (*Federal* is also capitalized when it refers to a historical architectural style, to members of the original Federalist party, or to adherents of the Union in the Civil War.)

> Federal Election Commission   National Security Council
> a federal commission   national security
> Federalist principles

21. The word *administration* is sometimes capitalized when it refers to the administration of a specific U.S. president, but is more commonly lowercased. Otherwise, it is lowercased except when it is a part of the official name of a government agency.

> the Reagan administration *or* the Reagan Administration
> the administration *or* the Administration
> from one administration to the next
> the Social Security Administration

22. Names of political organizations and their adherents are capitalized, but the word *party* is often lowercased.

> the Democratic National Committee
> the Republican platform
> the Christian Coalition
> most Republicans
> the Democratic party *or* the Democratic Party
> party politics

Names of less-distinct political groupings are usually lowercased, as are their derivative forms.

the right wing
the liberals
the conservative agenda
but often
the Left
the Right

23. Terms describing political and economic philosophies are usually lower-cased; if derived from proper names, they are usually capitalized. Consult a dictionary for doubtful cases.

authoritarianism	fascism *or* Fascism	social Darwinist
democracy	nationalism	Marxist

Historical periods and events

24. The names of some historical and cultural periods and movements are capitalized. When in doubt, consult a dictionary or encyclopedia.

Bronze Age	New Deal	Victorian era
Middle Ages	Fifth Republic	age of Pericles
Prohibition	Third Reich	the baby boom
the Renaissance	the atomic age	

25. Century and decade designations are normally lowercased.

the nineteenth century
the twenties
the turn of the century
a 12th-century manuscript
but
Gay Nineties
Roaring Twenties

26. The names of conferences, councils, expositions, and specific sporting, cultural, and historical events are capitalized.

Fourth World Conference on Women	Cannes Film Festival
Council of Trent	Miss America Contest
New York World's Fair	San Francisco Earthquake
Super Bowl	Johnstown Flood

27. Full names of specific treaties, laws, and acts are capitalized.

Treaty of Versailles
the Nineteenth Amendment
the Bill of Rights
Clean Air Act of 1990
but
gun-control laws
an equal-rights amendment

28. The words *war, revolution,* and *battle* are capitalized when they are part of a full name. Official names of actions are capitalized. Descriptive terms such as *assault* and *siege* are usually lowercased even when used in conjunction with a place-name.

War of the Roses   between the two world wars
World War II   the American and French revolutions
the French Revolution   the siege of Leningrad
Battle of Gettysburg   Washington's winter campaign
Operation Desert Storm

Hyphenated Compounds

29. The second (third, etc.) element of a hyphenated compound is generally capitalized only if it is itself a proper noun or adjective. (For hyphenated titles, see paragraph 65 below.)

Arab-Israeli negotiations   Forty-second street
East-West trade agreements   twentieth-century architecture
French-speaking peoples

30. When joined to a proper noun or adjective, common prefixes (such as *pre-* or *anti-*) are usually lowercased, but geographical and ethnic combining forms (such as *Anglo-* or *Sino-*) are capitalized. (For details, see paragraphs 45 and 52 on pages 291 and 292.)

anti-Soviet forces
Sino-Japanese relations

Legal Case Titles

31. The names of the plaintiff and defendant in legal case titles are italicized. The *v.* (for *versus*) may be roman or italic. Cases that do not involve two opposing parties are also italicized. When the party involved rather than the case itself is being discussed, the reference is not italicized. In running text, a case name involving two opposing parties may be shortened.

Jones v. *Massachusetts*
Smith et al. v. Jones
In re Jones
She covered the Jones trial for the newspaper.
The judge based his ruling on a precedent set in the *Jones* decision.

Medical Terms

32. Proper names that are elements in terms designating diseases, symptoms, syndromes, and tests are capitalized. Common nouns are lowercased; however, abbreviations of such nouns are all-capitalized.

Alzheimer's disease   Schick test   mumps
Tourette's syndrome   black lung disease   AIDS

33. Scientific names of disease-causing organisms follow the rules discussed in paragraph 58 on page 271. The names of diseases or conditions derived from scientific names of organisms are lowercased and not italicized.

a neurotoxin produced by *Clostridium botulinum*
nearly died of botulism

34. Generic names of drugs are lowercased; trade names should be capitalized.

retinoic acid
Retin-A

Military Terms

35. The full titles of branches of the U.S. armed forces are capitalized, as are standard short forms.

U.S. Marine Corps	the Marines
the Marine Corps	the Corps

Those of other countries are capitalized when the precise title is used; otherwise they are usually lowercased. The plurals of *army, navy, air force,* and *coast guard* are lowercased.

Royal Air Force
the Guatemalan army
the tiny armies of both countries

The modifiers *army, navy, marine coast, guard,* and *air force* are usually lowercased; *naval* is lowercased unless it is part of an official name. The noun *marine* is usually lowercased.

an army helicopter	the first naval engagement
a career navy man	the Naval Reserves
the marine barracks	a former marine

Full or shortened names of specific units of a branch are usually capitalized.

U.S. Army Corps of Engineers
the Third Army
the Eighty-second [*or* 82nd] Airborne
the U.S. Special Forces, or Green Berets
. . . of the First Battalion. The battalion commander . . .

36. Military ranks are capitalized when they precede the names of their holders, or replace the name in direct address. Otherwise they are lowercased.

Major General Smedley Butler
Please be seated, Admiral.
The major arrived precisely on time.

37. The names of decorations, citations, and medals are capitalized.

Medal of Honor
Purple Heart

Numerical Designations

38. A noun introducing a reference number is usually capitalized. The abbreviation *No.* is usually omitted.

Order 704	Form 2E
Flight 409	Policy 118-4-Y

39. Nouns used with numbers or letters to refer to major reference entities or actual captions in books or periodicals are usually capitalized. Nouns that designate minor reference entities and do not appear in captions are lowercased.

Book II	Title VI	paragraph 6.1
Volume 5	Section [*or* section] 8	question 21
Chapter 2	page 101	
Table 3	line 8	

Organizations

40. Names of organizations, corporations, and institutions, and terms derived from those names to designate their members, are capitalized.

the League of Women Voters	the University of the South
General Motors Corporation	the Rotary Club
the Smithsonian Institution	all Rotarians

Common nouns used descriptively or occurring after the names of two or more organizations are lowercased.

enrolled at the university
Yale and Harvard universities
   but
the Universities of Utah and Nevada

In legal documents, common nouns referring to organizations named in the document are usually capitalized.

an employee of the Company
the Institute's plan

41. Words such as *agency, department, division, group,* or *office* that designate corporate and organizational units are capitalized only when used as part of a specific proper name. (For governmental units, see paragraph 16 on page 263.)

head of the Sales Division of K2 Outfitters
a memo to the sales divisions of both companies

42. Nicknames for organizations are capitalized.

the Big Six accounting firms
referred to IBM as Big Blue
trading on the Big Board

People

43. The names and initials of persons are capitalized. If a name is hyphenated, both elements are capitalized. Particles forming the initial elements of surnames (such as *de, della, der, du, l', la, le, ten, ter, van,* and *von*) may or may not be capitalized, depending on the practice of the family or individual. However, the particle is always capitalized at the beginning of a sentence. The prefixes *Mac, Mc,* and *O'* are always capitalized.

Cecil Day-Lewis	Walter de la Mare
Agnes de Mille	Mark deW. Howe
Cecil B. DeMille	Martin Van Buren

   . . . of van Gogh's life. Van Gogh's technique is . . .

44. A nickname or epithet that either is added to or replaces the name of a person or thing is capitalized.

Babe Ruth	Billy the Kid	Deep Throat
Stonewall Jackson	the Sun King	Big Mama Thornton

A nickname or epithet placed between a person's first and last name is enclosed in quotation marks or parentheses or both. If it precedes the first name, it is sometimes enclosed in quotation marks but more often not.

>Charlie "Bird" [*or* ("Bird") *or* (Bird)] Parker
>Mother Maybelle Carter

45. Words of family relationship preceding or used in place of a person's name are capitalized; otherwise, they are lowercased.

>Uncle Fred   her uncle's book
>Mother's birthday   my mother's legacy

46. Words designating languages, nationalities, peoples, races, religious groups, and tribes are capitalized. Designations based on color are usually lowercased.

>Spanish   Muslims
>Spaniards   Assiniboin
>Chinese   both blacks and whites
>Asians   white, black, and Hispanic jurors

47. Corporate, professional, and governmental titles are capitalized when they immediately precede a person's name, unless the name is being used as an appositive.

>President John Tyler
>Professor Wendy Doniger of the University of Chicago
>Senator William Fulbright of Arkansas
>Arkansas's late former senator, William Fulbright

48. When corporate or governmental titles are used as part of a descriptive phrase to identify a person rather than as part of the name itself, the title is lowercased.

>Marcia Ramirez, president of Logex Corp.
>the president of Logex Corp., Marcia Ramirez
> *but*
>Logex Corp.'s prospects for the coming year were outlined by President Marcia Ramirez.

49. High governmental titles may be capitalized when used in place of individuals' names. In minutes and official records of proceedings, corporate or organizational titles are capitalized when used in place of individuals' names.

>The Secretary of State objected.
>The Judge will respond to questions in her chambers.
>The Treasurer then stated his misgivings about the project.
> *but*
>The report reached the senator's desk yesterday.
>The judge's rulings were widely criticized.
>The co-op's treasurer, it turned out, had twice been convicted of embezzlement.

50. The word *president* may be capitalized whenever it refers to the U.S. presidency, but more commonly is capitalized only when it refers to a specific U.S. president.

It is the duty of the president [*or* President] to submit a budget to Congress.
The President's budget, due out on Wednesday, is being eagerly awaited.

51. Titles are capitalized when they are used in direct address.

Is it very contagious, Doctor?
You may call your next witness, Counselor.

Religious Terms

52. Words designating the supreme being are capitalized. Plural forms such as *gods, goddesses,* and *deities* are not.

Allah	Yahweh	in the eyes of God
Brahma	the Almighty	the angry gods
Jehovah	the Trinity	

53. Personal pronouns referring to the supreme being are often capitalized, especially in religious writing. Relative pronouns (such as *who, whom,* and *whose*) usually are not.

God gave His [*or* his] Son
Allah, whose Prophet, Muhammad I

54. Traditional designations of apostles, prophets, and saints are capitalized.

the Madonna	Moses the Lawgiver	St. John of the Cross
the Prophet	the Twelve	John the Baptist

55. Names of religions, denominations, creeds and confessions, and religious orders are capitalized, as are adjectives and nouns derived from these names.

Judaism	Society of Jesus	Jesuit teachers
Church of England	Eastern Orthodox	a Buddhist
Apostles' Creed	Islamic	

Full names of specific places of worship are capitalized, but terms such as *church, synagogue,* and *mosque* are lowercased when used alone. The word *church* is sometimes capitalized when it refers to the worldwide Catholic Church.

Hunt Memorial Church	Beth Israel Synagogue
the local Baptist church	services at the synagogue

56. Names of the Bible and other sacred works, their books and parts, and versions or editions of them are capitalized but not italicized. Adjectives derived from the names of sacred books are capitalized, except for the words *biblical* and *scriptural*.

Bible	biblical
the Scriptures	Talmud
Revised Standard Version	Talmudic
Old Testament	Koran *or* Qur'an
Book of Revelation	Koranic *or* Qur'anic

57. The names of prayers and well-known passages of the Bible are capitalized.

| the Ave Maria | the Our Father | Sermon on the Mount |
| Lord's Prayer | Ten Commandments | the Beatitudes |

Scientific Terms

58. Genus names in biological binomial nomenclature are capitalized; species names are lowercased, even when derived from a proper name. Both names are italicized.

> Both the wolf and the domestic dog are included in the genus *Canis*.
> The California condor *(Gymnogyps californianus)* is facing extinction.

The names of races, varieties, or subspecies are lowercased and italicized.

> *Hyla versicolor chrysoscelis*
> *Otis asio naevius*

59. The New Latin names of classes, families, and all groups above the genus level in zoology and botany are capitalized but not italicized. Their derivative nouns and adjectives are lowercased.

| Gastropoda | gastropod |
| Thallophyta | thallophytic |

60. The names, both scientific and informal, of planets and their satellites, stars, constellations, and other specific celestial objects are capitalized. However, except in technical writing, the words *sun, earth,* and *moon* are usually lowercased unless they occur with other astronomical names. A generic term that follows the name of a celestial object is usually lowercased.

Jupiter	Ursa Major	life on earth
the North Star	the Little Dipper	a voyage to the moon
Andromeda	Mars, Venus, and Earth	Halley's comet

Names of meterorological phenomena are lowercased.

> aurora australis
> northern lights
> parhelic circle

61. Terms that identify geological eons, eras, periods, systems, epochs, and strata are capitalized. The generic terms that follow them are lowercased.

Mesozoic era	in the Middle Ordovician
Upper Cretaceous epoch	the Age of Reptiles
Quaternary period	

62. Proper names that are elements of the names of scientific laws, theorems, and principles are capitalized, but the common nouns *law, theorem, theory,* and the like are lowercased. In the names of popular or fanciful theories or observations, such words are usually capitalized as well.

Mendel's law	Einstein's theory of relativity
the Pythagorean theorem	Murphy's Law
Occam's razor	the Peter Principle

63. The names of computer services and databases are capitalized. Some names of computer languages are written with an initial capital letter, some with all letters capitalized, and some commonly both ways. When in doubt, consult a dictionary.

America Online   Pascal *or* PASCAL
World Wide Web   BASIC
CompuServe   Internet *or* internet
Microsoft Word

Time Periods and Dates

64. The names of the days of the week, months of the year, and holidays and holy days are capitalized. Names of the seasons are lowercased.

Tuesday   Ramadan
June   Holy Week
Yom Kippur   last winter's storm
Veterans Day

Titles of Works

65. Words in titles of books, magazines, newspapers, plays, movies, long poems, and works of art such as paintings and sculpture are capitalized except for internal articles, coordinating conjunctions, prepositions, and the *to* of infinitives. Prepositions of four or more letters are often capitalized. The entire title is italicized. For sacred works, see paragraph 56 on page 270.

Far from [or *From*] *the Madding Crowd*
Wolfe's *Of Time and the River*
Publishers Weekly
USA Today
the original play *A Streetcar Named Desire*
All about [or *About*] *Eve,* with Bette Davis
Monet's *Water-Lily Pool,* in the Louvre
Rodin's *Thinker*

The elements of hyphenated compounds in titles are usually capitalized, but articles, coordinating conjunctions, and prepositions are lowercased.

The Post-Physician Era: Medicine in the Twenty-First Century
Politics in Early Seventeenth-Century England

66. The first word following a colon in a title is capitalized.

Jane Austen: A Literary Life

67. An initial article that is part of a title is capitalized and italicized. It is often omitted if it would be awkward in context.

The Oxford English Dictionary
the 20-volume *Oxford English Dictionary*

68. In the titles of newspapers, the city or local name is usually italicized, but the preceding *the* is usually not italicized or capitalized.

reported in the *New York Times*
last Thursday's *Atlanta Constitution*

69. Many periodicals, especially newspapers, do not use italics for titles, but instead either simply capitalize the important words of the title or, more commonly, capitalize the words and enclose the title in quotation marks.

> the NB. column in the Times Literary Supplement
> The Nobel committee singled out Walcott's book-length epic "Omeros."

70. The titles of articles in periodicals, short poems, short stories, essays, lectures, dissertations, chapters of books, radio and television programs, and novellas published in a collection are capitalized and enclosed in quotation marks. The capitalization of articles, conjunctions, and prepositions follows the rules explained in paragraph 65 above.

> an article on Rwanda, "After the Genocide," in the *New Yorker*
> Robert Frost's "Death of the Hired Man"
> O'Connor's story "Good Country People"
> "The Literature of Exhaustion," John Barth's seminal essay
> last Friday's lecture, "Labor's Task: A View for the Nineties"
> *The Jungle Book*'s ninth chapter is the well-known "Rikki-tikki-tavi."
> listening to "All Things Considered"
> watched "Good Morning America"

71. The titles of long musical compositions are generally capitalized and italicized; the titles of songs and other short compositions are capitalized and enclosed in quotation marks, as are the popular names of longer works. The titles of compositions identified primarily by their musical forms (such as *quartet, sonata,* or *mass*) are capitalized only, as are movements identified by their tempo markings.

> Mozart's *The Magic Flute*
> Frank Loesser's *Guys and Dolls*
> "The Lady Is a Tramp"
> Beethoven's "Für Elise"
> the Piano Sonata in C-sharp minor, Op. 27, No. 2, or "Moonlight" Sonata
> Symphony No. 104 in D major
> Brahms's Violin Concerto in D
> the Adagietto movement from Mahler's Fifth Symphony

72. Common titles of book sections (such as *preface, introduction,* or *index*) are usually capitalized when they refer to a section of the same book in which the reference is made. Otherwise, they are usually lowercased. (For numbered sections of books, see paragraph 39 on page 267).

> See the Appendix for further information.
> In the introduction to her book, the author explains her goals.

Trademarks
73. Registered trademarks, service marks, collective marks, and brand names are capitalized. They do not normally require any further acknowledgment of their special status.

Frisbee	Jacuzzi	Levi's
Coke	Kleenex	Vaseline
College Board	Velcro	Dumpster
Realtor	Xerox	Scotch tape
Walkman	Band-Aid	Teflon

Transportation

74. The names of individual ships, submarines, airplanes, satellites, and space vehicles are capitalized and italicized. The designations *U.S.S., S.S., M.V.,* and *H.M.S.* are not italicized.

> *Challenger*
>
> *Enola Gay*
>
> H.M.S. *Bounty*

OTHER STYLING CONVENTIONS

1. Foreign words and phrases that have not been fully adopted into English are italicized. In general, any word that appears in the main section of *Merriam-Webster's Collegiate Dictionary* does not need to be italicized.

> These accomplishments will serve as a monument, *aere perennius,* to the group's skill and dedication.
>
> "The cooking here is *wunderbar!*"
>
> The prix fixe lunch was $20.
>
> The committee meets on an ad hoc basis.

A complete foreign-language sentence (such as a motto) can also be italicized. However, long sentences are usually treated as quotations; that is, they are set in roman type and enclosed in quotation marks. (For details, see paragraph 6 on page 252.)

> The inscription *Honi soit qui mal y pense* encircles the seal.

2. In nonfiction writing, unfamiliar words or words that have a specialized meaning are set in italics on their first appearance, especially when accompanied by a short definition. Once these words have been introduced and defined, they are not italicized in subsequent references.

> *Vitiligo* is a condition in which skin pigment cells stop making pigment. Vitiligo usually affects . . .
>
> Another method is the *direct-to-consumer* transaction, in which the publisher markets directly to the individual by mail or door-to-door.

3. Italics are often used to indicate words referred to as words. However, if the word was actually spoken, it is usually enclosed in quotation marks instead.

> Purists still insist that *data* is a plural noun.
>
> *Only* can also be an adverb, as in "I *only* tried to help."
>
> We heard his warning, but we weren't sure what "repercussions" meant in that context.

4. Italics are often used for letters referred to as letters, particularly when they are shown in lowercase.

> You should dot your *i*'s and cross your *t*'s.

If the letter is being used to refer to its sound and not its printed form, slashes or brackets are used instead of italics in technical contexts.

> The pure /p/ sound is rarely heard in the mountain dialect.

A letter used to indicate a shape is capitalized but not italicized. Such letters are often set in sans-serif type.

an A-frame house	Churchill's famous V sign
the I beam	forming a giant X

5. Italics are often used to show numerals referred to as numerals. However, if there is no chance of confusion, they are usually not italicized.

> The first *2* and the last *1* are barely legible.
> Anyone whose ticket number ends in 4 or 6 will win a door prize.

6. Italics are used to emphasize or draw attention to words in a sentence.

> Students must notify the dean's office *in writing* of any added or dropped courses.
> It was not *the* model for the project, but merely *a* model.

7. Italics are used to indicate a word created to suggest a sound.

> Its call is a harsh, drawn-out *kreee-awww*.

8. Individual letters are sometimes italicized when used for lists within sentences or for identifying elements in an illustration.

> providing information about *(a)* typing, *(b)* transcribing, *(c)* formatting, and *(d)* graphics
> located at point A on the diagram

9. Commas, colons, and semicolons that follow italicized words are usually italicized.

> the Rabbit tetralogy *(Rabbit Run, Rabbit Redux, Rabbit Is Rich,* and *Rabbit at Rest); Bech: A Book; S;* and others

However, question marks, exclamation points, quotation marks, and apostrophes are not italicized unless they are part of an italicized title.

> Did you see the latest issue of *Newsweek*?
> Despite the greater success of *Oklahoma!* and *South Pacific*, Rodgers was fondest of *Carousel*.
> "Over Christmas vacation he finished *War and Peace*."
> Students always mistake the old script *s*'s for *f*'s.

Parentheses and brackets may be italicized if most of the words they enclose are also italicized, or if both the first and last words are italicized.

> *(see also Limited Partnership)*
> [German, *wunderbar*]
> *(and* is replaced throughout by *&)*

10. Full capitalization is often used in legal documents for the names of parties and legal papers.

> hereinafter called the LENDER
> THIS AGREEMENT, made this 3rd day of November, 1997

11. The text of signs, labels, and inscriptions may be reproduced in various ways.

> a poster reading SPECIAL THRILLS COMING SOON
> a gate bearing the infamous motto "Arbeit macht frei"
> a Do Not Disturb sign

a barn with an old CHEW MAIL POUCH ad on the side
the stop sign

12. *Small capitals,* identical to large capitals but usually about the height of a lowercase *x,* are commonly used for era designations and computer commands. They may also be used for cross-references, for headings in constitutions and bylaws, and for speakers in a dramatic dialogue.

The dwellings date from A.D. 200 or earlier.

Press ALT+CTRL+PLUS SIGN on the numeric keyboard.

(See LETTERS AS LETTERS, page 162.)

SECTION IV. The authority for parliamentary procedure in meetings of the Board . . .

LADY WISHFORT. O dear, has my Nephew made his Addresses to Millamant? I order'd him.

FOIBLE. Sir Wilfull is set in to drinking, Madam, in the Parlour.

13. *Underlining* indicates italics in typed material. It is almost never seen in typeset text.

14. *Boldface* type has traditionally been used primarily for headings and captions. It is sometimes also used in place of italics for terminology introduced in the text, especially for terms that are accompanied by definitions; for cross-references; for headwords in listings such as glossaries, gazetteers, and bibliographies; and for page references in indexes that locate a specific kind of material, such as illustrations, tables, or the main discussions of a given topic. (In mathematical texts, arrays, tensors, vectors, and matrix notation are standardly set bold as well.)

Application Forms and Tests Many offices require applicants to fill out an employment form. Bring a copy . . .

Figure 4.2: The Electromagnetic Spectrum

The two axes intersect at a point called the **origin.**

See **Medical Records,** page 123.

antecedent: the noun to which a pronoun refers

appositive: a word, phrase, or clause that is equivalent to a preceding noun

Records, medical, **123-37,** 178, 243

Referrals, **38-40,** 139

Punctuation that follows boldface type is set bold when it is part of a heading or heading-like text; otherwise it is generally set roman.

Table 9: Metric Conversion

Warning: This and similar medications . . .

Excellent fourth-quarter earnings were reported by the pharmaceutical giants **Abbott Laboratories, Burroughs Wellcome,** and **Merck.**

Plurals, Possessives, and Compounds

This section describes the ways in which plurals, possessives, and compounds are most commonly formed.

In regard to plurals and compounds, consulting a dictionary will solve many of the problems discussed in this section. A good college dictionary, such as *Merriam-Webster's Collegiate Dictionary,* will provide plural forms for any common word, as well as a large number of permanent compounds. Any dictionary much smaller than the *Collegiate* will often be more frustrating in what it fails to show than helpful in what it shows.

PLURALS

The basic rules for writing plurals of English words, stated in paragraph 1, apply in the vast majority of cases. The succeeding paragraphs treat the categories of words whose plurals are most apt to raise questions.

Most good dictionaries give thorough coverage to irregular and variant plurals, and many of the rules provided here are reflected in the dictionary entries.

The symbol → is used here to link the singular and plural forms.

1. The plurals of most English words are formed by adding *-s* to the singular. If the noun ends in *-s, -x, -z, -ch,* or *-sh,* so that an extra syllable must be added in order to pronounce the plural, *-es* is added. If the noun ends in a *-y* preceded by a consonant, the *-y* is changed to *-i* and *-es* is added.

voter → voters	blowtorch → blowtorches
anticlimax → anticlimaxes	calabash → calabashes
blitz → blitzes	allegory → allegories

Abbreviations

2. The plurals of abbreviations are commonly formed by adding *-s* or *-'s;* however, there are some significant exceptions. (For details, see paragraphs 1–5 on page 296.)

yr. → yrs.	M.B.A. → M.B.A.'s
TV → TVs	p. → pp.

Animals

3. The names of many fishes, birds, and mammals have both a plural formed with a suffix and one that is identical with the singular. Some have only one or the other.

bass → bass *or* basses	lion → lions
partridge → partridge *or* partridges	sheep → sheep
sable → sables *or* sable	

Many of the animals that have both plural forms are ones that are hunted, fished, or trapped; those who hunt, fish for, and trap them are most likely to use the unchanged form. The *-s* form is often used to emphasize diversity of kinds.

caught three bass	a place where antelope feed
but	*but*
basses of the Atlantic Ocean	antelopes of Africa and southwest Asia

Compounds and Phrases

4. Most compounds made up of two nouns—whether they appear as one word, two words, or a hyphenated word—form their plurals by pluralizing the final element only.

courthouse → courthouses
judge advocate → judge advocates
player-manager → player-managers

5. The plural form of a compound consisting of an *-er* noun and an adverb is made by pluralizing the noun element only.

runner-up → runners-up   diner-out → diners-out
onlooker → onlookers   passerby → passersby

6. Nouns made up of words that are not nouns form their plurals on the last element.

show-off → show-offs   tie-in → tie-ins
pushover → pushovers   lineup → lineups

7. Plurals of compounds that consist of two nouns separated by a preposition are normally formed by pluralizing the first noun.

sister-in-law → sisters-in-law   chief of staff → chiefs of staff
attorney-at-law → attorneys-at-law   grant-in-aid → grants-in-aid
power of attorney → powers of attorney

8. Compounds that consist of two nouns separated by a preposition and a modifier form their plurals in various ways.

snake in the grass → snakes in the grass
justice of the peace → justices of the peace
jack-in-the-box → jack-in-the-boxes *or* jacks-in-the-box
will-o'-the wisp → will-o'-the-wisps

9. Compounds consisting of a noun followed by an adjective are usually pluralized by adding *-s* to the noun. If the adjective tends to be understood as a noun, the compound may have more than one plural form.

attorney general → attorneys general *or* attorney generals
sergeant major → sergeants major *or* sergeant majors
poet laureate → poets laureate *or* poet laureates
heir apparent → heirs apparent
knight-errant → knights-errant

Foreign Words and Phrases
10. Many nouns of foreign origin retain the foreign plural. However, most also have a regular English plural.

alumnus → alumni   appendix → appendixes *or* appendices
genus → genera   concerto → concerti *or* concertos
crisis → crises   symposium → symposia *or* symposiums
criterion → criteria

11. Phrases of foreign origin may have a foreign plural, an English plural, or both.

pièces de résistance → pièces de résistance
hors d'oeuvre → hors d'oeuvres
beau monde → beau mondes *or* beaux mondes

Irregular plurals

12. A few English nouns form their plurals by changing one or more of their vowels, or by adding -*en* or -*ren*.

foot → feet	man → men	tooth → teeth
goose → geese	mouse → mice	ox → oxen
louse → lice	woman → women	child → children

13. Some nouns do not change form in the plural. (See also paragraph 3 above.)

series → series	corps → corps
politics → politics	species → species

14. Some nouns ending in -*f*, -*fe*, and -*ff* have plurals that end in -*ves*. Some of these also have regularly formed plurals.

elf → elves	wife → wives
loaf → loaves	staff → staffs *or* staves
scarf → scarves *or* scarfs	

Italic Elements

15. Italicized words, phrases, abbreviations, and letters are usually pluralized by adding -*s* or -*'s* in roman type. (See also paragraphs 16, 21, and 26 below.)

three *Fortune*s missing from the stack	used too many *etc.*'s in the report
a couple of *Gravity's Rainbow*s in stock	a row of *x*'s

Letters

16. The plurals of letters are usually formed by adding -*'s*, although capital letters are often pluralized by adding -*s* alone.

p's and q's
V's of migrating geese *or* Vs of migrating geese
dot your *i*'s
straight As *or* straight A's

Numbers

17. Numerals are pluralized by adding -*s* or, less commonly, -*'s*.

two par 5s *or* two par 5's
1990s *or* 1990's
in the 80s *or* in the 80's *or* in the '80s
the mid-$20,000s *or* the mid-$20,000's

18. Written-out numbers are pluralized by adding -*s*.

all the fours and eights
scored three tens

Proper Nouns

19. The plurals of proper nouns are usually formed with -*s* or -*es*.

Clarence → Clarences
Jones → Joneses
Fernandez → Fernandezes

20. Plurals of proper nouns ending in -*y* usually retain the -*y* and add -*s*.

Sunday → Sundays
Timothy → Timothys
Camry → Camrys

Words ending in -*y* that were originally proper nouns are usually pluralized by changing -*y* to -*i* and adding -*es*, but a few retain the -*y*.

bobby → bobbies   Tommy → Tommies
johnny → johnnies   Bloody Mary → Bloody Marys

Quoted Elements
21. The plural of words in quotation marks are formed by adding -*s* or -'*s* within the quotation marks, or -*s* outside the quotation marks. (See also paragraph 26 below.)

too many "probably's" [*or* "probablys"] in the statement
one "you" among millions of "you"s
a record number of "I can't recall"s

Symbols
22. When symbols are referred to as physical characters, the plural is formed by adding either -*s* or -'*s*.

printed three *s
used &'s instead of *and*'s
his π's are hard to read

Words Ending in -*ay*, -*ey*, and -*oy*
23. Words that end in -*ay*, -*ey*, or -*oy*, unlike other words ending in -*y*, are pluralized by simply adding -*s*.

castaways
donkeys
envoys

Words Ending in -*ful*
24. Any noun ending in -*ful* can be pluralized by adding -*s*, but most also have an alternative plural with -*s*- preceding the suffix.

handful → handfuls   armful → armfuls *or* armsful
teaspoonful → teaspoonfuls bucketful → bucketfuls *or* bucketsful

Words Ending in -*o*
25. Most words ending in -*o* are normally pluralized by adding -*s*. However, some words ending in -*o* preceded by a consonant take -*es* plurals.

solo → solos   cargo → cargoes *or* cargos
photo → photos   proviso → provisos *or* provisoes
tomato → tomatoes   halo → haloes *or* halos
potato → potatoes   echo → echoes
hobo → hoboes   motto → mottoes
hero → heroes

Words Used as Words

26. Words referred to as words and italicized usually form their plurals by adding -'s in roman type. (See also paragraph 21 above.)

> five *and*'s in one sentence
>
> all those *wherefore*'s and *howsoever*'s

When a word referred to as a word has become part of a fixed phrase, the plural is usually formed by adding -s without the apostrophe.

> oohs and aahs
>
> dos and don'ts *or* do's and don'ts

POSSESSIVES

Common Nouns

1. The possessive of singular and plural common nouns that do not end in an *s* or *z* sound is formed by adding -'s to the end of the word.

> | | |
> |---|---|
> | the child's skates | this patois's range |
> | women's voices | people's opinions |
> | the cat's dish | the criteria's common theme |

2. The possessive of singular nouns ending in an *s* or *z* sound is usually formed by adding -'s. A less common alternative is to add -'s only when it is easily pronounced; if it would create a word that is difficult to pronounce, only an apostrophe is added.

> | | |
> |---|---|
> | the witness's testimony | the prize's recipient |
> | the disease's course | rickets's symptoms *or* rickets' symptoms |
> | the race's sponsors | |

A multisyllabic singular noun that ends in an *s* or *z* sound drops the -*s* if it is followed by a word beginning with an *s* or *z* sound.

> for appearance' sake
>
> for goodness' sake

3. The possessive of plural nouns ending in an *s* or *z* sound is formed by adding only an apostrophe. However, the possessive of one-syllable irregular plurals is usually formed by adding -'s.

> | | |
> |---|---|
> | dogs' leashes | buyers' guarantees |
> | birds' migrations | lice's lifespans |

Proper Names

4. The possessives of proper names are generally formed in the same way as those of common nouns. The possessive of singular proper names is formed by adding -'s.

> | | |
> |---|---|
> | Jane's rules of behavior | Tom White's presentation |
> | three books of Carla's | Paris's cafes |

The possessive of plural proper names, and of some singular proper names ending in an *s* or *z* sound, is made by adding just an apostrophe.

> | | |
> |---|---|
> | the Stevenses' reception | New Orleans' annual festival |
> | the Browns' driveway | the United States' trade deficit |
> | Massachusetts' capital | Protosystems' president |

5. The possessive of singular proper names ending in an *s* or *z* sound may be formed by adding either -'*s* or just an apostrophe. Adding -'*s* to all such names, without regard for the pronunciation of the resulting word, is more common than adding just the apostrophe. (For exceptions see paragraph 6 below).

> Jones's car *or* Jones' car
> Bliss's statue *or* Bliss' statue
> Dickens's novels *or* Dickens' novels

6. The possessive form of classical and biblical names of two or more syllables ending in -*s* or -*es* is usually made by adding just an apostrophe. If the name has only one syllable, the possessive form is made by adding -'*s*.

> Socrates' students   Ramses' kingdom   Zeus's warnings
> Claudius' reign   Elias' prophecy   Cis's sons

The possessives of the names *Jesus* and *Moses* are always formed with just an apostrophe.

> Jesus' disciples
> Moses' law

7. The possessive of names ending in a silent -*s*, -*z*, or -*x* are usually formed with -'*s*.

> Des Moines's recreation department
> Josquin des Prez's music
> Delacroix's painting

8. When the possessive ending is added to an italicized name, it is not italicized.

> *East of Eden*'s main characters
> the *Spirit of St. Louis*'s historic flight
> *Brief Encounter*'s memorable ending

Pronouns

9. The possessive of indefinite pronouns is formed by adding -'*s*.

> anyone's rights   somebody's wedding
> everybody's money   one's own
> someone's coat   either's preference

Some indefinite pronouns usually require an *of* phrase to indicate possession.

> the rights of each
> the inclination of many
> the satisfaction of all

10. Possessive pronouns do not include apostrophes.

> mine   hers
> ours   his
> yours   theirs
> its

Miscellaneous Styling Conventions

11. No apostrophe is generally used today with plural nouns that are more descriptive than possessive.

weapons systems   steelworkers union
managers meeting   awards banquet
singles bar

12. The possessive form of a phrase is made by adding an apostrophe or -'s to the last word in the phrase.

his father-in-law's assistance   from the student of politics' point of view
board of directors' meeting   after a moment or so's thought

Constructions such as these are often rephrased.

from the point of view of the student of politics
after thinking for a moment or so

13. The possessive form of words in quotation marks can be formed in two ways, with -'s placed either inside the quotation marks or outside them.

the "Marseillaise"'s [*or* "Marseillaise's"] stirring melody

Since both arrangements look awkward, this construction is usually avoided.

the stirring melody of the "Marseillaise"

14. Possessives of abbreviations are formed like those of nouns that are spelled out. The singular possessive is formed by adding -'s; the plural possessive, by adding an apostrophe only.

the IRS's ruling   Eli Lilly & Co.'s chairman
AT&T's long-distance service   the HMOs' lobbyists
IBM Corp.'s annual report

15. The possessive of nouns composed of numerals is formed in the same way as for other nouns. The possessive of singular nouns is formed by adding -'s; the possessive of plural nouns is formed by adding an apostrophe only.

1996's commencement speaker
the 1920s' greatest jazz musicians

16. Individual possession is indicated by adding -'s to each noun in a sequence. Joint possession may be indicated in the same way, but is most commonly indicated by adding an apostrophe or -'s to the last noun in the sequence.

Joan's and Emily's friends   her mother and father's anniversary
Jim's, Ed's, and Susan's reports   Peter and Jan's trip *or* Peter's and Jan's trip

COMPOUNDS

A compound is a word or word group that consists of two or more parts that work together as a unit to express a specific concept. Compounds can be formed by combining two or more words (as in *double-check, cost-effective, farmhouse, graphic equalizer, park bench, around-the-clock,* or *son of a gun*), by combining prefixes or suffixes with words (as in *ex-president, shoeless, presorted,* or *uninter-*

ruptedly), or by combining two or more word elements (as in *macrophage* or *photochromism*). Compounds are written in one of three ways: solid (as in *cottonmouth*), hyphenated *(screenwriter-director),* or open *(health care).* Because of the variety of standard practice, the choice among these styles for a given compound represents one of the most common and vexing of all style issues that writers encounter.

A good dictionary will list many *permanent compounds,* compounds so commonly used that they have become permanent parts of the language. It will not list *temporary compounds,* those created to meet a writer's need at a particular moment. Most compounds whose meanings are self-evident from the meanings of their component words will not be listed, even if they are permanent and quite widely used. Writers thus cannot rely wholly on dictionaries to guide them in writing compounds.

One approach is to hyphenate all compounds not in the dictionary, since hyphenation immediately identifies them as compounds. But hyphenating all such compounds runs counter to some well-established American practice and can therefore call too much attention to the compound and momentarily distract the reader. Another approach (which applies only to compounds whose elements are complete words) is to leave open any compound not in the dictionary. Though this is widely done, it can result in the reader's failing to recognize a compound for what it is. A third approach is to pattern the compound after other similar ones. Though this approach is likely to be more complicated, it can make the compound look more familiar and thus less distracting or confusing. The paragraphs that follow are intended to help you use this approach.

As a general rule, writing meant for readers in specialized fields usually does not hyphenate compounds, especially technical terminology.

Compound Nouns
Compound nouns are combinations of words that function in a sentence as nouns. They may consist of two or more nouns, a noun and a modifier, or two or more elements that are not nouns.

Short compounds consisting of two nouns often begin as open compounds but tend to close up as they become familiar.

1. noun + noun Compounds composed of two nouns that are short and commonly used, of which the first is accented, are usually written solid.

farmhouse	lifeboat	football
hairbrush	paycheck	workplace

2. When a noun + noun compound is short and common but pronounced with nearly equal stress on both nouns, it is more likely to be open.

fuel oil	health care
park bench	desk lamp

3. Noun + noun compounds that consist of longer nouns and are self-evident or temporary are usually written open.

costume designer
computer terminal
billiard table

4. When a noun + noun compound describes a double title or double function, the compound is hyphenated.

> hunter-gatherer
> secretary-treasurer
> bar-restaurant

Sometimes a slash is used in place of the hyphen.

> bar/restaurant

5. Compounds formed from a noun or adjective followed by *man, woman, person,* or *people* and denoting an occupation are normally solid.

> anchorman   spokesperson
> congresswoman   salespeople

6. Compounds that are units of measurement are hyphenated.

> foot-pound   column-inch
> kilowatt-hour   light-year

7. **adjective + noun** Most adjective + noun compounds are written open.

> municipal court   hazardous waste   nuclear medicine
> genetic code   minor league   basic training

8. Adjective + noun compounds consisting of two short words are often written solid when the first word is accented. However, some are usually written open, and a few are hyphenated.

> notebook   shortcut   steel mill
> bluebird   dry cleaner   two-step

9. **participle + noun** Most participle + noun compounds are written open.

> landing craft   sounding board   preferred stock
> frying pan   barbed wire   informal consent

10. **noun's + noun** Compounds consisting of a possessive noun followed by another noun are usually written open; a few are hyphenated. Compounds of this type that have become solid have lost the apostrophe.

> fool's gold   Queen Anne's lace   foolscap
> hornet's nest   cat's-paw   menswear
> seller's market bull's-eye

11. **noun + verb + *-er* or *-ing*** Compounds in which the first noun is the object of the verb or gerund to which the suffix has been added are most often written open but sometimes hyphenated. Permanent compounds like these are sometimes written solid.

> problem solver   street-sweeping   air conditioner
> deal making   fund-raiser   lifesaving
> ticket-taker   gene-splicing

12. **object + verb** Noun compounds consisting of a verb preceded by a noun that is its object are written in various ways.

fish fry	bodyguard
eye-opener	roadblock

13. **verb + object** A few, mostly older compounds are formed from a verb followed by a noun that is its object; they are written solid.

cutthroat	carryall
breakwater	pickpocket

14. **noun + adjective** Compounds composed of a noun followed by an adjective are written open or hyphenated.

sum total	president-elect
consul general	secretary-general

15. **particle + noun** Compounds consisting of a particle (usually a preposition or adverb) and a noun are usually written solid, especially when they are short and the first syllable is accented.

downturn	outpatient	afterthought
outfield	undertone	onrush
input	upswing	

A few particle + noun compounds, especially when composed of longer elements or having equal stress on both elements, are hyphenated or open.

on-ramp	off year
cross-reference	cross fire

16. **verb + particle; verb + adverb** These compounds may be hyphenated or solid. Compounds with particles such as *to, in,* and *on* are often hyphenated. Compounds with particles such as *up, off,* and *out* are hyphenated or solid with about equal frequency. Those with longer particles or adverbs are usually solid.

lean-to	spin-off
trade-in	payoff
add-on	time-out
start-up	turnout
backup	hideaway

17. **verb + -er + particle; verb + -ing + particle** Except for *passerby,* these compounds are hyphenated.

runner-up	listener-in	talking-to
diners-out	carrying-on	falling-out

18. **letter + noun** Compounds formed from a single letter (or sometimes a combination of them) followed by a noun are either open or hyphenated.

T square	T-shirt
B vitamin	f-stop
V neck	H-bomb
Rh factor	A-frame
D major	E-mail *or* e-mail

19. **Compounds of three or four elements** Compounds of three or four words may be either hyphenated or open. Those incorporating prepositional phrases are more often open; others are usually hyphenated.

editor in chief	base on balls	give-and-take
power of attorney	right-of-way	rough-and-tumble
flash in the pan	jack-of-all-trades	

20. **Reduplication compounds** Compounds that are formed by reduplication and so consist of two similar-sounding elements are hyphenated if each element has more than one syllable. If each element has only one syllable, the compound is often written solid. Very short words and newly coined words are more often hyphenated.

namby-pamby	crisscross	sci-fi
razzle-dazzle	singsong	hip-hop

Compound Adjectives

Compound adjectives are combinations of words that work together to modify a noun—that is, they work as *unit modifiers*. As unit modifiers they can be distinguished from other strings of adjectives that may also precede a noun.

For instance, in "a low, level tract of land" the two adjectives each modify the noun separately; the tract is both low and level. These are *coordinate* (i.e., equal) *modifiers*. In "a low monthly fee" the first adjective modifies the noun plus the second adjective; the phrase denotes a monthly fee that is low. It could not be revised to "a monthly and low fee" without altering or confusing its meaning. Thus, these are *noncoordinate modifiers*. However, "low-level radiation" does not mean radiation that is low and level or level radiation that is low, but rather radiation that is at a low level. Both words work as a unit to modify the noun.

Unit modifiers are usually hyphenated, in order to help readers grasp the relationship of the words and to avoid confusion. The hyphen in "a call for more-specialized controls" removes any ambiguity as to which word *more* modifies. By contrast, the lack of a hyphen in a phrase like "graphic arts exhibition" may give it an undesirable ambiguity.

21. **Before the noun (attributive position)** Most two-word compound adjectives are hyphenated when placed before the noun.

the fresh-cut grass	a made-up excuse
its longer-lasting effects	his best-selling novel
her lace-trimmed dress	projected health-care costs

22. Compounds whose first word is an adverb ending in *-ly* are usually left open.

a privately chartered boat	its weirdly skewed perspective
politically correct opinions	a tumultuously cascading torrent

23. Compounds formed of an adverb not ending in *-ly* followed by a participle (or sometimes an adjective) are usually hyphenated when placed before a noun.

the well-worded statement   their still-awaited assignments
more-stringent measures   her once-famous uncle
his less-exciting prospects

24. The combination of *very* + adjective is not a unit modifier. (See also paragraph 33 below.)

    a very happy baby

25. When a compound adjective is formed by using a compound noun to modify another noun, it is usually hyphenated.

    a hazardous-waste site   a roll-call vote
    the basic-training period   their problem-solving abilities
    a minor-league pitcher

    Some familiar open compound nouns are frequently left open when used as adjectives.

    a high school diploma *or* a high-school diploma
    a real estate license *or* a real-estate license
    an income tax refund *or* an income-tax refund

26. A proper name used as a modifier is not hyphenated. A word that modifies the proper name is attached by a hyphen (or an en dash in typeset material).

    the Civil War era   the splendid *Gone with the Wind* premiere
    a New England tradition   a Los Angeles-based company
    a *New York Times* article   a Pulitzer Prize-winning author
    the Supreme Court decision   pre-Bull Run skirmishes

27. Compound adjectives composed of foreign words are not hyphenated when placed before a noun unless they are hyphenated in the foreign language itself.

    per diem expenses   a comme il faut arrangement
    an ad hoc committee   the a cappella chorus
    her *faux-naïf* style   a ci-devant professor

28. Compounds that are quoted, capitalized, or italicized are not hyphenated.

    a "Springtime in Paris" theme   his AMERICA FIRST sign
    the book's "I'm OK, you're OK" tone the *No smoking* notice

29. Chemical names and most medical names used as modifiers are not hyphenated.

    a sodium hypochlorite bleach
    the amino acid sequence
    a new Parkinson's disease medication

30. Compound adjectives of three or more words are hyphenated when they precede the noun.

    step-by-step instructions   a longer-than-expected list
    state-of-the-art equipment   turn-of-the-century medicine
    a wait-and-see attitude

31. **Following the noun** When a compound adjective follows the noun it modifies, it usually ceases to be a unit modifier and is therefore no longer hyphenated.

> instructions that guide you step by step
> a list that was longer than expected

However, a compound that follows the noun it modifies often keeps its hyphen if it continues to function as a unit modifier, especially if its first element is a noun.

> hikers who were ill-advised to cross the glacier
> an actor too high-strung to relax
> industries that could be called low-tech
> metals that are corrosion-resistant
> tends to be accident-prone

32. Permanent compound adjectives are usually written as they appear in the dictionary even when they follow the noun they modify.

> for reasons that are well-known
> a plan we regarded as half-baked
> The problems are mind-boggling.

However, compound adjectives of three or more words are normally not hyphenated when they follow the noun they modify, since they usually cease to function as adjectives.

> These remarks are off the record.
> medical practice of the turn of the century

When compounds of three or more words appear as hyphenated adjectives in dictionaries, the hyphens are retained as long as the phrase is being used as a unit modifier.

> The candidate's position was middle-of-the-road.

33. When an adverb modifies another adverb that is the first element of a compound modifier, the compound may lose its hyphen. If the first adverb modifies the whole compound, however, the hyphen is retained.

> a very well developed idea
> *but*
> a delightfully well-written book
> a most ill-timed event

34. Adjective compounds that are color names in which each element can function as a noun are almost always hyphenated.

> red-orange fabric
> The fabric was red-orange.

Color names in which the first element can only be an adjective are often unhyphenated before a noun and usually unhyphenated after.

> a bright red tie   reddish orange fabric *or* reddish-orange fabric
> the pale yellow-green chair The fabric was reddish orange.

35. Compound modifiers that include a number followed by a noun (except for the noun *percent*) are hyphenated when they precede the noun they modify, but usually not when they follow it. (For details on measurement, see paragraph 42 on page 317.)

the four-color press
a 12-foot-high fence
a fence 12 feet high
a 300-square-mile area

an area of 300 square miles
but
a 10 percent raise

If a currency symbol precedes the number, the hyphen is omitted.

an $8.5 million deficit

36. An adjective composed of a number followed by a noun in the possessive is not hyphenated.

a nine days' wonder
a two weeks' wait
but
a two-week wait

Compound Adverbs

37. Adverb compounds consisting of preposition + noun are almost always written solid. However, there are a few important exceptions.

downstairs
uphill
offshore
overnight
but
in-house

off-key
on-line

38. Compound adverbs of more than two words are usually written open, and they usually follow the words they modify.

here and there
more or less
head and shoulders
hand in hand

every which way
once and for all
but
a more-or-less certain result

A few three-word adverbs are usually hyphenated, but many are written open even if the corresponding adjective is hyphenated.

placed back-to-back
met face-to-face
but
a word-for-word quotation

quoted word for word
software bought off the shelf

Compound Verbs

39. Two-word verbs consisting of a verb followed by an adverb or a preposition are written open.

follow up
roll back

strike out
take on

run across
set back

40. A compound composed of a particle followed by a verb is written solid.

overlook	undercut
outfit	download

41. A verb derived from an open or hyphenated compound noun is hyphenated.

double-space	water-ski
rubber-stamp	field-test

42. A verb derived from a solid noun is written solid.

mastermind	brainstorm
highlight	sideline

Compounds Formed with Word Elements

Many new and temporary compounds are formed by adding word elements to existing words or by combining word elements. There are three basic kinds of word elements: prefixes (such as *anti-, non-, pre-, post-, re-, super-*), suffixes (such as *-er, -fold, -ism, -ist, -less, -ness*), and combining forms (such as *mini-, macro-, pseudo-, -graphy, -logy*). Prefixes and suffixes are usually attached to existing words; combining forms are usually combined to form new words.

43. prefix + word Except as specified in the paragraphs below, compounds formed from a prefix and a word are usually written solid.

anticrime	reorchestration	transnational
nonaligned	subzero	postdoctoral
premedical	superheroine	

44. If the prefix ends with a vowel and the word it is attached to begins with the same vowel, the compound is usually hyphenated.

anti-incumbent	co-organizer	intra-arterial
de-escalate	semi-independent	pre-engineered

However, there are many exceptions.

reelect
preestablished
cooperate

45. If the base word or compound to which a prefix is added is capitalized, the resulting compound is almost always hyphenated.

pre-Victorian
anti-Western
post-Darwinian
non-English-speaking
   but
transatlantic
transalpine

If the prefix and the base word together form a new proper name, the compound may be solid with the prefix capitalized.

Postimpressionists
Precambrian
   but
Pre-Raphaelite

46. Compounds made with *ex-*, in its "former" sense, and *self-* are hyphenated.

ex-mayor   self-control
ex-husband   self-sustaining

Compounds formed from *vice-* are usually hyphenated. Some permanent compounds are open.

vice-chair   vice president
vice-consul   vice admiral

A temporary compound with *quasi(-)* or *pseudo(-)* may be written open (if *quasi* or *pseudo* is being treated as a modifier) or hyphenated (if it is being treated as a combining form).

quasi intellectual *or* quasi-intellectual
pseudo liberal *or* pseudo-liberal

47. If a prefix is added to a hyphenated compound, it may be either followed by a hyphen or closed up solid to the next element. Permanent compounds of this kind should be checked in a dictionary.

unair-conditioned   non-self-governing
ultra-up-to-date   unself-confident

48. If a prefix is added to an open compound, the hyphen is often replaced by an en dash in typeset material.

ex-campaign treasurer
post-World War I era

49. A compound that would be identical with another word if written solid is usually hyphenated to prevent misreading.

a re-creation of the setting
shopped at the co-op
multi-ply fabric

50. Compounds that might otherwise be solid are often hyphenated in order to clarify their formation, meaning, or pronunciation.

tri-city   re-oil   anti-fur
de-iced   non-news   pro-choice

51. When prefixes are attached to numerals, the compounds are hyphenated.

pre-1995 models
post-1945 economy
non-19th-century architecture

52. Compounds created from proper ethnic or national combining forms are hyphenated when the second element is an independent word, but solid when it is a combining form.

Anglo-Saxon	Sino-Japanese	Francophone
Judeo-Christian	Anglophile	Sinophobe

53. Prefixes that are repeated in the same compound are separated by a hyphen.

re-refried
post-postmodern

54. Compounds consisting of different prefixes or adjectives with the same base word which are joined by *and* or *or* are shortened by pruning the first compound back to a hyphenated prefix.

pre- and postoperative care	early- and mid-20th-century painters
anti- or pro-Revolutionary sympathies	4-, 6-, and 8-foot lengths
over- and underachievers	

55. word + suffix Except as noted in the paragraphs below, compounds formed by adding a suffix to a word are written solid.

Fourierism	yellowish	custodianship
benightedness	characterless	easternmost

56. Compounds made with a suffix or a terminal combining form are often hyphenated if the base word is more than two syllables long, if it ends with the same letter the suffix begins with, or if it is a proper name.

industry-wide	American-ness	Hollywood-ish
recession-proof	jewel-like	Europe-wide

57. Compounds made from a number + *-odd* are hyphenated. A number + *-fold* is written solid if the number is spelled out but hyphenated if it is in numerals.

fifty-odd	tenfold
50-odd	10-fold

58. Most compounds formed from an open or hyphenated compound + a suffix do not separate the suffix with a hyphen. But combining forms that also exist as independent words, such as *-like, -wide, -worthy,* and *-proof,* are attached by a hyphen.

self-righteousness	a Red Cross-like approach
middle-of-the-roadism	a New York-wide policy
bobby-soxer	

Open compounds often become hyphenated when a suffix is added unless they are proper nouns.

flat-taxer
Ivy Leaguer
World Federalist

59. combining form + combining form New terms in technical fields created with one or more combining forms are normally written solid.

cyberworld
macrographic

Abbreviations

Abbreviations may be used to save space and time, to avoid repetition of long words and phrases, or simply to conform to conventional usage.

The contemporary styling of abbreviations is inconsistent and arbitrary, and no set of rules can hope to cover all the possible variations, exceptions, and peculiarities encountered in print. The form abbreviations take—capitalized vs. lowercased, punctuated vs. unpunctuated—often depends on a writer's preference or a publisher's or organization's policy. However, the following paragraphs provide a number of useful guidelines to contemporary practice. In doubtful cases, a good general dictionary or a dictionary of abbreviations will usually show standard forms for common abbreviations.

The present discussion deals largely with general, nontechnical writing. For information about abbreviations used in legal citations, see pages 318–23, especially pages 322–23, and Chapter 13, "The Law Library," especially pages 422–33.

Abbreviations are almost never italicized. An abbreviation consisting of single initial letters, whether punctuated or not, never standardly has spacing between the letters. (Initials of personal names, however, normally are separated by spaces.)

The first reference to any frequently abbreviated term or name that could be confusing or unfamiliar is commonly spelled out, often followed immediately by its abbreviation in parentheses. Later references employ the abbreviation alone.

PUNCTUATION

1. A period follows most abbreviations that are formed by omitting all but the first few letters of a word.

cont. [*for* continued]	Oct. [*for* October]
enc. [*for* enclosure]	univ. [*for* university]

   Former abbreviations that are now considered words do not need a period.

lab	photo
gym	ad

2. A period follows most abbreviations that are formed by omitting letters from the middle of a word.

govt. [*for* government]	bros. [*for* brothers]
atty. [*for* attorney]	Dr. [*for* Doctor]

   Some abbreviations, usually called *contractions*, replace the omitted letters with an apostrophe. Such contractions do not end with a period. (In American usage, very few contractions other than two-word contractions involving verbs are in standard use.)

ass'n *or* assn. [*for* association]	nat'l *or* natl. [*for* national]
dep't *or* dept. [*for* department]	can't [*for* cannot]

3. Periods are usually omitted from abbreviations made up of single initial letters. However, for some of these abbreviations, especially uncapitalized

ones, the periods are usually retained. No space follows an internal period.

GOP [*for* Grand Old Party]   CEO *or* C.E.O. [*for* chief executive officer]
PR [*for* public relations]   a.m. [*for* ante meridiem]

4. A few abbreviations are punctuated with one or more slashes in place of periods. (For details on the slash, see the section beginning on page 257.)

c/o [*for* care of]   w/o [*for* without]
d/b/a *or* d.b.a. [*for* doing business as] w/w [*for* wall-to-wall]

5. Terms in which a suffix is added to a numeral are not genuine abbreviations and do not require a period. (For details on ordinal numbers, see the section on page 305.)

1st   3d
2nd   8vo

6. Isolated letters of the alphabet used to designate a shape or position in a sequence are not abbreviations and are not punctuated.

T square
A1
F minor

7. When a punctuated abbreviation ends a sentence, its period becomes the terminal period.

For years she claimed she was "the oldest living fossil at Briggs & Co."

CAPITALIZATION

1. Abbreviations are capitalized if the words they represent are proper nouns or adjectives.

F [*for* Fahrenheit]   Amer. [*for* American]
IMF [*for* International Monetary Fund] LWV [*for* League of Women Voters]
Jan. [*for* January]

2. Abbreviations are usually all-capitalized when they represent initial letters of lowercased words. However, some common abbreviations formed in this way are often lowercased.

IQ [*for* intelligence quotient]   FYI [*for* for your information]
U.S. [*for* United States]   f.o.b. *or* FOB [*for* free on board]
COLA [*for* cost-of-living allowance] c/o [*for* care of]

3. Most abbreviations formed from single initial letters that are pronounced as words, rather than as a series of letters, are capitalized. Those that are not proper nouns and have been assimilated into the language as words in their own right are most often lowercased.

OSHA   NAFTA   sonar
NATO   snafu   scuba
CARE   laser

4. Abbreviations that are ordinarily capitalized are commonly used to begin sentences, but abbreviations that are ordinarily uncapitalized are not.

Dr. Smith strongly disagrees.

OSHA regulations require these new measures.

Page 22 [*not* P. 22] was missing.

PLURALS, POSSESSIVES, AND COMPOUNDS

1. Punctuated abbreviations of single words are pluralized by adding -*s* before the period.

   yrs. [*for* years]

   hwys. [*for* highways]

   figs. [*for* figures]

2. Punctuated abbreviations that stand for phrases or compounds are usually pluralized by adding -*'s* after the last period.

M.D.'s *or* M.D.s	LL.B.'s *or* LL.B.s
Ph.D.'s *or* Ph.D.s	v.p.'s

3. All-capitalized, unpunctuated abbreviations are usually pluralized by adding a lowercase -*s*.

IRAs	CPAs
PCs	SATs

4. The plural form of a few lowercase one-letter abbreviations is made by repeating the letter.

ll. [*for* lines]	vv. [*for* verses]
pp. [*for* pages]	ff. *or* ff [*for* and the following ones *or* folios]
nn. [*for* notes]	

5. The plural form of abbreviations of units of measurement (including one-letter abbreviations) is the same as the singular form. (For more on units of measurement, see the section beginning on page 317.)

10 cc *or* cc. [*for* cubic centimeters]	24 h. [*for* hours]
30 m *or* m. [*for* meters]	10 min. [*for* minutes]
15 mm *or* mm. [*for* millimeters]	45 mi. [*for* miles]

   However, in informal nontechnical text several such abbreviations are pluralized like other single-word abbreviations.

lbs.	qts.
gals.	hrs.

6. Possessives of abbreviations are formed like those of spelled-out nouns: the singular possessive is formed by adding -*'s*, the plural possessive simply by adding an apostrophe.

the CEO's speech	the PACs' influence
Apex Co.'s profits	Brown Bros.' ads

7. Compounds that consist of an abbreviation added to another word are formed in the same way as compounds that consist of spelled-out nouns.

   an FDA-approved drug

   an R&D-driven company

   the Eau Claire, Wisc.-based publisher

Compounds formed by adding a prefix or suffix to an abbreviation are usually hyphenated.

pre-CD recordings	a CIA-like operation
non-IRA deductions	a PCB-free product

SPECIFIC STYLING CONVENTIONS

A and *An*

1. The choice of the article *a* or *an* before abbreviations depends on the sound, rather than the actual letter, with which the abbreviation begins. If it begins with a consonant sound, *a* is normally used; if with a vowel sound, *an* is used.

a CD-ROM version	a U.S. Senator	an M.D. degree
a YAF member	an FDA-approved drug	an ABA convention

A.D. and B.C.

2. The abbreviations A.D. and B.C. and other abbreviated era designations usually appear in books and journals as small capitals; in newspapers and in typed or keyboarded material, they usually appear as full capitals. The abbreviation B.C. follows the date; A.D. usually precedes the date, though in many publications A.D. follows the date as well. In references to whole centuries, A.D. follows the century. (For more on era designations, see paragraph 12 on page 311.)

A.D. 185 *but also* 185 A.D.

41 B.C.

the fourth century A.D.

Agencies, Associations, Organizations, and Companies

3. The names of agencies, associations, and organizations are usually abbreviated after being spelled out on their first occurrence in a text. If a company is easily recognizable from its initials, the abbreviation is likewise usually employed after the first mention. The abbreviations are usually all-capitalized and unpunctuated. (In contexts where the abbreviation will be recognized, it often replaces the full name throughout.)

Next, the president of the Pioneer Valley Transit Authority presented the annual PVTA award.

. . . at the American Bar Association (ABA) meeting in June. The ABA's new officers . . .

International Business Machines released its first-quarter earnings figures today. An IBM spokesperson I

4. The words *Company, Corporation, Incorporated,* and *Limited* in company names are commonly abbreviated even at their first appearance, except in quite formal writing.

Procter & Gamble Company *or* Procter & Gamble Co.

Brandywine Corporation *or* Brandywine Corp.

Ampersand

5. The ampersand (&), representing the word *and,* is often used in the names of companies.

H&R Block
Standard & Poor's
Ogilvy & Mather

It is not used in the names of federal agencies.

U.S. Fish and Wildlife Service
Office of Management and Budget

Even when a spelled-out *and* appears in a company's official name, it is often replaced by an ampersand in writing referring to the company, whether for the sake of consistency or because of the writer's inability to verify the official styling.

6. When an ampersand is used in an abbreviation, there is usually no space on either side of the ampersand.

The Barkers welcome all guests to their B&B at 54 West Street.
The S&P 500 showed gains in technology stocks.
The Texas A&M Aggies prevailed again on Sunday.

7. When an ampersand is used between the last two elements in a series, the comma is omitted.

Jones, Kuhn & Malloy, Attorneys at Law

Books of the Bible
8. Books of the Bible are spelled out in running text but generally abbreviated in references to chapter and verse.

The minister based his first Advent sermon on Matthew.
Ye cannot serve God and mammon.—Matt. 6:24

Compass Points
9. Compass points are normally abbreviated when they follow street names; these abbreviations may be punctuated and are usually preceded by a comma.

1600 Pennsylvania Avenue[,] NW [N.W.]

When a compass point precedes the word *Street, Avenue,* etc., or when it follows the word but forms an integral part of the street name, it is usually spelled out.

230 West 43rd Street
50 Park Avenue South

Dates
10. The names of days and months are spelled out in running text.

at the Monday editorial meeting
the December issue of *Scientific American*
a meeting held on August 1, 1995

The names of months usually are not abbreviated in datelines of business letters, but they are often abbreviated in government and military correspondence.

business dateline: November 1, 1995
military dateline: 1 Nov 95

Degrees and Professional Ratings

11. Abbreviations of academic degrees are usually punctuated; abbreviations of professional ratings are slightly more commonly unpunctuated.

> Ph.D.
>
> B.Sc.
>
> M.B.A.
>
> P.LS *or* P.L.S. [*for* Professional Legal Secretary]
>
> CMA *or* C.M.A. [*for* Certified Medical Assistant]
>
> FACP *or* F.A.C.P. [*for* Fellow of the American College of Physicians]

12. Only the first letter of each element in abbreviations of degrees and professional ratings is generally capitalized.

> D.Ch.E. [*for* Doctor of Chemical Engineering]
>
> Litt.D. [*for* Doctor of Letters]
>
> D.Th. [*for* Doctor of Theology]
> > *but*
>
> LL.B. [*for* Bachelor of Laws]
>
> LL.M. [*for* Master of Laws]
>
> LL.D. [*for* Doctor of Laws]

Geographical Names

13. When abbreviations of state names are used in running text immediately following the name of a city or county, the traditional state abbreviations are often used.

> Ellen White of 49 Lyman St., Saginaw, Mich., has been chosen . . .
>
> the Dade County, Fla., public schools
> > *but*
>
> Grand Rapids, in western Michigan, . . .

Official postal service abbreviations for states are used in mailing addresses.

> 6 Bay Rd.
>
> Gibson Island, MD 21056

14. Terms such as *Street, Road,* and *Boulevard* are often written as punctuated abbreviations in running text when they form part of a proper name.

> an accident on Windward Road [*or* Rd.]
>
> our office at 1234 Cross Blvd. [*or* Boulevard]

15. Names of countries are usually spelled in full in running text.

> South Africa's president urged the United States to impose meaningful sanctions.

Abbreviations for country names (in tables, for example), are usually punctuated. When formed from the single initial letters of two or more individual words, they are sometimes unpunctuated.

> | Mex. | Ger. | U.K. *or* UK |
> | Can. | Scot. | U.S. *or* US |

16. *United States* is normally abbreviated when used as an adjective or attributive. When used as a noun, it is generally spelled out.

the U.S. Department of Justice

U.S. foreign policy

The United States has declined to participate.

17. *Saint* is usually abbreviated when it is part of a geographical or topographical name. *Mount, Point,* and *Fort* may be either spelled out or abbreviated. (For the abbreviation of *Saint* with personal names, see paragraph 25 below.)

St. Paul, Minnesota   *or*   Saint Paul, Minnesota

St. Thomas, U.S.V.I.   *or*   Saint Thomas

Mount Vernon   *or*   Mt. Vernon

Point Reyes   *or*   Pt. Reyes

Fort Worth   *or*   Ft. Worth

Mt. Kilimanjaro   *or*   Mount Kilimanjaro

Latin Words and Phrases

18. Several Latin words and phrases are almost always abbreviated. They are punctuated, lowercased, and usually not italicized.

etc.	et al.	c. *or* ca.
i.e.	ibid.	fl.
e.g.	op. cit.	et seq.
cf.	loc. cit	
viz.	q.v.	

Versus is usually abbreviated *v.* in legal writing, *vs.* otherwise.

Da Costa v. *United States*

good vs. evil   *or*   good versus evil

Latitude and *Longitude*

19. The words *latitude* and *longitude* are abbreviated in tables and in technical contexts but often written out in running text.

in a table: lat. 10°20′N *or* lat. 10-20N

in text: from 10°20′ north latitude to 10°30′ south latitude

      or from lat. 10°20′N to lat. 10°30′S

Military Ranks and Units

20. Official abbreviations for military ranks follow specific unpunctuated styles for each branch of the armed forces. Nonmilitary writing usually employs a punctuated and less concise style.

in the military: BG Carter R. Stokes, USA

      LCDR Dawn Wills-Craig, USN

      Col S. J. Smith, USMC

      LTJG Carlos Ramos, USCG

      Sgt Bernard P. Brodkey, USAF

outside the military: Brig. Gen. Carter R. Stokes

      Lt. Comdr. Dawn Wills-Craig

      Col. S. J. Smith

      Lt. (j.g.) Carlos Ramos

      Sgt. Bernard P. Brodkey

21. Outside the military, military ranks are usually given in full when used with a surname only but abbreviated when used with a full name.

Major Mosby
Maj. John S. Mosby

Number
22. The word *number,* when followed by a numeral, is usually abbreviated to *No.* or *no.*

> The No. 1 priority is to promote profitability.
> We recommend no. 6 thread.
> Policy No. 123-5-X
> Publ. Nos. 12 and 13

Personal Names
23. When initials are used with a surname, they are spaced and punctuated. Unspaced initials of a few famous persons, which may or may not be punctuated, are sometimes used in place of their full names.

> E. M. Forster
> C. P. E. Bach
> JFK *or* J.F.K.

24. The abbreviations *Jr.* and *Sr.* may or may not be preceded by a comma.

> Martin Luther King Jr.
> *or*
> Martin Luther King, Jr.

Saint
25. The word *Saint* is often abbreviated when used before the name of a saint. When it forms part of a surname or an institution's name, it follows the style used by the person or institution. (For the styling of *Saint* in geographical names, see paragraph 17 above.)

> St. [*or* Saint] Teresa of Avila   St. Martin's Press
> Augustus Saint-Gaudens   St. John's College
> Ruth St. Denis

Scientific Terms
26. In binomial nomenclature, a genus name may be abbreviated to its initial letter after the first reference. The abbreviation is always capitalized, punctuated, and italicized.

> . . . its better-known relative *Atropa belladonna* (deadly nightshade).
> Only *A. belladonna* is commonly found in . . .

27. Abbreviations for the names of chemical compounds and the symbols for chemical elements and formulas are unpunctuated.

> MSG   Pb   NaCl
> PCB   O   FeS

28. Abbreviations in computer terms are usually unpunctuated.

> PC   I/O   Ctrl
> RAM   DOS   ASCII
> MB   Esc   EBCDIC
> CD-ROM   Alt

Time

29. When time is expressed in figures, the abbreviations *a.m. (ante meridiem)* and *p.m. (post meridiem)* are most often written as punctuated lowercase letters, sometimes as punctuated small capital letters. In newspapers, they usually appear in full-size capitals. (For more on *a.m.* and *p.m.*, see paragraph 39 on page 316.)

> 8:30 a.m. *or* 8:30 A.M. *or* 8:30 A.M.
>
> 10:00 p.m. *or* 10:00 P.M. *or* 10:00 P.M.

Time-zone designations are usually capitalized and unpunctuated.

> 9:22 a.m. EST [*for* eastern standard time]
>
> 4:45 p.m. CDT [*for* central daylight time]

Titles and Degrees

30. The courtesy titles *Mr., Ms., Mrs.,* and *Messrs.* occur only as abbreviations today. The professional titles *Doctor, Professor, Representative,* and *Senator* are often abbreviated.

> Ms. Lee A. Downs
>
> Messrs. Lake, Mason, and Nambeth
>
> Doctor Howe *or* Dr. Howe

31. Despite some traditional objections, the honorific titles *Honorable* and *Reverend* are often abbreviated, with and without *the* preceding the titles.

> the Honorable Samuel I. O'Leary *or* [the] Hon. Samuel I. O'Leary
>
> the Reverend Samuel I. O'Leary *or* [the] Rev. Samuel I. O'Leary

32. When an abbreviation for an academic degree, professional certification, or association membership follows a name, no courtesy or professional title precedes it.

> Dr. Jesse Smith *or* Jesse Smith, M.D. *but not* Dr. Jesse Smith, M.D.
>
> Katherine Fox Derwinski, CLU
>
> Carol W. Manning, M.D., FACPS
>
> Michael B. Jones II, J.D.
>
> Peter D. Cohn, Jr., CPA

33. The abbreviation *Esq.* (for *Esquire*) often follows attorneys' names in correspondence and in formal listings, and less often follows the names of certain other professionals, including architects, consuls, clerks of court, and justices of the peace. It is not used if a degree or professional rating follows the name, or if a courtesy title or honorific (*Mr., Ms., Hon., Dr.,* etc.) precedes the name.

> Carolyn B. West, Esq. *not* Ms. Carolyn B. West, Esq. *and not* Carolyn B. West, J.D., Esq.

Units of Measurement

34. A unit of measurement that follows a figure is often abbreviated, especially in technical writing. The figure and abbreviation are separated by a space. If the numeral is written out, the unit should also be written out.

> 15 cu. ft. *but* fifteen cubic feet
>
> What is its capacity in cubic feet?

35. Abbreviations for metric units are usually unpunctuated; those for traditional units are usually punctuated in nonscientific writing. (For more on units of measurement, see the section beginning on page 317.)

14 ml	50 m	4 sec.
12 km	8 ft.	20 min.

Numbers

The treatment of numbers presents special difficulties because there are so many conventions to follow, some of which may conflict in a particular passage. The major issue is whether to spell out numbers or to express them in figures, and usage varies considerably on this point.

NUMBERS AS WORDS OR FIGURES

At one style extreme—usually limited to proclamations, legal documents, and some other types of very formal writing—all numbers (sometimes even including dates) are written out. At the other extreme, some types of technical writing may contain no written-out numbers. Figures are generally easier to read than spelled-out numbers; however, the spelled-out forms are helpful in certain circumstances, and are often felt to be less jarring than figures in nontechnical writing.

Basic Conventions

1. Two alternative basic conventions are in common use. The first and more widely used system requires that numbers up through nine be spelled out, and that figures be used for exact numbers greater than nine. (In a variation of this system, the number ten is spelled out.) Round numbers that consist of a whole number between one and nine followed by *hundred, thousand, million,* etc., may either be spelled out or expressed in figures.

> The museum includes four rooms of early American tools and implements, 345 pieces in all.
> He spoke for almost three hours, inspiring his audience of 19,000 devoted followers.
> They sold more than 700 [*or* seven hundred] TVs during the 10-day sale.
> She'd told him so a thousand times.

2. The second system requires that numbers from one through ninety-nine be spelled out, and that figures be used for all exact numbers above ninety-nine. (In a variation of this system, the number one hundred is spelled out.) Numbers that consist of a whole number between one and ninety-nine followed by *hundred, thousand, million,* etc., are also spelled out.

> Audubon's engraver spent nearly twelve years completing these four volumes, which comprise 435 hand-colored plates.
> In the course of four hours, she signed twenty-five hundred copies of her book.

3. Written-out numbers only use hyphens following words ending in -*ty*. The word *and* before such words is usually omitted.

twenty-two
five-hundred ninety-seven
two thousand one hundred forty-nine

Sentence Beginnings

4. Numbers that begin a sentence are written out. An exception is occasionally made for dates. Spelled-out numbers that are lengthy and awkward
are usually avoided by restructuring the sentence.

>   Sixty-two new bills will be brought before the committee.
>   *or* There will be 62 new bills brought before the committee.
>   Nineteen ninety-five was our best earnings year so far.
>   *or occasionally* 1995 was our best earnings year so far.
>   One hundred fifty-seven illustrations, including 86 color plates, are contained
>   in the book.
>   *or* The book contains 157 illustrations, including 86 color plates.

Adjacent Numbers and Numbers in Series

5. Two separate figures are generally not written adjacent to one another in
running text unless they form a series. Instead, either the sentence is
rephrased or one of the figures is spelled out-usually the figure with the
shorter written form.

>   sixteen ½-inch dowels
>   worked five 9-hour days in a row
>   won twenty 100-point games
>   lost 15 fifty-point matches
>   By 1997, thirty schools . . .

6. Numbers paired at the beginning of a sentence are usually written alike. If
the first word of the sentence is a spelled-out number, the second number
is also spelled out. However, each number may instead be styled independently, even if that results in an inconsistent pairing.

>   Sixty to seventy-five copies will be required.
>   *or* Sixty to 75 copies will be required.

7. Numbers that form a pair or a series within a sentence or a paragraph are
often treated identically even when they would otherwise be styled differently. The style of the largest number usually determines that of the others. If one number is a mixed or simple fraction, figures are used for all the
numbers in the series.

>   She wrote one proposal and thirteen [*or* 13] memos that week.
>   His total record sales came to a meager 8 [*or* eight] million; Bing Crosby's, he
>   mused, may have surpassed 250 million.
>   The three jobs took 5, 12, and 4½ hours, respectively.

Round Numbers

8. Approximate or round numbers, particularly those that can be expressed
in one or two words, are often spelled out in general writing. In technical
and scientific writing, they are expressed as numerals.

>   seven hundred people *or* 700 people
>   five thousand years *or* 5,000 years

four hundred thousand volumes *or* 400,000 volumes *but not* 400 thousand volumes
but in technical writing
200 species of fish
50,000 people per year
300,000 years

9. Round (and round-appearing) numbers of one million and above are often expressed as figures followed by the word *million, billion,* and so forth. The figure may include a one- or two-digit decimal fraction; more exact numbers are written entirely in figures.

the last 600 million years
about 4.6 billion years old
1.2 million metric tons of grain
$7.25 million
$3,456,000,000

Ordinal Numbers

10. Ordinal numbers generally follow the styling rules for cardinal numbers. In technical writing, ordinal numbers are usually written as figure-plus-suffix combinations. Certain ordinal numbers—for example, those for percentiles and latitudes—are usually set as figures even in nontechnical contexts.

entered the seventh grade
wrote the 9th [*or* ninth] and 12th [*or* twelfth] chapters
in the 21st [*or* twenty-first] century
the 7th percentile
the 38th parallel

11. In figure-plus-suffix combinations where the figure ends in 2 or 3, either a one- or a two-letter suffix may be used. A period does not follow the suffix.

2d *or* 2nd
33d *or* 33rd
102d *or* 102nd

Roman Numerals

12. Roman numerals are traditionally used to differentiate rulers and popes with identical names.

King George III
Henri IV
Innocent X

13. When Roman numerals are used to differentiate related males with the same name, they are used only with the full name. Ordinals are sometimes used instead of Roman numerals. The possessive is formed in the usual way. (For the use of *Jr.* and *Sr.*, see paragraph 24 on page 301.)

James R. Watson II
James R. Watson 2nd *or* 2d
James R. Watson II's [*or* 2nd's *or* 2d's] alumni gift

14. Lowercase Roman numerals are generally used to number book pages that precede the regular Arabic sequence (often including a table of contents, acknowledgments, foreword, or other material).

    on page iv of the preface
    See Introduction, pp. ix–xiii.

15. Roman numerals are used in outlines; see paragraph 23 on page 314.

16. Roman numerals are found as part of a few established scientific and technical terms. Chords in the study of music harmony are designated by capital and lowercase Roman numerals (often followed by small Arabic numbers). Most technical terms that include numbers, however, express them in Arabic form.

blood-clotting factor VII	vii_6 chord
quadrant III	*but*
the cranial nerves II and IX	adenosine 3′,5′-monophosphate
HIV-III virus	cesium 137
Population II stars	PL/1 programming language
type I error	

17. Miscellaneous uses of Roman numerals include the Articles, and often the Amendments, of the Constitution. Roman numerals are still sometimes used for references to the acts and scenes of plays and occasionally for volume numbers in bibliographic references.

    Article IX
    Act III, Scene ii   *or*   Act 3, Scene 2
    (III, ii)   *or*   (3, 2)
    Vol. XXIII, No. 4   *but usually*   Vol. 23, No. 4

PUNCTUATION

These paragraphs provide general rules for the use of commas, hyphens, and en dashes with compound and large numbers. For specific categories of numbers, such as dates, money, and decimal fractions, see "Specific Styling Conventions," beginning on page 309.

Commas in Large Numbers
1. In general writing, figures of four digits may be written with or without a comma; including the comma is more common. If the numerals form part of a tabulation, commas are necessary so that four-digit numerals can align with numerals of five or more digits.

    2,000 cases   *or less commonly*   2000 cases

2. Whole numbers of five digits or more (but not decimal fractions) use a comma to separate three-digit groups, counting from the right.

    a fee of $12,500
    15,000 units
    a population of 1,500,000

3. Certain types of numbers of four digits or more do not contain commas. These include decimal fractions and the numbers of policies and contracts,

checks, street addresses, rooms and suites, telephones, pages, military hours, and years.

2.5544	12537 Wilshire Blvd.	1650 hours
Policy 33442	Room 1206	in 1929
check 34567	page 145	

4. In technical writing, the comma is frequently replaced by a thin space in numerals of five or more digits. Digits to the right of the decimal point are also separated in this way, counting from the decimal point.

28 666 203
209.775 42

Hyphens

5. Hyphens are used with written-out numbers between 21 and 99.

forty-one years old
his forty-first birthday
Four hundred twenty-two visitors were counted.

6. A hyphen is used in a written-out fraction employed as a modifier. A non-modifying fraction consisting of two words only is usually left open, although it may also be hyphenated. (For details on fractions, see the section beginning on page 312.)

a one-half share
three fifths of her paycheck *or* three-fifths of her paycheck
  but
four five-hundredths

7. Numbers that form the first part of a modifier expressing measurement are followed by a hyphen. (For units of measurement, see the section on page 317.)

a 5-foot board
a 28-mile trip
an eight-pound baby
  but
a $6 million profit

8. Serial numbers, Social Security numbers, telephone numbers, and extended zip codes often contain hyphens that make lengthy numerals more readable or separate coded information.

020-42-1691
413-734-3134 *or* (413) 734-3134
01102-2812

9. Numbers are almost never divided at the end of a line. If division is unavoidable, the break occurs only after a comma.

Inclusive Numbers

10. Inclusive numbers—those that express a range—are usually separated either by the word *to* or by a hyphen or en dash, meaning "(up) to and including."

spanning the years 1915 to 1941   pages 40 to 98
the fiscal year 1994–95   pp. 40–98
the decade 1920–1929

Inclusive numbers separated by a hyphen or en dash are not used after the words *from* or *between*.

from page 385 to page 419 *not* from page 385–419
from 9:30 to 5:30 *not* from 9:30–5:30
between 1997 and 2000 *not* between 1997–2000
between 80 and 90 percent *not* between 80–90 percent

11. Inclusive page numbers and dates may be either written in full or elided (i.e., shortened) to save space or for ease of reading.

pages 523–526 *or* pages 523–26
1955–1969 *or* 1955–69

However, inclusive dates that appear in titles and other headings are almost never elided. Dates that appear with era designations are also not elided.

England and the French Revolution 1789–1797
1900–1901 *not* 1900–01 *and not* 1900–1
872–863 B.C. *not* 872–63 B.C.

12. The most common style for the elision of inclusive numbers is based on the following rules: Never elide inclusive numbers that have only two digits.

24–28 *not* 24–8
86–87 *not* 86–7

Never elide inclusive numbers when the first number ends in 00.

100–103 *not* 100–03 *and not* 100–3
300–329 *not* 300–29

In other numbers, do not omit the tens digit from the higher number. *Exception:* Where the tens digit of both numbers is zero, write only one digit for the higher number.

234–37 *not* 234–7
3,824–29 *not* 3,824–9
605–7 *not* 605–07

13. Units of measurement expressed in words or abbreviations are usually used only after the second element of an inclusive number. Symbols, however, are repeated.

ten to fifteen dollars
30 to 35 degrees Celsius
an increase in dosage from 200 to 500 mg
    but
45° to 48° F
$50–$60 million *or* $50 million to $60 million

14. Numbers that are part of an inclusive set or range are usually styled alike: figures with figures, spelled-out words with other spelled-out words.

> from 8 to 108 absences
>
> five to twenty guests
>
> 300,000,000 to 305,000,000 *not* 300 million to 305,000,000

SPECIFIC STYLING CONVENTIONS

The following paragraphs, arranged alphabetically, describe styling practices commonly followed for specific situations involving numbers.

Addresses

1. Numerals are used for all building, house, apartment, room, and suite numbers except for *one*, which is usually written out.

6 Lincoln Road	Apartment 609	Suite 2000
1436 Fremont Street	Room 982	One Bayside Drive

When the address of a building is used as its name, the number in the address is often written out.

> the sophisticated elegance of Ten Park Avenue

2. Numbered streets have their numbers written as ordinals. Street names from First through Tenth are usually written out, and numerals are used for all higher-numbered streets. Less commonly, all numbered street names up to and including One Hundredth are spelled out.

> 167 Second Avenue
>
> 19 South 22nd Street *or less commonly* 19 South Twenty-second Street
>
> 145 East 145th Street
>
> in the 60s *or* in the Sixties [streets from 60th to 69th]
>
> in the 120s [streets from 120th to 129th]

When a house or building number immediately precedes the number of a street, a spaced hyphen may be inserted between the two numbers, or the street number may be written out, for the sake of clarity.

> 2018 - 14th Street
>
> 2018 Fourteenth Street

3. Arabic numerals are used to designate highways and, in some states, county roads.

Interstate 90 *or* I-90	Texas 23
U.S. Route 1 *or* U.S. 1	County 213

Dates

4. Year numbers are written as figures. If a year number begins a sentence, it may be left as a figure but more often is spelled out; the sentence may also be rewritten to avoid beginning it with a figure.

> the 1997 edition
>
> Nineteen thirty-seven marked the opening of the Golden Gate Bridge.
>
> *or* The year 1937 marked the opening of the Golden Gate Bridge.
>
> *or* The Golden Gate Bridge opened in 1937.

5. A year number may be abbreviated to its last two digits when an event is so well known that it needs no century designation. In these cases an apostrophe precedes the numerals.

> the blizzard of '88
> class of '91 *or* class of 1991
> the Spirit of '76

6. Full dates are traditionally written in the sequence month-day-year, with the year set off by commas that precede and follow it. An alternative style, used in the military and in U.S. government publications, is the inverted sequence day-month-year, which does not require commas.

> *traditional:*   July 8, 1976, was a warm, sunny day in Philadelphia.
>   the explosion on July 16, 1945, at Alamogordo
> *military:*   the explosion on 16 July 1945 at Alamogordo
>   the amendment ratified on 18 August 1920

In legal documents, the day is often spelled out and the year is occasionally spelled out.

> February eighth [*or* this eighth day of February]
> nineteen hundred and ninety-nine

7. Ordinal numbers are not used in full dates. Ordinals are sometimes used, however, for a date without an accompanying year, and they are always used when preceded in a date by the word *the*.

> December 4, 1829
> on December 4th *or* on December 4
> on the 4th of December

8. All-figure dating, such as 6-8-95 or 6/8/95, is usually avoided except in informal writing. For some readers, such dates are ambiguous; the examples above generally mean June 8, 1995, in the United States, but in almost all other countries mean August 6, 1995.

9. Commas are usually omitted from dates that include the month and year but not the day. The word *of* is sometimes inserted between the month and year.

> in October 1997
> back in January of 1981

10. References to specific centuries may be either written out or expressed in figures.

> in the nineteenth century *or* in the 19th century
> a sixteenth-century painting *or* a 16th-century painting

11. The name of a specific decade often takes a short form, usually with no apostrophe and uncapitalized. When the short form is part of a set phrase, it is capitalized.

> a song from the sixties
>   *occasionally* a song from the 'sixties *or* a song from the Sixties
> tunes of the Gay Nineties

The name of a decade is often expressed in numerals, in plural form. The figure may be shortened, with an apostrophe to indicate the missing numerals; however, apostrophes enclosing the figure are generally avoided. Any sequence of such numbers is generally styled consistently.

> the 1950s and 1960s *or* the '50s and '60s
> *but not*
> the '50's and '60's
> the 1950s and '60s
> the 1950s and sixties

12. Era designations precede or follow words that specify centuries or numerals that specify years. Era designations are unspaced abbreviations, punctuated with periods. They are usually typed or keyboarded as regular capitals, and typeset in books as small capitals and in newspapers as full-size capitals. The abbreviation B.C. (before Christ) is placed after the date, while A.D. (*anno Domini*, "in the year of our Lord") is usually placed before the date but after a century designation. Any date given without an era designation or context is understood to mean A.D.

> 1792-1750 B.C.
> between 600 and 400 B.C.
> from the fifth or fourth millennium to c. 250 B.C.
> between 7 B.C. and A.D. 22
> c. A.D. 100 to 300
> the second century A.D.
> the 17th century

13. Less common era designations include A.H. (*anno Hegirae*, "in the year of [Muhammad's] Hegira," or *anno Hebraico*, "in the Hebrew year"); B.C.E. (before the common era; a synonym for B.C.); C.E. (of the common era; a synonym for A.D.); and B.P. (before the present; often used by geologists and archeologists, with or without the word *year*). The abbreviation A.H. is usually placed before a specific date but after a century designation, while B.C.E., C.E., and B.P.,. are placed after both a date and a century.

> the tenth of Muharram, A.H. 61 (October 10, A.D. 680)
> the first century A.H.
> from the 1st century B.C.E. to the 4th century C.E.
> 63 B.C.E.
> the year 200 C.E.
> 5,000 years B.P.
> two million years B.P.

Degrees of Temperature and Arc

14. In technical writing, a quantity expressed in degrees is generally written as a numeral followed by the degree symbol (°). In the Kelvin scale, neither the word *degree* nor the symbol is used with the figure.

> a 45° angle   0° C
> 6°40′10″N   Absolute zero is zero kelvins or 0 K.
> 32° F

15. In general writing, the quantity expressed in degrees may or may not be written out. A figure may be followed by either the degree symbol or the word *degree;* a spelled-out number is always followed by the word *degree.*

> latitude 43°19″N
> latitude 43 degrees N
> a difference of 43 degrees latitude
> The temperature has risen about thirty degrees.

Fractions and Decimal Fractions

16. In nontechnical prose, fractions standing alone are usually written out. Common fractions used as nouns are usually unhyphenated, although the hyphenated form is also common. When fractions are used as modifiers, they are hyphenated.

> lost three quarters of its value   *or* lost three-quarters of its value
> had a two-thirds chance of winning

Multiword numerators and denominators are usually hyphenated, or written as figures.

> one one-hundredth of an inch   *or* 1/100 of an inch

17. Mixed fractions (fractions with a whole number, such as 3½) and fractions that form part of a modifier are usually expressed in figures in running text.

> waiting 2½hours
> a 7/8-mile course
> 2½pound weights

Fractions that are not on the keyboard or available as special characters on a computer may be typed in full-sized digits; in mixed fractions, a space is left between the whole number and the fraction.

> a 7/8-mile course
> waiting 2 3/4 hours

18. Fractions used with units of measurement are usually expressed in figures, but common short words are often written out.

> 1/10 km   7/8 inch   a half-mile walk
> 1/3 oz.   half a mile   a sixteenth-inch gap

19. Decimal fractions are always set as figures. In technical writing, a zero is placed to the left of the decimal point when the fraction is less than a whole number; in general writing, the zero is usually omitted. Commas are not used in numbers following a decimal point.

> An example of a pure decimal fraction is 0.375, while 1.402 is classified as a mixed decimal fraction.
> a .22-caliber rifle
> 0.142857

20. Fractions and decimal fractions are usually not mixed in a text.

> weights of 5½ lbs., 3¼ lbs., and ½ oz.
>   *or* weights of 5.5 lbs., 3.25 lbs., and .5 oz.
>   *not* weights of 5.5 lbs., 3¼ lbs., and ½ oz.

Lists and Outlines

21. Both run-in and vertical lists are often numbered. In run-in numbered lists—that is, numbered lists that form part of a normal-looking sentence—each item is preceded by a number (or, less often, an italicized letter) enclosed in parentheses. The items are separated by commas if they are brief and unpunctuated; if they are complex or punctuated, they are separated by semicolons. The entire list is introduced by a colon if it is preceded by a full clause, and often when it is not.

> I will try to establish (1) the immediate historical background, (2) the chronological sequence of events in the critical two days, and (3) the likely cause-and-effect relations of the key decisions and actions.

> The new medical dictionary has several special features: *(a)* common variant spellings; *(b)* examples of words used in context; *(c)* abbreviations, combining forms, prefixes, and suffixes; and *(d)* brand names for drugs and their generic equivalents.

22. In vertical lists, each number is followed by a period; the periods align vertically. Run-over lines usually align under the item's first word. Each item may be capitalized, especially if the items are syntactically independent of the words that introduce them.

> The English peerage consists of five ranks, listed here in descending order:
> 1. Duke (duchess)
> 2. Marquess (marchioness)
> 3. Earl (countess)
> 4. Viscount (viscountess)
> 5. Baron (baroness)

The listed items end with periods (or question marks) when they are complete sentences, and also often when they are not.

> We require answers to the following questions:
> 1. Does the club intend to engage heavy-metal bands to perform in the future?
> 2. Will any such bands be permitted to play past midnight on weekends?
> 3. Are there plans to install proper acoustic insulation?

Items that are syntactically dependent on the words that introduce them often begin with a lowercase letter and end with a comma or semicolon just as in a run-in series in an ordinary sentence.

> The signed consent may be given by
> 1. the patient,
> 2. a legally qualified representative (such as a parent or guardian) of the patient,
> 3. an executor or administrator of an estate, or
> 4. an agency designated by the court as a guardian.

A vertical list may also be unnumbered, or may use bullets (•) in place of numerals, especially where the order of the items is not important.

> Chief among the important advances in communication were these 19th-century inventions:
> Morse's telegraph
> Daguerre's camera
> Bell's telephone
> Edison's phonograph

This book covers in detail:
- Punctuation
- Capitalization and italicization
- Numbers
- Abbreviations
- Grammar and composition

23. Outlines standardly use Roman numerals, capitalized letters, Arabic numerals, and lowercase letters, in that order. Each numeral or letter is followed by a period, and each item is capitalized.

    I. Using health information
      A. Confidentiality
      B. Insurance billing
        1. Requirements for health information
        2. Diagnosis coding
        3. Procedure coding
   II. Managing health information
      A. Storage and retrieval
        1. Filing systems
          a. Numerical
          b. Color-coded
        2. Retrieval systems
      B. Record disposal

Money

24. A sum of money that can be expressed in one or two words is usually written out in running text, as is the unit of currency. But if several sums are mentioned in the sentence or paragraph, all are usually expressed as figures and are used with the unspaced currency symbol.

The scalpers were asking eighty dollars.
Grandfather remembered the days of the five-cent cigar.
The shoes on sale are priced at $69 and $89.
Jill wanted to sell the lemonade for 25¢, 35¢, and 45¢.

25. Monetary units of mixed dollars-and-cents amounts are expressed in figures.

$16.75
$307.02

26. Even-dollar amounts are often expressed in figures without a decimal point and zeros. But when even-dollar amounts appear near amounts that include cents, the decimal point and zeros are usually added for consistency. The dollar sign is repeated before each amount in a series or inclusive range.

They paid $500 for the watercolor.
The price had risen from $8.00 to $9.95.
bids of $80, $90, and $100
in the $80-$100 range

27. Sums of money in the millions or above rounded to no more than one decimal place are usually expressed in a combination of figures and words.

a $10-million building program
$4.5 billion

28. In legal documents a sum of money is usually written out fully, often capitalized, with the corresponding figures in parentheses immediately following.

> Twenty-five Thousand Dollars ($25,000)

Organizations and Governmental Entities

29. Ordinal numbers in the names of religious organizations and churches are usually written out.

> Seventh-Day Adventists
> Third Congregational Church

30. Local branches of labor unions and fraternal organizations are generally identified by a numeral, usually placed after the name.

> Motion Picture Studio Mechanics Local 476
> Loyal Order of Moose No. 220
> Local 4277 Communications Workers of America

31. In names of governmental bodies and electoral, judicial, and military units, ordinal numbers of one hundred or below are usually written out but often not.

> Second Continental Congress
> Fifth Republic
> First Congressional District
> Court of Appeals for the Third Circuit
> U.S. Eighth Army
> Twelfth Precinct *or* 12th Precinct
> Ninety-eighth Congress *or* 98th Congress

Percentages

32. In technical writing, and often in business and financial writing, percentages are written as a figure followed by an unspaced % symbol. In general writing, the word *percent* normally replaces the symbol, and the number may either be written out (if it does not include a decimal) or expressed as a figure.

> *technical:*   15%
>   13.5%
> *general:*   15 percent
>   87.2 percent
>   Fifteen percent of the applicants were accepted.
>   a four percent increase *or* a 4% increase

33. In a series or range, the percent sign is usually included with all numbers, even if one of the numbers is zero.

> rates of 8.3%, 8.8%, and 9.1%
> a variation of 0% to 10% *or* a 0%–10% variation

Plurals

34. The plurals of written-out numbers, including fractions, are formed by adding *-s* or *-es.*

> at sixes and sevens   ever since the thirties
> divided into eighths   still in her thirties

35. The plurals of figures are formed by adding *-s* or less commonly *-'s*, especially where the apostrophe can prevent a confusing typographic appearance.

in the '80s
since the 1980s [*or less commonly* 1980's]
temperatures in the 80s and 90s [*or* 80's and 90's]
the *1*'s looked like *l*'s

Ratios

36. Ratios are generally expressed in figures, usually with the word *to;* in technical writing the figures may be joined by a colon or a slash instead. Ratios expressed in words use a hyphen (or en dash) or the word *to.*

odds of 10 to 1	a 3:1 ratio	a fifty-fifty chance
a proportion of 1 to 4	29 mi/gal	a ratio of ten to four

Time of Day

37. In running text, the time of day is usually spelled out when expressed in even, half, or quarter hours or when it is followed by *o'clock*.

around four-thirty	now almost a quarter to two
arriving by ten	arrived at nine o'clock
planned to leave at half past five	

38. Figures are generally used when specifying a precise time.

an appointment at 9:30 tomorrow morning
buses at 8:42, 9:12, and 10:03 a.m.

39. Figures are also used when the time of day is followed by *a.m.* and *p.m.* These are usually written as punctuated lowercase letters, sometimes as small capital letters. They are not used with *o'clock* or with other words that specify the time of day.

8:30 a.m. *or* 8:30 A.M.	home by nine o'clock
10:30 p.m. *or* 10:30 P.M.	9:15 in the morning
8 a.m. *or* 8 A.M.	eleven in the evening

With *twelve o'clock* or *12:00*, it is helpful to specify *midnight* or *noon* rather than the ambiguous *a.m.* or *p.m.*

The third shift begins at 12:00 (midnight).

40. Even-hour times are generally written with a colon and two zeros when used in a series or pairing with any times not ending in two zeros.

started at 9:15 a.m. and finished at 2:00 p.m.
worked from 8:30 to 5:00

41. The 24-hour clock system—also called *military time*—uses no punctuation and omits *o'clock, a.m., p.m.* or any other additional indication of the time of day. The word *hours* sometimes replaces them.

from 0930 to 1100
at 1600 hours

Units of Measurement
42. In technical writing, all numbers used with units of measurement are written as numerals. In nontechnical writing, such numbers often simply follow the basic conventions explained on page 303; alternatively, even in nontechnical contexts all such numbers often appear as numerals.

> In the control group, only 8 of the 90 plants were affected.
> picked nine quarts of berries
> chugging along at 9 [*or* nine] mules an hour
> a pumpkin 5 [*or* five] feet in diameter
> weighing 7 pounds 9 ounces
> a journey of 3 hours and 45 minutes

The singular form of units of measurement is used in a modifier before a noun, the plural form in a modifier that follows a noun.

> a 2- by 9-inch board *or* a two-inch by nine-inch board *or* a two- by nine-inch board
> measured 2 inches by 9 inches *or* measured two inches by nine inches
> a 6-foot 2-inch man
> is 6 feet 2 inches tall *or* is six feet two inches tall
> is six feet two *or* is 6 feet 2

43. When units of measurement are written as abbreviations or symbols, the adjacent numbers are always figures. (For abbreviations with numerals, see the section on page 302.)

> 6 cm $4.25   4'
> 1 mm   67.6 fl. oz.   98.6°

44. When two or more quantities are expressed, as in ranges or dimensions or series, an accompanying symbol is usually repeated with each figure.

> 4" × 6" cards
> temperatures of 30°, 55°, 43°, and 58°
> $450–$500 suits

Other Uses
45. Figures are generally used for precise ages in newspapers and magazines, and often in books as well.

> Taking the helm is Colin Corman, 51, a risk-taking high roller.
> At 9 [*or* nine] she mastered the Mendelssohn Violin Concerto.
> the champion 3[*or* three]-year-old filly
> for anyone aged 62 and over

46. Figures are used to refer to parts of a book, such as volume, chapter, illustration, and table numbers.

> vol. 5, p. 202
> Chapter 8 *or* Chapter Eight
> Fig. 4

47. Serial, policy, and contract numbers use figures. (For punctuation of these numbers, see paragraph 3 on page 306.)

Serial No. 5274
Permit No. 63709

48. Figures are used to express stock-market quotations, mathematical calculations, scores, and tabulations.

Industrials were up 4.23.
$3 \times 15 = 45$
a score of 8 to 2   *or*   a score of 8-2
the tally: 322 ayes, 80 nays

Legal Citations

A citation is a reference to a legal authority that is used as a support for a statement made within a text; it may also be used to identify the souse of a quotation. These References are usually cited to statutory sources (constitutions, statutes, codes, and regulations), to reports of cases in official and unofficial reporters, and sometimes to secondary sources such as encyclopedias, books, and periodicals. (See Chapter 13, "The Law Library," for a description of legal sources.) While the lawyer or legal assistant is normally responsible for the content of a citation—determining which sources to cite and the order in which to list them—the legal secretary is responsible for double-checking, or *verifying*, all parts of the citation before keyboarding it, and ensuring that it is consistent with those in other documents produced by the office and also with any rules laid down by state or federal courts.

A legal citation is conventionally designed to give a great amount of information in concentrated form so that the reader may easily find the source and determine its relative authority. Both *consistency of form* and *absolute accuracy* are essential. Citation forms are complex enough that whole books are devoted to the matter. The most widely used citation manual is *The Bluebook: A Uniform System of Citation*, published by the Harvard Law Review Association (Cambridge, Mass.). The section that follows is designed to give the secretary a familiarity with basic citation forms though it is by no means a thorough presentation of this complex subject.

CITATION TO STATUTORY SOURCES

Statutory sources of law include constitutions, statutes, codes, and administrative regulations. Citation to each type are described here.

Constitutions
1. Citations to constitutions have four parts: (1) the jurisdiction or name of the constitution, usually abbreviated, (2) the article or amendment number, usually in Roman numerals preceded by the abbreviation *art.* or *amend.*, (3) the section, chapter, or clause number, if applicable, in Arabic numerals, and (4) the date of the constitution in parentheses if it is no longer in force.

U.S. Const. amend. XIII
Ind. Const. art. III, § 2, cl. 4
Mich. Const. art. Vi, § 6 (1850)

Note that punctuation is minimal; frequently no comma separates the name of the constitution and the article or amendment number. Some alternative stylings capitalize *Art.* and *Amend.* Instead of the section symbol, the abbreviation *Sec.* is occasionally used.

Federal Statutes

2. Federal statutes appear in both codified and uncodified form (as described in Chapter 13). Those statutes in *slip law* form (that is, those that have not yet been published in the *Statutes at Large* or in the *United States Code*) are usually cited in the following order: (1) name of statue if known, (2) public law number, (3) chapter and section number if applicable, (4) (sometimes) the congress that passed the law, (5) published source, if the slip law itself is not available, and (6) date of enactment in parentheses, if necessary.

   Trade Agreements Act, Pub. L. 96-235, § 12, 105th Cong., 1st Sess. (July 26, 1999)

3. When the statute is found in the *Statutes at Large,* the information is listed in the citation as follows: (1) name of statute if applicable, (2) chapter and section number of the statute if applicable, (3) volume number of the *Statutes and Large* in Arabic numerals, (4) official abbreviation *Stat.,* (5) number of the page on which the law begins (but *not* the word "page" or its abbreviation), and (6) date of the *Statutes at Large* edition in parentheses.

   Parental Kidnapping Prevention Act of 1980, § 33, 94 Stat. 3569
     or 94 Stat. 3569 (1980)

4. Federal statutes that have been codified—i.e., published in the *United States Code* in a subject-matter arrangement—are usually cited in the following order: (volume number of the code, in Arabic numerals, (2) name of the code abbreviated—U.S.C. or U.S.C.A., (3) section number of the code, (4) date of the codification or date of the code volume, when necessary, in parentheses, (5) any needed supplementary information, including identification of amendments to the code and the name of the code publisher.

   28 U.S.C. § 17
   28 U.S.C. § 17 (1964)
   28 U.S.C. § 17 (1964, as amended (Supp. II, 1966)

State Statutes

Forms of citation for both state session laws and state code compilations vary from state to state. In many of the state code compilations the publishers give the accepted citation form at the front of each code volume; some states have uniform citation rules promulgated and recognized by the courts. *The Bluebook* also provides guidelines and examples for each state.

5. A complete citation to the *session laws* of a state might include the following items: (1) year of the session, usually not followed by a comma, (2) name of the state compilation, properly abbreviated, (3) chapter, title, or section number of the law (only the abbreviation *No.* for *Number* is normally capitalized), (4) page number, usually preceded by the word *at* if it immediately follows a section number, and (5) additional information, if needed, in parentheses.

   1922 Ark. Acts No. 198, at 45 (expired 1940)

6. Citations to state *code compilations* typically follow this order: (1) name of the compilation, properly abbreviated, (2) section number, (3) date of the compilation, usually in parentheses, and (4) additional information as needed.

> Miss. Code Ann. § 5 (1989)

When citing the statutes of the states in which they practice, lawyers may omit the name of the state: instead of the proper form *Minn. Stat. § 289.23*, for instance, a Minneapolis lawyer might use *Stat. § 289.23*.

Administrative Regulations

7. The regulations of federal administrative agencies are cited to the *Code of Federal Regulations* (C.F.R.), to the *Federal Register* (Fed. Reg.), or to the exact form in which they were originally issued.

> 32 C.F.R. § 199 (1994)
> 43 Fed. Reg. 54221 (1978)
> Treas. Reg. 118, § 28.04 (1953)

The numbers preceding *C.F.R.* and *Fed. Reg.* in the examples above refer to the volume numbers of those two sources; the number following *Fed. Reg.* is the page on which that statute begins in volume 43.

CITATIONS TO CASES

Court decisions are cited to either official reporters or unofficial reporters. Segments of case citations are described in the following paragraphs.

Case Title

1. The case title is italicized whether or not the case involves two opposing parties.

> *Surner v. Kellogg*
> *In re Watson*

2. Only the surnames of individuals are included in the case title, but the full names of corporations and other organizations are used, although they may be abbreviated. The first word of a litigant's name, however, is never abbreviated.

> *Cramdon v. National Labor Relations Board* [*or* N.L.R.B.]

3. When it is a party to an action, *United States* is always spelled in full.

> *Marston v. United States*

Reporter Source

4. The names of the reporters in which court decisions are found refer to the jurisdiction of the courts included in those reporters (such as *Minn.* for *Minnesota Reports* and *S.W.* for *South Western Reporter*). The reporter in which the case is found is always identified in this order: (1) volume number, (2) official abbreviation of the reporter title, (3) page number at which the opinion begins, and (4) year of publication in parentheses.

> *Johnson v. California* 267 Cal. Rptr. 180

5. When more than one reporter cites the same case, the two citations are separated by a comma.

> *A Minor v. State,* 85 Nev. 323, 454 P.2d 895 (1969)

CITATIONS TO SECONDARY SOURCES

Interpretive or analytical sources that may be cited include legal encyclopedias, periodical articles, and books and treatises on law.

Legal Encyclopedias

1. Citations to major legal encyclopedias include the following segments: (1) volume number of the encyclopedia, in Arabic numerals, (2) official abbreviation for the publication (such as *C.J.S.* for *Corpus Juris Secundum* or *Am. Jur. 2d* for the second edition of *American Jurisprudence*), (3) title of the article cited, (4) page and section numbers, and (5) date of the edition

> 88 C.J.S., *Trial* § 192 (1955)

Periodical Articles

2. Citations to articles in legal periodicals—typically law reviews—include the following order elements: (1) full name of the author, (2) title of the article, (3) volume number of the periodical, or year if the volume number is not known, (4) name of the publication, typically abbreviated, (5) page number at which the article begins, and (6) year of publication, in parentheses, unless it already appears in place of the volume number.

> William Owen, Punitive Damages in Product Liability Litigation, 74 Mich. L. Rev. 1257 (1976)

Sometimes the citation is to a law review article written anonymously by a student. In these cases, the author's name is omitted and the article is called "Note," "Comment," or some such title.

There are numerous variants in the styling of citations to law reviews and other periodicals. You may see the title of the article italicized and the title of the periodical printed in all-capital letters. Or the article title may be roman, perhaps also enclosed in quotation marks, while the periodical title is italicized.

Books and Treatises

3. The styling of citation to texts, like that of citations to legal periodicals, differs from the styling used for bibliographies in nonlegal fields. The normal order of the segments of these citations is (1) volume number, if applicable, in Arabic numerals, (2) last name of the author or, if needed, only the first initial and the last name, (3) title of the book, *unabbreviated,* (4) section or page number if needed, and (5) (sometimes) edition and date of publication. A subtitle that follows a colon may be omitted if it would make the title unduly long. The book title is usually italicized to make it stand out in the citation, but many lawyers prefer to have the entire citation, including the title, printed in roman.

> C. Wright, *Handbook of the Law of Federal Courts* § 50, at 29 (Supp. 1972)

ABBREVIATIONS USED IN CITATIONS

The following is a list of standard abbreviations for reporters and other publications, states, months of the year, and textual subdivisions, all as commonly used in legal citations.

Reporters and Other Publications

American Jurisprudence, Second Edition	Am. Jur. 2d
American Law Reports Annotated	A.L.R.
American Law Reports Annotated, Second Series	A.L.R.2d
American Law Reports Annotated, Third Series	A.L.R.3d
Atlantic Reporter	A.
Atlantic Reporter, Second Series	A.2d
Bankruptcy Reporter	B.R.
California Appellate Reports	Cal. App.
California Appellate Reports, Second Series	Cal. App. 2d
California Appellate Reports, Third Series	Cal. App. 3d
California Reporter	Cal. Rptr.
Code of Federal Regulations	C.F.R.
Corpus Juris Secundum	C.J.S.
Federal Cases	F. Cas.
Federal Register	Fed. Reg.
Federal Reporter	F.
Federal Reporter, Second Series	F.2d
Federal Rules Decisions	F.R.D.
Federal Supplement	F. Supp.
Illinois Decisions	Ill. Decs.
Lawyers' Edition, U.S. Supreme Court Reports	L. Ed.
Lawyers' Edition, U.S. Supreme Court Reports, Second Series	L. Ed. 2d
Lawyers Reports, Annotated	L.R.A.
Lawyers Reports, Annotated, New Series	L.R.A. (n.s.)
New York Criminal Reports	N.Y. Crim.
New York Supplement	N.Y.S.
New York Supplement, Second Series	N.Y.S.2d
North Eastern Reporter	N.E.
North Eastern Reporter, Second Series	N.E.2d.
North Western Reporter	N.W.
North Western Reporter, Second Series	N.W.2d
Pacific Reporter	P.
Pacific Reporter, Second Series	P.2d
South Eastern Reporter	S.E.
South Eastern Reporter, Second Series	S.E.2d
South Western Reporter	S.W.
South Western Reporter, Second Series	S.W.2d
Southern Reporter	So.
Southern Reporter, Second Series	So. 2d
Supreme Court Reporter [United States]	S. Ct.
United States Code	U.S.C.
United States Code Annotated	U.S.C.A.
United States Code Service	U.S.C.S.
United States Statutes at Large	Stat.
United States Supreme Court Reports	U.S.

States

Ala.	Ill.	Mont.	R.I.
Alaska	Ind.	Neb.	S.C.
Ariz.	Iowa	Nev.	S.D.
Ark.	Kan.	N.H.	Tenn.
Cal.	Ky.	N.J.	Tex.
Colo.	La.	N.M.	Utah
Del.	Md.	N.C.	Vt.
D.C.	Mass.	N.D.	Va.
Fla.	Mich.	Ohio	Wash.
Ga.	Minn.	Okla.	W.Va.
Haw.	Miss.	Or.	Wis.
Idaho	Mo.	Pa.	Wyo.

Months of the Year

Jan.	Apr.	July	Oct.
Feb.	May	Aug.	Nov.
Mar.	June	Sept.	Dec.

Textual Subdivisions

amendment(s)	amend., amends.
appendix(es)	app., apps.
article(s)	art., arts.
book(s)	bk., bks.
chapter(s)	ch., chs.
clause(s)	cl., cls.
column(s)	col., cols.
folio(s)	fol., fols.
footnote(s)	n., nn.
number(s)	No., Nos.
page(s)	p., pp. [*or* at]
paragaph(s), subparagraph(s)	para., paras., ¶, ¶¶
part(s)	pt., pts.
section(s), subsections(s)	§, §§ [space before number]
series, serial(s)	ser.
title(s)	tit., tits.
volume(s)	vol., vols.

Chapter 9

Dictation and Transcription

In the job descriptions for legal secretaries, the ability to handle dictation is often the first or second requirement, indicating the importance of this skill in the legal-work environment. This chapter covers the basics of taking and transcribing dictation, and offers advice on choosing and using dictation equipment, avoiding common problems involving dictation, and improving transcription accuracy and quality.

Live versus Machine Dictation

In the past, secretaries worked for one or perhaps two attorneys and the volume of the work was considerably less than today. Oral dictation was the norm. As lawyers and secretaries were asked to handle more work, they began to search for tools that would give them greater flexibility and efficiency. Dictating equipment was one answer. With it, the lawyer could dictate at home, on the plane, and in the car, and the secretary didn't need to be present. It permitted recording one's thoughts and revising them before the material was handed to the secretary for transcription. The lawyer could also add to existing material or drop one project and go to another.

Today dictating machines are in use in almost all law offices, though undoubtedly there is still an office here and there using secretaries to take oral dictation exclusively. Dictating equipment allows a lawyer to dictate two to three times faster than live dictation. The secretary can transcribe twice as fast from machine dictation as from shorthand notes, and more accurately. The cost of producing a single machine-dictated letter is about 25 percent less than that for a similar letter dictated to a secretary taking shorthand. Additionally, while the lawyer is dictating into the machine, the secretary can be working on other tasks.

Despite the economic advantages of machine dictation, live dictation does have its merits, so most law offices have at least one secretary who can take live dictation. That secretary can be pressed into service when documents need to be changed in an ongoing conference or meeting where several people must collaborate on the changes to be dictated. The secretary may also be asked to take dictation over the telephone. While it is possible to record both conferences and telephone messages, not all law offices have the necessary equipment, and the lawyers may simply prefer to have the secretary personally involved in such dictation. In these circumstances, a secretary with shorthand skills will be a valuable asset to the firm.

In a live-dictation session, the secretary may be used as a "sounding board" or be expected to contribute to the document. Live dictation can give the attorney a means of trying out new ideas or determining how another person—a nonlawyer—interprets statements. When two people have worked together for a while and have handled a volume of work, the lawyer can simply mention that he or she wants to include a certain paragraph used in a recent document prepared for "John Smith" and the secretary will know where to go for the material and which paragraph to use. If there is a question about the material, it can be answered at the time of dictation rather than later, when the lawyer may not be available. Grammatical errors can also be corrected immediately in live dictation.

In one-on-one sessions, the secretary has an opportunity to see the material the lawyer is using for dictation. If the material is handed to the secretary at the conclusion of the dictation, he or she can check the spelling of names and addresses, check the dates dictated against the documentation, and clarify the words being used. (The secretary should become expert in document production. He or she will be expected to know correct spelling, proper sentence construction, and the meaning of the words being used.) An advantage of live dictation is that the secretary can ask questions before beginning transcription.

Today, however, most schools train their secretarial students in machine transcription only. Although there are a few disadvantages connected with machine dictation—mostly involving poorly maintained equipment or inattentive dictators—in the opinion of most lawyers and administrators the advantages of this mode of transcription far outweigh the disadvantages. Secretaries handling work for more than one lawyer have found that machine dictation allows them to structure their workdays. They can identify and handle priorities more easily, and, if pressed for time, delay transcription of documents that have no deadline.

Evaluating Dictation Equipment

Dictation equipment must be evaluated from both the dictator's and the transcriber's points of view. With any dictation equipment, the quality of sound and convenience of the machine for both transcriber and dictator are important. While a few lawyers may learn to use all of a machine's features, far more adopt a method of dictating that matches their way of working and leave it up to the secretary to determine the best method of handling transcription. Thus the secretary's input on choice and operation of equipment is important.

High-quality dictating units allow the dictator to fast-forward, rewind, correct dictation, mark the end of documents, and indicate priority work. The volume is adjustable and most models can record at two speeds. (Speech recorded at the slower speed does not have the quality of that recorded at the faster speed, but a tape recorded at slow speed can hold about twice as much dictation.) Most good dictating units can record straight dictation or be set for recording conferences in a medium-sized room.

In some cases a single unit can serve multiple purposes: when a microphone is attached to it, it becomes a dictating unit; when a foot control is attached, it becomes a transcriber. In other cases these units are separate. In any case the transcribing unit at the secretary's desk should include such features as earphones, on/off foot controls, rewind ability, an indexing system to indicate the length of the documents, controls for dictation corrections and insertions, and adjustments for speed, volume, and tone. Home entertainment equipment seldom has the features needed by office professionals, and the constant starting and stopping places great stress on the equipment.

The office that chooses equipment on the basis of price alone will probably end up spending a considerable amount on repairs and on temporary rental equipment to replace the faulty machinery. Like most office equipment, dictation equipment must be capable of running all day, every day. Units designed for casual usage cannot withstand such punishment and will have to be repaired or replaced more often than professional-quality equipment.

Thus, such products must be carefully considered before purchase, and the secretary should be an active participant in the selection process. Determine what you need the equipment to do. Do you want it to handle the work of one person, or many? Is it to be used for dictation only, or both dictation and transcription? Will it be used for voice mail as well? Do you need voice-activated machinery or is manual control sufficient? One of the most important questions of all is who will service the equipment when it breaks down or presents problems. In general it is best to contact a local vendor with a good reputation for sales and service. The number of features on dictation equipment is limited only by the amount of money a law firm wishes to spend. Features that won't be used are luxuries and may be sources of future repair problems. Evaluators should secure a guarantee of service on the equipment for a reasonable length of time.

Desktop Dictation Machines

For the lawyer who spends his or her day in the office, a desktop dictation machine is a good choice. The equipment is more durable than the portable models, and usually comes with more features that can enhance the quality of the dictated material and in general facilitate a smooth dictation-to-transcription process.

Portable Dictation Machines

The lawyer who does part of his or her work at home, while traveling, or in a meeting with a client outside the office will probably choose a portable dictation machine. These units are about the size of a deck of cards and fit easily into a pocket or briefcase. They are also, unfortunately, relatively easily lost or damaged. In general portables require more service than desktop models.

Central Dictation Systems

In an office with many attorneys, paralegals, and support personnel, the volume of dictation may indicate the need for a dictation system with a central recorder and several extension microphones. Some central dictation systems use endless-loop recorders; others use a group of cassettes. Central systems can receive input by private or public telephone from local or long-distance sources. A machine with an endless-loop system can also accept dictation at the same time the secretary transcribes from it. However, even though dictation and transcription can occur simultaneously, usually only one dictator may input at a time.

New digital equipment, which records on computer disks rather than tape, enables the secretary to type during dictation, identify priority jobs, calculate the length of each document, and preview changes before beginning transcription. The sound quality of digital recording is a distinct advantage, since it results in improved accuracy, thus speeding transcription.

Such equipment is now combined with voice mail, which not only allows lawyers to call in and dictate to the secretary, but permits clients to leave long messages for the lawyer. Such messages can be accessed from outside the office and can then be transcribed by the secretary to be reviewed by the lawyer or placed in the client's file. This equipment allows two listeners or dictators to access the equipment at the same time.

Giving and Taking Dictation

It is unfortunate that dictation is sometimes undertaken without the proper preparation and attention to detail. Dictators often pick up their dictating equipment and start talking with little thought about what they want to accomplish or how the secretary will interpret their instructions. Secretaries may begin work without the proper materials at hand. Interrupted work causes mistakes and delays. Both the dictator and transcriber must therefore take a few minutes to prepare for dictation. The preparatory steps enumerated in the next two sections should aid both the secretary and the dictator.

Giving Dictation

The dictator can reduce the amount of time needed to dictate (and ultimately transcribe) his or her work by observing the following points:

1. Plan ahead. Dictating early in the day allows more time for the finished product to be returned to you. Designate high-priority items.
2. Gather the documents you intend to address. If you are dictating pleadings, for example, have the full file at hand.
3. Begin your dictation by identifying what you are dictating—for example, "This is a letter to . . .." or "This is a motion to quash in . . .." If it is a first draft, identify it as such.
4. Specify special handling—for example, "Send this by fax and follow up with regular mail" or "Send this by express mail [*or* next-day delivery *or* hand delivery]." Letters and documents to be mailed will go by ordinary mail unless otherwise specified. If copies are to be sent to others, indicate who will get the copies. Are recipients to be noted on the correspondence, or are blind copies preferred? Are there any other special instructions?
5. Avoid rustling papers, tapping pencils, or moving things around on the desk. Such noises are picked up by the dictation equipment and may hinder transcription.

6. Forgo dictating punctuation unless necessary for clarity in special circumstances. The voice should indicate what is to be done: a pause for a comma, a stop for a period, and so forth. Long and involved sentences require clear dictation. Pronounce complex medical and legal words carefully—syllable by syllable if necessary. You many need to supply the secretary with a list of unusual words along with the tape. (This is particularly useful in the medical malpractice field).

Taking Live Dictation

There are times when the lawyer who regularly uses a recording device may wish to dictate a short memo or even a long document directly to the secretary. Frequently the secretary is also asked to take notes at a meeting. In such cases, the following procedures should be observed:

1. Organize your materials in advance. A separate notebook for each attorney or paralegal is necessary. In addition, pencils, sticky notes, and other writing supplies should be at hand. All these items can be arranged in a folder or portfolio.

2. If the attorney tends to make lengthy corrections or changes, use only the left-hand side of a shorthand or other notebook, reserving the right side for corrections. Some secretaries skip a line between dictated sentences to allow for insertions and to make the material easier to read.

3. Determine how you will identify rush projects. You and the lawyer may institute a system that uses color coding—for example, red means immediate, blue means by noon, green means by the end of the day and yellow means at your convenience. A numerical system (1, 2, 3, etc.) or sticky notes can be used the same way.

4. Date the page where the dictation begins. The date may be important for documentation in the future or when trying to locate dictation in your notebook. Word-processing programs automatically date the document and re-date it when it is revised on the computer; a dictation notebook should have the same controls.

5. Identify specific dates that are to be calendared and mark them off when they have been transferred to the docketing system or the appropriate calendar.

6. Develop a system for labeling inserts and additions. For example, use an X to indicate where an insert is to go, then make another X a page or so beyond the dictated material and record the insert. Further inserts can then be identified as *X2*, *X3*, and so on.

7. In the event that a word is omitted from your notes, or there is reason to question the dictator about the material, leave a conspicuous mark (e.g., a question mark in a circle) or a blank space to serve as a reminder. Many dictators do not want to be interrupted but allow time at the end of a session to answer questions. If questions are not resolved during or immediately following the dictation, transcription will be interrupted as answers are chased down.

Recording meeting notes   The second most common type of dictation a secretary may be asked to take is to record events at a meeting between clients and attorneys or at in-house staff meetings. In such cases, word-for-word accuracy is not needed, but a summary record similar to the one shown in Fig. 9.1 should be made.

Fig. 9.1   An Informal Meeting Summary

CONFIDENTIAL   SUMMARY

Pelham Insurance Corp.

Personal-Injury Division Meeting

November 23, 19–

Attendance	Messrs. Foster, Rudinov, Purdy; Mss. Grafton, Tsing-Carter
New Report Form	Mr. Rudinov discussed the effect of revised legislation and submitted a proposed new reporting form for personal-injury cases.
Database Options	Ms. Grafton presented a final summary of the two database systems under consideration, recommending the LinkLine system.
Decisions	The proposed reporting form was adopted. It was determined that, before choosing LinkLine, a final test over the local network should be conducted.

Recording question-and-answer (Q & A) sessions   Secretaries in the modern law office are seldom called upon to take deposition dictation. Court reporters are used when speed and accuracy are crucial. The average dictation rate is 90 to 110 words per minute, while deposition speeds can exceed 150 words per minute. However, secretaries with good shorthand skills and speed can take dictation in a question-and-answer (Q & A) format with the cooperation of the parties involved.

If you are asked to take dictation at a Q & A session, you should set up the pages of your notebook to accommodate this format. Divide each page into three equal-width columns. The questions of the examining attorney will be recorded in the left-hand column; the answers of the person giving evidence (i.e., the deponent) will be recorded in the center column; and the opposing counsel's questions will be recorded in the third column. Attorneys using secretaries to record a question-and-answer session should be asked to slow down if the exchange gets too fast. The testimony must be both taken and transcribed verbatim, even if it is grammatically incorrect.

Legal Terminology

Every profession uses terms with special meanings, and this may be especially true of the legal profession. A word like *continuance* may have one meaning in general usage and quite another in legal phraseology. Special compound words, unfamiliar foreign words and phrases, set phrases and clauses, and capitalized introductory words and phrases are all a part of the specialized legal terminology that a legal secretary should know. Compile a list of special words and phrases as you encounter them for the first time. If you take shorthand, you will also need to make your own brief forms for these words so you can move smoothly through dictation.

Compound words   Legal terminology includes many compound words that have precise meanings. *Aforesaid* (said or named before or above), *hereinafter* (in the following part of this document), *herewith* (with this, enclosed with this), *therein* (in that place), and the *undersigned* (the person who signs his or her name at the end of a document) all have precise meaning for lawyers. Always transcribe these words exactly as they are dictated.

Introductory words and phrases   In legal documents, recognition of introductory, closing, and special paragraphs is accomplished by using introductory words or phrases such as *In witness whereof* (usually typed in all-capital letters). You should become familiar with these legal words and phrases and how they sound when dictated.

Sound-alike words   Poor enunciation by the dictator, particularly in machine dictation, is the secretary's most common problem and can lead to difficulty in notetaking and transcription. Many words are misrecorded because they sound like other words. In taking and transcribing dictation, be aware of the sound-alike words. A list of easily confusable words appears in Appendix II.

Reference books   Just as a lawyer relies on law books, the legal secretary will require the use of general and specialized reference works. You should keep the following reference books near your desk:

> A good general dictionary
> A standard law dictionary
> A medical dictionary
> A handbook of legel citation
> A handbook of English
> A word-division manual
> A secretarial manual
> A thesaurus
> A book of standard legal forms

The experienced legal secretary will usually have his or her own set of reference and form books. The beginner will have fewer books and will need to rely on the office for material; however, with increasing time in service he or she will begin to assemble materials that help solve problems and make the job easier.

Standard word processors include general spell checkers. The secretary handling medical matters is well advised to have a medical spell-check program as well. Most spell-check programs allow new words to be added. Documents run through the spell checker will be automatically compared to both the regular and new-words lexicons.

Even with the best tools, the secretary must be vigilant. A correctly spelled but misued word will not be flagged by the spell checker. For example, the words *effect* and *affect* will both pass through a spelling program, but their correct usage should be checked by the secretary using a dictionary.

Transcription

Transcription from handwritten notes of machine dictation is an important part of the secretary's duties. The production of accurate, professional papers, both letters and legal documents, is the major goal of all transcribers. It is also what determines the transcriber's potential for advancement in many firms. An alert secretary combines knowledge, skill, and intellect to attain success in transcription.

Preparation

Take a few minutes to arrange the equipment before beginning your work. Position the desk and chair to allow full access to the transcription equipment and the supplies needed. When transcribing from written notes, place the notebook on a copyholder where it is easily viewable and free of visual distractions.

Review the materials forming the basis for the dictation and place them in the same order as the dictation. That means reviewing written notes or listening to the dictation on tape before beginning transcription. If you are unfamiliar with the lawyer's dictating style, listen to a recorded dictation for several minutes before beginning keyboarding. Get a feel for how the dictator marks the end of a document. Determine how changes are indicated. Are they clearly marked, or must you be alert to subtle changes in voice? The experienced secretary can often tell from the tone of voice whether the dictator is questioning or about to change the dictation.

Unless you are working in a pool environment, in which you are expected to type anything that comes across the desk exactly as presented, you should take a few minutes before beginning work with a new lawyer and inquire about his or her special likes and dislikes. Good communication will make it easier for you and the lawyer to work together through the orientation period. The lawyer may prefer a particular style for correspondence or other documents or other documents. Knowing these preferences will make the transcription work go much faster—although beginning secretaries are often reluctant to take time away from their transcription.

Type materials in draft form for the first few times. In the long run, it will probably be faster. Do not yield to the temptation to alter the attorney's language until you have worked together long enough to have earned his or her confidence. If the dictation is not clear or pronunciation is garbled, leave a space and call it to the attention of the dictator.

Transcription Quality

The modern secretary has the advantage of word-processing programs. Such programs allow mistakes to be corrected before the document is printed, or revisions to be made and material reprinted without the whole document having to be retyped. Even with the best equipment, though, documents must be carefully proofread.

Following is a list of transcription quality standards useful in any law office:

1. Type everything that is dictated. Do not change, reword, delete or add to any dictated material.
2. Make absolutely sure that all words are spelled correctly.
3. Do not hyphenate the last word on a page in a legal document.
4. Do not hyphenate proper names in legal documents. If possible, do not separate first and last names.
5. Correct all typographical errors. (If using a typewriter, there should be no strikeovers.)
6. Make corrections to printed documents only if it can be done undetectably. Never try to correct proper names, dates, or sums of money in a printed legal document, as this may jeopardize the legality of the document. Instead, retype or reprint the page.
7. Style all abbreviations according to the dictionary designated by the attorney.
8. Use the formats preferred by the lawyer for any documents you produce.

As a rule, lawyers are fluent dictators and have a good command of grammar. However, occasionally a mistake will occur or the dictator will call the plaintiff the defendant or vice versa. The secretary is responsible for catching such errors. If the sentence is complex, read each part independently and then determine how they are linked together. If you are transcribing correspondence, you may, *with permission,* correct the sentence. Legal documents should be changed only at the direction of the dictator. Most secretaries will put a note on a transcribed document calling the attorney's attention to any changes made, or will see the attorney in advance of transcribing the document for clarification.

Post-Transcription Tasks

Before the document is handed to the lawyer it must be carefully proofread. The following are a few suggestions that will help the transcriber become a good proofreader.

1. Confirm that the correct format and style have been used. This includes consideration of the paper size used. Recently some courts, both federal and state, have switched to letter-sized paper rather than the traditional legal-sized. Creating a pleading on the wrong-sized paper may result in its not being accepted for filing at the court.
2. Use a ruler or other straightedge to focus attention on each successive line as you read.
3. Read for content. Have the proper words been used? Are any words missing or duplicated? (The spell-check program will tell you if a word has been duplicated but will not know if a word is missing.) Are there any grammatical errors or other problems of meaning?
4. Check punctuation and capitalization. Is the document properly punctuated? Are hyphens in the correct place? If specific words are to be capitalized, is the practice followed consistently throughout the document?
5. Check names, unfamiliar terms, and figures carefully, character by character, against the handwritten or dictated original document.

6. If you are checking legal descriptions, complex contracts, and the like, enlist the aid of another secretary. One should read aloud while the other checks the typewritten material. All elements should be read aloud including punctuation marks, abbreviations, and capital letters.
7. Review your work before submitting it to the attorney.

Meeting Minutes

Serving as recording secretary and taking minutes or notes at meetings and conferences may be a major portion of your responsibility. Unless the attorney requests it, full minutes need not be taken of in-house staff meetings, but a summary record should be made, distributed to the participants, and filed. The format could be similar to that of the meeting summary shown on page 329 (Fig. 9.1). Formal meetings such as stockholders' or corporate committee meetings require the preparation of a formal record in conventional minute form.

Preparing for the Meeting

You should arrive early at the meeting so that you can organize the area where you will be taking minutes. For manual note-taking, you will want a sufficient number of pens, pencils, and notebooks and a supply of paper. Tape recorders are often used to supplement note-taking when verbatim minutes are required, in which case you will need to have a number of blank cassette tapes of the proper size. Test the recorder in the room beforehand to determine the best placement and volume setting.

If you are not familiar with the names of the meeting's participants, devise a numbered seating chart so that you can identify by number those who make motions. The presiding officer can give you their names afterward.

The presiding officer and you should discuss the materials that will be needed. Be sure you know which materials you must bring; these might include the minutes books, the bylaws, the membership and committee lists, extra copies of the agenda and printed minutes, and a reference book on parliamentary procedure.

If you are a corporate secretary you will need to take some or all of the following items to the annual stockholders' meeting, directors' meetings, and other special meetings:

Current meeting file (current papers relating to the meeting)

Record of proxies received

Minutes books

Corporate seal

Copy of published meeting notice to stockholders, with a notation of the mailing date

Copy of corporation laws of the state in which the firm is incorporated

Copy of the certificate of incorporation, including amendments

Copy of the corporate bylaws, plus amendments

Meeting regulation information, if any

Blank forms for affidavits, oaths, and other purposes

Following Meeting Procedures

Having adequate knowledge of meeting procedures is essential. Reading and referring to previous minutes and talking with secretaries who have taken notes at similar meetings will aid you in your own note-taking. Before a meeting, it is also a good idea to consult the presiding officer about how to have motions or statements clarified or repeated when necessary.

Meetings may be conducted formally or informally. At informal meetings the presiding officer joins in the discussion, and some of the formalities of parliamentary procedure are waived. Such is usually the case in committee meetings. Formal meetings, on the other hand, call for strict adherence to the rules of parliamentary procedure and the bylaws governing the meeting. (See *Merriam-Webster's Rules of Order* for details.)

A meeting agenda or order of business may or may not be used at informal meetings; however, it is required for formal meetings, and it is a great help to both the presiding officer and the recording secretary.

The items in an agenda follow a set pattern established by the official group or organization. A comprehensive list of possible agenda items follows.

Agenda (Order of Business)

1. Call to order
2. Roll call or verification of participants present
3. Minutes of the previous meeting (changes/approval)
4. Reading of correspondence
5. Report of treasurer
6. Report of board of directors
7. Report of officers
8. Report of standing committees
9. Report of special committees
10. Unfinished business (from previous meetings)
11. New business (normally items submitted in advance to the presiding officer)
12. Appointment of committees
13. Nominations and elections
14. Program, if appropriate
15. Announcements (including date of next meeting)
16. Adjournment

It is essential to record the following basic facts concerning a meeting:

1. Date, time, and location of the meeting.
2. Name of the presiding officer.
3. Kind of meeting (such as regular, special, board, executive, or committee).
4. Names of members present and absent, for small groups of under 20 persons. A quorum check is needed for larger groups. (Majority representation at stockholders' meetings is usually based upon shares of stock rather than the number of stockholders. Thus, it is necessary to know the number of shares owned by each stockholder.)
5. Order of business as indicated on the agenda.

6. Motions made, their adoption or rejection, how the vote was taken (show of hands, voice etc.), whether the vote was unanimous, and the names of the originators of the main motions. (It is not necessary to record the names of those who second motions unless requested to do so.)

It is normally unnecessary to record details of discussion. Minutes should concentrate on actions taken, not topics discussed. However, when you need to summarize an important discussion, use one side of your notebook for the main speaker and the other side for incidental speakers. Use paper clips or gummed tags to mark any action that must be taken following the meeting.

Transcribing Minutes

Typing the minutes of any meeting is an important responsibility. Because minutes serve as the official record of a meeting, accuracy is essential. Tape recorders are of great value in checking the precise wording of motions. Though meetings vary in degree of formality, it is always imperative that the wording of minutes be factual, brief, and devoid of editorial comment. Acceptable minutes capture the gist or subtance of the meeting and follow the agenda closely; as a rule, a verbatim record is made only of main motions and resolutions.

When your superior is the presiding officer, he or she will frequently want to see a rough draft of the minutes before the final copy is typed. If the minutes are dictated to you by the corporate secretary, you should similarly submit a rough draft for review, because it is essential that there be no errors in the final copy.

Minutes should be typed while the meeting is still fresh in your mind. A little forethought is needed before beginning the actual typing; being well organized will make the task easier and save time and effort. The following items should be assembled:

A copy of the agenda
Attendance information
Previous minutes
Copies of reports and materials distributed
A copy of motions and/or resolutions
A copy of the organization's constitution and/or bylaws
An up-to-date dictionary
Reference books on style and parliamentary procedure
Official stationery and continuation sheets, or plain 20-pound bond paper
Other data pertinent to the minutes

Since the format of the minutes is usually dictated by the organization itself, carefully examine the format of past minutes. Some organizations provide printed stationery designed especially for the first page of the minutes, along with special continuation sheets. Official minutes are frequently printed on 28-pound bond intended for printing on both sides. If special printed paper is not available, high-quality plain white bond should be used. Minutes are filed in a notebook, either a regulation locking type or an ordinary loose-leaf notebook. Pages are usually numbered sequentially throughout, with an index to facilitate reference to important decisions.

The arrangement of the minutes should closely parallel the agenda or order of business. Common elements include the following:

Name and address of organization or group

Type of meeting

Call to order: time, date, presiding officer

Attendance information: names of individuals, or a statement that a quorum was present

Previous minutes: reading and corrections

Reports: by whom, title, subject

Unfinished business (if any): motions, by whom, votes

Program, including speakers' names and titles

Announcements, including time and place of next meeting

Adjournment, time

See sample minutes in Fig. 9.2. Reports from officers and committee chairs are frequently attached to the minutes as an appendix, and a notation such as "Mr. Hedley read the Finance Committee report, a copy of which is appended to these Minutes" is made in the body of the minutes. Resolutions, especially lengthy ones and ones recorded on printed forms, may be handled in the same manner.

The first rule for typing minutes is to be consistent with the format of previous minutes of the organization. If you are free to adopt your own format, some suggested guidelines for minutes—especially those that are to be typed on plain paper—are as follows:

1. Leave a 2″ top margin.
2. Type the title in capital letters and center it on the page.
3. Center the date two lines beneath the title. Leave two blank lines below the date.
4. Use side headings to provide easy reference. Choice of side-heading style will vary according to organization guidelines; compare the side headings on the meeting summary and sample minutes in Figs. 9.1 and 9.2.
5. Single-space the text paragraphs, unless your organization prefers them double-spaced.
6. Type sums of money in both words and figures when they are mentioned in motions and resolutions.
7. Number each page at bottom center.
8. Provide blank underlines for your signature and the chairperson's.
9. Make the necessary copies for distribution and filing.

Corporate titles and the names of specific entities within a corporation or organization are usually capitalized in minutes; for example, "the Chairman," "the Comptroller," "the Board," "the Company," "the Board of Directors," "Common Stock," "the Corporate Bylaws," "the Annual Meeting of the Corporation." However, lowercase letters are preferred by some executives. Some secretaries type the text of all motions entirely in capital letters in order to facilitate reference to them; for example, "Roger Clark moved THAT THE ORGANIZATION DONATE THE SUM OF TWO HUNDRED DOLLARS ($200.00) TO . . ."

Fig. 9.2   Minutes of a Board Meeting

```
                                                          122
                                                          19-- #3


              C O M M U N I C O M   I N T E R N A T I O N A L ,   I N C.

                              Directors' Meeting

MINUTES OF JANUARY 8, 19--                      REGULAR MEETING, NO. 3

                  A regular meeting of the Board of Directors of Communicom
                  International, Inc., was held on Tuesday, January 8, 19--. The
                  meeting was called to order by Steven J. Morton, Chairman, at 10
                  a.m. in the Founder's Conference Room of the Corporate Office on
                  Center Street in Houston, Texas.

PRESENT           Thirteen members of the Board were present: Grant Appleby,
                  Samuel Cleveland, Jeffrey Conningsworth, Philip Esposito, Harrison
                  Flynn III, Jonathan Jalisco, Roslyn La Guardia, Andre Paradis,
                  Heather Pearlmutter, Roderick Rizzo, Peter Salisbury, Herbert
                  Smith Jr., and Monica Zelasky. These members constitute a quorum.

ABSENT            One member was absent: Richard Rodriguez.

MINUTES           The minutes of the December 5, 19--, special Directors' meeting
APPROVED          were read and approved.

CHAIRMAN'S        The chairman reported on the growth in sales during the last
REPORT            quarter, especially in international business. For that period,
                  the company enjoyed a 12 percent increase as compared with a year
                  ago. However, mention was made of the increasing difficulties in
                  bidding for large projects against strong and affluent domestic
                  and foreign competitors.

                  A plan for Organizing for Growth was briefly outlined and
                  submitted to the Board for study. It was decided that the plan
                  will be taken up in detail at the next meeting.

TREASURER'S       Arlin Sebesky, Treasurer, submitted a quarterly profit and loss
REPORT            statement, dated December 31, 19--, showing a net profit of
                  $12,757,000. The surplus available for dividends is $4,443,000, as
                  determined by a general balance sheet, dated March 31, 19--. These
                  reports were accepted and placed on file.

ADJOURNMENT       A motion for adjournment was made by Mr. Esposito and seconded
                  by Ms. Pearlmutter. The meeting was adjourned at 11:30 a.m.




        _____          _____
        Maura McGrudin, Secretary        Steven J. Morton, Chairman
```

Resolutions are formal expressions of the opinion, will, or intent of the body. Most secretaries follow conventional forms in typing resolutions. Formal resolutions use language such as the following:

WHEREAS it has become necessary . . . : Therefore be it

RESOLVED, That . . . ; and be it

RESOLVED further, That . . .

An informal resolution might be phrased more simply:

     RESOLVED, That . . .

Corrections

Corrections (such as those pointed out at the next meeting) should be written in ink above the line or in the margin. Major corrections and additions may be typed on a separate page and attached, with a note in the margin of the original page drawing attention to the attachment. Never discard the original minutes, no matter how many mistakes they may hold. You may retype a page only if you attach it to the original, uncorrected page.

Chapter 10

Preparing and Executing Legal Documents

Often the sole end of a legal matter is the creation of a legal document, a formal piece of writing sanctioned as authoritative under the law. The legal secretary will encounter many different such documents in today's law office, though more and more this area is becoming a specialization handled by paralegals or experienced legal assistants. The content and style of a particular type of document may vary considerably depending on the state in which the lawyer practices or even the specific court with which the document is to be filed. For this reason, it is not possible to give detailed guidance in this book on filling out specific forms or documents; you must instead follow local practice as spelled out in books of rules and procedures issued by state judiciary bodies or the office of the court clerk. Nevertheless, the general guidelines presented in this chapter should be useful to the novice secretary or legal assistant unfamiliar with the handling of legal papers.

The chapter describes the essentials of preparing and handling legal forms, from establishing a stock of standard forms (either printed forms or computer templates) to using form paragraphs and other elements of content and style to executing legal documents—that is, obtaining the proper signatures, filing the documents with the court, serving legal papers, and so on.

Obtaining and Maintaining Legal Forms

Printed legal forms—commonly called "law blanks" because they have blank areas that are intended to be filled in—are frequently used in the law office for routine business transactions and court proceedings. Nowadays computer forms or templates are just as likely to be used in place of the older printed forms. The use of such forms or templates saves time and effort because the proper format is already in place and only the filled-in portions need to be supplied by the attorney, paralegal, or legal secretary. The experienced legal secretary should be able to complete these forms with only limited instructions from the attorney, once the facts of the case have been provided (either by the attorney or by material in the case file).

Obtaining Forms

All forms must comply in both format and style to state and local regulations and conventions. Often the court or state bar association (or similar judiciary body) will itself make available the proper *court forms,* or forms used for filing with the court. Check with the clerk of the court in your jurisdiction. Since most business operations are controlled by state or local regulations, locally printed *commercial forms,* or forms used for business transactions, are indispensable in many law firms. See your Yellow Pages under "Legal Forms." Government bodies also issue a wide variety of *government forms,* to be used in conducting business with the government. Finally, a number of nationally recognized law and professional publishers offer various *form books* that contain many useful practice forms (i.e., forms used in different areas of law practice). The major categories of forms and their sources may be summarized as follows:

1. *Court forms* These are used for filing with the court. Each court or jurisdiction will often have its own requirements; you must be familiar with these requirements and use only the correct and most current version of each form. Printed court forms may be obtained, usually free of charge, from the office of the clerk of the court. Widely used court forms include pleadings, depositions, jury instructions, subpoenas, summonses, writs, notices, and affidavits of service.

2. *Commercial (business) forms* Law-form printers publish catalogs listing the titles and identification numbers of the commonly used business or commercial forms they print. Hundreds of different types of law blanks may be obtained from these printers (see "Legal Forms" in your Yellow Pages) or by mail and at office supply stores. Agreements, bankruptcy forms, powers of attorney, contract forms, bills of sale, promissory notes, deeds, and rental forms are commonly purchased in this way. Some are sold as pads in lots of from 25 to 100. Sometimes the firm's name and address may be printed on the stock forms. Special business forms are also supplied, free of charge, by banks, insurance companies, and title and abstract companies.

3. *Government forms* Government forms are usually supplied free of charge by agencies of the federal, state, and local governments. State tax forms may be obtained from the state division responsible for collection of taxes; the IRS supplies forms for federal taxes. State and local police departments and courts supply accident report forms. Federal agencies such as the Social Security Administration, Securities and Exchange Commission, Small Business Administration, and Veterans Administration supply forms frequently used in law offices.

4. *Form books (practice forms)* These usually come in the form of loose-leaf binders that hold sets of original or reproducible forms. A subscription to an update service serves to keep the books current. Virtually every practice area is covered by one or another of the publishers that offer these products. Among the largest form-book publishers are Matthew Bender & Co., Inc. (New York; 800-833-9844), Butterworth Legal Publications, Inc. (Salem, N.H.; 603-890-6001), Clark Boardman Callaghan (New York; 800-422-2101), and Warren Gorham & Lamont, Inc. (Boston; 800-950-1210). (See also "Form Books and Loose-Leaf Services," pp. 432–33.)

You should become familiar with all the forms that your attorney uses so that you can find and help fill out the required form quickly and easily. Some attorneys rely on their secretary or paralegal to know which form is to be used when and how it is to be filled out and filed. The more you can demonstrate expertise in this area the greater your chances for advancement.

Forms on computer   Many of the court forms and other documents required under local rules are increasingly available as software packages, either in CD-ROM or floppy-disk format. These programs provide templates that are called up and filled in using the computer almost as a typewriter. Electronic or print indexes are usually also provided and should be stored on or at the computer for ease of reference. These software programs are often bought on a subscription basis so that updates can be received as they are published. The advantage of such programs is that you are assured access to the most current forms and the material takes up far less space than do form books or form files. Most of the law and professional publishers listed above (item no. 4) offer electronic as well as print editions of forms.

Maintaining Forms

In order to make it easier for the attorney and you to do your work, it is important to maintain an efficient and effective legal-forms inventory system. You may be responsible for maintaining an adequate supply of forms and re-ordering them when necessary (in cases where they are not reproducible or become out-of-date). Implementing a forms inventory control system will ensure that forms are available when needed and will eliminate the extra cost and effort of processing rush orders. Such a system may be as simple as keeping a list of the forms your office uses, including the title and identification number, the source of each form, the price, the quantity last obtained, and the date last obtained. Similar information should be kept for electronic products in case additional units or licenses are needed. Computerized inventory control systems may be appropriate for large offices that traffic in many different forms. Ask your local software vendor for information.

Before using, filing, or ordering any form, it is important to check both its title and its identification number (usually supplied by the printer or publisher). Many forms are similar in appearance and can be easily confused. In cases in which the titles of two forms are the same but their identification numbers differ, the contents of the forms may not be identical. Check with the lawyer, court clerk, or publisher if you are not sure you are using the correct form.

Printed forms   Printed forms should be segregated from other filed material and publications, assigned titles and/or identification numbers, and arranged according to general categories such as tax forms, real estate transactions, wills, trusts, personal property transactions, corporations, and so on. Each general category may be broken down into subcategories. For example, real estate transactions may be further divided into deeds, mortgages, leases, documents of sale, and so on. In the case of reproducible forms, a "master" should always be retained and properly identified so that it is available when needed.

Most legal forms today are letter-sized (8½" × 11") rather than legal-sized (8½" × 14") and may be stored in regular filing cabinets, wall files (sometimes called "pocket files"), or loose-leaf binders. The subject categories should be indicated on tabbed dividers and exterior labels. Color coding may aid in identifying the proper file, each general category (including the subcategories) being given its own color.

An index of forms should be kept in the front of the file or binder for reference. It should list the forms by subject, title, and identification number. It is also useful to include the publisher and the date of publication.

Computer templates Master forms created from computer templates should be stored on the computer's hard drive in a "forms" directory, with subdirectories for different categories of forms and a separate file for each form. A printout of the directory structure and contents will also prove useful.

Preparing Legal Forms

The legal secretary is responsible for the careful preparation of many legal documents. These may be documents prepared from printed (or reproducible) legal forms, forms stored electronically on disk or on the computer, or even documents such as leases, agreements, or contracts created entirely through word processing. The attorney is ultimately responsible for the content of all legal documents, but their preparation and final appearance are the responsibility of the legal secretary. The attorney may dictate the information to go into the specific blanks on a legal form, or he or she may complete a draft copy and pass it on to the legal secretary to put into its final form. In either case, if you are unfamiliar with the form being used, be sure to obtain a copy of a completed form to use as a model.

General Guidelines

Size and type of paper As noted above, it is common today for legal documents to be letter-sized ($8\frac{1}{2}'' \times 11''$) rather than legal-sized ($8\frac{1}{2}'' \times 14''$). This varies from state to state and region to region, however. The choice is often determined as much by the style of the attorney as by local customs and rules.

Bond paper is typically used for the document original and a lighterweight paper (often designed for photocopying) for copies. Sometimes the attorney will ask for two (or more) originals, in which case both should be on bond paper. Some courts are beginning to require that recycled paper be used for documents filed with the court. Check your local rules.

Legal cap Some word-processing programs have "pleadings" or "legal cap" templates that may be formatted according to local rules by addressing a series of queries posed by the program. Legal software programs also commonly contain such templates. Blank legal cap may also be purchased at a good office supply store.

Legal cap (*cap* from the *cap* in *foolscap,* a watermarked paper) is a white bond paper for legal use that is usually $8\frac{1}{2}''$ and 13″ or 14″ long and is often ruled or lined. It typically has a wide vertically ruled left margin ($1\frac{1}{4}''$) and a narrow ruled right margin (½″)—but this can vary from jurisdiction to jurisdiction. In some states legal cap has numbers along the left margin indicating individual lines of text. This type of paper is often used in pleadings and briefs.

Drafts   It is often necessary to type a draft of a legal document so that the attorney can review it and make any necessary alterations. The word DRAFT (or FIRST DRAFT, SECOND DRAFT, etc.) should be typed across the top of the page so that the draft will not be mistaken for the final document. The draft should be double- or triple-spaced, depending on the preference of the attorney. Extracts copied directly from another source may be double- or single-spaced. After the draft has been checked and the final document typed, the draft should be presented to the attorney along with the final copy so that he or she can compare it with the original if desired.

Margins   Local rules may dictate the size of the margins, depending on what type of document is being prepared. Generally margins of at least one inch in width should be allowed at the top and bottom and at the left and right sides of a legal document.

Line spacing   Most legal documents are double-spaced. Certain material such as property descriptions and lengthy quotations are usually set off as single-spaced indented text, with triple spacing above and below.

Paragraphs   Standard paragraph indents of one-half inch to one inch (five o ten letter spaces) are used in most legal documents. Paragraphs in long documents are often numbered. Usually the attorney has a preference in style for the numbering of paragraphs. A paragraph that falls at the bottom of a page and must be divided, should have at least two lines of text at the end of the page and at least two lines at the top of the next page. To ensure continuity between pages of a document, it is best not to end a paragraph on the last line of a page but rather to carry over two or more lines of the paragraph to a new page. A three-line paragraph should not be divided.

Form paragraphs   Much of the language in legal documents is repetitive. Whether you are working with printed forms or computer templates, it is helpful to have a backlog of form paragraphs—commonly called "boilerplate"—readily available. Form paragraphs include specific clauses that can either be used without change or provide a starting point for a draft. In either case, ready access to such material will result in a reduction of effort and time. Many attorneys combine form paragraphs and specially written or dictated paragraphs to draw up documents such as wills, leases, complaints, answers, motions, and notices that tend to follow a standard pattern. The attorney can select the appropriate form paragraphs and add the special material required. Form paragraphs are typically stored in computer files, but it is useful to have a printout contained in a notebook as well.

Page numbers   Again local rules or office custom may come into play when applying page numbers. Otherwise pages may generally be numbered at the top right or bottom center of the page.

Signature lines   Lines are normally included for signatures on all legal documents—a separate line for each signer. (See also "The Testimonium Clause," p. 347.) Signature lines are usually placed to the right of the center of the page and continue to the right margin. Below each line appears the name of the signer, centered and typed exactly as it is to be signed but often fully capitalized. The style of the signature must agree with the name of the party as it appears in the document. Instead of the party's name, some attorneys prefer to indicate the capacity in which the person is signing—as Seller or Purchaser for example, whichever terms are used in the text of the document. (In these cases usually only the initial letter of the term is capitalized.) Four or five spaces should be allowed between the signature line and the line above it to accommodate large signatures.

_____

Seller

_____

Purchaser

Corporate signatures   Corporate signatures require that you type first the name of the corporation in solid capitals, and below it a signature line frequently preceded by the word *By:* to indicate that an officer will sign for the corporation. The corporate officer's title is typed immediately below the signature line, centered and capitalized. If the signer is a member of a partnership rather than an officer of a corporation, the signature line is typed as for a corporate signature but the title is omitted.

The secretary of the corporation is frequently required to attest to the fact that the imprinted seal is the actual seal of the corporation. When a corporate seal is to be attested (the testimonium clause [see p. 347] will indicate if it is to be attested), the word ATTEST is typed on the left side of the page and below the signature line, as shown here. The corporate secretary signs above the word *Secretary*.

XYZ CORPORATION

[corporate seal]   By _____

ATTEST:

Secretary

Spacing   A signature line should never appear alone on the final page of the document. At least two lines from the body of the document in addition to the testimonium clause should be carried over. This prevents the unauthorized substitution or inclusion of additional pages. Furthermore, the signatures should all be on one page unless there are a great many signatures.

Z-marks   Sometimes a printed legal form will provide more space than is needed to complete it. In order to prevent the addition of unauthorized information, some attorneys require that you draw what is known as a *Z-mark,* as illustrated at the end of this paragraph, to fill the space.

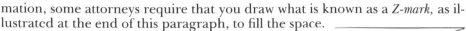
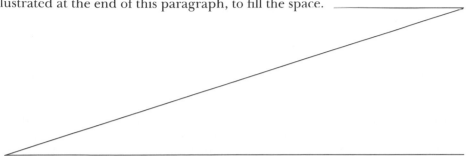

Attachments, riders, exhibits In instances where there is too little space provided on a printed legal form, it may be necessary to use an addendum, known variously as an attachment, rider, or exhibit, to complete the information. This is often the case when long property descriptions are involved. When such information is continued on an addendum, the language used to link the addendum to the original, or face, document may read as follows: "See Exhibit 'A' attached hereto and incorporated herein by this reference as though fully set forth." An attachment, rider, or exhibit should list pertinent information at the top that will identify it as part of the face document. Such information may include (1) the term "Rider" or "Exhibit" or "Attachment" centered and positioned about one inch from the top, (2) the name of the document, (3) the date of the document, and (4) either the names of the parties to the document or the street address of the property concerned.

Proofreading Accurate proofreading is extremely important in a law office. Of course, word-processing programs will catch simple typographical and spelling errors, but various other errors, such as missing or misused words, will not be caught by a spell-check program. The document must instead be read through completely. This is often done in connection with the many drafts a document may go through on its way to becoming a completed legal instrument. It is important that a legal secretary comprehend what he or she is keyboarding, as this will increase the accuracy of the work product. In some cases it may be helpful to have another secretary double-check a document to ensure that it is accurate.

Corrections and insertions In the age of word processing, corrections to a document can be made quickly and easily. Although correction fluid is still sometimes used for making typewritten (or handwritten) changes, photocopying machines have made it possible to produce fresh "originals" that show no visible signs of having been altered in this way. In some cases, interlinear insertions will be necessary; this is often the case with printed forms or documents prepared by another office (but which the parties wish to complete and sign). Interlinear insertions can be a word, a sentence, or more, depending on the situation. Oftentimes such obvious changes have to be initialed by the parties involved.

Number of copies   The attorney will usually state how many copies of a document are to be prepared. The instruction is often given in the form of "two plus four," meaning an original, a duplicate original, and four copies; or "one plus two," meaning one original and two copies. In general, when preparing court papers, copies should be made as follows: one original for the court, one copy for each attorney party to the action, one file copy, and one copy for the client. For other documents, make originals for each party in the action, a copy for each attorney, and one file copy.

Collating   Collating is the process of assembling the pages of a document, or sets of pages in multiple documents, in the proper order. Many photocopying machines have a collating feature that can facilitate this process. However, when preparing multiple documents with various exhibits, attachments, and so on, it is often still necessary to collate manually. In all cases the order of pages should be double-checked.

Legal backs   Some states require that certain documents such as wills or deeds be backed by a heavy sheet of paper called a *legal back*. The top inch of the legal back is folded down and the document is inserted (and sometimes stapled) under the flap. The entire assembly is then usually folded vertically into thirds to create a tall, slim packet with a thick protective cover (i.e., the folded legal back). Identifying information is then usually written on the cover. Specific rules regarding the application and use of legal backs vary from state to state, and these rules should be consulted.

Printed forms   If you are using a printed form, the following guidelines will help you produce an accurate, legible, and attractive document:

1. Margins for inserts of typed material should match the margins of the lines printed on the form. An exception is land descriptions; see guideline 8 below.
2. If there are no ruled or dotted lines below the blank spaces, the typed line should be perfectly aligned with the printed line.
3. If the fill-ins must be made on ruled or dotted lines, the bases of the typewritten characters should appear slightly above those lines. The tails of the letters *g, j, p, q,* and *y* will rest on the ruled or dotted line.) A small bit of white space between the typed words and the underlining increases legibility.
4. The form should be inserted into the typewriter so that fill-ins do not appear slanted upward or downward.
5. Care must be taken to fill in *all* of the small blanks, many of which call for only one or two letters. In most law blanks these are not underlined but are indicated by a small space. Many of these spaces call for letters to complete words which describe the person or persons signing the document. For example, a printed lease might include the following: "And the lessee   hereby covenant   with the lessor   and   heirs. . . ." If there is only one lessee, *s* is added to covenant; if there is only one lessor, *his* (or *her*) is filled in before *heirs*. If there is more than one lessee, *s* is added to *lessee*; if there is more than one lessor, *their* is filled in before *heirs*. The dictator will normally not bother with these details but expect the secretary to take care of them.
6. If phrases or words are to be deleted, type x's over them. Occasionally, a substitute word must be typed in above the x'd portion.

7. When a large space is deliberately left blank, two or three hyphens, centered on the space, should be typed to indicate to the reader that dictator and typist have not simply forgotten to fill in this space with information.

8. Quotations, including land descriptions, are usually indented and single-spaced.

9. It is important to check to see if the form is continued on the back of the paper. Two-sided forms may also cause problems when you are photocopying.

Executing Legal Documents

A legal document is not valid until it is executed. The word *executing* is used informally in law offices to refer only to the signing of a document, but in formal terms execution includes everything necessary to make the document valid including, where appropriate, signature, seal, attestation, acknowledgment, verification, notarization, and delivery.

Once a document has been properly signed, the legal secretary's responsibilities are far from over. It is the secretary who prepares letters of transmittal to accompany the document for filing or recording and who arranges delivery to the office of the clerk of court or the recorder. In addition, the secretary may be expected to prepare certificates of mailing, instructions for service, and other accompanying papers without further instruction from the attorney. If a filing fee, recording fee, or other fee is needed, the secretary draws the check, keeps a record for client billing, and places the check, forwarding letter, signed instrument, and other required enclosures on the attorney's desk for signature.

The remainder of this chapter reviews the secretary's responsibilities in the execution of legal documents: seeing that they are properly signed and, where required, acknowledged, witnessed, or verified; and ensuring that they are properly recorded as legal instruments, filed with the court, or served on the parties involved in court actions.

Testimonium Clause

In many legal instruments or client documents a testimonium clause immediately precedes the signature block. The testimonium clause is a declaration by the parties to the instrument that their signatures are affixed in testimony of the contents of the instrument. The introductory phrase of the testimonium clause is usually capitalized, as in the following examples:

IN WITNESS WHEREOF, the parties hereto have hereunto set their hands the day and year first above written.

IN TESTIMONY WHEREOF, [Named Corporation] has caused its corporate seal to be affixed hereto and attested by its secretary, and these presents to be signed by its president, this fifth day of June, 19—.

A styling similar to the first example is normally used when the date appears in the first paragraph of the document. The secretary must note whether the testimonium clause mentions a seal; if it does, there must be a seal next to the signature. Testimonium clauses should be inserted in the secretary's form file for future reference.

Signature

By the act of signing a legal document, the signer gives it effect as his or her act and avows knowledge, approval, acceptance, and/or obligation. The parties to a legal instrument normally sign it, and in most cases the body of the instrument will indicate who is to sign. Court documents, on the other hand, are usually signed by the attorney or, in the case of court orders and judgments, by the judge in accordance with state statutes or the rules of the court. You should become familiar with the signature requirements for each type of document you prepare, and your form file should contain examples of the proper signature blocks for all types of legal documents.

The legal secretary assumes the following responsibilities for the signing of legal documents:

1. making certain that the papers are correctly prepared for signing
2. determining exactly who is to sign the document so that the number of signature lines is accurate and the parties correctly identified
3. typing the party's name below the signature line, if required, exactly as it appears in the document
4. helping the attorney ensure that the document is signed exactly as the names appear in the document
5. typing *SEAL* or *L.S.* at the end of the signature line if required
6. ensuring that corporate seals are imprinted where needed
7. if attestation is required, ensuring that witnesses actually witness the signature
8. ensuring that the correct number of copies are signed
9. following the attorney's instructions concerning the acknowledgment or verification of the document

In some states, corporations are required to use a corporate seal or to state on corporate documents that the corporation has no seal. The seal is an engraved metal plate with which an imprint may be made on paper.

How to Conform Legal Documents

It is important to make a practice of conforming all copies of documents to the originals immediately after the originals are signed. If postponed, conforming may be unintentionally neglected.

Many law offices simply make photocopies of the executed document so that the signature, date, and additional notations are picked up automatically on the copies. If the copies are to be conformed manually, you must type or write on each copy all pertinent information from the original that was added after the document was typed; this includes signatures, seals, dates, initials, and any material added in the margins or between the lines.

To conform signatures, type or write in the signature space /s/ (or /S/, or S/) followed by the name to indicate that that is where and how the person signed the document.

/s/   Nicole Robbins

NICOLE ROBBINS

To indicate that a document has been sealed, type "[Corporate Seal]," "[Notarial Seal]," or "[Official Seal]" (in brackets) at the appropriate location.

Sometimes copies made on photocopiers or word processors are of such high quality that they could be mistaken for originals. It is a good idea to prevent any mix-ups by typing or stamping COPY across the top of each copy at the time they are conformed, if it has not already been done.

Executed Copies

Legal documents must often be prepared with duplicate or triplicate original copies. In the case of a multiparty contract, for example, each signatory receives an "original" that is signed by all parties to the contract. With photocopying machines and word processors in use it is seldom necessary to keyboard more than one copy. Each subsequent copy can then be treated as an executed copy by having the signers sign the required number of duplicate originals.

Executed copies differ from conformed copies in that an executed copy of an instrument is a valuable legal document and should be kept in a safe place. A conformed copy does not have the same legal value and need not be as carefully safeguarded.

Acknowledgment

Acknowledgment of an instrument is a formal declaration before an authorized official—who may be a notary public, judge, clerk of court, or other public officer—that the instrument is the free act of the person who executed it. Documents that must be recorded, such as deeds, mortgage notes, liens, and leases, require acknowledgment with an acknowledgment clause, or certificate of acknowledgment, annexed to the document. The form of an acknowledgment varies from state to state. Check your local rules.

Acknowledgments are of two kinds: individual and corporate. The acknowledgment on an instrument executed by a corporation usually must contain the name of the corporation, the corporate office held by the person or persons signing the instrument, and a statement that the corporation has authorized that person to execute the instrument on behalf of the corporation.

Authentication   It is sometimes necessary to acknowledge an instrument in one state and file it in another. In these cases, some states require a certificate of authentication that certifies the validity of the notary public's commission. The notary may obtain the proper forms, when necessary, from the local courthouse.

Attestation

Some client documents require that signatures be witnessed. An attestation clause is used to introduce the witnesses' signatures. This clause is a brief statement by the witnesses that the instrument was executed before them; it is signed by the witnesses at the request of the party signing the instrument. The attestation clause is sometimes necessary to make the instrument legal, and its form varies; it may be simply "In the presence of:" or it may be in the lengthy style commonly used in wills. The secretary must determine before typing the document whether attestation is required in order to plan the spacing of the signature page.

Verification

A verification is a sworn confirmation of the truth or authenticity of a writing, most commonly a pleading. It is accomplished by affidavit, oath, or deposition. In some jurisdictions, all litigation pleadings which contain new affirmations must be verified, in which case the verification is usually made by a party to the litigation but may in certain instances be made by the party's agent or attorney. Whenever a complaint is verified, the answer must also be verified. The format of a verification varies, but it almost always contains the *venue* (the political subdivision in which the document was executed) and a *jurat* (statement of when, before whom, and where verification was made).

Affidavit

An affidavit is a written statement of fact designed to help prove that fact. It must be sworn to in the presence of a notary public or a bonded public officer qualified to administer such oaths. The officer verifies only the validity of the signature, not the contents of the statement. The person who makes the affidavit is called the "affiant" or "deponent." Affidavits and acknowledgments are sometimes confused by inexperienced secretaries. An affidavit is a sworn statement that asserts the truth or validity of the statements contained in it; it is signed by the deponent as well as by the person giving the oath. An acknowledgment, on the other hand, verifies only the signature on a document and is signed by a notary public. An acknowledgment is an appendage to another document; an affidavit is a separate legal instrument.

The Notary Public

Since many legal documents require notarization, legal secretaries usually obtain notarial commissions. Information on how to become a notary public is available from the secretary of state or a similar designated state official. A bond is required in some states, which is usually paid for by the employing law firm. Some states have additional requirements such as passing a written examination.

Once you have been commissioned, you may purchase a notary's kit which includes a seal bearing your name, license number, the county in which you are commissioned, and the expiration date of your commission. The seal may be either a rubber stamp or a metal plate. Some states now allow the use of a rubber stamp in place of the engraved plate traditionally used in sealing documents. The rubber stamp is, of course, less expensive and easier to carry, but many notaries public still prefer the formality and official appearance of the imprint made by an engraved metal plate.

The notary public must register a new commission with the county clerk or other designated official. Then, whenever the notary's signature and commission need to be authenticated for use in another state, the clerk can issue the required certificate of authentication.

The powers and duties of a notary public are governed by state statute. They generally include administering oaths and affirmations and taking acknowledgments, depositions, verifications, and affidavits. When a notary administers an oath to the signer of an affidavit, verification, or deposition, the oath is documented in the form of a jurat. To *notarize* a document, on the other hand, means to attach a certificate of acknowledgment that the signature on a document is authentic. Acknowledgments are not made under oath and therefore do not require the jurat. Both the jurat and the certificate of acknowledgment require the notary's signature.

When notarizing a document, the secretary should (1) check to make sure that a seal is included with the signature if required; (2) date the acknowledgment with the correct date; (3) check to make certain that any blanks are filled in where required, such as the date of the expiration of the notary's commission; (4) check to see if an authentication is required; and (5) take the acknowledgment: that is, ask the person if he or she signed the instrument in question. It is important to adhere to the statutes governing the taking of acknowledgments. For example, the person making the acknowledgment must appear personally before the notary to attest that the signature on the document is genuine; acknowledgments should not be taken over the telephone. If the person making the acknowledgment is not a client and is a stranger, the notary should ask for evidence of identity. Some states require that husband and wife make separate acknowledgments.

A notary public may act only within the territory (usually a state or county) authorized by the statutes and may be required to keep a record of instruments acknowledged. Most states set maximum notarial fees and require that a notarial seal or stamp be impressed on documents authenticated by a notary public. Some states also require that the notary's name and the date of expiration of the notary's commission be printed or typed below the notary's signature.

There are civil and criminal penalties for errors, omissions, or misconduct in the official duties of a notary public, and the bonding company as well as the notary may be held liable. You should become thoroughly familiar with the statutes governing notaries public in your state. Whenever possible, notarize documents only when they have been signed in your presence. Only then will you be able to testify (as you may be called upon to do) that the signature is genuine. You must also be sure that the date is accurate.

The notarial duties of a legal secretary most often involve verifications and acknowledgments.

Recording Legal Documents

The prompt recording of certain legal instruments after execution is an important secretarial responsibility. Recording documents is the act of entering them in the public land records to preserve authentic evidence of their existence and thus to protect the interests of those involved. Promptness in recording is essential, because an unrecorded conveyance of title may be void. These records are kept by the county recorder, who may also be known as the register of deeds.

The recorder's office records each instrument by making a photocopy or microfilm record and placing that copy in its official records. The date and the page and volume numbers that indicate where it is entered in the record book are noted on the original document, which is then returned to the person who presented it for recording. Certain documents in certain states, for example a divorce judgment affecting real property, may be recorded in abstract form. Valuable documents such as deeds, however, are recorded in full so that if the original is lost it may be replaced by a photocopy upon application to the recorder's office.

Papers which *must* be recorded are those having an effect on ownership of real property, including both land and buildings—such as transfers of title, mortgages, easements, liens, and any court judgment affecting ownership of property. Articles of incorporation may also have to be recorded in a local government office.

Documents are recorded in the county in which the property is located, regardless of the residence of the parties or where the papers are executed.

When preparing a document for recording, remember that in order to be recorded a document must first be acknowledged before a notary public or other public officer. Note on the face of the document the name and address of the party to whom the recorded document is to be returned, or, if the document is in a legal back, write above the firm's name and address printed on the endorsement: "Please record and return to _____." Deliver or mail it by certified mail (return receipt requested) to the appropriate recorder's office with a letter of transmittal and a check for the recording fee. Recording fees are fixed by state statute. The fee normally depends on the length of the document and the number of party names to be indexed. A telephone call to the recorder's office is the simplest way to determine the amount of the fee. (As always, keep a record of the fee for client billing.) When mailing documents to be recorded, use certified mail as described in Chapter 5.

When the document is returned by the recorder's office, *immediately* conform on all copies the numbers stamped on it by the recorder. Then forward the original to the client, again by certified mail, and keep a conformed copy for your file.

Filing Legal Documents with the Court

Filing legal papers is simply placing them in the custody of a court through delivery to the clerk of court. Whereas legal instruments are recorded to preserve them in order to establish ownership, documents are filed with the court to begin and maintain litigation and to preserve a record of legal actions. And while the registry of deeds keeps only copies of original documents, the court retains the originals.

Filing the Initial Pleadings

A lawsuit is commenced by filing an initial pleading (which may be termed a claim, complaint, petition, declaration, or libel) with the court of proper jurisdiction and serving it, with a summons, on the defendant. An attorney decides in which court to commence a lawsuit after considering the subject matter of the lawsuit, the amount of money at issue, and the residence of the parties. Subsequent pleadings and supporting papers are also filed with the court.

When the first pleading is filed with the clerk of court, the clerk notes on the document the date it was received, assigns an index, docket, or case number to the lawsuit, and returns to the attorney a copy of the pleading marked with the date of receipt and the index number. The original is retained in the clerk's office, where it may be inspected by concerned parties.

Filing fees for litigation are set by statute or court rules. They often differ from court to court and are subject to change. Questions concerning the fee can be answered by a telephone call to the clerk of court. You should keep a current list of fees of the courts in which the lawyers in the office practice; you will find it convenient to add to that list the standard witness fee, the mileage rate for subpoenaed witnesses, and the other fees you often pay.

When the copy of the initial pleading is returned to you, or when the attorney is served a pleading that requires an answer, you should make a record of the index or case number assigned to the case by the clerk of court. If you do not know the number, ask the clerk for it and immediately note it on your copy of the pleading. That number *must* appear on all pleadings and papers filed in the action and should be given in any telephone calls to the clerk of court about the case.

As courts have computerized, they have required more information on the parties filing law suits and those representing the parties. Some jurisdictions require that each attorney authorized to practice in that jurisdiction apply for an identifying attorney number and that all documents filed in a matter have that number affixed following the attorney's name.

Calendaring   The legal secretary's calendaring responsibilities begin even before the case is filed. As soon as a prospective case is received in the law office, the date on which the statute of limitations runs out should be determined and noted in the case file, in the case progress record or suit register, and on the attorney's calendar. Once the action is commenced, the date of service of the papers determines the date on which the response is due. Refer to a practice manual or the rules of the court for the number of days in which the response is due and the method for computing the days. If the due date falls on a Sunday or holiday (or in some jurisdictions on Saturday), the response is due the next working day. Take care to note the date of receipt of any legal documents which are delivered to the law office and the date of mailing (the postmark) of any legal documents served by mail, since several days are usually added to the time for response to documents served by mail. Immediately calculate the date on which the response is due and calendar it. See Chapter 11, pp. 358–68, for a description of calendaring methods and techniques for reminding the lawyer of upcoming matters.

Summons and complaint   A summons is usually prepared on a form available from and to be signed by the clerk of the court, although in some instances it is prepared and signed by the plaintiff's attorney. In the latter case, the summons and complaint may have to be authenticated by the court before they are served on the defendant. While in some instances only the summons is served to commence an action and the plaintiff then "demands" a copy of the complaint either from the court or from the attorney for the filing party, most jurisdictions require that the summons and complaint be served together. A check for the filing fee must accompany the summons and complaint when they are filed with the court.

Some courts require a cover sheet to be filed with the initial papers. Cover sheets are forms that provide a description of the lawsuit; they are available from the clerks of courts which require them. They are filed only with the court and are not served on the defendant.

Once filed with the court, the summons and complaint are then served on the defendant (except in those jurisdictions where only the summons is served). Clerks of court are usually willing to deliver to the server of process the copies of the summons and complaint which are to be served on the defendant, but many law offices prefer to deliver these pleadings to the process server themselves.

Checklist of Filing Procedures

Even if your office files all actions by mail or employs messengers to deliver them, you should file at least one action with the court yourself so that you will be familiar with the procedure. Before a summons and complaint leave your office, make sure that all these steps have been taken:

1. The complaint must be properly signed, dated, and, if necessary, verified.
2. The summons must be signed by the plaintiff's attorney in jurisdictions where it is necessary.
3. Sufficient copies must be made: the original (and sometimes more) for the court; one copy to be served on each defendant; one copy to which the process server will attach the certificate of service in those jurisdictions where it is required; one copy for the client; and one copy for your files.
4. All exhibits must be attached to the complaint.
5. Legal backs, if required in the jurisdiction, should be attached to the copies that will be filed and served.
6. A check must be written to the order of the clerk of the court in the amount of the filing fee.
7. A letter or memo of instructions for serving should be prepared.
8. A check for advance payment of service fees must be written if the process server requires advance payment.

After the proper preparations have been made, you are ready to file the papers:

1. Take the original summons and complaint to the office of the clerk of court along with the check for the filing fee.
2. Obtain from the clerk a receipt for the filing fee.
3. Note the case number and, in some courts, the name of the judge to whom the case is assigned.
4. In jurisdictions where it is required, present copies with the original. The clerk will authenticate them and immediately return them to you.
5. Deliver copies of the initial papers to the process server with a check for advance payment of fee, if required, and instructions for service.

The initial pleadings may also be mailed by certified mail to the clerk of court with a letter of transmittal and a stamped, addressed envelope. The clerk will often forward to the process server the copies to be served.

Papers subsequent to the initial pleading are served on the other party first, then filed with the court along with an affidavit of service where required. There are exceptions to this rule; for instance, in some jurisdictions sufficient copies of the papers are filed with the clerk of the court, who then serves them on other parties. You should check a practice manual or ask the attorney for the correct procedure in your jurisdiction.

Serving Court Documents

Service of court documents gives notice to concerned parties of the actions that involve them. Service is accomplished by giving a conformed copy of the court document to the party in question (who may be an individual or an agent of a corporation or association) and by returning to the court a form stating that the papers were properly delivered to that party at a particular time. Summonses, complaints, and subpoenas are served directly on the party, while other litigation papers subsequent to the complaint are ordinarily served on the party's attorney.

As suggested in the preceding section, local practice regulations govern service of the initial papers in a lawsuit. In most jurisdictions, copies of the summons and complaint are served together, the summons stapled to the top of a copy of the complaint. In others only the summons is served, and the party served is required to pick up a copy of the complaint at the clerk's office. In still other jurisdictions, the complaint is filed *after* the summons is served on the defendant.

Process Servers

The server of process may be a public officer such as a U.S. marshal or deputy marshal or a sheriff or deputy sheriff; or it may be a professional process server.

Public officers It is usually the legal secretary's responsibility to obtain a process server. In federal jurisdictions, the U.S. marshal nearest the court in which the action is filed serves process within his or her jurisdiction and forwards papers to be served outside his or her jurisdiction to the U.S. marshal in the area in which the paper is to be served. An advance fee is usually required by the U.S. marshal. In state and local actions, the sheriff may serve legal documents, although in some jurisdictions the sheriff's department does so only for criminal actions.

Professional process servers Professional process servers may serve legal papers in most jurisdictions, and you should have a list of dependable professional process servers in your area. If you need to serve a paper in another geographical area, local process servers can usually give you names of authorized process servers in other places. You can also go to the public library to check the Yellow Pages of telephone books for other cities. If all else fails, you can call a legal secretary at a law firm in the area where the paper is to be served to request the name of a dependable process server. When serving a subpoena duces tecum, which requires the recipient to provide certain documents as evidence, professional process servers are sometimes authorized to obtain those papers, copy them, notarize and deliver the copies to the attorney, and return the originals.

The Secretary's Responsibilities

When delivering papers to a process server, you should advise the server how and where to serve the papers. You should furnish the addresses of the recipient's residence and place of employment and any information you have about working hours or probable location at any specific time. Let the process server know if the party is to be served as the representative of a corporation. Be sure to state the time limits within which service must be made, and follow up to ensure that service is accomplished before that date.

The server of process may require advance payment of part of the service fee. Each time you forward papers to be served, you should find out whether an advance is necessary and, if so, attach a check for that amount to the papers.

In some jurisdictions, the certificate of service contains a statement to the effect that the "attached" document was served. In such cases, an extra copy of the paper to be served must be included with the papers sent to the process server.

You should be aware that some states have special laws for serving certain parties. For instance, in some states an insurance company or a defunct corporation is served by serving the secretary of state. A fee for this service is payable to the office through whom service is made, and an extra copy is usually required.

Proof of Service

After service of process has been made, the process server returns a proof of service (often called a certificate or affidavit of service) to the court or to the attorney. When proof of service is returned, it is your responsibility to check it carefully to be sure that it is filled out properly. You may need to notarize the signature. The affidavit of service may be made directly on a copy of the document served, or it may have to be attached to a copy of that document.

The returned proof of service will be accompanied by a statement for the server's fee. These statements should be paid promptly and a record kept for client billing.

Dates of service should be recorded at once on your calendar, since the time for response begins to run on the date of service. Compute the date on which the response is due and calendar it. If the response does not arrive on or before that date, notify the attorney immediately.

Make a photocopy of the proof of service for your files, and file the original with the clerk of court.

Service by Publication

In most cases, actual personal delivery of an initial pleading is required in order to effect service. However, when a party cannot be found through proper diligence, sufficient notice of a lawsuit may be made by publishing the summons in an officially designated newspaper. The intervals and the duration of publication are designated by statute. Notice by mail to the last known address of the party may also be required.

To accomplish service by publication, the summons is mailed to the newspaper designated in the state statutes with a letter setting forth the dates and number of times it should be published and asking the newspaper to return a proof of publication. When the proof of publication is returned, check it carefully, make a copy for your files, and file the original with the court. If the proof of publication is not promptly received, contact the newspaper and ask that it be sent.

Papers Subsequent to the Summons and Complaint

Copies of pleadings and other court documents subsequent to the summons and complaint are served on the attorneys for the parties rather than directly on the parties. Some jurisdictions require that a certificate of service accompany these documents when they are filed with the court. Other jurisdictions consider that filing the document with the court constitutes certification that a copy has been timely served on all parties required to be served. Answers and subsequent documents may be delivered to the opposing attorney's office in person, or they may be mailed. Process servers are not required to deliver these papers in most jurisdictions.

Service by personal delivery   When an answer is served on the opposing attorney, the recipient (who is often the attorney's secretary) may be required to write or stamp on the back of the original document a notation that indicates (1) the date the copy was received, (2) the name of the recipient firm, and (3) the name of the client represented by the firm. A form for this purpose may already be printed on the legal back. Many attorneys advise their secretaries who receive preprinted forms to read them carefully and cross out any words such as "timely" or "due and proper" service before signing the form. After receiving the document, the secretary should immediately calendar the date.

Service by mail   Court papers that follow the summons and complaint are frequently served by mail. Certificates of mailing—formal affidavits that are required in many jurisdictions—are signed by the person who mailed the documents and should be notarized. A typical form contains a list of the names and addresses of all parties to whom the papers were sent together with a sworn statement that the papers were sent. A printed form such as the one reproduced on the following page may also be used. The secretary who mails a document requiring such an affidavit must adhere to the terms of the affidavit, which usually require that the affiant—the secretary or a messenger—deposit the document "in the United States Mails"—*not* in an OUT box to be picked up by someone else.

Copies of legal papers in a lawsuit are served on attorneys for *all* parties in the action, whether they represent opposing parties or coparties. When serving papers by mail, send them with a short transmittal letter stating the name of the action, the case number, and the titles of the documents being served.

You will need to conform all copies of the document, record the date served, and calendar the date on which response is due. After service is completed and the certificate filled in, the original is then mailed or delivered to the clerk of court for filing, together with the proof of mailing.

Chapter 11

Docket Control and Records Management

If you are an administrative secretary, you must be familiar with your office's docketing (calendaring) system and with all records containing information that the attorney may need. Keeping an accurate register (docket) of cases to be tried, and being able to locate all the relevant material when called upon to do so, are two of the legal secretary's most important responsibilities.

This chapter covers the key elements of docket control and records management, including calendar systems, tickler files, docket reports, general filing systems and equipment, and records storage and retrieval. It discusses both computerized and manual systems and applications.

Docket Control

One of the most important responsibilities of a legal secretary is the maintenance of a good docket-control system. If you are new in the legal field, the term *docket control* will probably be foreign to you, but it represents a key element in the operations of any law firm. A *docket* is a calendar of matters to be acted on. In a law office, docket *control* means a system for ensuring that important legal deadlines are met—a reminder system for lawyers and other personnel of specific time schedules and dates for filing documents, making court appearances, and other similar duties.

A poorly maintained docket-control system may result in failure to carry out any of the following actions on time:

- filing pleadings
- appearing in court
- filing tax returns and related information
- meeting a statute-of-limitations deadline
- answering interrogatories

- filing motions and notices
- filing appeals and briefs

Missing a statutory deadline can result in malpractice proceedings, monetary damage to the client and the lawyer, loss of clients, and personal embarrassment.

Malpractice claims against lawyers are increasing, and as a result professional liability insurance premiums have become very expensive. Agents are reluctant to write coverage for a law firm with a record of missed filing dates that have resulted in judgments against it. Explanation of the firm's docket-control system is usually required on applications for liability coverage, and some insurance companies require an in-house physical inspection of the system prior to writing coverage.

A docket-control system does not have to be elaborate and expensive. Requiring little work itself, such a system should function as a simple and efficient tool to help the lawyer dispose of matters on a timely basis. It should help prevent last-minute rushes to meet deadlines, requests to the court for extension, needless tensions in the office, and the need to explain additional delays to the client.

All law offices should have copies of the rules of procedure for the courts and districts in which the lawyers practice, which are usually printed by the courts and obtainable from the clerk of each court. In addition, it is helpful to prepare a reference book for your office by compiling a court-by-court list of all important documents to be filed, the number of copies required, and the time and place for filing. Use a three-ring loose-leaf notebook so that, as statutes or rules change, new pages may be easily inserted to ensure an up-to-date reference.

A good docket-control system will require the secretary to calendar all dates that create deadlines. In a firm that has a docket-control clerk, you will be responsible for routing information promptly to the docket clerk.

System Requirements

A good docket-control system has four requirements:

1. Calendaring must be *immediate and automatic*. As soon as an appointment has been made over the telephone, it should be calendared. All incoming and outgoing mail, faxes, and other documentation should be automatically checked for dates at the time they are sent or received.

2. Every system should have a *double* or even a *triple check*. Lawyer and secretary can check each other with duplicate systems. A third person should be assigned to check each calendar in case both lawyer and secretary are absent at the same time. (For this reason, all information must be legible and understandable.) The docket clerk should have a backup employee to double-check the entire system. New employees should receive thorough training in docket control.

3. The system should provide *plenty of lead time* to meet the requirements of each appointment. It may also require a series of reminders as a deadline approaches.

4. A *follow-up check* needs to be provided for to ensure that the work has been done.

It is the secretary's responsibility, alone or together with a docket clerk, to keep the lawyer informed of calendared events. In some cases, even written reminders are insufficient. Do not hesitate to orally remind the lawyer of an appointment or deadline, even though normal calendaring procedures have been followed. In the course of regular lawyer-secretary meetings to discuss files and appointments, upcoming deadlines and verification of compliance with recently passed deadlines should be reviewed.

As you become familiar with the docket-control system in your office, watch for ways to improve it and suggest them to the lawyer or office manager. Whether your system is computerized or manual, the principle is the same: you must have a date-accounting system and a way of disseminating the information to the appropriate people in a timely fashion. If nothing falls through the cracks, it is a good system; if an appointment or deadline is missed, search for the problem area and fortify your system. As the law practice changes and laws themselves are revised, your calendaring will also change. Compare your system with others, and always search for improvements.

Software Programs

Electronic case- or time-management programs can put facts at your fingertips. The information in your desktop calendar, appointment book, and other such organizing devices can be recorded and retrieved quickly using these programs. Depending on which software you purchase, an electronic program will generally include the following components:

- An appointment calendar
- A tickler (reminder) file
- A listing of "to-do" items
- A project-planning schedule
- A notepad (for memos and notes)
- A time-management assistant
- An address book (for names, addresses, and telephone numbers)

These programs can be used both as docketing aids and as trial notebooks to help organize cases, prepare witness and exhibit lists (including dates), and maintain outlines of depositions and records of conversations. They can also help you to build a basic address list and keep track of calls made to clients and court officers. The best programs have graphical interfaces (as in Windows or the Macintosh) and are easy to use, though they need an abundance of RAM to run properly. If you plan to use one on your portable computer, make sure you have enough RAM and a sufficiently large hard disk drive.

General Docketing Guidelines

Whether you use a computerized system, a manual one, or some combination of both, the following general suggestions for calendaring and docketing apply:

- When recording a date, whether in a memo, telephone message, or note, always write the month, day, *and year* in your notation.
- Don't carry docketing information in your head; rather, write it down so as to get it into the system.

- Remember that, in addition to computerized and manual docketing, you should always communicate dates orally.
- If necessary, develop your own personal docketing system that ties into the regular office system.
- Don't discard telephone logs and calendars, as these can be used as references in compiling docketing information.
- Ask the lawyer for docketing information whenever he or she returns from court or out-of-office appointments.
- Note in the margins of any written documents from which docketing information has been obtained (e.g., pleadings, letters, court orders) that you have entered the date(s) into the docketing system (e.g., "Deadline noted" or "Noted on calendar").
- Always enter the statutory limitation into the office docketing system upon the client's first visit, as this date will be extremely important for all subsequent actions.
- Leave a paper trail of documentation that is complete with regard to dates, times, and names. As a safeguard, you may want to keep a file at your desk that contains copies of all your memos concerning docketing.

Calendar Systems

Daily calendars There are any number of calendars and diaries that can be purchased for recording daily appointments. The one-day-at-a-time desk calendar is useful for jotting down items that require little attention and do not have legal deadlines. Simple reminders for routine office matters (ordering supplies, calling repairmen, etc.) obviously do not merit a place in the docket-control system. Notations on this daily calendar of events can be reviewed and transferred later to a more permanent reminder system if they develop importance. The secretary and the attorney may keep duplicate calendars, but the attorney's copy will not normally contain the routine office tasks that are noted in the secretary's copy.

To-do lists To ensure that your work is done in a timely fashion, prioritize your work every morning by keeping a daily "to-do" list. Some items on your list will be "must-dos"; others will be less essential but should serve as reminders of how to budget your time.

The double diary When a weekly or monthly calendar is used in conjunction with the daily calendar, a double-diary system is created. An 8½" × 11" week- or month-at-a-glance calendar seems to be the most popular and practical for scheduling the lawyer's daily appointments and activities. Appointments, hearings, trial dates, directors' meetings, deposition dates, seminars, vacations—these and all other scheduled events should be noted on this calendar for the lawyer, with a duplicate at the secretary's desk. Block out in advance any times that appointments cannot be made, such as holidays and vacations. If you have to reschedule or cancel an appointment, cross out rather than erase the old date and enter the new one. Calendars are permanent records, and it is necessary that they reflect changes as well as events that took place on time. Making duplicate entries on both the secretary's and the lawyer's calendars ensures that each acts as a check on the other.

The double-diary system of daily and weekly/monthly calendars is easy to keep and use. It fits well with the docket-control system of larger law firms, since court matter on the calendar can be referred to the docket-control clerk, thus creating a triple check, while personal reminders and the lawyer's appointments are retained on the diary.

Pocket calendars To supplement the secretary's and lawyer's calendars, the lawyer should always carry a pocket calendar or diary with pages for an entire year or more. Events scheduled on the desk calendar should be transferred regularly to the pocket calendar and vice versa. Many times when a lawyer is at the courthouse, in another office, at lunch, or at meetings of professional associations, clubs, or corporate directorships, an appointment will be made orally and noted on the pocket calendar. The secretary should daily check the pocket calendar and transfer these appointments to the office calendars.

Wall calendars A large wall calendar is a helpful supplement, especially for the legal assistant. Filing dates, deposition dates, investigation times, pretrial

Fig. 11.1 Docket-Entry Request Form

```
        DOCKET ENTRY REQUEST

    Date:_____

    Please enter the following
    matter on the Docket:

    Event Date:_____

    File No.:_____

    Client/Case:_____

    Atty:_____

    Event:_____

    _____

    _____

    _____


    Tickler Reminder:

    Yes:_____    No:_____



           DOCKET CONTROL
    Date Docketed:_____

    _____
           Operator
```

dates, and trial dates are recorded on the wall calendar and marked off when completed. Scheduled out-of-town trips to other courts will also be reflected here. This calendar is an excellent reference when scheduling events, such as travel, that will take up blocks of time.

Noting Deadlines

Deadlining should be done routinely from a variety of documents. Incoming and outgoing mail, faxes, and phone calls should be reviewed for any deadlines they contain. Notices of trial settings, depositions, and all matters in litigation should be automatically calendared before being filed or processed. Litigation items should be calendared well in advance so that there is ample time for both the lawyer and the secretary to prepare the necessary documents.

If, in a larger firm, all documentation is not screened for docketing information by a single person (such as a docketing clerk) but rather is handled separately by a variety of staff members, it will be necessary to communicate to the docketing clerk or individual legal secretary the required information. A form similar to the one shown in Fig. 11.1 may be used for this purpose.

Checklists   Docketing entries can be made from file folder checklists (and vice versa). These checklists, which itemize in chronological order the procedures, documents, and deadlines for each case, are usually kept attached to the front inside cover of a file folder. The checklist should indicate:

1. The documents or actions required
2. The name of the person responsible
3. The times and dates due
4. The dates filed or completed

Timetables   Many state bar associations publish procedure manuals that include deadlines and reminder dates for various areas of legal practice. In addition, law offices may prepare their own timetables according to local court rules. Figure 11.2 (p. 364) is a table of important general deadline dates incorporated into the docket-control system of a litigation firm representing a plaintiff in the state of Iowa.

Calendaring financial items   In offices where the secretary is also the bookkeeper, calendaring is essential for scheduling financial matters. The lawyer may depend entirely on you to take care of deposits, accounts payable, quarterly tax reports, payroll, banking, and other financial matters relating to the day-to-day operation of the law office. If you are responsible for these activities and reports, you should schedule them wisely, calendaring all deadlines for your attention and planning ahead by comparing these tasks with your other calendar entries.

If your financial responsibilities are extensive, you may need to keep a separate bookkeeping calendar, using, for instance, a month-at-a-glance calendar to record all bookkeeping reminders and due dates. Preparing complicated legal documents is far more important than routine bookkeeping duties, and when a crisis develops in the office (which will happen with some regularity), you will be able to produce a better legal document under less stress if you have already completed your bookkeeping obligations.

Fig. 11.2   Sample Timetable

Document	Deadline
Petition	Prior to Statute of Limitation
Defendant's Answer to Petition	(In most cases) 20 days from the date of service of Petition
Defendant's Pre-Answer Motions	Prior to filing of Answer, 20 days from service of Petition
Resistance to Motions	Consult local rules
Answer to Interrogatories; Requests for Admission; Requests for Production	60 days from receipt, if filed and served with Petition; 30 days, if filed subsequent to filing of Petition
Answer to Counterclaim	20 days from filing of Counterclaim
Designation of Experts (when Petition filed against a lawyer, doctor, CPA, or hospital)	30 days after defendant's Answer; 15 days after plaintiff's Designation
All Discovery, Motions, Designation of Experts, Trial Briefs, Jury Instructions	As stated in Court Scheduling Order
Notice of Appeal	30 days from final disposition of case or verdict

Corporation calendars   The secretary whose office has a variety of corporate responsibilities may need to keep a separate corporation calendar, supplemented by a tickler system such as that described later in this chapter. This calendar would remind the lawyer of such things as meetings of directors and stockholders, renewal and expiration dates of contracts and other documents, tax deadlines, annual stockholders' reports, and reports to state and federal authorities.

Timekeeping diaries   Many lawyers prefer to use daily appointment calendars that divide the day into half- or quarter-hour increments. This is a very good system for keeping track of time billable to clients. As secretary, you may be expected to construct a daily time sheet from the lawyer's daily calendar. If you are assigned to assist in keeping track of the lawyer's time, remember that accurate records are important. Check the lawyer's diary and calendar for items noted there but not reflected on the time form to ensure that all chargeable time is actually billed to the client.

Pull dating   Many firms use a system of noting a *pull date* on each client's file folder. This date is determined by the lawyer and penciled on the folder and the lawyer's desk calendar. (If the date is extremely important, a red pencil may be used.) The secretary then calendars the pull date and returns the file to storage. Each day, the files with pull dates for that day are removed from the file cabinet and placed on the lawyer's desk for action. Files are never returned to storage without a new pull date being entered on the file and calendared. If no action is necessary, the file is marked for monthly or quarterly review, depending on the nature of the matter. On these review dates the client can be advised of the status of the file. This type of system will also ensure that clients' files are never overlooked.

Tickler Files

One type of calendar that is used in many law offices is called the *tickler file*, because it tickles your memory. It is designed to remind its users of recurring events and deadlines—annual meetings, tax deadlines, and the like—rather than day-to-day appointments, though day-to-day items may be recorded there. Your firm may want to have reminders for matters several years in the future, and this can be accomplished with little effort and cost by using the tickler system.

Setting up the system   As noted, electronic tickler files are available; but many offices still rely on the tried-and-true manual method. To set up a manual system, you will need the following:

1. A 3″ × 5″ × 12″ *file box*
2. A set of 12 3″ × 5″ *guide cards* (tabbed index cards) marked "January" through "December"
3. At least two sets of 3″ × 5″ *numerical guide cards* (tabbed index cards) numbered 1 through 31
4. A supply of 3″ × 5″ *blank guide cards* (tabbed index cards) on which will be noted the years following the current year
5. A supply of 3″ × 5″ *tickler cards*
6. A *deposit tray* or small box in which to place tickler cards to be processed by the docket clerk

You now have the necessary equipment for the tickler file. The month and day on which the system is started will be reflected in the first guide cards in the tickler box. Suppose, for example, that you begin using the system on January 1. The first guide card will be the "January" card, and it will be followed by numbered guide cards for days 1 through 31. Cards marked "February" through "December" will follow. A second set of numerical guide cards (1–28) will fill out the "February" section, and more sets for subsequent months may also be used if necessary; otherwise, the two sets of numerical cards can be recycled as the dates pass. The "December" section will be followed by blank guide cards labeled for the following year and each year thereafter up to 10 years or more. Ticklers for future years are simply filed behind the designated year, to be moved into monthly and daily sections as that year approaches.

Tickler cards   The tickler cards may be made in your office and customized to fit its needs (see Fig. 11.3). They can also be purchased from legal suppliers in single pages or as carbonless-copy sets. Cards may vary in the amount of information they are designed to contain. Color-coded cards can be assigned to specific deadline matters or to particular attorneys. Carbonless sets are extremely useful when a number of lawyers are receiving ticklers for the same

Fig. 11.3   Sample Tickler Card

Client/Case:_____   Matter No. _____

Event: _____

_____

Date of Event _____

Reminder Dates: _____ _____ _____

Attorney Responsible: _____

Statute of Limitations Date: _____

Notes: _____

_____

file. Such sets are also useful in a dual tickler system—that is, when ticklers are filed alphabetically as well as chronologically. A dual system requires a second box and a set of A–Z guide cards. When alphabetized by client/matter, the copy ticklers will serve as a double check against the chronological file.

Information on the tickler card should be brief but must contain enough information so that the lawyer will know to what case or client it refers and exactly what is expected. The tickler should contain only one matter per entry and include the following information:

1. Deadline date
2. Date deadline is met
3. Attorney to whom deadline is directed
4. Client's file number
5. Client's name
6. Client's matter
7. Subject matter of the deadline
8. Source of the information (e.g., court order, notice, pleading received or filed, letter, phone call, fax) and its date

Ticklers made for dates in the distant future should be particularly specific as to the action to be taken, and should contain additional information such as the location of closed files or where information might be located if files have been destroyed during the interim years.

Ticklers should be prepared for all recurring deadlines (monthly payments, retainer bills, annual accountings, annual corporate meetings, tax returns, annual court reports, etc.). Information for ticklers will come from correspondence, faxes, and documents sent and received. It is useful to prepare a

Fig. 11.4   Docket-Control Report

DOCKET CONTROL REPORT

JANUARY 2, 19—   PREPARED BY ᴍᴅᴋ

DATE	ATTY	FILE NAME	NO.	AS PER	ACTION REQUIRED	SOL	DONE (DATE)
19—/01/02	TCR	Grady	4234	12/2/— Defendant's filed Interrogs & Req. for Production	Our response		
19—/01/02	KCR	Pemberton	4456	5/14/— Intake memo		SOL	
19—/01/02	BGF	Blakely	4523	12/22/— Motion for separate trials	Our response		
19—/01/03	ISZ	Klokowski	4354	4/3/— Intake memo		SOL	
19—/01/03	RHT	Chester	4578	9/18/— Order	Brief – Additional Parties		
19—/01/03	JKL	James	4074	7/5/— Intake memo		SOL	
19—/01/04	MNO	Handke	4222	12/5/— Pre-trial Order	Respondent to take tele depos of ABC Electric president		
19—/01/07	TCR	Jones	4424	11/7/— Notice from Court	Pick up Exhibits (or they will be destroyed)		
19—/01/09	JKL	Meenhan	4048	2/9/— Intake memo	Note: Declination letter sent 2/9/—	SOL	
19—/01/10	GHI	Friedrich	4679	11/11/— Notice from Court	Pick up Exhibits (or they will be destroyed)		
19—/01/11	MNO	Van Blythe	4456	12/5/— Pre-trial Order	Claimant and Respondent to exchange witness lists		
19—/01/16	GHI	Wallace	4141	12/5/— Pre-trial Order from Court	Witnesses not already disclosed made available for tele depo		
19—/01/16	LKJ	IATL Mtg.	—	1/6/— Letter from Green	Seminar outline due		
19—/01/18	GHI	Blackmore	4745	1/11/— Letter to Aldrin	Acceptance of Settlement		
19—/01/21	RHT	Hiller	4343	11/29/— Pre-trial Order	Joint Appendix and Brief		
19—/01/21	RKT	Fishman	4321	12/5/— Pre-trial Order	Brief – Points & Authorities		
19—/01/23	ISZ	Slater	4889	1/12/— Letter to Ralston	Answer, Third Party Action		
19—/01/24	LKJ	Peel	4650	10/30/— Intake memo	(Possible Med Mal) Declination letter sent 11/1/—	SOL	
19—/01/25	TCR	Vladin	4790	Petition served 1/5/—; Hammar Petition filed 1/5/—	Answer due		
19—/01/27	BGF	Farmer	4887	12/5/— Pre-trial Order	Rebuttal Brief		
19—/01/27	RKT	Barton	4002	10/27/— Order	Plaintiff to establish jurisdiction in Maine state court		

tickler for each piece of outgoing correspondence that requires a reply. Date it for an appropriate future time so that you can check to see if a follow-up letter is needed.

Using the system   The docket clerk or other designated person should be responsible for processing all ticklers. The file should remain at a designated location. The ticklers will be removed on the appropriate dates (i.e., sufficiently in advance of the event) and distributed to the responsible lawyer. A conspicuous location in the lawyer's office should be selected and the ticklers should always be placed there.

After the docket clerk has pulled the ticklers for the day, the date guide for that day is placed behind the last daily guide in the tickler system so that it may begin working forward again. This will also be done for the month and year guides in their turn, providing a perpetual calendar system.

The docket-control report   From the tickler cards, a master docket-control report or reminder sheet is typed and circulated to all responsible parties to advise them of upcoming deadlines (see Fig. 11.4). This docket report can be typed into a word-processing file and updated daily. The report will serve as a convenient summary on which notations can be made as actions are completed. The docket-control clerk or secretary responsible for the reminder sheet should be advised of any corrections, additions, or deletions.

A tickler system centralizes important due dates, providing a backup for the lawyer's and secretary's daily and monthly calendars. Given that both manual and computerized systems are in use, often in combination, it may be necessary to experiment a bit to arrive at the most practical and effective method for your office.

Records Management

Virtually every action in a law office results in some form of documentation, from simple notes of telephone messages to important appeal briefs, and a good management system is indispensable for the proper storage and retrieval of these records. In a small law firm, a secretary usually has control over every facet of records management. Primary tasks include opening files, filing incoming documents as well as documents generated in the office, keeping an index and cross-reference to the files, retrieving records, checking records to see that items are correctly placed, purging records at intervals, and destroying or transferring records to other storage areas at the proper time. In addition, the secretary may be asked to develop retention schedules that state when to dispose of records. Depending on the size of the firm, the secretary could also be responsible for personnel and accounting files as well as legal files.

The secretary in a large law firm or corporation usually works in conjunction with a records department that services the entire firm, and its records are housed in a central files facility. If the records department is set up to maintain control over all active cases, the secretary merely sees to it that all documents are correctly prepared and routed to the appropriate file by filling out a special filing form. When a document or file is requested by the attorney, the secretary calls the records department and gives it the information necessary for retrieval. The records-management staff in this case will assume responsibility for the filing, while the secretary retains only those documents or copies of documents that the attorney wishes to keep at hand. Thus, even in large firms with central records departments, the legal secretary may be responsible for the short-term management of a large number of active files.

The secretary who has control over all the attorney's files is in a position to control the speed and accuracy of a document's retrieval. This is done by creating a primary index and a cross-index system, by selecting suitable equipment and supplies, and by transferring or destroying records when appropriate. As a records manager, the secretary has three major duties:

1. ensuring that filing operations are systematized and uniform,
2. seeing that all information is easily located, and
3. carefully filing the documents.

Although attorneys frequently help to design the records-management system used in their offices, it is the secretary, file clerk, or central records department that normally assumes full responsibility for the daily maintenance of office files.

Computerized File Management

The future of records management for the law office rests with computer applications. The computer has already advanced word processing, legal research, and accounting in law offices. Now the management of legal records is being improved by linking microfilm and computers, by using computers for indexing, and by storing file information in data banks.

Using a *document-management program* you can name, file, and retrieve a wide variety of electronic documents, including files containing graphics, spreadsheets, databases, text documents, and other work products. Document-management programs enable you to store and retrieve all your documents quickly and easily; they can help you (1) keep track of commonly used forms; (2) track information from separate databases, such as marketing and cases in trial; (3) organize documents by client/matter number or by type of document; and (4) monitor document-preparation costs for the purposes of cost recovery or internal accounting.

Using these programs helps save time because you can locate a document without using the path or file name, do full-text search and retrieval, automate archival operations (deletions and restorations), group documents according to the method best suited to your law office, use a report writer to detail documentation, use long character strings to name a document, and ensure document security.

Computers also play a crucial role in litigation support, the process of preparing a case for trial. In complex and protracted litigation, documents collected can run into the millions. The gathering of data on such a large scale has resulted in the development of computer techniques to control it. Past procedures—using trial notebooks, tab locators, card indexes, and the like—have proved inadequate to handle discovery materials in many antitrust, product-liability, class-action, and labor-discrimination cases.

A computer can categorize and give instant access to the vast numbers of documents that contain evidentiary material relevant to a case at considerable savings in time and cost over older methods. Entire documents may be stored, keyed, indexed, and cross-referenced in computers. Documents may be reviewed by either a full-text or index method. In the full-text method, the entire text of each document is coded into the computer. In the index method, only key words from documents are coded on a database to assist a searcher in finding a document.

The cost of a computer litigation-support system is substantial, but expenses per document decrease as the number of documents increases. Small firms involved with document-heavy litigation usually share a computer system. In-house computer litigation-support systems are usually found only where the amount of litigation work with excessive documentation justifies the cost.

Confidentiality

You should assume that *all* the documents law firms generate are confidential. The Model Rules of Professional Conduct of the American Bar Association require that attorneys and all law-firm employees treat all information regarding a client with the utmost confidentiality. In addition to the canons of the ABA rules, there are federal regulations governing the release of certain kinds of information. The Securities and Exchange Commission, for example, may penalize law-firm employees found guilty of insider trading—that is, using confidential information to personal advantage by buying or selling securities. Furthermore, private companies that hold government materials are required by the Department of Defense to assign special control numbers to all classified documents kept on the company's premises. When a law firm represents one of these companies, any papers regarding the classified information also require control numbers, and a legal secretary should be aware of the importance of properly handling these documents.

Handling physical documents   Special procedures for handling classified or highly confidential material may be required. Documents marked with government terms such as "Limited Access" should be stored in locked cabinets or a safe. The attorney may direct a secretary to mark documents with a stamp noting "Attorney-client privilege, Confidential." Special codes could be affixed to files that contain confidential documents, or these documents could be separated from the main set of files in locked cabinets or on premises with limited access. Another method of protecting confidential client files or classified government papers is to microfilm them and place them in a bank for safekeeping. Each law office sets its own standards for the security of such documents. Some offices routinely lock most of their client files to prevent their easy removal. Locked files, however, are impractical for storing unclassified records that are frequently requested by attorneys.

Special procedures designed to ensure confidentiality may seem to prevent a filing system from reaching maximum efficiency. But in the law office, wherever efficiency conflicts with a client's trust, the latter always takes precedence.

Computer systems   Of special concern in today's law office is the safeguarding of confidential documents within the computer system. There are a variety of ways to ensure that unauthorized individuals do not have access to private documents. *Electronic theft of information is a very real and present danger.* No matter how much security you employ, if your document is stored on your computer, a determined individual will probably be able to circumvent your security. If a file's security has been compromised, you will usually be unaware of the theft. Very few electronic procedures will alert you to any previous access to the file. The only way to ensure absolute security is to provide complete physical protection of the document. For all practical purposes, this means putting the document on a floppy disk and storing it under lock and key.

Stand-alone computers Stand-alone desktop computers offer many excellent features built right into them. Depending on the level of security needed, you may find one of the following methods acceptable.

1. *Disk Storage* This is perhaps the most secure method available. All computer records and files of the classified document are stored on a floppy disk. (NOTE: Do not store a copy of the file. Store the actual file on the floppy disk.) After the document is safely transferred to the disk, the disk can then be stored in an appropriate manner under one of the methods discussed earlier. One of the biggest drawbacks to this type of storage is that it makes bringing up the computer record and storage of the document cumbersome and time-consuming. However, if you need absolute security, you must remove the document from the electronic environment.

2. *Passwords* Most computers will allow you an option in the initial setup sequence that requires a password to be input every time the unit is turned on. This provides an excellent first level of protection. One consideration with this type of protection is the number of people that need to have access to the computer. If more than one person will be using the computer on a regular basis, the opportunity for a security breach becomes greater with each person who knows the password.

3. *Key Locks* Most personal computers come with a lock-and-key mechanism. This mechanism neutralizes the keyboard command portion of the computer's startup routine. When powered up with the keyboard locked, the computer is fooled into thinking there is a system failure and will not activate itself.

Network systems Confidentiality on a network system becomes all the more difficult to maintain in that several users will have electronic access to the same information. You can apply the stand-alone techniques to your individual computer; however, in a network environment, anyone with terminal access to the network will have access to your information. Security measures beyond those available for a desktop computer are available to most network users, and if you are serious about protecting your documents you need to become familiar with some of the following options:

1. *Network Security* Your network administrator should be able to provide you with a personal password that you need to enter into the computer every time you log on. This password tells the computer what information you have access to. Regardless of where you log on to a system, your password will make all your information available to you. Conversely, information that you are not authorized to access will be suppressed.

2. *Document Security* Most programs that allow you to produce, store, and retrieve information will offer some form of document password security. In order for a user to call up a particular file, the software asks for a password. Unless the proper password is supplied, access to the information is denied.

3. *Encryption Software* A new development in document protection is the use of encryption programs. A user creates a document in a particular software,

and before saving it to a computer disk or hard drive runs the file through an encryption program. No one can retrieve the file without the decoding portion of the encryption program and the password to activate the process. As with most software programs, there are varying degrees of sophistication in encryption programs. You will certainly pay a little more for a top-level program, but if security is a top concern, such a program may be a wise investment.

The Records Manual

The filing system selected by an office should be followed by everyone on the staff. Disparate systems will work only as long as files at one secretarial station are never commingled with files from another. Uniformity is achieved by creating standard procedures and policies and teaching them to the staff. This is where a records manual becomes necessary. The manual typically is planned and written by the firm's management in cooperation with secretaries and filing staff. All aspects of a firm's records operations should be included in the manual, from file creation to microfilm recording. A records manual should include the following information:

1. Statement of objectives
2. Description of the filing system and procedures
3. Description of filing equipment
4. List of items to be considered as records
5. List of terminology used to describe file contents
6. Retention schedules
7. Transfer and destruction requirements and procedures
8. Special procedures for extraordinary material
9. Facsimiles of all filing forms, retention slips, charge-out forms, etc., that the office uses

The records manual, which may be incorporated into the firm's general office manual, helps new employees—both attorneys and support staff—learn the firm's records-management system. For this reason, a manual is useful in law firms of every size. The manual should be durable, and its contents should be clearly stated. Seminars may be held to introduce it to the staff and to answer questions about filing procedures and policies. Everything must be done to ensure that the manual is taken seriously. This is a necessity; effective records management requires the total cooperation of the law-office staff. The manual should be periodically reviewed and revised.

Types of Law-Office Files

Different kinds of records are maintained in every law office. The secretary must learn the categories in order to file documents accurately and retrieve them speedily. A new secretary should first review the manual, then survey existing files to become familiar with the subject areas of the law practice and the common types of documents. If no manual exists, the secretary may prepare a computerized list or card index containing all the file subjects and the document types with the appropriate terminology. This index will provide the standard for classifying current and future documents.

When a new document is ready to be filed, the secretary must classify it. The categories most commonly used in law offices include client files, legal-opinion and memoranda files, form files, office-administration files, the attorney's personal files, miscellaneous correspondence files, and files for catalogs and bulletins. Additional, separate files may also be maintained for such subjects as client histories, legislative histories, time summaries, and collections.

Client Cases and Matters

Client files are the most frequently handled files in a law office. To make large numbers of client files more manageable, most firms keep separate cabinets for active and inactive files. Client files are generally grouped according to the name of the client, with each case or matter assigned a separate file. For example, a law firm representing the XYZ Corporation might have a dozen or more files for matters such as annual meetings, stock divestiture, or Federal Trade Commission matters—each of which is filed separately under the XYZ name. In many offices, client files are routinely divided into nonlitigation and litigation matters, with the nonlitigation matters sorted alphabetically by subject and litigation matters alphabetically by opposing party or by plaintiff. Nonlitigation matters may be further divided into specific fields of law such as contracts, real estate, bankruptcy, and the like. If a client file includes a very large number of cases, they may be sorted according to the lawyer handling the case, with cases or matters further subdivided within the lawyer grouping.

A basic fact sheet, often called a *client-intake form* or *new-matter sheet,* is usually prepared prior to the opening of a file and attached to the outside or to the inside front of each case/matter folder (see Fig. 6.2, p. 135). This sheet prevents unnecessary searches through the file for certain data. It may include the client's address and telephone number, the name and address of the opposing party, a summary of the progress of the case with dates, how and when the client is to be billed, and other information such as a statute of limitations or the opposing attorney's name. Cross-indexes should be maintained for all client files (see below, pp. 381–84).

Contents of a client case/matter file Client files contain all the documents that relate to the client's affairs, categorized first according to the particular case or matter, then to subjects and document types. These categories are often separated by file dividers within the case/matter folder. The particular arrangement varies widely from office to office and is not nearly as important as the practice of arranging papers in the same order in every client file. Case/matter folders generally have two major divisions, correspondence and formal papers, with correspondence placed first. But if there is a large number of records, the following categories may be used with additional folders or folder dividers:

1. *Correspondence* This file can be divided into correspondence with the client and correspondence with others concerning the matter. If the correspondence covers several years, it may be further subdivided chronologically. Because of the volume of letters written and received, it is often helpful to create these categories.

2. *Conference Memoranda* This file contains notes on attorney-client discussions made in meetings and in telephone conversations. It may also include telephone messages.

3. *Investigations* Discovery material—i.e., case inquiries, examination of accident details, medical reports, character examinations, interviews with prospective witnesses, and other documents generated by exploratory, fact-finding work-is placed in this file. If investigations are extensive, the material should be subdivided.

4. *Legal Research* The research file includes copies of relevant cases, statutes, issues, rules, and regulations; printouts of computerized legal research; and other information pertinent to the legal aspects of a case.

5. *Memoranda of Law* Formal statements of law or other questions pertinent to a case should be maintained in a separate memoranda-of-law section. Because a legal memorandum prepared for one case may have value in another case, the different subjects covered by the memorandum should be listed in a cross-reference index. Memoranda of law are frequently removed from a client file when they become inactive and placed in a separately maintained memoranda file in the firm's library.

6. *Formal Papers* Significant documents such as wills, trusts, agreements, and copies of court pleadings are normally placed in a separate section for formal papers. If certain types of papers such as pleadings or motions are numerous, separate folders should be made for them, with attached checklists of their contents. It is especially important that original papers be protected from excessive handling.

7. *Billing* The billing file is always separate. It contains recorded transactions concerning the attorney's billable progress on a case. It includes bills and invoices, receipts, time and work summaries, copies of checks, disbursement cards, telephone slips, and all other documents relevant to charging for the work performed in the client's behalf. The items in this file may be transferred to the accounting department if that is office policy, but having them in the client file is helpful to an attorney when a client requests information about the legal expenses involved in his case.

8. *Miscellaneous Documents* This category may include, among other things, the exhibits needed for litigation.

These eight categories are among those frequently used. Categories will, however, vary a great deal. Firms that handle many personal-injury cases, for instance, might routinely include a divider tabbed for medical bills, while a divorce action might include a category for the inventory of assets. Being familiar with the office manual and the different types of documents in the client files will enable a secretary to devise standard classification terms for uniform filing and efficient retrieval.

Other Filing Categories

In addition to their client case/matter files, most law firms use separate file cabinets or drawers for various other categories of documents. The following are the most common file types:

1. *Opinion Files* Copies of each important brief, court opinion, court decision, and law-firm opinion generated in the course of handling a client matter may be placed in a separate filing cabinet. These documents are preserved

because they might be needed as references in a similar case in the future. To make these documents accessible for future reference, their contents should be recorded in a file-management database or a cross-reference index.

2. *Memoranda-of-Law Files* Each memorandum of law written by the firm should be maintained in a file for future reference. The secretary or records department must create a retrieval system for them. As in the case of opinion files, an index should be made to categorize the memoranda. Two file copies may be made of the original memorandum, one for the client file and one for the memoranda file. To avoid duplication, a single file copy could be placed in the client file with a cross-reference guide in the memoranda file that indicates the location of the document.

3. *Form Files, Physical* The form file stores standard documents that contain "boilerplate" language—that is, paragraphs or whole pages that are used repeatedly and therefore have permanent value. Examples of formal documents such as standard contracts, motions, and pleadings may be stored in this file. Using these standard documents as models for the preparation of similar documents saves time for both lawyer and secretary and results in a lower fee to the client. In addition to boilerplate, this file may also be used to store sample legal blanks—tax, court, government agency, and other forms—although a few copies of frequently used forms may also be kept at the attorney's or secretary's desk. A forms index should be maintained.

4. *Form Files, Computerized* The computer system lends itself well to maintaining boilerplate forms and generating documents for the client from these forms.

5. *Client Histories* Many law firms keep separate files of documents relating to the history of a corporate client. Papers concerning a corporation's formation and financial background, annual reports and other company publications, and a history of all work performed for the client can be helpful. Information about individual clients, on the other hand, is ordinarily kept in the client's case/matter file.

6. *Legislative Histories* Although usually found on library shelves, materials relating to legislative histories (hearing reports, floor debates, bills, committee reports) may be placed in separate files, tabbed, and indexed. If a firm specializes to such an extent that certain laws are frequently researched, it may help the attorney if a secretary, legal assistant, or librarian assembles and maintains a ready-made file of all historical material pertaining to those laws.

7. *Office Staff Matters* This file contains records regarding personnel and office maintenance, including interoffice memoranda, equipment purchase and repair records, and the like. Depending upon the size of the office, these files may be kept by the secretary or by the office administrator.

8. *Personal Matters* The personal files of an attorney might contain information about bar-association activities, community affairs, and family financial matters as well as personal correspondence. This file is arranged alphabetically and needs no indexing.

9. *Reading Files* A special file is set up in some offices for the attorney's daily correspondence. A copy of every letter sent and received, arranged in chronological order and separated by year and month, is placed in this "chron" file so that the attorney may periodically review them. However,

such a file requires extra copies of correspondence and is not necessary if a calendaring system such as that described in the first part of this chapter has been set up with built-in ticklers.

10. *Time Summaries* Each attorney keeps daily records of his or her billable and nonbillable time. These should be collected and filed. Weekly, biweekly, or monthly time summaries may then be prepared for use by the firm's management.

11. *Collections* When the number of commercial collections that a firm handles becomes significant, a separate collections file may be set up. A separate file is helpful because of the constant attention that must be paid to collections.

12. *Publications* A file devoted to items such as suppliers' catalogs, brochures, and bulletins may be set up. However, to be useful, it must be strictly organized and periodically purged of outdated publications.

13. *Miscellaneous Correspondence* The letters in this file are arranged alphabetically by the name of the correspondent.

Types of Filing Systems

Centralized, Decentralized, and Combination Systems

Record storage can be either centralized, decentralized, or a combination of the two.

In a *centralized* system, the firm's records are kept in a central filing facility until the retention schedule or the responsible attorney directs their destruction or transfer to outside archives. Certain staff members are authorized to remove or refile records and other resource material. Large law offices generally maintain centralized systems in order to ensure prompt and convenient delivery of all files to all users. In a centralized system, the legal secretary requests documents, photocopies of documents, or whole files for the attorney's use from the records-department staff.

Small firms generally keep *decentralized* files because usually only one attorney works on a single case. In a decentralized system, the secretary has complete control over the files. Any requests for records are directed to the secretary rather than to a clerk in a central records area. Active files are maintained near the secretary's workstation. A secretary's office or workstation usually includes vertical or lateral file cabinets, while other means of storage-open shelves, electrically operated mobile units, microfilm, computer tape-are likely to be found in central records.

Many law firms have found that a *combination* of centralized and decentralized records-management systems increases efficiency. In these cases, the secretary typically keeps all active files at the workstation but, when a file is closed, sends it to the central facility. This procedure allows the attorney to control the active files. By checking with the attorney, the secretary can constantly monitor the amount of space needed for new files and arrange the transfer of less active files to the central location.

The decision to adopt a centralized or decentralized filing system or a combination of the two depends on a number of factors. The size of the law firm, the volume of files it generates, the number of people who handle the documents, and the availability of time for a secretary to maintain an individual filing system will all affect this decision.

Computerized Filing Systems

Computerized document-storage systems must address how information is going to be stored to help facilitate quick and easy retrieval at a later date. Although computers don't lose documents by themselves, you can easily lose a document in the computer system if you don't have a systematic approach to naming and storing your documents. The following three things should be considered when developing such a system:

1. The type of *directory structure* to be used
2. The type of *document labeling system* to be used
3. The feasibility of using a *software-driven system* for document labeling and storage

Directory structure   Directory structure within the computer is the equivalent of the filing system commonly used for physical files. Refer to your computer manual for specific procedures in creating directories. The key consideration is that all personnel who will be creating and storing documents on the system should be properly trained in its use.

Usually you will create an electronic directory to store frequently used documents. These are called form directories. The following is an example of a form directory for family-law documents:

I. Family-Law Forms.
   A. Dissolution
   B. Adoptions
   C. Guardianship/Conservatorship
   D. Paternal
   E. General Forms

This, of course, is just one type of directory. Each firm would design and maintain many different directories for their documents.

Labeling system   After you have developed your directory structure, you need to consider how you will label your documents. The labeling system you use should identify the date the document was created and the directory in which it is filed. For example, in the label *95JUN127.PEP* the first part of the label (*95Jun*) indicates the year and month the document was created, the second part (*127*) is the directory number, and the part following the period (*PEP*) indicates the author of the document. The specific elements used in labels will differ from office to office, but in general it is a good idea to include the date and directory number and to apply the labeling system consistently to all documents in use.

Software-driven labeling   A number of software-driven labeling systems are available that will automatically label and store your documents. These systems are particularly effective when they are automatically activated each time a new document is created on the system. The sophistication of the labeling software you use will depend on the number of documents you store and the need to create multiple directories.

Alphabetic and Numeric Filing

Alphabetic Filing

In alphabetically arranged files, information can be retrieved directly, simply by going to the correct alphabetic sequence in the files. The office staff, however, must adhere to a strict alphabetic sequence, and all personnel must have a clear understanding of the rules of alphabetizing.

Client files in an alphabetic system are arranged by the individual client's surname and by the company's corporate name. In many instances, a client will have two or more cases or matters in the file. The file arrangement most commonly used by law firms contains the following sequence, each in alphabetic order: client name, case or matter name(s), and subject(s). For example, the XYZ Corporation might have separate files for matters involving separate government agencies such as the Federal Trade Commission and the Occupational Safety and Health Administration. A legal matter might be filed under the following guides:

> Client name: XYZ CORPORATION
> Case or matter: FTC
> Subject: FLAMMABILITY STANDARDS

Files may also be broken down alphabetically within major categories of a client file such as litigation and nonlitigation. In those files where a subject (such as a point of law or the name of a case) rather than a proper name is the unit of reference for filing, the subjects are filed alphabetically.

Alphabetic files make retrieval time short because information can be located directly without the use of a separate index. However, misspelled names and errors in alphabetizing can cause retrieval problems. A more serious problem with alphabetic files is the difficulty in planning for expansion; the secretary must leave enough space in the cabinets in the appropriate alphabetic sequences to accommodate the attorney's future client files.

Alphabetizing names of individuals   The following guidelines should be used to alphabetize individual names:

1. Alphabetize the names of individuals by surname + given name or initial + middle name or initial.

   > Jones, M. Arthur
   > Jones, Mary Ann

2. Alphabetize letter by letter to the end of the surname, then the given names and initials.

   > Morison, John A.
   > Morison, John Thomas
   > Morrison, John Andrew

3. Treat hyphenated or compound names as one word.

Fitzgerald, Marcia	Foster-Brown, James	Vandella, James
Fitz Smith, Patrick	Fosteri, Arnold	van der Meer, Howard
		Van Dyne, Helen

4. Disregard titles such as *Dr., Mrs., Captain,* or *Senator* when alphabetizing. However, these designations may be included to provide additional identifying information.

   Nyhus, Lloyd (Dr.)
   Smith, Walter (Senator)

5. Treat religious titles (such as *Reverend* and *Sister*) similarly.

   Raphael, Mary (Sister)
   Smith, John (Reverend)

6. Alphabetize abbreviated elements (such as *St.*) as if they were spelled out *(Saint).*

   St. Peter, Joanne
   Saint-Simon, Paul
   Sarris, Eleanor

7. Disregard designations such as *Jr., Sr.,* or *2nd* in filing.

   Smith, John T. (Sr.)
   Smith, John Thomas (Jr.)

8. Use the legal signature of a married woman when filing. Her husband's name may be cross-referenced if desired.

   Poulet, Marie Anne (Mrs. Paul Poulet)

9. File "nothing" before "something' if initials are used for a given name.

   Peters, J.
   Peters, J. G.
   Peters, John

10. Arrange surnames having prefixes such as *de, La,* and *Mac* just as they are spelled.

Macdonald, Rose	Deforest, Charles R.	Lapierre, Rita R.
MacDougal, John	DeMarco, Hector	LaRosa, Dino and Fay
McDonough, Mary	de Vries, Philip	La Salle, Kenneth H.

11. If you are uncertain which name is the surname, file under the last name given and provide a cross-reference for any other possible surname.

    Hop, Chin Sing [with cross-references at *Chin* and *Sing*]
    Hope, Genevieve Carson [with a cross-reference at Carson]

Alphabetizing names of organizations or businesses When indexing the names of organizations or businesses, rules similar to those just described are observed. For example, in a company name beginning with the full name of an individual, the name is inverted so that the surname appears first. In the name *Ted Corvair, Inc.,* the first unit becomes *Corvair* and the second unit becomes *Ted.* When no complete name of an individual is used—for example, *Corvair Construction Company*—the company name is indexed as it is ordinarily written. Companies operating under two different names are indexed under the name used most often and cross-referenced under the other name. Compound words and hyphenated names are treated as single units. Compound geographical names are treated differently, however. *The Palo Alto Trust* would be filed under *Palo* as first unit, *Alto* as second unit, and *Trust* as third unit; the initial *The* should be ignored (but any *internal* articles, prepositions, or conjunctions would be included as elements for alphabetization). Punctuation is also ignored: *Smith's Grocery* would be alphabetized as *Smiths.*

Single letters in names such as those used in radio or television stations are treated as separate units; thus, *KXYZ* would be filed near the beginning of the *K* section. Names of companies beginning with numbers in figure form are filed in numerical order at the front of the entire file. If the numbers are spelled out, however, the name is filed alphabetically. For example, *21st Century Corp.* would be filed in the front section of the complete files, while *One Main Street* would be filed alphabetically under the *O*'s. Names of foreign firms are filed as they are normally written unless elements of them are identifiable as surnames, in which case they are treated like their English counterparts.

Schools name for their geographical location are indexed by the geographical name; for example, *Tulsa, University of.* In an alphabetical listing, *Tulsa Junior College* would follow *Tulsa, University of.* (Since *Tulsa* is the only unit that precedes the comma, the rule of "nothing before something" applies.)

Alphabetizing governmental and political entities   When indexing government correspondence, use the most important word. Many companies file according to the rule that the first three units are always *United States Government,* followed by the name of the department, bureau, or commission. The same approach is taken with states and cities: the official name of the state is used first (e.g., *Texas, State of* or *Virginia, Commonwealth of*), followed by the applicable department, bureau, or division within the state government. Military installations are first filed under *United States Government* and then under the name of the installation (fort, station, base, etc.). Foreign governments are treated like states and cities; a record from a department of the government of South Korea would be filed first under *Korea, Republic of (South Korea)* and then under the department's name.

Although the alphabetization rules provided here are widely observed, you must primarily follow any particular indexing system used by your firm. The records manager should be able to brief you on established guidelines.

Numeric Filing

A second filing system is the numeric. It is commonly used by firms that require records to be continually added for new clients and new matters. In a numeric filing system, each file is given a number and arranged sequentially. The first numbered file is for the first client; as new folders are required, new numbers are added in strict numeric sequence. The maintenance of numeric files is time-consuming because of the additional procedures needed. For example, an accession register that houses a record of the numbers assigned must be maintained. The register is a complete list of clients in numeric order beginning with 1; it may be in book or card form. It requires only three columns: (1) the numbers, (2) the clients' names, and (3) the dates of assignment. The purpose of the register is to prevent the same number from being given to two different clients. It may also be used to record the date at which the file is transferred to inactive status.

In addition to the accession register, a cross-index must be maintained. The cards in the cross-index are arranged alphabetically by client name. Separate cross-reference cards are prepared under the matter name or adverse party name, each giving the file number. Consulting the index before locating the file takes extra time, but this disadvantage is generally thought to be offset by the advantages of the numeric system, which include the following:

1. Papers may be refiled rapidly and accurately and the number of misfiles reduced, since people are less likely to file numbers out of sequence than names.
2. Orderly expansion is possible through the use of additional numbers.
3. Speedy retrieval is possible because it is unnecessary to search through several files labeled with the same surname in order to find the right full name.
4. Numbered labels give a client's files an extra measure of privacy.

Moreover, in the case of files frequently referred to, once the number of the file is determined and noted by the secretary or attorney, the file can be requested or retrieved directly by number.

In a numeric filing system, clients are each given a master or key number. Each case or matter of the client is given a subnumber or number-letter combination. For example, a file for the XYZ Corporation/FTC might be given the code 4300-01NL (nonlitigation), while XYZ Corporation/OSHA is given the number 4300-02L (litigation). Many coding variations are possible. Litigation and nonlitigation cases can be assigned special numbers instead of identifying letters, or litigation case files can assume the court docket numbers. Many offices arrange files numerically according to the year the case was opened, along with a series number; thus 95-001 would be the first case opened in 1995. Some law offices reserve a series of numbers for certain types of cases; for example, 1–200 for tax, 201–400 for real estate, and so forth. In these cases the numeric system for filing often matches with the numeric system used by the accounting department of the firm.

When it is time to transfer a file to inactive status or to place it in storage, it should be assigned a special inactive status or transfer number. Index cards for these files should be either so marked or else removed to a separate index-card file for inactive cases.

Indexing and Cross-Reference

Indexing is used to show where a record has been filed so that it can be found when needed. If a computerized document-management system is not used in your office, a file containing index cards may serve the same purpose. Whichever system is used, individual index entries should be structured as simply as possible. Any information that will expedite record retrieval and make filing more efficient should be entered; any other information should be omitted.

The index entry for a client matter may contain the following information: name of client, case/matter designation, file number and location, list of principal subjects, list of principal documents with dates, retention period, transfer and destruction dates, and other data needed for the office filing system (see Fig. 11.5).

An index entry prepared from an appeal brief might contain the following information: subject of law, identification of case, name of document, and location of document (see Fig. 11.6). In some cases, an index entry may refer to

Fig. 11.5   Index-file Entry for Client Matter

Client: Harkness, John M.	*File No.:* 100-02-H	
Case/Matter: U.S. v. Harkness, Attempted Burglary		
Classification	*Location*	*Retain Until*
Docket File, Correspondence, 19--	Shelf 2 Section 2	Until case is settled

Remarks:

Since the pleadings in this case will be of further use in drafting similar documents in the future, transfer the pleadings in the DOCKET FILE to the FORMS FILE when the case is completed.

Fig. 11.6   Index-file Entry for Appeal Brief

Issue: Title VII Racial Discrimination
West Key Number Digest Classification: 43XX-D
Case: Ray v. Home Corp. (2d Cir. 1969)
Document: Brief for Appellants
Location:

File Cabinet 1, Shelf 2, Opinions, File 1, Tab A |

Fig. 11.7   Cross-reference Entry (Index File)

```
Client:  Domestic Fence Company

See Also:       Association of Chain Link Fence
                      Companies
                The "Chain Link" Report
                B&L Fencing, Inc.
                High Post Fencing Companies
```

several briefs in which the same question of law appears. If the documents are filed by case title, subject entries are prepared as cross-references to the case title; if filed by subject, case-title entries are used as cross-references. The opinion-files index can be set up either alphabetically by subject or case title or numerically in accordance with a numbering system such as West Publishing Company's key-number digest classification (see in Chapter 13) or one of original design.

If there is any chance that a file might be requested under a title other than the one under which it is filed, a cross-reference index entry should be prepared for the alternative title, referring searchers to the proper location. Cross-reference entries should always be prepared for litigated cases in the name of both plaintiff and defendant, and may also be made with names of opposing attorneys. Cross-referencing is also helpful when one cannot recall how

Fig. 11.8   Cross-reference Sheet (Regular Files)

```
Client:  Domestic Fence Company

See Also:  Incorporation

Partner-in-Chief:  Ralph P. Kittredge

Date Opened:   9/1/--

Date Closed:   _____

File Number:   122-01   NL

Adverse Party: None

See following clients or titles:
        Association of Chain Link Fence Companies
        The "Chain Link" Report
        B&L Fencing, Inc.
        High Post Fencing Companies
```

to properly index the name of a government agency or court, or when a client company is referred to by an abbreviated form such as an acronym. A copy of a legal-periodical article filed under its title may be cross-referenced under the subject or the periodical name to save time in searching for it.

A simple cross-reference entry for a client matter is shown in Fig. 11.7; some firms also prepare more comprehensive cross-reference sheets and place these in the files (see Fig. 11.8)

Handling and Storage of Records

Filing Equipment

Your workstation will usually house vertical or lateral filing cabinets. Other means of storage such as open shelves, card files, microfilm, and computer tape are likely to be found in central records. Only the records necessary for day-to-day operations—records used at least once a month—should be kept in the office. All other material is generally considered inactive and should be moved to central storage, from which it can be retrieved by request when needed.

Vertical and lateral cabinets   Vertical storage cabinets may be from two to five drawers in height. Each drawer should be labeled to indicate its contents and should also contain file guides to provide quick reference and adequate physical support for the folders. Each drawer should have from 20 to 25 guides. Letters should be filed left side down in folders, with the most recent letters at the front of each folder. No folder should contain more than 50 sheets of paper.

The order of the guides and folders in a typical drawer is shown in Fig. 11.9: main guide, individual folders, "Out" guides or folders, special name guides, permanent cross-reference guides, and a miscellaneous folder at the end of the section for material not yet considered active. (Some records managers think miscellaneous folders should not be used at all. If they are used, no more than five pieces on a given subject should be allowed to accumulate there before an individual file is set up.

In vertical cabinets, hanging folders may be used. The sides of hanging folders have hooks which enable the folders to hang from a frame inserted in the file drawer. Hanging folders can hold larger numbers of records than regular folders and the tab may be moved to different positions.

Lateral filing cabinets generally permit speedier storage and retrieval than vertical cabinets. The length of the cabinet lies against the wall and the drawers pull out only about one foot. The fronts of the folders face the left side of the drawer. The back ledge of the cabinet may be moved to accommodate either letter-size or legal-size folders. Like vertical cabinets, lateral cabinets may be from two to five drawers in height.

Open-shelf storage   Open shelves have become popular because of the savings in space over normal cabinets (up to 50 percent) and the quick and easy reference they offer for highly active files. Only where there is neither air-condi-

Fig. 11.9   Guide and Folder Arrangement for Cabinet Files

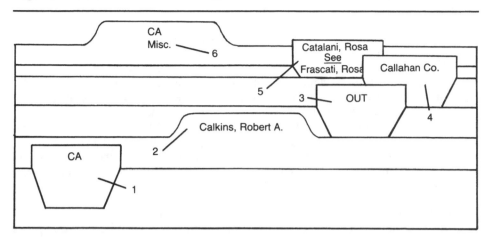

1. *Alphabetical caption guide* The guide tabs usually are positioned on the left.
2. *Individual account folder* Most account correspondence and data regarding a company's clients are kept in such folders.
3. *Out guide* "Out" guides or substitution cards, with tabs at center right, record the identity and location of folders that have been removed.
4. *Special name guide* Special guides can be inserted at the far right for very active accounts that have more than one folder or that require special handling.
5. *Permanent cross-reference guide* These guides direct the user to a folder at another location.
6. *Miscellaneous folder* These folders, placed at the end of each letter-caption category, hold material not yet of sufficient quantity to require an individual folder.

tioning nor air filtration would the use of open-shelf storage be questionable, since dust and humidity can be harmful to records. Open shelves are sometimes constructed on tracks for movability, requiring less floor space and making filing and retrieving even easier.

Automated systems An automated storage and retrieval system offers the advantages of optimum convenience, rapid retrieval, concentration of vast amounts of file material in a small amount of floor space, and superior control over records. Automated units are rotating, electronically driven carriers up to 30 feet high which present the operator with the desired tray at the touch of a button. Some machines can automatically sort and retrieve individual files or cards, thus reducing the handling of material and protecting it against excessive wear. Automated storage and retrieval systems also handle microfilm and are adaptable to computer applications. However, mechanized filing operations are extremely expensive and thus are economical only for users with a high daily volume of filing and a minimum amount of space.

Card cabinets Information for basic reference can be filed in card cabinets of various sizes. The most common card sizes are $3'' \times 5''$, $4'' \times 6''$, $5'' \times 8''$, and

$6'' \times 9''$. The most sophisticated card cabinets are those in automatic retrieval units.

Visible card cabinets are small desktop cabinets with numerous flat traylike drawers. Racks in these drawers hold cards (usually $6'' \times 4''$ or $8'' \times 5''$) in an overlapping arrangement that permits very rapid access. They are commonly used for indexes to the location and status of other records.

Tickler files—described in detail above (pp. 365–68)—usually use $3'' \times 5''$ cards and contain reminders for following up projects or meetings. When the tickler file takes the form of a tub file on wheels instead of a card file, guides and folders (12 guides for the months and 31 folders for the days) are arranged in a similar way. Letters that need following up are placed in folders behind the dates or months on which action must be taken. Special folders are also available with sliding tabs that indicate the dates on which action should be taken.

Microfilm storage   The use of microfilm—a method for miniaturizing records on film—can markedly reduce storage space requirements. When hard copy is converted to microfilm (usually by a professional microfilming service), only two percent of the space taken up by the original material is necessary for the microfilm. Microfilm can be filed on 16-mm. and 35-mm. rolls in color or in black and white, and housed in cartridges or magazines. Other microfilm forms, or *microforms*, include microfiche (card-sized pieces of film), ultrafiche (reduced-image microfiche), and computer-output microfilm (a direct computer-to-film technology). Storage cabinets, binders, and small tubs are available for storing microforms.

Computer tape storage   Computer tapes can hold a tremendous amount of information, save large amounts of space, and afford fast information retrieval. A special closed cabinet or a rack kept in a closed area can be used to store these tapes. There are also storage boxes designed so that the tapes slide forward as one is taken out, thus facilitating retrieval. The tapes are indexed, and a record is kept of the location of each tape so that information can be located fast.

Optical disks   The electronic-imaging industry was spawned with the invention of the laser optical disk. The disk offers a high-density, long-lasting alternative to other methods.

Folders, Labels, and Guides

Folders   Plain file folders come in a variety of shapes and sizes. A set of folders will normally include equal numbers of folders with tabs at the left, center, and right, permitting the user to stagger them in the file for maximum tab visibility. On "1/3 cut" folders, the tabs are one-third the width of the entire folder; on "1/5 cut" folders, one-fifth the width; and so on.

End- or side-tabbed folders are designed for use in lateral file cabinets or on open shelves. Accordion or expandable file folders (sometimes secured with string) are used to hold a large number of documents; they may have tabs on either the top or the side. Ring folders have two-pronged fasteners that securely attach the records, which must be punched before filing. Folders also may be purchased with several attached inserts, each with its own fastener, or with plain dividers.

Hanging folders, as described earlier, hang from racks inserted in (or built into) the files drawer, by means of hooks at either end of the top of the folder. Since they slide easily along the rack and do not sag even when full, they permit easy access to their contents. They are stronger but more expensive than standard folders.

Folders are commonly made of four types of material:

- *Manila* The most common and least expensive folder material. Available with wax or Mylar coating for extra durability, and available in various colors (though "manila" frequently refers only to sand-colored folders).
- *Kraft* Heavier; brown; quite durable; does not soil easily. More expensive than manila; should be used only for folders subjected to much wear and tear.
- *Pressboard* Expensive, durable material; more suitable for guides than for folders.
- *Vinyl or other plastic* Very durable, thus suitable for holding papers of permanent value, but quite expensive. Very smooth in texture, hence slippery and not good for stacking. Available in a variety of colors.

Law offices frequently use specially printed file folders for client matters so that information about the case may be filled in on the outside of the folder. This allows for quick perusal of the file's contents as well as a review of the history of the case. Printed folders with lines for fill-ins may be custom-printed or purchased from law-office supply companies. Law-office supply companies also provide preprinted envelopes for storing specific types of documents. Litigation filing envelopes, multipurpose court-docket envelopes, and docket envelopes designed for real estate or contract matters are examples. Prenumbered and color-coded folders are also commercially available.

Labels All folders that are not preprinted should be identified with pressure-sensitive (self-adhesive) labels typed neatly and consistently. The caption should be typed as close as possible to the top of the label for greatest visibility. Runovers are usually indented, and sub-captions are blocked with the caption. If the label includes both an index number and a name, adequate space should separate the two. The primary indexing units should precede any secondary units.

> 6.78 Schwartz, Howard M., Inc.
> Footwear Division

Color-coded labels marked with letters or numbers provide an excellent system for files, because one can instantly see if a file is out of sequence by noticing that the colors do not match. A color system may work in one of several ways. A particular color may denote the first two or three letters of a name (e.g., "Co" in Fig. 11.9); labels may be used to indicate each large grouping of files; or a single color may be used for a given year.

Guides To expedite filing and retrieving, guides should be placed throughout the files to separate the cards or folders into groups. In card files, one guide should be placed after 25 cards.

When purchasing guides, remember that durability and visibility are the most important considerations. The tab on each guide should project far enough above the folders to be completely visible. In straight numeric files, new guides must be added regularly; in alphabetic files, the guides are usually permanent. Guides should be made of pressboard or vinyl. Pressboard is generally preferable because most records need heavy guides for support; vinyl guides are satisfactory for card files. Since guides are sold in sets based on the size of the files, consider potential growth in your files when purchasing guides.

"Out" guides, special name guides, and permanent cross-reference guides should also be used. Guides may be color-coded like labels to differentiate alphabetic and numeric sections or divisions.

Steps in Filing

An important issue in handling records is determining how long they should be kept. Retention schedules—set up with the cooperation of the records administrator or attorney in charge—are a necessity in maintaining control over records. A retention schedule lists categories of records, the attorney or division responsible for the originals, retention periods, the place where the records are to be stored, microfilming instructions where relevant, and sometimes an indication of the method of destruction.

Documents should be filed daily to reduce the chance of their being misplaced. Procedures to be observed when preparing for the storage of records include the following:

1. Read or scan the document.
2. Be sure that a *release mark* (initials, date, or stamped code), indicating that the document is ready for storage, appears on it.
3. If your system permits it, place a numerical file code or a name or subject code in an upper corner of the document to indicate where the material should be stored. (Some records administrators prefer to do this themselves.)
4. Place on the document another code that will indicate how long it must be retained. (Again, some records administrators prefer to do this themselves.)
5. Check to see whether the record needs cross-referencing. If it might be called for by a title other than the one it is filed under, write "X" in the margin and prepare a cross-reference index entry for it.
6. Arrange the material in the order in which it will be stored.
7. Prepare any necessary follow-up notations for a tickler file.
8. Remove unnecessary paper clips to eliminate bulk and prevent damage to the documents. Mend torn pages and smooth out wrinkles.
9. Place documents in the proper sections of the folder, left side down, with the most recent records toward the front.
10. If certain documents are too large to fit in the folder, insert a cross-reference sheet that refers readers to a special area for oversized documents.

Approximately 25 percent of the records crossing your desk each day can probably be destroyed or recycled immediately or passed on to some other person for disposition.

Reading, scanning, and coding   Look for the most important name or subject, and underscore or circle it in pencil, or write or code it onto the letter if it is not mentioned in the text itself. The code will include numbers or letters or both, depending on the filing system being used. Care should be taken to select the proper code or subject heading. Some records administrators prefer that the secretary not code records that are being sent to central records, as the records personnel will be more familiar with the storage categories. You can, however, always code the records that you will store yourself.

Indicate to the filing personnel that the record is ready to be filed by initialing it or by stamping it "File" or "Release," typically in the upper right corner.

Retention codes   As a help to the filing personnel, each document should be marked with a code indicating the retention period of the material (30 days, 60 days, one year, etc.). The retention schedule will indicate whether the records are then to be transferred to inactive storage, microfilmed, or placed in computer storage in accordance with established company policy.

Follow-up   If an attorney expects to want to see a given record in the near future, you or the attorney should indicate on the record the date when it should be returned. If the record is being sent to the records center, you or the records personnel should add a card to the tickler file as a reminder.

Controlling Documents in Storage

No matter how or when records are stored, a system for controlling their location and movement must be established and observed by all personnel. If there is no control, records may be missing when they are needed or may fall into the wrong hands. When you have accepted a record for safekeeping, every precaution must be taken to protect that record so that it will be available when needed. A simple method of protecting firm records is to permit only authorized personnel to withdraw material from the files.

Charge-out procedures   Removal of a record from the files should not be permitted until it has been properly charged out. A record can be charged out to a person who officially requests it for a specific length of time using a special form. This requisition, which should include a description of the record (including whatever information appears on the label or tab), the date of release, and the person's signature, can often also serve as a charge-out form. The form should be inserted into a pocket on the Out guide. If only one record is removed, then an Out guide or substitution card can replace the charged-out record in the file. Consider using an Out folder rather than a guide when an entire folder has been charged out; the Out folder will serve to hold new records that arrive temporarily.

An "On Call" guide may replace the Out folder. The On Call guide directs the filing personnel to send the folder on to the person listed on the guide itself when the folder is returned. Only when the material is back in its place can the Out or On Call guide be removed for reuse.

Confidential and classified materials   Special precautions must be exercised when highly confidential or classified documents are in your possession or stored in the records center. In addition to the normal protection just mentioned, a firm can use a safe or a built-in vault large enough for holding document-storage equipment. Another method of protecting confidential or classified documents is to duplicate or microfilm the material and then give it to a bank for safekeeping.

Firms that deal with the government are required by the Department of Defense to assign special control numbers to any classified documents kept on company premises, as well as communications (such as letters and memorandums) regarding these contracts or projects. Although the responsibility for maintaining records for these classified documents will be in the hands of knowledgeable attorneys within the firm, you must be aware of the necessity for control numbers and any other identification that may be placed on classified documents.

In addition to following special storage procedures for confidential and classified documents, take care not to leave them uncovered on desks; be sure that they have cover pages and are kept in drawers or locked areas when not being used. Classified documents may not be released to a person unless proof has been furnished that the individual is cleared to handle the documents.

Transferring records   Records that are no longer useful should be sent to central records or to an inactive storage area. You or the records personnel will be responsible for preparing material for transfer. Transfer boxes, transfer forms, and instructions for labeling should be available from the storage center. Transfer boxes will generally accommodate either letter- or legal-size papers. Transfer forms should indicate which records are scheduled to be moved, their codes, inclusive dates or series, and the length of time that the records are to be kept in the inactive area. The transfer boxes and transfer forms should have labels and identification that conform to the requirements of the records administrator.

If a special transfer code is assigned to the transferred files, that code should also be noted on all pertinent index cards. You may even want to move these cards to a separate file box for inactive or transferred files. Whether you take an active part in the transfer or not, you must be aware of the various methods of transfer and storage and the specific transfer process. You need to know where every record in the office is and, if it is not accessible within 30 seconds, what has happened to it. Is it being used by someone in the office? Has it been transferred to the records center on a certain date with a specific location code? Was it transferred to the records center for a definite length of time for storage? Or was it destroyed on a certain date?

Retention schedules   A retention schedule is a form that lists specific kinds of records and specifies how long each type should be kept. It also provides instructions for disposal-whether the papers are to be transferred to inactive or archival storage, destroyed, microfilmed, or placed in computer storage. The retention schedule is generally drawn up by the records administrator and is approved by a senior attorney. (Retention of medical records is generally determined by state law.) Copies of the schedule should be in the hands of everyone involved in the handling of firm records. The secretary should have a copy of this schedule and be aware of any changes that have been made in it.

Records disposal   The retention schedule may also provide for disposal or destruction of records. Some records that are no longer valuable can simply be discarded in a wastebasket or recycled. Others may need to be shredded, either at your desk or in the records center. Still others may carry instructions for disposal by other means, such as burial or chemical decomposition. The retention schedule could also require that certain records be microfilmed before the originals are discarded.

The destruction of confidential or classified records must be witnessed by the records administrator and, in some cases, a senior partner. Signed forms must indicate that the records were destroyed and that proper approval for destruction was given beforehand. Companies having government contracts, and especially contracts with the Department of Defense, must be very careful when disposing of miscellaneous paper in connection with classified documents, since such paper must be destroyed in a manner that renders the information absolutely unreadable.

Chapter 12

Accounting and Bookkeeping

This chapter will introduce you to the main features of financial record keeping in use in law offices today. A general understanding of accounting and bookkeeping terminology will help you to assist the attorney in managing the operations of the firm. You may be called upon to keep financial records, handle client billing, create financial statements, or process payroll. These important financial duties are executed using specialized computer programs or, particularly in small firms, various manual bookkeeping systems. This chapter will outline both of these systems.

It is highly recommended that the law firm's accountant be consulted to obtain detailed information on accounting and bookkeeping matters. Proper financial-accounting procedures are critical to the operation and success of any attorney or law firm. Every area of accounting consists of forms and procedures that must be followed precisely to work effectively and satisfy government regulations. All procedures should be documented to prevent any confusion or oversight. Again, it is advisable to work with an accountant. Many books on the subject are also available (see Appendix III).

Accounting Procedures

The role of secretaries in the accounting matters of law firms varies directly with the size of the firm. Medium-sized and large firms normally have a separate accounting department that handles all the day-to-day accounting transactions. In small firms, where it is not economically possible to maintain such a staff, the accounting functions may be handled by a secretary (usually the secretary to a senior lawyer) or they may be divided among several secretaries within the firm. This section focuses on the accounting functions that are common to law firms and highlights the procedures and systems that are utilized to perform these functions.

Financial Records

Below are defined various accounting terms to help you understand how financial transactions occur and what accounting procedures must take place.

Chart of accounts   Every financial transaction in the modern law office must be assigned an account, or a particular financial category. Each of these categories or accounts is summarized in what is normally called the *chart of accounts*. The chart of accounts is divided into four major categories: (1) assets, (2) liabilities, (3) capital, and (4) income and expense. Each major activity of the firm is categorized into one or more of these accounts.

1. *Assets* are those items that are owned by the law firm. They include cash, accounts receivable, fixed assets, and advances to clients.
2. *Liabilities* are items owed by the law firm. They consist primarily of loans taken for various expenditures which are being repaid to a lending institution, money held in trust for others, and other obligations payable to outside parties.
3. *Capital* represents the ownership interest by the partners or owners of the firm. In a partnership, it is normally the individual partners' capital; in a professional association or corporation, it is the equity of the stockholders.
4. *Income and expenses* refers to the fees the firm collects for its services and the expenses that occur (e.g., salaries, rent, supplies, taxes) as a result of rendering these services.

The income-and-expenses section of a sample chart of accounts for a large firm is illustrated in Fig. 12.1.

As shown in the chart, separate accounts are usually given numerical designations. For example, the 100 numbers might be given to cash accounts, 200 to accounts receivable, 400 to income, 500 to compensation (payroll) and taxes, and 600 and 700 to expenses. The extent to which the chart of accounts is organized will depend on the size of the firm, the number of different account classifications desired, and the information that the firm wishes to subject to management control. Some accounts are very broad and contain a multitude of transactions. Others are created in order to obtain financial information on specific activities. For example, "Continuing Legal Education" could be a specific expense category within the chart of accounts. The firm may decide that it wishes to divide this into two separate classifications, one for courses sponsored by the local bar association and one for courses taken at a college or business school. The account "Office Supplies and Services" may be divided into specific types of supplies and services such as copying paper, equipment maintenance, and cleaning services. The key is to establish a chart of accounts that is flexible—one that can be expanded rapidly without affecting the overall numbering scheme. It should also be designed so as to be compatible with any computerized accounting system the office may be using.

Setting up a chart of accounts is the first step in establishing an effective accounting system. Any accounting firm or any company dealing in accounting systems for law firms can provide a chart. Every transaction must be catego-

Fig. 12.1   Classifications within a Chart of Accounts: Income and Expenses

Gross Income

400	Net Fees Collected
401	Retainer Fees Received
410	Interest Income
415	Other Income

Compensation

510	Compensation—Associates
512	Compensation—Law Clerks
513	Compensation—Secretaries
514	Compensation—Non-Secretary—Legal
515	Compensation—Non-Secretary—Administrative
516	Overtime—Secretaries
517	Overtime—Non-Secretary—Legal
518	Overtime—Non-Secretary—Administrative
519	Compensation—Other

Payroll Taxes

530	FICA Taxes
531	Unemployment Insurance Taxes
532	Other Taxes

Other Personnel Costs

560	Temporary Office Service
561	Hospitalization
562	Medical and Major Medical
565	Pension Plan
570	Other Employee Insurance
580	Other Personnel Costs

Depreciation and Amortization

600	Depreciation Control
601	Depreciation Expense—Office Furniture and Fixtures
602	Depreciation Expense—Office Equipment
603	Depreciation Expense—Library
608	Amortization Expense

Other Occupancy Costs

610	Rent Expense
620	Records Storage
630	Moving Expenses
640	Alterations and Redecorations
650	Maintenance and Repairs—Furniture and Equipment
660	Minor Items of Furniture and Equipment
670	Parking
675	Other Occupancy Costs

Professional Expenses

710	Meetings—Professional Organizations
711	Continuing Legal Education—Bar Association
712	Continuing Legal Education—Other
713	Meetings—Bar Association
715	Dues and Fees—Professional Organizations

718	State and Federal Registration Fees

Business and Community Activities

722	Entertaining Clients
724	Club Dues and Assessments
725	Dues—Business and Community Associations
726	Meetings—Business and Community

Recruiting Expenses

730	Recruiting Expenses—Recruiters
731	Recruiting Expenses—Candidates
733	Ads and Agency Fees
734	Miscellaneous Recruiting Expenses

General Staff Expenses

740	Partners' Luncheons and Dinner Meetings
742	Firm Outings and Parties
744	Administrative Travel
746	Messenger Service
747	Messenger Service—Credits
749	Other Expenses Incurred by Staff

Staff Reference Materials and Supplies

750	CCH, P-H, and Other Services
751	Library Books and Periodicals
752	Other Reference Material
753	Staff Supplies
755	Microfilm Reference Service

Office Supplies and Services

760	Office Supplies and Stationery
761	Reproduction—Supplies
762	Reproduction—Equipment Rental
763	Reproduction—Credits
764	Equipment Rental
765	Office Canteen Services

Telephone and Telegraph

770	Telephone, Telex and Cables
771	Telephone, Telex and Cables—Credits
772	Postage and Express
773	Postage and Express—Credits

Other Operating Expenses

780	Contributions
781	Insurance
783	Other Taxes—State and Local
784	Interest Expenses
785	Professional Fees
788	Sundry Expenses
789	Guaranteed Payments

Outside Data Processing Services

790	Timekeeping System
791	General Accounting
796	Other Data Processing Charges

Fig. 12.2   General Ledger (Simplified)

ACCOUNT/NO. *Staff expenses*					SHEET NO. *7*		
DATE 19*96*		DESCRIPTION	PR	DEBITS		CREDITS		BALANCE
–	–	*Balance from p.6*	–	–	–	–	–	*7400*	–
Nov	*10*	*Partners' lunch*	*40*	*220*	–			*7180*	–
"	*11*	*Messenger*	*46*	*30*	–			*7150*	–
"	*12*	*Hotel overcharge*				*100*		*7250*	–

rized within the chart of accounts and posted to a ledger on a regular basis as the transactions that affect the accounts occur.

General Ledger   The *general ledger* is the firm's main accounting document. It lists each of the accounts from the firm's chart of accounts and provides columns for posting or recording the various financial transactions that take place in each account (see Fig. 12.2). The transactions are usually posted on a monthly basis from the summary journals, which are described below. While general ledgers are often in computerized forms, the transactions are still posted manually in many small law firms. The typical ledger includes the following information:

1. *Account/Number* The account name (and, if applicable, the number from the chart of accounts).
2. *Sheet Number* The ledger page number.
3. *Date* The last two digits of the year entered in the column heading, and repeated at the top of each new page. The month of the year entered in the left side of the column, and the day of the month in the right side.
4. *Description* The titles of the individual acounts involved in the transactions.
5. *Posting Reference (PR)* A reference number indicating the account or ledger from which (or to which) the transaction has been posted.
6. *Debit* The amount that is debited to (subtracted from) an account.
7. *Credit* The amount that is credited (added) to an account.
8. *Balance* A tally of debits and credits.

Cash receipts   As the term implies, cash receipts are all the receipts in the form of cash or checks received by the law firm. Receipts normally include the payments on account by clients for professional services rendered and for expenses advanced, moneys received on behalf of clients to be held in trust or placed in escrow accounts, and miscellaneous cash receipts such as repayment of loans or advances by employees. The cash receipts are posted on a daily basis to the cash-receipts journal (see Fig. 12.3). The journal is summarized daily; it provides the information for the bank deposit. Each month the journal is

Fig. 12.3   Cash-Receipts Journal

ACCOUNT/NO. *Cash receipts*					SHEET NO. *1*	
DATE 19**96**		DESCRIPTION	PR	DEBITS	CREDITS	BALANCE
Apr	1	Zweig retainer	401		2500 ⁻	2500 ⁻
"	1	IRS bill rectification	-	200 ⁻		2300 ⁻
"	2	Mallory payment	15a		1800 ⁻	4100 ⁻

summarized and the individual column totals are posted to the corresponding accounts within the general ledger.

Cash disbursements   Cash disbursements are those items that are paid out or disbursed by the firm for expenses such as salaries and office supplies, filing fees, copies of medical records, and depositions, as well as for disbursements made from client trust funds in escrow-account transactions. The source of information for the cash-disbursements journal will be the various checkbooks. For example, one checkbook may be for payroll checks, a second checkbook for other expenses, and a third for trust-account funds. All checks are posted to a cash-disbursements journal under the column corresponding to the nature of the disbursement (see Fig. 12.4). Those disbursements made regularly throughout the month are each given a separate column, and a general ledger column is used for those disbursements that are made infrequently. The cash-disbursements journal is summarized monthly, and the individual column totals are posted to the specific accounts within the general ledger. By determining the cash receipts, cash disbursements,

Fig. 12.4   Cash-Disbursements Journal

ACCOUNT/NO. *Cash disbursements*						SHEET NO. *3*	
DATE 19**96**		PAYEE	CH. NO.	DEBITS	CREDITS	BALANCE	
-	-	Balance from p.2	—	—	—	8300 ⁻	
Oct	7	County Clerk-fee	178	250 ⁻		8050 ⁻	
"	8	ABA - dues	179	250 ⁻		7800 ⁻	
"	8	Subscription svc. rebate			175 ⁻	7975 ⁻	

and prior cash balances, the accountant or bookkeeper can keep daily cash balances and maintain an effective program of cash management. The typical cash-disbursements journal includes the following information:

1. *Account/Number* The account name (and, if applicable, the number from the chart of accounts).
2. *Sheet Number* The ledger page number.
3. *Date* The last two digits of the year entered in the column heading, and repeated at the top of each new page. The month of the year entered in the left side of the column, and the day of the month in the right side.
4. *Payee* The names or titles of the individuals or accounts involved in the transactions.
5. *Check Number* The number of the check used in the transaction.
6. *Debit* The amount that is debited to (subtracted from) an account.
7. *Credit* The amount that is credited (added) to an account.
8. *Balance* A tally of debits and credits.

Financial Statements

The result of all the entries that record all the transactions during a certain period is a set of financial statements from which the general condition of the firm can be assessed. Three such statements should be prepared: (1) the balance sheet, (2) the income statement, and (3) the cash-flow analysis.

Balance sheet The balance sheet is nothing more than a listing of all the accounts within the general ledger with their corresponding balances. It provides a statement of the firm's financial position as of a given date, usually the end of the month. It lists in summary form the firm's assets, liabilities, and capital accounts, and thus can indicate the net worth or value of the firm. This value is indicated by *net assets*, which are the total assets minus the liabilities or claims against the assets. If a firm has a negative net worth—that is, if its liabilities are greater than its assets—it is possible that it may be on the verge of going out of business. A sample balance sheet appears in Fig. 12.5.

Income statement The *income statement*, or *profit-and-loss statement*, summarizes the activity of the firm with respect to its income and expenses over a certain period of time, normally a calendar year. This statement is important because it presents a net income or profit picture that can be compared to budgeted income amounts. Where possible, the income statement should contain a comparison with amounts for the previous year so that unusual fluctuations may be highlighted for review. The success of a law firm is often judged not only by its ability to generate profits in a given year but also by trends that indicate sustained profits over a period of several years. A sample income statement is illustrated in Fig. 12.6.

Cash-flow analysis A cash-flow analysis is perhaps the most important statement that can be prepared for a law firm—although it is probably the least understood and most neglected. Many lawyers tend to view the firm's net income not only as an indicator of profitability but also as an indicator of cash flow. However, there are many transactions that affect cash balances but are not part of the income statement and therefore have no effect on profit. The most sig-

Fig. 12.5 Sample Balance Sheet

Sanford & Jovonis, P.L.C.
Balance Sheet
December 31, 19--

Assets

Cash in bank	79,652	
Unbilled client expenses	3,280	
Billed client expenses	4,833	
		87,765

Fixed Assets

Furniture and fixtures	28,500		
Less depreciation	(4,778)		
		23,722	
Library capital	16,200		
Less depreciation	(3,114)		
		13,086	
Leasehold improvements	10,332		
Less depreciation	(1,578)		
		8,754	
			45,562
			133,327

Liabilities and Partners' Equity

Bank loan/line of credit	23,327	

Partners' Equity

Draw account—Sanford	55,000	
Draw account—Jovonis	55,000	
		133,327

nificant examples are the purchase of fixed assets such as office furniture and equipment and the repayment of debt obligations.

There are also categories which, although part of the income statement, do not affect the cash balance. The most significant example is depreciation—listed as an expense in the income statement but without cash-flow implica-

Fig. 12.6   Sample Income Statement

Sanford & Jovonis, P.L.C.
Income Statement
January 1–December 31, 19–

	Current Year	Previous Year
Income		
Fees collected	442,800	412,088
Miscellaneous income	1,450	1,150
Total Income	444,250	413,238
Expenses		
Personnel		
Staff	56,800	51,200
Associates	65,615	61,587
Legal Assts./Paralegals	28,306	26,904
Law Clerks	10,000	9,200
Other		
Employee insurance	6,720	6,245
Pension plan	8,011	6,816
Payroll taxes	12,302	11,344
Rent expenses	13,621	12,160
Maintenance and repairs	3,218	2,800
Depreciation	2,430	2,016
Library	9,646	7,998
Telephone	12,817	12,360
Insurance	11,205	10,272
Taxes	4,826	3,960
Office supplies	19,250	16,736
Meetings	3,076	2,544
Miscellaneous	1,650	1,536
Total Expenses	269,493	245,679
Net Income (Income – Expenses)	174,757	167,560

tions. Even though net income is reduced by the amount of the depreciation, the cash balance is not affected.

The cash-flow statement reflects the source and application of cash and provides information not directly provided in the income statement. The analysis is an important supplement to traditional financial statements. In ad-

Fig. 12.7   Sample Cash-Flow Analysis

Sanford & Jovonis, P.L.C.
Cash-Flow Analysis
January 1–December 31, 19--

Balance beginning of year	56,700
Additions	
Net income	174,757
Depreciation	2,430
Capital	16,200
	193,387
Deductions	
Partner compensation	160,220
Fixed asset additions	8,135
Loan repayment	3,195
	171,550
Other	
Increase (decrease) in other assets	(6,438)
Balance end of year	72,099

dition to indicating current cash-flow needs, it provides a basis for determining long-term cash requirements, specifically additions to the partners' capital or to the stock of a professional corporation. Projections of future cash needs can be made only through the careful preparation and examination of the cash-flow analysis on a monthly basis. An example of cash-flow analysis appears in Fig. 12.7.

Banking and Cash Transactions

The business activities of a law firm are so intertwined with banking that the secretary must be aware of how bank services are used by the firm. Secretaries in small to moderate-sized firms are often called on to perform such duties as writing checks, depositing funds, paying bills, handling petty-cash transactions, and processing payroll.

Checking Accounts

A checking account is opened at a commercial bank upon deposit of funds and the completion of bank forms listing the bank's rules and regulations. A signature card containing the signature(s) of anyone empowered to sign checks for the firm must be completed. The depositor is known as the *drawer,* the bank is the *drawee,* and the company or individual to whom a check is made out is the *payee.*

Deposit slips   Funds deposited in the bank are accompanied by a deposit slip listing the types and amounts of money being deposited. This money includes coins, bills, checks, and money orders. A duplicate copy is retained by the depositor.

The checkbook   Checkbooks come in a variety of forms. Some hold three checks per page, with prenumbered stubs attached by perforation to prenumbered checks; others are fully computerized. In any case, information about the check—date, payee, amount, and reason for the disbursement—is written both on the check and in a permanent record of payment (such as a stub or check registry). Checks may be typed, printed, or written in ink. The signature should be written or stamped in facsimile. Erasures and deletions are not permitted. If an error is made, the word "VOID" should be written on both the stub and the check. In large firms, checks may be printed by computers that store information about the checks internally for quick reference. Checkwriters—machines that print check amounts so that they are difficult to change—may also be used to reduce the time it takes to write checks.

Voucher checks   Checks may be printed with attached stubs that contain information about the checks. The stubs (vouchers) are used by the payees for recording and reference purposes.

Overdrafts   Despite the best of intentions, or through an oversight, a firm's checks may occasionally be written for sums greater than the amount on deposit. As a customer service, the bank may honor the overdrawn check and ask the firm to deposit sufficient funds to cover it. On the other hand, it may refuse to honor the checks. Since the latter action can cause great embarrassment to the firm, overdrafts should be treated seriously, and good relations with the bank should be cultivated. Dishonored checks may be returned to a depositor with a bank notice indicating the reason for its return.

Stop payments   Should a depositor want to stop payment on an issued check, the bank must be notified immediately. However, the bank cannot stop the check if it has already been cleared. Stop payments are usually requested on stolen or lost checks and on those that are discovered to contain errors. To make a stop payment on a check, immediately telephone your bank and inform them of your request, providing the date of the check, the amount, the check number, and the name of the payee. Follow up this telephone conversation with a letter listing the same information.

Check endorsements   In order to negotiate a check, the payee must endorse it on its reverse side. When endorsed *in blank,* only the payee's name appears as the endorsement. This may be done by a payee who is a private individual. The payee should endorse the check just before depositing it, since any bearer of the endorsed check can cash it or negotiate it further. A *full* or *special* endorsement contains the name of the company or person to whom the check is being given, followed by the payee's signature: for example, "Pay to the order of George Dean—[signed] John R. Sanford." Only the new payee (George

Dean) can negotiate the check further. A *restrictive* endorsement indicates the condition of endorsement and limits the negotiability of the check: for example, "For Deposit Only—[signed] John R. Sanford." The words "For Deposit Only" followed by the payee's signature mean that the check is to be deposited in the payee's bank account. It cannot be negotiated again. In all cases, it is advisable to write or stamp the depositor's account number below the endorsement.

Bank Statements and Bank Reconciliations

Depositors receive monthly statements from their banks that indicate the previous month's beginning balance, deposits made and checks written during that month, other charges or additions, and the ending balance. Because it is likely that certain transactions have not been entered on both the bank's and the depositor's books by the last day of the month, their respective end-of-month balances will not coincide. A *bank reconciliation statement* must be prepared, indicating the reasons for the disparity. The statement is prepared by the computer, an accountant, or a bookkeeper.

Canceled checks   These are checks that have been paid by the bank and are returned in the envelope containing the bank statement. Many banks have developed computerized systems that eliminate the return of canceled checks, but they will supply them to depositors upon request.

Outstanding checks   If a depositor's check has not cleared the bank by the end of the previous month, it is considered outstanding. All outstanding checks must be considered when comparing the bank statement with the firm's books.

Deposits-in-transit   Depositors may enter receipt amounts in their records that do not reach the bank as deposits by the last day of the previous month and are therefore not included on the bank statement. Such deposits are said to be late or in transit.

Bank service charges and bank memos   Banks may charge depositors for services such as the collection of notes and stop payments. These charges are listed on the bank statements. In addition, deductions and additions indicated on bank statements are sometimes explained in debit and credit memos sent along with the statement to the bank customer.

Other Bank Services and Features

The secretary should be acquainted with the variety of services offered by banks. Such information is invaluable for use in assisting a busy lawyer. Bank officials are usually glad to explain how to take advantage of the bank's services.

Cashier's check   A bank customer who does not have a checking account may purchase a cashier's check from the bank by paying the amount of the check plus a service charge. Also known as a *treasurer's check* or an *official check*, it is written by the bank on its own funds. The check is used in the same manner as an ordinary check, but the payee recognizes that the check is guaranteed.

Bank draft   Similar in purpose to a cashier's check, a bank draft is a check written by a bank on funds it has in another bank. The customer pays the amount of the draft plus a service charge.

Personal money order   For customers requiring small sums, banks sell money orders similar to those sold by post offices. These bank money orders are negotiable and serve the same purpose as business or personal checks.

Certified check   Should a payee require guaranteed payment, a bank will certify that a depositor's account contains sufficient funds to pay for the check. The amount is subtracted from the depositor's balance and the check is stamped "Certified."

Certificate of deposit   Banks pay interest on short-term deposits (a minimum of 30 days) to customers who do not want cash to lie idle. The bank issues a promissory note to the depositor that can be negotiated with other parties or cashed at the end of the time period.

Short-term checking account   A depositor can open a temporary checking account for a particular purpose. As soon as that purpose has been accomplished, the account is closed.

Bank discounting   If a company wants to secure cash for a draft or note it is holding, it may do so by discounting the instrument at a bank. After deducting interest, the bank gives the company the proceeds and collects on the instrument at the specified time.

Foreign payments   Firms doing business in foreign countries may send funds through banks in the form of cable money orders, bank drafts, mail payments, and currency. Electronic transfer of funds may also be available.

Safe-deposit box   A firm or an individual may rent a safe-deposit box from a bank for the storage of valuable papers and other items. The rental fee varies according to the size of the box.

Petty-Cash Fund

Since it is impractical to pay small expenses by check, firms maintain petty-cash funds for small items. Items such as taxi fares, postage, and small quantities of office supplies are often paid from the fund. To start the fund, a check is written and cashed. The cash is kept in a locked office drawer or box and is maintained by the person designated to disburse the funds (frequently the secretary). The amount of the fund depends on the size of the office and the frequency of small payments. A disbursement from the fund is recorded on a petty-cash receipt (written authorization) which indicates the date, matter number/case name (if appropriate), amount, and purpose of the expenditure, and is signed by the person receiving the money (see Fig. 12.8) The receipts are kept in the petty-cash box, so that at all times the total of cash paid out and receipts equals the original amount. Where a bill has been received, it is attached to the petty-cash receipt. When the fund is low, a check is cashed to restore the fund to its starting amount. The petty-cash receipts are entered in the appropriate accounting records on a regular basis.

Fig. 12.8 Petty-Cash Receipt

PETTY CASH REQUEST

Date: _12/6/98_   Amount: $ _150.00_

Client No. _I 324_   Matter No. _____

Case/Matter: _Irving_____

Purpose: _process server_____

Requested by (signature): _____LKW_____

Trust Accounts

Perhaps one of the most difficult and also potentially dangerous accounting functions performed in law firms is the handling of client trust funds—that is, advances by clients for expenses, collections made for clients, and estates and trusts of which the firm is executor or trustee. These funds entrusted to the attorney by the client must be segregated and accounted for to avoid any semblance of impropriety on the part of the lawyer.

Separate Trust Accounts

Misappropriation of client funds, or failing to exercise proper care in accounting for them, is a major problem in the legal profession, particularly for lawyers with smaller practices. The penalties for mishandling these funds range from private reprimand to revocation of license to imprisonment.

Procedures for handling of trust funds are delineated by American Bar Association rules, with the principal intent of preserving the identity of a client's funds and property. Basically the rules state that, with certain exceptions, "all funds of clients paid to a lawyer or law firm, other than advances for costs and expenses, shall be deposited in one or more identifiable bank accounts maintained in the state in which the law office is situated and no funds belonging to the lawyer or law firm shall be deposited therein." They also state that the lawyer must notify the client promptly of the receipt of his or her funds, maintain complete records of all the funds, and promptly pay or deliver to the client as requested the funds, securities, or other properties in the possession of the lawyer that the client is entitled to receive. These measures were adopted to guard against the possible misuse or loss of client funds.

This section describes the various kinds of funds coming into a law firm's possession that are subject to the rules of rendering accountings to clients. Also discussed are ways to account effectively for trust funds, and some auditing procedures that can help prevent problems. Although this discussion concerns cash funds, the same rules apply to securities or other of the client's assets.

Trust accounts   A separate bank account should be set up for all trust funds. This is a relatively simple procedure: one goes to the bank and has it set up a separate account under the firm's name with the notation "Trust Account" (as opposed to "Attorney's Account") as part of the account name. It is then necessary to have separate checks printed for that particular account and to authorize certain persons to sign the checks. Two signatures should be required, one of them being that of an attorney not working on the matter. The attorney assigned to the matter may decide to set up separate accounts for separate types of transactions. For example, there may be one account set aside strictly for real-estate transactions, another for collection matters, another for various types of closings such as loan financings, and perhaps yet another for those in which the firm is acting in a fiduciary capacity.

Account ledger   Next it will be necessary to set up an individual ledger account card for each client to record the transactions that occur. A sample escrow-account ledger is illustrated in Fig. 12.9. This is a relatively simple form with columns for receipts, disbursements, and a balance. As receipts and disbursements occur they are posted to the ledger card, which is kept with copies of the check and other pertinent details of each transaction. Each month a trial balance should be taken off the individual ledger cards and reconciled with the bank statement. A trial balance is nothing more than a listing of all the trust accounts with a total that agrees with the bank reconciliation. This enables you to immediately determine the outstanding balance in each of the trust accounts and to answer questions clients might ask about their balances. These accounts should be reviewed periodically to make certain that, whenever there are balances after a transaction is completed, appropriate refunds are made.

Interest-bearing accounts   When a large amount of money is held in trust, it is tempting to put it in a short-term interest-bearing account rather than in a regular checking account. The American Bar Association has stated that a lawyer receiving money under circumstances that require him or her to account to another for such money would be violating Canon 9 of the Code of

Fig. 12.9 Escrow-Account Ledger

DATE 19 **96**		DESCRIPTION	PR	DEBITS		CREDITS		BALANCE	
2–	9	Retainer	123			3000	–	3000	–
2–	11	Filing fee	cc1	55	–			2945	–
3–	9	Firm fees	4x	950	–			1995	–

ACCOUNT/NO. *Karen L. Trapp – T0194*   SHEET NO. *1*

Professional Responsibility should the money be placed in an interest-bearing account and the interest kept for the lawyer's personal use, unless specifically authorized by the client to do so. The normal procedure is for the client to give written permission to have the money deposited in an interest-bearing account, normally in a savings account or as certificates of deposit, which are relatively free of risk. The client's tax-identification number is obtained so that the interest earned accrues to the client rather than to the lawyer. Records should be kept on a separate ledger card to show the disposition of the funds and the fact that they are kept in a separate interest-bearing account.

Cash advances and retainers   Another potential problem is the handling of advances on behalf of clients: should advances be made from trust accounts or from the attorney's own funds? Obviously funds cannot be disbursed for one client from the trust funds belonging to another; these cash advances must be made from the attorney's own funds.

Cash advances can create a serious cash drain on the law firm. All too often clients have become accustomed to using a firm's funds to finance their transactions. In many cases, it is appropriate for the lawyer to ask for a retainer to cover anticipated expenses. This money is placed in the trust accounts; checks are disbursed and accounts controlled just as for other trust moneys. If the balance gets low, the client should advance more funds. Retainers are now becoming more popular and have helped the cash-flow problems of many firms. Retainers are also an answer to the fee-collection problem because time expended can be applied against the retainer. If a client sends a check, part of which is for payment of fees and the remainder for subsequent advances, the amounts should be deposited into two separate accounts, the regular account and the trust account.

Commingling of Funds Within a Trust Account

The commingling problem must be examined not only as it pertains to setting up trust accounts separate from the regular disbursing accounts of the lawyer, but also with respect to the commingling of funds within the bank accounts themselves. There are two factors in this problem: one is the business risk involved in issuing checks on uncollected funds; the other is the ethics of paying out of the funds of one client for the account of another.

The ethical prohibition against commingling client funds with law-firm funds was adopted primarily to prevent loss of a client's funds through their personal use by the attorney or through the claims of the attorney's creditors. In addition, the lawyer must always be able to promptly deliver the money to the client upon request. The lawyer cannot do this unless the funds of that client are actually in the account and can be drawn upon. It is unethical to put the funds of the other clients at risk or make them unavailable should one client demand all his or her escrow funds.

Collected funds   Ethical codes do not address themselves to the mechanics of handling the cash flow of an account that contains the funds of many different clients. For example, there is no requirement that there actually be *collected* funds in the bank on which the check is drawn. Under Disciplinary Rule 9-102, therefore, you may conceivably draw a check against an escrow account even though the mechanical steps of depositing the funds to the account have not been completed. Furthermore, the code of ethics lists no requirements as to the types of banks or other financial institutions into which escrow funds should be deposited. It can be assumed, therefore, that failure of the depository is an acceptable risk. Consequently, a certified or a cashier's check, even when not yet deposited or classified as collected funds, should be valid, since the only risk of those funds is the solvency of the bank upon which the funds are drawn. Similarly, checks drawn on other institutions such as savings and loan associations and insurance companies would also be valid. The lawyer is apparently given latitude to exercise reasonable judgment as to the soundness of the depository and the soundness of the drawer's check.

Collectibility of Checks

In addition to ethical considerations, there is the question of business risk in using trust funds. On the one hand, all checks may be presumed uncollectible until notification by the depository that the funds are available. On the other hand, all checks may be presumed to be good and be drawn against at once. Most law firms take the latter view, although the individual lawyer or business manager must make a subjective decision in each case.

In most cases, the firm takes no real risk of collection on cashier's checks on a local bank, on checks certified by local banks, on checks drawn on local banks by local savings and loan associations, and on checks drawn by similar lending institutions and by some law firms. Similarly, the firm normally takes no real risk of collection on cashier's or certified checks on certain reputable city banks. Your firm normally takes a minimal risk of collecting on the checks drawn by the major corporations.

Time lags   There is an additional consideration, however. Even if the risk of collection is assumed, the way in which the depository collects the funds will affect the timetable upon which checks may be drawn against the funds. The time lag involved in clearings through the banking system varies among different banks. Sometimes there is confusion between the terms *good or available funds* and *collected funds*. Good funds are available for use or investment but are not necessarily collected. Collected funds are those funds, represented by checks, that have physically been paid by the client's bank—that is, matched against funds on deposit of the drawer. A check always provides good funds in no more than two days, but it can take as long as seven days to provide collected funds. The following guidelines may be used:

1. Checks drawn on the depository become collected funds on the second day; these may be drawn upon without affecting the status of other client funds in the bank account. A certified check may also be drawn on these funds on the second day.
2. Checks drawn on local banks other than the depository are collected funds on the third day after the check is deposited.
3. Clearance of checks on out-of-town banks varies, depending on such things as distance, Federal Reserve districts, and the nature of the funds. Generally speaking, checks drawn on banks in your own Federal Reserve district but outside your immediate area will become collected in three days. If drawn on out-of-state banks, they will become collected in five days. It should be noted that using certified or cashier's checks may reduce the risk of collec-

tion but does not appreciably speed up the clearing process. As a practical matter, however, time can be saved because you do not have to await word from the depository that the check has cleared.

Determining the collectibility of a check   It is essential to designate a specific person or persons in the firm to make decisions on the acceptability of particular client checks as they are received.

For example, suppose that your office is involved in a $100,000 real-estate transaction and you receive a check from a bank in New York. If this check is not certified, it will take at least five days for the check to clear and for the funds to become collected funds in, say, a Philadelphia bank. This means that if funds are disbursed from that account on the date the check is received, moneys belonging to other clients in that escrow account are being used for this transaction. Should the check that you receive in connection with the closing not turn out to be collected, then another client's money has been improperly used since that client's funds cannot be made immediately available upon request.

However, as mentioned previously, there is also a prudent businessperson's approach to the problem that involves making a subjective evaluation of each check. Your office could prepare a list of preferred corporations, lending institutions, law firms, and other groups whose checks up to a certain amount will automatically be considered collected funds. Checks above that amount would have to be certified. It should not be embarrassing to ask a client to have a check certified; in fact, it is a normal business practice.

Electronic transfer of funds   There are certain methods now available to expedite and ensure the collectibility of funds. One of the most popular is electronic transfer.

Electronic transfer is one way of determining that there are collected funds in an account because a bank will not transfer money electronically unless it first makes sure that the funds are in the drawer's account. The easiest way to take advantage of electronic transfer is to have various bank accounts at banks throughout the area and to call upon one person, normally the bank transfer officer, to transfer funds when necessary. As an alternative, the firm's bank could be used and the client instructed to transfer funds into this account. Electronic transfer results in funds being immediately available for disbursement. It relieves the problems of collectibility and of having cash tied up for long periods of time.

Cashier's and certified checks   A *cashier's check*, as explained earlier in this chapter, is a check drawn by a bank on itself. The check does not represent collected funds, so it must go through the same process as regular checks to be collected and available for disbursement. A *certified check* is drawn by a bank after examination of the drawer's account to make sure that funds are available; the funds are subtracted from the drawer's account when the check is written. In most cases a bank will certify against a cashier's check if it knows the customer, and against a bank if there is no chance that it will fail as a depository. Both certified checks and cashier's checks guarantee collectibility; the only risk is the failure of the depository.

Audits

Bar associations studying the problems of trust funds have proposed that periodic audits be made of attorney trust accounts. An audit usually consists of nine basic steps:

1. Direct confirmation of the balance of the account or accounts is made with the bank. This is done with a standard confirmation form sent to the bank, signed, and returned directly to the auditor.
2. The reconciliation of the bank account(s) as of the date of the audit is examined and correlated with the confirmed account balances.
3. The auditor examines canceled checks, determines whether the proper person signed the checks, and reviews endorsements for unusual items.
4. The auditor reviews canceled checks that came in after the cutoff date in order to check the accuracy of the list of outstanding checks on the reconciliation.
5. On a spot-check basis, the auditor reviews the client files to see that the proper client accounts are being charged for disbursements.
6. The auditor may check to see if the amounts are being disbursed from collected funds.
7. Cash receipts are reviewed to ensure that all receipts were properly deposited and recorded to the proper client.
8. Trial balances of client accounts are examined and explanations obtained as to why certain accounts have long-term balances that have not been refunded.
9. The auditor reviews the internal control procedures concerning the receipt and disbursement of funds.

These procedures are a normal part of every audit performed by independent accountants. A legal secretary should be prepared to accept the auditing procedures and assist the auditors in performing an audit that will meet the standards of the accounting profession as well as the ethical standards of the legal profession.

Summary

The following procedures for handling trust accounts should be instituted in your office to ensure that the lawyer's Code of Professional Responsibility is not violated.

1. Set up a bank account for all client trust funds separate from the account used for the firm's normal transactions. Use separate checks for the trust account and identify these checks on your books.
2. Keep separate ledger cards for each client, recording all receipts and disbursements and noting the balance.
3. Reconcile all escrow funds monthly, and make trial balances. Have a responsible individual within the firm periodically review the accounts to see that the transactions are proper and that funds are available to clients upon demand.
4. Establish procedures for disbursing funds that are not collected funds at the time of the transaction.
5. When feasible, use electronic transfers and certified checks to speed up transactions and to avoid spending uncollected funds. This is particularly

important in major transactions where funds are disbursed on the same day they are received.

6. Educate all lawyers and staff as to the proper procedures and the ethics of handling escrow accounts.

Payroll

The secretary in a small law firm who is responsible for preparing the payroll must understand that, to an employee, few things are more sacred than his or her paycheck. With federal and state tax rules and guidelines ever increasing, it is recommended that payroll be outsourced to a qualified payroll-service organization. (Look in your Yellow Pages under "Payroll Preparation Service.") Otherwise you may want to consider purchasing a payroll-preparation software program for your computer. If neither of the above options are available in your office, then preparing accurate and timely payrolls that meet federal and state tax regulations necessitates a thorough understanding of the method by which payroll is computed, disbursed, accounted for, and coordinated with the various taxing authorities.

Computing and Recording the Payroll

Payroll periods Traditionally, payroll periods are either biweekly, semimonthly, or monthly. Although there are still some law firms that pay on a weekly basis, you will find that semimonthly payment is probably the most popular for the nonpartners or nonowners, with a monthly payment for the partners or owners of the firm. Payment is normally made on or close to the 15th and the last day of the month (if the pay period falls on a Saturday, Sunday, or holiday, the payroll is distributed on the last working day before the normal pay date). Biweekly payrolls are prepared in some cases; however, letting pay periods go past the last day of the month or the last day of the year creates certain accounting and administrative problems that do not occur when the firm is on a strict semimonthly or monthly pay schedule.

Salary computation Most employees of a law firm are on an annual salary with their annual pay divided into 12 or 24 equal amounts, and this amount is the same each pay period unless there are circumstances—such as leaves of absence, sick pay, and overtime—that add to or subtract from the normal pay. Depending on the number of prescribed hours per week, most employees are paid their hourly rate up to 35 or 40 hours per week, with an overtime rate of one-and-a-half times the normal pay for all hours over the norm. The attorney will examine overtime pay regulations in your state or locality to make sure that you are adhering to them.

Payroll forms and records There are three major forms associated with the preparation of the regular payroll:

1. *Payroll check* The check given to the employee is normally in two parts. The employee deposits or cashes the check portion and keeps the payroll stub as

a record of gross wages, deductions, and net pay. Most stubs also contain the year-to-date information for these items.

2. *Employee's earnings card* This is a record of the total wages and deductions for each person in the firm over the course of a 12-month period. It is an important record for preparing various tax returns. It contains the employee's name, address, social security number, number of exemptions claimed, date of birth, marital status, rate of pay, hours worked, earnings, deductions, net pay, check numbers, year-to-date earnings, date of hire, and termination date.

3. *Payroll journal* The payroll journal is a listing of all the employees who are being paid in a specific pay period. It indicates gross pay, deductions, net pay amount, and the number of each check written for the net pay.

Payroll Taxes

Deductions   The normal deductions from pay are federal withholding taxes, state withholding tax, FICA (Federal Insurance Contributions Act, or social security) tax, Medicare tax, and in some parts of the country, county payroll tax. The social security amount—the percentage as well as the base on which this percentage is applied-varies from year to year. The actual deduction for an employee can be determined from FICA tax tables supplied by the government or purchased from stationers. With regard to FICA and Medicare tax, the law requires employers to match a like amount. If, for example, a person's gross compensation is $100, the FICA tax is 6.2%, and the Medicare tax is 1.45%, the total FICA and Medicare tax withheld from the employee would be 7.65% of $100, or $7.65; the employer, or firm, is required to match that amount as well. Federal withholding tax refers to the income taxes that employers must withhold from their employees' salaries as the money is earned. The withheld funds are then deposited at any banking institution that is a federal withholding agent. The federal withholding deduction is based on the employee's gross pay for the payroll period and the number of exemptions (primarily dependents) claimed. Some states have their own income-tax programs and require employers to deduct these taxes from salaries and wages. The Internal Revenue Service (IRS) publishes *Circular E: Employer's Tax Guide,* and state tax agencies publish booklets that list the deductions at various levels of pay.

If your firm is a partnership, the individual partners do not have federal, state, or social-security deductions. Partners are treated differently from employees for tax purposes. They pay their taxes directly to the IRS on an estimated basis and do not have taxes withheld from their paychecks.

Other deductions may be made for U.S. Savings Bonds, health insurance, loans, 401(k) plans, pension funds, company-stock purchase plans, and charitable contributions.

Tax returns   It is important to be familiar with the various tax returns that must be filed on a periodic basis with local, state, and federal taxing authorities. The following paragraphs describe the major federal tax forms that a legal secretary may be required to process for filing with the IRS.

Federal Tax Deposit (Form 8109)   This form (see Fig. 12.10) is filed at a commercial bank along with funds withheld for FICA and FWT. Tax regulations re-

Fig. 12.10 Federal Tax Deposit Coupon (Form 8109)

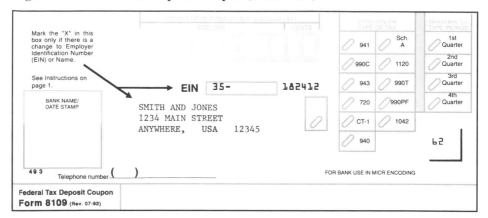

quire that employers deposit withheld income tax and FICA taxes with an authorized commercial bank depository or a Federal Reserve bank. New law firms will need to obtain Form SS-4 from an IRS or Social Security Administration (SSA) office. Complete this form in order to obtain a nine-digit Employer Identification Number (EIN). The EIN will be used on all forms and correspondence with the IRS and SSA. The IRS will then send a Federal Tax Deposit (FTD) coupon book. The FTD coupon book will contain 24 copies of Form 8109, one of which must be completed each time the firm deposits withheld payroll taxes. The IRS will keep track of the number of FTD coupons used and will send a new booklet of coupons when needed.

Employer's Quarterly Federal Tax Return (Form 941)   Amounts remitted with Forms 8109 plus amounts not yet remitted are summarized on Form 941, which is filed during the month following the payroll quarter. The form also reports taxable FICA wages and deductions for federal withholding and FICA taxes.

Whether your firm is required to make deposits depends on the amount of the liability at the end of each pay period or at the end of each quarter. The IRS office in your area can provide information about filing the payments and the amount that must be deposited. The IRS is very strict on the timely preparation and submission of these returns. It is important that you understand the requirements and make your deposits on time.

Employee's Withholding Allowance Certificate (Form W-4)   The W-4 form (see Fig. 12.11) is completed by individual employees to authorize the federal and state income-tax deductions that are made from their pay. This form indicates whether the employee is married or single and how many exemptions he or she claims; this information determines the amount of deductions from the check. W-4 forms should be kept in the individual employees' personnel files.

Wage and Tax Statement (Form W-2)   This statement (see Fig. 12.12) is sent by employers to employees no later than January 31 of each year; it lists the previous year's gross pay, federal income taxes withheld, FICA taxes withheld, and total FICA wages paid. Where state income taxes are deducted, an addi-

Fig. 12.11 Employee's Withholding Exemption Certificate (Form W-4)

Form **W-4** Department of the Treasury Internal Revenue Service

Employee's Withholding Allowance Certificate

▶ For Privacy Act and Paperwork Reduction Act Notice, see reverse.

OMB No. 1545-0010 **1994**

1 Type or print your first name and middle initial — Last name — 2 Your social security number

Home address (number and street or rural route) — 3 ☐ Single ☐ Married ☐ Married, but withhold at higher Single rate.
Note: *If married, but legally separated, or spouse is a nonresident alien, check the Single box.*

City or town, state, and ZIP code — 4 If your last name differs from that on your social security card, check here and call 1-800-772-1213 for more information . . . . ▶ ☐

5 Total number of allowances you are claiming (from line G above or from the worksheets on page 2 if they apply) . — 5

6 Additional amount, if any, you want withheld from each paycheck . . . . — 6 $

7 I claim exemption from withholding for 1994 and I certify that I meet **BOTH** of the following conditions for exemption:
- Last year I had a right to a refund of **ALL** Federal income tax withheld because I had **NO** tax liability; **AND**
- This year I expect a refund of **ALL** Federal income tax withheld because I expect to have **NO** tax liability.

If you meet both conditions, enter "EXEMPT" here . . . . ▶ 7

Under penalties of perjury, I certify that I am entitled to the number of withholding allowances claimed on this certificate or entitled to claim exempt status.

Employee's signature ▶ — **Date ▶** , 19

8 Employer's name and address (Employer: Complete 8 and 10 only if sending to the IRS) — 9 Office code (optional) — 10 Employer identification number

tional copy is sent. The employee files a copy of the W-2 statement attached to the federal income-tax form by February 28. Refer to IRS publication 393 for instructions on completing Form W-2.

Unemployment tax The federal government and most states also impose an unemployment-compensation tax on all earnings up to certain maximum amounts. The state unemployment-compensation return is filed on a quarterly basis, normally by the last day of the month following the end of the quarter.

Fig. 12.12 Wage and Tax Statement (Form W-2)

a Control number 22222 — Void ☐ — **For Official Use Only ▶ OMB No. 1545-0008**		
b Employer's identification number	1 Wages, tips, other compensation	2 Federal income tax withheld
c Employer's name, address, and ZIP code	3 Social security wages	4 Social security tax withheld
	5 Medicare wages and tips	6 Medicare tax withheld
	7 Social security tips	8 Allocated tips
d Employee's social security number	9 Advance EIC payment	10 Dependent care benefits
e Employee's name (first, middle initial, last)	11 Nonqualified plans	12 Benefits included in box 1
	13 See Instrs. for box 13	14 Other
f Employee's address and ZIP code	15 Statutory employee ☐ Deceased ☐ Pension plan ☐ Legal rep. ☐ 942 emp. ☐ Subtotal ☐ Deferred compensation ☐	

16 State	Employer's state I.D. No.	17 State wages, tips, etc.	18 State income tax	19 Locality name	20 Local wages, tips, etc.	21 Local income tax

Cat. No. 10134D — Department of the Treasury—Internal Revenue Service

Form **W-2 Wage and Tax Statement 1994**

For Paperwork Reduction Act Notice, see separate instructions.

Copy A For Social Security Administration

Federal unemployment-tax returns are filed annually; however, deposits are normally made quarterly and are credited against the final tax liability at the end of the year. The base upon which both the state and federal tax is computed changes periodically and varies from state to state. Therefore, you should obtain information locally about this tax at the time you are given the responsibility for preparation of the payroll. Employers must also file and/or deposit federal unemployment (FUTA) taxes. At the time of publication, FUTA tax is paid only on the first $7,000 of compensation received on each employee. The multiplier is .008; therefore the maximum amount of FUTA tax paid for each employee would be $56 per year. Refer to the IRS publication *Circular E* to determine when deposits of FUTA tax are required. FUTA taxes are deposited by using a Form 8109 coupon. The box should be filled in, indicating that you are depositing 940 return funds with a federal-withholding agent.

Billing and Collections

It is important to bill clients on a current basis and to adequately follow up on accounts that become past due. Legal secretaries can be very helpful in this area. Once the attorney becomes confident of the secretary's skills, the entire billing-and-collection process may be turned over to the secretary. However, no matter how much financial responsibility a secretary is given, the determination of billing rates is always the attorney's decision, and the secretary is warned *never to discuss fees with a client.*

Time accounting is a key to the financial success of any law firm. Surveys have shown that those lawyers who keep close track of their time normally generate more income than those who do not. However, timekeeping is of no value unless the time can eventually be converted into cash through the billing-and-collection process. In those firms that do keep time, lawyers are assigned billing rates that, when multiplied by the total hours expended, form the basis for the bill to the client.

Fig. 12.13 Disbursement Card

EXPENSE VOUCHER

Date: 6/7/97   Amount: $ 85.00   Check #238   Cash _____

Client No. — Matter No. F 46 -X

Client Name: Pesci

Purpose: Court filing fees

Your Name (signature): Lawrence Kendrake

In addition, the firm normally passes on to each client those disbursements or expenses that can be readily identified as pertaining to that client's matter. Disbursement cards are commercially available, frequently in carbonless-copy sets (see Fig 12.13). They may be used to record client expenditures, both billable and nonbillable, for work on a case. The card should list the name of the client and the case or matter, the corresponding docket number or reference number, the responsible attorney, the file number, the date, a description of the work done, and the amount of expenditure. Expenses that might be detailed on client disbursement cards include filing fees, toll calls, travel expenses, copying and printing charges, expert witness fees, local counsel expertise, and miscellaneous out-of-pocket expenditures.

The Billing Statement

The actual format of the bill will vary from firm to firm, and from client to client within the firm. Clients normally wish to receive a bill that adequately describes (1) the work performed, (2) the period of time covered by the work, and in some cases (3) the individuals who performed it, with the hours, billing rates, and total value of each person's work listed. The sample bill illustrated in Fig. 12.14 provides the information most clients request.

The advent of computerized timekeeping has assisted law firms in preparing bills. In many cases, information that is stored in the computer becomes the basis for the bill itself. Computerized systems can perform all steps in producing the bill, with the lawyer performing primarily an editing function before the bill is sent to the client. There are a number of software programs specifically written for law firms to handle timekeeping and billing functions. These programs are often cost-effective and should be considered.

Collection

Once the bill has been rendered, it becomes an "account receivable" of the firm until the client makes payment and the receivable is converted into cash. Billings should be rendered as early as possible after the completion of the work or, if it is an ongoing matter, at frequent intervals—preferably every month. Bills that are sent promptly tend to be paid promptly. When the bill is submitted, it normally is posted to the client's accounts-receivable ledger (see Fig. 12.15). By examining this particular ledger, the lawyer is able to see at a glance when the bills were rendered, when they were paid, and the balance owing. By examining the entire group of client ledgers, the lawyer can take appropriate action to collect long-outstanding balances. This action may include first a friendly reminder, then perhaps a stronger letter, and finally, after all other means of collection have been exhausted, legal action. (For examples, see pages 225–26.)

If a statement is not paid within 60 days, chances of collecting the amount owed diminish. Collection of the firm's accounts receivable is the responsibility of the managing attorney. The legal secretary can assist in this effort by preparing a monthly list of unpaid accounts separated into "aging" categories: for example, accounts that have been outstanding for up to 90 days, from 90 to 180 days, from 180 days to a year, and over a year. The attorney can then focus on those accounts that have been outstanding for long periods of time and take whatever action is required to collect them. Another way that the secretary can

Fig. 12.14 Billing Statement

Graves & Whittier
Law Offices

November 24, 19--

Bill for services through 11/15/--

Bill number SDS-00352-002 MCG

FOR PROFESSIONAL SERVICES RENDERED

DATE	ATTY	DESCRIPTION	RATE	FEE
11/14/--	MCG	Prelim research	1hr @ $100/hr	100.00
11/14/--	MCG	Prep court papers	1hr @ $100/hr	100.00
11/15/--	MCG	Execute/file papers	1hr @ $100/hr	100.00
		Total fees for this matter		$300.00

DISBURSEMENTS

11/15/--	MCG	Court filing fee		75.00
		Total disbursements for this matter		$ 75.00

BILLING SUMMARY

Total attorney fees		300.00
Total disbursements		75.00
TOTAL CHARGES FOR THIS BILL		$375.00

---

help make collections more efficient is by making an extra copy of each bill and putting it in a separate file or notebook that is kept by the lawyer responsible for collection. When payment is received, this copy of the bill is destroyed.

Once the moneys are received, the cash is deposited each day at the firm's designated bank. It is essential that the money belonging to the attorney be segregated from the money belonging to the client and deposited in the firm's es-

Fig. 12.15   Client Accounts-Receivable Ledger

ACCOUNT/NO. *Morgan Enterprises - M0425* SHEET NO. *1*					
DATE 19_99_	BILL NO.	DEBITS	DATE 19_	PAYMENT	CREDITS
5- 17	M0425- 001	475 69	6- 7	CK#144	475 69
6- 20	" -002	1022 77	7- 1	CK# 188	1022 77
7- 18	" -003	850 41			

crow accounts. As moneys are received, the amount is posted to the client ledger so that a continuing running balance of the client's account can be maintained.

Computerized Accounting

Computerized accounting software is available for a number of different applications, from billing to check disbursement. Often such software comes in "modules" that may be used singly or in combination to form an integrated system.

Choosing Software

When considering accounting software, the basic issue is ease of use. You should ask for a demo disk to take back to your office to review at your own pace; don't settle for a "canned" demonstration designed to make a system look easy. When you have questions, write them down and ask a sales representative for an explanation. A reputable company should have a support system to handle questions or problems. Obtain a list of users and contact them to ask their opinion of the software. Check to see whether the company continues to update its programs as technology changes.

Applying Programs

The sections below review some of the basic programs and applications.

General ledger   Computers have automated the process of keeping a general ledger, or a book containing accounts to which debits and credits are posted from books of original entry. A computerized ledger can automatically post entries made in your accounts-payable and accounts-receivable software modules. The general-ledger menu typically contains such selections as *journal* (or *account book*) *entry/maintenance, journal posting, journal printout, trial balance, report balance,* and *chart of accounts.*

In reviewing general-ledger programs, you should look to see how simple or complicated it is to create a profit-and-loss statement and a balance-sheet report. How easy it is to make changes in these statements? What steps are necessary to close the accounts at the end of the year? Does it provide you with a detailed trial balance showing each transaction? Can you print any report at any time during the month and not just at month's or year's end?

Accounts payable   With this program (or module), you can enter invoices for office supplies, bills, and notices of court fees. Such entries are called *vouchers*. The menu for accounts payable will typically offer such choices as *voucher entry, voucher lookup, processing, form-1099* (interest and dividends) *processing, vendor master, check printing,* and *reports.*

In examining accounts-payable software, you should ask the following: Is it easy to create and delete vendors? How simple is it to prepare and print checks? Can a check be printed quickly in case of an emergency? Is the transfer of data from accounts payable to general ledger easy or difficult? Do you get a detailed printed report showing what is going to be transferred to general ledger? Will the system automatically print Form 1099s at year's end? If you are using accounts-payable software in conjunction with a timekeeping and billing program, does the accounts-payable program interface smoothly with the other program? Is the transfer of information accomplished easily? Can you get a report showing a vendor history that tells you how much you've spent with a particular vendor and when you last sent them a check?

Cash disbursements and payroll   Check writing and tracking may be handled through a separate program or module called *cash disbursement,* which is essentially an automated checkbook. The menu selections in such a module typically include *check writing, check printing, check processing, audit trails, check reconciliation, check register, check listing,* and *trust detail.*

For payroll applications, check for easy entry of employee data and printing of payroll checks. Check to see if it is difficult to set up and change tax tables. Does the program provide useful reports, such as the amount of time worked by employees, compensation earned by month, quarter or year-to-date? How easy is it to print W-2s? Look at the procedure to set up payroll-deduction accounts for health-insurance premiums, 401(k) funds, and disability premiums. Finally, does the payroll program interface with your general-ledger program?

Time and billing   Time-and-billing software performs two functions: recording attorney work time and generating client billing. The time feature of the software typically includes such menu choices as *time entry, time adjustment, time audit, timekeeper rates, time inquiry,* and *report.* The billing side of the software would include such functions as *select matter, pre-billing, billing trail, processing, bill calculation, print,* and *report.*

In considering a time-and-billing package, you should ensure that it allows flexibility with bill formats and management reports, and provides client lists by practice area, attorney, or alphabetically. How easy is it to enter time and make necessary corrections? Can bills be printed at any time and can corrections or changes be made? Can you get an aged accounts-receivable report and an aged unbilled-time and/or -expense report?

Chapter 13

The Law Library

The first chapter of this book summarized the sources of American law—constitutions, statutes, regulations, and case law. This "law," created by legislative and judicial bodies, is disseminated through a variety of legal publications. Law books and electronic publications are extremely important tools for the practice of law, and the information they contain is organized and identified in a manner unlike that of the publications of most other professional disciplines. Today's law librarian (or person in the firm designated as librarian) must be proficient in the handling of legal publications and the use of basic legal research tools. This chapter describes the tools and practices of this important field. (For information about legal citations, see pp. 318–23.)

The Electronic Revolution

With the advent of computer-assisted legal research (CALR) in the mid-1970s, a long tradition of relying exclusively on printed books to locate cases and statutes began to decline—though books are far from fading from the scene. Before the 1970s a small number of government agencies and commercial book publishers made available to legal professionals the vast array of court and legislative decisions that are used in the practice of law. One commercial publisher in particular, West Publishing Company of St. Paul, Minn., so dominated legal book publishing that its system of organizing cases and statutes for publication became the industry standard. Today West's "Coordinated State and Federal Research System" remains definitive for finding and citing the law in printed books. However, the system has come under challenge by other publishers and, above all, by the emergence of computerized legal databases.

The company that originated computer-assisted legal research, LEXIS, quickly became the leading electronic publisher serving the legal community; however, West soon followed suit and developed its own on-line service, known as WESTLAW. Today both of these services cover the full range of judicial, legislative, administrative, and scholarly legal sources that lawyers must have access to. LEXIS is widely used because of its full-text presentation of original legal sources and its precision search capabilities; WESTLAW is popular because of its use of case annotations ("headnotes") and a numbering system ("key numbers") that derive from West's standard print publications (although LEXIS has recently added comparable annotations, and WESTLAW now offers most of its sources full-text). The two companies continue to enhance their products as the legal market expands and technology changes.

You must receive training on either or both of these databases from representatives of the individual companies if you are to carry out research using them. You should find it easy to learn to use LEXIS or WESTLAW, and there are many guides to the use of these systems available. A good place to begin is the book *Using Computers in Legal Research* by Christopher G. Wren and Jill R. Wren (1994).

Manual Versus Computer-Assisted Legal Research

The initial issue in deciding whether to use CALR or traditional manual research is cost, with speed being a related factor. If the traditional method of using law books is fast and effective in light of the total cost to the client, CALR may not be the best option. Both LEXIS and WESTLAW are relatively expensive services. If, on the other hand, there is no efficient way for the lawyer to locate hard-to-find information (e.g., the opinions of a specific judge or cases involving specific individuals or attorneys), then CALR may be cost-effective. In many areas of the law, specialized loose-leaf publications or digests are available (see below). These printed resources are arranged in such a way as to yield results quickly, leaving little practical advantage to using the computer. But if your attorney seldom works in a specialized subject area (e.g., tax law, patent and trademark law), the cost of purchasing these resources may be higher than that of making the occasional computer search.

CD-ROMs CD-ROMs provide much of the flexibility of computer searching without the pay-as-you-go expense of connecting with a remote on-line database. One disk, identical with a music CD, can contain tens of thousands of pages of information. Various publishers are bringing out CD products that are intended to cover all your research needs for a particular subject area. Many of the comments regarding on-line research compared to traditional print material apply equally to the use of CDs. You may pay from a few hundred to a few thousand dollars per year for a particular CD library, but you can search and download to word processing as much material and as often as you like. CDs are typically updated either by print, floppy-disk, or on-line supplements. Your computer will need a CD-ROM drive to read the information on the disk.

Types of Legal Sources

Most legal publications can be divided into two broad categories known as *primary* and *secondary sources*. Primary sources consist of statutory material, administrative regulations, and court decisions. Secondary sources are generally interpretive, analytical, theoretical, philosophical, or practical publications. The distinction is important because primary sources are said to be authoritative or mandatory; that is, legislative enactments and/or judicial decisions within a given jurisdiction *must* be applied to resolve legal conflicts unless strong circumstances warrant a departure from them. Secondary sources are merely persuasive, although they can and often do influence the drafting of statues and the application of statutory provisions and judicial decisions.

Official and Unofficial Publications

Legal publications can also be divided into *official* and *unofficial sources.* Official sources are those whose publication has been sanctioned or approved by a governmental or judicial body. For example, the *United States Statutes at Large* is the official source of all the statutory enactments of the U.S. Congress. These same statutes are also found in the *United States Code Congressional and Administrative News* (West Pub. Co.), but because the latter is a commercial publication, it is not considered an official source. Similarly, the *United States Reports* is the official edition of the cases and decisions of the U.S. Supreme Court. Two other publications, the *Supreme Court Reporter* and *United States Supreme Court Reports, Lawyers' Edition,* contain the same decisions, but again, because these are published commercially (by West and Lawyers Cooperative Publishing, respectively), they are considered unofficial.

These publications are all *primary* source materials, even though some are official and others are unofficial. The two ways of classifying should not be confused: the primary/secondary distinction applies to the *contents* of the publications, while the official/unofficial distinction applies to their *publisher.*

Updating Law Publications

Legal publications require continuous updating and supplementation, since legal precedents, whether statutory or judicial, are always subject to change. The United States is a common-law country, which means that legal precedent is a cornerstone of its legal system. As a common-law country, it historically retains and applies the pronouncements of its judicial and legislative bodies so long as circumstances do not mandate a change. However, when these principles no longer provide equitable resolutions to legal conflicts, they do change. Publications that contain legal information must therefore be adaptable in order to accept frequent changes.

You should learn about publications in slip form, pocket parts, advance sheets, loose-leaf services, electronic media, and citators and their importance to legal research and legal materials, all of which are discussed in the following pages. The lawyer must always be aware of what has occurred in the past, what the current status of the law is, and what new developments may augur for the future, and the legal secretary must likewise develop a sensitivity to the past, the present, and the future of American law.

Primary Source Materials

This section deals chiefly with the primary materials that relate to the federal government. The scheme that emerges, however, is generally applicable to state materials as well. The section describes the standard printform documents and includes notes, where applicable, regarding more recent electronic formats.

Federal Statutes

The U.S. Congress passes all federal legislation. Once a bill becomes a law, it is published in three different forms: first in *slip* form (hence the expression "slip law"); next in the official, chronologically arranged *United States Statutes at Large;* and finally in three *code* editions.

Slip laws and *Statutes at Large* As a slip law, a statute is published all by itself. A subscription to the slip laws is available from the Government Printing Office (GPO) in Pittsburgh, PA. When the law is later incorporated into a volume of the *Statutes at Large*, it is listed there in chronological order according to its public law number. Today the public law number, which is an important identifier, consists of two parts. For example, Pub. L. No. 103-1, a proper form of citation, refers to the first law (-1) enacted in the 103d Congress (103); Pub. L. No. 103-465 happens to be the last law passed in that Congress. The first example appears in 107 Stat. 3 and the latter in 108 Stat. 4809, which are the proper, official citations to a federal law once it is published in the *Statutes at Large*. Note that the volume number of the *Statutes at Large* does *not* correspond to the number of the Congress in which the public law was enacted.

Because the publication of each *Statutes at Large* volume is quite slow, it is useful to know about a commercial publication, the *United States Code Congressional and Administrative News* (West Pub. Co.), which since 1941 has been the unofficial equivalent of the *Statutes at Large*. It contains the identical text of the public laws arranged in the same chronological order, but its publication is faster. (It is also available on WESTLAW, while the official *Statutes at Large* is accessible through LEXIS.)

Code formats The publications described above are arranged and numbered chronologically. Another way to arrange U.S. statutes is in code form. Codes employ the numeric designations but primarily provide a *subject* arrangement of all the laws currently in force in the jurisdiction that the code covers. At the federal level there are three code editions: the *United States Code* (U.S.C.), which is the official edition (and is accessible through LEXIS); and two unofficial, annotated editions, the *United States Code Annotated* (U.S.C.A.; West Pub. Co., available on WESTLAW) and the *United States Code Service* (U.S.C.S.; Lawyers Cooperative Publishing, available on CD-ROM). These three editions are described below.

There are important reasons why a subject arrangement of the laws is needed. For one thing, researching applicable law through a myriad of chronologically arranged volumes is cumbersome and time-consuming. Also, changes in the law are not easy to trace in chronologically arranged volumes. What the lawyer needs is a publication that brings together all the relevant law on a particular subject and that can also accommodate changes as they occur.

The United States Code The *United States Code*, the official, unannotated edition, is divided into 50 titles that designate the broad subject categories into which the various federal statutes fall. A list of these titles appears on page 4 of this book. A proper citation to the code looks like this: 20 U.S.C. § 236 (1988). The number preceding *U.S.C.* signifies the title (not the volume, because Title 20 happens to be in volume 5), and § (section) 236 is a particular provision of that title. The year in parentheses indicates the edition of the *United States Code*.

This date is important because the code is republished in a new edition every six years. Annual supplements, designated in Roman numerals, are issued between editions to update the basic material. If pertinent statutory language is taken from a supplement, it is so indicated in the citation. For example, 20 U.S.C. § 236 (Supp. V 1993) indicates that the provision appears in the fifth supplement, dated 1993.

Unofficial codes   The two unofficial code compilations are virtually identical in content to the *United States Code* but have added features that enhance their value as research aids.

For one thing, they are *annotated*. This means that any case decisions that have interpreted, applied, analyzed or distinguished provisions in the code will be referred to in the annotations, thus alerting the user to relevant cases. Both unofficial publications also offer brief case summaries, comprehensive word indexes, and cross-references to related statutes, administrative publications, and secondary source material.

Another very important research feature of the annotated codes is that all the volumes in these editions are supplemented by annual pocket parts (or monthly electronic updates) and additional supplementary pamphlets that incorporate new legislation and changes in or repeal of existing statutes. *Pocket parts* are pamphlets intended to be inserted in a pocket constructed in the back of each code volume. Pocket parts are almost always updated annually. When they become too numerous, the publisher issues a new edition of the volume that incorporates the supplements. To locate or verify a statutory citation, therefore, you must consult not only the basic code volumes but also the latest supplemental material in order to be certain that your information is current. The checking is not difficult, because the arrangement remains the same from one supplementary source to another; that is, after locating 20 U.S.C.A. § 236 or 20 U.S.C.S. § 236, you simply check for the same citation number in the pocket parts of both editions and in their respective supplementary pamphlets. In the case of on-line or compact-disk updates, changes are automatically integrated into the main body of the code.

Federal Administrative Regulations

Administrative regulations are, in a sense, a by-product of statutory enactments. They are promulgated by the myriad of federal administrative agencies, agencies such as the Security and Exchange Commission, the Internal Revenue Service, and the Federal Trade Commission. These agencies were created by statutory enactments of Congress that define the scope of their respective authority and the nature of the functions they may exercise. Some agencies are strictly regulatory bodies, but most are hybrids, exercising quasi-judicial powers (rendering decisions) as well as quasi-legislative powers (promulgating regulations).

The *Code of Federal Regulations*   Administrative regulations function and are applied in much the same way as statutes; however, the publications in which they are located are a bit more difficult to manipulate and are not as easy to update. Federal administrative regulations currently in force are located in a subject compilation called the *Code of Federal Regulations* (C.F.R.). It constitutes primary source material, and it is official. It is available on-line through

WESTLAW and LEXIS, or on CD-ROM from Lawyers Cooperative Publishing.

Like the federal codes, the C.F.R. is divided into 50 titles, but there is *not* a one-to-one correspondence between its titles and those of the *United States Code.* Of all the printed volumes in the C.F.R., you should become most familiar with title 3, "The President," and the last volume, the "Index and Finding Aids." The presidential volume is important because in a small library it is the one place where you can locate the proclamations and executive orders of the nation's chief executive officer. Inside the cover of the latest annual volume you will find a listing of all the title 3 compilations, which date back to 1936. Executive orders and proclamations can also be found in *United States Code Congressional and Administrative News* and in U.S.C.S., but they are most conveniently located in the C.F.R.

The Index and Finding Aids volume is one key to learning how to use the C.F.R. (Other, electronic indexes are described below.) One of the most important elements that you should become familiar with is Table 1, Parallel Table of Statutory Authorities and Rules. It lists all the sections of the *United States Code* and the *Statutes at Large* that together are the authority for both the regulations promulgated in the C.F.R. and the presidential proclamations or executive orders. There is also an alphabetical list of all the agencies named in the C.F.R. and where their regulations will be found.

The *Federal Register*   Regulations, like statutes, may be amended, revised, or repealed. Since the C.F.R. titles are revised only once each year, another source must be consulted to update the information found in the annual volumes: the *Federal Register,* a government publication issued daily (Monday through Friday) by the National Archives and Records Service of the General Services Administration. A subscription may be placed with the Superintendent of Documents at the GPO.

The cover of each issue features a "Highlights" listing of the most important regulatory information contained within, followed by a full table of contents. Presidential documents such as proclamations and executive orders are always given first in both lists. There is also, at the front of each issue, a compilation of the C.F.R. titles and sections affected by the regulations in the issue at hand; at the back of each issue this information is cumulated for the days in a given month. This "List of CFR Sections Affected" (or LSA) also appears in quarterly cumulative pamphlets containing updated references to C.F.R. titles and sections that may have been changed subsequent to their annual revision dates. Monthly pamphlets are also issued between the quarterlies. The overall intent is to provide a finding tool that the researcher can use to identify the most recent form of an administrative regulation.

Suppose, for example, that you wish to check a particular regulation in the C.F.R.—for example, 24 C.F.R. § 571.100 (revised as of 4-1-94). Since Title 24 has been revised as of April 1, 1994, you should check this citation in the "List of CFR Sections Affected" (LSA) for dates after that date through the latest quarterly cumulation and monthly pamphlet of the LSA. If you should happen to find a reference to 24 C.F.R. § 571.100, you would note the page references to the *Federal Register.* You would then check your page references against those listed in the "Table of Federal Register Issue Pages and Dates," found at the back of each LSA pamphlet, in order to get the exact date of the *Federal Register* in which the new information will be found.

If in the above example the latest quarterly cumulation was through June 1994 and the latest monthly pamphlet was July 1994, you would check for changes to 24 C.F.R. § 570.100 in those pamphlets first, jot down what you found, and get the dates of the *Federal Register* for your pages. If you were searching in the month of September, you would next go to the *last* issue for the month of August and the last daily issue available to you in the month of September. In the last daily issue of August you would find the LSA cumulated for all of August. After checking it you would then go to the latest daily issue of September, where you would find the LSA cumulated for September through that date. If the latest monthly issue of the LSA was August 1994, you would check it and then check the latest daily for September.

Having recorded your references to the *Federal Register,* or having found none, you would have completely verified your C.F.R. citation right up to the date of your search.

To summarize:

1. Find the regulation in C.F.R. and note the pamphlet's revision date.
2. Check the regulation in the latest quarterly and latest monthly issues of the LSA subsequent to its revision date.
3. Check the regulation in the LSA in the last daily issue of each month of the *Federal Register* as necessary.
4. Check the regulation in the last daily issue of the *Federal Register* preceding the date on which the searching is done.

The route will cover either all four steps or just the first, second, and fourth, depending on the dates of the publications being consulted.

For a more detailed explanation see *The Federal Register: What It Is and How to Use It,* published by the Office of the Federal Register, which also offers user workshops. Otherwise you may simply wish to access both the *Federal Register* and the C.F.R. through LEXUS or WESTLAW, both of which include useful electronic indexing functions.

Congressional Information Service   An alternative method of accessing government administrative publications is to subscribe to a set of serially issued commercial indexes, the *CIS Federal Register Index* and the *CIS Index to the Code of Federal Regulations,* both published by the private Congressional Information Service (CIS; New Providence, N.J.). The CIS publications are updated on a timely basis and index geographic locations as well as agencies and subjects. They are considered by many to be easier to use than the government's indexing system. CIS also publishes numerous Congressional documents—e.g., bills and resolutions, committee reports, transcripts of floor debates and hearings—in microfiche along with comprehensive indexes. These Congressional documents are used by lawyers in compiling *legislative histories* to shed light on how statutes should be interpreted.

Federal Case Law

The hierarchical structure of state and federal courts is described in the first chapter of this book. A case begins in a lower court that has original jurisdiction, and it can end in an appellate court. Usually a case will proceed to an intermediate appellate court before going up to the highest court of appeal, but under certain circumstances the intermediate step can be bypassed.

Law reports The opinions of all these courts and others discussed here are published in printed volumes called *law reports*. There are many series of law reports; some cover many courts in one jurisdiction, and some cover several jurisdictions. The official/unofficial distinction discussed in connection with statutory publications applies in some but not all cases of law-report publishing.

The decisions of the U.S. district courts are found in a set of law reports called the *Federal Supplement* (F. Suppl.; West Pub. Co.). Although considered unofficial because of its commercial publication, it is the only place where these decisions are consistently published. The opinions of the U.S. courts of appeals are published in a single set called the *Federal Reporter* (F., F.2d, or F.3d), which is also commercially produced (West) and therefore unofficial. An important point to remember is that the *Federal Reporter* is now in a third series (hence the *3d* in the title abbreviation).

Decisions of the U.S. Supreme Court constitute an exception because, as mentioned above (page 421), they are reproduced in three different series of reports: one official—*United States Reports* (U.S.)—and two unofficial—*United States Supreme Court Reports, Lawyers' Edition* (L. Ed, or L. Ed. 2d), and *Supreme Court Reporter* (S. Ct.). The unofficial editions have indexes, tables, and annotations that enhance their value as research tools, and thus they are more popular than the official reports; they are also available on CD-ROM.

Slip opinions Before being published in bound editions as law reports, the opinions of the U.S. Supreme Court, like statutes of the U.S. Congress, are first published in "slip" form, as are the decisions of many other federal and state courts. This means that the opinion is printed individually so that it may be filed either by date of decision or by a docket or index number.

The *docket number* is an important identifier for any case decision even after it has been reported and printed in a law report series. A docket number is assigned to a case when it is filed in a particular court; each court has its own docketing system. The case is then placed on a calendar, where its status is periodically updated as it moves closer to hearing and disposition by the court. A federal case may have several docket numbers: one in a U.S. district court, one in a U.S. court of appeals, and one in the U.S. Supreme Court. All documents filed with the court relating to the case will be identified by its docket number, and usually will forever be filed under that number in the archival depositories of the court.

Most law-office libraries subscribe to the slip opinions of the U.S. Supreme Court and perhaps also to those of the U.S. court of appeals for the circuit in which they are located; they may also subscribe to the slip opinions of a state court. Cost is often a determining factor, because slip opinion subscriptions can be very expensive.

Advance sheets A sequence of slip opinions is cumulated to appear eventually in what is called an *advance sheet*. Advance-sheet publications generally accompany each law-report series. Advance sheets also are eventually cumulated and superseded by bound volumes of law reports, at which time the sheets can be discarded. Advance-sheet services can be subscribed to by themselves or as part of a subscription to the bound volumes. Some of the larger law offices arrange to get multiple subscriptions to the advance sheets for circulation to various attorneys so that they can keep current on the decisions of certain courts.

Citations to Cases in Law Reports

Citations to cases are determined by the law reports in which the cases are reported. As a general rule, all parallel citations to a case (different citations to the *same* case) should be given, with the official citation (if there is one) indicated first. The following are illustrations of citations to federal court cases:

U. S. District Court
Name of case: Jones v. Buffalo
Citation: 867 F. Supp. 1155 (W.D.N.Y. 1994)
U.S. District Court docket number: No. 92-CV-3455

U.S. Court of Appeals
Name of case: Barker v. Shalala
Citation: 40 F.3d 789 (6th Cir. 1994)
U.S. Court of Appeals docket number: No. 93-6122

Name of case: Sweet Home Chapter v. Babbitt
Citation: 17 F.3d 1463 (D.C. Cir. 1994)
U.S. Court of Appeals docket number: No. 92-5255

U. S. Supreme Court
Name of case: Crusan v. Missouri Dept. of Health
Official citation: 497 U.S. 261 (1990)
Unofficial citations: 110 S. Ct. 2841 (1990)
                     111 L. Ed. 2d 224 (1990)
                     58 U.S.L.W.* 4916 (U.S. Sept. 5, 1990)
U.S. Supreme Court docket number: No. 88-1503

The numbers preceding the abbreviations for all law-report series indicate the *volume* in which the decision will be found; the numbers following the abbreviation designate the *page* at which the case begins. The abbreviated information in parentheses at the end of a citation identifies the specific federal district or appeals court in which the case was decided and the year of the decision. For instance, *W.D.N.Y.* refers to the U.S. District Court for the Western District of New York, and *6th Cir.* refers to the U.S. Court of Appeals for the Sixth Circuit. The docket number does not appear in the citation but may be found in the prefatory material preceding the actual text of the decision.

Searching and verifying citations to a case requires precision. A slip of the finger can alter the information and send the reader to the wrong sources. Judges, law clerks, and supervising attorneys do not excuse such errors lightly. Accuracy is critically important in identifying legal sources, especially primary ones such as law reports.

State Statutes and Administrative Regulations

Federal statutory publications have their equivalents at the state level. The following paragraphs discuss features common to all or most state materials; however, keep in mind that there are 50 jurisdictions and that each state's body of law is different. In researching state law, if the general principles given here do not seem to apply, seek the assistance of someone familiar with the state's system and its publication sources.

State statutory publications State statutes, like federal statutes, are published both in chronological/numeric order and in a subject compilation or code. The

---

United States Law Week—publishes U.S. Supreme Court and other court opinions

chronological/numeric series is generally called *session laws* (in some states it is called *public acts, general laws,* or something similar). In addition, all states have at least one code representing a subject arrangement of the law currently in force. You should become familiar with those in your own state.

State code compilations vary in the number of volumes in each set, the subject headings used, and the way in which the subjects are broken down. Most state codes include sections on topics like agriculture, civil procedure, and taxation. California's code includes a segment on water because that topic is subject to much legislation in California. All the state codes are supplemented regularly, mostly by annual pocket parts inserted at the end of each volume and additional pamphlets issued during the course of a state legislative session. All have some sort of numeric breakdown—title, chapter, section, etc.—for their code material.

All state session laws are primary source materials, as are all state codes. However, the distinction between official and unofficial publications is not so clear-cut. The attorney should advise you as to which form of citation is required or preferred. You may also consult your handbook of legal citation.

It is occasionally necessary to consult statutes of other states, for which purpose the irregularly supplemented *Subject Compilation of State Laws* or the annually published state law summary in the *Martindale-Hubbell Law Directory* (see below) are useful. WESTLAW and LEXIS also offer access to the full text of state statutes and some state session laws.

State administrative regulations   Most sources of state administrative regulations are not well organized, though many jurisdictions have published administrative codes and some of these are updated by weekly or monthly supplements. A good source of information about these publications is Mary L. Fisher's *Guide to State Legislative and Administrative Materials,* a loose-leaf publication updated regularly.

State Law Reports

Law reports at the state level are numerous because they represent the judicial product of fifty jurisdictions. Another problem is that the distinction between official and unofficial publications applies to some state law-report series but not to others.

With some exceptions, such as *New York Miscellaneous Reports* (Misc., Misc. 2d), decisions of the state courts where cases originate are generally not published in any formal law-report series. A local legal newspaper, however, is likely to print the text of the more important cases from lower courts, or at least summaries of the cases. At the intermediate appellate level, in a considerable number of the more litigious states (New York, Pennsylvania, California, Illinois, Ohio, etc.) there are many law-report series, and most states publish official reports of their supreme appellate court decisions. However, some states have found it too expensive to maintain official editions of these opinions.

At least two commercial vendors provide published sources for state court decisions. One set is called the National Reporter System; the other is known as *American Law Reports* (A.L.R.).

The National Reporter System   The National Reporter System, as developed in the nineteenth century by West Pub. Co., is comprehensive in that it contains decisions of the supreme appellate courts of all the 50 states. It is subdivided into seven regional reporters and three individual state reporters. The three separate reporters are the *New York Supplement* (N.Y.S., N.Y.S.2d), the *California Reporter* (Cal. Rptr.), and *Illinois Decisions* (Ill. Decs.). The regional reporters are the *Atlantic* (A., A.2d), *North Eastern* (N.E., N.E.2d), *North Western* (N.W., N.W.2d), *Southern* (So., So.2d), *South Eastern* (S.E., S.E.2d), *South Western* (S.W., S.W.2d), and *Pacific* (P., P.2d). Their geographic breakdown is as follows:

Atlantic:	Connecticut, Delaware, District of Columbia, Maine, Maryland, New Hampshire, New Jersey, Pennsylvania, Rhode Island, Vermont
North Eastern:	Illinois, Indiana, Massachusetts, New York, Ohio
North Western:	Iowa, Michigan, Minnesota, Nebraska, North Dakota, South Dakota, Wisconsin
Pacific:	Alaska, Arizona, California, Colorado, Hawaii, Idaho, Kansas, Montana, Nevada, New Mexico, Oklahoma, Oregon, Utah, Washington, Wyoming
South Eastern:	Georgia, North Carolina, South Carolina, Virginia, West Virginia
Southern:	Alabama, Florida, Louisiana, Mississippi
South Western:	Arkansas, Kentucky, Missouri, Tennessee, Texas

Note that, in addition to the individual state reporters, California is also covered by the Pacific and New York and Illinois by the North Eastern reporters. Hence there may be at least three places where texts of court decisions in these states can be found: in the official state reports (all three have several), their individual reporters, and the regional reporters.

Court decisions in the National Reporter System are initially published in advance-sheet pamphlets, which are then cumulated and superseded by bound volumes. These commercially published law reports are all considered to be unofficial sources of case decisions, even in those states that have abandoned official editions.

American Law Reports   *American Law Reports* (A.L.R.; Lawyers Cooperative Publishing) is a much less comprehensive law-report series, although it spans many volumes (it is now in its fifth series) and has a distinguished history as a research tool. The difference in coverage between A.L.R. and the National Reporter System lies in A.L.R.'s selectivity. Of the thousands of reported cases decided in the courts of the 50 states, its editorial board selects those that illustrate a unique application or development of a legal principle of interest to lawyers beyond the jurisdiction of the rendering court. The selected cases are carefully evaluated by legal experts, and their analyses are published as annotations to the cases chosen. These annotations are often lengthy pieces of documentary research, and they are sometimes revised and updated. Though a small law library may not subscribe to A.L.R., attorneys are well aware of its usefulness and may often request volumes from a neighboring law library.

Updating A.L.R. and using its index can be somewhat difficult. However, a CD-ROM edition offers some improvements, including links to LEXIS search queries and West's key numbers.

Secondary Source Materials

Beyond primary sources such as statutes and law reports are a number of essential research tools that attorneys use and that the legal secretary should be familiar with. These tools are secondary source materials: indexes and citators, form books, loose-leaf services, legal periodicals, textbooks, encyclopedias, and miscellaneous reference works.

Indexes and Citators

Given the array of legal publications that must be consulted when researching a point of law, and the attorney's continuing need for reliable and current information, the necessity of sophisticated indexing tools becomes clear. Some of these indexes—both printed and electronic—have been mentioned above. Below are described two other major indexing tools frequently used by lawyers.

The American Digest System Indexes to printed publications, especially to those on case law, are chiefly in the form of *digests*. The most important one is West's American Digest System, which accompanies West's National Reporter System as described in the last section. It is cumulated over ten-year periods; thus, with the exception of the earliest and the most current ones, its volumes are identified as *Decennial Digests.* The initial volumes, covering the period 1658–1895, are known collectively as the *Century Digest*. Volumes that are currently being cumulated are called the *General Digests*. So far there have been ten decennial cumulations beyond the *Century* edition.

What the digest system does is to break down the large body of published law into a series of general topics such as bankruptcy, constitutional law, evidence, liens, and torts. These topics are then broken down into specific subheadings, each of which is assigned what is popularly know as a "key number." The *key* derives from the fact that the publisher uses a trademarked symbol of a key preceding the numerical classification given to each subheading; thus, once a researcher has identified the key number assigned to the subject area being analyzed, he or she can then consult the digest volume containing listings of the relevant cases and scan *squibs* (abstracts) of these cases to determine which ones address the particular point of law that is of interest. Once the cases have been identified, the full texts of the decisions can be located in one (or more) of the national reporters by using the same key-number system.

There are a few additional volumes in the Digest that enhance its utility and make access to the system easier. The *Descriptive-Word Index* indexes factual and legal terminology used in the cases digested. The *Table of Cases* is an alphabetical listing of all the cases covered for a particular period, with their key numbers. So, for example, if an attorney learned that a particular unfamiliar case might be relevant to the problem at hand, he or she would look up the case in the Table of Cases to get its citation and also all the key numbers under which it has been digested. The digest could then be consulted under those key numbers for additional information about the case.

The most significant research contribution that the American Digest makes is its universality. All case law, regardless of its originating jurisdiction, is digested by the application the same general subject headings and the assignment of specific key-numbered subheadings. This feature is augmented by the publication of four regional digests that correspond to four of the seven regional reporters of the National Reporter System (omitted are separate digests for the North Eastern, Southern, and South Western regional reporters). In addition, there are key-number digests for a majority of the states. At the federal level, there is one covering all the federal courts—the *Modern Federal Practice Digest* with its successive editions, up to *Federal Practice Digest*, 4th. Another *U.S. Supreme Court Digest*, covers the decisions of the U.S. Supreme Court.

Understanding how this digest system works requires hands-on experience. The key numbers under which each case reported in the National Reporter System is digested always appear preceding the full text of the cases in both the advance sheets and the bound volumes. For practice, you can pick a case at random and examine the entries listed under it in the digest volume for your state or geographic region or in any of the decennial volumes. Check the case in any of the Tables of Cases appearing after its date of decision and see what information you find. The more experience you get in looking up cases in these indexes, the easier it will become to use digests efficiently.

Shepard's Citations   From the moment a case is decided by some court or a statute is enacted by some legislature, it becomes subject to the process of change. The decision of the court may be applied identically again and again to similar situations, or it may be distinguished, modified, or even reversed in whole or in part. The same is true of a statute: it may stand for a long time or be amended or repealed in whole or in part. Such changes in the law occur daily; thus, whatever legal authority an attorney locates to support a legal argument has to be tested to see if it is still "good law." The tool that allows the lawyer to do that is a citator, and the publication whose title is virtually synonymous with legal citators is Shepard's Citations (published by Shepard's/ McGraw-Hill, Colorado Springs, CO), so much so that the process of updating a case or statute is known as Shepardizing.

Shepardizing a case or statute involves finding all the references to it in subsequent cases. These subsequent citations are then analyzed as to their effect on the judicial precedent that the case or statute represents. Shepardizing provides a historical summary of the case or statute from the date of its rendition to the present.

The simple mechanics of Shepardizing are explained at the front of every Shepard's citator. There are many individual citators in the Shepard's system: there is one for every unit of the National Reporter System and for all the reports and statutes of the federal system, including a number of administrative-agency report series and the *Code of Federal Regulations*. There are also citators for each of the 50 states, covering both statutory and case law. A key point to remember in the case of state citators is that intrastate citations are covered in the individual state volumes, whereas only *interstate* citations are covered in the regional volumes.

In order to Shepardize a case, statute, or federal regulation using the traditional manual method, you must have an *accurate* citation with which to start. One wrong digit could lead to the wrong item and cause you to miss noting that a case has been reversed or a statute repealed. For purposes of illustration, take the citation to the *Bakke* case: 438 U.S. 265 (1978). Since it was decided in 1978, we must consult volume 1.8 of *Shepard's United States Citations*, which is in the Case Edition (1994). Because we are working with the official citation, we turn to the first section, covering *United States Supreme Court Reports,* and look for "Vol. 438" on the upper outside corner of the page. Having located it on page 112 of the citator, we now look for 265, the starting page for the case, which is on page 127. Immediately below 265, we see in parentheses the two alternative unofficial citations to *Bakke:* 57 LE2d 750 and 98 SC 2733. (Note that the abbreviations for the *Lawyers' Edition* and *Supreme Court Reporter* are different from the ones recommended earlier in this chapter. That is because Shepard's uses its own forms of abbreviations; they are *not* to be used in citing any legal writing.)

Following the alternative citations you will see a string of citations to cases that have cited *Bakke.* Some have small letters preceding them; the significance of these letters and of all symbols used in the citator is explained at the front of the volume. After you have checked the bound volume (if it was your starting point), you must check the citation in any supplementary pamphlets that may be available. *You must verify the status of the case as good law through the most current pamphlet.*

You can also begin Shepardizing with one of the two unofficial citations *if it is correct.* Always remember to check your information and to exercise the utmost care when copying it out for the attorney.

The following steps summarize the process of Shepardizing for the legal secretary:

1. Find the Shepard's citator that corresponds to your citation. Also locate all the supplementary pamphlets you will need.
2. Find the series, volume number, and page number corresponding to your citation.
3. Copy all the information following the page number exactly as you see it.
4. If the attorney wants to see the cited materials, assemble and present them as instructed.

Shepardizing statutes requires the same procedure as Shepardizing cases except that you begin with a different kind of citation. Keep in mind that, whereas a case citation never changes, a statute may be recompiled and thus renumbered, or it may even be transferred to another section in the code. Therefore, you must be especially careful in dealing with statutory citations.

Electronic Shepardizing   Shepard's offers a CD-ROM edition that contains the texts of its principal citators and automatically checks the accuracy and validity of citations. Automatic Shepardizing supplies the name of the case, the date and place of the decision, the official citation, any parallel citations that exist, and citations to cases that directly affect the validity of the case. You can also keep electronic records ("user trails") and keep track of time spent on Shepardizing for billing purposes. Most of the same Shepard's services are available on-line through WESTLAW and LEXIS. These on-line companies offer up to four "levels" of citation verification, including overnight or near-overnight services for last-minute checking of the most recent decisions.

Form Books and Loose-Leaf Services

A good portion of a lawyer's time is spent drafting legal documents. Whether these forms are substantive (a contract, will, or trust agreement) or procedural (a motion, affidavit, or complaint), the attorney will frequently check sample forms whose substance and style are generally accepted.

Two general, multivolume sets of form books commonly used by attorneys are *American Jurisprudence Legal Forms,* 2d ed. (20 vols.; Lawyers Cooperative Publishing) and *American Jurisprudence Pleading and Practice Forms* (25 vols.). The first set contains substantive legal forms and the second covers procedural forms; both sets include floppy disks containing form templates or can be purchased as CD-ROMs. In addition to these publications, the jurisdiction in which the attorney practices may have published form books dealing exclusively with forms accepted and recognized by its courts. Also, volumes of forms often accompany texts or treatises on certain legal subjects such as probate or tax law (see also "Loose-leaf services," below). The attorney (and the many publishers' sales representatives) will most likely call these to your attention.

Loose-leaf services   A loose-leaf service is a form of publication well adapted to supplying current information in a particular field of law. A publication in loose-leaf form makes it easy to continually insert new or revised pages into its basic text. At least one and often several loose-leaf services exist for every legal specialty. A list of loose-leaf publishers and the abbreviations to use in referring to them is included in most of the standard citation manuals.

Each service reprints the full texts of statutes, regulations, and court opinions that affect a particular area of the law, together with commentary, news about pending legislation, and other pertinent items. A subscription to a loose-leaf service will provide you with the basic text or treatise along with weekly updates. The service should also supply introductory material that states the extent of its coverage and gives detailed explanations on how to use it. The weekly updates should come with precise, easy-to-understand filing instructions printed on numbered transmittal sheets to make checking, verifying, and filing simple.

Many loose-leaf publications can now be purchased as CD-ROMs, which offer even more advantages than the printed publications. Some publishers offer comprehensive "topical libraries" in certain specialized subjects, allowing the user to electronically access cases, statutes, regulations, and supplementary material such as treatises, legislative histories, and forms with the click of a mouse.

Encyclopedias, Treatises, Periodicals, and Newspapers

Among the many secondary sources important in the practice of law are legal encyclopedias, treatises (texts), and legal periodicals.

Legal encyclopedias   There are two major legal encyclopedias: *Corpus Juris Secundum* (C.J.S.; West Pub. Co.) and *American Jurisprudence, 2d edition* (Am. Jur. 2d; Lawyers Cooperative Publishing). They are similar to general encyclopedias except that their coverage is devoted to legal subjects. Both are filled with references to cases and statutory sources, and both present extensive explanatory material that elucidates generally accepted legal principles. They provide good starting points for initial research into unfamiliar areas: the emphasis of C.J.S. is on cases, while that of Am. Jur. 2d is on statutes and regulations. *American Jurisprudence 2d,* which is available on CD-ROM, is somewhat more efficiently cross-referenced and indexed and offers occasional loose-leaf and bound supplements covering new topics.

Many of the states also have encyclopedic sets covering the development of legal principles within their own jurisdictions; the word jurisprudence is usually part of their titles, as in *Texas Jurisprudence, Ohio Jurisprudence,* and *California Jurisprudence III.*

Treatises   Single- and multivolume legal treatises (texts) are numerous. They are written by legal academics for use by lawyers, judges, and other professionals in comprehending the basis of laws. All the major legal publishers will, upon request, provide catalogs listing the most significant texts they sell, or you can consult *Legal Books and Serials in Print.* Among the most widely used law texts are the following:

> *Administrative Law,* by Kenneth Culp Davis, et al.—a standard text that is supplemented irregularly.
>
> *Collier on Bankruptcy*—a multivolume, periodically updated loose-leaf text.
>
> *Model Business Corporation Act Annotated*—a three-volume work that is supplemented irregularly.
>
> *A Treatise on the Law of Contracts,* by Samuel Williston—supplemented with annual pocket parts and popularly known as "Williston on Contracts."
>
> *Evidence in Trials at Common Law,* by John Henry Wigmore—supplemented with annual pocket parts and popularly known as "Wigmore on Evidence."
>
> *American Jurisprudence: Proof of Facts,* 3d series—a multivolume text supplemented with annual pocket parts.
>
> *Personal Injury: Actions, Defenses, Damages,* edited by Louis R. Frumer, et al.—a multivolume, loose-leaf text.
>
> *The Law of Trusts and Trustees,* by George Gleason Bogert—supplemented with annual pocket parts and popularly known as "Bogert on Trusts."
>
> *Page on the Law of Wills,* by William H. Page—supplemented with annual pocket parts.
>
> *Restatement of the Law,* 1st and 2d—a multivolume set resembling a legal encyclopedia but confined to certain subject areas. It is nevertheless an important, highly recognized, and much used research tool.

The items listed above represent a very small sampling of the large number and variety of legal texts available. There are many other single-volume casebooks, hornbooks, and handbooks that are equally of value and importance to attorneys. The contents of a law-office library will reflect the areas of the firm's practice and the personal preferences of its lawyers. Catalogs of lawbook publishers are good sources of information about basic legal publications.

Legal periodicals and periodical indexes   Other valuable research publications include legal periodicals and periodical indexes. Most legal periodicals are known as *law reviews,* since their primary function is to review legal developments in a variety of subjects, and originate at law schools; for example the *Cornell Law Review, Duke Law Journal,* and *University of Chicago Law Review.* Some law reviews concentrate on specific subject areas such as urban law, civil rights, and employee relations. There are several private publishers of legal periodicals as well.

There are several indexing tools for searching legal periodicals. The oldest is the *Index to Legal Periodicals,* which is available in print, on-line, or on CD-ROM. Two others are the *Index to Periodical Articles Related to Law* and the *Harvard Current and Annual Legal Bibliography.* The youngest is the *Current Law Index,* which is available in print, microfilm, on-line, and on CD-ROM.

Legal newspapers   Legal newspapers are also fairly numerous. Most of them are local, published primarily for readers in particular cities or states. The best known of these are the *New York Law Journal* and the *Los Angeles Daily Journal.* In addition, there are now several national legal newspapers, including the *Legal Times,* the *National Law Journal,* and the *American Lawyer.* These newspapers focus on the practice of law and on trends, developments, and people in the profession.

Directories, Dictionaries, and Other Reference Tools

Other secondary source materials are legal directories, dictionaries, and various government-information publications.

Directories   Of the legal directories, the *Martindale-Hubbell Law Directory* (Martindale-Hubbell, New Providence, N.J.) is best known and is found in almost every law office of any size. Published annually, it is a multivolume/CD-ROM publication that lists names of practicing attorneys throughout the United States and selected countries abroad. The printed volumes are organized alphabetically by location, so you must know the state and city where an attorney is practicing in order to find the listing. Each of the main volumes has a biographical section in which lawyers are listed individually and by firm, and a services-and-supplies section in which various legal services (e.g., expert witnesses, title-search companies, private detectives) are listed by type. Other volumes in the set include listings by area of practice, information on corporate and government lawyers, and digests of the most important statutory and common-law provisions of each jurisdiction. The latter volumes are very useful when you want to check information such as the statute of limitations for a given matter in a particular jurisdiction (which nevertheless must be verified by consulting the original state code). The CD-ROM edition allows you to search by location, practice area, attorney, firm, or other criteria—including combinations (so that you could locate, for example, "sole-practitioner bankruptcy attorneys in Seattle"). The same *Martindale-Hubbell* services are also available through LEXIS.

For subscribers of WESTLAW, West's Legal Directory (WLD) is available on-line. This directory covers much the same information as *Martindale-Hubbell,* but is a newer publication. A CD-ROM version of WLD has also been released.

In addition to these directories, many state lawyer directories are published by bar associations, often as supplements to bar publications. These directories may carry other useful information such as the state's code of conduct for lawyers and judges, a list of important public officers, and much other information needed in the daily practice of law.

Dictionaries   The best-known legal dictionaries are *Black's Law Dictionary* (West) and *Balentine's Law Dictionary* (Lawyers Cooperative). Both have pronunciation guides along with the definitions, which are based on case law, and both supply lists of standard abbreviations. *Black's* has extensive coverage of definitions of legal maxims, which are sometimes difficult to find. In addition, it features examples of usage (with citations), though these can sometimes be dated. A citation-based dictionary based on current (and historical) usage is *Merriam-Webster's Dictionary of Law.*

Words and Phrases (West) is another research tool that attorneys find useful when dealing with legal terms or general phrases that may develop legal connotations in case law. It is basically a 46-volume annotated dictionary whose definitions are based on judicial interpretations of the terms. If, for example, you wanted to know whether the expression "about one year" had ever been judicially interpreted or defined, you could check the phrase in this set. *Words and Phrases* is supplemented annually by pocket parts.

Government information   Every law office should have a copy of the latest *United States Government Manual,* which can be purchased from the G.P.O. It is the single most comprehensive source of information on all three branches of the federal government, including the many executive and independent agencies functioning in each branch. It lists key personnel and telephone numbers, provides organization charts, describes functions and authority, and refers to statutes creating and governing each of the agencies. You might also wish to have the latest edition of the *Statistical Abstract of the United States,* prepared by the Bureau of the Census (and available from Bernan Associates, Wash., D.C.).

If the lawyers in your office have regular business with congressional personnel, one or two additional publications may be useful: the latest *Congressional Staff Directory* (published by Congressional Staff Directory, Inc.) and the *Congressional Directory* for the present Congress, available from the GPO.

Three publications that may be useful if you have need of out-of-state information are the current editions of (1) *Book of the States,* which contains much official information on government structure and organization for the fifty states; (2) *State Administrative Officials Classified by Function,* which supplies information about many state administrative agencies; and (3) *State Elective Officials and the Legislatures.* All three are published by the Council of State Governments (Lexington, KY).

News and Business Information

Many law firms have begun to subscribe to general news and business information services (on-line) to meet the increasing need of lawyers for corporate and financial data. The three most popular services are NEXIS, DIALOG, and Dow Jones.

NEXIS   The NEXIS component of the LEXIS-NEXIS service offers a wide variety of individual information sources, including news and business publications (e.g., *The New York Times, The Washington Post, Business Week, Fortune*), cable television and public radio feature stories, international wire service reports (e.g., Associated Press, Reuters), and other information such as brokerage house findings, SEC filings, company market-share information, and stock quotes from all the major domestic exchanges. Another service allows you to access current information on individual countries. Unlike some of the other business databases, most of what is available on NEXIS is full-text, allowing you to print individual articles or reports without having to track down the originals. One of the efficiency features of NEXIS is its grouping of material into topical libraries (e.g., banking and finance, computers and communications, energy) so that you receive all the information you need on a given subject.

DIALOG   DIALOG (Knight-Ridder Communications, Inc., Mountain View, Cal.) is another on-line information service that many law firms subscribe to, often as an optional component of WESTLAW (DIALOG on WESTLAW). The DIALOG service is really a collection of 350 individual database services, containing over 260 million bibliographic records of books, articles, conference proceedings, news, and statistics in a wide variety of fields, from science and technology to business and finance. The material in DIALOG is increasingly available as full text, but for many of the individual databases the contents are bibliographic records only. This arrangement generally allows for less-expensive searching and practically always permits you to see summaries or abstracts before deciding to retrieve an article. Typically you can order a copy of the article for next-day delivery at a reasonable cost. Otherwise you can get much current information on-line by using a "dial menu" function that permits you to search a particular subject in all the databases or in specified databases only. You can also subscribe to an "alert" service that will provide you with immediate updates on developments in a given field.

Dow Jones   This news retrieval service (headquartered in Princeton, N.J.) is also widely used in law offices, again frequently accessed through WESTLAW or subscribed to independently. Dow Jones offers general business, financial, and economic news (including full-text access to *The Wall Street Journal, Barron's,* and other periodicals); current information from various business wire services; company and industry information; stock quotes and statistics; and general services such as E-mail, on-line brokerage, movie reviews, travel services, and weather information. One popular feature is a "quick search" that permits you to retrieve information about a specific publicly-held company gathered from a number of different databases using only the stock-ticker symbol.

Other resources   While you may not ordinarily require access to all or any of these resources, you should be aware of them in case they become relevant to a particular project or to your practice generally. One good source of information about these and other such services is *Full Text Sources On Line* (Bibliodata, Needham Heights, Mass.), a directory issued twice a year which lists sources by category such as government, banking, environment, labor, medicine, and so on.

Managing the Law Library

A good law library, regardless of its size or type, is distinguished by three qualities: order, system, and discipline. There must be *order* to permit the user to locate material quickly and easily, and the order must be based on a *system*—a scheme that brings like materials together in a reasonable way. Finally, *discipline* is needed to ensure that order and system prevail and that the library client is properly served.

When a law collection approaches about 10,000 volumes, many law firms hire a professional librarian. Until such a professional is hired, however, it is often the secretary who administers the library. With initiative and the will to learn, it is possible for the secretary to maintain the law-firm library quite effectively.

This section introduces the essentials of the subject, leaving many of the details to more specialized publications on librarianship.

Sources of Information

If you are responsible for the law library, you should become familiar with three publications: (1) a book or manual on legal research, (2) a handbook of legal citation, and (3) a book on operating a law library (see the Appendix for specific titles). Although you may not be expected to read these works from cover to cover, the more you refer to them the more familiar you will become with legal publications and the management of a law library.

Other sources of information are courses in legal bibliography and legal research, which are frequently offered as part of paralegal or legal-secretarial education programs. In addition, a visit to the library of a law school, bar association, or court, or even a nearby law firm will give you an excellent opportunity to see the variety of law books being published and the method of their arrangement.

There may be a chapter of the American Association of Law Libraries (AALL) or some other locally organized group of law librarians in your city or state. Although professional requirements may prevent full membership, it may be possible to attend the meetings, seminars, and workshops of these organizations as a guest so as to benefit from the expertise of those who address their full energies to law-library administration and service. A call to the librarian at the nearest law library should supply the information you need regarding existing organizations. In addition, you can get a wealth of information from the *Directory and Handbook of the American Association of Law Libraries* (AALL) (published by Commerce Clearing House, Chicago, Ill.), available from AALL headquarters, 53 West Jackson Boulevard, Chicago, Il.

Establishing Order

The first task of the new law librarian is to inventory the firm's information resources: on-line services, CD-ROMs, audiovisual materials, and books in the library, attorneys' offices, and conference rooms. If the material is not already well organized, it should be arranged in a clear-cut and rational manner so that items can be located easily and properly reshelved when a user is finished with them.

One method is to group material by jurisdiction, then by type or format, then by subject. That is, all federal materials should be shelved together, with primary statutory sources first, followed by case-law sources, related digests, and *Shepard's Citations*. All state materials should be similarly organized. Treatises should be grouped together and arranged by author, or, if there are many titles, by subject and then by author. Periodicals and loose-leaf services should be grouped together and arranged by title or author. Legal encyclopedias, form books, dictionaries, and the like can be grouped to form the core of a secondary-reference collection. The attorneys' preferences will usually dictate the arrangement scheme, but you should try to see that it is logical, responsive to their needs, and easy for you to implement and maintain.

The next step is to check the currency of your materials and make a note of items with missing pocket parts or advance sheets. Find out if anyone has maintained records of the materials. If any missing materials turn up, check them against your inventory of the physical holdings and attempt to assess their usefulness and currency.

Cataloging and Maintaining Records

Cataloging a law collection is a highly technical and demanding undertaking best left to trained professional librarians who can handle the many problems that will arise. If you must undertake the job yourself, you will have to study the topic thoroughly before you begin. Two books are recommended, but with the caution that their contents are not easy to assimilate: (1) Elizabeth Finley's *Manual of Procedures for Private Law Libraries,* and (2) *Akers' Simple Library Cataloging,* by Arthur Curley and Jana Varlejs (originally by Susan Grey Akers). Another approach you might consider, after you have inventoried your holdings and recorded them as completely as possible, is to visit another law library in your area whose collection is already cataloged and replicate its system and style with modifications to meet your needs.

A record must be made and filed for each publication in the library. While a card file may be sufficient to catalogue a very small library, for larger libraries placing the library inventory on a computer file is more effective. There are several library software programs available for use in the law office. These programs provide search screens, lists of titles, bibliographic information, and book status (in/out).

You should generally record the following information for each title:

1. Author (personal or corporate)
2. Title (as complete as possible)
3. Publisher, place of publication, and date
4. Number of volumes; number of pages for single-volume titles
5. Format and method of supplementation (i.e., periodical, loose-leaf, pocket parts, advance sheets/pamphlets, bound volume, floppy disk, CD); frequency of publication, if indicated
6. Call number (as determined by cataloging procedures)
7. Price
8. Miscellaneous information

Much of this data should come from the publications themselves. Data for items that you order will be supplied by a publisher's representative. In addition to the eight items listed, you will want to record the date on which you order an item and reserve space for recording the date when the item is received. You might also add an entry for "Requested by" where you can record the name of the attorney requesting the material.

Continuations records   The vast majority of legal publications are updated at some time, and receipt of the additional volumes and supplements must be carefully recorded. Record systems may be as simple as 3″ × 5″ cards alphabetized by titles on which you write the volume and issue number (or release number, for loose-leaf reports) of each new item, and perhaps a check mark when it has been paid for. Otherwise computer software documentation will assist you in developing such records.

Financial records   As with continuation records, keeping track of what has been paid for is crucial to ensure that subscriptions don't lapse. For small collections, it should be easy to create a manual log or a simple computerized spreadsheet with a separate page for each publisher or vendor that lists titles you have acquired from them, with columns for payment amounts and what the payments cover.

Circulation

You will need to have a circulation system in order to know where a given item is at any given moment. The most effective method is to use a computer-based circulation or inventory-control program involving the use of bar codes. When a book is charged out, you merely scan the bar code and type in the name of the patron (or scan a bar-coded user card) to update the computerized catalog. In smaller libraries, traditional charge cards and back-of-the-book pockets can achieve the same purpose. For details, consult a book on library circulation.

Appendix I:

Expressions (Clichés) to Avoid in Business Writing

The following is a list of expressions that you should avoid if you seek more clarity, brevity, and originality in your business writing.

above   While this word may properly be used as a noun ("see the above"), an adjective ("the above figure"), and an adverb ("see above"), overusing it within a document can distract a reader. Consider alternative expressions:

> See the figure on page 27.
> This figure . . .
> See the material illustrated earlier.

above-mentioned/aforementioned/aforesaid   The use of these words is on the wane in legal contexts, and they can sound pompous in general business communication. They can usually be replaced by *this, that, these,* and *those.*

> *not:*   The aforementioned company . . .
> We must reach a decision regarding the aforesaid dispute.
> *instead:* This company . . .
> The company in question . . .
> The company mentioned earlier . . .
> We must make a decision about this (that) dispute.

acknowledge receipt of/in receipt of   This expression can be replaced by the shorter *have received.*

> *not:*   We acknowledge receipt of your check.
> *instead:* We have received your check.

afford (one) the opportunity   This wordy expression can usually be replaced with *allow* or *permit.*

> *not:*   This ruling affords us the opportunity to move ahead.
> *instead:* This ruling allows us to move ahead.

and etc.   This phrase is redundant, because the Latin *et cetera* means "and the rest." Omit the *and.*

> *not:*   calls, letters, faxes, and etc.
> *instead:* calls, letters, faxes, etc.

and/or   This expression is best restricted to use between two alternatives: "A and/or B" means "A or B or both." In "A, B, and/or C," *and/or* will likely be either ambiguous or unnecessary.

any and all   This phrase is sometimes unavoidable in legal documents, but in most correspondence it should be shortened to either *any* or *all.*

as per   This expression has been overworked when meaning "as," "in accordance with," and "following."

     not: As per your request of . . .
                As per our telephone conversation of . . .
                As per our agreement . . .
     instead: As you requested . . .
                According to your request . . .
                In accordance with your request . . .
                As a follow-up to our telephone conversation . . .
                As we agreed . . .

as regards/in regard to/with regard to   These expressions can often be replaced with *concerning, regarding,* or *about.*

     not: We wrote to them several times in regard to their unpaid balance.
     instead: We wrote to them several times about their unpaid balance.

at an early (a later) date   This phrase can usually be replaced by *soon (later).*

     not: We expect to be able to present our case at an early date.
     instead: We expect to be able to present our case soon.

at this juncture   This is best used only sparingly when referring to an important or crucial point ("At this critical juncture in the prosecution of the case"). It can usually be replaced by *at this point, now, currently,* or *at present.*

     not: I advise you to remain silent at this juncture.
                At this juncture we are considering our options.
     instead: I advise you to remain silent at this point.
                Currently we are considering our options.

at this point in time/at this time   These phrases may be replaced by *now, currently,* or *at (the) present.* Similarly, *at that point in time* and *at that time* may be replaced by *then.*

at this writing   This may be replaced by *currently, now,* or *at present.*

at your earliest convenience   This expression can often be replaced by the more direct *as soon as you can.* Other alternatives include *immediately, by* (date), and *within* (number) *days.*

attached/enclosed hereto/herewith   These phrases in business correspondence are rather formal, and the sentences in which they occur can often be recast.

     not: Attached hereto is a list . . .
     instead: Attached is/are . . .
                We are attaching . . .
                I have enclosed . . .
                You'll find enclosed . . .

awaiting your instructions   This phrase can usually be replaced with *please let us know.*

> *not:*   We are awaiting your instructions regarding this matter.
> *instead:*   Please let us know how you would like us to handle this matter.

basic fundamentals   This redundant term can be shortened to *basics* or *fundamentals.*

dated   The word *dated* may sometimes be omitted.

> *not:*   your letter dated June 1
> *instead:*   your letter of June 1

deem (it)   This rather stiff word can often be avoided.

> *not:*   We deem it advisable that you . . .
> *instead:*   We advise you to . . .
>   We think it in your best interest to . . .

despite the fact that   Substitute *although* or *though.*

due to/due to the fact that   Substitute *because (of)* or *since.*

duly   This word is usually unnecessary and can almost always be omitted.

> *not:*   Your request has been duly forwarded.
> *instead:*   Your request has been forwarded.
>   We have forwarded your request.

during the time that/at the time when   These expressions can usually be replaced by *while, when,* or *as.*

> *not:*   During the time that the injunction was in force . . .
>   At the time when she was suffering from seizures . . .
> *instead:*   While the injunction was in force . . .
>   When she was suffering from seizures . . .

each and every   Shorten to either *each* or *every.*

endeavor   This formal verb can be replaced by *try* or *attempt.*

> *not:*   We shall endeavor to . . .
> *instead:*   We will attempt to . . .
>   We will make every effort to . . .
>   We will do everything we can to . . .

for the purpose of   This expression may often be shortened to *for.*

> *not:*   necessary for purposes of accounting
> *instead:*   necessary for accounting

for the reason that   Substitute *because* or *since.*

forward . . . on   Shorten to simply *forward.*

> *not:*   We have forwarded your complaint on to the proper authorities.
> *instead:*   We have forwarded your complaint to the proper authorities.

hold in abeyance   This expression often sounds stilted and can usually be avoided.

> *not:*   We are holding our final decision in abeyance.
> *instead:*   We are deferring our final decision.
>   We are delaying our final decision.
>   We are holding up our final decision.

I (we) call your attention to   This phrase can usually be replaced with *please note* or *note*.

> *not:*   I call your attention to paragraph 15.
> *instead:*   Please note paragraph 15.
>   Note the wording in paragraph 15.

if and when   This phrase retains some standing in legal documents, but it can often be shortened to either *if* or *when*.

in a . . . manner   This phrase can usually be replaced by an adverb ending in *-ly*.

> *not:*   He approached his work in a careless manner.
> *instead:*   He approached his work carelessly.

in connection with   This is usually a wordy way of saying *about, on,* or *concerning*.

> *not:*   They received numerous compliments in connection with their efforts.
> *instead:*   They received numerous compliments on their efforts.

in many cases   This can usually be replaced by *often* or *frequently*.

> *not:*   In many cases you can avoid litigation.
> *instead:*   Often you can avoid litigation.

in order that   This can usually be replaced with *so that*.

> *not:*   . . . in order that we may process your case.
> *instead:*   . . . so that we may process your case.

in the amount of   This is a long way of saying *for*.

> *not:*   We are sending you a check in the amount of $50.95.
> *instead:*   We are sending you a check for $50.95.

in the case of (X v. Y)   This can usually be shortened to *in* (X *v.* Y).

in the course of   The more concise *during* may often be substituted.

> *not:*   In the course of the deposition . . .
> *instead:*   During the deposition . . .

in the event that   This phrase may often be replaced by *if* or *in case*.

> *not:*   In the event that you cannot meet with me next week, . . .
> *instead:*   If you cannot meet with me next week, . . .

in the process of   This overworked phrase can usually be replaced with *currently* or *now*.

>   *not:*   We are in the process of taking depositions.
>   *instead:* Currently we are taking depositions.

in view of the fact that   This expression can be replaced by *because (of)* or *since*.

>   *not:*   In view of the fact that he is now president . . .
>   He was terminated in view of the fact that he had been negligent.
>   *instead:* Since he is now president . . .
>   He was terminated because he had been negligent.

in view of the foregoing   This expression can often be replaced by *thus, therefore,* or *consequently*.

>   *not:*   In view of the foregoing, we cannot accept the terms of the
>   agreement.
>   *instead:* Therefore, we cannot accept the terms of the agreement.

it has been brought to our notice   Substitute one of the following:

>   We note . . .
>   We notice . . .
>   We see . . .
>   We have learned . . .

it is incumbent upon   The thought here is more easily expressed as *I/we must, you must,* or *he/she/they must*

it is interesting to note that   This expression can often be either dropped or replaced with a transitional word or short phrase.

>   *not:*   It is interesting to note that, by this time last year, all January orders
>   had been met.
>   *instead:* By this time last year, all orders received in January had been met.
>   Moreover, by this time last year, all January orders had been met.

it may be said that   This phrase can often be omitted.

>   *not:*   Indeed, it may be said that without the support of this department,
>   this project would not have succeeded
>   *instead:* Indeed, without the support of this department, this project would
>   not have succeeded.

kindly   This expression can be replaced with *please*.

make the necessary inquiries/make inquiry   This hackneyed expression can usually be replaced with *look into, research,* or *investigate*.

>   *not:*   We will make the necessary inquiries for you.
>   *instead:* We will look into the matter for you.
>   We will research the matter for you.

meet with one's approval   This stiff phrase can often be avoided by recasting the sentence.

> *not:*   If the plan meets with your approval . . .
>
> *instead:*   If the plan is acceptable to you . . .
>   If you approve . . .

note that   Expressions with *note* are often unnecessary.

> *not:*   We note that your prospectus states . . .
>   You will note that the amount in the fourth column . . .
>
> *instead:*   Your prospectus states . . .
>   The amount in the fourth column . . .

notwithstanding the fact that   This wordy phrase can be replaced with *although* or *even though*.

> *not:*   . . . notwithstanding the fact that she has no claim to the property.
>
> *instead:*   . . . even though she has no claim to the property.

of a . . . nature/of this nature   This phrase can usually be avoided by using an adjective or by recasting the sentence.

> *not:*   The court does not normally hear cases of a probate nature.
>
> *instead:*   The court does not normally hear probate cases.

of the opinion that   This stiff phrase can often be avoided.

> *not:*   We are of the opinion that . . .
>
> *instead:*   We think (*or* believe) that . . .
>   Our opinion is that . . .
>   Our position is that . . .

on a . . . basis/on the basis of   These phrases are somewhat long-winded and can often be avoided.

> *not:*   On the basis of what we have learned so far, . . .
>   They accepted the case on the basis of its merits.
>   We will provide services on an as-needed basis.
>
> *instead:*   From what we have learned so far, . . .
>   They accepted the case because of its merits.
>   We will provide services as needed.

However, these phrases are sometimes useful, and there often is no good way to avoid them.

on or about   While this phrase has some legitimate legal applications, it can often be shortened to either *on* or *about*.

period of time   This can often be shortened to either *period* or *time*.

> *not:*   During this period of time . . .
>
> *instead:*   During this period . . .

pursuant to   This stiff phrase unfortunately occurs at the very beginning of many follow-up letters and memorandums. It can be replaced with *According to, Following up, As a follow-up to,* or *In accordance with.*

    not: Pursuant to discussions held in this office on June 1, . . .

    instead: Follwing up our June 1 meeting . . .

reason is because   This redundant expression should be replaced with *The reason is that.*

receipt . . . is acknowledged   This impersonal passive construction can be replaced by *We received* or *We have received.*

reduce to a minimum   This phrase may be replaced by *minimize.*

    not: This tack reduces to a minimum the possibility of appeal.

    instead: This tack minimizes the possibility of appeal.

refuse and decline   Shorten to either *refuse* or *decline.*

    not: We must refuse and decline any further dealings . . .

    instead: We must refuse any further dealings . . .

                  We must decline to have any further dealings . . .

regarded as being   Omit *being.*

    not: The witness is regarded as being hostile.

    instead: The witness is regarded as hostile.

reiterate again   Omit *again,* which is redundant here.

said   This adjective is standard in legal documents but sounds stiff in other contexts. Use *the, this, that, these,* or *those* instead.

    not: a discussion of said matters

    instead: a discussion of these matters

same   This is often an awkward substitute for *it* or *them,* or for the noun it replaces.

    not: We have your check and we thank you for same.

                  Your July 2 inquiry has been received and same is being researched.

    instead: Thank you for your check.

                  Your July 2 inquiry has been received and is being researched.

subsequent to   This phrase may usually be replaced by one beginning with *after* or *following.*

    not: Subsequent to her acceptance of the job . . .

    instead: After accepting the job . . .

therefor/therein/thereon   These words are commonly used in legal documents but sound stiff in general business contexts.

> *not:*   The order is enclosed herewith with payment therefor.
> The safe is in a secure area with the blueprints kept therein.
> Enclosed please find Forms X, Y, and Z; please affix your signature thereon.
>
> *instead:*   We're enclosing a check with our order.
> The blueprints are kept in the safe, which is located in a secure area.
> Please sign the enclosed Forms X, Y, and Z.

to all intents and purposes   This phrase can usually be replaced by *in effect* or *really.*

> *not:*   Their response was, to all intents and purposes, no response at all.
> *instead:*   Their response was, in effect, no response at all.

until such time as   This legalism may usually be replaced by *until* or *unless.*

> *not:*   Until such time as we receive new instructions from you . . .
> *instead:*   Until we receive new instructions from you . . .

up to the present writing   This stilted expression should be replaced with briefer alternatives.

> *not:*   Up to the present writing, we do not seem to have received your answer.
> *instead:*   We have not yet received your answer.
> We still haven't received your answer.
> To date, we have not received . . .

we would appreciate your advising us   This phrase can usually be replaced by *please let us know.*

> *not:*   We would appreciate your advising us of any changes . . .
> *instead:*   Please let us know of any changes . . .

whosoever/whomsoever   These highly formal words can be replaced by *whoever/whomever* or *anyone who.*

with reference to/with respect to   These phrases can usually be replaced by *as to, concerning,* or *about.*

> *not:*   He called with reference to a complaint that was received.
> With respect to the evidence in the case . . .
> *instead:*   He called about a complaint that was received.
> Concerning the evidence in the case . . .

with the exception of   This phrase can usually be replaced by *except* or *except for.*

> *not:*   With the exception of SoundStorm, all parties have agreed in principle.
> *instead:*   All parties except SoundStorm have agreed in principle.

within (one's) power to   This is a lengthy way of saying "We can," "We are able to," or (in the negative—i.e., with *not*) "We cannot," "We are unable to."

> *not:*   It is not within our power to pursue such a questionable goal.
> *instead:*   We cannot pursue a questionable goal.

would   This verbal auxiliary should not be unnecessarily repeated.

> *not:*   I would think that our chances would improve if we accepted arbitration.
> *instead:*   I think our chances would improve if we accepted arbitration.

Frequently Confused and Misused Words

abjure to reject solemnly
adjure to command

abrogate to nullify
obrogate to alter or repeal
arrogate to claim

abstruse hard to understand
obtuse not sharp

accede to agree
exceed to go beyond

accent to emphasize
ascent act of moving
assent to agree to something

acceptor one who accepts an order or bill
exceptor one who objects

access right or ability to enter
excess intemperance

ad advertisement
add to join to something; to find a sum

adapt to adjust to something
adept highly skilled
adopt to take as one's child; to take up and practice

addenda additional items
agenda list of things to be done

addition part added
edition form in which a text is published

adept *see* ADAPT

adherence act of adhering
adherents followers

adjoin to be next to
adjourn to suspend a session
adjure *see* ABJURE

adopt *see* ADAPT

adverse unfavorable
averse disinclined

advice counsel or information
advise to give advice

affect to act upon or influence
effect *n* result; *vb* to bring about

agenda *see* ADDENDA

alimentary relating to nourishment
elementary simple or basic

allegation positive assertion
alligation binding together

allocator person who allocates
allocatur kind of writ

allude to refer indirectly
elude to evade

amenable accountable, agreeable
amendable capable of being amended

amend to alter in writing
emend to correct

ante- prior to or earlier than
anti- opposite or against

antimony chemical element
antinomy contradiction between laws

aphasia loss of speech
asphyxia suffocation
atasia inability to stand

appraise to set a value on
apprise to give notice of
apprize to appreciate or value

approximate *adj* nearly correct or exact; *vb* to approach
proximate very near or direct

arraign to bring before a court
arrange to come to an agreement

arrogate *see* ABROGATE

ascent *see* ACCENT

assent *see* ACCENT

asphyxia *see* APHASIA

assay to test for valuable content
essay to try tentatively

assure to give confidence to
ensure to make certain
insure to guarantee against loss

atasia *see* APHASIA

atone to make amends
attain to reach or achieve
attorn to agree to be tenant to a new landlord

aural relating to the ear or hearing
oral relating to the mouth, spoken

averse *see* ADVERSE

avert to anticipate and ward off
overt not concealed

bail security given
bale bundle of goods

biannual usu. twice a year; sometimes every two years
biennial every two years

bloc group working together
block tract of land

boarder one that boards
border boundary

born produced by birth
borne *past participle* of BEAR

breach infraction of law
breech a fetus presented breech first

breadth width
breath air breathed in or out

by law according to law
bylaw, byelaw local or corporate rule

callous hardened
callus hard area on skin

cannon artillery piece
canon accepted principle or rule

canvas strong cloth; oil painting
canvass to solicit votes or opinions

capital city that is the seat of government
capitol building where a state legislature meets
Capitol building where the U.S. Congress meets

carat unit of weight for precious stones
caret mark showing where something is to be inserted

carpus wrist
corpus body

casual not planned
causal relating to or being a cause

casually by chance or accident
casualty one injured or killed

censor to examine writings for improper content
censure to express disapproval of

cession a yielding
session meeting

chalcosis copper in body tissue
chalicosis industrial lung disease

cite to summon; to quote
sight payable on presentation
site piece of land

cliental relating to clients
clientele body of clients

collaborate to work or act jointly
corroborate to confirm

collision act of colliding
collusion secret cooperation for deceit

coma unconscious state
comma punctuation mark

commensurate equal in measure or extent
commiserate sympathize

complacent self-satisfied
complaisant amiable

complement something that completes
compliment flattering remark

concert to act in harmony or conjunction
consort to keep company

concurso legal proceeding
concursus religious doctrine

condemn to censure; to pronounce sentence against
contemn to scorn

consul diplomatic official
council administrative body
counsel *n* legal representative; *vb* to give advice

corespondent joint respondent
correspondent one who communicates

corpus *see* CARPUS

corroborate *see* COLLABORATE

council *see* CONSUL

counsel *see* CONSUL

councillor member of a council
counselor lawyer

courtesy something allowed or accepted
curtesy husband's right in dead wife's
land
curtsy slight bow

credible worthy of being believed
creditable worthy of praise

currant raisinlike fruit
current *n* stream; *adj* belonging to the
present

curtesy *see* COURTESY
curtsy *see* COURTESY

cynosure one that attracts
sinecure easy job

debar bar from something
disbar expel from the legal profession

decedent deceased person
dissident one who disagrees

decent conforming to a standard
descent transmission of an estate by
inheritance
dissent difference of opinion

decree official order
degree extent or scope

defuse to make less harmful
diffuse to pour out or spread widely

deluded misled or deceived
diluted weakened in consistency or
strength

demean to behave
demesne landed property
domain territory possessed and governed

demur to protest
demure shy

depositary one who receives a deposit
depository place where something is
deposited

deprecate to disapprove of
depreciate to lower the worth of

deraign to prove
derange to disarrange or upset

descent *see* DECENT

desperate having lost hope
disparate distinct

device piece of equipment or tool
devise to invent; to plot

diffuse *see* DEFUSE

diluted *see* DELUDED

diplomat one employed in diplomacy
diplomate one certified as qualified

disassemble to take apart
dissemble to disguise feelings or intentions

disbar *see* DEBAR

disburse to pay out
disperse to scatter

discreet capable of keeping a secret
discrete individually distinct

disparate *see* DESPERATE

disperse *see* DISBURSE

dissemble *see* DISASSEMBLE

disseminate to spread widely
dissimilate to make or become dis-
similar
dissimulate to hide under a false appearance

dissent *see* DECENT

dissident *see* DECEDENT

dissimilate *see* DISSEMINATE

dissimulate *see* DISSEMINATE

domain *see* DEMEAN

edition *see* ADDITION

effect *see* AFFECT

elementary *see* ALIMENTARY

elicit to draw or bring out
illicit not lawful

eligible qualified to have
illegible not readable

elude *see* ALLUDE

emanate to come out from a source
eminent standing above others in
some respect

immanent inherent
imminent ready to take place

emend *see* AMEND

emigrate to leave a country
immigrate to come into a place

eminence prominence or superiority
immanence restriction to one domain
imminence something imminent

engross to prepare a text; to purchase in quantity
in gross existing independently

ensure *see* ASSURE

enumerable countable
innumerable too many to count

envelop to surround
envelope paper container for a letter

equable free from unpleasant extremes
equitable fair

erasable removable by erasing
irascible hot-tempered

essay *see* ASSAY

exceed *see* ACCEDE

exceptor *see* ACCEPTOR

excess *see* ACCESS

ex mora because of delay
ex more according to custom

extant currently existing
extent size, degree, or measure

flounder to struggle
founder to sink

forego to precede
forgo to give up

formally in a formal manner
formerly at an earlier time

gage a security deposit
gauge to measure

gager giving of a gage
gauger one that gauges

gait manner of walking
gate opening in a wall or fence

gauge *see* GAGE

gauger *see* GAGER

generic general
genetic of or relating to the genes

guarantee to promise to be responsible for
guaranty something given as a security

hail to greet
hale *vb* to compel to go; *adj* healthy

hearsay rumor
heresy dissent from a dominant theory

humerus long bone of upper arm
humorous funny

illegible *see* ELIGIBLE
illicit *see* ELICIT

immanence *see* EMINENCE

immanent *see* EMANATE

immigrate *see* EMIGRATE

imminence *see* EMINENCE

imminent *see* EMANATE

immure to enclose within walls
inure to accustom to something undesirable

impracticable not feasible
impractical not practical

inapt not suitable
inept unfit or foolish

incite to urge on
insight discernment

incredibility unbelievableness
incredulity disbelief

incurable not curable
incurrable capable of being incurred

indict to accuse formally
indite to put in writing

inept *see* INAPT

inequity lack of equity
iniquity wickedness

infirmation invalidation
information knowledge received

ingenious very clever
ingenuous innocent and candid

in gross *see* ENGROSS

inherent being an essential part of something
inherit to receive from an ancestor

iniquity *see* INEQUITY

in jure according to law
injure to do harm to

innumerable *see* ENUMERABLE

in re in the matter of
in rem against a thing

insight *see* INCITE

install to set up for use
instill to impart gradually

insure *see* ASSURE

interment burial
internment confinement or impounding

interpellate to question formally
interpolate to insert words in a text

interstate involving more than one state
intestate leaving no valid will
intrastate existing within a state

inure *see* IMMURE

irascible *see* ERASABLE

it's *contraction:* it is
its *possessive form* of IT

larynx upper part of the trachea
pharynx space between the mouth and esophagus

lean to rely on for support
lien legal claim upon property

lesser smaller
lessor grantor of a lease

levee embankment to prevent flooding
levy imposition or collection of a tax

liable obligated by law or equity

libel *vb* to make libelous statements; *n* false and damaging publication

lien *see* LEAN

lumbar relating to vertebrae of the lower back
lumber *n* timber ready to use; *vb* to move clumsily

malfeasance wrongful conduct
misfeasance improper performance of a legal act
nonfeasance failure to do what ought to be done

mandatary one holding a mandate
mandatory obligatory

material *adj* having relevance or importance; *n* matter
matériel equipment and supplies

mean *n* middle point; *adj* stingy or malicious; *vb* intend
mesne intermediate or intervening
mien appearance

median middle value in a range
medium *adj* intermediate in position or degree; *n* means of communication

meet to come into contact with
mete to allot

meretricious falsely attractive
meritorious deserving reward or honor
meticulous extremely careful about details

mesne *see* MEAN

mete *see* MEET

meticulous *see* MERETRICIOUS

mien *see* MEAN

miner mine worker
minor *n* one of less than legal age; *adj* not important or serious

misfeasance *see* MALFEASANCE

moot having no practical significance
mute *n* a person unable to speak; *vb* to tone down or muffle

mucous relating to mucus
mucus secretion from membranes

mute *see* MOOT

myatonia muscular flabbiness
myotonia tonic muscular spasm

naval relating to a navy
navel belly button

nonfeasance *see* MALFEASANCE

obliger one who obliges
obligor one who writes a surety bond

obrogate *see* ABROGATE

obtuse *see* ABSTRUSE

oral *see* AURAL

ordinance law, rule, or decree
ordnance military supplies
ordonnance compilation of laws

overt *see* AVERT

oyer hearing of a document read in open court
oyez Hear ye!—a call for silence in court

parlay to bet again a stake and its winnings
parley discussion of disputed points

parol oral statement
parole conditional release

pedal relating to the foot or a pedal
peddle to travel about and sell goods

peer one of equal standing
pier bridge support

penal relating to punishment
penile relating to the penis
pineal relating to or being the pineal gland

penance act to show repentance
pennants flags or banners

peremptory ending a right of action, debate, or delay
preemptory preemptive

perpetrate to be guilty of
perpetuate to make perpetual

perquisite a right or privilege
prerequisite a necessary preliminary

persecute to harass injuriously
prosecute to proceed against at law

personal relating to a particular person
personnel body of employees

personality distinctive personal quality
personalty personal property

perspective view of things
prospective relating to the future
prospectus introductory description of an enterprise

perspicacious very discerning
perspicuous easily understood

pharynx *see* LARYNX

pier *see* PEER

plaintiff the complaining party in litigation
plaintive expressive of sadness

plantar relating to the sole of the foot
planter plantation owner

plat plan of a piece of land
plot small piece of land

pole long slender piece of wood or metal
poll sampling of opinion

pore to read attentively
pour to dispense from a container

portend to give an omen or sign of
portent something that foreshadows a coming event

practicable feasible
practical capable of being put to use

precede to go or come before
proceed to go to law

precedence priority
precedents previous examples to follow

preemptory *see* PEREMPTORY

prerequisite *see* PERQUISITE

prescribe to assert a prescriptive right or title
proscribe to put outside the law

presence fact of being present
presents the present legal instrument

presentiment premonition or prejudgment
presentment offering of something to be dealt with

preview advance view
purview part or scope of a statute

principal main body of an estate; chief person or matter
principle basic rule or assumption

proceed *see* PRECEDE

pro rata proportionately
prorate to divide proportionately

proscribe *see* PRESCRIBE

prosecute *see* PERSECUTE

prospective *see* PERSPECTIVE

prospectus   *see* PERSPECTIVE

prostate   gland
prostrate   to put oneself in a submissive position

proximate   *see* APPROXIMATE

pubes   pubic hair or region
pubis   pubic bone

purpart   purparty
purport   *n* meaning; *vb* to claim or intend

purview   *see* PREVIEW

raise   to lift, to increase
raze   to destroy or tear down

reality   the quality or state of being real
realty   real property

rebound   to spring back or recover
redound   to have an effect

recession   ceding back
recision   cancellation
rescission   act of rescinding or abrogating

reclaim   to reform or better
re-claim   to claim back

recognizer   one that recognizes
recognizor   one obligated under a recognizance

recover   to obtain a right in court
re-cover   to cover again

redound   *see* REBOUND

reform   *vb* to amend; *n* amendment
re-form   to form again

release   to give up
re-lease   to lease again

relic   something remaining
relict   widow

rescission   *see* RECESSION

reserve   to keep back
re-serve   to serve again

residence   place where one lives
residents   those who reside in a place

resign   to relinquish
re-sign   to sign again

resume   to take up again
résumé   summary

revendicate   to recover something
revindicate   to vindicate again

role   part, function
roll   bread

session   *see* CESSION

settler   one who settles something or somewhere
settlor   one who makes a settlement

shear   to cut off
sheer   very thin or transparent

sight   *see* CITE

sinecure   *see* CYNOSURE

site   *see* CITE

specie   coined money
species   class of individuals

stationary   still
stationery   writing material

statue   piece of sculpture
stature   natural height or achieved status
statute   law enacted by a legislature

subordination   placement in a lower rank
subornation   crime of procuring perjury

tack   course of action
tact   sense of the proper thing to say or do

tare   weight allowance
tear   to pull apart by force

tenant   one who occupies a rental dwelling
tenet   principle
tenere   to possess
teneri   clause in a bond
tenor   general character or sense
tenure   act or right of holding property

therefor   for that
therefore   thus

tort   wrongful act
torte   rich cake or pastry

tortious   involving tort
tortuous   lacking in straightforwardness
torturous   very painful or distressing

track path or course

tract stretch of land; system of body organs

trustee one entrusted with something

trusty convict allowed special privileges

tympanites swollen abdomen

tympanitis ear inflammation

venal open to bribery

venial excusable

veracity truthfulness

voracity greediness

waive to give up voluntarily

wave to motion with the hands

waiver act of waiving a right

waver to be irresolute

warrantee person to whom a warranty is made

warranty guarantee of integrity

wave *see* WAIVE

waver *see* WAIVER

wheal welt or raised patch on the skin

wheel circular frame capable of turning

Appendix III

Further Reading

Automation and Technology

Access: A Resource Guide to Legal Automation. Chicago, Ill.: American Bar Association, 1991.

American Library Association Staff. *PC LAN Systems for the Small Law Firm.* Dubuque, Iowa: Kendall-Hunt, 1993.

American Library Association Staff. *Software Selection—Law Firms.* Dubuque, Iowa: Kendall-Hunt, 1993.

American Library Association Staff. *Telephone and Peripheral Systems for Law Firms.* Dubuque, Iowa, Kendall-Hunt, 1993.

Arentowicz, Frank, and Ward Bower. *Law Office Automation and Technology.* New York: Mathew Bender, 1980 (updated regularly).

Automating the Small Law Office and Solo Practice. New York: Practicing Law Institute, 1992.

Ayres, James J. *Law Office Software.* New York: Wiley, 1990.

Designing Your Law Office. Chicago: American Bar Association, 1989.

Braeman, Kathryn M., and Fran Shellenberger. *From Yellow Pads to Computers.* Chicago: American Bar Association, 1991.

Kartson, Despina C., and Norman F. Strizek. *Computerized Litigation Support.* New York: Wiley, 1993.

Robbins, Richard L. *The Automated Law Firm.* Englewood Cliffs, N.J.: Prentice-Hall, n.d.

Ween, Peter G. *Every Manager's Guide to Information Technology.* Cambridge, Mass.: Harvard Business School Press, 1995.

Bookkeeping and Accounting

Burke, William J, and Carl W. Bradbury. *Accounting Systems for Law Offices.* New York: Mathew Bender, 1978 (updated regularly).

Covington, J. S., Jr. *Beginning Accounting in Law.* Houston, Texas: John Marshall, 1990.

Quinn, John P. *Law Firm Accounting.* New York: New York Law Publishing, 1986.

Rachlin, Robert, and Allen Sweeny. *Accounting and Financial Fundamentals for Nonfinancial Executives.* New York: Amacom, 1996.

Siegel, Joel G., and Jae K. Shim. *Accounting Handbook,* 2d ed. Hauppauge, N.Y.: Barron's, 1996.

Computers

Aker, Sharon Z. *The Mac Almanac.* New York: Ziff-Davis, 1994.

Biow, Lisa. *How to Use Your Computer.* New York: Ziff-Davis/Macmillan, 1996.

Computer Fundamentals for Legal Professionals, 4th ed. Dallas, Texas: Pearson Publications, 1991.

DiNucci, Darcy, et al., eds. *The Macintosh Bible,* 5th ed. Berkeley, Calif.: Peachpit Press, 1994.

Engst, Adam C, Corwin S. Low and Stanley K. Orchard. *Internet Starter Kit.* New York: Hayden Books/Macmillan, 1995

Ghazi, Juliane K. *Computer Use for the Legal Assistant.* St. Paul, Minn.: West Publishing, 1994.

Hahn, Harley. *The Internet Complete Reference,* 2d ed. New York: Osborne/McGraw-Hill, 1996.

Heid, Jim. *MacWorld New Complete Mac Handbook,* 4th ed. Foster City, Calif.: IDG Books, 1995.

Knorr, Eric. *The PC Bible,* 2d ed. Berkeley, Calif.: Peachpit Press, 1995.

Levine, John R., and Margaret Levine Young. *Internet for Dummies,* 2d ed. Foster City, Calif.: IDG Books, 1996.

Mason, Mary A., and Robert Harris. *Using Computers in the Law,* 3d ed. St. Paul, Minn.: West Publishing, 1993.

Pike, Mary Ann, et al. *Using the Internet.* Indianapolis, Ind.: QUE, 1996.

Sadler, Will, et al. *Using Internet E-Mail.* Indianapolis, Ind.: QUE, 1995.

Turley, James L. *PCs Made Easy,* 2d ed. New York: Osborne/McGraw-Hill, 1993.

Dictation and Transcription

Eskew, Mike, and Nancy Patterson. *Legal Procedures and Terminology for Court Reporters and Paralegals.* Englewood Cliffs, N.J.: Prentice-Hall, 1992.

Gonzalez, Jean, and Margaret Cline. *Computer Aided Transcription.* Huntington Beach, Cal.: Middleton-Wasley Publications, 1992.

Good, C. Edward. *Citing and Typing the Law,* 2d ed. Charlottesville, Virginia: Blue Jeans Press, 1987.

Hewitt, William E., and Jill B. Levy. *Computer Aided Transcription.* Williamsburg, Virginia: National Center for State Courts, 1994.

Lyle, Linda, and Howard Doty. *Legal Transcription.* St. Paul, Minn.: Paradigm, 1994.

Dictionaries

Black's Law Dictionary, 6th ed. St. Paul, Minn.: West Publishing, 1990.

Burton, William C. *The Legal Thesaurus,* 2d ed. New York: Macmillan, 1991.

Merriam-Webster's Dictionary of Law. Springfield, Mass.: Merriam-Webster, 1996.

Prince, Mary M. *Bieber's Dictionary of Legal Abbreviations,* 4th ed. Buffalo, N.Y.: William S. Heine, 1993.

Directories

Encyclopedia of Legal Information Sources, 3d ed. Detroit: Gale Research, 1996.

Fisher, Mary L. *Guide to State Legislative and Administrative Materials,* 4th ed. Littleton, Col.: Rothman, 1988 (updated).

Heels, Erik J. *The Legal List: Internet Desk Reference.* Rochester, N.Y.: Lawyers Cooperative Publishing, 1995.

Martindale-Hubbell Law Directory. New Providence, N.J.: Martindale-Hubbell, 1996 (updated annually).

Ethics and Human Relations

Center for Professional Responsibility. *Model Rules for Professional Conduct.* Chicago: American Bar Association, 1992.

Graves, Dana L., et al. *How to Survive in a Law Firm.* New York: Wiley, 1993.

Lynton, Jonathan, and Terri M. Lyndall. *Legal Ethics and Professional Responsibility.* Albany, N.Y.: Delmar, 1994.

Morrison, Laura L., and Gina DeCiani. *Legal Ethics for Paralegals and the Law Office.* St. Paul, Minn.: West Publishing, 1994.

Orlik, Deborah K. *Ethics for the Legal Assistant,* 2d ed. La Canada, Cal.: Marlen Hill Publications, 1990.

Smith, Charlotte. *Law Office Dynamics.* Dallas, Texas: Pearson Publications, 1992.

Etiquette

Baldridge, Lettitia. *Lettitia Baldridge's Complete Guide to Executive Manners.* New York: Rawson Associates/Macmillan, 1993.

Post, Emily. *Emily Post on Business Etiquette.* New York: HarperCollins, 1990.

Stewart, Marjabella Young, and Maria Faux. *Executive Etiquette.* New York: St. Martin's, 1994.

Forms and Documents

American Jurisprudence Legal Forms. Rochester, N.Y.: Lawyers Cooperative Publishing, 1991.

American Jurisprudence Pleadings and Practice Forms. Rochester, N.Y.: Lawyers Cooperative Publishing, 1993.

Federal Procedural Forms. St. Paul, Minn.: West Publishing.

Atwood, Illa W. *Law Office Documents.* Westerville, Ohio: Glencoe, 1993.

Law Library and Legal Research

Cohen, Morris L., and Kent C. Olson. *Legal Research in a Nutshell,* 5th ed. St. Paul, Minn.: West Publishing, 1992.

Cohen, Morris L., et al. *Finding the Law,* 9th ed. St. Paul, Minn.: West Publishing, 1993.

Curci-Gonzalez, Lucy, and Sharon K. French. *Managing the Private Law Library.* New York: Practicing Law Institute, 1991.

Curley, Arthur, and Jana Varlejs. *Akers' Simple Library Cataloging,* 7th ed. Metuchen, N.J.: Scarecrow, 1985.

Elias, Stephen. *Legal Research,* 3d ed. Berkeley: Nolo, 1992.

Evans, James. *Law on the Net.* Berkeley: Nolo, 1995.

Finley, Elizabeth. *Manual of Procedures for Private Law Libraries.* Chicago: American Association of Law Libraries, 1966; Supplement 1984.

Gurdak, John A. *Computer-Assisted Research for Legal Personnel.* Dallas, Texas: Pearson Publications, 1988.

Jacobstein, J. Myron, and Donald J. Dunn. *Legal Research Illustrated,* 6th ed. Westbury, N.Y.: Foundation Press, 1994.

Hazelton, Penny. *Computer Assisted Legal Research.* St. Paul, Minn.: West Publishing, 1993.

Moys, Elizabeth M., ed. *Manual of Law Librarianship,* 2d ed. New York: Macmillan, 1987.

Mueller, Heinz P., et al. *Law Librarianship.* Littleton, Col.: Rothman, 1983.

Panella, Deborah S. *Basics of Law Librarianship.* Binghamton, N.Y.: Haworth Press, 1991.

Walston-Dunham, Beth. *Legal Research.* St. Paul, Minn.: West Publishing, 1994.

Wren, Christopher G., and Jill R. Wren. *Using Computers in Legal Research.* Madison, Wisc.: Adams & Ambrose, 1994.

Legal Citations

The Bluebook: A Uniform System of Citation, 15th ed. Cambridge, Mass.: Harvard Law Review Association, 1991.

Mair, Elaine C. *How to Prepare a Legal Citation.* Hauppauge, N.Y.: Barron's, 1986.

Raistrick, Donald. *Index to Legal Citations and Abbreviations,* 2d ed. New Providence, N.J.: Bowker-Saur, 1994.

University of Chicago Manual of Legal Citation. Rochester, N.Y.: Lawyers Cooperative Publishing, 1989.

Letters and Writing

Fatooh, Audrey, and Barbara Mauk. *Style and Sense for the Legal Professional.* Palm Springs, Cal.: ETC Publications, 1996.

Garner, Bryan A. *The Elements of Legal Style.* New York: Oxford University Press, 1991.

Gordon, Mary Elizabeth. *The Deluxe Transitive Vampire.* New York: Pantheon, 1993.

Hodges, John C., ed. *Harbrace College Handbook,* 12th ed. San Diego, Cal.: Harcourt Brace, 1993.

Merriam-Webster's Guide to Business Correspondence, 2d ed. Springfield, Mass.: Merriam-Webster, 1996.

Magazines and Newsletters

The Docket. Tulsa, Okl.: National Association of Legal Secretaries.

Law Office Administrator. Atlanta, Georgia: Law Office Administrator.

Law Office Computing. Costa Mesa, Cal.: James Publishing.

Legal Assistant Today. Costa Mesa, Cal.: James Publishing.

Legal Automation News. Coral Gables, Fl.: Executive Data Systems.

Mail

U.S. Postal Service Publications. Washington, D.C.: U.S. Postal Service
  Consumer's Guide to Postal Services and Products
  Designing Letter Mail

Domestic Mail Manual
National ZIP Code and Post Office Directory
Ratefold

Parliamentary Procedures

Keesay, Ray E. *Modern Parliamentary Procedure*. Washington, D.C.: American Psychological Association, 1994.

Robert's Rules of Order, 11th ed. New York: HarperCollins, 1991.

Rozakis, Laurie. *Merriam-Webster's Rules of Order.* Springfield, Mass.: Merriam-Webster, 1994.

Records Management

Guide to the Management of Legal Records. Prairie Village, Kansas: Association of Records Managers and Administrators, 1987.

Secretarial Skills

Atwood, Illa W. *Law Office Procedures.* Westerville, Ohio: Glencoe, 1993.

De Vries, Mary A. *Legal Secretaries Complete Handbook, 4th ed.* Englewood Cliffs, N.J.: Prentice-Hall, 1992.

Estrin, Chere B. *Everything You Need to Know About Being a Legal Assistant.* Albany, N.Y.: Delmar, 1995.

Garrett, Vena. *Introduction to Legal Assisting.* Westerville, Ohio: Glencoe, 1992.

Lee, Jo Ann, and Marilyn L. Satterwhite. *The Irwin Law Office Reference Manual.* Burr Ridge, Ill.: Irwin Professional Publishing, 1995.

Lynton, Jonathan, et al. *Law Office Management for Paralegals.* Albany, N.Y.: Delmar, 1991.

National Association for Legal Assistants, Inc., Staff. *NALA Manual for Legal Assistants.* St. Paul, Minn.: West Publishing, 1991.

National Association of Legal Secretaries. *The Career Legal Secretary,* 3d ed. St. Paul, Minn.: West Publishing Co., 1993.

Training and Education

Law Office Staff Manual: Model Policies and Procedures. Chicago: American Bar Association, 1992.

Wills, Mike. *Managing the Training Process.* New York: McGraw-Hill, 1993.

INDEX